The NEBI YEARBOOK 1998

North European and Baltic Sea Integration

Springer-Verlag Berlin Heidelberg GmbH

The NEBI YEARBOOK 1998

North European and Baltic Sea Integration

General Editors:

Lars Hedegaard
and
Bjarne Lindström

Co-editors:

Pertti Joenniemi
Anders Östhol
Karin Peschel
Carl-Einar Stålvant

Springer

Lars Hedegaard
Nordregio/North
Nyhavn 38, 5 floor
DK-1051 Copenhagen K
Denmark

Bjarne Lindström
Department of Statistics
and Economic Research in Åland
Box 60
FIN-22101 Mariehamn
Åland Islands

ISBN 978-3-540-64210-7 ISBN 978-3-642-58886-0 (eBook)
DOI 10.1007/978-3-642-58886-0

Originally published by Springer-Verlag Berlin Heidelberg New York in 1998

SPIN 10669911 43/2202-5 4 3 2 1 0 – Printed on acid-free paper

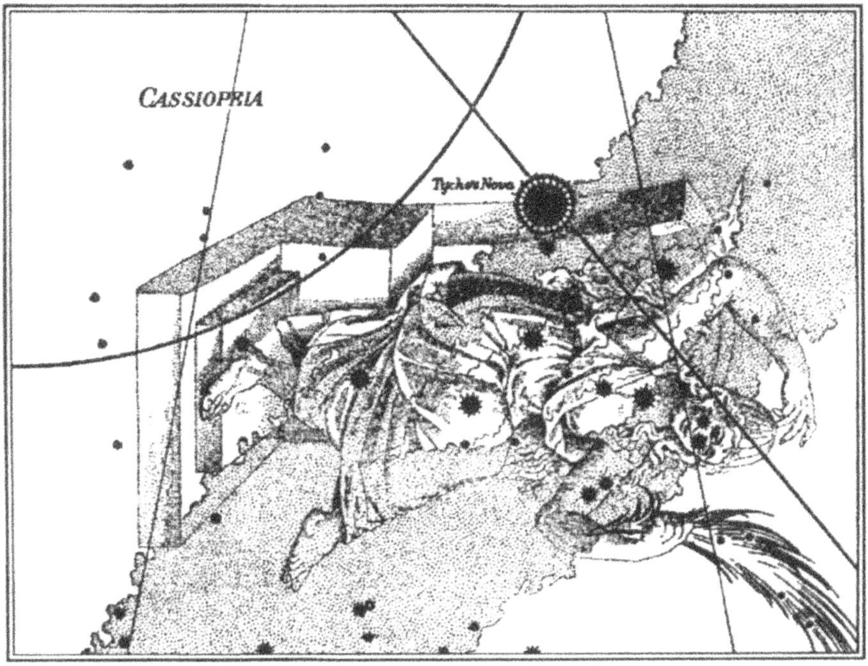

The computer-enhanced photo on the cover shows six bright stars in Cassiopeia and – in the top left-hand corner – the Polar Star. With its characteristic W-shape, Cassiopeia is among the most easily identifiable constellations in the NEBI area's night sky. Its name comes from *Quassio-peaer*, meaning Rose-Coloured Face in Phoenician and being the name of a queen who reigned over a world far from Greece. Ptolemy attributed to Cassiopeia the qualities of Saturn and Venus, meaning power, respect and command. When the combination was negative, however, it generated exaggerated pride and great presumption. Among countless depictions throughout the centuries is the above from Bayer's *Cassiopeia* (1603). *Tycho's Nova* is the famous exploding star discovered by the Danish astronomer Tycho Brahe on 11 November 1572 and described in his book *De nova stella* (1573). The new star quickly dimmed, and in March 1574 it could no longer be seen.

The Editors wish to acknowledge the kind assistance provided by the Tycho Brahe Planetarium, Copenhagen.

Cover design: Rita Baving, Delta Grafisk, Copenhagen

Foreword

Thorvald Stoltenberg

Ambassador
Chairman of the Editorial Advisory Board

Most of us have been overwhelmed by the speed and extent of the changes that have been taking place in Europe since the late 1980s. Over the span of a few years, we have witnessed the collapse of the Soviet Union and the unification of Germany. This process has had far-reaching implications for Northern Europe: the Baltic states have attained independence, and with the establishment of the Baltic Sea regional co-operation and the Barents co-operation, a new type of East-West relations has come into being.

The process of change continues. Its latest manifestation is the agreement between Russia and NATO, and NATO and EU enlargement is expected to take place over the next few years.

With such far-reaching transformations, we need to reflect on what is happening. We need a more coherent picture of the new situation in Northern Europe and of where we are heading.

This Yearbook is an attempt to fulfil this need. I would like to thank the editors for taking this initiative, which has been long awaited by those of us who have been actively interested in the improved relations between the former East and the old West that have been made possible by the end of the Cold War – and particularly in the new opportunities for cross-border co-operation and integration in the North European and Baltic space.

As the title indicates, the Yearbook focuses on the North European area, from the Barents region in the north to the Baltic Sea in the south. It expressly aims to cover important elements of integration over a wide range of fields: economics, politics, cross-border regional co-operation, the environment and infrastructure, foreign and security policy and the state of the civil society.

The Yearbook is also aimed at a wide range of readers, not only students of European affairs and actors in government, education and the media, but also the business community and a growing number of citizens from all parts of the area whose interest in new opportunities for co-operation and development has been awakened by recent events.

As Chairman of the Yearbook's Editorial Advisory Board I am particularly pleased that the editors have managed to combine solid links to the predominant economic and political actors and leading academic institutions with editorial independence.

As the editors point out in Chapter 1, for the first time in this century, the entire North European area is free from regimes bent on military aggression against their neighbours. This is the basic cause behind the lifting of the Iron Curtain which divided East and West from approximately 1947 to 1989. And whereas democracy and the rule of law may not be irreversibly or universally ensured throughout the area, there are at present no openly repressive or totalitarian regimes along the coasts of the Barents and Baltic Seas.

But there are a number of challenges. New conflicts often arise as the old order collapses, as we have seen in the Balkans, and it is vital to resolve them before they have gone too far. The zone extending from the Barents region via the Baltic and the Balkans towards the Black Sea and Northern Africa to the south contains the potential for a number of political, environmental and ethnic conflicts. Moreover, it is crucial to prevent the Iron Curtain from being replaced by a Silk Curtain that divides the haves from the have-nots in Europe. Unless we succeed in forging a Europe which is truly 'whole and free,' we shall have failed to take advantage of a historic opportunity. I consider it vital to prevent NATO and EU enlargement from creating new dividing lines in Europe.

This Yearbook is an encouraging sign that an impressive network of researchers from a broad spectrum of the social sciences has taken the new challenges seriously. And as the list of partners testifies, the Yearbook is very much a collective effort by leading agents of integration in the region.

A Yearbook, as the name indicates, is meant to appear every year. If it meets with the response we anticipate, it is our intention to continue the work.

Contents

Foreword vii
Thorvald Stoltenberg

1. The North European and Baltic Opportunity 3
Lars Hedegaard and Bjarne Lindström

PART I: ECONOMIC INTEGRATION
Edited by Karin Peschel

2. Core Elements of Successful Reform in Baltic Rim Countries 33
Klaus Schrader and Claus-Friedrich Laaser

3. The Importance of Social and Political Stability for Integration into Europe: Lithuania's Case 47
Kazimira Prunskiene

4. Current Trends in Economic Integration 55
Lars Lundqvist and Lars Olof Persson

5. Trade Potentials in Northern Europe and Consequences for Traffic Flows 73
Stefan Callsen

6. Foreign Direct Investment: Problems in Deepening the Integration of the Baltic Sea Region 87
Urpo Kivikari

7. Sustainable Investment Policies in the Murmansk Region 99
Vladimir Didyk and Ulf Wiberg

8. Labour Force Mobility in the Baltic Sea Area and the Transition Economies: With Special Reference to Economic Integration 115
J. Ilari Karppi

9. The CAP: An Obstacle to EU Enlargement? 131
Ewa Rabinowicz

10. Estonian Entrepreneurship: Towards Western Markets and Operating Patterns 145
Erik Terk and Juhan Teder

PART II: SPATIAL PLANNING AND THE ENVIRONMENT

Edited by Carl-Einar Stålvant

11. VASAB 2010: A Critical Analysis 163
Ralph Westermann

12. Transboundary Environmental Problems: Risk Analysis and Practical Lessons 187
Gunnar Sjöstedt

13. European Transport Corridors along the Eastern Baltic Shores: International and National Interests 199
Garri Raagmaa, Raik Vürst, Kalle Pungas and Härmo Haljaste

14. Development and Implementation of Baltic Sea Pollution Commitments: The Case of Sweden 217
Ronnie Hjorth

15. Poland's Economic Recovery and Its Implications for Energy Use and Air Pollution 233
Jürgen Salay

16. The New Berlin: Towards the Sustainable Capital? 251
Christof Ellger and Kai Richter

17. The Development of Kaliningrad in the Light of Baltic Co-operation 267
Malgorzata Pacuk and Tadeusz Palmowski

PART III: TRANSBORDER REGIONAL CO-OPERATION

Edited by Anders Östhol

18. Cross-Border Co-operation after World War II 285
Viktor Frhr. von Malchus

19. A Norden of the Regions? 297
Harald Baldersheim and Krister Ståhlberg

20. Spatial Development and Planning between 'High' and 'Low' Politics: Interreg II C in the Baltic Sea Region 309
Ib Jørgensen and Jan Nielsen

21. Transborder Co-operation along the EU's External Borders and the Turnabout of Regional Development Policies: A Mediterranean Perspective 323
Riccardo Cappellin

22. Cross-Border Co-operation in the Barents Region 337
Hallgeir Aalbu

23. Business and Politics in the Barents Region 349
Bo Svensson

PART IV: POLITICAL INTEGRATION, TERRITORIAL GOVERNANCE AND SECURITY
Edited by Pertti Joenniemi

24. Security around the Baltic Rim: Concepts, Actors and Processes .. 363
Kari Möttölä

25. Military Command Structures in the Baltic Sea Area 405
Bertel Heurlin

26. CFE and the Baltic Rim 423
Jane M.O. Sharp

27. Settled and Remaining Border Issues around the Baltic Sea 437
Tuomas Forsberg

28. The Security Policy Doctrines in the Nordic and Baltic Countries: Stability and Change 449
Clive Archer and Øyvind Jæger

29. Russia's Security Policies in the Baltic Sea Area 465
Alexander A. Sergounin

30. Poland's Security Policies in the Baltic Sea Area 485
Wojciech Kostecki

31. Germany's Security Policies in the Baltic Sea Area 503
Axel Krohn

32. 'Internal' Security in the Baltic States 521
Joan Löfgren and Helena Mannonen

33. The Tackling of Minority Issues in the Baltic Sea Region in the Context of OSCE and CBSS 537
Hanne-Margret Birckenbach

NORTH EUROPEAN AND BALTIC STATISTICS 551
Compiled by Jüri Köll, Statistics Sweden

List of Abbreviations 619
List of Figures 623
List of Tables 625

Index 627
About the Authors and Editors 649
List of Partners 653

The NEBI YEARBOOK
1998

1 The North European and Baltic Opportunity

Lars Hedegaard and Bjarne Lindström

A New Place in a New World

Eight years after the fall of the Berlin Wall and six years after the demise of the Soviet Union, the entire North European and Baltic Sea area is still very much in a process of transformation brought about by the largely unexpected collapse of the Soviet state and its dependencies in the region, Poland and the German Democratic Republic.

Given the enormity of the challenges to primarily the old 'Eastern' parts of the area but which have also forced the old 'Western' countries and regions to change strategies and policies and in general rethink their place in the world, it is hardly surprising that the North European and Baltic Sea area is still in a state of flux.

As will become evident from the contributions to this volume, few if any durable patterns of area-wide interaction, to say nothing of integration, have yet emerged across the old East-West divide or, for that matter, between the new transformation countries and regions that formerly belonged to the Eastern Bloc.

Regardless of where one looks – to basic economic development, foreign trade, foreign investments, the structure of labour markets, migration, tackling environmental challenges, creating adequate soft and hard infrastructures, political and institutional reforms, the state of the civil society, human and minority rights, cross-border regional co-operation, providing for military and societal security, finding a place within the growing network of alliances, institutions and agreements that make up the emerging European-Transatlantic-Russian world – the North European and Baltic Sea area as a whole is still groping with new patterns of co-operation, economic interaction and so forth.

Although many developments within the fields just mentioned have been slow and sometimes hesitant, uneven and contradictory, it seems fair to say that the immediate crisis of the first couple of years after the Communist collapse is over. We are, it would appear, in an intermediate phase between the passing of the acute crisis and the establishment of a new normalcy.

What this new normalcy is eventually going to look like economically, politically, or in terms of security arrangements or nature and extent of intra-area integration cannot be predicted with any degree of confidence if one looks ten or twenty years ahead. Which is not the same as saying that the area lacks structuring features even in the present phase of transition – a point to which we shall return.

One fundamental and indisputable fact, however, stands out: For the first time in this century, the entire North European and Baltic Sea area is free of regimes bent on military aggression against their neighbours. That is the basic cause of the lifting of the Iron Curtain that divided East and West from approximately 1947 to 1989. And whereas democracy and the rule of law may not be irreversibly or universally ensured throughout the area, there are at present no openly repressive or totalitarian regimes operating along the coasts of the Barents and Baltic Seas. For the first time this century, therefore, a real possibility exists to create a region that is 'whole and free' – to quote NATO's slogan from the early 1990s.

That is the opportunity. What the actors in the area have done to take advantage of it and what has been accomplished so far are central themes in this Yearbook on North European and Baltic Sea integration.

The NEBI Area

There is no commonly accepted name that covers the area whose internal interaction, integration and links to the outside world are in focus here. The core area under consideration covers vast stretches of Northern Europe: the Nordic countries, Denmark, Finland with Åland, Norway and Sweden; republics, regions and areas of the Russian Federation bordering on Norway and Finland and on the Baltic Sea, i.e. in practice most of the area covered by Russia's north-western 'economic association' (see Figure 1.3); Estonia, Latvia and Lithuania; the maritime provinces of Poland; and the German *länder* of Mecklenburg-Vorpommern, Schleswig-Holstein and Hamburg . The region has a population of 55 million (for a map of the area, see the Statistical Section in this volume).[1]

Admittedly, the selection of regions does not rest on any hard and fast criteria. This is true even if one considers the two seas – the Barents and the Baltic – that provide the area with some of its geographically and economically distinctive features.

In particular, it is questionable whether Hamburg should be included given the fact that the city state's trade appears weakly linked to rest of the region. In 1995, the share of Hamburg's exports going to other countries wholly or partly inside the NEBI area was only 10.8 per cent (down from 15.4 per cent in 1992). Similarly, the NEBI countries' share of the city's imports was a paltry 10.5 per cent and exactly the same as in 1992 (Statistical Section). However, Hamburg's unquestionable importance to the neighbouring Schleswig-Holstein appears to warrant its inclusion.

Another problem in this context is the concept of 'region'. By and large, it has two different meanings in this volume. Contributors with a regional policy background tend to interpret a region as an administrative or industrial-economic unit at the subnational or – as is increasingly the case – transnational level. Authors with roots in the security policy tradition, on the other hand, take region to mean a coherent structure of security policy actors, of which the sovereign state is the most important. Within the regional policy discourse, therefore, the region's primary basis is its spatial and economic function, and within the security discourse it is its institutional and political function. This is not the place to embark on any conceptual exegesis. We will point out, however, that it is possible as well as necessary to analyse the NEBI area as defined above from both perspectives, i.e. as an economic as well as political unit.

Our apology for the cumbersome term 'North European and Baltic Sea Integration' – giving rise to yet another acrostic (NEBI) in a Europe already constipated by an unwholesome fare of alphabet soup – is that we could think of no acceptable alternative. Outside the Nordic countries, 'North European' is often taken to mean 'Scandinavian.' On the other hand, people in the Barents area – which is very much a part of our focus – would have little patience with a book placing their region under the heading 'Baltic Sea Integration.'

Apart from a shared interest in the peaceful and sustainable development of all countries and regions along the Barents and Baltic Seas, a defining characteristic of the NEBI area – and one which constitutes it as a unit deserving of being considered jointly – is that the regions belonging to it are collectively threatened by peripheralisation, both in the socio-economic and political sense. It is desirable for the area to reach some degree of internal, transnational and transregional integration and develop some overarching co-operative structures and integrationist regimes providing it with a voice in Europe and the world. If not, there is a danger that future globalisation and, in particular, a widening and deepening of the European Union will create relations of dependency rather than co-operation between this geographical periphery and the economic, technological and political core of Europe (Eskelinen and Snickars 1995).[2]

It is true that despite their 'geometric' peripherality, at least the Nordic countries do not currently evidence some of the problems that are often attributed to peripheral status, such as a low GDP per capita, low quality of life, dependency and exploitation. Historically, however, this is a rather novel situation. Well into the present century, countries such as Finland, Norway and Sweden were poor by European comparison (Illeris 1995).

The Case for Economic Interdependency: Recent Trends

Within a framework of modern market economics, there is hardly any alternative to increased interaction and an enhanced division of labour between the NEBI area's inhabitants, enterprises and institutions. Greater intra-area interaction may, of course, assume different expressions and may lead to different types of competition and in a worst-case scenario to open conflict. The point is, however, that growing regional interaction is unavoidable. This is true of the NEBI area, Europe and, for that matter, any other part of the world. In the long run, there is no turning back from growing economic and political interdependency (Tsoukalis 1993; Amin and Thrift 1995; Gamble and Payne 1996).

Following the economic and political collapse of the Soviet Union, expectations concerning developments in the Baltic Sea area have oscillated between unmitigated optimism and the darkest pessimism. Immediately after the liberation around 1990, optimistic prognoses were predominant: like a so many phoenixes, the eastern parts of the Baltic Sea area would rise out of the ruins of five and in some places seven decades of malgovernment and become integrated into the economically and politically advanced structures of Western Europe.[3]

However, as the full implications of the Eastern regions' economic, infrastructural, ecological, social and political problems gradually dawned on Western observers, optimism turned into its antithesis: all that one could observe was a witches' brew of social, economic and ecological collapse, political instability, chaos and underdevelopment.

As evidenced by even a cursory survey of recent economic developments, neither the most optimistic nor the most pessimistic scenarios have been confirmed.

Following a decline in total production (GDP) in some of the area's established market economies (Finland and Sweden) at the beginning of the 1990s and an even stronger downturn in all transformation economies (i.e. the former communist economies), which was a direct result of the old system's collapse, recovery has been noticeable. Parts of the NEBI area have experienced a growth which is considerable by international comparison – not least Poland and Finland with growth rates above the OECD average (Statistical Section). Recently, Estonia has joined the league of high growth achievers. Newly published, preliminary figures indicate an increase in GDP of more than 7 per cent from the fourth quarter of 1995 to the fourth quarter of 1996 (Statistical Office of Estonia 1997). The worst growth problems are concentrated in certain Russian regions which are still affected by severe structural impediments.

The same picture applies to transnational investment flows in the form of foreign direct investments (FDI). Investment activities have been particularly noteworthy in Estonia and Latvia, whose economies have been strengthened by inflows not least from developed economies in the NEBI area, primarily Finland and Denmark. Since 1990 the stock of foreign capital in these countries has multiplied (Kivikari in this volume). In Estonia, FDIs accounted for 5-10 per cent of GDP over the years 1993-95 (Statistical Section). Even St Petersburg has experienced considerable development with substantial investment flows from the Nordic countries (primarily Finland and Sweden) and Germany (Borsos and Erkkilä 1995a). Other Russian NEBI regions, however, are still not receiving foreign investments of any consequence (Kivikari; Didyk and Wiberg; Pacuk and Palmowski in this volume).

Until now, investment flows in the area have been one-sided, with practically all investments going from developed Western countries to the new Eastern transformation economies. The bulk of NEBI-internal investment capital appears to come from Germany, Finland and Sweden, with Denmark and particularly

Norway playing a more modest role (Borsos and Erkkilä 1995b). Significantly, initial fears that investments would be accompanied by massive transfers of enterprises and jobs from the area's Western regions towards the low-wage economies in the East have not been substantiated. For example, Finnish investments in Estonia and St Petersburg have tended to complement rather than out-compete comparable activities at home (Borsos and Erkkilä 1995a).

Trade in the NEBI area has also expanded greatly in recent years. This is true of trade with external partners as well as internal trade (Statistical Section). In 1995, internal trade accounted for somewhat more than one-fifth of the total trade in the area. The most extreme case is that of Latvia – more than 80 per cent of whose trade is with other parts of the NEBI area.

The area's internal trade volume is, however, hampered by the fact 90 per cent of Germany's trade – that is the trade of the most powerful economy by far – is directed towards areas outside the NEBI area (Callsen in this volume). Nevertheless, between 1994 and 1995, NEBI-internal trade grew in almost all countries. The only exceptions to the rule that intra-Baltic trade grows as a percentage of the countries' total foreign trade were Estonia and Finland with a slight, *relative* decline (Callsen in this volume). In absolute figures, however, the two countries' NEBI-internal trade has increased strongly. This is particularly the case if one considers their bilateral trade, which has almost doubled every year from 1993 through 1995 (Borsos and Erkkilä 1995a).

Open borders and more trade have also paved the way for an increase in travel, both for business and leisure. If we take Estonia again as the clearest example of this development, the number of visiting ships and passengers grew by close to 50 and 70 per cent, respectively, between 1992 and 1995 (Statistical Section).

So far, increased mobility has not led to any significant, open, trans-Baltic migration (Karppi in this volume). Following a slight increase at the beginning of the 1990s, today's net migration between the economies of the NEBI area is generally inconsequential. In the three Baltic republics, total net out-migration is about 20,000 persons per year (Statistical Section). However, regional variations are considerable. The Murmansk region, for example, has experienced a net population decline of close to one-tenth during the 1990s (Didyk and Wiberg in this volume).

Of course, mobility in the NEBI area depends to a great deal on local economic and social conditions. The general standard of living is still low in the transformation economies and in some cases, e.g. Murmansk, the Karelian Republic and Kaliningrad, it is very low. And clearly, social problems have been aggravated during the process of structural change – as may be directly inferred from the statistics on life expectancy. In every single North European member unit of the former Soviet Union, life expectancy has fallen since the end of the 1980s. From 1995, however, there are signs of a change for the better. Decline has been replaced by a slight upturn – even in Kaliningrad and Murmansk (Statistical Section).[4]

Despite some positive economic trends in recent years, there are good reasons to warn against exaggerated optimism.

NEBI-integrationist forces are still weak, not least as a consequence of the northern German and Polish economies' strong links to the rest of Germany and Central Europe. And although economic disparities may be assumed to further the division of labour and thus integration (see the next section), the economies in parts of the NEBI area are so underdeveloped that even under the most auspicious circumstances, it will take decades for them to reach the basic level required for meaningful integration with the region's more advanced economies (Callsen; Kivikari; Didyk and Wiberg; Lundquist and Persson in this volume). According to the 's recent analysis of the economies of ten Central and Eastern European candidates for EU membership, GDP per capita in the three Baltic republics is no more than about a fifth of the EU average, and in Poland it is about a third (Commission 1997: 'Summary and Conclusions').

As several contributions (Svensson; Laaser and Schrader; Prunskiene; Terk in this volume) make clear, the institutional and cultural problems related to the transition to developed market economies are far from solved. In addition, there is great uncertainty concerning the integrationist impact of EU enlargement and the extension of its institutional structures, including the common agricultural policies (Rabinowicz in this volume). This applies particularly to the two countries in the NEBI area with whom the Commission's document *Agenda 2000* proposes to start immediate membership negotiations, i.e. Estonia and Poland (Commission 1997: 'Summary and Conclusions'). A future EU border between these two applicants and their Baltic neighbours will undoubtedly bring about a novel situation with many new elements of uncertainty.

In conclusion, it would appear prudent to regard the NEBI area as a volatile zone of transformation whose future economic architecture must remain obscure.

NEBI Peculiarities

Though the increasing pressures towards more economic interaction are by no means specific to the NEBI area – but are indeed European and global – there are a number of particular traits and complications that apply especially to the North European area.

Perhaps the most important special characteristic is the area's dramatic recent history caused by the collapse of the Soviet Union and the ensuing political and economic 'vacuum.' The upshot has been that despite promising historical antecedents, such as the ancient Pomor trade in the Barents region and the old Hanseatic League in the Baltic Sea area, integration has in reality had to begin from scratch.

Being forced to start from zero may, of course, have its attractions. For one thing, this situation means that any change represents some sort of development compared to conditions prior to 1991. In addition, the absence of long-established (and so perhaps mossgrown) institutions is likely to provide greater freedom and room for innovative thinking when it comes to building new co-operative structures in the area. On the other hand, there is no denying that the area lacks most fundamental 'infrastructural' prerequisites, in the widest sense, to even commence any transnational integration process worth the name (Borsos and Erkkilä 1995a; Kivikari; Schrader and Laaser; Raagmaa et al. in this volume).

Another peculiarity of the NEBI area is its unique geographical position between some of Europe's heaviest economic and political structures.

As will be apparent from Figure 1.1, the NEBI area is situated in the midst of a zone defined by overlap between the EU's industrial core, the sparsely populated but economically well-developed Nordic countries and the new transformation economies of the ex-Soviet Union and its dependencies. To the north (the Barents region), it holds Europe's perhaps richest reserves of valuable minerals and fossil energy (NordREFO 1993). The Barents region is also interesting from the point of view of transportation. If technical obstacles can be overcome, the North-East

Figure 1.1: The economic geography of the NEBI area

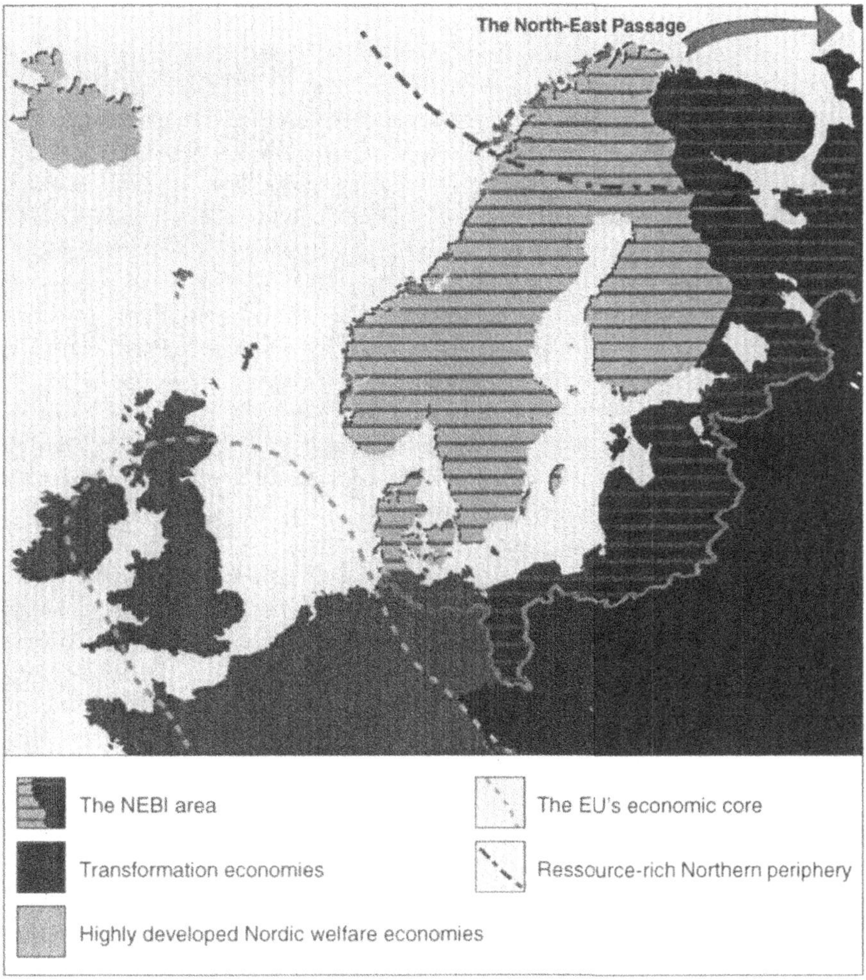

maritime passage from Western Europe to the important markets of East Asia may become an attractive alternative to the much longer routes through the Suez Canal or round the southern tip of Africa. To the south, the area touches the world's single biggest consumer market, i.e. the densely populated core areas of the European Union.

Since the time of Adam Smith and David Ricardo, differences in productive structures and markets have been viewed as conducive to economic specialisation, technical development, the exchange of ideas, migration and trade. Or more simply put: as the very basis of economic progress and social integration. If this classical assumption still holds, the prerequisites of long-term economic integration in the NEBI area would appear to be at hand.

Figure 1.2: The geopolitical position of the NEBI area

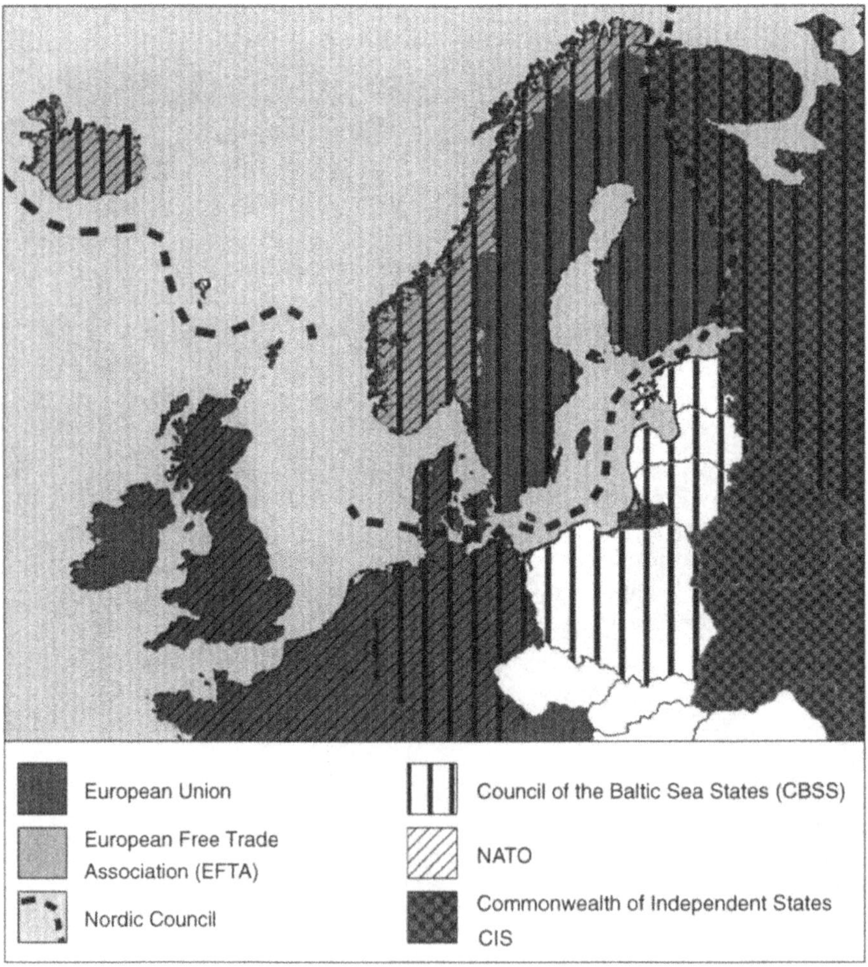

The area's geopolitical position is equally interesting. As shown in Figure 1.2, the NEBI area encompasses most of the political constructions of space known in today's world. It contains classical territorial states (Sweden, Poland, Estonia, Latvia and Lithuania), federations (Russia and Germany), 'federacies' (Finland-Åland and the 'Unity of the Realm' of Denmark, the Faroe Islands and Greenland) and a confederation, i.e. the European Union, whose member units in the area are Germany, Sweden, Finland with Åland and Denmark – but not the other parts of the Danish federacy, the Faroes and Greenland.[5] As a consequence of its unique, internationally guaranteed home rule, Åland had the option of staying outside the EU but decided to join following an independent referendum.[6] A further anomaly in the area is presented by the strange Russian enclave of Kaliningrad, which is not contiguous with the rest of the Russian Federation (Pacuk and Palmowski in this volume).

The NEBI area is also a place where practically all of Europe's transnational co-operative structures come together: the EU, the EEA (the European Economic Area), EFTA (the European Free Trade Association), the Nordic Council, the CBSS (the Council of the Baltic Sea States), NATO, PfP (Partnership for Peace), the OSCE (the Organisation for Security and Co-operation in Europe) and many more. In addition the area also encompasses a number of neutral states.

Through Denmark – and to some extent Norway – with their strong historical connections to Iceland and the autonomous territories of the Faroe Islands and Greenland, the NEBI area is further linked to Canada and the United States, not least as a consequence of the dominant position of the Greenlandic Inuit in relation to Inuit in Canada and Russia.

To make the area even more interesting from a European and global perspective, the NEBI area is the only place where EU territory (Finland) borders directly on Russia.

A New Approach to Integration

It is a distinct feature of most writings on regional development and regional integration that they are ahistorical and acultural. Most often they are also apolitical except in a rather narrow sense having to do with the administrative aspects of territorial governance. Many a grandiose scheme for regional development and integration – whether produced by regions, nations, organs of intergovernmental co-operation or the EU – takes as its point of departure little more than a few recent statistics on the areas to be developed or linked. The regions' population is thus thought of as a *tabula rasa* with no historical, cultural or political stamp worth considering, with no fears, animosities, deep-rooted aspirations or cultural or moral norms and values of any concern to researchers, planners, bureaucrats or politicians. This approach is futile and bound to lead to disappointment and embarrassment.[7]

The explanation is not only the compartmentalising traditions within the different branches of economics, social and political science, geography, regional policy research etc. Part of the blame must be put on the 'diplomatic' approach that is usually imposed on regional development and integration schemes. No national government and no trans- or supranational body would dare point to the need of overcoming internal deficiencies in any region having to do with social or political norms, with any burden of history or with the quality of its civil society.

It will, however, require a lot more than desk-top plans, transfers of money and the creation of formal institutional structures to bring about regional development and cross-border integration. First and foremost, it is essential to realise that for people to be willing to integrate with their neighbours, they must be secure. They must feel reasonably safe from foreign take-over, domination or penetration. And they must have confidence in the strength of their civil society if they are to trust their own ability to compete successfully in and benefit from any politico-economic regime whether regional or transregional (Putnam 1993).

This realisation has prompted the editors and authors of the NEBI Yearbook to consider far more integrationist and disintegrationist factors than are usually taken into account by literature on regional development, planning and integration.

The Rupture of 1989-91

So where do the NEBI regions come from, what is the nature of their historical experience and where do they stand today?

Every passing year without any relapse into totalitarianism, autarchy or the closing of borders in the post-communist states along the eastern and southern shores of the Baltic Sea and along the Finnish and Norwegian borders increases the likelihood that the area's transformation during the years 1989-91 was indeed a fundamental break with many decades of perverse development – if development is the right word.

To gauge the utter discontinuity – and fundamental novelty – of the situation obtaining today compared with conditions prevailing in Russia, Estonia, Latvia, Lithuania, Poland, and the former GDR less than a decade ago, it is perhaps helpful to briefly reconsider the legacy of twentieth-century history as it applies to the Baltic Sea and Barents areas – and to re-examine our mental construction of the major events of the past eight decades.

Whereas contemporaries of such cataclysmic occurrences as World War I, World War II, the Cold War balance of terror, the National Socialist and Communist dictatorships would tend to view them as separate events, each with its own specific set of causes – that will probably not be the verdict of future historians.

If it turns out that the failed August 1991 coup in the Soviet Union followed by the temporary abolition of the Bolshevik-style Communist Party and the demise of the Soviet Union in December of that year was, in fact, the last gasp of a discredited order – and not just a lull before a return to totalitarianism and oppression – it appears a reasonable assumption that the entire span of years from the outbreak of war in 1914 till the collapse of the Soviet Union and the loss of most of its empire will come to be viewed as one long debacle with a common internal dynamic.

The Apotheosis of Modernity

A number of historians have long realised that World War I and World War II were not discrete phenomena but rather different acts in the same drama. Unfinished business or business created by the war of 1914-18 had to be fought over again from 1939 to 1945.[8]

Nor were Hitler's National Socialism and Stalin's Socialism in One Country (and in one contiguous empire) only antagonists – as the proponents of these ideologies would have their followers believe – but rather exemplars of complementary revolutionary and modernising impulses. Whereas National Socialism died with Hitler in 1945, the communists managed to hold out for another 46 years and were thus able to impose their mark on much of the post-World War II world. This was pre-eminently the case in the NEBI area, which has had the misfortune of being in the direct firing line between the two competing absolutist empires and has had to bear the full brunt of their ideological schemes – in some cases, unfortunately, with the support and participation of segments of the population.[9]

Until we have a better name for the age of 1914-1991, the Apotheosis of Modernity seems to capture its essence. Capitalism's break with all customary societal relations and concepts – so evocatively expressed by Karl Marx and Friedrich Engels in the Communist Manifesto – was not nearly as radical as that which was to follow in the wake of the fateful summer of 1914. World War I inaugurated an age characterised by a belief in the absolute sway and omnipotent capacity of political power to manipulate and transform not only society and economics but nature and man himself – and in the need to do so.[10]

In the worldview of National Socialism and Leninist-Stalinist Communism – undoubtedly the two most radical regimes ever to come to power in Europe – man was viewed as raw material[11] – like so much petroleum, iron ore or cattle – to be moulded, bred, improved, moved around, expended, discarded and, if need be, eliminated.

From a perspective of regional development and spatial governance it is important to stress that the Apotheosis of Modernity was equally the high point of the centralised, territorial state claiming for itself exclusive and uniform sovereignty not only over every bit of the national territory but over all spheres of life within its borders (Lindström 1997).

The implication was that any regional initiative not expressly initiated, sanctioned and supervised by central government was either discouraged or expressly forbidden as it would invariably be interpreted by the national capitals as an intolerable infringement of their territorial prerogative. Of course, this stance was most zealously upheld in the totalitarian states. In fact, it was one of the defining features of both the Nazi and Soviet regimes.[12]

Of course, the political and ideological purposes of centralisation in totalitarian states bear no comparison with the benevolent and humanistic endeavours of, e.g., the Nordic welfare states. Nevertheless, it is interesting to observe that centralisation was by no means unknown in the democratic countries of the NEBI area.

For a long time, the Nordic countries have been strongly centralised unitary states with few or no politically countervailing forces able to withstand or in any way challenge the central power of the national capitals. This was perhaps most pronounced in Finland. With the exception of autonomous Åland, there was, until the beginning of the 1990s, absolutely no political power at the regional level apart from the state's own representatives (Lindström 1996).

In a recent evaluation of the implementation of Structural Fund initiatives in the new member states, Austria, Finland and Sweden, the EU's Committee of the Regions was very critical, pointing to state interference or downright state monopoly with regard to important decisions, especially in Sweden (Baldersheim and Ståhlberg in this volume).

If anything, the welfare-state character of the Nordic countries – with their massive, centrally initiated transfers of tax revenue for the purposes of social and regional equalisation – has tended to underline their centralisation (NordREFO 1994).

NEBI 'Hot Spots' and the Legacy of History

Many of the 'hot spots' or problem areas identified in planning documents on the Baltic Sea and Barents regions as impediments to integration (e.g. VASAB 2010, 1994) result directly from the policies of totalitarian, centralising and modernising regimes. This is not the place to go through the entire, lamentable catalogue of human, economic, political or environmental disasters. A few examples must suffice.

The challenge to social and political harmony posed by the presence of sizeable ex-Soviet minorities in Estonia and Latvia (Birckenbach in this volume) is a result of Soviet policies imposed against the will of the two countries.[13] In the Baltic republic most affected by immigration from other parts of the Soviet Union, Latvia, the percentage of ethnic Latvians, which stood at 75 per cent before the war, had fallen to a bare majority of 50.7 per cent by 1989 (Hiden and Salmon 1991).

Similarly, some of the gravest examples of environmental degradation in the NEBI area are directly caused by the utter disregard of the consequences of economic schemes evidenced by communist command economies. Particularly enlightening in this regard is the economic history of the Soviet Union's, now Russia's, Murmansk region, whose disturbing combination of economic depression and ecological crisis may be traced back to the centralised investment policies of former Soviet authorities concentrating on the rapid development of 'cheap' regional resources (Didyk and Wiberg in this volume).[14]

The enormous economic differences between countries and regions found in the NEBI area are also largely an outcome of political malgovernance. The area's lack of economic cohesion is among the most glaring in Europe. According the 1993 EU index of the Community's 25 richest and 25 poorest regions (measured in terms of GDP per capita in purchasing power standards), the NEBI area contains three of the richest, including *the* richest, Hamburg, with 189 per cent of the Union average, Åland with 127 per cent and Stockholm with 119 per cent. Mecklenburg-Vorpommern ranks as the EU's ninth poorest region with just 52 per cent and Brandenburg as the eighteenth poorest with 57 per cent of the Union average. Mecklenburg-Vorpommern's ranking is particularly remarkable as it is the only North European region among the bottom ten, five of which are overseas departments of France or Portugal (Commission 1996b).

If the EU statistic had encompassed all regions of the NEBI area, including Norway, the Baltic republics and the relevant parts of Poland and Russia, the gaps in wealth would be even more astonishing.

It is futile to speculate on what economic development might have been realised in the north-western regions of Russia in the absence of war, revolution and central planning.[15] However, concerning Estonia, Latvia and Lithuania, we do have information relating to their years of independence between the World Wars. They indicate that their economic performance relative to, e.g., the Nordic countries was incomparably better than it became after the Soviet occupation. The pre-war development levels of Estonia and Finland were nearly equal, and by 1939, the Estonian standard of living was approximately on par with – if not slightly higher than – that of Finland, and Latvia was not far behind (Kukk 1991; Lieven 1993). A rough calculation based on figures presented in the Statistical Section of this volume shows that by 1995, the discrepancies in GDP per capita had reached the order of ten to one in the case of Finland and Estonia and fifteen to one in the case of Finland and Latvia.[16]

More indicative than the EU regional statistic quoted above is the chilling realisation that by 1995, the GDP of Åland, with 25,000 inhabitants, was 25 per cent of Estonia's (1.5 million), 20 per cent of Latvia's (2.5 million) and 15 per cent of Lithuania's (3.75 million).

Sad as the record of economic, political and ecological failure may appear, it also provides reasons for optimism. The current state of underdevelopment in depressed regions of the NEBI area – and consequently their difficulties in co-operating with other, more advanced regions on an equal basis – has little to do with any inherent natural impediments or human deficiencies but can be traced directly back to policies imposed by the totalitarian ideology of a centralised empire.

Much the same may be said of the quality of their civil society. When Western visitors to former Soviet regions are struck by a perceived lack of efficiency and initiative (Svensson in this volume) and in some cases by an all-pervasive lethargy typified by a new species of man called the 'Homo Sovieticus,' one would do well to remember that this outcome was precisely what the rulers in Moscow did their utmost to achieve. During the Stalinist regime, the political leaderships, the local bureaucracies, the intellectual elites and the industrial cadres of every single Soviet province, republic or area showing the slightest signs of any capacity for independent action were purged and purged again – to secure the kind of docility deemed desirable. Russia's second city, Leningrad, for example, underwent almost unbroken waves of purges from 1934 till the death of Stalin (Conquest 1990).

The Demise of Territorial Centralism

In his farewell address to the Wehrmacht Officer Corps of early May 1945, Hitler's successor, Grand-Admiral Dönitz encouraged his 'comrades' to keep a zealous watch over the 'greatest boon that has been given us by National Socialism – our unity' (Wheeler-Bennett 1967: 698-9). But unity in the territorial sense was precisely what the Germans did not preserve – and were not permitted to preserve by the occupying powers. Rather the much admired constitution of 1949 reinstituted federalism, providing strong constitutional guarantees of the rights of länder. This federal constitution enabled the länder to pursue their individual interests – not only vis-a-vis the federal government but also, to a certain extent, in relation to cross-border co-operation.[17] Among the most famous examples of regional activism was Prime Minister Björn Engholm's Baltic initiatives at the onset of the 1990s.[18]

By constituting the new Germany as a federal republic, its framers created powerful allies of European integration and consequently of North European and Baltic Sea integration. In contradistinction to the Bund, which can only loose power as a result of increased Europeanisation, the länder would, on balance, appear to increase *their* influence through the process (Scharpf 1990). It should, however, be stressed that Germany's federal authorities appear far from uniformly devoted to the strong central state.[19] In fact, the Federal Republic has assumed the role as the primary spokesman of regional interests in the European Union, e.g. during the difficult negotiations leading up to the creation of the Committee of the Regions, which was set up in accordance with Articles 198a-c of the Maastricht Treaty (Saether, Schmidt-Nissen and Lorenz 1997).

In Russia – the other great Baltic power, whose attitudes and potentials will necessarily become major determinants in Baltic Sea and Barents integration – the straight jacket of centralism was kept on until the Soviet Union's final breakup in 1991. The same was true, of course, of the Soviet Union's imperial dependencies in the area.

Given this very recent legacy and the immensity of the problems left behind by the communist regime, it was not to be expected that Russia's ride towards normalisation would be a straight or smooth one. Nor should it surprise that Russian politics, economy, institutions and civil society must still be characterised as being in a state of flux, with few discernible patterns having emerged.

From a regional integrationist perspective, however, it has been interesting to observe a changing balance of power in favour of the Russian Federation's 89 components (among them 47 regions, called *oblasts, krais* and autonomous *okrugs*, and 21 'ethnic republics' claiming quasi-sovereign power) and away from the central government (*The Economist* 1997a).

Russia's new constitution of 1993 and a subsequent law obliging local leaders to be elected by the end of 1996 have led to a great many old-style local power-holders being replaced by more reform- and independent-minded people. One effect has been a transformation of the upper house of the Russian parliament, the Federation Council, where local leaders sit, into a less tractable body. Probably the recent changes will make it difficult for the central government to fire governors who are seen to exceed their powers. Instead, the Kremlin will have to negotiate with them, especially the ones representing regions with relatively strong economies.

It is a distinct possibility that the regions, particularly the economically more successful ones, will want to move in the direction of the republics, gradually acquiring quasi-sovereign powers. Russia's foreign ministry is especially worried that the regions will seek to usurp its exclusive prerogative to conduct foreign policy by entering into private diplomacy and negotiating trade and investment treaties abroad for their own benefit, but not necessarily that of the country.

To increase their influence further, the regions, republics and areas have entered into 'economic associations' – eight in number and covering the entire territory of the Russian Federation (see Figure 1.3). Of particular interest from a Baltic and Barents perspective is the north-western regional association encompassing the Republics of Karelia and Komi; the regions of Arkhangelsk, Vologda, Kaliningrad, Kirov, Leningrad, Murmansk, Novgorod and Pskov; the Nenets area; and St Petersburg City.

Figure 1.3: Russia's regional associations

1. Central Russia
2. Black Earth
3. Greater Volga
4. North-West (Republics of Karelia and Komi; Arkhangelsk, Volodga, Kaliningrad, Kirov, Leningrad, Murmansk, Novgorod and Pskov regions; Nenets area; St Petersburg City)
5. Urals
6. North Caucasus
7. Siberia
8. Far East

Source: The Economist (1997a: 27).

When speaking of the integrationist pressures released by the fall of the Berlin Wall and the subsequent liberation of countries under communist control, observers often forget that this pressure is not only directed towards the eastern parts of the NEBI area but also towards its western parts.

The security policy status of Finland and Sweden have changed dramatically (Heurlin; Möttölä in this volume). Economic integration under the auspices of supranational bodies such as the EU has influenced the relative position of the nation states involved. The area's large cities, and not least the national capitals, are no longer in a position where they can simply lean on their role as national centres. They must increasingly seek a new footing within a framework of a multifaceted pattern of urban networks encompassing the entire Baltic Sea region (Vartiainen 1997).

Finally, Finland and to a lesser extent Sweden have realised the need to adjust their legislation concerning local government and administration to European Union systems and programmes (Baldersheim and Ståhlberg in this volume).

In the case of Finland, an entirely new non-state authority with rather broad political responsibilities has been created at the regional level. Similarly, Sweden recently decided to initiate a process of cautious regionalisation through a time-limited experiment designed to strengthen regional political influence in certain parts of the country (Lindström 1996).

The Transnational Imperative

It has been pointed out that the activist, even interventionist foreign policies of some of the Western countries bordering on the Baltic Sea towards the emerging nations on the eastern shore – in particular that pursued by the Danish Foreign Minister Uffe Ellemann-Jensen from 1989 to the beginning of the 1990s and with an early culmination in the Ellemann-Genscher initiative of the Council of the Baltic Sea States in 1992 – were close to being audacious (Archer and Jæger in this volume). And undoubtedly, Denmark's – and Iceland's – early recognition of Baltic independence together with its express willingness to receive Baltic refugees in case of a Soviet attack may be interpreted as proof of a concrete commitment. Whether the Danish government was also committed to a regional vision beyond traditional inter-state relations is an entirely different question.

According to observers who have closely monitored the diplomatic history of Baltic Sea co-operation, Prime Minister Engholm's initiative from 1989-90 to set up a Baltic Council modelled on the non-statist historical antecedent of the mediaeval Hansa was not at all well received in Bonn. In fact, Foreign Minister Hans Dietrich Genscher sent a letter to Björn Engholm complaining that Kiel's plans for a New Hansa infringed on the foreign policy prerogative of the Federal Republic. In the view of insiders, Bonn subsequently encouraged Foreign Minister Ellemann-Jensen – who was not keen on any regional commitment – to take the lead in setting up the Council of the Baltic Sea States. The move was pre-emptive.

The idea was to create a council of traditional state actors with almost no budget and no permanent staff.

As it now turns out, the ailing CBSS infant has grown to be a promising adolescent (Joenniemi 1997). From a historical perspective, this will undoubtedly be interpreted to mean that Baltic Sea integration was a necessity imposed on the nation states by events beyond their control. Given their inescapable dependency on peace and a modicum of normalcy in their near abroad, there was no way that the Germans and Nordics could have opted out of it.

It was equally clear that integration could only come about on Western terms – despite talk in some circles that a continuation in democratic guise of segments of the old autarchic economy would have been less painful and caused fewer disruptions and dislocations.

To argue in this manner is forgetting that the root cause of the Soviet collapse was the failure of autarchy to deliver the goods. It is also tantamount to neglecting the intimate links between political or 'class' control of the 'commanding heights' of industry and dictatorial rule.

The Norwegian government's policy in the Barents region was, to be sure, politically less ambitious – as it would have to be given the fact that the primary partner on the other side of the border was not some hitherto oppressed nation seeking independence but the very successor state of the Soviet Empire. Nevertheless, the Barents initiative contains clear elements of damage control and benevolent containment. It does, of course, also emphasise vast opportunities in terms of economic, environmental, cultural and people-to-people contacts. But that does not detract from the fact that regional co-operation in the Barents area is essentially foreign and security policy by other means and in a different wrapping (Aalbu in this volume). In the absence of the ingenious Norwegian scheme of cross-border regional co-operation sanctioned and made legitimate by the central governments and attracting outside guarantor powers such as the EU, some other policy aimed at solving the same problems would have had to be devised.

Transnational integration is also imposed on the NEBI area by its attachment to the European Union. This attachment has not only come about as a result of the membership of Denmark, Germany, Finland and Sweden and Norway's and Iceland's entry into the European Economic Area (EEA) but through a steadily growing network of treaties and agreements between the Union and all non-member states in the area. Particularly important from a regional integrationist perspective is the anticipated effects of the Interreg II C Programme, which is intended to promote transborder regional co-operation (Jørgensen and Nielsen in this volume).

Towards New Integrationist Regimes?

Some form of spatial integrationist regime is necessary if political, social and economic interaction is to reach its optimal potential. It does not, however, necessarily have to assume EU-like dimensions so as to be formally and specifically designed to promote ever closer area-wide convergence of political and economic structures. Ad hoc regimes or regimes aiming at a more limited approach and overtly less ambitious in their long-term objectives may well serve the immediate needs.

But this optimal development towards NEBI-wide structures is by no means the only possibility. Another possibility is spatial fragmentation along lines defined by resurgent security-policy blocs or intra-area economic competition, which may be intensified by other disintegrationist factors such as social instability, threats against the civil society or ethnic conflict. In the worst case, the outcome may be regional 'Balkanisation' or perverse regionalisation.

To a considerable extent, the shape and direction of future NEBI integration will depend on what actors take the lead – traditional, top-down territorial states or 'post-national,' 'region-building' regimes.[20] If the territorial states maintain their grip on the integration process, it is likely to proceed in accordance with traditional principles of intergovernmental co-operation. Some of the important integrationist schemes, such as the Barents co-operation, the Council of Baltic Sea States and VASAB 2010, must be characterised as nation-state initiatives (Aalbu; Westermann in this volume) – which is not the same as saying that they will continue to be dominated by states or that some of their tasks may not be taken up by other types of actors.

An entirely possible alternative or complement to traditional intergovernmental co-operation is the emergence of political-territorial co-operative regimes focusing on cross-border *region-building* and entailing a situation where traditional state actors are gradually replaced or complemented by a number of new ones. These actors may be supranational, e.g. the EU, they may be subnational, e.g. various types of regional actors, or they may be 'non-national' or rather non-territorial, e.g. networks of cities, universities or interest organisations, such as chambers of commerce or industrial associations.

Figure 1.4 attempts to illustrate the various scenarios that may result from combinations of actors and types of interaction.

None of the regimes indicated in Figure 1.4 can be excluded from a picture of Northern Europe's future. In fact, even today there are elements of all four in the

Figure 1.4: Conceivable interactionist regimes

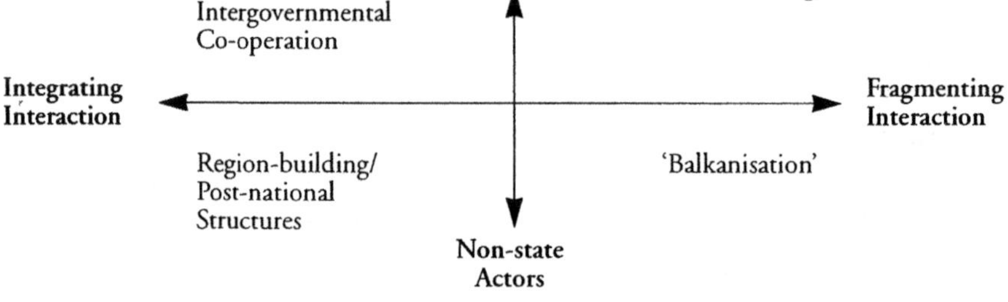

area, and there are many signs that this will remain the case in the foreseeable future.

Given its functional complexity and economic pluralism combined with relative political stability – not least due to the influence of such organisations as the EU, NATO and Nordic bodies – it is no wonder that a major study of the area pronounced it an ideal laboratory in which to test alternative models of Europe's future political-territorial architecture (NordREFO 1993).

Emerging Trends on a Kaleidoscopic Background

In general, 1996 and 1997 have been characterised by an avalanche of overlapping political initiatives, by attempts at transnational institution-building and by gradually increasing but regionally uneven economic integration. The complex and to some extent disparate nature of these developments is hardly surprising in view of what has just been said of the area's geopolitical and economic structure.

The fact that developments must be characterised as multifaceted and, frankly, hard to grasp does not, however, imply that they are entirely devoid of structuring elements. Two overlapping policy areas appear to be emerging from the expanding web of co-operative initiatives.

In traditional political science parlance, the first area would be characterised as dealing with 'low policy.' It has to do with initiatives and processes whose aim is to increase social and economic interaction through an exchange of ideas, knowledge, experience, models of organisation, culture, goods and services etc. Today it is possible to identify two main *loci* of this type of integrationist initiative: an ever more active *regional level* and a growing number of *functional networks.*

The regional interactionist 'leg' is very much tied to a specific territory and involves the commitment of regional and local actors to take part in cross-border co-operation. The explosively growing activities in this field complement, and in some respects make inroads into the nation states' former monopoly on co-operation between political territories. At the moment, transregional co-operation varies in dignity from uncommitted declarations of intent and twinned city relations (Johansson and Stålvant 1997) to more serious attempts to create integrationist political and economic structures at the transnational regional level (Joenniemi 1993; Veggeland 1994; Council of the Baltic Sea States 1996).

As already indicated, functional networks – the other leg of low policy interaction – are not primarily based on any concept of territory or geopolitics (Törnquist 1997). Their central feature is the creation of functional relations among groups of professionals, economic associations, industrial unions, various types of institutions, organisations etc., who believe that their social, commercial, professional or other types of interests will be furthered by more interaction across state borders (Lundqvist and Persson 1995).[21]

At present, both regional integration and functional networks are in an initial phase of development. National programmes, regional and local resources and, not least, a number of EU programmes such as Interreg, PHARE and TACIS may eventually help to create and strengthen long-term and resourceful co-operative structures of both a territorial and functional character (Commission 1996a). There can be little doubt that the proposed enlargement of the EU as a result of the entry of Estonia and Poland – and soon perhaps Latvia and Lithuania (Commission 1997. 'Summary and Conclusions') – will improve the financial and economic preconditions for a more intimate collaboration between the NEBI area's many low policy actors.

The other main structuring force in NEBI integration is initiatives and processes aimed at developing the area's geopolitical architecture – i.e. the field of 'high policy.' Less than ten years ago, geopolitics in the North European and Baltic Sea area was exclusively determined by the heavy hand of national interests organised in competing military and economic alliances which largely prevented any meaningful cross-border integration. Today the situation is substantially changed. Gone is the old bipolarity and with it the former subservience of such concerns as economic development, quality of life and direct contacts between countries, regions and populations to the demands of militarily defined security policy structures. The late 1990s are dominated by the efforts of a growing number of transnational actors – EU, NATO, Council of the Baltic Sea States with various offshoots, such as the Baltic Sea States Subregional Co-operation (BSSSC) – to establish regional integrationist regimes where security in the military sense is underpinned by socio-economic stability and development (Möttölä in this volume).

To achieve this aim, high policy has increasingly had to combine with low policy. In practice, traditional geopolitical interests can only be secured through increased focusing on the sub- or transnational regional level and on the new structures of functional networks (Cappellin in this volume). It is no longer sufficient that national capitals co-operate with each other. If the concrete problems of the Barents and Baltic Sea regions are to be solved, it is not enough for, say, Oslo to maintain good relations with Moscow or Stockholm with Warsaw or Bonn because such a limited approach is not conducive to the direct involvement of the regional populations and interests that must be mobilised if area-wide integration is to move beyond the sphere of paper schemes. In the same vein, some observers, e.g. Möttölä in this volume, have claimed that in all likelihood the integrationist development in the NEBI area will become a 'test of the extent to which regionalism as a phenomenon and region-building as a policy may have a primary or subsidiary role in producing security for states.'

Traditionally the concept of security has tended to operate according to a logic of its own that does not mix easily – if at all – with departures that are less fixed on sovereign territories such as regionality, region-building and cross-border regional co-operation. Until recently, the relationship between security and region-building was mostly one of either/or (Joenniemi 1997). However, the encounter in the Baltic Sea area between regionality and security policy appears to have inspired the latter – i.e. the high policy field *par excellence* – to develop a great number of rather distinct low policy features. One might even say that the Baltic Sea area is well on its way to becoming a *locus classicus* for the unfolding of an impressive array of security- and confidence-building schemes in the military field that cross old divides between members of Western and Eastern alliance systems and which also includes the neutral countries. Most notable have been such initiatives as joint military exercises and consultations, the creation of the Baltic Battalion (BALTBAT) and the Baltic naval unit (BALTRON), joint peace-keeping efforts in ex-Yugoslavia and a host of other measures under the concept of Partnership for Peace.

The Baltic Rim is thus giving evidence that security in post-Cold War Europe is 'increasingly defined, challenged and constructed locally and regionally' and through 'regional measures – undertaken by regional actors or targeted at regional conditions' (Möttölä in this volume). Somewhat ironically, the new unipolar world order with the United States being the ultimate 'pacifier' of Europe has led to increased regionalisation as the superpower acts with and through a network of selected allies willing and able to execute the 'new world order' policy and as states flock around the unipole in an attempt to impress on it that their region is of particular importance to world peace and stability (Heurlin in this volume).

Even the now assured prospect of NATO enlargement need not detract from the general trend towards security policy regionalisation in the Baltic Sea area, nor is it necessarily destined to change Russia's determination to be part of all the inclusive organisations and institutions that are promoting comprehensive security in the region, such as the CBSS and the OSCE. Under auspicious conditions, the process of NATO enlargement may even strengthen the regionalist features of the Baltic Sea area (Joenniemi 1997).

However, as the contributions to this volume by Sharp and Archer and Jæger would seem to indicate, the jury is still out on the likely effects of future security arrangements. The two non-NATO states Finland and Sweden have expressed concern that NATO enlargement could undermine security throughout the region as it might lead to new divisions between ins and outs. Archer and Jæger even surmise that there may be little incentive for the Baltic states to use subregional institutions to strengthen their security for fear that this would undermine their fundamental drive for NATO and EU membership.

Interestingly, the endeavours of the EU in the area are primarily intended to promote cross-border regional co-operation, e.g. through the Interreg programme (Jørgensen and Nielsen in this volume), and many CBSS and Nordic Council activities aim to strengthen functional networks, e.g. among universities and enterprises. It is also noteworthy that a typical low policy issue like the environment has turned out to be one of the most important arenas for rapidly growing Baltic co-operation in the 1990s (Sjöstedt in this volume).

Overcoming Obstacles

As noted earlier, public sentiments surrounding the outlook for further integration in the North European and Baltic Sea area have been prone to abrupt swings – from a sense of elation at the beginning of the 1990s towards a mood of despondency a few years later when it turned out that everything was not moving in a straight line from the bad old days towards a bright future.

Most of the recent pessimism, and in some quarters cynicism, stems from the uncomfortable realisation that developments are contradictory. Yes, 'the evil empire' has indeed tumbled, but among its ruins we detect not only glimpses of hope but also social and political malaise.

Much has been said and written about the problems of crime and corruption in some areas of the former Soviet Union and its dependencies. There has been a sense that some countries or regions are so mired in criminal behaviour, sleaze – to borrow a British expression – and mafia control, that they will remain beyond redemption for some time to come. Consequently, it is claimed, it is time to stop all lofty talk of meaningful integration between the old West and the old East.

But how one should view the unquestionable existence of crime in some parts of the NEBI area – and consequently the rather tenuous hold of the rule of law – is really a matter of historical perspective.

A number of observers would argue that the reason why there was little mentioning of crime and corruption in the Soviet era was that society itself was permeated by such criminal structures as the Party and the state apparatus (Davies 1996).[22] The issues of the rule of law and the need of democratically accountable institutions do not arise in totalitarian states because everybody is well aware that whatever legal protection may be on the books is ideological window dressing destined to be disregarded when it suits the purposes of those in power.

The very fact that crime and institutional deficiencies stand out today is therefore a demonstration that a presumption of the rule of law has been established, which is the first prerequisite for a successful fight against crime and corruption (Löfgren and Mannonen in this volume).

Concerning the extent of social malaise, it should come as no great surprise that sections of populations brought up under the old totalitarian regimes and having to bear the consequences of their economic, social and environmental failings have little trust in the rule of law. The struggle to raise societal conditions in some formerly communist-ruled regions to the level of, say, the Nordic countries is therefore bound to be a long one, and help in the shape of transnational police co-operation and exchange of administrative and institutional experience is called for. It would be unfair to expect decisive results after the few years which the new democratic governments have had at their disposal.

Another anomaly affecting some of the new democracies – not so much noted by the general public but the more so by planners and regional policy analysts – is the contradictory outcome of the demise of the communist central states in the NEBI area – most notably in the cases of Poland and the three Baltic republics.

At first glance, it appears ironic that the removal of Moscow's hegemony has led to an, from a Western perspective, out-moded build-up of traditional central states.

As of this writing, Poland is yet to pass an administrative and political reform paving a way for regional governments that can stand on their own feet. The absence of a functional administrative and politically autonomous regional level has also been noted by the European Commission in its recent opinion on Poland's capacity to participate in the EU's structural and cohesion policies (Commission 1997: 'Opinion on Poland's Application'). The problem is not only the lack of suitable counterparts in connection with the Union's future structural actions. The absence of strong regional actors is a general impediment to the development of cross-border regional co-operation in this part of the NEBI area.

Similarly, Estonia, Latvia and Lithuania seem to have embarked on a policy of nation-building reminiscent of processes that took place in nineteenth-century Western Europe, and often with results that strike foreign observers as decidedly ludicrous and counterproductive to cross-border co-operation.[23]

If NEBI-wide integration is to proceed and reach its main goal – which is to prevent the area from becoming a socio-economic and political backwater of Europe – such political expeditions into the past, unavoidable as they may be given the area's recent history, must cease.

Notes

1 Depending on the future orientation of the new German capital, Berlin and Brandenburg may be added. Little is said in the present volume about Western or North Atlantic Norden, i.e. the independent nation of Iceland and the home rule territories of the Faroe Islands and Greenland (both belonging to the Danish Realm), but they may well feature more prominently in future editions due to their age-old ties to the rest of Norden. The same may be the case for Scotland, which has recently been forging closer links with the Nordic countries in the field of regional development co-operation (Imset 1997). The basic principle is that areas outside the North European and Baltic core will be considered depending on their importance and contribution to NEBI integration.

2 Undeniably, the view that geographical peripherality may easily lead to socio-economic peripherality unless positive measures are undertaken to counteract it, is open to questioning. In a recent leading article, *The Economist*, commenting on the remarkable economic performance of Ireland, stated: 'Two things Ireland does show beyond doubt. First, small countries on the fringe of rich trading areas can prosper mightily. The curse of the periphery is a myth. Second, "globalisation", taken at the flood, is the fastest course to wealth' (*The Economist* 1997b). After reviewing a number of potential factors (such as the importance of Ireland's English language and the far-flung Irish Diaspora) behind Ireland's economic growth, a substantive article on Europe's 'Tiger economy' in the same issue concluded, however, that Ireland 'is more of a special case than its fans abroad realise.' Our point is not that individual regions within the NEBI area may not benefit from linking up with the global market with little or no concern for NEBI-wide cohesion, but that such a strategy may well lead to even wider disparities between advantaged and disadvantaged regions of the area than today.

3 Iver B. Neumann (1992: 67) has penned the following characteristic of a great many, rather speculative contributions to a vast 'Baltic' literature produced during the first few years of the 1990s: 'A number of these programmes took the Baltic Sea as their geographical base, and

were presented under labels such as the new *Hansa*, the Baltic Sea Region, Mare Balticum, the Euro-Baltic Region and the Scanno-Baltic Space. A tightly knit epistemic community of "Nordic" foreign policy intellectuals played a conspicuous role in producing the knowledge that was used to prop up these several ideas. Their battle-cry was that under the prevailing post-modern conditions, state sovereignty is relativised in favour of a new European mediaevalism where different political issues are settled on different political levels.'

4 However, even the good demographic news out of Russia may have a sinister explanation. The reason why life expectancy for men may have risen slightly in recent years could be that the most vulnerable young people have already died. A recent report (1997) to President Yeltsin suggests that if new health and education initiatives are not adopted soon, the population of Russia will decrease by as much as 30 million in the next 50 years (Specter 1997).

5 The defining characteristic of a federation is that the most important institutions managing shared government are directly elected by all citizens, as in Germany. Confederations differ from federations in one defining aspect: institutions managing shared rule consist of representatives of the unit governments and are not directly elected by all citizens, as in the European Union, whose most powerful institution is the Council. Federacies are structures of shared rule entered into by a large unit (in the NEBI area, Denmark and Finland) and smaller units (the Faroe Islands and Greenland and Åland, respectively). They differ from another possible construction – associated states – in one important respect: federacies cannot be dissolved except by agreement among all member units. This categorisation follows Ronald Watts as outlined in Hedegaard (1996). The Faroes' status as an autonomous territory within the Danish 'Unity of the Realm' dates back to 1948 – that of Greenland to 1979.

6 Together with Finland, Åland was conquered by Russia in 1809 and subsequently separated from Sweden. By the middle of the eighteen hundreds, the Åland archipelago was demilitarised through international agreement, and in 1921 the League of Nations gave it status as an autonomous territory under Finnish sovereignty (Barros 1968).

7 A case in point showing the importance of the historical legacy and the state of the civil society is Prunskiene's contribution to this volume. An excellent example of what consequences it may have to disregard history is the uncertain fate awaiting the 'Euroregion Schleswig' encompassing the Danish County of South Jutland and northern parts of Schleswig-Holstein. An acrimonious public debate on the Danish side has clearly demonstrated that old fears of a German take-over fuelled by the two Schleswig Wars of the nineteenth century and the experience of Danes under Prussian and later Nazi occupation are still very much a part of their collective consciousness (*North* 1997).

8 This interpretation is stated with admirable succintness by Norman Davies (1996), especially p. 900. In the same vein, Furet (1995: 34-35): 'La guerre de 1914 a tout changé à la vie de l'Europe, frontières, régimes, dispositions d'esprit, mæurs même. Elle a laboré si profond dans la plus brillante des civilisations modernes qu'elle n'en laisse aucun élément qui ne soit transformé. Elle marque le début de son déclin comme centre de la puissance du monde en même temps qu'elle inaugure ce siècle féroce dont nous sortons, tout empli de la violence suicidaire de ses nations et de ses régimes.'

9 See, for example, the assessment of Hiden and Salmon (1991: 118): 'The record of Baltic collaboration in the murder of their Jewish fellow citizens is a shameful one. Yet there is little in their previous records to suggest that it would have taken place without German instigation.'

10 Francois Furet (1995: 48) speaks of the desire of twentieth-century Europeans to 'reinvent' their political world in the wake of the horrors of World War I: 'ils ont voulu réinventer leur monde politique sur les deux grandes figures de la culture démocratique, l'universel et le national. Avec ces religions complémentaires et antagonistes (i.e. Bolshevism and Fascism, ed.), ils fabriqueront une catastrophe.'

11 Hitler was rather specific on this point: 'Why need we trouble to socialise banks and factories? We socialise human beings' (Davies 1996: 974). Similarly, the Soviet Party never tired of preaching the virtues of a 'new man' devoted to such edifying activities as 'Soviet love.'

12 Among the first sweeping acts of Nazi *Gleichschaltung* was the dissolution of state governments and parliaments and the abolition of the Weimar Republic Federal Council (*Reichsrat*).

The process was begun as early as March 1933 and culminated on 30 January 1934 with the Gesetz über den Neuausbau des Reiches, which in effect declared the federal principle of government that had been in existence since 1867 null and void. The states' sovereign rights were transferred to the Reich, and henceforth they were to be governed by *Statthalter* under the supervision of the Reich Minister of the Interior (Craig 1978).

In stark contravention of its 1922 and 1936 constitutions, the Soviet Union, with all its independent 'republics,' 'autonomous areas' etc., was in fact a thoroughly centralised empire, whose government did everything in its power to discourage unsupervised contacts between its citizens and regions and those of neighbouring states. As the Soviet Empire spread to Estonia, Latvia and Lithuania in 1940/1944-45 and on the Poland and the German Democratic Republic, Moscow's centralist regime was expanded and the tightest possible control imposed on the internal affairs and foreign relations of those countries.

Although a policy of territorial decentralisation of economic management was conducted over the years 1957-64, imperial interests reasserted themselves after Krushchev's fall and remained the dominant philosophy practically till the collapse of the Soviet Union (Kukk 1991).

13 Deportations from the three Baltic republics began immediately after their forced inclusion into the Soviet Union in early August 1940. It is estimated that the total number of those killed or deported in 1940-41 was 34,250 for Latvia, nearly 60,000 for Estonia and 75,000 for Lithuania. After the Soviet reoccupation of these countries following the German collapse, deportations resumed. The estimated number of deportees in 1944-52 is 124,000 for Estonia, 136,000 for Latvia and 245,000 for Lithuania. The deportees were allowed to return after 1956, but many had not survived their stay in Siberia (Hiden and Salmon 1991). Whether the subsequent influx of Russians and other people from the Soviet Union was part of a deliberate policy of Russification of Estonia and Latvia or just an unintended outcome of industrialisation policies is still moot. Rein Taagepera (1993: 82) maintains that 'imperialist considerations often outweighed the economic. Industrialization offered a path to colonize the country (Estonia) ... as a prelude to ... total assimilation' (see also p. 87).

14 See also the instructive case of the environmentally disastrous development of the Estonian oil-shale industry, which consumed over half of all industrial investments 1946-50, and whose intent was to turn Estonia into an economic annex of Leningrad (Kukk 1991).

15 Some figures on the social, cultural and economic development in pre-revolutionary Russia do seem to indicate that the country's potential was not as hopeless as claimed by the Bolsheviks – particularly not in its culturally and economically most advanced city, St Petersburg/Petrograd. For example, in the period 1900-1913, the output of Russia's heavy industry grew by 74.1 per cent. Perhaps more surprisingly, in 1915, 51 per cent of all children between 8 and 11 went to school, and 68 per cent of military conscripts could read and write (Heller and Nekrich 1982).

16 This calculation and the following comparing Åland with Estonia, Latvia and Lithuania must be taken with a grain of salt. They are only meant to indicate orders of magnitude as no reliable figures respecting purchasing power parities exist for 1995.

17 Which is not the same as saying that the German federal government has necessarily approved of cross-border initiatives by länder deemed to be infringing on Bonn's foreign policy prerogatives. See later concerning Björn Engholm's Baltic initiatives.

18 See below in this chapter. Also Engholm (1990: 58): 'In consequence of European integration, Schleswig-Holstein no longer considers itself a peripheral area of Europe but as Norden's South.'

19 By far the strongest protector of the perceived interests of pan-German 'nationhood' is the Federal Constitutional Court (*Bundesverfassungsgericht*), whose November 1993 decision on the constitutionality of the Maastricht Treaty has given rise to considerable controversy. For a highly critical view of the Court's disposition, see Weiler (1995).

20 For an explanation of the concept of 'region-building,' see Lindström (1996).

21 See Stålvant (1996) for a survey of the most important actors.

22 It will be recalled that following the failed August 1991 coup, Boris Yeltsin forced Mikhail Gorbachev to dissolve the Communist Party with reference to it being a 'criminal organisation.'

[23] For example, many Western visitors to the Baltic Republics are puzzled at having to wait at borders controls for hours while the personnel is visibly engaged in such activities as drinking coffee or playing chess.

References

Amin, Ash and Thrift, Nigel (1995). 'Living in the Global' in Amin, A. and Thrift, N. (eds.). *Globalization, Institutions and Regional Development.* New York, Oxford University Press.

Barros, J. (1968). *The Åland Islands Question: Its settlement by the League of Nations.* New Haven.

Borsos, Julianna and Erkkilä, Mika (1995a). 'Regional Integration in the Baltic Rim: FDI and Trade-based Integration in the Triangle of Finland, Estonia and St Petersburg,' *ETLA Discussion Papers*:539, Helsinki.

Borsos, Julianna and Erkkilä, Mika (1995b). 'Foreign Direct Investment and Trade Flows Between the Nordic Countries and the Baltic States,' *ETLA Discussion Papers*:540, Helsinki.

Commission of the European Communities (1996a). 'Baltic Sea Region Initiative,' Communication from the Commission, SEC(96) 608 final, Brussels.

Commission of the European Communities (1996b). *First Cohesion Report.* 06.11.1996. COM(96) 542 final, Brussels.

Commission of the European Communities (1997). 'Agenda 2000: Summary and Conclusions of the Opinions of the Commission Concerning the Applications for Membership to the European Union Presented by the Candidate Countries' (DOC/97/8) and 'Commission Opinion on Poland's Application for Membership of the European Union' (DOC/97/16). Brussels, 15 July 1997.

Conquest, Robert (1990). *The Great Terror: A Re-Assessment.* London.

Council of the Baltic Sea States (1996). *Cross-border Cooperation in the Baltic Sea States Region: Summary Report.* Karlskrona, The Baltic Institute.

Craig, Gordon A. (1978). *Germany 1866-1945.* New York, Oxford University Press.

Davies, Norman (1996). *Europe: A History.* New York, Oxford University Press.

The Economist (1997a).'Russia's Regions: Fiefs and Chiefs,' 25-31 January, pages 27-28.

The Economist (1997b). 'Ireland Shines' and 'Green is Good,' 17-23 May, pages 15-16 and 23-26

Engholm, Björn (1990). 'Mare Balticum,' *Nord Revy* 1990:1.

Eskelinen, Heikki and Snickars, Folke (eds.) (1995). *Competitive European Peripheries.* Berlin, Springer-Verlag.

Furet, Francois (1995). *Le Passé d'une illusion: essai sur l'idée communiste au XXe siècle.* Paris, Robert Laffont/Calmann-Lévy.

Gamble, Andrew and Payne, Anthony (eds.) (1996). *Regionalism and World Order.* London, Macmillan.

Hedegaard, Lars (1996). '"Glocalisation": Wave of the Future' (interview with Ronald Watts), *Nord Revy* 1996:5/6

Heller, Michel and Nekrich, Aleksandr (1982). *L'utopie au pouvoir: Histoire de l'U.R.S.S. de 1917 à nos jours.* Paris, Calmann-Lévy.

Hiden, John and Salmon, Patrick (1991). *The Baltic Nations and Europe: Estonia, Latvia and Lithuania in the Twentieth Century.* London and New York, Longman.

Illeris, Sven (1995). 'Peripherality and European Integration: The Challenge Facing the Nordic Countries,' pages 115-30 in Eskelinen, Heikki and Snickars, Folke (eds.). *Competitive European Peripheries.* Berlin, Springer-Verlag.

Imset, Øystein (1997). 'Scotland, Nordics Join Forces in Regional Development,' *North* 1997:1, pages 8-9.

Joenniemi, Pertti (ed.) (1993). *Cooperation in the Baltic Sea Region.* Washington, Taylor & Francis.

Joenniemi, Pertti (1997). 'Security and Regionality: Post-Enlargement Options around the Baltic Sea.' Background paper for a seminar organised by the Lund Academic Officer's Society and the Lund Association for Foreign Affairs, 16 May, 1997.

Johansson, T. and Stålvant, Carl-Einar (1997). 'The Twinning of Cities: A Code for Neighbourhood Cooperation in the Baltic Sea Area?' in Wellmann, Christian (ed.). *From Town to Town: Local Authorities as Transnational Actors.* Münster, Lit Verlag.

Kukk, Kalev (1991). 'On Economic and Geographical Development of Estonia in 1945-1990,' *Publications of the Estonian Geographical Society.*6.

Lieven, Anatol (1993). *The Baltic Revolution: Estonia, Latvia, Lithuania and the Path to Independence.* New Haven and London, Yale University Press.

Lindström, Bjarne (1992). 'Nationalstaten, regionerna och det framtida Europa. På väg mot en ny integrationsmodell' in *Regionalpolitikken utfordres.* Copenhagen, NordREFO 1992:2.

Lindström, Bjarne (1996) (with Lars Hedegaard and Noralv Veggeland). *Regional Policy and Territorial Supremacy: Nordic Region Building and Institutional Change in the Wake of European Integration.* Copenhagen, NordREFO 1996:2.

Lindström, Bjarne (1997). 'Towards a Post-Sovereign Political Landscape?' Paper presented at the NARF seminar, University of Greenland, 20-22 March.

Lundqvist, Lars and Persson, Lars Olof (eds.) (1995). *Baltic Regions and Baltic Links.* Copenhagen, NordREFO 1995:2.

Neumann, Iver B. (ed.) (1992). *Hva skjedde med Norden?* Olso, Europaprogrammet and Cappelen.

NordREFO (1993). *Impact of the Development of the Nordic Countries on Regional Development and Spatial Organisation in the Community.* (A study undertaken on behalf of the Commission of the European Communities, Directorate-General for Regional Policies). Copenhagen.

NordREFO (1994). *Välfärdsstatens framtid och regionerna.* Copenhagen, NordREFO 1994:5

North (1997). 'Know-Nothing Nationalism,' *North.*1997:1.

Putnam, Robert D. (1993) (with Robert Leonardi and Raffaella Y. Nanetti). *Making Democracy Work: Civic Traditions in Modern Italy.* Princeton, New Jersey, Princeton University Press.

Saether, Arild, Schmidt-Nissen, Nicola and Lorenz, Kerstin (1997). 'The Role of the Region in the European Union: The Future of the Committee of the Regions,' pages 87-109 in Peschel, Karin (ed.). *Regional Growth Policy Within the Framework of European Integration.* Heidelberg, Physica-Verlag.

Scharpf, Fritz W. (1990). 'Regionalisierung des europäischen Raums. Die Zukunft der Bundesländer im Spannungsfeld zwischen EG, Bund und Kommunen' in von Alemann, Ulrich, Heinze, Rolf G. und Hombach, Bodo (Hg.): *Die Kraft der Region: Nordrhein-Westfalen in Europa.* Bonn, Verlag J.H.W. Dietz.

Specter, Michael (1997). 'Russian Demography: A Case for Dostoyevsky,' *International Herald Tribune,* 9 June.

Statistical Office of Estonia (1997). 'Press Release on National Account.' Tallinn, 29 April.

Stålvant, Carl-Einar (1996). *Actors around the Baltic Sea: An Inventory of Infrastructures: Initiatives, Agreements and Actors.* Stockholm, Ministry of Foreign Affairs.

Taagepera, Rein 1993). *Estonia: Return to Independence.* Boulder, Westview Press.

Tsoukalis, Loukas (1993). *The New European Economy: The Politics and Economics of Integration.* New York, Oxford University Press.

Törnquist, Gunnar (1997). *Människa, teknik och territorium.* Copenhagen, NordREFO 1997:4.

Vartiainen, Perttu (1997). 'The Advantages of Baltic Cities.' Paper presented at the Council of Europe's conference 'The Challenges Facing European Society with the Approach of the Year 2000: Strategies for Sustainable Development of the Northern States in Europe.' Helsinki, 22-23 May.

VASAB 2010 (1994). *Vision and Strategies around the Baltic Sea 2010: Towards a Framework for Spatial Development in the Baltic Sea Region.* Copenhagen.

Veggeland, Noralv (1994). *Regionbygging over grenser i det nye Europa: aktører, arenaer og regimer.* Copenhagen, NordREFO 1994:6.

Weiler, Joseph H.H. (1995). 'The State "über alles": Demos, Telos and the German Maastricht Decision,' *Harvard Jean Monnet Working Paper* 1995:7.

Wheeler-Bennett, J.W. (1967). *The Nemesis of Power: The German Army in Politics 1918-1945.* London, Macmillan and St. Martin's Press (first edition: 1953).

Part I

Economic Integration

2 Core Elements of Successful Reform in the Baltic Rim Countries

Klaus Schrader and Claus-Friedrich Laaser

The Baltic Rim as a Northern European Integration Area

Since the early 1990s the Baltic Sea has been increasingly transformed into an inland sea within the European Union (EU). As a result of the treaty establishing the European Economic Space, important parts of the EU's Single Market Programme were extended to the EFTA countries in 1993. This process continued through a second northern enlargement of the EU with Sweden and Finland joining the Union in 1995. Even the eastern and south-eastern Baltic Rim countries may become part of the EU in a few years. After the signing of an association agreement between Poland and the EU in 1991 (a so-called Europe Agreement) and the three Baltic states Estonia, Latvia, and Lithuania catching up with Poland in this respect in 1995, the integration of the Baltic Rim economies into the European Single Market is close to completion.

What makes the difference between the new Northern members of the EU and the potential candidates in the South and East of the Baltic Rim is the fact that the latter belong to the group of economies in transition from centrally administered to market economies. The advantages of the EU option[1] for the transforming countries are obvious: the EU may serve as an anchor of political stability and ensure political independence; access to the European market and integration into the European division of labour promise welfare gains; last but not least substantial transfers from the EU distribution system may be expected to flow into Poland and the Baltic economies (Tangermann 1995; 1996). In view of these prospects it is not surprising that not only Poland but also the three newly independent Baltic states with their close historical ties to the Western European economies try to participate in the European integration process.[2]

But the reform countries on the southern and eastern Baltic Rim face the challenge of reintegrating into a world economy which has undergone fundamental structural change in the past decades. Needless to say, the realisation of the EU option depends on a number of preconditions which the Baltic states have to fulfil. They include, first of all, the creation of a suitable economic policy framework for a market economy, thorough macroeconomic stabilisation and effective steps towards structural change. The reforms necessary for creating the legal framework of a functioning market economy may be viewed as the basic precondition for carrying through a drastic but necessary structural change in the economy. This process must lay the foundation for a sound competitive economy which should enable Poland and the Baltic states to successfully reintegrate into the world economy.

One should, however, distinguish between the core elements of a functioning market economy on the one hand and the formal preconditions for joining the EU as full member on the other hand. The latter have been elaborated in detail by the European Commission in its White Paper of 1995 (KOM 1995a; 1995b).[3]

The focus of our analysis will be the core preconditions for setting up a functioning market economy in the reform countries at the southern and eastern shores of the Baltic, which is indispensable if they want to build up internationally competitive economic structures.[4] We shall also examine to what extent Poland and the Baltic states exhibit serious bottlenecks in complying with these preconditions in addition to the countries' status quo and prospective relationship with the EU.

Core Elements of a Functioning Market Order

As an analytical tool we shall use a catalogue of criteria based on the essential elements of a liberal market economy. The catalogue refers to the basic paradigms of a market economy and is neither oriented towards the actual conditions in Western economies nor, as already mentioned, towards the precepts of the European Commission's White Paper. Our criteria are: (i) the legal base and the rule of law, (ii) the state of private property, (iii) competition rules and liberty of the markets, (iv) macroeconomic stabilisation and (v) economic openness. This catalogue serves two purposes: On the one hand it defines an ideal economic policy framework of a market economy ('how it should be'), on the other hand it is an instrument to determine the current state of the reform process ('how it is'). By comparing ideal and reality it becomes possible to identify reform deficits and to develop adequate reform proposals.

The Legal Base

The indispensable prerequisite of a functioning market is a clearly defined and properly working legal order which ensures basic human rights and freedoms; protects individuals against political arbitrariness; guarantees the market order itself; and ensures the enforceability of claims from private contracts.

Such a legal order serves as a mechanism to formulate and enforce the rules which are necessary to stabilise a society. Both the legal order and the complementary enforcement mechanism are necessary for the working of a market economy, because producing goods and services and exchanging them in the market involve bargaining and enforcing contracts. In a market economy the state thus provides and enforces a legal system as a public good which is a prerequisite to the production of private goods. A market system can only work, if engaging in economic activities is guaranteed by law without any discrimination and if the rule of law prevails.[5] To actively take part in production, contracting and exchange, individuals must be free from coercion. The legal system must guarantee basic human liberty not only formally but also in daily practice. For this purpose there must be strong public authorities who can provide proper safeguards. However, in exercising their natural monopoly on power, public authorities themselves have to be controlled in order to avoid political arbitrariness.

Control of the basic legal and state order itself is accomplished by two mechanisms. The first relates to political freedom and political competition, the second ensures control of power by division of powers. Concerning political freedom, a liberal democratic system seems to be the one that is most consistent with a constitutional state and a market economy. The democratic order is itself tied to the rule of law and has to safeguard minority rights (e.g. Hoppmann 1994; Watrin 1994). With respect to the second issue, the legal order must protect the individual from political arbitrariness. This is most easily obtained if the constitutional order provides for power-sharing with mutual control, if the legal system is independent of government and parliamentary patronising and if administrative and legislative decisions are subject to judicial examination (Hayek 1953: 50 ff.; 1968: 5 f.). For this purpose, independent courts are indispensable.

At the micro-level, the legal system must also guarantee the liberty of private contracting, which constitutes the essence of a market order. A mechanism of sanctions is necessary to enforce contractual fidelity. That is the task of civil law and the corresponding court system.

Thus the legal base is axiomatic to a functioning market order. It should be noted, however, that such an order cannot be created at short notice because the underlying way of thinking must be learned by the members of the political and juridical institutions. A sound legal tradition needs time to develop.

The latter aspect is of major importance when assessing the actual development in the Baltic Rim reform countries. After winning back independence, all the Baltic states adopted new constitutions that established a pluralistic democracy and a system of checks and balances. In contrast to the other Soviet successor states, the Baltic states could profit from their historical inter-war experience when rebuilding their legal systems. They did not have to introduce a legal infrastructure or legal instruments completely new to them. Latvia, e.g., re-established the constitution of 1922 and the civil code of 1937. However, the new institutions lack the necessary routine and effectiveness, most notably the administrative and judicial experience of a long-established civil service. In particular, the state administrations and the court systems are not yet adequate or reliable, which makes it difficult for citizens to enforce their legal claims. It will certainly require a new generation of public servants, judges and lawyers – more trustworthy than the old generation educated under the Soviet system – to handle the new legal instruments. Under these circumstances, many legal provisions will only be enforced to a limited extent during the coming years. Despite these shortcomings, the legal base of each of the Baltic states appears to be strong enough to guarantee political stability (Schrader 1997b).

In Poland the basic elements of a legal order have been also introduced in principle. However, the reservations concerning a smooth working of the legal and political system are valid for Poland as well. A special feature of the Polish legal system contributing to uncertainty is the fact that the constitution is still only a provisional arrangement, whose main problem lies in the incomplete division of powers between president, government and parliament. This has already caused some disputes about competencies.

The Property Question

A consistent market order needs to define the role of private property. Private ownership – especially of the means of production, but also of real estate – is a necessary precondition for the efficient resource allocation in an economy.

Private property means that the proprietor enjoys of a bundle of rights. He has the exclusive right to use and transfer his property and to realise returns guaranteed by law. In addition the stability of the property rights structure must be ensured. To serve this end, property rights have to be allocated exclusively and consistently. Under these conditions, the proprietor has incentives to allocate his property efficiently to the various opportunities of usage and to spend parts of his return for the maintenance of his assets (Coase 1960: 2 ff.; Demsetz 1975: 23 ff.; Schüller 1988: 168 f.).

In a market economy, property rights serve as an incentive for the individual to make rational use of his disposable resources. The function and utility of property rights can be best demonstrated by considering the effect of their absence in the former centrally planned economies. When state or social property dominates, the incentives normally provided by property rights are largely missing because the user's property rights are severely restricted and the user's income is independent of the realised returns. In the absence of proper incentives, resource users will not care much about the efficient allocation and maintenance of public property. Where dominate, society had to refer to altruism in order to keep intact the economy's productive potential. Altruism, however, is a rather scarce commodity in any social relationship. The case of the centrally planned economies in Eastern Europe reveals the disastrous effects of the dominance of public property: With no regard for costs or the maintenance of the industrial substance, they tried to keep the production running. The result was decline and a continuous consumption of the basic capital stock.

Even in a market economy there are several cases where private property rights have to be restricted. In instances where the public welfare is at stake, expropriation may be appropriate, but because the term public welfare lacks operability, the entire market system could be unhinged if its invocation – combined with the right of court appeal and compensation – is not constrained by law to the exceptional case (Hayek 1971: 281 f.). It also seems justified to restrict private property rights to avoid negative externalities which would infringe on the private property rights of others. Although private property must dominate in a market economy, a certain share of public property is necessary to provide restrictively defined genuine public goods.[6]

This suggests, in conclusion, that the private share of national productive property is an important indicator of the degree of capitalism and therefore decisive for a country's wealth. It therefore seems relevant for an evaluation of transition economies to what extent the formation and free disposition of private property are really guaranteed and by what kind of measures the transformation of public into private property is proposed or realised. In the transformation debate, the question of privatisation is usually split into 'small' and 'large' privatisation, which refers to either small entities in the service and handicraft sector or to large entities mostly in industry. Privatisation of former state property is indeed crucial to the transformation process. It should be added, however, that the stress lies on the creation of private property rights, because in many cases newly founded private enterprises may substitute public enterprises that are incapable of being reorganised..

It is not surprising that the privatisation of large state-owned enterprises poses one of the severest challenges to reform policy in the Baltic Rim reform countries – as is the case in most transition economies. In the majority of these countries the privatisation process has become a never-ending story due to the influence of branch ministries, old management structures, trade unions or distribution policy, to mention just some of the major obstacles.

Nevertheless at least the Estonian efforts have proved that large-scale privatisation is not necessarily a mission impossible but an excellent opportunity to write a success story. After a less successful trial and error process, it was decided to offer state enterprises for international tenders and to establish the Estonian Privatisation Agency as the sole institution responsible for the whole privatisation process. This approach followed the German Treuhand model and resulted in the privatisation of the majority stakes in about 95 per cent of industrial enterprises by the summer 1996. In addition even the privatisation of transport and public utility enterprises, typical areas of public production, are planned.

In view of this successful development, the Latvian government started to imitate the Estonian privatisation process in 1994, but after wasting plenty of time on half-hearted efforts, Latvian privatisation is still lagging way behind.

In Lithuania the government has tried to leave the dead end of domestic voucher privatisation but the mixture of Estonian privatisation methods, the exclusion of 'strategic' enterprises from privatisation and the still influential branch ministries is not paving the way for substantial privatisation.

After a paralysing discussion, the Polish mass privatisation programme finally got under way in 1995. Otherwise it would have only been a question of time before the Polish economy would have been privatised by the formation of new private enterprises (Schrader and Laaser 1997: 13 ff.; Schrader, 1997a).

It can be concluded that the formation of private property is progressing in the Baltic Rim reform countries. But in most of these countries the missing political will to introduce this core element of a market economy without any compromises has decidedly slowed down the economic catching-up process.

The Liberty of the Markets and Competition Rules

The incentive and control mechanism of private property rights can guide the individuals' decisions to allocate resources and efforts if the price mechanism serves as an information and co-ordination system. Free markets are characterised by individual planning and sovereign decisions by sellers and buyers: It is up to the sellers to calculate the prices of their goods according to the (opportunity) costs incurred, and it is up to the buyers to determine the relevant price of their demand according to their valuation of individual utility functions. The price mechanism then co-ordinates supply and demand at an equilibrium price. In this way a system of relative prices emerges which carries information about the relative scarcities of goods and services and helps to allocate the available resources efficiently (Eucken 1952: 254; Luckenback 1986: 111 ff.). The famous notion of the invisible hand of the price mechanism (Adam Smith) which is responsible for the decentral co-ordination of the economy can work only as long as state authorities relinquish their power to restrict the sovereignty of sellers and buyers. The experience of the Eastern European socialist economies clearly demonstrates that a central system of administered prices cannot realise an equilibrium of supply and demand in the various markets. The exchange of information by supply and demand through the price mechanism cannot be substituted by a central mechanism – neither quantitatively nor qualitatively. A central planning authority is not able to collect or work up a comparable amount of information. This is even more valid if dynamic aspects of growth, structural change and investment are considered.[7] For a transformation towards a market economy, a system of relative prices free of public and administrative interventions is indispensable.

To make the price mechanism work, every potential supplier must be permitted to offer goods and services whenever he assumes to possess a comparative advantage, i.e., on the one hand, the entry to the markets must be guaranteed without any exception (freedom of trade), on the other hand, suppliers and buyers must be free to bargain mutual contracts according to their individual utility and cost considerations (contractual freedom) (Hayek 1967: 29; Eucken 1952: 278). Complementary to the free access to markets is the market exit of marginal suppliers, which must be ensured to prevent resources being bound in suboptimal utilisation. This end can be served by a properly working bankruptcy regulation (Gröner 1984: 253 ff.; Hax 1985: 89 ff.).

Already by opting for the freedom of trade, the indispensability of openness and competition has been acknowledged. The more an economic system is bound to the principle of competition, i.e. the more the openness of the markets is guaranteed and the abuse of economic power is chastised, the more efficient the allocation of a country's resources will be. Competition serves as a combined incentive and control mechanism which ensures efficient cost control and maximum productivity (Röpke 1957: 442) because competition forces enterprises and individuals to permanently look for new products, processes and locations of production – a behaviour which is a typical feature of a growing economy. In the view of von Hayek (1968: 3 ff.), competition can be characterised as a discovery procedure.

Competition, however, is a permanently endangered good because suppliers often tend to arrange agreements or to form cartels restricting competition. In most of the Western countries rules exist which prohibit such agreements and the abuse of economic power. The institutionalised control of competition, however, differs, considerably from country to country corresponding to the criteria which define the market dominance of an enterprise, the abuse of economic power, the activities which can be viewed as restricting competition and even the underlying concepts of competition.[8] It should be noted that a complementary (and in the absence of experienced institutions of competition policy: a substitutive) mechanism is provided by an opening of the domestic markets to foreign competitors, which appears to be the better instrument to stimulate competition. Openness means that domestic monopolies will at least be subject to foreign competition. Whereas it takes some time to introduce institutionalised domestic competition control, foreign competition would be effective immediately.

Of course it has been widely discussed in competition theory and policy that a number of specific markets may not be suited to be governed by competition because the price mechanism and the competitive principle may not work properly. One of the most prominent cases is that of the natural monopoly, which must be publicly regulated. It can be shown, however, that most sectors exempted from competitive governance can be spared from public control if markets are opened up for substitutional or monopolistic competition, even from abroad. Even in those cases where good theoretical grounds for regulation may exist (because the natural monopoly seems to be protected from all kinds of competition by the existence of sunk costs at the moment), public regulation may become redundant over time. The practical experience in Western countries with deregulating markets being exempted from competition for long times clearly shows that the bulk of long-term regulations has proved counterproductive.[9]

The prices of goods and services have been substantially liberalised in all of the Baltic Rim reform countries. Some price controls, however, have remained in force, namely in branches like energy, transport, telecommunication, housing and public services, where state monopolies or special market access regulations exist. On the labour and capital markets the pricing is free with the exception of minimum wages and regulations affecting state enterprises. This means that a further liberalisation of the labour markets is closely connected with the progress of the privatisation process. This is also true for the commercial banking systems because in all reform countries the state still holds majority or minority stakes in the most important commercial banks.

None of the reform countries has established a politically independent competition authority with exclusive responsibility for competition policy and the protection of competition. The competition laws even permit exemptions from the general ban on cartels: cartel agreements can be approved if they serve goals like improving international competitiveness, product quality or market supply. It should be obvious that such rules contain the germ for an abuse of discretion.

Whereas the reform countries' entry barriers to markets for goods and services are comparable to those in Western countries, their legislation on market exit generally does not conform with the requirements of a market economy. Especially in Latvia bankruptcy seems to be regarded as a destructive element, and it is not realised that bankruptcy offers the opportunity of an efficiency-improving reorganisation of the economy. Poland is the only reform country where the liquidation of small and medium-sized state enterprises has developed into a successful privatisation method (Schrader and Laaser 1997: 26 ff.; Schrader 1997a).

Macroeconomic Stabilisation

The macroeconomic stabilisation task in the course of the reform process is, among other things, a matter of regulating and stabilising the monetary system. The necessity of providing a stable monetary order stems from the fact that the price mechanism can play its allocational function only if relative prices are not distorted by price level fluctuations (Eucken 1952: 256 f.). It is a widely held view that this task can best be performed by an independent central bank which is constrained to pursue the goal of price level stability.[10]

Another public task is to provide sound financing of the public expenditures. A restrictive definition of public tasks helps to avoid significant expenditures like sectoral subsidies which only cause welfare losses through a distorted allocation. In addition the revenues must be based on a simple system of taxes and fees which the taxpayers do not regard as disincentives to work.

Other elements of a sound fiscal policy are limitations on public liabilities and a strict separation of the state budget from the authority to print money. If no control of the expenditures exists and the printing press is abused to finance the budget deficit, monetary stability will be considerably jeopardised. In view of the close connection between a sound fiscal policy and monetary stability, it is important to prohibit the financing of the state budget by central bank credits. It is especially for this reason that the independence of a central bank obligated to pursue monetary stability is crucial to macroeconomic stability.

Macroeconomic stabilisation has been initiated in all of the Baltic Rim reform countries. In Latvia and Estonia the introduction of national currencies has been rather successful with regard to monetary stabilisation, at least compared to other Soviet successor states although the approaches are different. Latvia, the Baltic state with the lowest annual inflation rate, decided to establish an independent central bank solely obliged to keeping price stability. Estonia preferred a currency board system, having tied the Estonian Crown to the German Mark. The shortcoming of this model is that the central bank cannot serve as a lender of last resort because it lacks the necessary instruments to control money supply. Nevertheless the introduction of the Estonian model in Lithuania in 1994 resulted in a considerable improvement in monetary stability. Before this radical change, the Lithuanian central bank was not obliged to pursue price stability and lacked independence from political lobbyists. The Polish central bank is still marred by this flaw: a higher degree of political independence is the missing element in the central bank law.

With respect to fiscal discipline, it is again Estonia which stands out from the other reform countries. In recent years Estonia's efforts to balance the state budget have been quite successful although in 1996 the problem arose that local governments increased their deficits significantly. In Latvia, Lithuania and Poland the disciplinary pressure of the IMF was necessary to stop extensive deficit spending. In all the reform countries, the shortcomings of the tax administrations pose a serious threat to fiscal stability. Although the countries have tried to improve the effectiveness of their tax administrations, it has not yet been possible to enforce the new Western-style tax systems (Schrader and Laaser 1997: 33 ff.; Schrader 1997a).

The Open Economy

The reform countries' degree of devotion to integrating their economies into the European Single Market and the world market may be determined by the degree to which their national economies are opened to foreign competition and tied to the international division of labour. Opening markets is the essence of integration.

The advantages of openness are evident: The free exchange of goods and services widens domestic bottlenecks and provides specialisation gains from trade; the unrestricted mobility of capital and labour enhances the spatial allocation of resources; in the end free trade guarantees an optimal supply; being involved in the international competition widens the scope for the disposal of scarce capital goods as a prerequisite for economic development, and domestic production keeps in contact with technical progress and entrepreneurial and managerial know-how. Domestic competition is enhanced and forces productivity gains (e.g. Haberler 1954; Baldwin 1992). Moreover, the reform countries' participation in the international division of labour makes it easier to find a market-conforming path of structural change and to bust the old monopoly structures. The new trade relations are qualitatively superior compared with the former intra-COMECON and intra-Soviet trade, which did not follow the principle of comparative advantages.

Openness means that the markets have to be opened for imports, which implies dispensing with tariff and non-tariff import barriers and policies of import substitution. The latter would require significant subsidies which would burden the state budget. This is also true of the export business. Tariffs, quotas and loans represent the old autarchy regime and can only result in a non-competitive economic structure which does not correspond to the real comparative advantages.

In addition the enterprises must be permitted to organise their foreign trade activities as they see fit. Any kind of foreign trade monopoly would be counter-productive.

A necessary element of foreign trade liberalisation on the monetary side is the free convertibility of the national currency and unrestricted private currency transactions. In this way citizens may independently decide on their participation in foreign trade and capital transfers, and domestic sellers and buyers may obtain undisturbed information about relative scarcities through the world market prices.

Finally, the reform countries are dependent on foreign direct investment to renew their physical capital and to acquire technical and entrepreneurial human capital from the capitalist countries. Therefore an attractive legal setting for foreign direct investments is indispensable.

Regarding foreign trade policy in the Baltic Rim reform countries, the picture is again diverse. The Estonian trade arrangement comes close to a perfect free trade regime whereas the other Baltic Rim countries maintain import tariff systems aimed at protecting various sectors of the economy. Especially agriculture is protected by a wall of high import tariffs. In some cases even quotas complete this protectionist picture.

Concerning convertibility, at least current account transactions are not restricted in the reform countries. But without any exception, the Baltic Rim reformers obviously do not trust in the quality of their reform policy to the extent that they would dare to give up controls of capital account transactions. The same is true of the exchange rate systems, none of which will dispense with exchange rates fixed to an anchor currency or currency basket.

In general, the legislation on foreign direct investment does not vary from the corresponding legislation in most of the other Central and Eastern European reform countries. There are no prohibitive approval or registration procedures, the repatriation of profits and incomes is not restricted, investments are protected by law and international agreements and wholly foreign-owned companies are permitted. Difficulties can arise when foreign investors intend to acquire land and other real estate. In Estonia no serious restrictions exist, in Latvia and Poland the acquisition of real estate can be prohibitively restricted while in Lithuania there is no better alternative than the 99 years option (Schrader and Laaser 1997: 44 ff.; Schrader 1997a).

Conclusions

When going ahead in reforming their legal and economic framework, the Baltic Rim states should be aware that the diverse features of a market economy as described above are mutually interdependent and thus exhibit certain network characteristics. This could easily be demonstrated if in a hypothetical experiment any one of the criteria were to be taken away and the interaction of the remaining were to be studied.[11]

Of course the practical implementation of the various measures may require compromises, and a certain sequencing of reforms may be dictated by actual bottlenecks whose relevance may vary from country to country, but in essence the mutual interdependency of all the elements of a market order gives clear advice in terms of reform strategy: Gaps left open due to actual shortcomings have to be closed as soon as possible. What is called for is a consistent and systemic approach.

Even if the individual core elements of successful reforms and the whole programme taken together may look rather ambitious, it should be clear that any attempt by the reform countries to integrate into the European Union must be based on a strict reform concept as described above. Welfare gains from integrating into the European Union's Single Market can only be absorbed if the future applicants from the Baltic Rim have done their homework in developing their own market economy. Prosperity begins at home. This conclusion may be drawn from the different integration stories of the Mediterranean countries Greece, Portugal, and Spain, who joined the Union during the so-called southern enlargement in the eighties. While Spain and later on Portugal tried to enhance their competitiveness by reforming and opening up markets in the course of accession, Greece largely relied on the Union's transfers and neglected reforms even as a member state. Whereas Spain and Portugal were able to make use of the chances of integration and managed to catch up after becoming member states, Greece fell behind.[12] This should be a lesson to all applicants for European Union membership, especially for those at the Baltic Rim.

Notes

1 For the transforming countries it could be a complementary integration strategy to re-intensify their trade relationships with the Community of Independent States (CIS), now on a competitive basis. The geographical location of Poland and the Baltic states and their experience in doing business with the CIS might enable them to serve as a bridge between Western Europe and the CIS, especially the Russian Federation. But the very slow transformation process and the lack of political stability in the Russian Federation make this option appear a long-term perspective, at least for the time being.

2 For details, see Laaser and Schrader (1992: 191).

3 Cf. also Baldwin (1994) and Hare (1996).

4 To be sure, having a market economy is also a precondition for the accession of any candidate country as stated by Art. 3a and 102a EGV, but the criteria are not nearly as clearly defined as for the other basic precondition, the realisation of a democratic constitutional state (Schrader and Laaser 1994: 147).

5 This view has not only been put forward by classical economists and philosophers like Aristotle, Adam Smith and John Locke (cf. Mises 1927), but also by the proponents of the modern constitutional economics like Buchanan and Hayek.

6 For the definition of public goods in terms of welfare economics, see Samuelson (1954: 387). Without any constraint, the public sector would tend to grow beyond the share suggested by efficiency considerations as is the case in many advanced and aged market economies. For public interventions via regulations in the case of Germany, cf., e.g., Soltwedel et al (1986); Boss, Laaser, Schatz et al. (1996). For an actual assessment of the degree of state intervention by subsidies, see Boss and Rosenschon (1997).

7 It is especially the failure of preserving and augmenting the socialist economies' capital stock and thus production potential that falsifies Oskar Lange's hypothesis of a perfect imitation of the price mechanism through the concept of 'competitive socialism' (cf. Giersch 1961: 165 ff.).

8 See, e.g., the so-called 'Hoppmann-Kantzenbach-controversy' in German competition policy, where Kantzenbach's concept of 'optimal intensity of competition' was challenged by Hoppmann's concept of 'competitive freedom' (Kantzenbach 1966; Hoppmann 1978).

9 See Soltwedel et al. (1986); Laaser (1991); Boss, Laaser, Schatz et al. (1996).

10 For an overview, see Clausen and Willms (1993).

11 For all the elements of the catalogue, this exercise has been performed in Schrader and Laaser (1992: 64 ff.) and Schrader (1997a).

12 See Schrader and Laaser (1994) and Laaser (1997) for an analysis of the southern enlargement.

References

Baldwin, Richard E. (1992). 'Are Economists' Traditional Trade Policy Views Still Valid?' *Journal of Economic Literature* 30:2, pages 804-29.

Baldwin, Robert E. (1994). *Towards an integrated Europe*. London.

Boss, A. and Rosenschon, A. (1997). 'Subventionen in der Bundesrepublik Deutschland – Bestandsaufnahme und Bewertung.' Institut für Weltwirtschaft an der Universität Kiel, Kieler Arbeitspapiere:793.

Boss, A., Laaser, C.-F., Schatz, K.-W., Bode, E., Böhme, H., Horn, E.-J., Rosenschon, A., Sander, B., Schmidt, R., Sichelschmidt, H., Stehn, J., Wolf, H. (1996). *Deregulierung in Deutschland. Eine empirische Analyse.* Kieler Studien:275. Tübingen.

Clausen, V., M. Willms (1993). 'Unabhängigkeit der Zentralbank,' *WiSt*:12, pages 605-10.

Coase, R. H. (1960). 'The Problem of Social Cost,' *The Journal of Law and Economics*:3, pages 1-44.

Demsetz, H. (1975). 'Toward a Theory of Property Rights,' pages 23-36 in Manne, H.G. (ed.). *The Economics of Legal Relationships: Readings in the Theory of Property Rights.* St. Paul.

Eucken, W. (1952). *Grundsätze der Wirtschaftspolitik.* Tübingen.

Giersch, H. (1961). *Allgemeine Wirtschaftspolitik*, Bd. 1, Grundlagen. Wiesbaden.

Glismann, H.-H. and Schrader, K. (1991). 'Zur ordnungspolitischen Situation in den Ländern Osteuropas,' *Die Weltwirtschaft*:2, pages 95-129.

Gröner, H. (1984). 'Marktsystem, Unternehmenskontrollen und Insolvenzen: Volkswirtschaftliche Überlegungen zur Reform des Insolvenzrechts,' pages 247-267 in *ORDO*, Bd. 35.

Haberler, G. (1954). 'Konvertibilität der Währungen,' pages 15-59 in Hunold, A. (Hrsg.). *Die Konvertibilität der europäischen Währungen.* Erlenbach-Zürich.

Hare, P.C. (1996). 'How Far is Eastern Europe from Brussels? Reform deficits in potential member states.' Paper presented at the Kiel Week Conference on 'Quo Vadis Europe?' at the Kiel Institute of World Economics on June 26 and 27, 1996.

Hax, Herbert (1985). 'Economic Aspects of Bankruptcy Law,' *Zeitschrift für die gesamte Staatswissenschaft*:141, pages 80-98.

Hayek, F.A. von (1953). 'Entstehung und Verfall des Rechtsstaatsideals,' pages 33-65 in Hunold, A. (Hrsg.). *Wirtschaft ohne Wunder.* Erlenbach-Zürich.

Hayek, F.A. von (1967). 'Grundsätze einer liberalen Gesellschaftsordnung,' *ORDO*:18, pages 11-33.

Hayek, F.A. von (1968). 'Der Wettbewerb als Entdeckungsverfahren.' Kieler Vorträge:56. Kiel.

Hayek, F.A. von (1971). *Die Verfassung der Freiheit.* Tübingen.

Hoppmann, E. (1978). 'Das Konzept der optimalen Wettbewerbsintensität. Rivalität oder Freiheit des Wettbewerbs: Zum Problem eines wettbewerbspolitisch adäquaten Ansatzes der Wettbewerbstheorie.' pages 235-93 in Teichmann, U. (Hrsg.). *Probleme der Wirtschaftspolitik.* Bd.1: *Zielfindung und politischer Entscheidungsprozess; Ordnungspolitik.* Darmstadt.

Hoppmann, E. (1994). 'Freiheitliche Wirtschaftspolitik und Verfassung,' pages 3-16 in Hasse, R.H., Molsberger, J. and Watrin, Chr. (Hrsg.). *Ordnung in Freiheit.* Stuttgart.

Kantzenbach, E. (1966). *Die Funktionsfähigkeit des Wettbewerbs.* Göttingen.
Kommission der Europäischen Gemeinschaften (1995a). *Vorbereitung der assoziierten Staaten Mittel- und Osteuropas auf die Integration in den Binnenmarkt der Union.* Weissbuch, vorgelegt von der Kommission, KOM (95) 163 endg., Hauptband. Luxemburg 1995.
Kommission der Europäischen Gemeinschaften (1995b). *Vorbereitung der assoziierten Staaten Mittel- und Osteuropas auf die Integration in den Binnenmarkt der Union.* Weissbuch, vorgelegt von der Kommission, KOM (95) 163, 2 endg., Add. Annexe, Luxemburg 1995.
Laaser, C.-F. (1991). *Wettbewerb im Verkehrswesen. Chancen für eine Deregulierung in der Bundesrepublik.* Kieler Studien:236. Tübingen.
Laaser, C.-F. (1997). *Ordnungspolitik und Strukturwandel im Integrationsprozess – Das Beispiel Griechenlands, Portugals und Spaniens.* Kieler Studien. Tübingen (forthcoming).
Laaser, C.-F. and Schrader, K. (1992). 'Zur Reintegration der baltischen Staaten in die Weltwirtschaft,' *Die Weltwirtschaft*:2, pages 189-211.
Luckenbach, H. (1986). *Theoretische Grundlagen der Wirtschaftspolitik.* München.
Mises, L. von (1927). *Liberalismus.* Jena.
Röpke, W. (1957). 'Eigentum als Säule einer freien Gesellschaft,' *Schweizer Monatshefte*:37, No 6, pages 441-47.
Samuelson, P.A. (1954). 'The Pure Theory of Public Expenditure,' *The Review of Economics and Statistics*:36, pages 387-89.
Schrader, K. (1997a). 'Ordnungspolitische Weichenstellungen für eine marktwirtschaftliche Entwicklung in mittel- und osteuropäischen Reformländern.' Unpublished manuscript. Kiel.
Schrader, K. (1997b). 'Knocking on the Door: The Baltic States Returning to Europe,' in Salvatore, D. and Orlowski, L.T. (eds.). *Trade and Payments in Central and Eastern Europe's Transforming Economies.* Westport.
Schrader, K. and Laaser, C.-F. (1992). 'Kompromisse statt Marktwirtschaft – Reformdefizite in der Russischen Föderation, der Ukraine, Weissrussland und den baltischen Staaten.' Institut für Weltwirtschaft, Kieler Diskussionsbeiträge:186/187.
Schrader, K. and Laaser, C.-F. (1994). *Die baltischen Staaten auf dem Weg nach Europa. Lehren aus der Süderweiterung der EG.* Kieler Studien:264. Tübingen.
Schrader, K. and Laaser, C.-F. (1997). 'Der Transformationsprozess in den baltischen Staaten: Ordnungpolitische fortschritte und strukturelle Anpassungsprozesse.' Institut für Weltwirtschaft an der Universität Kiel, Kieler Arbeitspapiere:783. Kiel.
Schüller, A. (1988). Ökonomik der Eigentumsrechte in ordnungstheoretischer Sicht,' pages 155-183 in Cassel, D., Ramb, B.-T. and Thieme, H.J. (Hrsg.). *Ordnungspolitik.* München.
Soltwedel, R., Busch, A., Gross, A. and Laaser, C.-F. (1996). *Deregulierungspotentiale in der Bundesrepublik.* Kieler Studien:202. Tübingen.
Tangermann, S. (1995). 'Osterweiterung der EU: Wird die Agrarpolitik zum Hindernis?' *Wirtschaftsdienst*:IX, pages 484-91.
Tangermann, S. (1996). 'Reforming the CAP: A Prerequisite for Eastern Enlargement.' Paper presented at the Kiel Week Conference on 'Quo Vadis Europe?' at the Kiel Institute of World Economics on June 26 and 27, 1996.
Watrin, Chr. (1994). 'Auf dem Weg zur Marktwirtschaft,' pages 3-19 in C. Herrmann-Pillath, C., Schlecht, O. and Wünsche, H.F. (Hrsg.). *Marktwirtschaft als Aufgabe: Wirtschaft und Gesellschaft im Übergang vom Plan zum Markt.* Grundtexte zur Sozialen Marktwirtschaft:3. Stuttgart.

3 The Importance of Social and Political Stability for Integration into Europe: Lithuania's Case

Kazimira Prunskiene

The re-establishment of the Baltic states (Lithuania, Latvia and Estonia) occurred simultaneously with the reformation of their political and economic systems. The move from a one-party communist system to a multi-party democratic one, and from a command economy to a market economy had to be accomplished under rather harsh external conditions. The resurrection of state borders and the reclaiming of property took place at a time when the Soviet Union had not yet collapsed (1990-91). In addition, the new states had to overcome their isolation from the rest of the world and join strange international integration processes of which they had little experience. The rejection of the Soviet political regime and the acceptance of the principles of a democratic system and a market economy did not automatically lead to democratic maturity nor to a rise in economic or social prosperity.

At least a decade will be required for democracy to gradually become deeply rooted in all corners of the body politic and for the economy to benefit from the new market conditions. The individual citizens, even those in elevated positions such as specialists, leaders and owners, and the whole civil society need to mature.

The processes of economic development and rapprochement toward Western Europe are constantly affected by various interwoven political, social, and psychological factors, whose influence is discussed in this chapter.

The Swings of the Political Pendulum

The most important historical turn in the life of Lithuania began with the appearance of the liberation movement Sajudis (1988), which eventually led to independence and reform. The internal process of revival and development was subject to many political upheavals and fluctuations and can be divided into four stages:

1) 1988-90: The maturation of reformist ideas and the first steps toward statehood and the transformation of a planned economic system to a market economy; intense dialogue with Moscow. This was a courageous decision to wreck the Soviet regime and create democracy in politics and economics. On 11 March, 1990, Lithuania declared independence, with Latvia and Estonia following suit later that same year.
2) 1991-92: International recognition; radical destruction of former structures and a sudden turn towards the right.

   In this period political interests began to dominate over economic interests, responsibility and competence. Economic ties with the East were rejected on ideological grounds, and trade with Russia was treated as betraying the homeland. Shock therapy was applied in areas which, objectively, could only be reformed gradually. However, there was no free choice between fast and gradual reform. There was no button to press for miracles to happen and a mature democracy and socially oriented market economy to appear.
3) 1992 to the beginning of 1996: Externally this period was dominated by intensive relations with Europe and international structures. Internally – as a result of the second democratic elections and the splitting and weakening of the centralist parties – the balance of political forces moved to the left (the voters were disappointed with the rightists), and right-wing extremism was stopped. Unfortunately, the political majority proved incapable of any systematic endeavour due to its lack of reform potential. At that time, the majority in the Lithuanian Parliament (Seimas) – the Lithuanian Democratic Labour Party (LDLP), which had promised to fight for workers' interests during the campaign, and, in part, won the elections due to this promise, turned out to be closely connected to the largest financial and industrial capitalists and often to shadowy interests. However, the parliamentary majority did not directly block essential reform.
4) The 1996 Seimas elections made the political pendulum swing back to the right and brought victory to the same forces who had held the majority back in 1991-92, still with a rather populist and internally un-co-ordinated programme. The rightist government programme promising fast economic and social prosperity quickly began to fall apart. The victory of the new right coalition of Conservatives' and Christian Democrats (both differing greatly from their analogous parties in Western Europe) was determined by the people's disillusionment with economic recession, the spread of crime and corruption and by the popular belief that the most adamant critics of the old government would be best able to quickly overcome all hardship and, most importantly, knew how to improve people's lives.

   Decline in patriotic enthusiasm (independence was already restored) and disappointment in authority resulted in a decrease in voting by more than 20 percentage points between the 1992 and the 1996 Seimas elections. In 1996 only 52.94 per cent of all voters participated – the majority being the most politically active rightist, often fanatically disposed, and seeking vengeance

> against their political competitors as well as their supporters. The citizens are still finding it hard to understand that they are themselves responsible for the quality of the government. Bad weather on the day of elections would seem to be a sufficient excuse not to go to the ballot boxes. Non-participation and apathy are still proudly presented as signs of defiance against a failing government and its unpopular decisions.

The wide swings of the political pendulum (at the 1992 Seimas elections, the LDLP received more than 50 per cent of the votes; in 1996 it got only 9.46 per cent) not only reflect the changing quality of political parties but also the motivational instability of the citizens as voters. What is stable is the fact that when the governing political forces are rejected because of unfulfilled 'miracles,' the voters rush over to the other side of the spectrum with new hope of something better. According to studies, the proportion of those voting for the established political parties was somewhat smaller than that of the 'politically homeless' and those with radically gyrating sympathies. This situation is also affected by the sudden collapse of the old economic structures and the resulting social instability: yesterday's civil servant becomes an employee of a private company, today's hired specialist may form a private company tomorrow, which may go bankrupt in no time and so forth.

A person going through such upheavals has no understanding of long-term considerations and does not connect his own unstable interests with political parties that are also trying to 'find themselves.' For the same reason it is difficult for political parties to form stable groups of supporters and voters in the electorate.

In Lithuania the competition between political parties for the role of the most patriotic and heroic party has lasted longer and been more intense than, for example, in Estonia. It is slow going to reach that stage of political maturity where all parties can agree upon the basic national goals and tasks (inviolability of statehood, foreign political priorities, principles of reform, free press etc.) and where they do not seek to profit from populist posturing.

In the present circumstances, a change of the political majority immediately leads to a change in personnel, essential regulations and means of formal expression in line with the controlling parties' conviction that they alone possess the worthwhile ideas. Leaders who are not supportive of the ruling party are held to be politically untrustworthy. This *modus operandi* is especially characteristic of the rightists.

Despite these obvious shortcomings of the new Lithuanian statehood, much has already been achieved. The most important accomplishments are:

- international recognition of the re-established statehood;
- the establishment of broad political and economic ties with the European Union and international structures;
- constant improvement of the legal and economic systems and integration (harmonisation) with the European Union;

- the creation of the most important prerequisites for internal democracy: free elections, a multi-party system, a multi-faceted and essentially free press.

The Socio-Psychological Climate of Economic Development

A civil society and democracy which emerged suddenly, with no long traditions, could not immediately have assumed a mature form. The people's mentality, formed during the Soviet era, and its lack of initiative are considerable impediments to making use of new opportunities and creating a stable social development. And such initiatives as are actually taken often appear deformed because they underestimate the reality and extent of risks. The outcome is often counterproductive and leads to losses. Understandably, the mature and the elderly have greater difficulties adapting to a new system and overcoming their lack of self-confidence.

The transformation of mentality has created some strange stereotypes and has in many cases caused the individual to hold diametrically opposed convictions. Thus, the average citizen still regards private businesses and businessmen with ill-will. In a society dominated by low wages and pensions and with 80 per cent of the population living on or below the poverty line, many people are primarily concerned about every-day worries. The recent appearance of opportunities to acquire property, to establish private businesses and accumulate capital, especially during the first years of independence, have had a negative effect upon the view of business and property. This negative attitude was formed in a political atmosphere in which the laws and traditions, the obligation to execute the laws, and indeed order itself were unsettled. In the midst of this troubled phase there arose several, essentially different processes of property and business formation: the return of private property lost during the Soviet era (land, houses), the privatisation of state property created during the Soviet era, the creation of new businesses – a process that was must impeded by the former two – and finally the creation of property through various illegal means.

Many people came to associate the return or acquisition of property with private business. The massive urge of people to divide state property, supported by many politicians, resulted in the passing of privatisation laws: workers' collectives were granted the privilege of acquiring up to 50 per cent of company property with vouchers. With this scheme came the illusion that the individual and the nation could prosper economically from dividends. All that a person needed after acquiring stocks would be to calculate his profits. There was little understanding that real estate, company buildings or equipment do not generate value in the absence of investments, business strategies and the production of goods and services.

In a majority of cases, small stockholders in large companies, investment firms or banks, having been completely kept away from control or influence, ended up loosing their property and the long-promised dividends. The swindling by crafty managers and large stockholders created a well-founded feeling of anger on the part of the victims This had ruinous effects on the civil society, solidarity, trust in the authorities and prospective business partners and vastly impeded the willingness to invest and create new companies, credit unions and co-operatives.

An especially heavy blow to civil and company trust in the authorities and the credit and finance institutions was dealt by the banking crisis of 1995-96 when several of the larger Lithuanian commercial banks were bankrupted (among others the "Lithuanian Stock Innovation Bank" and the Vakaru Bankas). Private deposits and company payment accounts were frozen, leading to a chain reaction that added to the economic and social crisis. All this occurred as a result of the ineffective credit policies of the government and the Bank of Lithuania, their involvement in shady transactions, their granting of loans for business projects with no serious guarantees (due to creditors' lack of resources) but with high interest (effectively over 30 per cent annually due to the stable exchange rate of the litas).

The government has received most of the blame for the banking crisis although the legal responsibility falls upon the Bank of Lithuania. By statute it has been confirmed as autonomous from government influence and in the legal sense, the government is absolved from any responsibility. An abstract moral obligation remains, however, and because of this, votes were lost.

The severity of the crisis created by the banking collapse has influenced the citizens to demand that the banks' losses be covered out of the national budget, i.e. by the taxpayers. This cannot help but reduce allocations for areas such as education, culture, health, welfare, police and so forth. The average citizen has not yet learnt that money allocated for some specific purpose will have to be deducted from some other purpose. This, in turn, forces the government to orient itself towards short-term decisions, thus strengthening the impression that a popular way out has been found, when, in reality, the true long-term effects are negative.

One of the most acute problems blocking Lithuania's path to Europe is the rise in crime and corruption. This is conditioned by several factors:

- The cost of living has more than doubled since 1990. At the same time, the shadow economy has created opportunities for criminals and racketeers to get rich quickly;
- Flaws in law and order combined with the high turnover among politicians have caused some of them to collaborate with the criminal underworld on occasion. There is an impression that it is not difficult to avoid punishment, even in cases of major crimes;
- As a result of the mentality formed in the Soviet era, that 'property which belongs to the state also belongs to the people,' there is little regard for the concept that property is inviolable.

Internal Discrepancies of Economic Reform

As a result of political instability, the fall of authority in the eyes of society and the immaturity of market economy traditions, Lithuania's economic reform exhibits several contradictory characteristics.

Despite rapid privatisation – by 1995 more than 70 per cent of the old state property had already been transferred to the private sector – there are still no owners or investors capable of making rational decisions, gaining trust as creditors or partners or actively working in the market. On the contrary, the lack of majority shareholders (controlling 50 per cent or more of the stock) have created conditions for the abuse of power. Having lost half of its capacity since 1990, Lithuania's industry is only half-way towards an economic system which coincides with the principles of a market economy.

Even more damage has been done to agriculture and rural residents. Reform ideas implemented with the intent of quickly wrecking the larger farms (former kolkhozes and state farms) have also succeeded in eliminating production as well as export potential. Property has been returned to pre-Soviet era landowners without any conditions for its use. Production factors such as agricultural equipment, buildings and the work force have been squandered in connection with the privatisation process. The rural areas are burdened by unemployment and a lack of living funds because job opportunities here present themselves at a slower pace than in the cities, and because the work force is older and less accustomed to new conditions.

Another problem is presented by the litas – the national currency introduced in 1993. It has remained tied to the US dollar (1 USD = 4 litas) despite an inflation rate of 45 per cent in 1994, 35 per cent in 1995 and 13 per cent in 1996. At the same time, the interest rate stands at over 20 per cent in 1997 – having reached 30-40 per cent in 1995-96. It can come as no surprise that the combination of the fixed dollar-litas relation and such high interest rates makes conditions impossible for businessmen, leads them to bankruptcy and creates a high risk of disastrous chain reactions. Neither the (Central) Bank of Lithuania nor the government has managed to introduce sound credit policies designed to at least limit the banks' margin. At the same time, competition from foreign bank affiliates has been limited. In violation of banking rules, the banks have granted many bad loans, thus not only showing a lack of competence, but criminal intent as well. Even loans from international credit institutions such as the World Bank, the EBRD and the ESB are channelled to the borrower via local commercial banks at great cost. Such overly expensive loans make the local investor non-competitive compared to foreign investors arriving with their own funds or less expensive credit.

A further problem is the inconsistency of general investment conditions. The right to own land is reserved for the state and private individuals and denied to foreign investors and local juridical persons. This impedes economic processes. Although foreign investors are allowed profit tax reductions, have the right to export profits and can benefit from importing investment capital, they are in no hurry to 'buy out Lithuania.'

It is planned that conditions for foreign and local investors will be equalised in 1997, but in the real world equality will be hard to achieve. One reason is the problem of investment funds and the local interest rates, which, even in 1997, will reach 18-20 per cent or more. Secondly, local investors do not have the international marketing experience of their foreign competitors. As a rule, local investors are content to create small and medium-sized businesses, whereas foreign investors have the ability to reach larger goals. This is particularly evident in the oil market, especially gas station construction.

A further inconsistency is the gap between import and export conditions. With a stable exchange rate for the litas and continuing domestic inflation and thus increasing production costs, export becomes complicated. This is why import conditions are more favourable than export conditions, which cannot be strategically beneficial to the state.

The government has been constantly changing the system of customs and licences thereby putting a burden upon foreign trade and investment. One of the most characteristic traits of Lithuanian economic policy has been the government's orientation towards short-term interests – primarily increasing budget revenues through higher taxes, while, at the same time, leaving many loopholes for tax evasion. Without really breaking with the short-term orientation of former governments, the new government formed after the 1996 Seimas elections has initiated strong measures to strengthen tax administration. A more complete collection of taxes, together with effective measures against illegal businesses and contraband, still remains one of today's most important legal and economic policy tasks.

Integration into Europe depends not only on the establishment of a legal foundation for the economy but also on its complete implementation and the elimination of loopholes. Our European partners must be convinced of our long-term stability and security and the legality and maturity of local businesses and their reliability in general transactions. This cannot be achieved through shock therapy but must proceed step by step.

4 Current Trends in Economic Integration

Lars Lundqvist and Lars Olof Persson

Integration Processes

Immediately after the break-up of the centrally planned economies in Eastern Europe, there were strong expectations of a rapid increase in foreign trade between the West and the East. These hopes were certainly strongest in countries sharing common borders. After a few years, however, it has become obvious that the optimism was somewhat exaggerated. Part of the explanation comes from the development in the East, not least the dramatic decrease in economic activity and industrial production, especially in Russia and the Baltic states. This, in turn was a result of the breakdown of COMECON and the trade between the Eastern countries, which had been based on a partly 'artificial' division of labour between these countries. Also, the political unrest increased the risks and uncertainties in both industry and trade. Obviously, the sudden exposition to direct international competition caused a shock to the formerly centrally regulated economies. Another part of the explanation is related to the simultaneous downturn of the business cycle in the West. Some countries even experienced a decline in gross production for short periods in the beginning of the 1990s.

The process is still in a turbulent phase. Although there is a consensus within the business and scientific communities and in the political spheres that we will witness continuos growth in the international trade in the Baltic Rim area, few seem to agree on which patterns and volumes are likely to develop in the long run. Trade between the East and the West is constantly searching for new and efficient transport routes.

This means that statistics describing the trade pattern and transport volumes are quickly found to be obsolete. In addition, the reliability and compatibility of such statistics are still questionable. Hence any empirically based analysis of the integration process will be uncertain. What seems to be emerging trends may quickly dissolve.

In addition, a theoretically founded analysis of changing trade patterns will prove to be difficult simply because of the uniqueness of these historical processes linking the highly developed post-industrial economies in the West with the developing economies in the East.

In the long run, integration through increased trade will lead to a more intensive regional and national specialisation. The comparative advantages of each region will be revealed more openly and stimulate structural change in regional and national economies. In the case of rapid institutional changes and improved accessibility this structural change is likely to be quite dramatic. The changing preconditions for trade in the Baltic region in the 1990's has already started this process of rapid structural change, though we have as yet only witnessed the very initial phase. With few exceptions, the economic imbalances between nations in the Baltic region are larger than between adjacent countries elsewhere in the world. Within this imbalanced region, international trade is currently increasing by about 10 per cent per annum on average.

Patterns of Economic Integration

Economic Imbalances in the Baltic Sea Region

The economic integration process during the 1990s between various parts of the Baltic Sea region starts from very different initial conditions and proceeds under very different phases of economic development and economic transition. Figure 4.1 clearly shows the dominance of Germany in terms of size: the German GDP is about three times that of Russia and about 10-20 times that of Poland and the

Figure 4.1: The size of the economy in terms of GDP, 1995, million USD

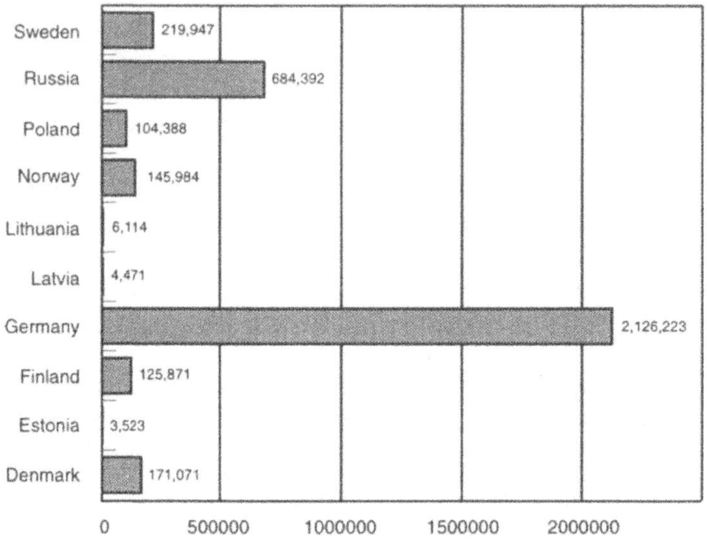

Source: *The World Economic Factbook 1996/97*, Euromonitor

Nordic countries. This picture is qualified if only the 'Baltic regions' in each country – i.e. regions directly facing the Baltic Sea – are considered. In that case the German, Polish and Russian economies would be reduced by about 80 per cent, 96 per cent and 93 per cent respectively. This would reduce the German Baltic regions to about double the GDP of Sweden, while the Polish Baltic regions would be comparable in GDP to the Baltic republics, and the Russian Baltic regions would have an economy about five times larger.

Concerning GDP per capita, Figure 4.2 indicates that Germany and the Nordic countries are leading (with Norway and Denmark on top) whereas all the remaining countries (previously belonging to the COMECON sphere) have per capita incomes of about 10 per cent of the German-Nordic level.

Economic growth during the 1980s and the first years of the 1990s was very uneven, as shown in Figure 4.3. Germany and the Nordic countries had positive GDP growth (with Germany and Norway in the lead). Poland was the only economy in the previous COMECON group showing positive growth. The Baltic republics and Russia (to a somewhat lesser extent) suffered from dramatic economic decline.

There are as yet few indications of increasing economic cohesion in the Baltic region. Figure 4.4 shows that the overall pattern of per capita income differences remained largely unchanged between 1993 and 1995. The changes which are

Figure 4.2: GDP per capita, 1995, USD

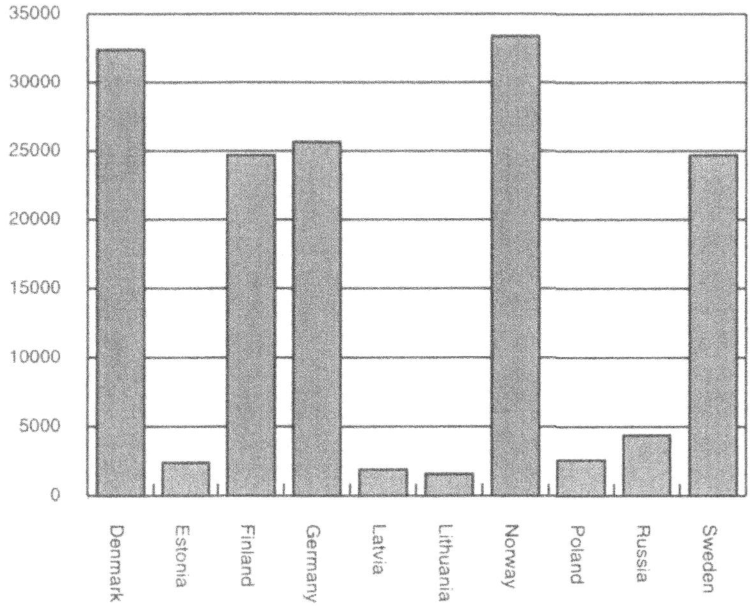

Source: *The World Economic Factbook 1996/97*, Euromonitor

Figure 4.3: GDP annual growth, 1980-93, percentages

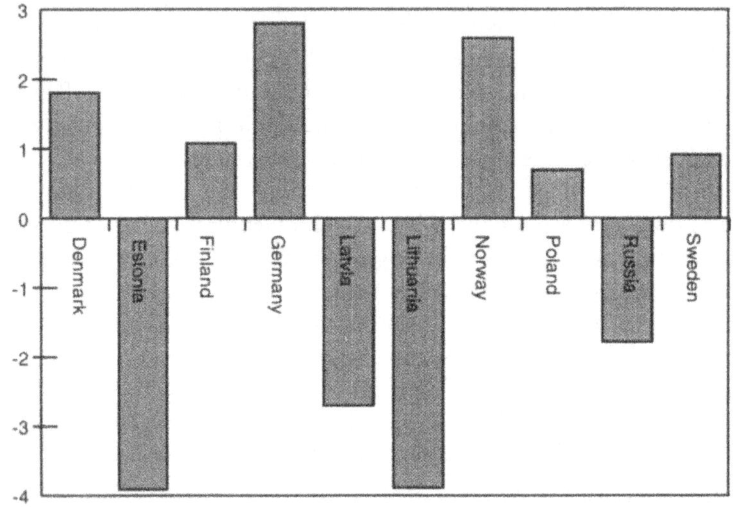

Source: World Bank 1995, published in *Human Development Report 1996*, UNDP

Figure 4.4: GDP per capita, 1993 and 1995 (index for Germany = 100 each year)

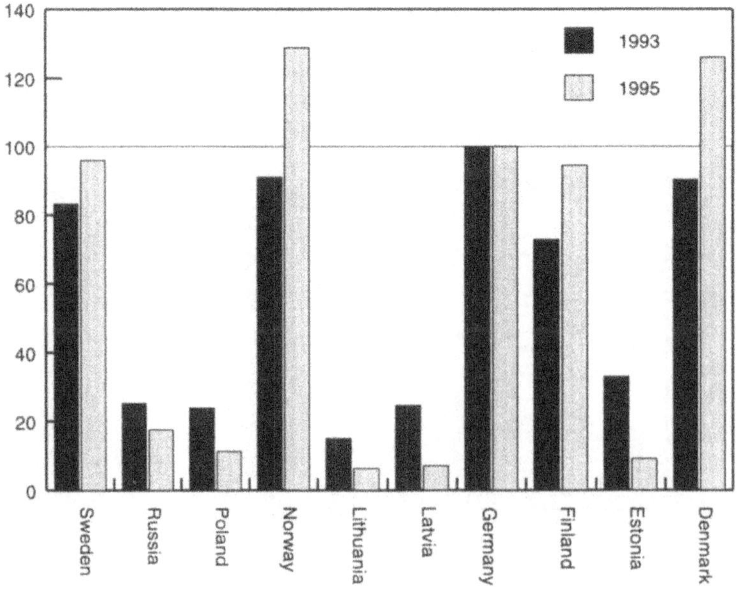

Source: *The World Economic Factbook 1996/97*, Euromonitor (for 1995) and *The World Bank Atlas 1995* (for 1993)

noticeable may very well be explained by the uncertain reliability of the underlying statistics. It should be observed that the values are expressed in index terms.

Finally, the economic imbalances can be described in terms of the sectoral structure of the economies in 1993, see Figure 4.5. In Russia and Lithuania, agriculture and manufacturing account for more than 60 per cent of GDP or about twice the corresponding share in Sweden and Denmark. Latvia and Poland are about halfway between these extreme levels.

Trade Patterns

The total trade dependency (import+export as a share of GDP) is around 55 per cent for the Nordic countries and around 45 per cent for Poland, see Figure 4.6. According to the World Bank, Russia and Germany have lower trade dependencies in 1993 (20-40 per cent). The three Baltic republics show considerably higher trade dependencies (around or above 100 per cent) during the 1992-95 period. This is due to the transit flows between Russia and the West. It seems that the importance of these flows are diminishing in Latvia and Lithuania and increasing in Estonia. The other differences can partly be explained by the size of the economies (larger economies tend to be less trade dependent) and partly by barriers between trade associations in the post-war period which cut through the Baltic Sea region.

Figure 4.5: The structure of the economy in terms of contributions to GDP by sectors, 1993, percentages

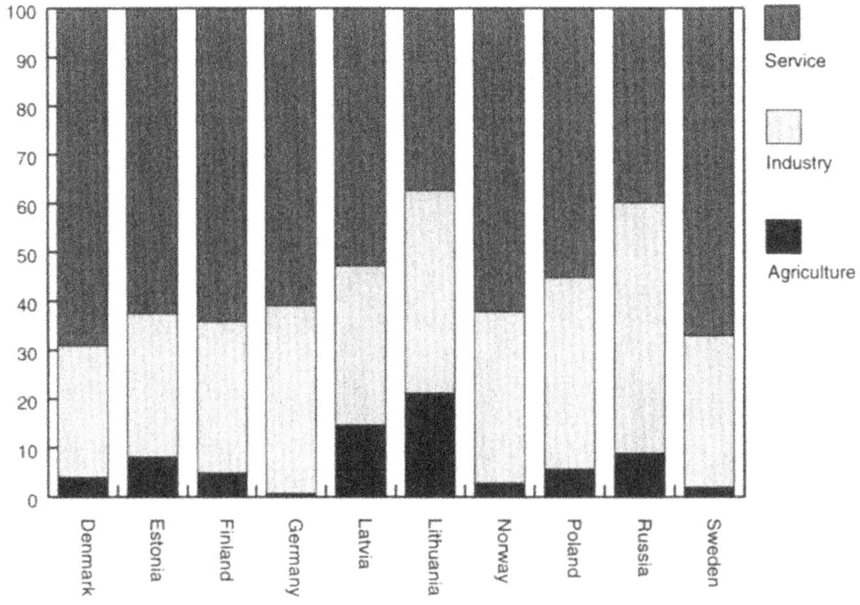

Source: World Bank 1995, published in *Human Development Report 1996*, UNDP

A summary picture of major export destinations and major import sources in Baltic region trade 1995 is presented in Figures 4.7 and 4.8. These are based on the more complete reports on export flows in all trade relations 1992 and 1995, which are provided in Tables 4.1 and 4.2. Strong and weak links can be identified, see Figure 4.9. The strong role of Germany in Baltic trade is easily seen. Germany accounts for around 30 per cent of all exports and imports within the region. Sweden holds a second position in total trade with Baltic countries, while the other Nordic countries, Poland and Russia exhibit 25-50 per cent lower levels and the Baltic republics show trade volumes amounting to 5-10 per cent of the Swedish level. Germany has strong links (here defined as exceeding 5 billion USD (exports + imports)) with all countries except the Baltic republics. Other strong links are identified between the Nordic countries (trade links between Denmark and Finland, Norway and Finland and to a lesser degree also Denmark and Norway are somewhat weaker than all other links) and between Finland and Russia and Poland and Russia. All remaining links are considerably weaker. However, exports from Finland to Estonia, from Sweden to Poland and from Russia to Latvia and Lithuania have increased rapidly and are approaching the category of strong links.

The volume of exports from the Baltic republics and Poland to other Baltic region countries has more than doubled in three years. Also exports from Finland and Germany to Baltic region countries have expanded faster than the average three-year growth of 26.5 per cent. Finland, Germany and Russia all have positive trade balances within Baltic region trade. The Baltic republics have big deficits in Baltic region trade (export/import ratios of 45-60 per cent), but also Sweden, Denmark and Poland are net importers in Baltic trade 1995.

Figure 4.6: Trade dependency, 1992 (for Latvia and Lithuania, 1993) and 1995 (import + export/GDP)

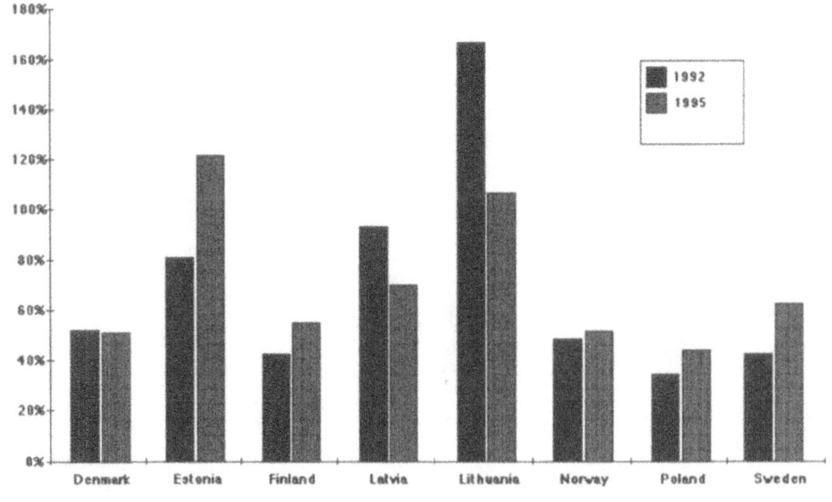

Source: Statistical Section in this volume

Figure 4.7: Export destinations from/to Baltic Sea countries, 1995, million USD

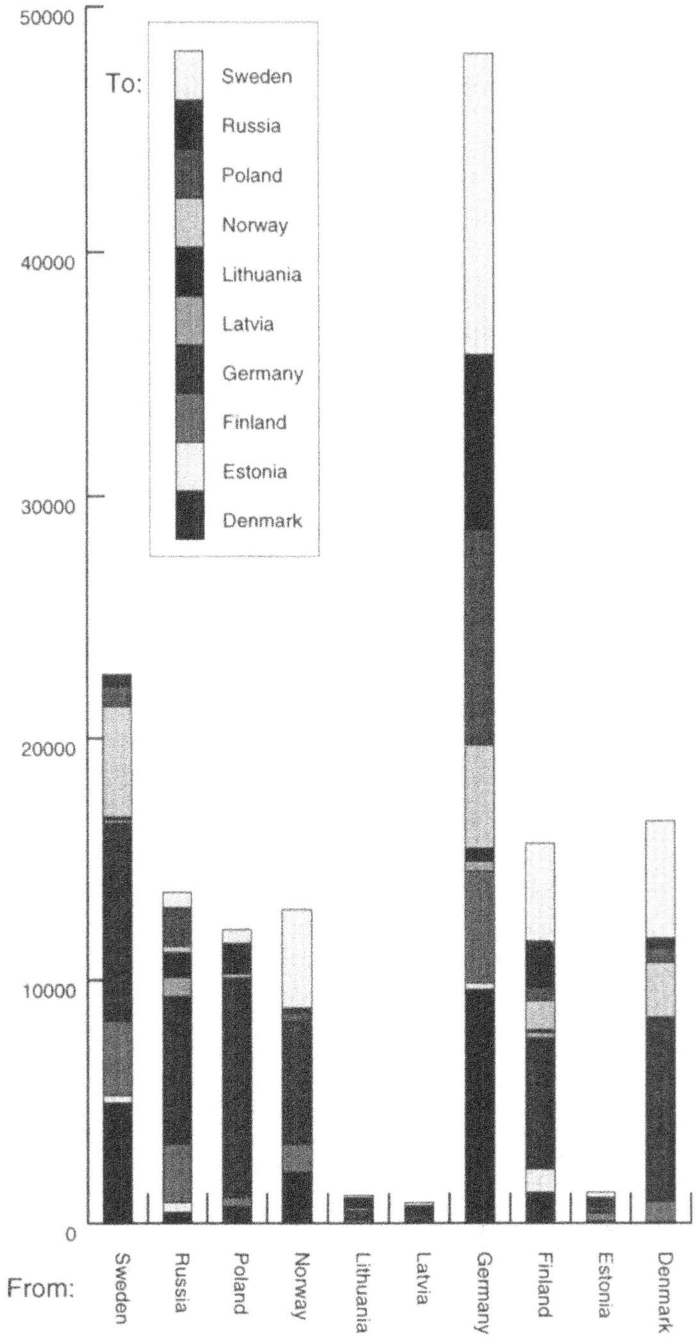

Source: *IMF Direction of Trade Statistics Yearbook*, 1996

Figure 4.8: Import sources to/from Baltic countries, 1995, million USD

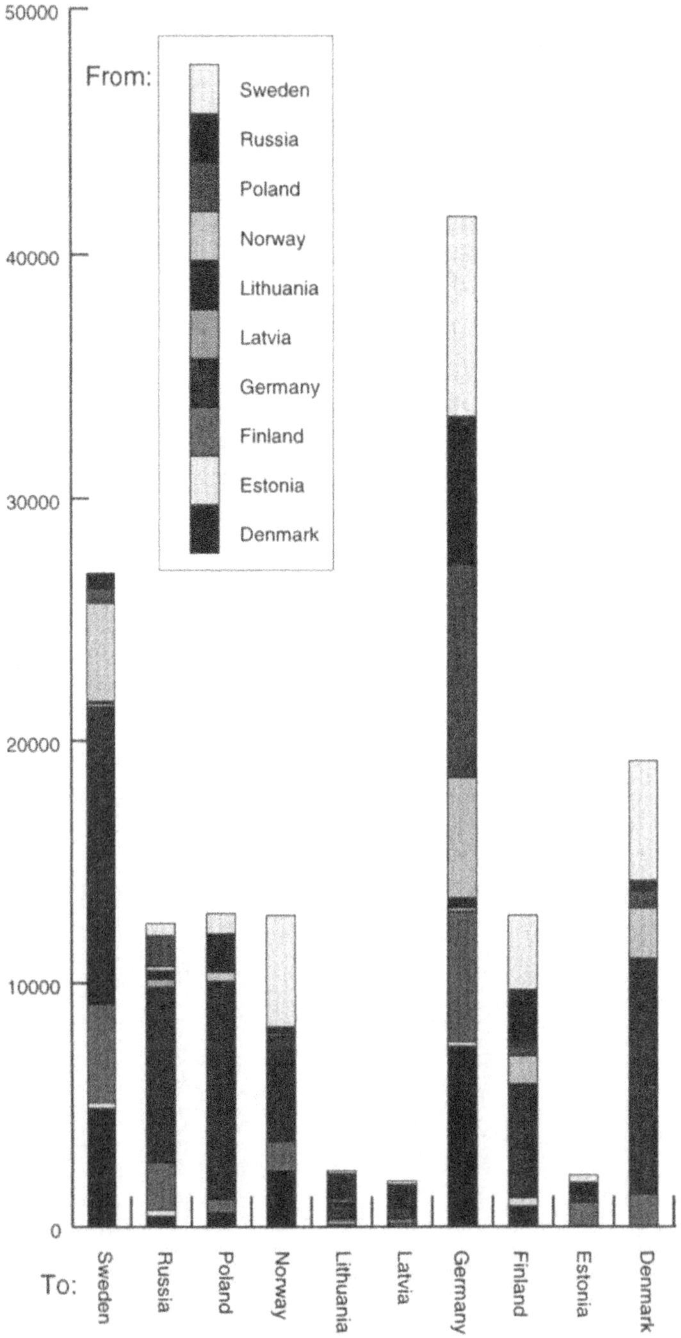

Source: *IMF Direction of Trade Statistics Yearbook*, 1996

The share of total exports going to other Baltic region countries is one measure of integration. For the period 1992-95, the average share for all Baltic countries has been stable at 18 per cent. The average share for Nordic countries has fallen from 38 per cent to 36 per cent. Higher shares are observed for the Baltic republics and Poland and lower shares are noted for Germany and Russia, see Table 4.3.

Other measures of integration can be calculated using entropy or minimum information indicators (Snickars and Weibull 1977). The entropy indicator measures the degree of dispersion of a statistical distribution. The minimum information indicator measures the 'distance' (in an information sense) between

Figure 4.9: Strong and weak links in Baltic region trade, million USD, exports + imports

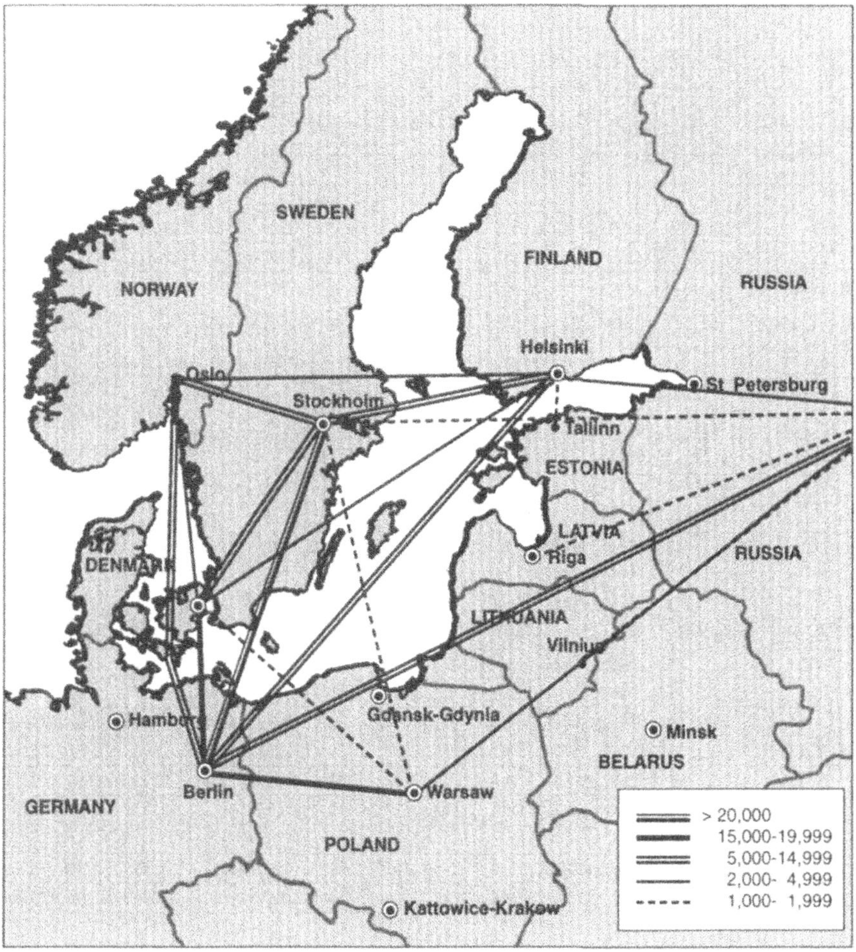

Source: *IMF Direction of Trade Statistics Yearbook*, 1996

two statistical distributions. We have computed the entropy indicator for each country reflecting the dispersion of trade in the Baltic region 1995. We have also computed the minimum information indicator for each country reflecting the deviation between the trade distribution and the GNP distribution 1995. These indicators are reported in Table 4.3.

Table 4.1: Exports to Baltic region countries in 1992 (or 1993 if not available), million USD

To: From:	DK	ES	SF	D	LA	LI	N	PL	R	S	Nor	Bal	World
DK	-	33	774	9218	25	38	2245	500	181	4113	7132	17127	38943
ES	17	-	109	46	69	30	7	8	182	87	220	555	805
SF	861	328	-	3752	45	27	843	367	670	3074	4778	9967	24997
D	8334	103	3625	-	131	167	3628	4688	6877	9383	24970	36936	424682
LA	6	19	29	62	-	28	2	18	202	59	96	425	774
LI	61	27	10	191	91	-	5	50	49	59	135	543	689
N	1906	3	899	4701	2	2	-	314	81	3289	6094	11197	35118
PL	330	5	259	4133	15	36	159	-	723	329	1077	5989	13186
R	281	83	1564	5873	180	299	225	1648	-	654	2724	10807	39742
S	4024	197	2897	8391	57	34	4733	374	282	-	11654	20989	56094
Nor	6791	561	4570	26062	129	101	7821	1555	1214	10476	29658	59280	155152
Bal	15820	798	10166	36367	615	661	11847	7967	9247	21047	58880	114535	635030

Source: *IMF Direction of Trade Statistics Yearbook*, 1996
Note: DK = Denmark; ES = Estonia; SF = Finland; D = Germany; LA = Latvia; LI = Lithuania; N = Norway; PL = Poland; R = Russia; S = Sweden; Nor = Nordic countries; Bal = Baltic region countries.

Table 4.2: Exports to Baltic region countries, 1995, million USD

To: From:	DK	ES	SF	D	LA	LI	N	PL	R	S	Nor	Bal	World
DK	-	52	854	7403	45	109	2246	577	439	4852	7952	16577	39256
ES	78	-	320	161	83	111	39	15	250	219	656	1276	1934
SF	1274	943	-	5380	224	117	1198	516	1933	4052	6524	15637	39995
D	9606	259	4616	-	414	537	4281	8876	7217	12279	30782	48085	509277
LA	24	41	42	178	-	72	23	32	320	122	211	854	1284
LI	37	77	29	388	91	-	26	61	352	93	185	1154	2558
N	2074	28	1147	4993	29	31	-	359	181	4063	7284	12905	41067
PL	688	16	353	8778	61	189	147	-	1274	581	1769	12087	22892
R	455	408	2377	6079	788	1024	254	1605	-	646	3732	13636	77389
S	4946	295	3072	8186	133	108	4575	827	497	-	12593	22639	67794
Nor	8294	1318	5073	25962	431	365	8019	2279	3050	12967	34353	67758	188112
Bal	19182	2119	12810	41546	1868	2298	12789	12868	12463	26907	71688	144850	803446

Source: *IMF Direction of Trade Statistics Yearbook*, 1996
Note: See Table 4.1.

In terms of entropy, the most concentrated trade pattern is observed for Poland, Norway and Denmark. In terms of the mininfo indicator, the least deviation from trade patterns proportional to the GNP distribution is found for Poland and Germany and the highest deviation is noted for Estonia. Three extremes can be observed. Estonia has a very high share of Baltic trade and a dispersed trade pattern with a big deviation from the GNP distribution of is neighbours. Germany has a small share of Baltic trade and a dispersed trade pattern closely related to the GNP distribution. Poland has a high share of Baltic trade and a concentrated trade pattern that is very close to the GNP distribution of its neighbours.

Table 4.3: Indicators of integration in Baltic region trade, 1995

	DK	ES	SF	D	LA	LI	N	PL	R	S
Baltic share	0.42	0.66	0.39	0.09	0.67	0.45	0.31	0.53	0.18	0.33
Entropy	1.42	1.95	1:76	1.83	1.80	1.76	1.29	1.04	1.71	1.61
Mininfo	0.43	1.08	0.49	0.27	0.67	0.58	0.59	0.08	0.68	0.61

Accessibility, Transport of Persons and Economic Integration

Accessibility

The major accessibility properties of rail and road infrastructure are very stable in a short to medium term perspective. Air and sea traffic are more flexible in terms of frequencies and levels of service provided that the terminal capacity is sufficient. Erlandsson (1991) conducted an extensive study of contact and travel opportunities between 98 European regions in the years 1976 and 1988. This study was later updated to 1992 (Erlandsson and Lindell 1993). The outbound contact indicator represents the total population that can potentially be visited from a certain region by day visits (starting after 6 a.m. and returning before 12 p.m.) of 4-8 hours duration (during at least three week days). A corresponding inbound contact indicator was computed representing the possibilities of visiting a certain region from all other regions. A detailed comparison of the changes in outbound contact opportunities of north European regions between 1976, 1988 and 1992 is reported in Table 4.4.

The contact opportunities from Nordic regions have increased over time and are very equally distributed, while the figures for east European regions have deteriorated over time. For some north German regions the contact opportunities seem to have peaked in 1988 (at least in relative terms). The pattern of inbound contact opportunities shows similar general properties. The index values are lower for all regions except Copenhagen and Moscow (due to their positions as major hubs), indicating that regions in the north European periphery are more difficult to reach than to leave in relative terms. The differences in relative terms between north European regions are smaller for inbound than for outbound contact opportunities with a less clear dichotomy between Nordic and east Baltic regions.

In a European context, the outbound accessibility values of Nordic capitals come very close to the accessibility levels of the 'European core regions' having index values above 60. Almost half of the 98 regions have relative accessibility levels lower than 30 and can be characterised as the European periphery. All the east Baltic and Polish cities belonged to this category in 1992. As noted above, the accessibility differences between cities in the Baltic region have increased over time.

Transport of Persons by Air and Sea

Dramatic changes in the orientation of air traffic from Baltic capitals occurred between 1988 and 1992 (Andersson 1992). In 1988, the air traffic of eastern Europe was characterised by a heavy focus on Moscow and by low frequencies. In 1992, direct connections to Western cities had emerged. At the same time, the frequen-

Table 4.4: Outbound contact opportunities 1976, 1988 and 1992 (index = 100 for Paris: 202.9, 237.3 and 258.1 respectively)

	1976		1988		1992	
	Value	Index	Value	Index	Value	Index
Stockholm	88.8	44	127.1	54	151.0	58
Gothenburg	89.2	44	108.2	46	136.1	53
Malmö	80.7	40	107.9	45	131.1	51
Oslo	85.7	42	119.0	50	147.5	57
Copenhagen	86.5	43	116.1	49	149.1	58
Århus	76.3	38	106.5	45	126.6	49
Helsinki	54.5	27	79.9	34	136.6	53
Moscow	67.7	33	57.5	24	62.0	24
St Petersburg	50.9	25	48.2	20	46.2	18
Tallinn	1.6	1	53.2	22	27.8	11
Riga	45.3	22	23.7	14	32.7	13
Vilnius	47.8	24	33.0	14	36.8	14
Warsaw	34.2	17	33.0	14	31.7	12
Gdansk	11.1	5	9.0	4	9.0	3
Poznan	11.7	6	15.7	7	12.2	5
Berlin	-	-	-	-	220.7	86
West	138.1	68	180.5	76	-	-
East	65.0	32	57.2	24	-	-
Hamburg	142.4	70	189.2	80	189.2	73
Bremen	86.0	42	153.2	65	125.3	49

Sources: Erlandsson (1991), Erlandsson and Lindell (1993)

cies to Eastern destinations had increased from the capitals of the Baltic republics. The pattern of Eastern destinations had been widened.

The frequency of direct air connections between Baltic cities 1994 and 1996 have been brought together in Figures 4.10 and 4.11. Over two years, the total number of weekly direct flights has increased by 44 per cent. Warsaw is the most interconnected city with direct flights to all the other 13 cities. The total frequency, however, is more than three times as high for Stockholm and Copenhagen. Riga and Tallinn have increased the total frequency by about 80 per cent from very low initial levels, leaving Vilnius and St Petersburg behind. The major impression is the very high frequencies between Nordic capitals and the strong position of Copenhagen.

Figure 4.10: Frequencies of direct air connections, January 1994, number of weekly return flights

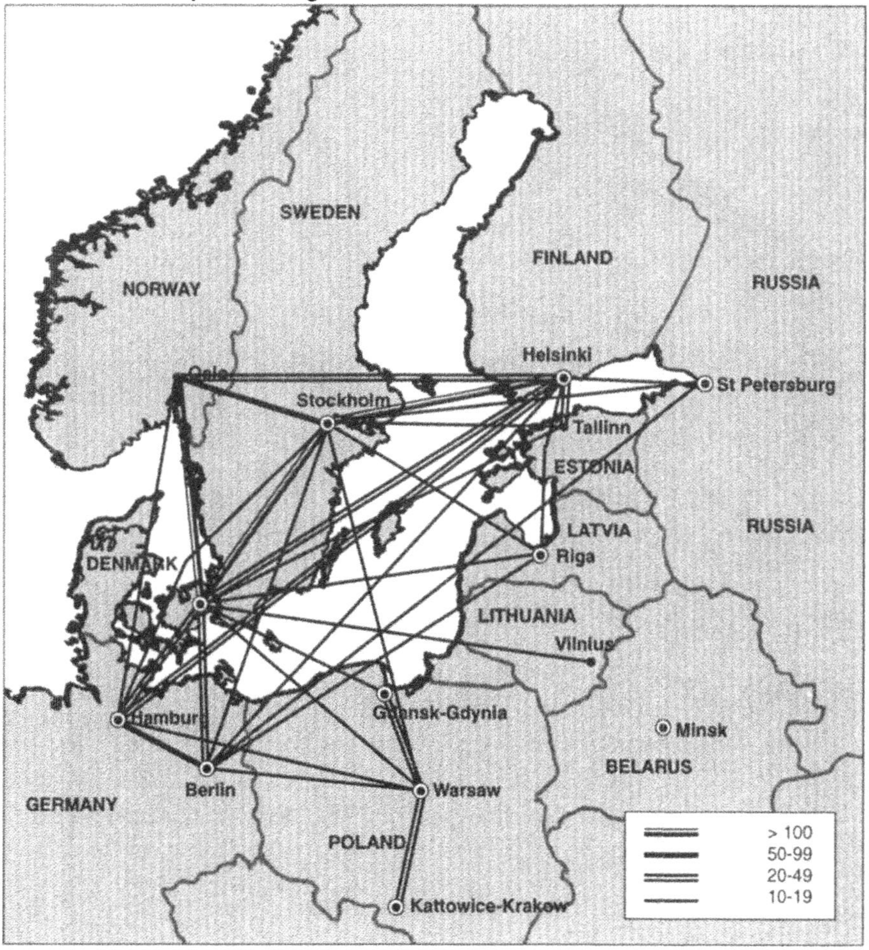

Source: *ABC Airways Guide*

Some parallels in the development of trade patterns and air connections may be observed. Air connections and trade with the eastern part of the Baltic region exhibit fast growth rates from low initial levels. The absolute growth is, however, greater in the western part. Regarding individual intercountry or intercity connections, there are, of course, exceptions to this general pattern. In the absence of passenger flow statistics, we have assumed that the supply of flights is reflecting the demand by gradual adjustments.

As an indicator of the changes in passenger flows by sea between Sweden and the other countries of the Baltic Rim we will report on statistics from 1970, 1980, 1990 and 1995. Table 4.5 contains the total volume and the percentage distribu-

Figure 4.11: Frequencies of direct air connections, February 1996, number of weekly return flights

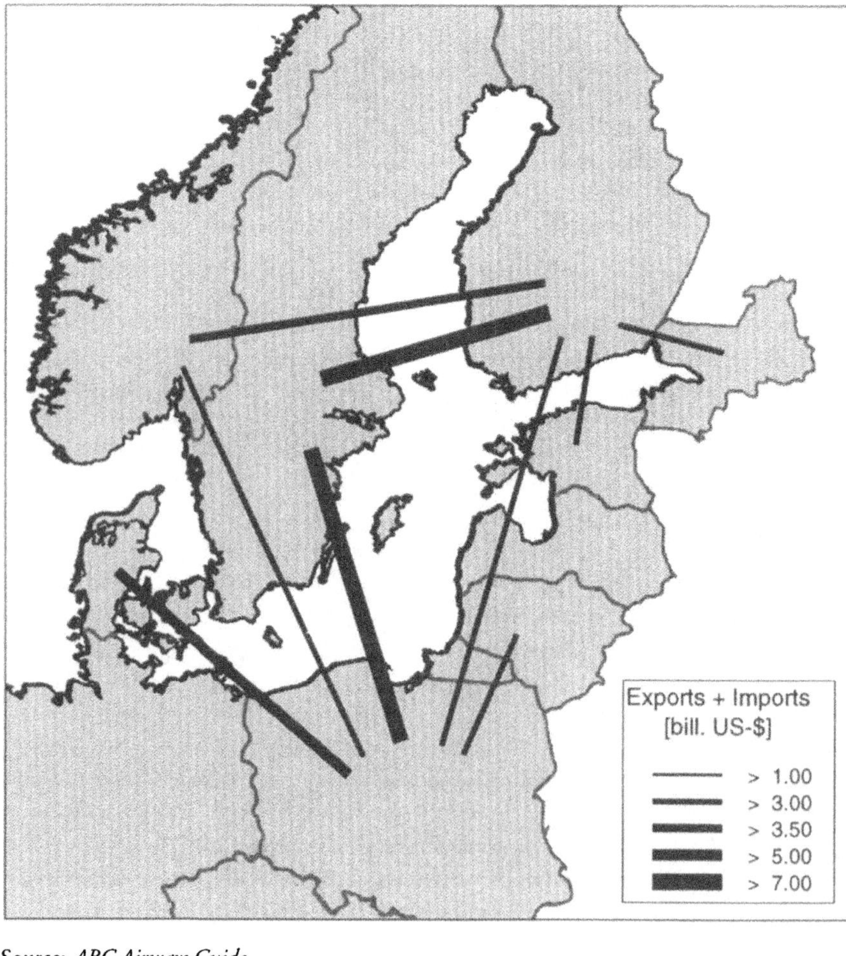

Source: *ABC Airways Guide*

tion over countries of passenger movements by sea during each of these four years. The completely dominating connections are with Denmark and Finland and, to some extent, with Germany.

The volume of passenger traffic with Denmark is about constant over time with a clear decline in the 1990s while the ferry traffic with Finland and Germany increases its share. The total market expanded in the period 1970-90 but has lost in the 1990s. Noticeable increases of volumes and shares are registered for the traffic with Norway, Poland and the former Soviet Union. After 1990 new connections with the Baltic republics have been established.

As a comparison, it may be mentioned that the total number of international air passengers entering and leaving Swedish airports in 1990 amounted to 8.8 million or about one-fifth of the total international passenger flows by sea in 1990. The total number of air passengers in 1990 was at the same level as the passenger flow by ferries between Sweden and Finland. Ninety-seven per cent of the international air passengers used the airports of Stockholm-Arlanda (74 per cent), Gothenburg-Landvetter (19 per cent) or Malmö-Sturup (4 per cent). In 1995 the total number of international air passengers had increased by 20 per cent to 10.6 million. During the same five year period, the total flow of sea passengers to Baltic region countries had decreased by about 9 per cent but was still about 3.5 times larger than the flow of air passengers.

Concluding Discussion

Depending on how the delimitation is done, the regions around the Baltic Rim cover a potentially integrated market with from 50 to about 100 million inhabitants.

Table 4.5: Passenger flows by sea between Sweden and the Baltic Sea countries, 1970, 1980, 1990 and 1995, 1000 passengers per year

	1970		1980		1990		1995	
To/from:	Volume	Prop.	Volume	Prop.	Volume	Prop.	Volume	Prop.
Denmark	26718	86.9	27512	78.5	26736	67.3	22670	63.5
Estonia	-	-	-	-	-	-	206	0.6
Finland	2719	8.8	5370	15.3	9135	23.0	8794	24.6
Germany	1073	3.5	1773	5.1	2886	7.3	2621	7.3
Latvia	-	-	-	-	-	-	40	0.1
Lithuania	-	-	-	-	-	-	3	0.0
Norway	138	0.5	201	0.6	391	1.0	824	2.3
Poland	84	0.3	184	0.5	418	1.1	508	1.4
Soviet Union	5	0.0	2	0.0	136	0.3	-	-
Russia	-	-	-	-	-	-	64	0.2
Total	30737	100.0	35042	100.0	39702	100.0	35730	100.0

Source: 'Sweden in the world,' *The Swedish National Atlas*, 1997

It has the potential of developing into one of Europe's most expansive regions, among other things depending on the rate of improvement of the infrastructure and the human capital. The common natural resource – the Baltic Sea – is also an important basis for co-operation along with a common economic development strategy. Nor should it be forgotten that trade and communication in the area have important historical antecedents.

In all these countries, there is at present generally strong political support for free international trade as a vehicle for economic growth. Hence, a likely long-term scenario is that major portions of the region will develop into an integrated part of the Single European Market. From this perspective, the main question is when this will be feasible. The strong links of trade and personal transport between the Nordic countries and between Germany and the Nordic countries may be seen as an indicator of the potential for future integration.

There are already strong political endeavours to reduce especially non-tariff obstacles to trade in the region. Crucial communication links – especially in the north-south direction – have been decided, are in the planning process or are being constructed. Several cross-border co-operation programmes have been launched as important elements in the integration strategy of the European Union. The need for visas has been eliminated between more and more of the countries.

The single most important factor when analysing the future pattern and structure of trade in the region is the probable enlargement of the European Union. This is by and large a political factor.

A second decisive factor is the accessibility and quality of the communication infrastructure. The development of this strategic factor for economic integration will certainly depend as much on decisions and actions by the private sector as by national and supranational authorities.

Furthermore, there is increasing interest and intensified activity in many cities of the Baltic region to enhance their role as import/export nodes – as 'gateway' or 'meeting place'. Such activities are often part of a strategy for urban competitiveness, ultimately aiming at attracting foreign investments and visitors. Due to such endeavours, there is an increasing tendency that regions become as – or even more – important in the economic integration process as the nation states.

The third – also largely political – factor is the degree of institutional stability in the different countries. The internationalisation process of firms and their willingness to invest in other countries are very sensitive to the real and perceived risks involved. Consequently, social and political stability and security in the Baltic region as a whole will directly influence the progress of cohesion between the various parts of the area.

Hence, the challenges of international and interregional co-operation in the Baltic Sea area are to – simultaneously – stimulate growth in all regions by introducing more competition, to increase international trade and human interaction and to enhance cohesion in this unbalanced part of Europe.

References

Andersson, J. (1992). 'The Route Goes Eastwards: About Air Traffic in the Baltic States 1988 and 1992.' Department of Social and Economic Geography, University of Lund. (In Swedish).

Erlandsson, U. (1991). 'Contact and Travel Opportunities in Europe 1976 and 1988.' Research Report 98, Department of Social and Economic Geography, University of Lund. (In Swedish).

Erlandsson, U. and Lindell, C. (1993). 'Contact and Travel Possibilities of Swedish Regions in Europe 1992.' Department of Social and Economic Geography, University of Lund. (In Swedish).

Snickars, F. and Weibull, J.W. (1977). 'A Minimum Information Principle: Theory and Practice,' *Regional Science and Urban Economics*:7, pages 137-68.

5 Trade Potentials in Northern Europe and Consequences for Traffic Flows

Stefan Callsen

Introduction

The opening up of Eastern Europe and the Northern enlargement of the European Union have entirely changed the economic conditions of northern Europe. Nowhere else in Europe are the discrepancies between the former centrally planned economies and the industrialised countries in such close geographical proximity as in northern Europe and around the Baltic Sea. The differences in income between the still declining Russia and the fairly poor Baltic states, on the one hand, and Denmark, Norway, Sweden and Germany as the countries with the highest income in Europe, on the other, are probably the biggest on the continent.

Even for the most successful reform states, the phase of catching up must surely be a long-term process. Beside direct foreign investment, one channel will be integration via foreign trade. During the catch-up phase, markets in the East European economies will grow significantly faster than those in Western Europe. While the opportunities for Eastern Europe are quite obvious, the possible benefits for the industrial countries have often been expressed in term of a 'new Hansa.' The hope is that Western businesses should benefit from the access to large and growing markets and that consumers might profit from lower prices and a wider selection of goods. Cultural affinities, geographical proximity and developments of the recent past give rise to the presumption that the nations around the Baltic Sea are natural trading partners.[1] This is borne out by annual double-digit growth rates in the region's trade volume, far exceeding the increase of overall trade of the countries.

Still, there are obvious trade distortions in northern Europe, which have to be seen in the light of some distinct limitations before the fall of the Iron Curtain. General barriers to economic integration can be identified in the spheres of political and social life, distance-bridging costs of transport and communication and in different political strategies among countries. Such trade impediments as explicit government policies, e.g. state monopolies on foreign trade, import licensing and foreign exchange restrictions have decisively distorted East-West trade. Furthermore, as trade tends to expand with respect to output and income, is is indirectly suppressed by the low income levels in the Eastern countries.

It is the aim of this chapter to forecast the future trade patterns of northern Europe. The analysis is based on certain scenarios in which the abolition of the above-cited trade distortions is assumed. Some qualitative conclusions about the resulting traffic implications, especially for north-western Europe, are added.

Trade Flow Projection

The trade estimates are made in the context of a gravity model developed by Johannes Bröcker and further applied by Olaf Jäger-Roschko at the Institute for Regional Research of the University of Kiel. Its predictive capacity has been proved in several ex-post analyses. Extensive use of the Bröcker model has been made in the prediction of East-West trade following the reforms in Central and Eastern Europe.[2] As a basis for the model, the Institute has developed two scenarios of the possible developmental paths the reform states may follow as they pursue further economic transformation and integrate themselves into the global division of labour.

The projection of trade flows cover all countries bordering the Baltic Sea. As earlier studies of the Institute indicate (Peschel 1990), the analysis of the Baltic area as an economic region has to include Norway due to its strong economic ties with the rest of the area. Regarding Russia, only the regions of Kaliningrad and St Petersburg will be considered.

Scenarios on the Future Economic Development of the Reform States

The first scenario, described in the following as the optimistic scenario, should correspond to the developments in case of successful reforms and complete macroeconomic stabilisation in Eastern Europe. The pessimistic scenario contrasts with the first scenario by portraying an economic development through the year 2010 which only just begins to approach Western European standards. Thus, a process is illustrated in which a far lower degree of economic development is attained in the transforming nations than in the optimistic case. A comparison between both scenarios illustrates the spectrum of effects on trade and transport flows expected from the introduction of a market economy system.

A calculation of income trends along with an elaboration of feasible developmental paths is central in trade models. The way chosen here was first introduced by Jäger-Roschko (1997). It determines a countries' relative position vis-a-vis a Western European reference country. In the optimistic scenario it was assumed that by the year 2010, among the group of Eastern European neighbours, the most developed country would have attained approximately the per capita income of Greece. In all probability, this will be Estonia. The country already has the highest per capita income of the states considered here, and in the opinion of most experts, it is making the greatest progress in transforming itself into a market economy. Poland and Latvia are placed immediately behind Estonia. Lithuania follows at some distance because its development has been less favourable. The two Russian regions appear at roughly the same level. At present, their progress toward economic transformation lags far behind the other regions reviewed here. Moreover, particular uncertainty prevails as to the continued political development of the Russian regions. The rank ordering given here is supported by prognoses up to the year 1998 by PlanEcon (1994) and is in line with comparable studies.[3] Externally generated GNP growth rates were used for Greece and the other countries in the western part of the forecast area.

Both scenarios produce the same rank ordering of countries. It is important to point out, however, that the values for per capita incomes in the pessimistic scenario are only between 50 and 60 per cent of those in the optimistic one. In addition to differences in income trends, two further differentiating factors between the two scenarios are included. In the first instance, differing EC membership structures are assumed, depending on the scenario. Thus, only in the optimistic scenario do the Baltic states and Poland become members of an eastwardly enlarged European Union. In the second instance, the optimistic scenario assumes that a tangible improvement of the transportation infrastructure occurs in North-eastern Europe, with the consequence that average travel and transport times will fall.

Trade Forecasts

The scenarios described above serve as the basis for an assessment of future trade integration in the Baltic Sea area. The findings must be regarded as speculative in so far as it is relatively difficult to gauge the reliability of many of the data required for the forecasts. Furthermore, the special situation of this economic area – with long-standing and new EU members on one the hand and former member states of the Soviet Union and Poland on the other – must be taken into account. In the next section only the general trends and most interesting findings will be highlighted.

The model distinguishes between a reference and a forecast area. Starting with the reference area – which includes the member states of the European Economic Area (EC and EFTA) in 1994 – an estimated model was used to investigate the manner in which a vector of factors determines trade flows. Hence, the gravity equations were expanded to include variables representing cultural distance factors, dummies for adjacency and variables representing resource endowments. The parameter values derived from the estimated model are used to draw up a prediction of future trade flows. The estimates are combined with projections of the model's exogenous parameters for the forecast time period. Once the forecasts of the model's exogenous parameters under both scenarios have been combined with the estimated regression model, international trade matrices can be built which describe flows within the Baltic Sea area. Admittedly, the forecasts take no account of limits to a country's ability to finance a foreign trade deficit. The matrices are established not just for total trade, but for each of five economic sectors as well (for the sectoral split, see Table 5.4). Each sector is the subject of an individually estimated model which incorporates specific traits pertaining to the particular situation of each economic domain.

The projected trade flows will be related to the most recent figures. In choosing the appropriate data ,it was assumed that most countries monitor their imports more carefully than their exports. Therefore, the analysis was carried out using data according to foreign exchange statistics of the importing country. The data were taken from the *Direction of Trade Yearbook* (IMF 1996) as the most commonly used source for trade economists. Trade figures for the regions of Kaliningrad and St Petersburg are based on data reported in Bolz and Polkowski (1995) and Reymann (1995) or stem from my own calculations.

Results

Overall Trends

In light of the results obtained from the model, it is to be expected that, in absolute terms, Germany and Sweden will dominate trade in the Baltic Sea area, followed by Denmark, Poland and Norway, and then by Finland. The dominant role of Germany and Sweden is indicated in Table 5.1, in which each country's volumes of exports and imports aggregated over all other Baltic sea countries are given for the year 2010. Accordingly, the increase in northern Europe's trade volume is mainly due to the trade expansion in the countries of the 'Western bloc.' In keeping with their small size, the Baltic states and the two Russian regions conduct far less foreign trade in the Baltic Sea area, but this does not imply that their share of trade in relation to national product is lower than that of the other countries.

The projected figures are related to actual exports and imports. It can be ascertained that Eastern Europe's *relative* change in the volume of trade will be substantially higher than that of the Western industrial countries, which is probably not a surprise. The increase in trade is especially pronounced for the imports of Eastern Europe. Whereas Germany and Norway show large export surpluses, all former COMECON states will show a significant foreign trade deficit by the year 2010. These countries will not have finished the process of catching up economically and will thus need to import more goods than they export. The tremendously high growth indices for the two Russian regions concerning imports are somewhat misleading. They mainly stem from the slump in present import figures.

The picture of high and still rising import surpluses in the Baltic has been observable in Estonia and Lithuania since 1993. This is, above other reasons, the outcome of the Baltic states' exchange rate system. In tying their currencies to the German mark or the US dollar, these countries will experience an overvaluation of their currencies with high inflation rates. Thus, from the Baltic states' viewpoint, Western imports are cheaper while the prices of their export goods are higher than in an equilibrium position. The question has to be raised whether (or how long) these exchange rate systems can be maintained.

Considering again the growth indices in Table 5.1, a significant increase in foreign trade in the Baltic Sea area is also forecast for the highly developed economies. By the year 2010, the observable growth rates will probably lead to national trade flows that are roughly three times higher than in 1994, except for Finland.

Comparing the Different Scenario Results

According to Table 5.2, the greatest divergence between the optimistic and the pessimistic scenario is forecast for the Baltic states and Poland. The smaller values – viewed in absolute terms – exhibited by the Russian areas can be explained by the assumption that Russia will not – even in the optimistic scenario – become a member of an expanded European Union. In contrast to the other countries, through the year 2010, totally free trade will not exist between Russia and the EU – even when the agricultural sector is excluded.

A further conspicuous result is that Finland and Germany are far more affected by developments in Eastern Europe than are Denmark, Norway and Sweden. This is indicated in the last two columns of Table 5.2, in which the percentage differences between both scenarios are calculated: Germany's and Finland's overall trade volume within northern Europe in the pessimistic case is about ten per cent lower compared to the optimistic case, while the trade figures for the other Western economies differ less than five per cent between both scenarios. An explanation for this can be found in these states' close geographical proximity to Eastern Europe. Furthermore, Germany and Finland traditionally conduct more trade

Table 5.1: Foreign trade projections in the Baltic Sea area,* optimistic scenario

	EXPORTS			IMPORTS		
	1994	2010	Index of growth 2010/1994 (1994=1)	1994	2010	Index of growth 2010/1994 (1994=1)
Denmark	13,730	46,207	3.4	15,192	54,486	3.6
Germany	36,356	147,206	4.0	40,984	103,161	2.5
Estonia	862	2,330	2.7	1,217	5,643	4.6
Finland	12,441	24,010	1.9	10,285	22,432	2.2
Latvia	897	2,267	2.5	821	6,483	7.9
Lithuania	931	2,753	3.0	1,647	6,124	3.7
Norway	12,537	50,514	4.0	11,548	30,550	2.6
Poland	8,849	22,809	2.6	9,253	46,644	5.0
Sweden	20,195	77,498	3.8	21,044	96,425	4.6
Kaliningrad	55	449	8.1	64	1,448	22.6
St Petersburg	342	1,490	4.4	175	4,137	23.6
Total	107,195	377,533	3.5	112,230	377,533	3.4

*In million USD, data source: IMF (1996)

Table 5.2: Scenario comparisons

	Optimistic scenario		Pessimistic scenario		Pessimistic scenario results in per cent of optimistic case	
	Exports*	Imports*	Exports*	Imports*	Exports	Imports
Denmark	46,207	54,486	44,323	53,501	95.9	98.2
Germany	147,206	103,161	124,162	92,216	84.3	89.4
Estonia	2,330	5,643	747	2,609	32.1	46.2
Finland	24,010	22,432	21,135	20,908	88.0	93.2
Latvia	2,267	6,483	759	2,961	33.5	45.7
Lithuania	2,753	6,124	867	2,525	31.5	41.2
Norway	50,514	30,550	48,773	29,932	96.6	98.0
Poland	22,809	46,644	9,046	21,240	39.7	45.5
Sweden	77,498	96,425	73,889	94,718	95.3	98.2
Kaliningrad	449	1,448	238	1,064	52.9	73.5
St Petersburg	1,490	4,137	808	3,071	54.2	74.2
Total	377,533	377,533	324,747	324,747	86.0	86.0

* Million USD in constant prices

with Eastern Europe than the remaining Western countries in the Baltic Sea area. It is therefore particularly essential for the Western countries just mentioned to support the transformation process among their Eastern European neighbours and thereby to ensure their future role as important partners in international trade.

Future Direction of Trade

The spatial pattern of foreign trade volumes (exports plus imports) in the year 2010 is depicted in Figures 5.1 and 5.2. In these figures different scales are used to present trade flows in the north-eastern part of Europe. For the purpose of better comparison, the trade flow between Finland and Sweden is depicted in both figures to indicate the different scales and different widths of the respective lines. Trade flows below one billion, respectively three billion US dollars were omitted.[4]

Apparently, most trade will be conducted in the western or south-western parts of the Baltic Sea area between Germany, Sweden, Norway and Denmark. Furthermore, the only significant trade flow between a former COMECON state and a country of the 'Western bloc' is between Poland and Germany. But it is questionable whether the total amount of German-Polish trade can be baptised 'Baltic trade' (see below).

A crucial question surely is whether a general orientation of all Baltic Rim countries towards northern Europe is likely in the future. Due to the fact that the estimated model is not a world trade model, we cannot relate the increase in internal Baltic trade to increases in world-wide trade by the year 2010. What we can do is to look at the actual significance of trade within northern Europe (Table 5.3). Although the period considered is fairly short, some important points shall be stressed here.

The last column in Table 5.3 gives an impression of the generally growing significance of trade in the area, indicated by increasing trade shares of northern Europe compared to overall trade. This is mainly due to an intensification of trade between all Scandinavian countries and Germany. But the present importance of trade within the Baltic Sea area should not be overestimated: Even the Scandinavian countries' shares are no more than roughly 40 percent. Important trading partners for all Scandinavian countries are Great Britain, France and the Benelux countries. Furthermore, Germany's share is only about 10 percent. This indicates that only the northern part of Germany is oriented towards northern Europe.[5] This is presumably also true for Poland. Of the two-thirds of Poland's 'Baltic' trade with Germany, probably only a small part is conducted in the northern regions of both countries. Only the Baltic states are predominantly oriented

Figure 5.1: Main trade links, 2010 (trade flows below 1 billion USD are omitted)

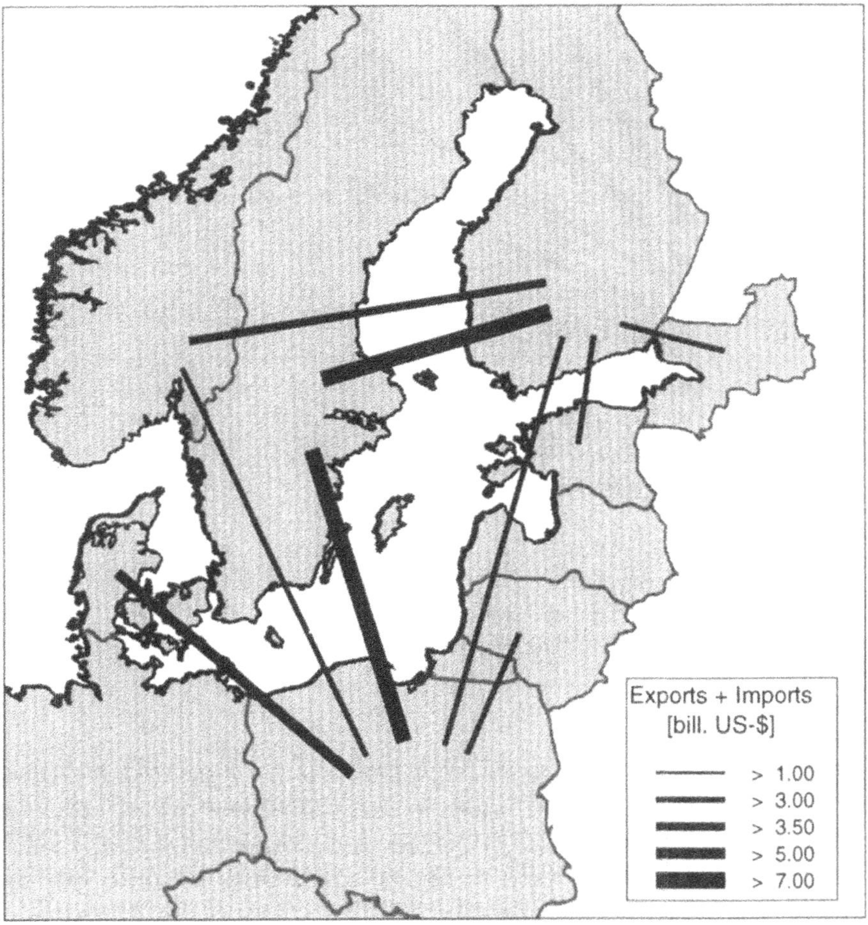

Figure 5.2: Main trade links, 2010 (trade flows below 3 billion USD are omitted)

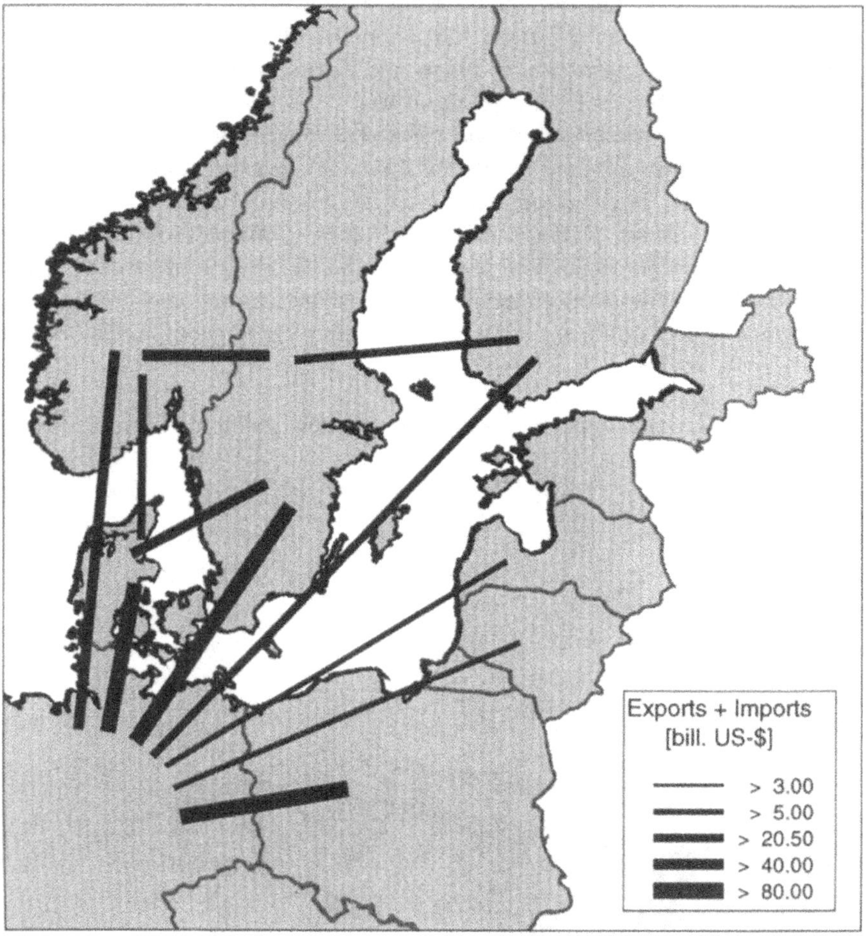

Source: *ABC Airways Guide*

towards the Baltic Sea region. However, the high value of all Baltic states' trade shares is a result of the inclusion of the whole of Russia, whereas the figures for the two Russian regions Kaliningrad and St Petersburg do not include internal Russian trade.

Sector Considerations

Some insights into the future spatial division of labour can be derived from looking at the sectoral split of foreign trade by the year 2010 in Table 5.4. The following trends can be identified: the main exporter of minerals and oil will be Norway, whereas the main importers will be Germany and Sweden. The main exporting countries for agricultural products are Denmark, followed by Sweden, Germany

Table 5.3: Significance and development of actual Baltic Sea trade

	1994			1995			
	Trade volume within the Baltic region*	Total trade volume*	Share of Baltic trade in per cent	Trade volume within the Baltic region	Total trade volume	Share of Baltic trade in per cent	Change in percentage points of Baltic trade share 94/95
Denmark	28,922	73,467	39.4	37,266	82,753	45.0	5.7
Germany	77,340	789,844	9.8	97,015	953,057	10.2	0.4
Estonia	2,079	2,965	70.1	3,514	5,029	69.9	-0.2
Finland	22,726	52,861	43.0	28,586	68,925	41.5	-1.5
Latvia	1,718	2,231	77.0	2,396	2,930	81.8	4.8
Lithuania	2,578	4,382	58.8	3,687	6,186	59.6	0.8
Norway	24,085	61,350	39.3	30,298	73,592	41.2	1.9
Poland	18,102	38,799	46.7	24,412	51,942	47.0	0.3
Russia	24,533	101,482	24.2	29,338	123,757	23.7	-0.5
– Kaliningrad	119	205	58.0	...	...	...	...
– St Petersburg	517	999	51.8	...	...	...	...
Sweden	41,239	112,641	36.6	52,278	131,216	39.8	3.2

* Exports and imports in million USD, data source: IMF (1996)

Table 5.4: Sector trade shares, 2010, optimistic scenario

	Minerals, quarrying, oil	Agriculture	Chemicals	Machinery and transport equipment	Other manu-facturing	Total*
	IN PER CENT OF NATIONAL AMOUNT					
Denmark	6.6	20.1	25.3	31.5	16.5	46,207
Germany	2.2	4.1	34.6	41.7	17.3	147,206
Estonia	8.1	15.2	29.0	19.8	28.0	2,330
Finland	6.2	11.2	9.5	27.4	45.6	24,010
Latvia	6.7	16.1	19.9	19.9	37.3	2,267
Lithuania	9.1	23.1	10.0	14.7	43.0	2,753
Norway	58.1	7.4	9.2	11.4	14.0	50,514
Poland	5.7	18.0	6.9	16.7	52.7	22,809
Sweden	11.6	13.4	10.0	32.5	32.6	77,498
Kaliningrad	6.5	29.8	16.2	12.5	35.0	449
St Petersburg	3.8	8.8	11.0	18.1	58.3	1,490
	IN PER CENT OF TOTAL AMOUNT					
Total	12.7	10.0	21.3	31.5	24.4	377,533

* Export figures in million USD at constant prices

and Poland. However, trade in these products will only be 10 per cent of all imports.

The Eastern European countries will have their relatively strongest export position in the sector 'other manufacturing,' i.e. manufacturing of textiles and wearing apparel, and iron and steel basic industries. As can be seen from the figures, the export share of agricultural products remains high in all Eastern European countries. And not surprisingly, their export share of machinery and transport equipment is low compared to the industrial countries.

Implications for Freight Transport

Our scenarios reveal that the changing international division of labour will have strong impacts on traffic and communications. This certainly holds only true on the assumption of successful reforms in Eastern Europe, which implies further dismantling of trade impediments between the states and the surmounting of infrastructure bottlenecks. While intra-industrial trade will grow, the traditional division of labour with finished industrial products flowing in one direction, raw and elemental materials and simple precursor products in the other, will decrease in significance. Correspondingly, the transport modalities – that is, the transport carriers – and the requisite information and communication flows have to be adapted: traffic via container and parcel transport, truck and rail carriage, and the combination of land and sea routes for technical products will increase not only in absolute, but also in relative terms, as bulk goods transport will decline in importance.

Connections Between Trade and Transport

Because the expansion of foreign trade goes hand-in-hand with an expansion of merchandise transport, private and public organisations throughout the Baltic Sea area face the challenge of ensuring that the transport of these goods proceeds smoothly. This implies that infrastructure must be adapted to the growing transportation demand. Not only improvements in the east-west direction are necessary to cope with increasing demand. The routes between the Scandinavian countries and Western Europe will become essential as well, which is obvious in light of the fact that this trade will increase most in absolute terms. Exact quantitative assessments of the consequences of changed trade flows on traffic levels and communications can only be performed by large-scale simulations. However, the following thesis can be formulated without requiring a basis in quantitative scenarios: the expansion of trade flows, posited in the optimistic scenarios, does not lead to proportionately higher traffic levels, because the volume of physical trade may rise slower than the value of the trade realised.

Quantitative assessments of the transport consequences of the future trade potential are based on considerations of the connection between trade in value and volume terms. The quotient of trade figures expressed in value and volume terms can be designated the value density of trade with the dimension 'unit of value per unit of weight' (e.g. USD/kg). In several studies (e.g. ECMT 1991; Andersson 1995) it has turned out that there are sometimes considerable differences between the value densities of a country's imports and exports. The same applies to differences between countries. These differences are, above all, due to the goods structure of trade. Since these proportions change over time, thevalue densities change as well. For Western European countries it can be observed that the value density of trade has risen significantly during the last twenty years. Accordingly, these trends show that the elasticity of trade in volume terms with respect to value terms is considerably less than unity, i.e. if the value of imports or exports increase by one unit, the corresponding volume of imports or exports increases by less than one unit. In covering seven Western European countries for the period 1978 to 1986, the ECMT (1991) calculated an elasticity of 0.65 for imports and 0.35 for exports. The estimated values reflect the still increasing share of intra-industrial imports. In the case of Eastern Europe's trade structure, it may also be assumed that – especially for its growing exports – the volume of transport will increase substantially less than the respective trade values – at least in a long-term perspective.

If we combine the above findings regarding transport elasticities with the presented projections of foreign trade (ranging from annual growth rates of approximately 5 to 10 per cent), we may very roughly estimate that freight transport in northern Europe is likely to increase at average annual growth rates of 2 to 4 per cent over time. This is not in line with studies examining the statistical link between transport and GDP.[6] According to these studies, transport demand in countries for which data are available[7] is likely to increase at average annual growth rates ranging from 1.5 to 2.8 per cent, if annual growth rates of real GDP of about 3 per cent are assumed. If one takes for granted that there is a given and continuing link between economic growth and transport which will surely hold true for all countries on average, one neglects an important point: the precise relation between increases in trade and rising transport demands.

Regardless of whether we rely on one figure or the other, it appears unrealistic to assume that the already planned expansion of rail and road infrastructure will suffice to prevent new bottlenecks in the traffic system of the Baltic Sea area. It is not to be expected that transportation logistics departments rely on a proportionate expansion of the infrastructure. They must rather increase their own flexibility, that is choose varying modes of transport routes and schedules.

Modal Split and Consequences for Future Traffic Policy

What can we say about future bottlenecks in the region? The Baltic Sea already has the densest sea traffic connections in the world with up to 300 million tons of shipments (i.e. 8 per cent of world-wide shipments). External traffic accounts for 60 per cent of these transports. The remaining internal freight transports are dominated by ferries and ro/ro-shipments which have experienced the highest annual growth rates in the nineties (3.5 per cent on average).[8] With respect to the modal split between road and sea transports, all recent figures indicate that overall sea transport will not lose much in significance compared to road transport.

As these considerations suggest, competition between current or future harbours along the southern Baltic shores will not take place on the basis of limited shipment opportunities. Rather, harbours will compete for a share of significantly growing shipments. And competition between harbours is certainly desirable. However, to overcome shortages and to maximise welfare effects of investments, there is a need for increased co-operation and shared decisions about traffic hubs and, particularly, harbour locations – at least on a regional scale.

Furthermore, it would be desirable to avoid a mentality rooted in nationalistic thinking. This holds especially true for the concept of a main port for shipments across the Baltic Sea. In view of the large investments required for harbour infrastructure, including access to harbours, and the growing opposition to extensive land use for harbours, none of the Baltic Sea ports is in a position to serve as a main port comparable to Rotterdam or Hamburg. Such a function would also necessitate substantial growth in road and rail traffic for the hinterland connections. But this exceeds by far the existing or anticipated capacity expansions along the Baltic traffic routes. Even today, the main constraint on meeting future transport demands is not the capacity of harbours themselves but the lack of hinterland connections. The perception that fixed links over the Great Belt and Øresund will satisfy the demand for fixed links in next few decades is probably erroneous in view of the rising transport demands in a highly integrated Baltic Sea region.

This calls for a co-ordinated expansion of communication and information networks between important production and sales locations and of traffic hubs – most notably the harbours' hinterland connections. In the conflict zone between the intensification of trade flows and increasing transportation bottlenecks, there is a need for intelligent, flexible traffic logistics, distributed over regions and locations in a harmonised fashion.

Summary

Transformation of the economic system and integration into the international division of labour offer the Eastern European countries tremendous opportunities. The first years after the demise of communism have already brought a strong expansion of trade with Western countries. This trend will continue into the year 2010 though economic potentials differ from one trading partner to another.

Both of our scenarios clearly show that it is absolutely necessary for the Eastern European economies to continue their reforms. Deviation from the reform path would result in a drastic slump in foreign trade ties and in the continued integration into the international division of labour. This surely is a crucial point for these countries, because foreign trade is an important means of funding their future development.

Finally, I would like to stress that economic integration manifests itself not only through increased trade flows of goods and services, but also in the area of investments, i.e. the movement of tangible and intangible forms of capital, such as finance, technology and the ownership or control of assets. In addition to foreign trade, one of the main driving forces behind further regional integration is foreign direct investments. Or, more precisely, the attraction of FDI goes hand-in-hand with the expansion of foreign trade. FDI not only brings production plants and equipment but it is usually linked to the transfer of production technologies, managerial skills and knowledge from one country to another. FDI thus leads to a further increase and diversification of trade – which is why the Baltic Sea reform countries should pursue it.

Notes

1 For a broader discussion on barriers to economic integration, see Peschel 1992; 1993.

2 The project's final report is found in Commission of the European Communities (1993), the empirical methodics are described in Bröcker and Jäger-Roschko (1996).

3 Among many studies, see for instance Rollo and Stern (1992) and Cohen (1992). A survey is found in Sheehy (1994).

4 This concerns especially the foreign trade of the Baltic states and of the Russian regions. For details of the Baltic states' respective split by trading partners, the reader is referred to Callsen and Jäger-Roschko (1996).

5 Germany's trade volume in 1995 with the small Benelux states – amounting to 130 billion USD – is approximately 40 per cent higher than aggregated trade with all countries considered here.

6 Among many studies, see, for instance, Voigt (1995).

7 For longer time periods, reliable data are only registered for western European countries.

8 For all figures the reader is referred to ECMT (1995).

References

Andersson, Å. (1995). 'Economic changes and transport,' pages 67-81 in European Conference of Ministers of Transport (ed.). *Transport: New Problems, New Solutions.* Luxembourg.

Baldwin, R.E. (1994). *Towards an Integrated Europe.* CEPR, London.

Bolz, K. and Polkowski, A. (1995). 'Der Wirtschaftsraum Sankt Petersburg – Wirtschaftliche und soziale Entwicklung im Herbst 1994 und Programme für die Zukunft.' Studie IV, *HWWA-Report*:149, HWWA-Institut für Wirtschaftsforschung, Hamburg.

Bröcker, J. and Jäger-Roschko, O. (1996). 'Eastern Reforms, Trade, and Spatial Change in the EU,' Papers in Regional Science, *The Journal of the Regional Science Association International*:75, pages 23-40.

Callsen, S. and Jäger-Roschko, O. (1996). 'Economic Growth and Trade Perspectives in the Baltic Basin: Two Scenarios,' *The Baltic Review*:11, autumn 1996, pages 10-12. Tallinn.

Commission of the European Communities (1993). Trade and Foreign Investment in the Communities Regions: The Impact of Economic Reform in Central and Eastern Europe,' *Regional Development Studies*:7. Brussels, Luxembourg.

Cohen, D. (1992). 'The Solvency of Eastern Europe,' *European Economy*, special edition No.2. Brussels.

Collins, S.M.and Rodrik, D. (1991). *Eastern Europe and the Soviet Union in the World Economy.* Washington, D.C, Institute of International Economics.

ECMT (1991) (European Conference of Ministers of Transport). *Prospects for East-West European Transport.* Paris, OECD Publications Service.

ECMT (1995) (European Conference of Ministers of Transport). *Annales statistiques de transport 1965-1990.* Paris, OECD Publications Service.

Fischer, M.M. and Johansson, B. (1994). 'Opening up International Trade in Eastern European Countries,' *WSG Discussion Papers*:40/94. Wien, Institut für Wirtschafts- und Sozialgeographie.

IMF (1996) (International Monetary Fund). *Direction of Trade Statistics,* Yearbook Vol. 31. Washington D.C.

Jäger-Roschko, O. (1997). *Internationaler Handel im Ostseeraum – Szenarien auf Basis eines Regressionsansatzes.* Schriftenreihe des Instituts für Regionalforschung:15. München, V. Florentz-Verlag.

Peschel, K. (1990). 'On the Spatial Structure of the World Economy since World War II,' pages 129-157 in Gehrels, F., Herberg, H., Schneider, H. and Vosgerau, H.J. (eds.). *Real Adjustment Process under Floating Exchange Rates.* Berlin, Heidelberg.

Peschel, K. (1992). 'European Integration and Regional Development in Northern Europe,' *Regional Studies*:26, No. 4, pages 387-397.

Peschel, K. (1993). 'Perspectives of Regional Economic Development around the Baltic' in Lundqvist, L. and Persson, L.O. (eds.). *Visions and Strategies in European Integration.* Berlin, Heidelberg.

PlanEcon (1994) *Review and Outlook: Analysis and Forecasts to 1999 of Economic Developments in Eastern Europe.* June 1994. Washington D.C., PlanEcon Inc.

Reymann, S. (1995). *Kaliningrader Gebiet – Wirtschaftsentwicklung und -politik im Herbst 1994.* HWWA-Report:150. Hamburg, HWWA-Institut für Wirtschaftsforschung.

Rollo, J.M.C. and Stern, J. (1992). *Growth and Trade Prospects for Central and Eastern Europe.* Working Paper:1. London, National Economic Research Associates (NERA).

Sheehy, J. (1994). 'CEEC's Growth Prospects for GDP and Manufacturing Trade with the EC: A Short Literature Survey,' *European Economy*:6, pages 3-16.

Voigt, U. (1995). 'Traffic Flow Trends.' pages 289-339 in *Transport: New Problems, New Solutions.* Luxembourg, European Conference of Ministers of Transport.

Wang, Z. and Winters, L.A. (1991). 'The Trading Potential of Eastern Europe,' *CEPR Discussion Paper*:610. London.

6 Foreign Direct Investment: Problems in Deepening the Integration of the Baltic Sea Region

Urpo Kivikari

The growth of intra-Baltic trade in the 1990s has laid the foundation for an economic region around the Baltic Sea. But commodity trade alone cannot unify a market, let alone furnish it with a distinctive identity. Rather, the intensification of integration is reflected in the increased mobility of factors of production. It is foreign direct investment that significantly promotes the formation of new networks and leads to a long-term convergence and integration of the national economies.

In developed market economies, foreign direct investment (hereafter FDI) is a conventional operation from which friction has recently been removed by the formation of the European Economic Area and the expansion of the European Union. By contrast, in the emerging market economies of the former socialist countries, FDI is still a fairly new phenomenon, in respect of which the expectations of both economic analysts and the enterprises have not been fulfilled. Direct investments in China have been thirty times as great as they have been in Russia, the principal heir of the Soviet Union. Direct investments in another Asian state, Malaysia, have been more than twice as great in this decade as they have been in Russia, Estonia, Latvia, Lithuania, and Poland together, even though in these countries, the total population is ten times that of Malaysia. As far as the outflow of FDI from the developed Western states of the Baltic region is concerned, the share that has gone to the five states mentioned above over the years 1991-95 was about 2 per cent from Finland and even less from other countries (IMF and World Bank staff estimates; World Development Report 1996: 64; Laurila and Hirvensalo 1996).

In order to further integration in the Baltic area, it is obviously important to find solutions to the problems of why the emerging market economies of the region have had so little success in attracting direct investments. In the following we shall, first and foremost, concentrate on the specific obstacles to FDI in the former socialist countries of the Baltic Sea region.

Background

In the era of the Cold War, the two basic factors that exerted a negative influence on the economic relations between the capitalist and socialist states were political rivalry and differences in economic systems. Commodity exports and imports directly reflected political relations. Where political antagonism existed, commodity trade was easily disturbed by a variety of restraints, such as heavy tariffs, embargo measures and restrictions on credit. Yet in the adoption of more developed operations in East-West trade, it was the friction caused by different economic systems that tended to grow, while the influence of political rivalry remained more in the background (see Table 6.1). Dissimilarities in accounting practice, pricing, marketing, risk-taking, i.e. in economic thinking and in the economic mechanism as a whole, proved to be much more real and embarrassing for joint ventures than was the case in commodity trade or in simpler industrial co-operation.

Table 6.1: The significance of obstacles arising from the peculiarities of East-West trade during the Cold War

Form of economic activity	Relative significance of the negative impact of:	
	a) political rivalry	b) differences in economic systems
Commodity trade	strong	slight
Industrial co-operation	moderate	moderate
Joint ventures	slight	strong

Source: Kivikari (1988)

More than five years ago, political antagonism between East and West passed into history in the Baltic Sea region as everywhere else in Europe, and Russia, Estonia, Latvia, Lithuania, and Poland began their transformation into market economies. The previous obstacles of a political nature were rapidly removed, but the important changes in the business environment needed for the promotion of FDI require a lengthier evolutionary process.

Motivation behind FDI

Even under the socialist regime, calculation of the pros and cons led to the adoption of FDI. Nowadays, its benefits to emerging market economies are more than ever evident. Apart from capital, FDI brings in new technology, management and marketing knowledge, as well as access to foreign markets. While FDI saves on import expenditure and risks, it contributes to competitive production at low opportunity cost and increases the export revenues of the host country. It exerts pressure for a new business culture and for institution-building. In the light of the favourable impacts of FDI on countries in transition, it is easy to believe that governments dedicated to developing a market economy are in earnest in their declarations of support for FDI and really do wish to combat obstacles to it.

The receptivity of the host country is a prior condition and an important attraction, but the decision to make the investment is, of course, in the hands of the foreign firm. No single theory exists about FDI, but there are several approaches to explaining why FDI constitutes an appropriate operation in the internationalisation of a firm. On one side of the theoretical spectrum, one finds political economists who state that FDI is an inevitable outcome of the capitalist system. At the other extreme, there is the approach of business analysts who are identifying, often empirically, the main factors that influence investment activity (Djarova et al. 1996: 9-17; Meyer 1995).

Concerning the investments made by Western firms in the emerging market economies, three particular groups of objectives can be distinguished: the market objective, the cost reduction objective and the 'pure investment' objective (Djarova et al. 1996: 24). FDI is a means of entering and serving local markets, of protecting a company's existing markets, or of preparing the host country to be a springboard for entry into third markets. In some cases, a combination of these three market objectives can be seen. As far as cost advantage is concerned, it becomes a real benefit only when it is not offset by low productivity. The objective of cost reduction can be attained also by other operations. Subcontracting with local companies is one such means. The 'pure investment' objective may exert an influence on the scope of the investor's own business when a small investment serves as 'a finger on the pulse.' Sometimes, simply the lucrative profit is the main motive for a (temporary) investment outside the investor's proper business.

Among the determinants exerting a positive influence on the Western company's attitude towards FDI are considerations of market size and prospects for growth. According to surveys, great importance is attached to a stable environment and to a political and economic climate favourable to foreigners. It is also clear that geographical, historical and cultural proximity promote business. However, the significance of low labour costs and an 'investment bonus,' that is incentives granted by governments, have generally not been viewed as particularly important determinants by Western investors (Djarova et al. 1996; Linderfalk 1996; Meyer 1995).

Obstacles to FDI[1]

Three different factors exert a negative influence on FDI in the Baltic region's emerging market economies. First, foreign firms always tend to be in an adverse position as compared with domestic firms. Among the 'natural' obstacles are higher transaction costs and unfamiliarity with language, culture, bureaucracy, networks etc. Secondly, there are some general obstacles which Western investors come up against in transition countries. Thirdly, Russia, Estonia, Latvia, Lithuania and Poland also have country-specific features that may impede their role as host countries to FDI.

Since foreign investment enterprise consists of production, sales, purchasing, transport, storage and other economic activities, any impediment to economic operations in the host country will at least indirectly affect FDI. And so, apart from factors that particularly obstruct FDI, obstacles to commodity trade are of relevance too. But in the following, consideration will primarily be given to obstacles to investment.

Physical Infrastructure

It is comparatively easy to make an objective and unambiguous assessment of defects in the physical structure. Correcting them is generally also regarded as fairly easy – provided that the requisite financing is available.

Telecommunications, both in capacity and quality, have been one of the most backward features of the legacy of socialism. Telecommunications are of crucial importance as an engine of economic development supporting both the decentralisation of the economy and the integration of the national market into the world economy. By improving the situation in this field, a marked alleviation of the obstacles on FDI in other fields may occur. FDI has a key role in enhancing the capacity and quality of telecommunications, but Western telecommunications firms have already experienced plenty of obstacles to FDI.

One of the greatest obstacles was revealed in a study based on interviews of representatives of Western telecommunications firms and their subsidiaries in St Petersburg, Estonia, and Latvia. It is the weakness and uncertainty of the market. The purchasing power of the consumers is weak, and even where the business segment is more viable, it remains unstable and chaotic. A regulatory environment, a policy of licensing, fragmented markets in which local operators hold a strong position – not to say one of de facto monopoly – have been found to be problematic both for foreign enterprises and for the general development of telecommunications sector. The role played by the authorities in telecommunications is at one and the same time both crucial and confusing, for they are often engaged in both the operation and regulation of telecommunications. The dual position of authorities, as well as conflicting interests and disputes between the different authorities, weakens the foreign investor's interest and confidence in the field. At the currently abnormally low tariff rates, the interest of outsiders in the sector falls off, and FDI is one-sidedly channelled into the most profitable segments only (Kaarre 1996: 172-78).

Institutional Infrastructure

Alongside problems of a technical nature, impediments often emerge from defects in the administration and other institutions. Concerning traffic questions, for example, the problems are only partly due to shortcomings in physical infrastructure. They may equally well be caused by administrative weaknesses. Due to its sluggishness and sheer incomprehensibility, the bureaucracy has frequently been experienced as a cause of delay and impediment. It is true that legislation has been amended, and in this respect the situation is continually showing signs of improvement. Nevertheless, problems of implementation remain. To take an example, it is often difficult to get exact information on the real content of environmental liabilities for investment. One stumbling-block is that legislation and its enforcement in regard to foreign ownership – especially land ownership – are still at the half-way stage (Gheciu 1996).

Many institutions of the market economy require for their development a longer time span than has actually passed on the road to democracy and the market economy. There are also weaknesses in banking and in the insurance sector which act as disincentives to FDI. The poor availability of investment funding also affects joint ventures and Western subsidiaries. The bankruptcy risk of local banks breeds instability in the market, and together with the bureaucracy, this impedes the entry of Western banks and the promotion of competition. In many respects, the insurance business is in its infancy, and the present need to mediate insurance from abroad increases costs. The size of the internal security markets remains modest, which is a hindrance to foreign investments of all kinds.

Structural Barriers in National Economies

As a result of system change, all the conditions of production have to be re-evaluated. The endowments of production, price formation, customer relations and almost all other factors in the economy are nowadays different from what they used to be. In Russia, the Baltic countries and Poland, it has been found necessary to re-organise the production plants, the financing systems, the exploitation of raw material resources, training and research as well as social policy. It is not always possible to know the sort of social obligations that may, in practice, fall on FDI, although the provision of housing, day-care facilities and recreational centres is no longer officially a function of the enterprise as was formerly the case. Nonetheless, enterprises may be confronted with the need to provide such services in cases where they have not otherwise been arranged locally or where competition for labour compels it.

In the West, successful companies often receive a back-up from related industries inn the shape of close-knit networks or clusters to which they themselves belong. For example, in Denmark the food industry benefits from companies in the field of biotechnology that also serve the pharmaceutical industry. In Finland and Sweden, the forest industry has engendered a flourishing paper-machine and pulp-equipment branch of manufacturing. In these countries, the forest industry has also stimulated a consultancy profession, whose services are nowadays crucial for the success of the forest industry (Hernesniemi 1996). In the eastern part of the Baltic region, a corresponding back-up, on which FDI could rely, is simply not there. The lack of related industry along with defective infrastructure and logistics may form an insuperable obstacle to FDI.

Political and Economic Climate

To a great extent, direct investments from the Western market economies have gone to countries in which democracy and the market economy are less developed than in the emerging economies of the Baltic Sea region. Confidence in the stability of the host country is sufficient for investors whereas incalculable uncertainty and instability are the worst possible poison for the potential investor. A lack of foresight on the part of local authorities has been a considerable obstacle. Reliable economic forecasts can only be made in countries with a stable system. Economic and political instability has clearly been the greatest cause of concern for Western firms, particularly with regard to investments in Russia (Borsos and Erkkilä 1996: 130). The fact that the investments by the Russians themselves find their way abroad in preference to being placed in their own country does not increase confidence among foreign investors in Russia.

At least outwardly, the official atmosphere generated has been favourable to FDI in all the emerging market economies of the region. However, the atmosphere is influenced by more factors than those proclaimed by the government. In reality, foreign-owned enterprises often bear a heavier burden as tax- and dues-payers than do domestic firms. Protectionism, too, has reared its head as the strong competitiveness of foreign firms arouses conflicting aspirations under difficult economic conditions. Firms feel it to be a threat when competition increases in their own field of business, whereas a foreign contribution in related industries is often welcomed as bettering the competitiveness of the firm in question and of the whole branch of business. In short, government and parliament have to be able to act in the interest of the economy as a whole, even when confronted by the turmoil of lobbying of many different kinds.

Especially in Russia, certain forces have fomented suspicion against foreign

Table 6.2: The appearance of problems in different forms of FDI

	Joint venture	Acquisition	Greenfield
Environmental liabilities	x	X	x
Restructuring costs	x	X	x
Valuation	X	X	x
Negotiation with government agencies	x/X	X	x/X
Ownership status of property	x	x	X
Supply and distribution networks	x	x	X
Integration into local economy	x	x	X
Cultural differences	X	X	x

X = relatively big problem; x = small problem/no problem at all

enterprises by claiming that they are stripping the country of its sources of wealth. Once foreign business activity becomes a pawn in local politics, firms that are considering investments – with the best of intentions – begin to feel uneasy. The connection between crime and business and the somewhat weak corpus of business ethics undoubtedly constitute further obstacles to FDI.

The Significance of the Form Taken by FDI

The obstacles FDI meets with vary according to the form of the business operations in question. Initially, in the socialist era, the only possibility was a minority stake in a joint venture (henceforth JV). The next stage was the possibility of becoming a majority holder in a JV. The foreign-owned firms that have functioned the longest are therefore JVs or at least firms that started out as such. Later on, the monopoly status of the JVs ended, and changes were also made in their legal position. Nevertheless, the JV is far from being a historical relic. Indeed, globally, it is in wide use in all kinds of countries.

Particularly in countries where the transformation to a market economy has proceeded fairly rapidly, acquisition as a form of FDI has spread most vigorously. Privatisation, a revolutionary process, has rendered this possible and provided large-scale opportunities for FDI. As a result of privatisation, whether initiated by the government or spontaneously by the enterprise, a significant number of state-owned enterprises – turned into joint stock or limited liability companies – have been acquired by foreign owners. Privatisation on a scale as vast as in the emerging market economies of the 1990s is a one-off phenomenon. Once this slackens off or ends, a crucial suction drawing in FDI is lost and in place of system-change, incentives for FDI have to be found in the dynamism of the national economy.

The third of the principal forms taken by FDI is greenfield investment. This occurs when a foreign firm establishes an entirely new enterprise. The most common grounds are that no hoped-for partner can be found in the host country and that there is no chance of buying an appropriate company there. Different investment forms may, of course, be combined. It may make sense for a Western company to greenfield a manufacturing process, and purchase supply and distribution channels. In a JV-acquisition, the Eastern partner contributes a plant or division to the new company, while the Western partner brings in capital, technology and know-how. Which form is chosen in each case depends on many factors (Gatling 1993: 44-7; Djarova 1996: 77-85). Table 6.2 illustrates the effect of obstacles that are clearly sensitive to the form taken by FDI.

Factors related to environmental protection are everywhere becoming of increasing importance for the location of production and for other planning. In greenfielding, it is easier to take environmental factors into consideration than it is in the acquisition of an already functioning enterprise. In a JV, the fact of there being a joint responsibility with the local owner for environmental liabilities eases the situation. Reconstruction costs are always a burden in an acquisition and cannot be accurately estimated when the acquisition is made. With FDI, expectations naturally arise of a positive rather than a negative effect on employment, and this may be something of a problem for a new owner of an overstaffed enterprise.

The special problems inherent in asset valuation as well as business valuation arise from the unfinished nature of system-change and from the difficulty of foretelling the future course. In greenfield investments these problems are, of course, smaller. Negotiations of every kind to ensure the success of the investment are most important, but they may also turn out to be laborious and time-consuming – at their worst creating so many obstacles that the FDI plan may even have to be abandoned. In the case of an acquisition, this is based both on governmental negotiation and often on negotiations with the management and employees of the enterprise, and even with other interested parties.

The issue of legislation and restitution having been partly solved, the ownership status of property is no longer as big an obstacle as it was some time ago. The potential number of claims has been somewhat higher in greenfield cases than in acquisition cases. The key motive in the choice of JV and acquisition is often the integration of production into the local economy. By contrast, when greenfield occurs, there is no ready supply and distribution chain; it is not part of a network, nor does it command an existing market share.

For foreign enterprises, cultural differences are always a cause of friction. In greenfielding, the chances of introducing the desired kind of enterprise culture into an FDI firm are, of course, greater.

Country-Specific Differences

Although the five emerging market economies of the Baltic Sea region have much in common in terms of incentives and obstacles, they clearly differ as to circumstances and performance. Table 6.3 gives data about the inflow of FDI that has already taken place. To get a comparative picture, the size of the country has been taken into account and, in consequence, the figures have been made proportional to the population and the GDP.

Table 6.3: Foreign direct investment flows into emerging market economies in the Baltic Sea region

	FDI inflow 1995			Cumulative FDI 1990-95	
	Total (million USD)	Per capita (USD)	Flow/GDP (per cent)	Stock (million USD)	Per capita (USD)
Estonia	205	138	8.8	638	420
Latvia	216	87	6.3	587	227
Lithuania	41	11	1.0	113	30
Poland	1 134	29	1.2	2 751	71
Russia	920	6	0.3	5 118	35

Source: *Economic Survey of Europe in 1995-1996*, pages 149-50

Of the countries that became independent after the break-up of the Soviet Union, it is Estonia that has most consistently followed a liberal policy of an open economy. Privatisation has been brisk and been aided by the direct sale of enterprises, and the participation of foreigners in all this has been encouraged. In proportion to its size, Estonia has obviously been the most successful recipient of FDIs, which are already having their effect on the country's economic development. Latvia, too, has made progress in its reforms, though at a somewhat slower pace than Estonia. The banking crisis in Latvia in 1995 undoubtedly created obstacles for all investment activity. In Lithuania, privatisation has actually proceeded more rapidly than it has in Latvia, but the part played by the sale of enterprises to outside interests has been very low, and this has acted as a brake on the widening of FDI. The economy of Lithuania was also overshadowed by a banking crisis in 1995 (Linderfalk 1996).

In Poland, the rather large markets, the shock therapy of a swift system change and the economic growth that began in 1992 have all served to promote FDI. On the other hand, the severe indebtedness of the country combined with a climate of political and economic uncertainty did retard foreign investments in the initial years of the transition. Until quite recently, most of these investments have been in the form of the JV, as favoured in the legislation. Poland offers great potential for the growth of FDI. Among the five coastal provinces, which specifically belong to the Baltic Sea region, Gdansk province has been most successful in attracting foreign investment with 13 per cent of all FDI, second only to Warsaw province.

The country with the greatest room by far for growth of foreign enterprise is Russia. At the moment, foreign investors there are facing uncertain property rights and contract law, inadequate law enforcement against criminal elements, unpredictable taxes and regulations that keep on changing. In the energy sector, FDI is hampered by jurisdictional disputes between local, regional, and federal authorities about the control of natural resources. Uncertainty still prevails in respect of the future line of policy. In the autumn of 1996, the media reproduced a statement made by General Aleksander Lebed according to which Russia will impose sanctions on foreign enterprises if NATO extends eastwards. These

Table 6.4: The investment ratings of emerging economies in the Baltic Sea region

	Euromoney country risk ranking		
	September 1996	March 1996	September 1993
Poland	55	58	72
Estonia	71	73	122
Latvia	75	89	132
Lithuania	59	85	130
Russia	86	100	137

Source: *Euromoney*, September 1993, September 1996

passing words, perhaps a result of thoughtlessness, will explain the level of FDI to Russia in 1997 better than its natural resources or any other endowment of the Russian economy. Still, quite an interest has been kindled in the West in the shares of some Russian companies. Perhaps direct investments will be accelerated in the wake of portfolio investment.

Russia's Baltic provinces' shares of FDI inflow in 1995 were St Petersburg 5.6 per cent, Leningrad province 0.7 per cent and Kaliningrad province 0.4 per cent. Of the FDI inflow to St Petersburg, 59 per cent was in food industry, 18 per cent in engineering and 8 per cent in transportation and telecommunications. After some years of uncertainty, Kaliningrad was in January 1996 declared a special economic zone, which immediately increased investors' interest in the enclave.

The difference between the two extreme cases of Estonia and Russia is illustrated by the fact that more capital has flowed from Finland to the more numerous foreign subsidiaries in Estonia than into the one-hundred times larger Russia. Both lands are neighbouring countries to Finland, but linguistically and culturally Estonia is closer. The experience of Finnish firms with regard to direct investments in Estonia and Russia has differed. At the behest of the Bank of Finland, this experiences has been collated repeatedly in a series of surveys since 1991. A questionnaire drawn up in 1995 was answered by 345 firms who had 184 subsidiaries operating in Russia and 235 in Estonia. Their answers certainly reflected an improvement in the situation in both countries if compared with the results of a survey made two years earlier. However, Estonia was increasingly favoured. In respect of Russia, the adjective most often used to characterise the business climate was 'tolerable.' In respect of Estonia, it was 'satisfactory.' Future expectations were fairly positive for both countries as far as Finnish businessmen were concerned. The difference between expectations seemed to be primarily due to the time-horizon. Businessmen felt that improvements could be expected to take place in the near future in Estonia, whereas in Russia everything was going to be put off to a more distant future (Laurila and Hirvensalo 1996). Parallel inferences can be drawn from some case studies of big Finnish companies (Hirvensalo 1996).

International business analysts regularly publish rating services listing the investment grade of different countries. In Table 6.4 gives the Euromoney country risk rating. It is based on appraisals made by economic and political analysts and on an array of quantitative data. The result is a sensitive measure of the level of the risk involved in investing in these countries. With regard to all five countries, a positive feature is that in 1996 their ranking among about 170 countries was much better than it was in 1993. For Poland, the investment risks are seen to be the smallest. Among the Baltic states, Lithuania has attained first place. The ranking of Russia has clearly risen after the presidential elections held in the summer of 1996.

Conclusions

In the 1990s Russia, Estonia, Latvia, Lithuania, and Poland began their transition to market economies and, as a part of this transition, embarked on a massive programme of privatisation. No comparable opportunity for FDI has ever previously been offered. Notwithstanding the fact that the enterprises of the advanced market economies have taken advantage of the situation, the eastward flow of FDI has nevertheless been smaller than anticipated.

It seems fairly evident that FDI would have been stimulated if ownership of enterprises had been more readily offered to foreigners than has been the case. More decisive nevertheless has been the general situation in these countries from the point of view of the foreign investor. Here it has to be said that so far the obstacles to FDI have exerted a stronger influence than any encouraging factor. This emerges most clearly in the case of Russia. Russia contains the greatest natural resources in the world, a consumer and labour potential of a population of 150 million and limitless investment opportunities from high technology to agriculture. But the truth is that the direct investments in Russia do not reflect these opportunities at all; what they reflect are the barriers which hinder the utilisation of these resources within the framework of the international division of labour. The persistent inadequacies have delayed the avalanche of investment which had been expected.

Some attempts have been made to attract direct investments by creating artificial advantages such as tax holidays, special economic zones and so forth. But tax exemption is not very attractive unless you are able to create something taxable, that is profit. The granting of special concessions to foreign firms has now been largely abandoned, which is a healthy development. It is far better when enterprises, whatever the composition of their ownership, are operating under competitive conditions that are as equal as possible.

The emerging market economies of the Baltic region have undoubtedly improved their globally competitive position in terms of ranking as host countries of investments. And there is reason for optimism about a further improvement in their position. The factors on which the attractiveness of these countries rests are rather well known. What is needed is the skill and drive to apply this knowledge.

Note

1 The obstacles FDI runs up against in transition economies have been dealt with in, among others, the following publications: Paliwoda 1994; Djarova 1996; Gatling 1993; Borsos and Erkkilä 1996; Kivikari 1996.

References

Borsos, J. and Erkkilä, M. (1996). 'Regional Integration in the Baltic Rim: FDI and Trade Based Integration in Finland, Estonia and St. Petersburg,' pages 85-166 in *Regional Integration and Transition Economies: The Case of Baltic Rim.* Centre for Co-operation with the Economies in Transition, OECD

Djarova, J. (1996). 'Foreign Investments in Central and Eastern Europe,' pages 55-88 in Djarova, J. (ed.). *Foreign Direct Investment in Central and Eastern Europe.* Erasmus University, Rotterdam

Djarova, J., Rietveldtand, O. and van Rossum du Chattel, O. (1996). Foreign Direct Investments: Survey on Theories and Determinants,' pages 55-88 in Djarova, J. (ed.). *Foreign Direct Investment in Central and Eastern Europe.* Erasmus University, Rotterdam.

Economic Survey of Europe in 1995-1996 (1996). UN Economic Commission for Europe.

Euromoney (1996). 'Asian Economies Start to Slip.' September, pages 200-205.

'From Plan to Market' (1996). *World Development Report 1996.* World Bank.

Gatling, R. (1993). 'Foreign Investment in Eastern Europe.' The Economist Intelligence Unit.

Gheciu, M. (1996). 'The Legal Framework of the Foreign Investment in Central and East-European Countries,' *Journal of East-West Business*:2 (3/4), pages 125-142.

Hirvensalo, I. (1996). *Strategic Adaptation of Enterprises to Turbulent Transitionary Markets.* ETLA, The Research Institute of the Finnish Economy, A 24 Series.

Kaarre, M. (1996). 'Foreign Direct Investments in Telecommunications in St. Petersburg and the Baltic States,' in *Regional Integration and Transition Economies: The Case of Baltic Rim.* Centre for Co-operation with the Economies in Transition, OECD.

Kivikari, U. (1988). 'Special Operations: Solution or Substitution in East-West Trade,' *Nordic Journal of Soviet & East European Studies*:5, No. 1, pages 55-62.

Kivikari, U. (1996). *The Legacy of Hansa: The Baltic Economic Region.* Otava Publishing Company.

Laurila, J. and Hirvensalo, I. (1996). 'Direct Investment from Finland to Eastern Europe: Results of the 1995 Bank of Finland Survey,' *Review of Economies in Transition*:5 , Bank of Finland, pages 5-25.

Linderfalk, B. (1996). 'Baltic Business: Foreign Investment Show the Way,' *The Baltic Times*, Dec. 19, 1996-Jan. 8, 1997, page 11.

Meyer, K.E. (1995). 'Direct Foreign Investment in Eastern Europe: The Role of Labor Costs,' *Comparative Economic Studies*:XXXVII, No. 4, pages 69-88.

Paliwoda, S.J. (1995). *Investing in Eastern Europe Capitalizing on Emerging Markets.* Addison-Wesley Publishing Company.

7 Sustainable Investment Policies in the Murmansk Region

Vladimir Didyk and Ulf Wiberg

Introduction

The debate about the definition and the meaning of the sustainable development concept has been going on for more than 20 years.[1] The most well-known definition concerns the problem in a global perspective, whereas the implications of the concept in a regional context may have some specific features. Nevertheless, the basic principles of sustainable development preserve their importance as a general guideline for the formulation of a policy at the regional level as well. These are demands for 1) ecological sustainability, which implies maintaining the economy at a scale that does not damage the ecological processes and functions; 2) improving the quality of life of the present generation without denying future generations a similar opportunity; 3) an efficient functioning of an economic system which is able to produce a surplus and technological knowledge in a self-contained way (WCED 1987; UNEP 1992; Costanza 1994: 393).

In recent years, this notion of sustainability has been extended in the regional development debate in Europe to refer to the maintenance of regional economic and social systems. For example, Bryden and Commins (1997) argue that 'it is through community organisation that people can reinforce attitudes and practices, and also institutionalise mutually agreeable strategies for sustainability.'

Investments play a critical role in providing environmental, social and economic sustainability. In this context investments should not be regarded in a narrow financial sense, but one which 'includes all human actions to realize intended changes in social organisation as well as accumulation of knowledge. ... It is a choice for the future' (Young 1992: 11). The aim of this article is to describe the current investment pattern in the Murmansk region ('oblast' in Russian) and to discuss future alternatives from a perspective of sustainability .

Changing Investment Patterns

The economy of the Murmansk region is characterised by the following factors which influence the pattern of investment activities: 1) the predominance of capital intensive, resource-extracting production, which is extremely dependent on a high regularity and level of investment; 2) severe climatic conditions, which cause much higher (50-100 per cent) per capita capital costs compared with corresponding production and social infrastructure in central Russian regions; 3) a heavy concentration of environmentally hazardous production and objects and of areas which are suffering from severe environmental damage.[2] There are obvious risks of irreversible degradation of sensitive Arctic ecosystems if measures for the protection of nature are not immediately integrated in investment strategies.

Neither the characteristics just mentioned nor some unique regional economic features were adequately taken into account in the centralised investment policy of the former Soviet authorities, who concentrated on the rapid development of 'cheap' regional resources (Luzin 1993: 129). Consequently, the Murmansk region has experienced a deteriorating regime of reproduction, especially in the mining industry. Needs for environmental protection and renewal at the technical level have been neglected. Not only specialised industries, but the entire regional economy is in a trough of an investment cycle that began in the late 1940s and early 1950s. A substantial renovation/reconstruction of most enterprises in the region is required.[3]

The transition from a centrally planned towards a market oriented economy that started in the early 1990s has been accompanied by a considerable decline

Figure 7.1: Industrial output, total capital investments and explicit environmental protection investments in the Murmansk region (deflated indexes, 1991=100 per cent)

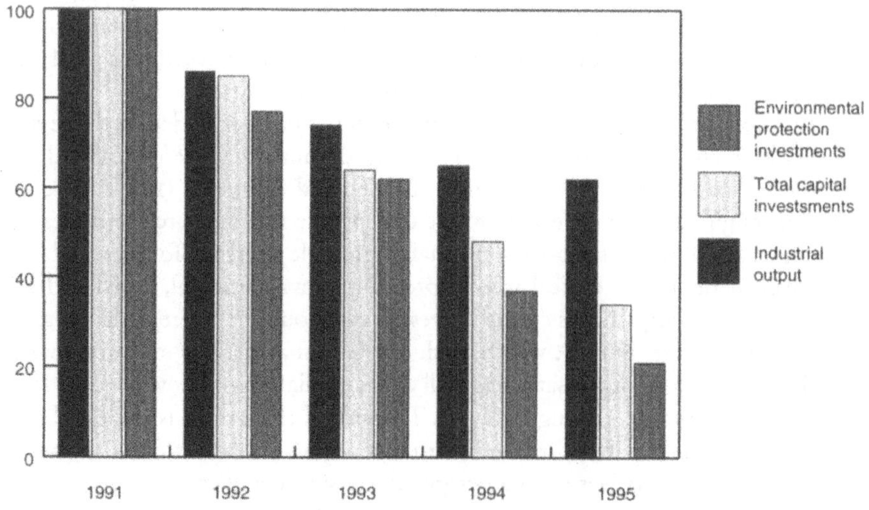

in production and investments in almost all regions and sectors of the Russian economy. Figure 7.1 shows industrial output and the capital investment pattern in the Murmansk region during 1991-95.[4]

From 1991 to 1995, the level of capital investments dropped much faster than the industrial production. It will also be noticed that the decline in investments for environmental protection was even more dramatic than the average decline of capital investments. The environmental protection investments in the figure represent, among other things, capital expenditures for recultivation of land, constructions for sewage treatment and facilities for controlling and detoxifying discharged gases. Between 1990 and 1995, the share of environmental protection investments in total capital investments declined from 2.5 per cent to 1.8 per cent. This has happened despite the introduction of a special tax to control pollution caused by industrial firms in accordance with the 'Russian Federation Law on the Protection of the Environment' (1992). In view of the specific characteristics of the region's economy, this collapse of investment activities will probably lead to more dramatically negative long-term consequences than in the regions further south.

The fall in production volume has not been accompanied by a proportional decline of harmful environmental impact in the Murmansk region. During the period 1991 to 1995, when industrial output decreased by almost 40 per cent (Figure 7.1), pollution decreased by only 20 per cent (Table 7.1).

As a consequence of economic decline, a significant migration out of the region has started. During 1991-95, the net out-migration was 88 000 persons, which represented almost 9 per cent of the population. Taking into account the harsh climatic conditions and the need for economic rationalisation and a reduction of the pressure on the environment, population decrease in itself could not evoke complaints. However, a negative consequence of the current out-migration is an increased share of retired and disabled people in the population. Obviously, from a perspective of social and economic sustainability, such a deformation of the population structure in a northern periphery is far from satisfactory. Despite the out-migration, the level of unemployment has risen more in the Murmansk

Table 7.1: Examples of pressure on the environment by economic activity in the Murmansk region

	1991	1992	1993	1994	1995
Extraction (million cubic m.)	2610	2318	2221	1763	2287
Discharge of polluted sewage (million cubic m.)	367	411	307	305	303
Pollution of atmosphere (thousand tonnes)	650	617	539	469	543

Source: *The Murmansk Region in Figures: Concise Statistical Handbook.* Goskomstat of the Russian Federation (1996: 32)

region (12.3 per cent in 1995) than in Russia as a whole (8.0 per cent in 1995). Under current market conditions, it is also unlikely that new labour-intensive industries will be established in the region unless especially favourable comparative advantages are involved.

Substantial structural changes are among the most important processes in the regional investment pattern during recent years. The most pertinent changes of the sources of investment funding (Table 7.2) have been a reduction in the share of spending from the federal budget alongside with expanded shares of financing from the enterprises' own resources and from other investment funds. It will also be noticed that the share of investment expenditures from local budgets has decreased. To a large extent, however, this shift is only a reflection of the privatisation of state-owned enterprises. A more problematic pattern is the reduction of the foreign investment share from 3.2 per cent in 1993 to 0.8 per cent in 1995. This small and declining share indicates a wait-and-see attitude among potential foreign investors.

Data on the structure of investments by type of ownership (Table 7.3) show that the share of state investments (which includes investments by state-owned enterprises) has declined considerably (from 94.7 per cent in 1990 to 51 per cent in 1994). However, the corresponding change for the whole of Russia was even more dramatic (a reduction to 38 per cent in 1994). It should also be noticed that the share of private and municipal investments is substantially lower in the Murmansk region compared with Russia in general. This illustrates the specific character of the regional economy, which is not very attractive for the expansion of private enterprise, and which has a weak public sector.

A striking feature of the sectoral structure (Table 7.4 compared with Figure 7.1) is that especially investments in geology and exploration, but also in agriculture and construction, have declined dramatically in comparison to other sectors, while investments in energy have increased. The high share of geology in 1990 is explained by the expenditure on oil and gas prospecting, which reached a peak that year. Noteworthy is also the deep relative and absolute decline of housing

Table 7.2: The structure of capital investment in the Murmansk region by source of financing, per cent

Financing from:	1992	1993	1994	1995
Federal budget	31.4	30.4	21.8	14.5
Local budgets	7.6	13.0	7.5	5.5
Investment funds	1.8	3.5	6.5	9.4
Own resources of enterprises	59.2	51.1	61.5	70.2
Resources of joint ventures and foreign companies	0.0	3.2	2.3	0.8
All sources	100	100	100	100

Source: Oblkomstat, 1993-1996

Table 7.3: The structure of capital investment in the Murmansk region and Russia by type of ownership, per cent

	1992 Murmansk region	1993 Murmansk region	1993 Russia	1994 Murmansk region	1994 Russia
State	92.7	63.4	53	51	38
Municipal	*	6.7	13	2.8	9.5
Private	4.1	6.4	14	8.7	16
Mixed without foreign participation	2.6	21.8	20	36.9	33
Mixed with foreign participation	0.0	1.5	n.a.	0.3	3.3
All types	100	100	100	100	100

* The phenomenon did not exist.
Source: Oblkomstat, 1993-1995; Goskomstat of the Russian Federation, 1995

construction, which is in marked contrast to the average tendency of expansion in Russia as a whole. Furthermore, it seems that the decrease in the region's housing construction will continue in the near future. There are two reasons for this hypothesis: First, out-migration from the region will continue due to the high structural unemployment, the unfavourable natural conditions and the high living expenses. Secondly, the cost of housing construction in the region is nearly twice as high as in the central parts of Russia.

Table 7.4: Sectoral distribution of capital investment in the Murmansk region, per cent

	1990	1992	1994
A. Productive sphere	73.2	60.5	68.0
of which:			
energy	1.8	4.6	16.1
geology and exploration	15.9	3.7	2.7
mining (metallurgical and chemical)	19.1	28.1	15.3
fish industry	9.4	3.8	8.2
agriculture	3.8	2.5	1.4
transportation	6.3	9.8	14.3
construction	4.3	1.5	0.9
other	12.5	6.5	9.1
B. Non-productive sphere	29.7	39.5	32.0
of which:			
housing construction	18.0	24.6	13.4
Total capital investment	100	100	100

Source: Oblkomstat, 1991-1995

From this discussion it may be concluded that the development in the Murmansk region, in the observed retrospective period, has been far from sustainable. With its legacy of problems, it is difficult to formulate a policy for a sustainable development in the region.

Several acute issues, directly and indirectly related to the subject of this article, will not be analysed here. For example, how could principles of sustainable development be implemented in financially insolvent districts of the region with an almost depleted resource base for large scale exploitation and operating with obsolete equipment? How could resource-user-pays and polluter-pays principles be adequately applied to enterprises whose sales prices have reached world market levels but are still showing no profit? Or when the bankruptcy of these enterprises might entail unemployment for thousands of people? How could capital flight be avoided during a period of high economic uncertainty, and how could capital be used in a socially desirable way for the region? Nevertheless, some basic elements of a regional investment policy are discussed in the next sections.

Investments from a Perspective of Sustainability

The share of extracting industries in the Murmansk region is approximately 42 per cent, whereas the average for Russia is less than 9 per cent (Luzin 1994: 80). According to Table 7.4, the sectoral structure of investments, even taking into account the dramatic decline in the real volume of investments, does not show any significant shift away from resource-based industries. During the current economic depression, we can hardly expect any significant structural change in the economy of the region and the related allocation of investments. There are plans to develop some large-scale investment projects, but they have little to do with any objective of sustainability. Obvious examples are extraction of the hydrocarbon deposit in the Barents Sea and the construction of a second complex at the Kola nuclear power station.

Table 7.5 illustrates how investments in the protection and rational use of land and forests, in the protection and reproduction of fish stocks, and in the creation of nature preserves have decreased dramatically, not to say been completely eliminated in recent years. Total investments in environmental protection in deflated prices have fallen by a factor of almost five between 1991 and 1995.

The Regional Government's Role in Promoting Sustainable Investment

According to the Russian Constitution of 1993, all 89 administrative regions (subjects of the Russian Federation), including the Murmansk region, have the right to pass their own legislation, but is must be in harmony with laws of Russia. There are also various potential levers and instruments of a direct and indirect character that influence the investment climate in a region. Regional investment policy is here defined as a set of measures that may be employed by governments at the national and regional level for the formation and use of investment resources aimed at maintaining, renewing and upgrading the collective and private assets in the regional economy.

It should be noted that there are still uncertainties concerning the division of power between federal and regional authorities in a number of areas (mainly those which the Constitution defines as issues of joint responsibility, such as the use of natural resources and tax policy). However, the Federal Government and some regions recently signed agreements on a relevant separation of powers. A similar document is now being prepared for the Murmansk region. It is intended to clarify the areas in which the bodies of regional government may embark on socio-economic policy planning

Success in regional development will depend on the choice and elaboration of objectives and strategy, the proper policy instruments and the mechanisms of organisational implementation.

Today the regional governments have no distinct policies for economic development and investments. One reason is that under the circumstances of the socio-economic crisis, local and regional authorities are mostly kept busy by every-day needs (fuel supply, financing of the public sector and so forth) rather than with formulating any long-term oriented policy. In addition, the regional representative body, the Oblast Duma – which is charged with the formulation of such a policy, has been in operation for just a couple of years and has not had enough time for this critical challenge.

The administration of the Murmansk region has taken some steps to encourage investments (e.g., prepared a draft of law 'On creation of favourable condition for investments in the Murmansk region,' and organised international investment conferences, 'Northern opportunities' in 1995 and 1996). However, these steps are far too insufficient to make any impact on the generally deteriorating investment

Table 7.5: Capital investment aimed at environmental protection in the Murmansk region, millions of roubles deflated to the price level of 1991

	1991	1992	1993	1994	1995
Protection of:					
water resources	22.5	17.3	11.5	6.9	3.7
atmosphere	4.4	2.9	11.6	12.0	6.5
land	-	-	-	-	0.1
forests	1.6	0.1	0.1	0.3	0.2
fish	-	0.5	-	-	-
mineral resources	25.6	20.9	10.2	0.8	0.3
creation of preserves	0.3	-	0.2	-	-
Total	54.4	41.7	33.6	20.1	11.3

Source: Oblkomstat, 1992-1996

climate or to promote sustainable investment in particular. The deterioration has happened despite a slight improvement in financial stability in 1995 compared with previous years (Soobschaet oblkomstat 1996) and an increase of the regional budget income by 20 per cent over the planned level (Ladan 1996).

As is illustrated in Table 7.6, the main internal potential sources of financing investments in the Murmansk region are profits and depreciation of enterprises and savings by households of the region. The sum of these sources compared with current capital investments financed from internal and external sources have gradually declined in recent years.

Another part of the problem is that due to inflation, the real physical volume of investment has decreased significantly. Thus the internal financing potential is increasingly unable to meet the need for investment capital in the region. This is confirmed by the following example. According to results of an international tender for reconstruction of the Pechenganickel smelter complex (aimed mainly to reduce the level of pollution), the project is estimated to cost $300m. This cost is almost as high as the total capital investment in the Murmansk region in 1995 (which was 1 611 billion roubles (Soobschaet oblkomstat 1996) or about $350m), and almost equal to the total after-tax profit per year of all industrial enterprises in the region. However, the output (in monetary terms) of the Pechenganickel plant has traditionally comprised only about 5 per cent of the total industrial output in the Murmansk region.

It is quite clear from the presented data that to a large extent, a resolution of the acute development problems in the Murmansk region depends on a stronger ability to attract investment capital from external sources. Hence an important task for an investment policy formulated by the regional government is to facilitate the growth of inward investment. Measures should include efforts to obtain

Table 7.6: Annual volume of capital investment compared with potential sources of financing in the Murmansk region, billions of roubles in current prices

	1991	1993	1994
1. Capital investment financed from all sources	1.9	253.5	891.4
2. Main potential sources of financing	4.8	421.7	1181.4
of which:			
– net profit of the region's enterprises and organisations	2.8	333.0	404.7
– depreciation of fixed assets	0.7	18.3	401.9
– population's savings in deposits and securities	1.3	70.4	374.8
Ratio (2:1)	2.5	1.6	1.3

Source: Oblkomstat, 1992-1995

support from the federal government, financing from domestic and international investment funds as well as the creation of a favourable investment climate. But first of all, it is necessary to design a regional investment policy with distinct objectives and priorities.

As already emphasised, a regional policy should serve the socio-economic interests of the inhabitants, with the ultimate goal of improving the quality of their lives. In view of the region's specific economic conditions, including its sensitive Arctic environment, the task of a regional investment policy becomes dual. On the one hand, a general improvement of the investment climate is needed to overcome the investment crisis. On the other hand, the regional government should oppose (at least not give subsidies to) investors in natural resources extraction or new industrial constructions which may cause further environmental damage.

Obviously, it is not enough to define preferable forms and directions of investments. There must be a system of measures aimed at realising the policy goals. In single-industry towns, which are predominant in the region, there are strong needs for broad investment programmes aimed at conversion and diversification. As Gronlund (1994) points out in a discussion concerning the restructuring of single-industry towns, various policy measures and transfer schemes carried out by central government often 'had not been able to delay or solve local problems' (ibid.: 162). In the Murmansk region, support from the central government is almost absent, which makes the elaboration and implementation of restructuring programmes more problematic. In addition, there are examples of actions taken by the regional government which have not exactly been conducive to restructuring or improvement of the local investment climate.

'Bodies of local government are practically deprived of the rights to independently formulate, approve and execute their local budget. ... Such a situation contradicts the Russian Federation law "On general guide-lines for the budget rights ... of local government bodies"' (Son 1995: 15, our translation). According to the law, a regional representative body is required to provide a stable basis for the local budgets for at least a five-year period. However, the real situation is quite different. For example, in the Kirovsk district of the Murmansk region, the local share of the total tax revenue accounted for 34.7 per cent in 1993. The share declined to 27.2 per cent in 1994 and to 20 per cent in 1995.[5] Thus, decisions on local budgets are still excessively centralised to the regional level.

The example reveals an 'opportunistic behaviour' by the regional government, which is one of three types of political risk that investors may face (Eliasson 1995: 6). This type of political risk refers to 'unpredictable behaviour on the part of governmental authorities in the form of changes in the institutions of the economy that regulate everyday economic behaviour, notably the property rights institutions, and the legal framework for contractual arrangements among firms' (Eliasson et al. 1994: 14). The other two types of political risk refer to the collapse of political and economic systems and are hence beyond the influence of regional government.

Alongside with measures to attract and stimulate investments, another important task for the regional government is to specify rules and guidelines concerning environmental safety, environmental liability and the protection of the rights and long-term interests of the local population. It would be useful to harmonise such environmental regulations with those of neighbouring regions in the Nordic countries.

Potential Alternatives

In this final section we will discuss potential investment alternatives and their possible consequences. The approach we suggest is to pay special attention to differences in the balance between domestic and international investment flows. The idea has been to demonstrate four extreme alternatives and their potential socio-economic and ecological consequences (Figure 7.2). Naturally, this approach is a rough qualitative estimation with a great deal of simplification. Nevertheless, the analysis may be a useful point of departure for the formulation of a governmental policy aimed at sustainable development.

The first alternative attempts to capture the current decline of investment flows and the passive behaviour among enterprises and governments. If this trend continues, it is likely to result in a further fall of industrial production and related revenues due to the deterioration of the capital stock. This alternative will have an obvious, unfavourable impact on the social life in the Murmansk region. First, there would be a decline in real income among most employees and a further

Figure 7.2: Matrix of potential investment alternatives and their consequences

International investment flows	Domestic investment flows: Low	Domestic investment flows: High
Low	– deteriorating assets constrain production; – decline in revenues; – out-migration of labour force; – aggravation of environmental problems. 1	– traditional pattern of production; – preservation of number and income of population; – high pressure on the environment. 2
High	3 – acquisition of modern technologies and skills – higher incomes of employees; – unemployment growth; – reduction of harmful environmental impact.	4 – growth of production; – growth of people's welfare; – high pressure on the environment.

polarisation of welfare levels. Secondly, there would be increased out-migration of the most mobile and well-trained inhabitants, with negative impact on the region's demographic structure. Thirdly, due to a scarcity of resources for restructuring programmes, social problems would be aggravated, especially in single-industry towns.

Despite the assumption in this alternative of a decrease in productive output, environmental conditions are likely to be further aggravated. The reason is that the existing productive apparatus of the region's major industries will continue to function for several years to come. With a low level of investment, the negative environmental impact of production will increase. Another reason is that a reduction in productive output will not automatically lead to a proportional decline of harmful environmental consequences, as was demonstrated above.

The conclusion of the first alternative is that a further depression and long-term stagnation of investments in the region from both domestic and international actors will likely lead to a vicious cycle of problems. This alternative means a development far removed from sustainability.

Our second alternative presupposes a significant recovery of domestic investment flows alongside with a further wait-and-see attitude of foreign investors. Such a one-sided flow may be conditioned by specific government policies to restrict the options of foreign investors. According to this alternative, investments will make possible the maintenance of the capital stock and the productive capacity at a level that will secure some profits. Out-migration may slow down significantly and living standards would be preserved. However, it is improbable that any isolationist policy will lead to a significant progress in environmental protection. Despite a wide-spread recognition of the urgent need to reduce harmful impacts on the environment, the problem cannot possibly be solved in the near future due to lack of appropriate technologies in the country. Consequently, exclusive reliance on domestic investment and technologies entails a high risk of further environmental degradation in the region. The second alternative, therefore, also contradicts the aim of sustainable development and should not be chosen as a strategy.

The third alternative assumes a considerable increase of international investments but very limited domestic investment flows. If foreign investments in the region are combined with transfers of modern technologies, it will stimulate economic efficiency and environmental safety. Higher efficiency will provide a potential for growing incomes among employees. However, the level of unemployment may increase significantly. In Western countries, people relegated from industrial production due to the growth of labour productivity have mostly been absorbed by a growing service sector. In the Murmansk region, there are less opportunities for expanding services to a level where they may absorb workers made redundant by radical industrial rationalisation.

Some additional aspects should be noted. First, positive (from a perspective of sustainability) results from foreign investment can be expected only if they are combined with an introduction of modern, environmentally sound technologies.

But this combination will not come about automatically. Specific policies are needed to attain the goal. Secondly, the probability of the third alternative depends on several conditions. Compared to domestic ones, foreign investment flows are much more sensitive to the level of comparative advantages including the existence of appropriate institutions and their efficient functioning (the investment climate) due to the additional risks involved in transborder joint ventures (Clegg 1992: 64). Furthermore, in the case of investments from Western countries in Russia, there is a significant barrier of cultural differences to consider (Svensson 1997). This barrier is difficult to overcome by any policy measure. Whereas the legal and institutional framework needed in emerging markets can be established through political and juridical change, cultural differences are usually very resistant to political decisions (ibid.: 107).

Regarding the third alternative, we may conclude that alongside with some potential benefits to regional development, there is a risk of unfavourable 'side effects,' like higher unemployment. The implementation is, furthermore, limited by significant constraints.

Our final alternative presupposes a most optimistic view concerning the recovery of domestic as well as growth of foreign investment. This alternative assumes a growing level of specialised economic activities in the Murmansk region due to a combination of comparative advantages for production and favourable market conditions for a majority of produced goods. The most obvious potential strengths of the region are huge natural resources in combination with access to cheap labour. As a consequence, the alternative indicates a growth of productive output that will lead to improvements in welfare. However, it is unlikely that an economic expansion in the region will reach a level where it will exceed the volume and value of production in the 1980s and the corresponding level of employment. Any further economic expansion which involves the use of existing technologies will unavoidably lead to an aggravation of the ecological situation in the region.

It is quite evident that none of the presented alternatives can guarantee a road towards sustainable development. A broad range of active policy efforts is needed to guide economic driving forces in a desirable direction. The basic guidelines for achieving ecological sustainability could be as follows:

> 'Harvesting rates of renewable natural resources should not exceed regeneration rate; waste emissions should not exceed the assimilative capacity of the environment; and non-renewable resources should be exploited, but at a rate equal to the creation of renewable substitutes' (Jansson et al. 1994: 5).

One form of non-renewable resource substitution might be the creation of regional financial funds for heritage and development (trust funds). These might be built on revenues generated from the exploitation of the region's natural resources. The funds might be used independently from the state in order to the benefit long-term interests of the local population (Pretes and Robinson 1992).

It should also be stressed that the mobilisation of local initiative and entrepreneurship is essential for achieving sustainability. Such a strategy is especially important for single-industry towns. Having synthesised case studies of local development initiatives in different parts of Europe, Stöhr (1990: 3-4) presented the following conclusion about successful restructuring initiatives in peripheral areas. They are well worth taking into account when discussing problems of development in the Murmansk region:

> 'The successful initiatives were oriented towards the broadening of local resources, combined with technological upgrading, training efforts, design and cultural activities, local financing and improved forms of local cooperation and information exchange. This not only helped to improve local employment and living conditions but also strengthened the local negotiating position with outside entrepreneurs, central government or international organizations.'

One lesson from these experiences is that the currently dominating top-down policy approach of the Murmansk regional government should be revised in favour of policies stimulating and supporting local initiatives and self-governance. Our impression is that the regional authorities are not using all options to improve the situation made available to them by the Constitution of 1993. There is an obvious absence of meaningful socio-economic policies.

As Eliasson (1995: 2-3) points out, institutions (legal code, conventions, ethical norms) define the investment climate. The most important among them are institutions supporting property rights, namely the right to manage property, to access and use the profits and to trade the property rights. Consequently, regional investment policies must place special emphasis on the development of an adequate institutional framework. Besides, this seems to be the only available way to stimulate investments as other standard policy instruments employing financial incentives for investors (tax breaks, cheap loans, investment grants, infrastructure aids) are very limited under the current economic depression.

Using the international experience, the creation of a Regional Inward Investment Agency (RIIA) as an element of a formal institutional structure for investment promotion might be suggested. Usually such an agency has the following functions: 1) policy formulation; 2) investment promotion and attraction; 3) investment approvals; 4) granting of incentives; 5) providing assistance; 6) monitoring, after-care (Young et al. 1994: 145). The argument in favour of an RIIA is that to overcome the current investment crisis, there is a need of specialised marketing skills that can only be effectively employed by a specialised organisation or at least in one which has a separate position from that of the government.

Notes

[1] For a review of the interpretation of the concept, see e.g. de Vries, 1994; Lyck, 1994.

[2] For more information about the economy in the Murmansk region, see Doiban et al., 1992; Luzin et al., 1994.

[3] This is one of the conclusions from the research project "Socio-economic diagnostics of the Kola region" which was conducted by scientists of the Leningrad Financial Economic Institute (now St.Petersburg Academy) and the Institute for Economic Problems of the Kola Science Centre in 1988-1989 (Dmitrieva et al., 1989).

[4] Most of the data presented in the article, unless otherwise indicated, are based on material from the official yearbooks of the The Murmansk regional Committee of State Statistics (Oblkomstat).

[5] The data are provided by A. Kuzin, head of the economic department of the Kirovsk district administration.

References

Bryden, J. and Commins, P. (1997). 'Rural Development: Policy Orientations and the Cork Declaration.' Paper presented at the 48th EAAE Seminar, Dijon, France 20-21 March 1997.

Clegg, J. (1992). 'Explaining Foreign Direct Investment Flows,' in Buckley, Peter J. and Casson, Mark (eds.). *Multinational Enterprises in the World Economy.* Vermont, Edward Eglag.

Costanza, R. (1994). 'Three General Policies to Achieve Sustainability,' in Jansson, A-M., Costanza, R. and Hammer, M. (eds.). *Investing in Natural Capital: The Ecological Economics Approach to Sustainability.* Washington, DC, Island Press.

Dmitrieva, O.G. and Associates (1989). *Report on Research Work.* Leningrad Financial Economic Institute. (In Russian).

Doiban, V.A., Pretes, M. and Sekarev, A.V. (1992). 'Economic Development in the Kola Region, USSR: An Overview,' *Polar Record*:28(164), pages 7-16.

Eliasson, G. (1995). *Investment Incentives in the Formerly Planned Economies.* Stockholm, Royal Institute of Technology.

Eliasson, G., Rybczynski, T. and Wihlborg, C. (1994). *The Necessary Institutional Framework to Transform Formerly Planned Economies.* Stockholm, The Industrial Institute for Economic and Social Research.

Gronlund, I.L. (1994). 'Restructuring One-Company Towns: The Norwegian Context and the Case of Mo i Rana,' *European Urban and Regional Studies*:1(2), pages 161-185.

Gubanov, S. (1995). 'Opyt i slozhnosti perekhoda k naukojomkoi ekonomike' (Experience and difficulties for transition toward scientific-intensive economy), *Ekonomist*:12, pages 12-21.

Jansson, A-M., Hammer, M., Folke, C. and Costanza, R.(eds.) (1994). *Investing in Natural Capital: The Ecological Economics Approach to Sustainability.* Washington, DC, Island Press.

Ladan, V. (1996). 'Strasti po biudzhetu' (Passion on Budget), *Kirovskii rabochii*, 23 March (newspaper). (In Russian).

Loginov, V. and Kulagin, A. (1995). 'Measures to Activate Innovation Policy,' *Problems of Economic Transition*:38(3), pages 78-89.

Luzin, G.P. (1993). 'Regional Policy and Economic Transition Process in Russia,' in Jussila, H., Persson ,L.O. and Wiberg U. (eds.). *Shifts in Systems at the Top of Europe.* Stockholm, The Royal Institute of Technology.

Luzin, G.P. (1994). 'The Economy of the Kola Peninsula and Its Significance for the Barents Region,' in Dellenbrant, Jan Åke and Olsson, Mats-Olov (eds.). *The Barents Region: Security and Economic Development in the European North.* Umeå, CERUM.

Luzin, G.P., Pretes, M. and Vasiliev, V.V. (1994). 'The Kola Peninsula: Geography, History and Resources,' *Arctic*:47(1), pages 1-15.

Lyck, L. (1994). 'Considerations on Sustainable Development in the Arctic,' in Greiffenberg, Tom (ed.). *Sustainability in the Arctic.* Aalborg, Aalborg University Press.

Pretes, M. and Robinson, M. (1992). 'Trust Funds in Alaska and Canada,' *ECO*:18, pages 125-133. (In Russian).

Soobschaet oblkomstat (1996). 'O social'no-ekonomicheskom polozhenii Murmanskoi oblasti v 1995 godu' (Information by the regional statistical committee 'On the socio-economic status of the Murmansk region in 1995'), *Murmanskii vestnik* (newspaper), 3 February.

Son (1995). 'Son v letn'uyu noch' (Dream in a summer's night), *Business*:8, pages 14-15.

Stöhr, W.B.(ed.) (1990). *Global Challenge and Local Response: Initiatives for Economic Regeneration in Contemporary Europe*. London and New York, Mansell Publishing Ltd.

Svensson, B. (1997). 'Managing Cultural Friction: Swedish Firms in Northwest Russia,' in Dellenbrant, Jan Åke and Wiberg, Ulf (eds.). *Euro-Arctic Curtains*. Umeå, CERUM.

UNEP (1992). *Agenda 21*. New York, United Nation Environmental Program.

Volkov, V. (1995). 'Rossiiskaya ekonomika na iskhode 1995 goda' (The Russian economy in 1995), *Ekonomist*:12, pages 35-44.

de Vries, B. (1994). 'Sustainable Development: A Guiding Principle in Search of Operationalization, in Science and Sustainability.' *Selected Papers on IIASA's 20th Anniversary*. Laxenburg, Austria.

WCED (1987). *Our Common Future: Report of the World Commission on Environment and Development*. Oxford: Oxford University Press.

Young, M.D. (1992). *Sustainable Investment and Resource Use: Equity, Environmental Integrity and Economic Efficiency*. UNESCO.

Young, S., Hood, N. and Wilson, A. (1994). 'Targeting Policy as a Competitive Strategy for European Inward Investment Agencies,' *European Urban and Regional Studies*:1(2),pages 143-159.

8 Labour Force Mobility in the Baltic Sea Area and the Transition Economies: With Special Reference to Economic Integration

J. Ilari Karppi

The 1985 *White Paper on Completing the Internal Market* proclaimed the four well-known liberties: free movement of goods, services, capital and labour. Quite a bit is known about the effects of trade and capital flows that cross the intra-EU borders. The same, however, cannot be said of the quantities of intra-EU labour force mobility.[1] Likewise, surprisingly little is known of the qualifications of international migrants (Fischer and Straubhaar 1996: 145). Yet labour force mobility is crucial for the flexible production strategy and the well-educated multi-skilled personnel of the post-Fordist, knowledge-intensive globalised economy (Ruigrok and van Tulder 1995).

The Nordic Common Labour Market and Beyond

Since the 1957 Treaty of Rome economic utilitarianism has been the basic philosophy underlying the development of supranational European policy frameworks. Thus it became natural for the intra-EU migration and social policy instruments to assume that emigrants were either employed or self-employed persons or their family members (Cohen 1988: 111-113; see also European Commission 1995b). Subordinating other aspects of integration to this logic exposes the original idea of European convergence as an extension of the modern industrial project (Alestalo 1992: 54-55).

The Nordic countries developed quite a different model of labour force mobility (Fischer and Straubhaar 1996: 103). In 1954 the governments of Denmark, Finland, Norway and Sweden formed a Nordic Common Labour Market (NCLM), based on a concept of free mobility remarkably wider than the one that was to be adopted by the then European Economic Community. Virtually from the beginning it encompassed all citizens of the Nordic countries, including pensioners, students and the unemployed.

A major milestone enabling the labour force mobility in the NCLM was the 1955 Nordic Social Security Convention (ibid. 121) which lowered the risk of failure embedded in the individual's decision to emigrate. At least one could count on the fact that social security systems within the NCLM did not put the citizens of other Nordic countries in an unequal position in relation to the natives. Moreover, labour market systems in all Nordic countries gave public institutions great intervention powers. This ensured an effective labour protection and enhanced, for example, women's participation in the labour market. This in turn made the decision to migrate easier for families in which two parents already held a paid job.[2] In addition, until the recession of the early 1990s, unemployment in the Nordic countries used to be below the European average. When these parameters of migratory decisions are added to the cultural similarities of the Nordic societies (as a factor lowering the information costs), it may be assumed that migration within the NCLM represented as minimal a risk to individuals and families as ever could be when international migration is concerned.

Despite few official and cultural obstacles, the de facto intra-Nordic labour force mobility has not been particularly intensive. The only exceptions to this rule have been some specific and relatively short periods. Furthermore, in these cases Finland has been the overwhelmingly most important sending country, and Sweden the main destination of emigrating Finns (see Table 8.1). Yet, Finland is the most atypical among the four countries discussed. Unlike the Scandinavian languages, Finnish is totally non-comprehensible to the speakers of Danish, Norwegian or Swedish.[3] Also geographically the core areas of Finland are remote from the main urban areas of the three other countries, separated from them by the sea. Secondly, Finland began its modernisation and urbanisation later than the other Nordic societies, thus preserving the agrarian values longer – the other Nordic societies again resembling each other more.

The main migratory flows within the NCLM have thus come from its most peripheral subarea to its geographical and economic centre. This supports some aspects of the traditional Heckscher-Ohlin-Samuelson equilibrium model of factor mobility (Södersten and Reed 1994: 456-58; Fischer and Straubhaar 1996: 31-2). Labour within the NCLM has reacted to the widest economic differences and migrated from relatively labour-abundant Finland to relatively capital-abundant

Table 8.1: Intra-Nordic migration balances between 1964 and 1988 in absolute numbers of migrants and percentages of total population

		Denmark	Finland	Norway	Sweden
Total NCLM balance		-5 084	-119 704	-13 559	138 347
As % of the whole population		-0.1	-2.5	-0.3	1.7
Breakdown	Denmark		-1 426	-359	6 869
by NCLM	Finland	1 426	-	2 919	115 359
countries	Norway	359	-2 919	-	16 119
	Sweden	-6 896	-115 359	-16 119	-

Source: Fischer and Straubhaar (1996)

Sweden. This exposes international migration as primarily and *economically induced phenomenon*, based on asymmetrical economic development and income gaps between different regions, and as individual and institutional mechanisms seeking to balance this asymmetry (Layard et al. 1992). The more the economies within the integrated Europe converge, the more internationally immobile is the labour force as a factor of production likely to remain.

The changes in North-West European migration from the 1960s to the 1980s are easiest to outline with the Finnish case. Within the NCLM, migration from Finland to Sweden has been the only migration movement clearly fluctuating over time (Fischer and Straubhaar 1996: 165). The number of Finns migrating to Sweden reached its peak from 1967 to 1970, with approximately 40 000 annual migrants. During that period Finland was undergoing profound structural change. Rapid urbanisation was taking place and manufacturing industries were still heavily increasing their share in the occupational structure. Thus, temporary slow-downs of the long-lasting continuous economic growth in the late 1960s effectively triggered migratory decisions of individuals and families who had already decided to leave their farming occupations or were seeking better paid jobs in industry. This wave of emigrants consisted mainly of less educated workers. Almost 73 per cent of them had only completed their basic education (ibid.: 146).

In the early 1970s the number of annual emigrants soon dropped to a figure between 10 000 and 15 000. In the late 1980s, with annual volumes only one-tenth of the past records, Finland began to receive more migrants from Sweden than the numbers migrating there. Transformations also took place in the qualifications of the migrating Finns. They were now far better educated, exceeding the national averages of educational level. Finland was now a net receiving country with much of the surplus made up of returning migrants, but an increasing share of the 15 000 to 20 000 annual immigrants had a nationality other than Finnish (Kultalahti 1994: 14-5).

These new patterns reflect the general changes in international labour force mobility. The global economy has grown increasingly interlinked, structured by dense organisational networks and demands for internationally transferable skills (Reich 1992). After the two oil crises of the 1970s, the 1980s witnessed a global liberalisation of Western financial and monetary policy regimes. Development of information, production and materials technology intensified the restructuring of Western economies. There was a new demand for highly specialised and well-paid professional services, but, due to the increased productivity, also for personal services of all kinds and at all levels. Large segments of the labour force had to be and must still be retrained from manufacturing to service jobs. The changes had international consequences. First, during the 1980s the structural gap differentiating market economies from the stagnating socialist bloc and the developing countries widened to new dimensions (Hettne 1996). Secondly, the number of the *traditional* jobs for the *traditional* migrants in their *traditional* destination areas began to diminish. Instead, *higher education now became an important factor increasing the individual's propensity to emigrate* (Fischer and Straubhaar 1996: 147;

Kultalahti 1994: 15-8). Simultaneously, some notable changes lessened the importance of intra-Nordic labour markets for Nordic international migrants.

For many Nordic corporations the 1980s was a decade of globalisation. Major mergers took place, for example the creation of the multinational ABB with its Swedish-Swiss core. Also Finnish corporations, such as Nokia, internationalised rapidly, first largely through direct investments, particularly through acquisitions of existing enterprises, for example German producers of consumer electronics. Some of the purchases were far from successful but they created a new option for many ambitious professionals: the internal labour markets (ILMs). Moving within the organisational structure of a transnationally operating enterprise, an employee could cross national borders without leaving his/her firm. When making the decision to migrate, an employee already knew for whom he or she would work in the destination area, and in some cases could even count on some repatriation programme after a few years. All these factors reduced the risk of failure as a migrant, making international migration a good alternative even to those who already had a good position in the country of their origin.

The above reflects an important phenomenon based on changing job opportunities for migrants from industry towards professional, white collar jobs. Push factors, such as high unemployment in the sending country, began to lose their importance as triggers of mass migration. Instead, pull factors, such as a dynamic and innovative regional economy in specialised European growth centres, now attracted professionals, either through internal labour markets or the traditional (or external) labour market (Fischer and Straubhaar 1996: 208). Emigration turned more selective. For example, the creation of the European Economic Area in 1994 and the 1995 EU membership of Finland and Sweden, as well as the need to establish extensive lobbying organisations near the EU institutions, had already in the late 1980s opened up new job opportunities for large groups of Nordic professionals.[4]

Other changes have taken place as well. After an extremely over-heated growth during the late 1980s, the Nordic economies faced a steep downturn. In the case of Finland and Sweden it was a question of real recession, as these economies declined much deeper than those of Western Europe in general. The traditional industrial jobs of the migrant labour force now diminished even faster. Simultaneously, the economies of Central and Eastern Europe suddenly opened, creating a crucially new situation.

Crossing the Borders: East-West Migration Pressures?

Since the opening-up of the socialist bloc, a much debated topic has been the expected demographic pressure from Eastern Europe to the EU area. The formation of new regional economic entities by integrating two previously separated regions would, it was assumed, increase human mobility. Special sources of unrest have been the interregional gap in living standards and the purchasing power of Western wage levels in the transition economies.

For the Western European countries, the new situation is paradoxical. During the Cold War, with Soviet leadership still keeping Central and Eastern Europe in its grip, freedom of emigration was one of the demands expressed by the Western democracies. After the changes of 1989, the West was given what it had asked for: Eastern and Central Europeans were free to go. After the first surprise, the EU countries made their move: closed the borders and imposed strict quotas on regular migrants from Central and East European countries. It was taken almost for granted that more people would be willing to migrate to the West than these restrictions allowed, and the concept of migration pressure caused by this asymmetry soon emerged as a catch-word illustrating the new relationship between the East and West of Europe.

But is there a specific East-West migration pressure to be afraid of? There are some pieces of evidence to calm down the worst fears of the Western politicians and administrators who have been most explicitly concerned about this possibility. The most convincing piece of evidence relates to migration as a global phenomenon. According to Straubhaar (1993: 10), only 2 per cent of the world's population is emigrants, with most of them eventually returning to the original sending areas. In other words, as a factor of production on a global scale, the labour force is as much as 98 per cent immobile. But Europe is not the entire world and the conditions here cannot be compared directly with the global conditions. However, there is another factor to be taken into account when analysing the effects the intensified East-West migration might have on the West.

It is far from obvious that large-scale East-West migration – should it occur – would have only negative effects. Layard et al. (1992: 8-9) point out that assuming the labour force participation rates in Western Europe remain at the 1985 levels, the trend of net entrants to the Western labour force will be strongly decreasing. For various reasons the participation rates in the EU have in fact *fallen* from 1985 to the mid-1990s (European Commission 1996: 41-52). Thus, the implication made by Layard and his colleagues is highly relevant. In the European division of labour, the transition economies may have a specific – even a primary – role as a source of young and youngish workers who may rescue the West from the looming labour shortage.

This approach clearly illustrates how Cohen's (1988) ideas of the regulated flow of migrants from specific labour reservoirs to the economic core areas fit in with the East-West scenario in Europe.[5] Simultaneously, it rephrases the entire question concerning the population movements from East to West: should the migration pressure be dealt with as a qualitative phenomenon and not as a question of volume? If so, the main points of interest should be which persons are able to migrate and what kind of input they could provide for the Western industries.

As an economic model based on demand theory, the migration pressure approach emphasises income gaps between two regions, thus seeking to reduce

analogies to the hydraulic models of containers and pipes, and taps blocking the free flow of liquid (Bruni and Venturini 1995: 379). Even if the pressure is seen to be caused by restrictive measures of the receiving country, there are some objective details not to be neglected while assessing the contexts of labour force flows. Among these are the volume of the labour reservoir in the sending area, the propensity of the potential emigrants to cross the border and the volume of the labour market in the receiving area. If we consider Denmark, Finland, Germany, Norway and Sweden as the area receiving the East-West labour force flows in the Baltic Sea area, we get an aggregate number of about 45.6 million employees in the labour market. Of this number 76.6 per cent are employed in Germany (see Table 8.2). In terms of unemployment the area is very heterogeneous, with Norway and Finland as the extremes.

Table 8.2: Potential receiving countries of the Baltic Sea area in terms of volume of labour market in the mid-1990s

1995	Employed [E] (1000)	Population [P] (1000)	E/P (%)	Unemployed (%)
Denmark	2 639	5 224	50.5	7.1
Finland	2 059	5 109	40.3	17.2
Germany	34 864	81 622	42.7	8.2
Norway*	2 034	4 348	46.7	5.2
Sweden	3 985	8 852	45.0	9.2
Total	45 581	105 155	43.3	8.5

* 1994
Sources: European Commission (1996); Central Statistical Bureau of Latvia (1996)

The sending part of the Baltic Sea area consists mainly of the three Baltic states, Poland and south-western Russia. It may be questioned whether or not all parts of Poland belong in this category – the question being relevant also in the case of Germany. From the viewpoint of physical geography, Poland is, however, clearly a part of the Baltic Sea basin. For the Poles, Germany is the primary orientation point in the EU area.

For most of the sending area there are available statistics on labour force and employment (see Table 8.3). North-western Russia is a different case, but some remarks may be made in regard to St Petersburg as the most important centre of the eastern Baltic Sea area. With the suburbs, the number of inhabitants of St Petersburg is a little less than five million, being on a slight decrease. The number of deaths per thousand inhabitants clearly exceeds the number of live births, and for the most part of the 1990s, the net migration rate has been negative. The share of people past working age[6] exceeds the number of children under 15. Thus, at least the demographic parameters do not point to immediate pressures that might trigger substantial migration flows from the main north-west Russian population centre.

Table 8.3: Potential sending countries of the Baltic Sea area in terms of volume of labour market in the mid-1990s

1994	Employed [E] (1000)	Population [P] (1000)	E/P (%)	Unemployed (%)
Estonia	517*	1 492	34.7	1.5
Latvia	1 205	2 530	47.6	6.5
Lithuania	1 675	3 718	45.1	4.5
Poland	14 658	38 544	38.0	14.4
Total	17 538	46 284	37.9	13.0

* Number of permanent job holders 1993
Sources: European Commission (1995a); Central Statistical Bureau of Latvia (1996)

Some implications can be made from Tables 8.1 and 8.2. The most basic one is that the transition economies of the Baltic Sea area that are culturally most West-oriented do not seem to contain any particularly large labour reservoir – one that could not, under favourable economic conditions, be swallowed by the labour markets of the receiving area. This is a simplified interpretation with two basic reservations. The first is the trustworthiness of the official figures – assuming that they *do* encompass phenomena relevant to the formation of migration pressure. The second is the reference to favourable economic conditions – which is not exactly the situation in most parts of Western Europe. Instead, what the aggregate numbers for the Western and Eastern subregions *do* indicate is relative labour-abundance in the Eastern region, mainly due the smaller share of population already employed. Yet, the subsequent remarks deserve to be taken into account.

The demographic pressure towards the West may not be highest from the area covered in Table 8.3. For example, the ethnic Germans living in the territory of the former Soviet Union form a population base that can be counted in millions who have a legal rights to migrate to Germany. It is also doubtful whether the true unemployment rates and the share of the employed of the total population are captured in Table 8.3. A great many people may be expected to remain behind the veils of the informal or hidden economy.

The figures do not include refugees who have gathered on the western edge of the transition economies in order to slip into the EU area. Excluded are also the many that have been smuggled through hidden routes – not only from Asia and Africa but also from Romania, Bulgaria and the former republics of the Soviet Union (Laufer 1996: 15). To expect no major labour force flows to occur from East to West, based on a strictly quantitative approach which assumes that the world only consists of the regions studied, would be to underestimate the situation which the Western governments should be aware of. Moreover, if the restructuring of West European economies does not lead to a new growth trajectory, there will obviously be no extra demand for even a slight increase in supply of immigrant labour force.

Actually, the new growth which is essentially knowledge-intensive leads to an increasing segmentation of the Western labour markets accompanied by growing income differentials. This may in turn result in extensive social exclusion of the less skilled. The post-Fordist idea of labour as a resource (Ruigrok and van Tulder 1995) may be applied to the educated and best skilled professionals, whereas the less skilled are to be treated primarily as a cost factor. This caveat is crucial where migration pressure is concerned. Low-priced labour (being conceivably a characteristic of East-West migrants) displaces more expensive Western labour. Thus it should be in the interest of the West to be determined in its attempts to succeed in the restructuring, to continuously enhance the qualifications of its labour force and, by so doing, to increase its knowledge-based productivity as a part of an all-European division of labour. A gloomy alternative may be underemployment as a long-lasting West European phenomenon worsened by East-West migration.

One obvious implication of this scenario is to emphasise the importance of changes in the West while seeking to solve problems related to the East-West integration. A revolutionary would be to openly admit that the East is not the sole region subjected to transition-related policies. The West may well need a transition policy of its own, linked especially to the breakthrough of the global economy and what it means to the more closely interlinked Europe.

A North-East European Model of Transition Economies

All transition economies are not alike. The Central European Visegrad[7] countries are further on their way towards the integrated Europe than countries that were either born or regained their independence due to the disintegration of the Soviet Union. In addition to various institutional factors, this feature can be seen on the level of individuals. The following text is based on data from more than 3000 questionnaires. It was collected from the employed labour force in four city regions. The survey was carried out during the spring and summer of 1996.[8] St Petersburg (Russia) and Tallinn (Estonia) represented the Baltic Sea area, and Prague (Czech Republic) and Bratislava (Slovakia) the Visegrad countries. Methodological aspects of the study are discussed in more detail elsewhere (e.g. Karppi and Rantala 1997).

The Visegrad area respondents tend to consider the possibility working abroad more often than do the respondents from the Baltic Sea area. This is the case in all age categories. In the Baltic Sea area, a pro-migration attitude prevails only among the youngest respondents. Table 8.4 shows how the Visegrad respondents who have thought about working abroad are distributed quite evenly among all age groups whereas in the Baltic Sea area, the potential migrants are predominantly young people.

So much greater reluctance by the Baltic Sea area respondents to consider working abroad is surprising. Income differentials between the two regions and their neighbouring countries would have led one to expect especially the Baltic Sea area respondents to tend to choose working abroad. Moreover, in the Visegrad

Table 8.4: Considerations about working abroad by age group in Visegrad and Baltic Sea areas

	Visegrad		Baltic Sea	
Age	Yes	No	Yes	No
-30	276	51	358	196
%	24.0	4.4	20.8	11.4
31-45	280	146	291	396
%	24.5	12.7	17.0	23.1
46-	214	181	137	338
%	18.6	15.8	8.0	19.7
Total	770	378	786	930
%	67.1	32.9	45.8	54.2
N	1148		1716	
%	100		100	

area the more equal income distribution (ibid.) allows more respondents to enjoy the fruits of economic development. In the following the differences between the Visegrad and Baltic Sea areas will be analysed through some cultural factors.

Cultural differences between the two regions (see Table 8.5) can be regarded both as a consequence of a longer historical heritage and the different positions of the case areas during the Cold War, resulting in varying degrees of isolation. The findings illustrate how the Central European countries were more influenced by their Western neighbouring areas than were the republics of the former USSR. In Tallinn it was possible to watch Finnish television,[9] and historically the Baltic countries used to be the most westernised of the Soviet republics. However, the

Table 8.5: Some factors perceived as barriers to migration in Visegrad and Baltic Sea areas

	Strange culture and way of living abroad		Insufficient language skills		Insufficient work skills	
	Visegrad	Baltic Sea	Visegrad	Baltic Sea	Visegrad	Baltic Sea
Not a barrier	349	257	194	217	388	225
%	29.6	15.6	16.3	12.8	32.8	13.6
A small barrier	564	554	399	470	484	485
%	47.8	33.7	33.5	27.7	40.9	29.3
A considerable barrier	205	433	379	536	238	556
%	17.4	26.3	31.8	31.6	20.1	33.6
A real barrier	72	402	218	475	73	387
%	6.1	24.4	18.3	28.0	6.2	23.4
Total	1181	1646	1190	1698	1183	1653
%	100	100	100	100	100	100

50 years under Soviet rule penetrated all strata of public life, effectively obliterating the Western traditions, whereas the citizens of the Visegrad countries had a better chance to preserve their cultural capital – an asset they are now able to make use of. Moreover, both the considerations of language and especially work skills seem to foster their readiness to migrate.

The question of language skills has quite an obvious explanation. During the Cold War Russian was both the official language of a superpower and the central language of the socialist bloc. This weakened the position of the Western languages, the most notable exception being German, which is shared by both the Western and (due to the former GDR) Eastern camp. Moreover, the Visegrad countries have recent historical ties to the German-speaking Europe. In addition, common religious traditions as well as social practises and institutions derived from them give Central Europeans a clear advantage in their attempts to redefine their place in Europe. However, the findings suggest that the leading position of the Russian language did succeed in increasing the mental distance between the Visegrad countries and Western Europe.

The differences are increased when it comes to the question of work skills. More foreign organisations have operated for a longer time in the Visegrad countries, spreading both knowledge and experiences to their citizens.[10] Presumably, denser pre-1989 organisational contacts also gave Central Europeans better opportunities to evaluate their own abilities in relation to Western demands and the need of extra training.

Another dividing line between the two areas can be drawn according to economic security. Central and Eastern European socio-economic regimes have a public image of laissez faire liberalism. However, the attitude of the regimes seems to be mirrored among the citizens, many of whom appear to view the prospect of unemployment with some equanimity. The responses given in Table 8.6 also imply an expectation of the efficiency of labour markets as a social institution.

The optimism among Visegrad area respondents compared to the Baltic Sea area respondents correlates strongly with their greater belief in the possibilities of being successful in the Western labour markets. The figures also suggest that at

Table 8.6: Expectations of economic difficulties caused by three months' unemployment

Economic difficulties	Visegrad	Baltic Sea
No	245	121
%	20.5	6.8
Some	598	743
%	50.0	41.8
Severe	354	914
%	29.5	51.4
Total	1197	1778
%	100	100

least some practices of the market economy are being embedded more firmly in the Visegrad than the North-East European area. The assurance that real labour markets do exist and create job opportunities gives rise to the assumption that if one becomes unemployed, there may be a chance of finding alternative employment. In malfunctioning labour markets one's current state of employment may instead be regarded as a unique event because all potential job opportunities are perceived as having been divided among the privileged few, i.e. among those who constitute the employed labour force.

The obvious difficulties in integrating especially the North-Eastern transition economies into the wider European framework must not be underestimated. Nor should one underestimate the mental assets that are likely to improve the chances of integrating the Central European countries. However, the integrationist path of the Baltic countries should not be seen only as a struggle from one hardship to another. In view of the perceived difficulties it would be better to emphasise the shared interest in making the Baltic Sea area function as one European region.

Conclusions: Future Challenges

In Central and East European countries the poor housing situation is a problem that has particularly reduced the willingness to move. For instance, transnational corporations (TNCs) operating in Tallinn or Prague may be frustrated in their efforts to post their local professionals to some provincial town in order to establish and run new branch offices. A position as a white-collar worker in some capital city organisation may well appear preferable to a managerial status with due benefits in some other location. Thus, the immobility of the labour force may be regarded as an all-European problem.

However, as regards *international* migration, East Europeans have a different tradition. Hegemonic interests of neighbouring nations have triggered numerous involuntary mass migrations from this multiethnic area, and this tradition has been kept alive long after the great West European migrations dried up. But where in Europe would migration flows lead?

In Tallinn, 60 per cent preferred the Western Baltic Sea area, in St Petersburg this figure was 40 per cent. In Tallinn, the question of geographical proximity seems to be important, allowing return migration to be kept as an open possibility. In this instance, migration may be perceived as a means to enhance the material standard of living rather than a life-long solution. In St Petersburg the entire question of long-term migration is more theoretical. The three most wanted destinations are large countries with notable economic importance and a high international profile, the two latter criteria applying also to Switzerland. Similarly, the next four countries share some of these qualities.

In Tallinn, 12.5 per cent of 1 979 randomly sampled respondents indicated some plans to emigrate. From a selected group of ca. 900 respondents,[11] only 6.5 per cent had at least one specific destination country in mind. In St Petersburg,

Table 8.7: Most wanted destination countries in Tallinn and St Petersburg

Tallinn		
Rank	Country	%
1	Germany	19
2	Sweden	17
3	Finland	11
4	Great Britain	8
5	Switzerland	7
6	Norway	7
7	Denmark	6
8	France	4
N	819	100

St Petersburg		
Rank	Country	%
1	Germany	20
2	France	14
3	Great Britain	13
4	Switzerland	10
5	Sweden	9
6	Finland	7
7	Italy	6
8	Denmark	2
N	593	100

the share of such respondents was 2.9 per cent. Large city regions are specific cases, and many socio-economic, cultural and personal factors further reduce the number of potential migrants. Thus, it would be an over-exaggeration to view the more open labour markets of the Baltic Sea area primarily as a threat to Western economies.

Many of the most preferred countries of the Baltic Sea area have also a negative image (see Table 8.8). Some historical experience seems to re-emerge but in a selective manner. For example, the German-Finnish axis related to the two World Wars seems to discredit these nations, but Denmark and Sweden, despite their historical expansionist interests in the Baltic Sea area, have unequivocally good records in the minds of respondents. Together Tables 8.7 and 8.8 create a rather confusing picture of which places are favoured by the labour force of the two cities and which ones they wish to avoid.

Table 8.8: Least wanted destination countries in Tallinn and St Petersburg (see also Table 8.7)

Tallinn		
Rank	Country	%
1	Russia	37
2	Finland	12
3	Poland	10
4	Albania	5
5	Germany	4
6	Romania	3
7	Italy	3
8	Turkey	2
N	689	100

St Petersburg		
Rank	Country	%
1	Albania	20
2	Germany	14
3	Poland	13
4	Romania	10
5	Italy	9
6	France	7
7	Finland	6
8	Great Britain	2
N	439	100

The problems of human resources mobility are wider than the ones related to East-West movements. Networking and mergers have turned TNCs into multicultural entities (Dowling et al. 1994: 13; Hofstede 1994). Going to new or previously unknown market areas increases the need of knowledge concerning local circumstances and (business) culture. As mentioned above, within the Baltic Sea area this is the case especially with the Baltic states and Russia, but to some extent also with Poland.

In the late 1990s, there is a broad public interest in solving these problems, for the national borders have ceased to regulate the functions important to the national economies. Thus, for instance, the Finnish Ministry of Labour has extended its research and development activities to areas where Finnish corporations operate, especially in the North-Eastern Baltic Sea area (Ministry of Labour 1996; Zabrodin 1996; Kauppinen and Heiskanen 1995). Such programmes may be regarded as important support systems for the most finely tuned instrument in integrating a regional economy through factor mobility: the international transfers of technological and managerial knowledge.

Direct West-East investments may have negative welfare effects in the Western part of the Baltic Sea area, transferring especially Western jobs in the manufacturing sector to the transition economies. Unimpeded East-West migration might worsen them, but with the migration propensity as discussed above this is not a certainty. Instead, tangible positive welfare effects may be expected due to the rising level of productivity in the transition economies – resulting in enhanced purchasing power and better functioning markets as a formal institution.

Thus, just like NAFTA, the US-Mexican (and Canadian) device to manage migration through welfare-creation, regional co-operation can be viewed as a far-reaching project to alleviate European East-West migration pressures. Welfare gains should be regarded as the ultimate source of legitimacy for economic integration. Well-functioning regional economies with various combinations of labour and capital have spread economic growth more effectively than strict borders that block such interaction. However, interaction on whatever terms should not be a goal. Qualitative aspects of operating new regional economies deserve to be taken into account, with a view towards giving the lagging subregion access to the means of modernisation. As pointed out by Södersten and Reed (1994: 474), any given combination of capital and labour produces less with a lower than with a higher level of know-how.

Notes

1 For instance, one of the recent reports published by the European Commission, Employment in Europe (1996), which gives a broad outlook on the challenges of the European labour markets, only occasionally mentions the intra-Union labour mobility – or mobility crossing the Union borders.

2 In European comparison, a typical feature for all NCLM countries has traditionally been women's high labour market participation rate (European Commission 1996: 42).

3 It is noteworthy that amongst the emigrants from Finland to Sweden, the share of Finland's Swedish-speaking minority has traditionally been nearly twice as high as its population share.

4 Of the Finns migrating to Belgium between 1987 and 1992, 46 per cent held a university degree, 53 per cent were male, and 59 per cent between 30 and 44 years of age (Kultalahti 1995: 70-3). Luxembourg and France show somewhat similar profiles, even if not so clearly.

5 For instance, the Europe Agreements guiding the process of how a country applying for membership becomes a member of the EU have such regulatory features. The Agreements set restrictions on the labour force mobility from the Central and East European applicant countries to the EU area. However, corporations that operate in the transition economies are allowed to select and 'import' the best and strategically educated specialists (e.g. in natural sciences) to the EU area. The non-specialists lack this opportunity, and only some special groups, like the ethnic Germans and Finns living in Russia, are collectively permitted to remigrate to their native countries.

6 Calculated according to the official retirement age in Russia: for women 55 and for men 60 years. It is worth noting that in 1994, the life expectancy at birth for men was lower than the retirement age, only 58.1 years. For women it was considerably higher, 70.7 years. The statistical data for St Petersburg are provided by the St. Petersburg Committee of State Statistics and published annually by Statistics Finland in a pocket-size statistical guide, St. Petersburg in Figures.

7 Referring to the Czech Republic, Hungary, Poland and Slovakia.

8 Research group financed by the Academy of Finland (Framework Programme for Russian and East European Studies), Project Social Changes in Eastern and Central Parts of Europe. Leader: Olli Kultalahti. Other members are Ilari Karppi, Heikki Rantala, Department of Regional Studies and Environmental Policy, University of Tampere, Finland.

9 Unlike Latvian and Lithuanian, both Finnish and Estonian are Finno-Ugric languages and closely related to the Baltic Sea Finnic languages with numerous common features.

10 An important issue contributing to the organisational presence are the market sizes. Unlike the Visegrad countries with their 'European' dimensions, the Baltic countries constitute a small and fairly unknown market area, whereas Russia is often considered strange and hard to manage – not only because of its geographical dimensions.

11 Selected from the random sample for a more detailed study by stressing the share of respondents having plans to migrate. The aim of this selection was to produce three groups sufficiently large for statistical analyses: 1) potential emigrants, 2) people having sometimes thought about emigrating, and 3) probable non-emigrants.

References

Alestalo, Matti (1992). 'Divergenssi vai konvergenssi? Länsi-Eurooppa pitkällä aikavälillä' (Divergence or Convergence? The Long-term Development of Western Europe), pages 51-73 in Kosonen, P. (ed.). *Euroopan integraatio, työmarkkinat ja hyvinvointivaltio* (European Integration, Labour Market and Welfare State). Helsinki, Gaudeamus.

Bruni, Michele and Venturini, Alessandra (1995). 'Pressure to Migrate and Propensity to Emigrate: The Case of the Mediterranean Basin,' *International Labour Review*.134, pages 377-400.

Central Statistical Bureau of Latvia (1996). *The Baltic and the Nordic Countries*. Riga.

Cohen, Robin (1988). *The New Helots. Migrants in the International Division of Labour.* Aldershot, Gower.

Dowling, Peter J., Schuler, Randall S. and Welch, Denice E. (1994). *International Dimensions of Human Resource Management.* Second Edition. Belmont, Ca., Wadsworth Publishing Company.

European Commission (1995a). 'Employment Observatory: Central and Eastern Europe,' *Employment Trends and Developments*:7, May 1995. Directorate-General for Employment, Industrial Relations and Social Affairs. Brussels.

European Commission (1995b). *Your Social Security Rights when Moving within the European Union: A Practical Guide.* Directorate-General for Employment, Industrial Relations and Social Affairs. Luxembourg.

European Commission (1996). *Employment in Europe.* COM(96) 485. Directorate-General for Employment, Industrial Relations and Social Affairs. Luxembourg.

Fischer, Peter A. and Straubhaar, Thomas (1996). 'Migration and Economic Integration in the Nordic Common Labour Market,' *Nord* 1996:2. Anniversary Issue: 40 Years of the Nordic Common Labour Market. Copenhagen, Nordic Council of Ministers.

Hettne, Björn (1996). *Development Theory and the Three Worlds: Towards an International Political Economy of Development.* Second edition. Harlow, Longman.

Hofstede, Geert (1994). *Cultures and Organisations: Software of the Mind.* London, Harper Collins.

Karppi, Ilari and Rantala, Heikki (1997). 'In Search of Strategic Groups from the Labour Market of European Transition Economies.' Tampere, forthcoming.

Kauppinen, Timo and Heiskanen, Aino (1995). *Workplace St. Petersburg. Development Programmes and Development in Action.* Publication of Labour Administration:102. Helsinki, Ministry of Labour.

Kultalahti, Olli (1994). 'Internationalization and Migration Pressure,' *Siirtolaisuus – Migration Quarterly*:3, pages 7-25.

Kultalahti, Olli (1995). Migration of Educated Finns to Western European Countries,' *Studi Emigrazione/Etudes Migrations*:XXXII, No 117, pages 66-77.

Laufer, Peter (1996). 'Schlepping into Paradise: A Push and Pull Between Good Diplomacy and Semi-Permeable Borders Between Poland and Germany,' *Pozor – News From Around the Bloc*:5, pages 12-17.

Layard, Richard, Blanchard, Olivier, Dornbusch, Rudiger and Krugman, Paul (1992). *East-West Migration: The Alternatives.* Cambridge, Ma., MIT.

Ministry of Labour (1996). *Workplace Finland-Workplace Europe Research and Development Programme.* Publication of Labour Administration:160. Helsinki.

Reich, Robert B. (1992). *The Work of Nations: Preparing Ourselves for 21st Century Capitalism.* New York, Vintage.

Ruigrok, Winfried and van Tulder, Rob (1995). *The Logic of International Restructuring.* London, Routledge.

Södersten, Bo and Reed, Geoffrey (1994). *International Economics.* Third edition. Basingstoke, Macmillan.

Staubhaar, Thomas (1993). 'Migration Pressure,' *International Migration*:1/XXXI, pages 5-41.

Winters, L. Alan and Wang, Zhen Kun (1994). *Eastern Europe's International Trade.* Manchester, Manchester University Press.

Zabrodin, Vadim (1996). *Työelämän suhteet Pietarissa. Työelämäan ja talouden rakenne ja dynamiikka.* Industrial Relations in St. Petersburg: The Structures and Dynamics of Working Life and Economy. Publication of Labour Administration:139. Helsinki, Ministry of Labour.

9 The CAP: An Obstacle to EU Enlargement?

Ewa Rabinowicz

Agriculture in the Baltic Region: Problems and Prospects

Would it be possible to extend the CAP (Common Agricultural Policy) to the countries in the Baltic region, Poland, Estonia, Latvia and Lithuania? What would be the impact of such policies? Are there any better alternatives? In this chapter an attempt is made to provide some answers to those questions.

Most of the problems the agriculture in the Eastern Europe is still struggling with are inherited from the past. Thus it may be appropriate to start with some basic facts about agriculture during the communist period.

Large differences existed between Poland and the Baltic states with respect to the agrarian structure. In the Baltic states arable land as well as other productive assets in agriculture were nationalised. The agrarian structure was bi-modal, consisting of large collective production units and small private plots (approximately 0.5 hectare) operated by the members of the collective farms. Labour productivity was considerably higher on privately operated land. The unique feature of the Polish agriculture was that is resisted the pressure of collectivisation. About 80 per cent of arable land was in hands of private farmers. The remaining 20 per cent was operated by state farms. The land used by those farms was owned by foreign nationals by before World War II and subsequently nationalised.

Productivity of agriculture in the region was considerably lower that in Western Europe. The yields per hectare were below West European levels. (This may to some extent be explained by lower quality of soils, especially in Poland).The region lagged even more behind in animal husbandry, though. This backwardness was (and still is) reflected in the breeds kept, animal hygiene and unfavourable feed utilisation rate (Csaki 1993).

The Baltic states were strongly integrated into the Soviet economy. All three countries were large exporters of agricultural products, in particular livestock products. When agricultural exports were at their peak in Latvia, agro-food products accounted for more than 25 per cent of total exports. The livestock exports were, however, to a large extent based on imported feed. Poland, on the hand was a net importer of food. The countries in the region were also dependent on import of (cheap) energy from the Soviet Union.

Due to substantial and persistent subsidisation, food consumption in Eastern Europe was considerably higher than might have been expected in view of income levels. This is particularly the case with the consumption of livestock products. Consumption of meat in Poland and in the Baltic states in the late 80s varied between 84 and 72 kilograms, which was significantly above the consumption level in Sweden or Finland at the time.

To summarise, the situation at the outset of the transition process was characterised by the following conditions: low efficiency in agricultural production due to a fragmented agrarian structure in Poland and low productivity of large-scale production in the Baltic states, a high level of consumption in relation to the level of incomes, dependence on CMEA (Co-operation for Mutual Economic Assistance, an economic organisation of the Soviet and the satellite countries, also called COMECON) for the agricultural trade and dependence on cheap imports of inputs such as energy, monopolised upstream and downstream industries and considerable macroeconomic imbalances (Brooks et al. 1991).

Looking at the process of privatisation and transformation in agriculture, it should be observed that it is more difficult to privatise and transform collective agriculture into production forms suitable for a market economy than is the case with many other sectors such as the production of services or even industry. In the latter cases there is no need of a major change in the way production is organised. Collective farms were originally designed as integrated production units, which make them difficult to divide. Indivisibility of assets is therefore a major problem in agricultural privatisation. Agricultural machinery suitable to operate large fields is not easy divided into small units. Huge cow stables cannot be transformed into several smaller ones (Rabinowicz and Swinnen 1997).

Considerable differences can be found between Poland and the Baltic states with respect to design of privatisation and transformation of agriculture. In the former case privatisation was a relatively minor problem for obvious reasons. The state farms in Poland were privatised by sale or lease of the land to private operators (often former employees of the farms). In the Baltic states the process was more complicated. Political and ideological considerations, such as a desire to undo historical injustice, appear to have played a more important role than economic considerations.

In short, arable land was privatised through its restitution – within historical boundaries – to former owners or their heirs. The property of collective farms was divided among former members of the state or collective farms, with the exception of property that had been restituted. Large shares of non-land assets were acquired by people of retirement age because the distribution was based on the number of years worked on the collective farms. There was a general tendency to privatise non-land assets separately from land. Often people who acquired machinery and equipment had no land. The settlement of land claims took a long time because of difficulties in establishing proper ownership titles and settle legal disputes over ownership and conflicts between different claimants. A lack of competent managers proved to be major constraint to the functioning of newly established enterprises. Privatisation in the food processing was generally lagging behind privatisation in agriculture. In the Baltic states, especially Latvia, privatisation methods in this sector favoured farm co-operatives.

Transition towards market economics has involved several systemic changes accompanied by macroeconomic stabilisation and efforts to restructure institutions and productive capacity. All countries in Eastern Europe have seen large falls in national income, industrial output and standard of living.

Poland was the first country in the region (as well as among all the Central and Eastern European Countries, CEECs) where the situation stabilised. Already in 1992 a modest growth of the gross domestic product could be observed. Since 1993 the Polish economy has exhibited strong growth (around 5 per cent per annum). The unemployment has remained high (15 per cent), however, and inflation is still considerable.

The Baltic countries have witnessed a much deeper decline in national incomes and a much longer period of recession. (Compared with 1989 the level of GDP was reduced by half in all three countries. Inflation reached 950 per cent in Latvia in 1992). In the second half of 1994 the Lithuanian economy showed the first signs of recovery. The upturn continued in 1995, when the economy grew by 3 per cent. In Latvia the economy started to grow in 1994 but a small decline of GDP could again be observed 1995. The Estonian economy began its upswing in 1995 with a growth of 3 per cent (data in this section are based on OECD 1996a; 1996b; 1996c).

Observers expected the liberalisation and transformation of agriculture in Eastern Europe to result in a fast growth of output, similar to the development in China. The result at the early stages of transition was, however, the exact opposite – a strong decline in production. A number of common factors underlying the collapse of agriculture can be identified.

The general economic collapse reduced the disposable income of the consumers. At the same time food subsidies were removed. As a result of both circumstances food demand fell substantially. (Meat consumption in Estonia, for instance, was reduced from 75 kilograms to 51). The persistence of monopoly food processors and distributors allowed the gap between farm-gate prices and retail prices to rise more than would be expected from the removal of the subsidies. Prices of farm inputs rose towards world prices for items such as energy and fertiliser. The cost-price squeeze evidently affected the economic performance of agriculture with big losses for large-scale farms, accumulating debts, bankruptcies and shortage of working capital. The restructuring of agriculture created considerable uncertainties for farming. The CMEA disintegrated, and the traditional Eastern markets were lost. In the case of Baltic states the collapse of the Soviet Union and the loss of markets in Russia were critical. Trade with countries in the former Soviet Union has, however, resumed strongly in case of Poland.

The pattern of development of agricultural production was again different between Poland and the three Baltic states. In the case of Poland we can observe a slow process of rationalisation towards a market economy but with a lower level of outputs, especially in the livestock sector. In 1996 Polish agricultural production (Gross Agricultural Production, GAO) stood at 85 per cent of the 1989 level. (Production has started to stabilise in 1992). Agriculture accounts for 6 per cent of the GDP. The employment in agriculture remained at a very high level with 25 per cent of the total labour force. Thus the productivity of labour in agriculture is very low (see Table 9.1).

Estonia, Latvia and Lithuania have witnessed a sharp decline of their agricultural production during the transition period. Livestock production has fallen most – in Lithuania shrinking by more than 50 per cent. A modest production growth in 1995. Agriculture's share in GDP is about 9 per cent, and it accounts for 23 per cent of employment. The decline was even stronger in Latvia, where in 1995 the GAO stood at 46 per cent of the 1986/89 level with production of livestock falling to 40 per cent of the pre-transition volume. The share of agriculture in Latvian GDP is 8 per cent and the share of employment 18 per cent. In Estonia 1995 GAO was down to 53 per cent compared with 1986. Share of agriculture in total employment is 8 per cent, approximately the same as the share of the GDP. With respect to trade all the Baltic states have significantly increased their imports of food and agricultural products (OECD 1996a; 1996b; 1996c).

A detailed description of agricultural policies cannot be given here. Since the initial stage of transition there have been many changes in policies. Poland started with a fairly liberal approach but became more protectionist over time. Estonia stands out as an exception not only among countries in the region but also from an international perspective. The country has pursued a liberal policy, and with very few exceptions there are virtually no import tariffs or any other restrictions on either imports or exports.

A useful way of summarising the level of support to agriculture is by using the concept of Producer's Subsidy Equivalent (PSE). PSE is intended to measure the value of monetary transfers to producers from consumers of agricultural products and from taxpayers. PSE is often expressed as 'percentage PSE,' i.e. the total value

Table 9.1: The importance of agriculture

	GDP/cap. USD	Population millions	Share of agriculture in GDP	Share of agriculture in employment	Share of food in people's expenditures
Estonia	938	1.6	10.4	8.2	39
Latvia	850	2.6	10.6	18.4	45
Lithuania	627	3.8	11	22.4	58
Poland	1907	38.7	6.3	25.6	40
EU	15572	369.7	2.5	5.7	22

Sources: CEC, *Agricultural Situation and Prospects in the Central and Eastern European Countries*, OECD

of transfers as a percentage of the total value of production at domestic prices (see Table 9.2). Estimates of PSE are available from calculations made by the OECD.

PSE for Poland has been estimated at 12 per cent (1992). In the case of Latvia the PSE was close to zero in 1994, rising to 3 per cent in 1995. A strong increase can be observed in Lithuania with PSE rising from -3 per cent to +13 per cent in 1995. Estonian agriculture was not subsidised but rather taxed, the PSE being -2 per cent in 1994, and -4 per cent 1995. Thus the level of support, if any, to agriculture is very low in the region and particularly in the Baltic countries, especially if one compares with the EU, whose support level has been 49 per cent during the last two years. It should also be observed that PSE calculations indicate that agriculture was heavily subsidised during the communist period in all countries in the region (OECD 1996a; 1996b; 1996c).

Table 9.2: Agriculture, arable land, yields and level of support

	Arable land million hectares	Arable land/ cap.	Yield of cereals metric tons/ha	Yield of milk tons/cow	PSE, per cent
Estonia	1.0	0.63	1.6	3.4	-2
Latvia	1.7	0.65	1.8	3	3
Lithuania	3.1	0.62	2	2.4	13
Poland	14.3	0.37	2.6	3.1	12*
EU	77.1	0.21	5.2	4.9	49

*The PSE figure for Poland is for 1992. The remaining figures are for 1995.

Sources: CEC, *Agricultural Situation and Prospects in the Central and Eastern European Countries*, OECD

Several trade agreements are in operation in the Eastern Europe. Poland is a member of CEFTA (Central European Free Trade Agreement). There is a growing interest from Lithuania and Latvia in becoming members of CEFTA as a step towards an all-European free market and EU membership. In the past free trade agreements often excluded agricultural commodities, but last June the Baltic states signed a free trade agreement including agriculture and food commodities which came into force as of January 1997. In December 1996 CEFTA's ministers of agricultural also agreed that all border restrictions between the five member countries will be lifted before January 1999.

To summarise, the region's major agricultural problems are related to the following aspects:

Agrarian structure: The major problem of Polish agriculture is fragmentation of land resulting in a very small average size of farms (5 hectares). Also in the case of the Baltic states the process of privatisation resulted in the establishment of many non-viable holdings. A large share of the land is occupied by small production units made up of enlarged plots originating from former collective farms. In

Lithuania such plots (2-3 hectares) cover 25 per cent of the land. The situation is similar in Estonia where small plots account for 26 per cent of land use and a high share of production (47 per cent of crop production, 30 per cent of livestock production). In Latvia part-time farms and subsidiary plots made up 53 per cent of the area sown in 1994.

As a more general comment on the future development of the agrarian structure in the Baltic states, it can be pointed out that the process will take a long time and that the future outcome is by no means certain. On the eve of the transition it was generally believed that the large collective farms would be promptly replaced by the more efficient family farms. This projection was, however, based on experience from the Western Europe, where collective forms of production in agriculture are rare. The experience from the east so far indicates that a multiplicity of different production forms will exist side by side.

Low productivity of agricultural labour: The low productivity is strongly related to the fragmented agrarian structure but also to hidden unemployment. In Latvia and Lithuania agricultural employment has increased in spite of falling production. Thus agriculture has absorbed the labour surplus emerging in urban areas. In the case of Poland labour was retained in agriculture due to a low demand for labour in other sectors of the economy and housing problems in urban areas. When 25 per cent of the labour force produces 6 per cent of the GDP (as is the case in Poland with an only slightly better situation in Latvia and Lithuania) the income of farmers must unavoidably be low.

Low efficiency in the upstream and downstream sector: The competitiveness of modern agriculture is critically dependent on efficient upstream and downstream industries. Low quality of products and bad hygienic conditions in processing as well as in agricultural production have been major impediments to export to Western markets. Another important problem is the monopolistic (monopsonistic) structure of the upstream and downstream industries. This cannot be remedied by privatisation, which would only turn state monopolies into private ones. Competition must be improved by restructuring and breaking up large units. Preferential treatment which has been accorded to farm co-operatives in the privatisation of food processing in the Baltic states may turn into an obstacle as this may deter other investors while farmers lack the know-how and capital needed to upgrade the quality of the equipment.

Market institutions: Modern agriculture is crucially dependent on a well-functioning institutional infrastructure for dealing with such problems as handling risks, providing credits, supplying market information and so forth. A lack of knowledge and experience of the functioning of market-oriented institutions is an obvious problem especially in the Baltic states. The main technical issue is the registration of land ownership. Farm inputs and capital markets remain underdeveloped. The establishment and active involvement of marketing and credit agencies in the transition economies are essential steps in order to meet the needs of private farmers.

Short Description of the CAP

The objectives of the Common Agricultural Policy are specified in the Treaty of Rome, Art. 39. Five objectives are identified but the aim of providing the farm population with a 'fair' income has beyond any doubt been the most important one. The present state of the policy is a result of a an evolutionary development which can be described as crisis-driven and oriented towards controlling the surplus and agricultural spending, the two being strongly interconnected. The latest reform of the CAP (MacSharry reform or 1992 reform) was also influenced by GATT and international pressures. Such pressures are expected to increase in the future (see below).

The process of evolution of the CAP has resulted in en ever-increasing degree of regulation, much more frequently adding new than removing old instruments. The outcome is a very complicated structure. The complicated nature of the CAP is also a result of the structure of decision-making. The CAP is supranational policy, but in reality it has been applied in a intergovernmental fashion due to a strong reliance on unanimity rather than on majority voting. It is difficult for a group of heterogeneous countries to reach a unanimous decision on complicated matters. In order to make this possible there has been a strong reliance on package deals making the agreements palatable to all parties involved. Thus the description below is oversimplified.

Major elements of the CAP are border protection, domestic intervention buying, direct payments, supply management measures (supply control) and structural policies oriented towards agricultural and rural development. One should perhaps also emphasise environmental measures, which have been introduced as accompanying measures in relation to the 1992 reform (based on regulation 2078/92). The structural policies are at the same time a part of the Structural Funds Objectives 5a and 5b as well as Objective 1. In the case of the Nordic countries, even the newly created Objective 6, covering extremely sparsely populated regions, can be involved.

Border protection restricts competition from foreign producers and may even, if not restricted, insulate the domestic market from the rest of the world. Until the signing of the GATT (General Agreement on Tariffs and Trade) agreement (see below), the border protection was mainly based on variable levies. The domestic intervention is used to prevent the prices from falling below certain specified levels. For some commodities (milk, most grains) the intervention is mandatory, in other cases it is optional.

A large step in the direction of the use of direct payments was taken by the 1992 reform, when the administrative price of grains (and to a lower extend beef) was lowered by 29 per cent and direct compensatory payments were introduced.

Such payments are also applied for oilseeds. After the reform direct payments account for a large share of the EU's agricultural budget, namely 42 per cent. The transition to direct payments shifts the burden of supporting farmers from consumers to taxpayers.

Supply control measures play an important part in the present CAP. The unwillingness to cut prices to avoid oversupply has forced the need to control the output by administrative measures. They are applied both in relation to agricultural output (production quotas for milk and sugar) and to inputs (limitation of land or animals which are eligible for support). The CAP expenditures are financed by the Agricultural Guarantee and Guidance Fund (EAGGF, the French acronym: FEOGA is more commonly used) consisting of two sections, Guarantee and Guidance, the latter being devoted to structural policies and being at the same time a part of the Structural Funds. The Guarantee section is used to finance market operations and uses 91 per cent of agricultural budget.

It may be observed that the CAP is a very heterogeneous policy. It can be described as a set of commodity regimes rather than as one single agricultural policy. Different instruments are relied upon for different commodities. A few examples will illustrate this point: Support for milk and sugar is based on border measures (price support). In the case of oil seeds there are no border measures, instead direct payments are used. When it comes to grains, both border measures and direct payments are applied. The same is the case for beef. However, in the latter instance the relative importance of direct payments and price support differs from the former cases. Also the degree of support as measured by PSE at commodity level varies strongly between the commodities, from 65 per cent for milk and sugar to 15 for eggs.

Prior to the Uruguay Round (UR) agriculture was in reality accorded a special status within the GATT. Agriculture was virtually exempted from disciplines which have been applied to trade with industrial products. As a result of the UR Agreement on agriculture, agricultural policies will – for the first time in the history of GATT (later replaced by the World Trade Organisation, WTO) – be subjected to legally binding measures. They relate to three major areas: import access, export competition and domestic support. With respect to market access, the Agreement requires tariffication, i.e. transformation of all non-tariff measures to bounded tariffs and a 36 per cent cut in tariffs. In regard to export competition, the Agreement requires a cutback of export subsidies by 21 per cent in volume and 36 per cent in spending. The commitment to domestic support reduction calls for a reduction of total support by 20 per cent . The reduction includes both product-specific and non-product-specific measures but excludes so-called 'green box' policies. These include general government services as well as certain form of 'decoupled' payments (OECD 1995).

The UR Agreement will have major implications for the future formation of agricultural policies in the Baltic Sea region. What may be of particular importance is the fact that there can be no export subsidies on products not subject to reduction commitments. Thus a country which has not subsidised export of a particular commodity before cannot embark on such a policy in the future. Since, as a rule, East European countries were not engaged in export subsidisation in the past, they will have little opportunity to subsidise future exports. This is clearly the case with Poland, which is already a WTO member and thus legally obliged by the Agreement. Estonia, Latvia and Lithuania are in the process of negotiating their membership. It is also clear that the future of the CAP will be affected by the Agreement (see below).

Present Relations between the EU and Countries in the Baltic Region

All countries in the Baltic Sea region have signed Association Agreements with the EU. In the case of Poland the agreement has been in operation since 1992. In general the agreements have developed into a great disappointment for the CEECs. The stated intention was to create an asymmetry in favour of the Eastern countries. The actual outcome so far indicates, however, an asymmetry to the advantage of the Union. Over the period in which the agreement has been in place, the trade balance in agricultural products between Poland and the EU has turned from a Polish surplus to a deficit. Moreover, the main benefits have accrued to the importing firms in the EU. Likewise, the Eastern countries' traditional exports to such markets as Russia have suffered competition from subsidised EU exports.

The bad performance of the Association Agreements has been attributed to several circumstances. In the case of agriculture they are based on trade liberalisation for limited quantities of products (so-called tariff quotas). If quotas are small in relation to the total trade, as it is the case here, the market prices will not be affected and the major benefit will accrue to those who are granted the right to trade (the quota) since this provides an opportunity to buy at lower prices and sell at higher ones. The quotas have been allocated to firms in the EU. In addition the concessions were based on historical trade figures and were not well adjusted to the present comparative advantages. Trade has also been hampered by the quality of East-European products and the lack of market information.

If EU enlargement is delayed, it would be desirable to make the agreement more generous by enlarging the quotas. The best solution, from the point of view of economic efficiency, would be to allocate the quotas through an auction procedure. The proceeds generated by such a procedure might be used for general assistance to countries in Eastern Europe (Rabinowicz 1996).

Impact of Extending the CAP to Eastern Europe

Assessments of the likely impacts of extending the CAP to the CEECs have been a popular subject of research and investigations. All studies indicate that it would be quite costly for the budget of the Union to extend the present CAP to the CEECs. The recent figures, such as the estimates made by the Commission – a price-tag of 12 billion ecu for including ten CEECs – are not as alarming as the first calculations (Baldwin 1994). Still it is a large sum of money, in particular considering the increasing scarcity of budget funds. Moreover, other studies have arrived at a somewhat higher figures (MAFF 1994). It should also be pointed out that estimates of the impact of the enlargement are genuinely difficult to make and therefore uncertain. Most of calculations are done for an aggregate of several countries. For Poland is has been estimated that the total impact on the EU budget of admitting the country would amount to 4.1 billion ecu, including the transfers through the Structural Funds and the Polish contribution to the budget (Kwiecinski 1995).

The major obstacle to Eastern enlargement is, however, not a problem of high budget costs. High food prices, which would result from extending the CAP to the CEECs, would make food much too expensive for consumers, in particular those with the lowest incomes. On average consumers in Poland spend on 40 per cent of their income on food. The figure for Lithuania is even higher, 58 per cent. The comparable figures for Latvia and Estonia are 45 per cent and 39 per cent respectively (see Table 9.1). The application of supply management, which is a cornerstone of the CAP, would be difficult and costly, particularly in Poland where the number of small farmers is very large (about 2 million). Supply management policies tend to freeze the existing production structure and reduce efficiency. This would be especially detrimental in Poland and the Baltic states since the process of transformation of production structures is not yet completed and the need to improve the agrarian structure is great (Rabinowicz 1996).

Also the use of arable land payments, which are a part of the MacSharry reform, may cause some concern. Since the payments are based on possession of land, they will increase land prices due to the supplementary land rent received by landowners. The distribution of the increased wealth in the CEECs would depend on the ownership structure of land. A substantial part of the transfers may, however, leek out of the sector since many owners of restituted land are no longer engaged in farming. In the short run, compensatory payments will improve CEECs farmers' ability to compete by providing an economic safety net and relieving credit constraints. Higher land prices may, however, hamper structural development in the long run (*European Economy* 1996)

Extending the CAP to Eastern Europe would affect not only agriculture. The high level of support would turn the agricultural sector into a so-called 'booming sector.' It is known from other countries affected by a sudden change of prosperity in one sector of the economy (such as discovery of energy resources) that export and import-competing industries are negatively affected. The major reason for the negative effect is a competition for resources in the domestic market. Thus it is important to assess the impact looking at the whole economy. (Such an analysis must incorporates some of the previously mentioned effects).

A recent attempt was made by a group of Danish researchers, who arrived at an estimate of the budgetary costs of 11.6 billion ecu for seven countries in Eastern Europe, including Poland but excluding the Baltic countries. Looking at impact on economic welfare the results indicate that extension of the CAP leads to income losses in both CEECs and the EU – as a result of higher taxes to finance extra costs as well as the loss of efficiency caused by suboptimal allocation of the factors of production and the pattern of consumption in both regions. In the CEECs, in particular, agriculture would expand but industry would shrink. The CEECs would, however, obtain significant gains in terms of trade as well as income transfers. The overall result would be a net loss for the EU of 13.7 billion dollars and a net gain for the CEECs of 11.4 billion dollars.

The above figures are of course uncertain but the order of magnitude appears reasonable as does the assessment of the overall effects. There is a net gain for the CEECs paid by the present members of the Union. The size of the sacrifice may constitute an obstacle to enlargement.

Enlargement 'on the Cheap'

A possibility which is sometimes discussed is not to make the CAP fully applicable to the CEECs. In particular, the idea of not extending the compensation payments to the countries in Eastern Europe is often advanced. (The idea is, inter alia, discussed in the *Agricultural Strategy Paper* (1995) and a 1996 study commissioned by the EU's DGVI). Since the major impact on the budget is due to the payments, the costs would be vastly alleviated. The other the negative effects mentioned above would, however, remain.

Different arguments are invoked against the payments: 1) that farmers in the CEECs have not experienced high prices and therefore have no need for compensation, 2) that farm incomes would become excessively high compared with those of other groups and therefore socially disruptive.

The first argument is based on a presumption that the compensations paid to the present beneficiaries in the Union are justified because the past policy has created expectations (or even entitlements to) of future support. The compensatory payments have been determined by calculating a hypothetical loss due to the reduction of prices. There is, however, no relation between the compensation and the actual injury since the prices have fallen much less than expected due to, inter alia, exchange rate realignments. Moreover, the regulations permit successors of the present generation of farmers to obtain the payments. It is difficult to invoke the compensation argument in relation to farmers who have entered farming after the 1992 reform. The task will not become simpler at the time of a possible accession of the CEECs, perhaps a decade after the reform. It could also be argued that the fact that even farmers in the new member states (Sweden, Finland and Austria) have been offered compensatory payments, has definitely transformed those payments from an adjustment measure to a part of the acquis.

The second line of arguing is based more on the need for transfers. It has been pointed out that a landowner in Lithuania with 20 hectares of land with a typical yield of only 2.5 tonnes per hectare might be entitled to payments of ecu 2250 or four times the country's GDP per capita in 1994. Such large payments would surely be socially disruptive. The same may, however, be claimed for the large sums which are paid in the present member states. In Sweden, where the data about distribution of payments are available, the 50 largest beneficiaries, almost all of them organised as limited liability companies, receive about 234 000 ecu on average. Such payments are also excessively high in relation to GDP and incomes of the average Swedish citizen.

There are further complications if payments are not applied in the CEECs. Producers in CEECs will be not obliged to apply set aside if compensatory payments are not offered to them. Moreover, since payments are not fully decoupled from production, they undoubtedly give competitive advantage to producers who receive them. If the CAP is not further reformed, the result will be a very unbalanced support structure.

We may summarise the discussion by pointing out that it is difficult to find convincing reasons for not giving agricultural payments to farmers in the CEECs. Most of the arguments advanced against such payments apply equally well to the present member countries. At the same time it easy to agree with the analysis made in the Strategy Paper (1995) that there are much more useful ways of spending money, namely by increasing disbursements to structural improvement, rural development and rural environment. It can be also observed that the CAP does not offer a direct remedy to major problems facing agriculture in the region as identified in first section.

What Kind of a CAP Reform Would Facilitate the Enlargement?

It is important to emphasise that the Eastern enlargement is only one, and not even the main reason, for a CAP reform. Even without the enlargement further changes in the CAP will be necessary in view of the anticipated further reduction of import protection, domestic supports and in particular allowable subsidised exports.

The volume and value constraints on subsidised exports constitute the stiffest challenge to the continuation of the current CAP. In the long run this leaves the Union with only two options. Either to give up the export position in the grain and dairy products market and employ tighter supply restrains, perhaps setting as much as 20 per cent of arable land aside, or to reduce prices to international levels to avoid the need to subsidise exports. The first option would have detrimental impacts on the European export industry, which is highly competitive.

Moreover, the internal legitimacy of the policy is in grave danger. The policy continues to disproportionally reward those with the largest farms and most wealth. It is widely recognised that intensive agriculture has a negative impact on the environment. Still, in spite of growing environmental concerns among the public, only a minor share (2 per cent) of the common budget is spent on environmental protection and rural development.

Thus agricultural policy must adjust to new social priorities and devote much more attention to the twin challenge of international competitiveness and environmental awareness. There is a need to push the CAP away from being a sectoral policy for agriculture to becoming part of a set of territorial policies for rural areas. The objectives of a new reformed CAP should be to ensure economically efficient and environmentally sustainable agriculture and to stimulate the integrated development of the Union's rural areas. A policy reform along these lines has been suggested by a group of researchers headed by Prof. A. Buckwell (Buckwell et al. forthcoming). The author of this chapter has been a member of the group.

Prices of agricultural commodities should be further reduced to the world market level. In order to protect against damage and depletion of rural resources and the cultural landscape of rural areas, farmers should be offered, when appropriate, environmental and cultural landscape payments. The reason for undertaking such payments is to counteract the risk of underprovision of such environmental benefits as biodiversity or landscape amenities provided by agriculture. In addition, rural development should be supported. This should include agricultural development but the main emphasis should be placed on stimulating opportunities for non-agricultural activities for farm resources and for resources released from agriculture. Existing compensatory payments should be transformed to a transitional adjustment assistance.

The idea of special income support to farmers, which is the major objective of the present CAP, is based on an assumption that agriculture has a general income problem and that this alleged problem should be solved by sectoral measures. The evidence points however, in the direction that income problems in agriculture are not of a general nature. Instead they are linked to a combination of socio-economic factors such as farm size, farmers' education, age, access to off-farm employment and so on. Such problems are more efficiently solved though social rather that sectoral measures. Accordingly, the new policy should not offer direct income support to farmers as an aim in itself. Rather it should encourage farmers to earn decent incomes by supplying private and public goods and by undertaking activities in rural areas.

A policy reform along these lines would enhance welfare in the enlarged Union as well as significantly facilitate the Eastern enlargement. Stimulating rural development would be especially beneficial in the CEECs and superior to the present CAP. Such policies are particularly important in Poland and the Baltic states due to the high share of employment and very low productivity of labour in agriculture. Moreover, such a policy would also be more equitable by avoiding high prices and distributing benefits to the entire rural population and not only to farmers. By eliminating supply management, structural change could proceed undisturbed. If compensatory payments are strictly decoupled from agricultural production and resource use and are, moreover, only temporary, it would be justified to exclude farmers from the East. The payments must, however, be designed in such a way that it is credible that they will not stay for ever.

References

Baldwin, R. (1994). *Towards Integrated Europe.* London, CERP.

Buckwell, A. et al. (forthcoming). *Common Agricultural and Rural Policy for Europe.*

European Economy (1996). 'The CAP and the Enlargement: The Economic Effects of Compensatory Payments.' No 2.

Brooks, K.C., Guasch, L.,Braverman, A. and Csaki, C. (1991). 'Agriculture and the Transition to the Market,' *Journal of Economic Perspectives*:5, No 4, pages 149-161.

Csaki, C. (1993). 'Transformation of Agriculture in Central and Eastern Europe and the Soviet Union: Major Policy Issues and Perspectives,' in Rayner, A.J. and Coleman, D. (eds.). *Current Issues in Agricultural Policy.* Macmillan.

Fischler, F. (1995). 'Study of Alternative Strategies for Developing Relations in the Field of Agriculture between EU and the Associated Countries with a View of Future Accession of Those Countries,' *Agricultural Strategy Paper.* COC.

Kwiecinski, A. (1995). *Integration of Polish Agriculture into the European Union.* Unpublished.

MAFF (Ministry of Food and Agriculture) (1994). 'Report 10 to the House of Lords: The Implication for Agriculture of the Europe Agreements.'

OECD (1995). 'Preliminary Evaluation of the Impact of the Agreement on Agriculture on the OECD Countries.' Paris.

OECD (1996a). *Agricultural Policies, Market and Trade: Country Study Estonia.* Paris.

OECD (1996b). *Agricultural Policies, Market and Trade: Country Study Latvia.* Paris.

OECD (1996c). *Agricultural Policies, Market and Trade: Country Study Lithuania.* Paris.

Rabinowicz, E. (1996). *EUs jordbrukspolitik och bönderna i öst.* Stockholm, SNS.

Rabinowicz, E. and Swinnen, J. (1997). 'The Political Economy of Privatisation and Decollectivisation of Central and East European Agriculture: Definitions, Issues and Methodology,' pages 1-31 in Swinnen, J (ed.). *The Political Economy of Agrarian Reform in Central and Eastern Europe.* Averbury.

10 Estonian Entrepreneurship: Towards Western Markets and Operating Patterns

Erik Terk and Juhan Teder

Re-establishing Entrepreneurship

During the Soviet period the Estonian economy was characterised by an extremely high degree of centralisation and concentration and a small variety of enterprises. Besides industry, concentration was characteristic of other spheres of economic activity as well, unlike in several other former socialist countries, also of agriculture and services.

Changes in the legislation concerning enterprises began step by step in the second half of the eighties. The first stage in the development of new types of enterprises was connected with the Soviet Union's *perestroika*, which was aimed not at a radical change of the structure of enterprises but at complementing it by new and more flexible elements predominantly in the shape of semi-private small businesses. Therefore it was not yet possible to introduce forms of enterpreneurship characteristic of market economies.

In 1986 the first so-called new co-operatives[1] were created in Estonia. Essentially they turned out not to be co-operatives in the Western sense but provided an opportunity to begin private business in the co-operative form.

From 1987 the founding of so-called state-owned small enterprises began in the first sectors of Estonian industry. This name was also somewhat deceptive. In practice the state-owned small enterprises were small businesses free from the restrictions of the state planned economy, operating on a contractual basis and with a free hand in the distribution of their profits. As to their form of ownership, they came neither under state nor private ownership. That issue had gone unregulated in their founding documents. Opportunities were expanded for private business in services, while in agriculture, private farms were being founded in the outlying areas of the large collective farms from 1988 onwards. The initial intention was that they would perform certain tasks on a contractual basis for the large farming enterprises, who could not practically solve them themselves due to their characteristic organisation of work.

Measured by production volumes, employment and use of main assets, the share of new forms of entrepreneurship did not amount to much by the end of the 1980s. In 1990 the co-operative and state-owned small enterprises provided full-time work for only approximately 4 per cent of Estonia's active labour force. The acreage sown by the private farms began to approach 10 per cent only in 1991. The actual importance of the new forms of business must, however, have been somewhat higher than indicated by the available official figures. The new co-operatives, for example, quite extensively employed labour that also worked full-time in the state sector. In addition, both legally and illegally, the new enterprises used such assets of the state-owned firms as production space and equipment. The profit margin of their activities was significantly higher than that of the state sector, but there are no reliable data about their profits.

The first joint ventures with Western capital also began operating in 1987. They brought new management methods and modern technology and thus provided a testing ground out of which grew a large part of the first wave of independent Estonia's entrepreneurs.

Since 1989, i.e. even before Estonia's independence was officially restored, the country's own legislation has been of prime importance in regulating entrepreneurship. The Law on Entrepreneurship and the Statute of Joint-Stock Companies, adopted in 1989, and the Statute of Economic Societies, passed in 1990, made the establishing of an enterprise very easy from the legal point of view. The number of new joint-stock companies began to rise very quickly in 1989. This form of enterprise later became the predominant in Estonia. The enterprise-establishing wave, which began in 1990, reached its peak two years later, and we may already speak of a subsequent stabilisation.

The electoral programme of the Popular Front government, which came to power in 1990 after the first free elections, supported not only an expansion of the forms of entrepreneurship but also direct privatisation of state-owned enterprises. Actual privatisation was begun while Estoniawas still formally a part of the Soviet Union. A law passed in December 1990 launched the so-called small-scale privatisation of state-owned services and trading firms. Later it was extended to include small enterprises in other sectors as the so-called experimental privatisation of the first list of large-scale enterprises was begun.

In July 1991, briefly before the restoration of Estonia's political independence, and after the first 44 small enterprises had been privatised, there existed approximately 1400 enterprises under full state ownership and control (Terk 1991). Some 150 of them – as a rule large enterprises – were so-called all-union enterprises, over which a legal conflict arose. Estonia considered them the property of the Republic, whereas Moscow claimed that they were the property of the USSR as a whole. Besides, there were some 130 leased enterprises (including those leased to the employees' collectives) or so-called popular enterprises, whose form of ownership was similar to lease, leaving the ratio of state property versus property controlled by employees or leaseholders rather vague.

In other words, state ownership of enterprises had begun to erode and merge with private ownership even before the beginning of the official privatisation, and it became necessary to clearly define the line between state and private property. In complex cases this took several years.

The privatisation of Estonia's large-scale enterprises was initially obstructed by the struggle between two concepts of privatisation, one concentrating on the sale for money and the other centred on restitution (i.e. return of property to the pre-war owners or sale of the enterprises' shares in exchange for so-called privatisation vouchers). After the establishment of the Estonian Privatisation Agency, the concept of sale for money began to dominate. But the restitution-centred approach remained predominant in the return of the pre-war land estates and buildings.

Privatisation for vouchers, typical of several other post-socialist countries, has been relatively marginal in the Estonian privatisation model. The basic principle has been the sale of enterprises for money to so-called core owners, either domestic or foreign. Similar to the example of the German *Treuhand*, the sales agreements oblige the new owners to make investments and to maintain employment. However, unlike the *Treuhand*, the Privatisation Agency does not administer the enterprises during the pre-sale period and is practically not involved in their pre-sale restructuring.

The Privatisation Agency managed to sell off the Estonian enterprises quite rapidly. The sale of large-scale enterprises, with the exception of the infrastructure enterprises, was practically completed by the summer of 1996. Even very large and quite problematical enterprises were sold, for example the Narva Kreenholm textile plant, one of the largest in Europe, which came under Swedish ownership. It had almost come to a standstill in the period before privatisation.

The Estonian business environment has been quite favourable to entrepreneurship, but direct support from the state (including to SMEs) has been rather limited.

Since 1989 the development of entrepreneurship in Estonia has been favoured by the simplicity of establishing enterprises. This has been conducive to a rapid growth of the number of firms.

The principles of the Law on Taxes do not favour any particular type of enterprise. At first the corporate tax was progressive. One of the aims was to create advantages to new firms, whose profits were, as a rule, lower at first. In addition, temporary tax deductions existed for firms with foreign capital involvement. The aim was to attract foreign investments into Estonia. The Income tax Law, valid until the end of 1993, was also aimed at the promotion of investments as it exempted 25 per cent of profits from tax if it was reinvested. Later on, the principle of equality of all firms has become predominant. The idea is to create a generally favourable climate for entrepreneurship rather than promoting certain groups of enterprises (including small firms).

Government support for entrepreneurship has been limited to extending credits on favourable terms and providing guarantees for credits through funds of target financing. Some funds have been established for the support of entrepreneurship (the Estonian Innovation Fund, the Fund for Crediting Agriculture and Rural Life, the Estonian Export Crediting Fund and the Fund for Crediting Small

Enterprises), but the capitalisation of these funds has been very limited. A positive role in promoting entrepreneurship is also played by business advisory services.

Capital and know-how from Western enterprises have contributed to the development of such Estonian infrastructure systems as communications, road and rail networks, gas supply and energy systems – often linked to wider North European infrastructure systems. This role will probably increase in the future.

The Structure of Entrepreneurship: Some Comparisons

Based on the number of registered enterprises, it may be estimated that Estonia has had approximately 40 per 1000 inhabitants in the recent years. This figure is about two-thirds of the number in some Western countries and lags behind the corresponding indicators for the European Union, but it appears to be somewhat higher than, for example, in Germany, Denmark or the Netherlands (accurate comparisons are complicated by different statistical methods). We may consequently conclude that thanks to the explosive growth of entrepreneurship in the first half of the 1990s, Estonia's entrepreneurial structure has become more or less comparable to that of the traditional European market economies. It must be remembered, however, that the peak of rapid increase of the number of enterprises has already passed in Estonia.

The most clearly defined areas of small- and medium-sized enterprises (SMEs) in Estonia are wholesale and retail trade, computer services, motor vehicle maintenance and sale, production and repair of office equipment, lending of home appliances and other equipment and the hotel and restaurant business. SMEs (we include here enterprises with up to 100 employees) employ 70-100 per cent of the labour in these fields. The average number of employees in the firms is below 14 in all of the above areas. The share of the SMEs is small (less than 25 per cent) in air and maritime transport, the production of vehicles, water supply, textile industry, communications, chemical industry and mining. Food production is also quite heavily dominated by large-scale industry, and SMEs account for only 28 per cent of employment.[2]

The regional distribution of enterprises reflects a general regional unevenness of economic growth. In the middle of 1995, 53 per cent of all registered enterprises were located in Tallinn. This percentage is notably higher than the percentage of the inhabitants of Tallinn in the total Estonian population.

The development of entrepreneurship is closely linked to the changes in unemployment. Former large-scale enterprises all over Estonia have dismissed a substantial number of their employees or have been shut down. An important question was therefore if the jobs created by the developing new firms would compensate for the loss of jobs in the old enterprises. In this respect there is great regional variation due to the different qualifications of the labour force, availability of capital, geographical attractiveness and several other factors. Foreign investments, generally beneficial to Estonian development, have also increased regional differences, since they are very unequally divided between regions.

Parallel to the rise in the number of enterprises, the share of small and medium-sized enterprises has also been rapidly increasing. This has been the result of the establishment of new enterprises, a reduction in the number of employees in the existing ones as well as the splitting up of large-scale enterprises.

Small and medium-sized enterprises have also increased their share of total employment (see Figure 10.1). The share of enterprises with less than 100 employees increased from 28.2 to 55.3 per cent of total employment during 1992-95.

Experts have expressed the opinion that the share of the medium-sized enterprises is too small. The previous system left a legacy of large enterprises, and numerous new small firms have cropped up. But they have not yet grown to medium size. This fact is reflected by a relatively small share of firms with 50-99 employees. At the beginning of the economic reforms, too much importance was attached to the development of small firms, which were often seen as a kind of magic wand for solving all economic problems. However, the situation differs among industries, and in several cases the market situation forces the enterprise to make use of economy of scale, i.e. move towards a more optimal size.

In several fields the number of enterprises is already too big. For example, the number of banks has already decreased, several newspapers have merged, and a drop in the number of wholesale firms is predicted. In certain cases Estonian firms will be forced to merge because of the entry of foreign firms to the Estonian market. A large number of small fuel firms will obviously be incapable of

Figure 10.1: Share of enterprises of different size in total employment, percentages

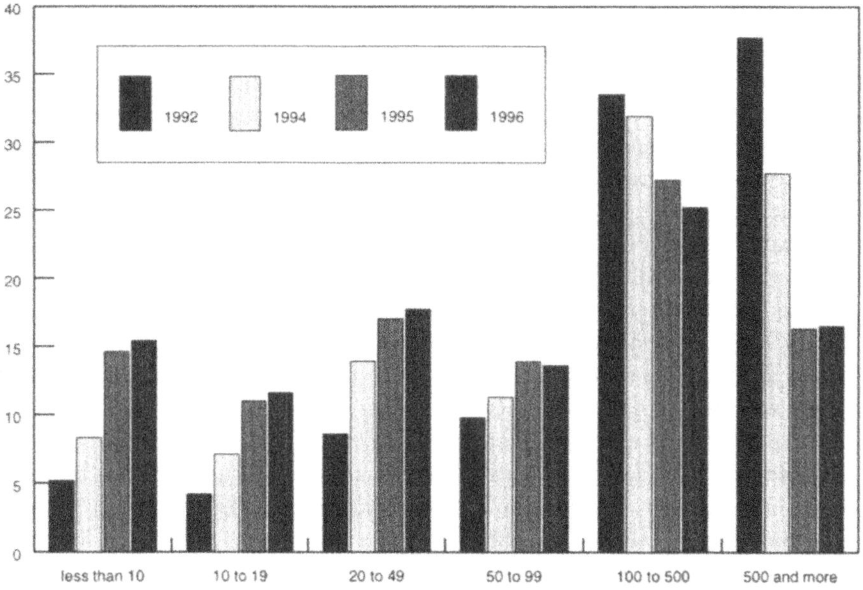

competing with foreign ones and will either have to merge or form an organisation covering all three Baltic states.

A Turn towards the West

If we judge the degree of openness/closedness of the economy according to the share of export and import in GNP, the Estonian economy could not be considered closed even during the Soviet period. It is another matter that the geographic structure of Estonia's foreign economic ties was deformed in the extreme – with most of the economic ties leading to the other Soviet republics within the planned economic framework and only a very small share to the world outside the USSR.

In principle, the enterprises had the right to produce for export outside the USSR, but since the Soviet foreign trade system was centralised, the enterprises' relations outside the USSR were limited and their incentives to export outside the USSR quite weak (as compared to the incentives to meet the so-called production target figures). The Estonian enterprises, consequently, had little interest in wider international relations, at least until the middle of the 1980s. As late as in 1987, Estonian imports (in real prices, rather than the prices calculated in the USSR by artificially lowering the exchange rate) comprised 31 per cent and exports 27 per cent of Estonia's gross material product. As far as industrial output is concerned, the corresponding indicators were even higher, 45 and 41 per cent, respectively. However, Estonia's imports from countries outside the USSR amounted to a mere 18.2 per cent and the corresponding exports to 7.3 per cent (Kukk 1992).

A significant increase in economic relations with the Western countries was a priority goal in Estonia beginning with the first projects for the independence of Estonia's economy and the transition to market economy in 1987. But progress was slow in the first years despite some successes in foreign investments in joint ventures, which were caused by the fact that during the second half of the 1980s, Western investors hoped to use Estonia as a springboard for access to the Russian market.

A sudden leap in the reorientation of economic ties to the West began after the liquidation of the USSR at the end of 1991. The abrupt rise in fuel prices during the first months of 1992 was a clear sign that Russia intended to conduct its trade with the independent Republic of Estonia according to world market prices. Besides, due to the economic collapse, the Russian market was not particularly solvent, and a large number of enterprises in Russia and Ukraine were failing to pay Estonian enterprises for goods delivered. In addition, as Alari Purju has pointed out, Estonia's trade with the CIS countries was complicated by differences in the speed of the transition of the pricing structure to the requirements of a market economy (Estonian Institute of Future Studies 1994). The result was that Estonian goods became too expensive for the markets with a slower transition (although Estonian goods were extremely cheap for the Western markets).

The turn to the West was significantly facilitated by the Estonian monetary reform in summer of 1992, when a relatively low exchange rate of the Estonian currency, the kroon, was established. This created very favourable starting positions for the enterprises exporting to the West because it reduced the cost of production inputs and led to an unprecedented, rapid rise in Finland's position as Estonia's main trading partner (replacing Russia), while Sweden's share was approaching that of Russia.

Independent Estonia has conducted a uniquely liberal foreign trade policy by avoiding import tariffs. Free-trade agreements with Finland and Sweden were signed quite rapidly, followed by a rather favourable agreement with the EU. The Estonian-EU free-trade agreement was signed in July 1994 and came into force on 1 January, 1995. It later became part of the Association Agreement concluded between Estonia and the EU.

Free-trade agreements have also been signed with Latvia and Lithuania. They initially covered all products with the exception of agricultural goods, which were included in 1996. Since 1996 Latvia and Lithuania have been invaded by successful new Estonian businesses which had exhausted the opportunities of the native market but were facing some difficulties in reaching the Western markets. Among the examples are banks, telecommunications, advertising and confectionery industries. Some of the Estonian firms have also been investors in these neighbouring Baltic countries.

In recent years nearly 60 per cent of Estonia's exports have gone to EU countries (after the admission of Finland and Sweden), who also account for approximately 75 per cent of Estonia's imports. It should be noted, however, that the statistics list goods imported from several other countries (Japan, for example) as having been imported from Finland (see Table 10.1).

Table 10.1: Main partners in Estonian foreign trade

	Estonia's main export partners (% of Estonia's exports)			Estonia's main import partners (% of Estonia's imports)		
	1994	1995	1996	1994	1995	1996
Finland	17.8	21.5	18.3	37.1	38.6	36.2
Russia	23.1	17.6	16.7	16.2	15.5	12.9
Sweden	10.8	10.8	11.5	9.5	9.0	8.4
Germany	6.8	7.2	7.0	8.8	8.4	8.9
Latvia	8.2	7.5	8.4	2.0	2.9	3.3
Denmark	3.4	3.3	3.6	2.9	2.9	3.0
Holland	3.1	4.7	2.9	3.5	3.5	3.7
Ukraine	3.1	3.8	5.1	1.6	1.0	1.6
Lithuania	5.4	4.7	5.8	2.9	2.0	2.3
UK	2.8	3.3	3.2	1.7	1.9	2.7

Source: Bank of Estonia

Russia's significance as a market for Estonian exports has decreased somewhat in recent years due to Russia's implementation of discriminating import tariffs (double tariffs) against Estonia . The importance of the Easterly neighbour is likely to increase should these tariffs be dropped.

The analysis of foreign investments is based on data from the top 50 Estonian enterprises which had received the most foreign investments as of the end of February 1997. As can be seen, Swedish and Finnish investors are leading here as well, especially thanks to the investments made in the Estonian communications and food industries. Unlike the geography of foreign trade, the position of the USA and Denmark is somewhat stronger among the foreign investors. Singapore's high placing is remarkable. It should also be noted that Russia's significance as an investor does not match the country's importance as a trader with Estonia.

Enterprises fully or partly owned by foreign capital play a very significant role in the Estonian economy, and foreign investors provide new capabilities, technology, training and access to Western markets. Yet more recent studies show that, as a whole, current R&D activities in newly established foreign-owned firms in Estonia are not very large (Borsos-Tostila 1997).

Table 10.2: Share of foreign investments in Estonian enterprises, by country

	Share of foreign investments in top 50 Estonian enterprises	Number of top 50 Estonian enterprises in which investors of the country particiate
Finland	40%	23
Sweden	20%	12
USA	12%	6
Singapore	7%	3
Holland	5%	2
Denmark	4.5%	3
Russia	3.3%	3
Germany	1.4%	2

Source: Calculations by Erik Terk based on data from the Estonian Foreign Investment Agency

Privatised Large Enterprises in Estonia: Status and Dynamics

A study of large privatised enterprises which had been operating under private ownership for at least a year – starting in 1993 or the beginning of 1994 – showed that sales and profits had not yet improved by 1995.[3] Positive changes did not come about until 1996, i.e. after the period studied and at a time of general improvement of the Estonian financial indicators.

A positive feature was that the liquidity of the privatised enterprises was quite good. Seventy-one per cent of the enterprises showed thoroughly satisfactory liquidity figures whereas only 9 per cent had serious liquidity problems.

Based on a success criterion of net profit and/or sales, Estonian investors from outside the enterprise had been the most successful.They were followed by foreign investors who had bought Estonian enterprises. The worst economic results were obtained by enterprises whose shares were dispersed among the staff and who had no core owner. For example, in 1994 as many as 80 per cent from this category were operating at a loss, and 50 per cent had serious liquidity problems. The management buy-out enterprises did not look too good either. Somewhat surprisingly, their economic results were roughly equivalent to those of agricultural processing companies (dairy and meat processing plants and so forth) purchased by co-operatives of agricultural producers.

The complications of interpreting the results mean that we cannot conclude beyond doubt that Estonian investors outside the enterprise have actually been more successful than the foreign investors. But we can certainly state with confidence that buyers outside the enterprise (either domestic or foreign) have been more successful than management and employee buy-outs.

Private capital in Estonia has, it may be concluded, been successful in purchasing enterprises and making them operate efficiently. This has not been a frequent phenomenon in most Central and Eastern European countries. In a number of countries the privatised enterprises have been predominantly divided between their managements and employees and foreign investors, while the role of domestic capital (from outside the enterprise to be sold) has remained quite marginal.

Two key words dominate in the list of problems presented by the managers: markets and investments. The problem of markets was stressed as very important by 69 percent of the managers. This includes the problem of Russian customs restrictions, which mainly concerns the food-producing enterprises. Enterprises privatised by owners outside the enterprise were more concerned with the lack of money rather than markets.

Figure 10.2: Dominant markets of Estonian large privatised enterprises

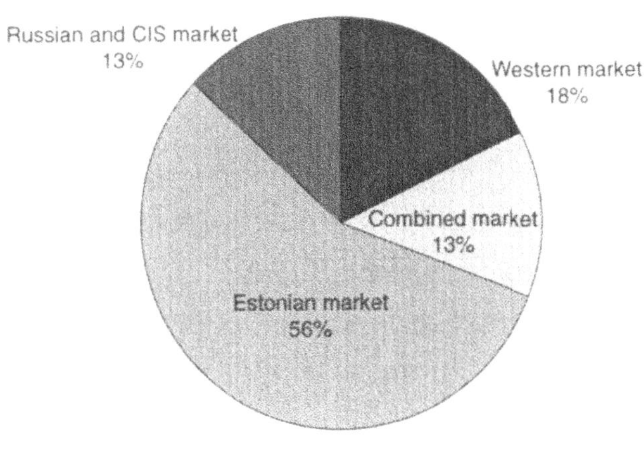

Owners of management buy-out firms are particularly confronted with difficulties of meeting their payments for the take-over and are exerting pressure on the Estonian government to have the terms amended, while other groups of enterprises generally do not consider the payment terms to be a major problem.

The privatised enterprises were also categorised according to their dominant markets. Among the enterprises oriented towards the Estonian market, bakeries, most of the dairy industry and trade enterprises are typical. But this segment also includes approximately half of the light industry and timber and furniture-producing enterprises. Most of the heavy industry is oriented towards the Russian and other CIS markets, although nearly all the enterprises in this category has also done some subcontract work for Western customers (predominantly Finland and Sweden). Other enterprises rely on combined markets (see Figure 10.2).

Job reductions have predominantly taken place in the privatised enterprises (and is still continuing in many of them, according to the managers), but they have been quite moderate. In 57 per cent of enterprises polled, the managers said that they had more or less the number of employees necessary, 39 per cent had more than they needed, and 4 per cent had less than necessary. The enterprises with too many workers considered an average of 15 per cent of the existing work force superfluous.

The problem is that the economically less successful enterprises do not want to, dare not or cannot (due to limits concerning employment) reduce their work force, while the more successful enterprises are more radical in that respect. The enterprises mainly producing for the Western market are reducing their work force quite steeply. At the same time, the enterprises of the so-called mixed markets (supplying the Western, Eastern and domestic markets) usually do not consider job cuts to be necessary.

The lack of investments is an important factor slowing down the development of privatised enterprises. The problem is not that it is totally impossibility for privatised enterprises to get loans in the banks but that the loan sums have been too small or the interest too high. The opportunities for involving extra capital via measures like the sale of shares in the stock market or using investment funds have been rather marginal for privatised enterprises.

The owners and management of the enterprises have a positive attitude towards the involvement of foreign capital. Nearly 70 per cent would even consider turning over part of the shares to a suitable foreign partner, but few would hand over a controlling interest to foreign investors.

Small and Medium-Sized Enterprises

Several studies concerning the small and medium businesses have been conducted in Estonia during the last 5-6 years, but their samples and results are unfortunately not directly comparable in a number of cases. We shall attempt to provide a general picture of the situation based on the results of three empirical studies.

The British researcher David Smallbone with his partner Urve Venesaar from the Estonian Institute of Economics conducted a comparative study of SMEs in the industry of the three Baltic states (Smallbone and Venesaar 1996). The study was done in the summer of 1995 and covered 300 enterprises, whose staff did not exceed 100 persons. The results were compared with conditions in Poland and the UK. It appeared that foreign markets were significantly more important to the Estonian industrial SMEs than to those of Latvia and Lithuania . The sales of the SMEs were also increasing more rapidly in Estonia than in Latvia or Lithuania.

Smallbone and Venesaar stress that in all three Baltic states, the owners of industrial SMEs are characterised by a very high educational level (significantly higher than in the British industrial SMEs), usually accompanied by some previous experience in the same industrial sector.

Tallinn-based enterprises have been somewhat over-represented in several studies of SMEs in Estonia conducted so far. Consequently, the results have shown the state and problems of entrepreneurship in the capital rather than the life of the Estonian SMEs as a whole. A pleasant exception is provided by a study conducted in the summer of 1996 by the Estonian Institute of Economics, EMOR Ltd and EIM International (*Regionaalne väikeettevõtete* 1996). The selection of the SMEs (enterprises with a staff of up to 80) was regionally representative and special attention was paid to the problems caused by the location of the SMEs in Estonia. The poll covered 1037 enterprises.

Out of the studied SMEs, 71 per cent were active in services and trade, 23 per cent in industry and 6 per cent in agriculture and forestry. Ninety per cent were under Estonian private owners, 5 per cent were municipal or state-owned. Another five per cent were foreign owned, and a further 8 per cent had foreign minority shareholders. Forty-three per cent of the firms were based on former enterprises from the socialist period, whereas the rest had no such antecedents.

It appeared that an average Estonian SME, especially outside the capital, is using predominantly local raw materials and semi-manufactured products, 76 per cent of them being purchased in Estonia, including 48 per cent in the county where the enterprise is located. Finland leads with 70 per cent among the foreign sources of raw material. Thirty-three per cent of the polled enterprises operate as subcontractors, either to other Estonian firms or foreign enterprises; 13 per cent of the Estonian SMEs receive most of their turnover from subcontracts. The domestic market is of greater importance for the sale of the products than for the purchase of raw materials and semi-manufactured goods.

Most of the enterprises (62 per cent) had increased their turnover as compared to the previous year. Fifty-eight per cent made a profit in 1995, 27 per cent were loosing money.

Among the main problems pointed out by the respondents were the small size and limited purchasing power of the Estonian domestic market, high interest rates and difficulties with making long-term loans. In the rural areas (and further away from the capital), the low quality of equipment and difficulties with obtaining new machinery are added as quite serious problems (this is primarily characteristic of agriculture, where the purchase of new equipment is largely limited by the low profitability of production and inadequate credit opportunities), as well as inadequacy of infrastructure (communications problems). A specifically urban problem is posed by the rent of production space, which has become too high for the SMEs.

The SMEs were grouped according to a so-called foreign relations index. Besides Tallinn and the surrounding Harju County, the foreign relations index is also high among the enterprises in Estonia's western regions: Lääne and Hiiu Counties (economic ties with Sweden are typical in both cases). But strong foreign ties are not necessarily tantamount to outstanding economic success. Whereas Tallinn and Harju Counties are successful and the south-eastern Estonian counties are backward, Estonia's second largest city Tartu with its surrounding county is showing good economic results (its foreign relations index is approximately the Estonian average). Hiiumaa, despite its high foreign relations index, has until now been relatively unsuccessful. Ida-Viru County with its industrial towns and predominantly Russian-speaking population is average according to the foreign relations index (relations with Russia), but weak in terms of SME success (as well as the number of SMEs per 10,000 inhabitants).

A third study approached the problems from a specific angle, namely stressing the motivation of the entrepreneurs (Aho et al. 1997).

Approximately 60 per cent of the entrepreneurs who started out in the period 1986-90 could be classified as 'enterprising individuals.' When the first opportunities for business emerged, the most enterprising individuals hastened to take advantage of them. As a rule, top executives and specialists of the existing enterprises continued to work in their previous posts, where the security was greater and the income was high. The 'professionals turned entrepreneurs' made up only 8 per cent of the businessmen who began in the years 1986-90. Entrepreneurs motivated by foreign factors were completely non-existent in the period when borders were still largely closed.

Immediately prior to the restoration of Estonia's independence, matters started to change. There were relatively many beginners due to privatisation in the period 1990-93. Approximately 80 per cent of the entrepreneurs motivated by foreign factors began operating in the 1991-93 period. The year 1991 was a turning point where a large part of the 'professional' entrepreneurs founded their businesses. This coincided with the period when a significant share of the former state-owned enterprises faced major difficulties, lost their previous suppliers and markets and had to cut their production volume and staff. But new opportunities also arose, and qualified specialists hurried to take advantage of them in private business. Seventy-five per cent of the private enterprises founded due to dire necessity were established in the years 1993-94. It may be presumed that after the members of the latter group began experiencing that their situation and income did not improve, despite the general economic upturn, they began to seek opportunities elsewhere.

Recently – 1994-95 – the share of the 'enterprising individuals' has again increased among the beginners. This was to be expected, since the 'professionals' have already found their new niche, the privatisation has been completed (with the exception of a few larger enterprises), the simpler ways of finding ideas from abroad to use in Estonia have been exploited, and the proceeds from a brief job abroad are no longer sufficient for starting a business in Estonia. The emergence of a new wave of 'professional' entrepreneurs may be predicted in the future.

Developing Legislation

The regulation of activities and requirements of different forms of entrepreneurship that was instituted by the laws and government resolutions adopted in 1989 and 1990 have become outdated. The original legal acts adopted to regulate entrepreneurship proved inadequate, and over the years it became evident that business needed thorough regulation. This is especially true of joint-stock companies and limited liability companies. The minimum amount of share capital initially required – 3,000 roubles (300 kroons after the monetary reform) – had become a ridiculously small amount of money due to the inflation. A large part of the registered firms did not operate, it was difficult to obtain reliable data on the them, several important areas (merger, division and transformation of enterprises) went unregulated, to mention some of the problems.

After long debates, amendments and changes, the parliament approved the Commercial Code on 15 February, 1995. It came into force on 1 September, 1995.

According to the Code, an entrepreneur shall be an individual for whom the sale of goods or services is a permanent activity (sole proprietor) and a commercial undertaking as enacted by the law. Commercial undertakings are general partnerships, limited partnerships, joint-stock companies and limited liability companies. Businesses are entered in the Commercial Register.

The Commercial Code includes requirements about the extent of liability and the minimum amount of capital required (the minimum required capital of joint-stock companies and limited liability companies was significantly increased). The law also regulated the formation, management, representation, accounting and allocation of profits, the winding up, beginning and ending of membership, as well as mergers, dissolution and transformation into a different kind of business.

The issue of the minimum capital was the object of the most heated debates. Due to the initially almost symbolic capital requirements, the joint-stock company had been the most popular form of business. In the summer of 1995, before the new Commercial Code came into force, there were 51,000 joint-stock companies, while the number of limited liability companies was less than 2000 and that of general and limited partnerships less than one hundred each. Under the new law the entrepreneurs will face the dilemma of whether they feel ready for full liability or should only invest enough capital to meet the minimum requirements.

After a certain time the enactment of the new legislation will be followed by significant changes in the proportions of different types of business. From 1 September, 1995 new businesses can be established only in accordance with the requirements set by the Commercial Code. An exception is that until 1 September, 1999 the share capital of a limited liability company shall be at least 10,000 kroons and that of a joint-stock company 100,000 kroons. From then on the minimum amount of share capital will be 40,000 kroons for a limited liability company and 400,000 kroons for a joint-stock company (8 Estonian kroons equal 1 DM). The already operating businesses must comply with the new rules by 1 September, 1997. For the joint-stock companies, for example, this means that they will have to increase their share capital, choose another form of business or close down. By the same term the businesses not allowed by the Commercial Code will have to wind up.

The adoption of the Commercial Code should ease Estonia's admission to the EU. European directives have been fully considered in the formulation of the Commercial Code, which has been fully harmonised with the EU legislation.

The Code is also expected to ensure an increased feeling of security among investors, including the foreign ones. Detailed regulation of the joint-stock companies will guarantee equal rights for all shareholders, definite control over the activities of the management, and protection of the minority shareholders' interests by making the investment in shares more attractive and less risky for the general public, including foreign investors.

The new requirements for the registration of enterprises and the coming into force of the Commercial Code are also expected to guarantee a higher reliability of the information on business and the registration of actually operating enterprises. The information, including data on the make-up of the management or the board of the enterprise, will be available to the public.

Notes

1. We use this term to differentiate them from the previously existing enterprises, which were formally co-operatives, but actually not unlike state property in view of the state regulation of their activities.
2. Calculations by J. Teder based on the Estonian Enterprises Register data.
3. The study was conducted by the Estonian Institute for Futures Studies and the firm Mainor-Trend during the first half of 1996. The study's main authors were Erik Terk and Ülle Pihlak. A total of 71 enterprises met the criteria (privatised in 1993 or the beginning of 1994, at least one year's operation under private ownership, a purchasing value of more than 5 million kroon at the time of privatisation). In 58 enterprises the development of financial indicators in the period after sale was studied. An additional interviewing of the management was conducted in 48 enterprises.

References

Aho, S., Piliste, T. and Teder, J. (1997). *Private Entrepreneurship in Estonia 1989-1996*. Tampere, University of Tampere.

Borsos-Torstila, J. (1997). 'Foreign Direct Investment and Technology Transfer: Results of a Survey in Selected Branches in Estonia,' *Discussion Papers of the Research Institute of the Finnish Economy*:580. Helsinki.

Estonian Institute for Futures Studies (comp.) (1994). *Estonia's Transition and Renewal: Overview to UNDP*. Tallinn.

Kukk, K. (1992). *Foreign Economic Relations of Estonia*. Tallinn.

Regionaalne väikeettevõtete uuring (1996). Tallinn, Majandusministeerium. (Regional Study of Small Enterprises. Tallinn, Ministry of Economic Affairs).

Smallbone, D. and Venesaar, U. (1996). 'Small and Medium Manufacturing Enterprises in the Baltic States: A Comparative Study,' *The Baltic Review*, Summer.

Terk, E. (1991). *Ettevõtlus Eestis*. IME bülletään:15, July. Tallinn, Eesti Majandusministeerium ja Eesti Majandusarengu Instituut. (Entrepreneurship in Estonia. IME Bulletin:15. Estonian Ministry of Economic Affairs, Estonian Institute for Economic Development).

Part II

Spatial Planning and the Environment

11 VASAB 2010: A Critical Analysis[1]

Ralph Westermann

1996 – The Big Push in Baltic Sea Regional Integration?

1996 saw a break-through in Baltic Sea regional (BSR) integration. At the Visby Summit of the heads of the riparian states in May of that year, it was clearly indicated that the primary objective of BSR co-operation is the constant improvement of the living and working conditions of BSR citizens within the framework of sustainable development (SD). In order to achieve this end with an action-oriented strategy, it was decided to draw up an Agenda 21 for the BSR (VASAB 1996c: 11). Moreover, for the first time really, the Baltic Sea region was acknowledged as independent actor on the European political scene, and has since then it has achieved a status similar to that of the Mediterranean region.

This process is underlined by the EU BSR Initiative which sets out how the EU contributes to and will continue to promote co-operation among BSR countries (Kommission der Europäischen Gemeinschaften 1996b). In line with the Visby Declaration, EU support actions can be grouped into three main categories, which were further elaborated at the meeting of the Council of Baltic Sea States (CBSS) foreign ministers in Kalmar:

- strengthening democracy and stability, including support of the civil society, the promotion of human rights and the fight against illegal activities,
- fostering economic development by developing bilateral relations and encouraging the transition countries in the Baltic Sea region to further develop relations among themselves, so that a larger economic area may provide better economic perspectives. This co-operation also includes the streamlining of legislative and administrative frameworks, the promotion of infrastructure and supply of energy as well as the promotion of sound environmental policies and practices,
- promotion of regional development as such. This includes co-operation among subnational regions across national borders, with the active involvement of local authorities.[2]

The Ministerial Conferences on the Environment and on Spatial Planning held in Stockholm in October 1996 took up these guidelines and developed a first draft of a regional Agenda 21 (Baltic 21). At the same time, the ministers adopted 'Common recommendations for spatial planning of the coastal zone in the Baltic Sea Region' (Committee for Spatial Development in the Baltic Sea Region 1996) and approved the VASAB 2010 action plan called 'From Vision to Action' (VASAB 1996a: 1).

As VASAB 2010 together with the HELCOM process may be viewed as the two major initiatives touching on the improvement of the BSR environment and having a truly riparian-wide target supported by an action programmes, it is the aim of this chapter to scrutinise how the comprehensive spatial planning initiative of VASAB 2010 meets the demands of a Baltic 21 and if and to what an extent it may contribute to its success (Hjorth; Ringius, both in this volume).

The chapter concentrates on an analysis of the VASAB 2010 institution by first deriving evaluation criteria for sustainable spatial planning from theoretical explanations of SD and Agenda 21, then describing the structure and process of the VASAB initiative and finally commenting critically upon its performance with regard to its compatibility with and support to a Baltic 21.

Sustainable Development in the Baltic Sea Region

At their Visby Summit, the governments of the Baltic Sea States agreed upon a path towards SD.[3] The next sections intend to clarify the contents of the sustainability concept and its implications for a Baltic Agenda 21.

Sustainable Development

SD can be defined as a form of development that will satisfy current needs without depriving future generations of the possibility to meet theirs (Hauff 1987: note 27). The demand for intergenerational justice has consequences for long-term economic growth and the unfolding of culture. An indispensable requirement is the protection of the environment and its manifold functions for mankind.[4]

The guiding principle of SD rests mainly on the three fundamental categories of retinity[5] (interwoven networks), dynamics and completeness. All three components are closely intertwined and represent pioneer knowledge for the development of a human society able to adapt to future challenges.[6]

The ethical category of retinity is essential for SD. It stands for the new insight that civilisations must conform with their underlying natural networks. This can only be achieved by a long-term harmonisation of dynamically growing economies and environmentally sound social developments. It is essential to understand that the carrying capacity of the natural environment sets the limits or thresholds which must not be overstepped if civilisation is to continue. The problem of interdependency therefore encompasses the problem of wealth distribution (SRU 1994b: 47).

The complexity of the retinity problem stems from the fact that nature and civilisation changes and develops at changing velocity. Nature may be considered a dynamic, evolutionary system changing continuously and abruptly at the same time. It is no fixed, static order but a highly complex construction of interdependent ecological systems. The apparent harmony of nature results from conflict-laden evolutionary processes and consequently has to be seen rather as a system which is simultaneously in equilibrium and in permanent flow. However, the ability of natural processes to respond or adapt to changes or disturbances from the cultural system are limited and connected to their own time cycles. The high velocity of developments undergoing exponential growth places an excessive burden on the recuperative capacity of natural counter-balancing mechanisms. Thus a fundamental law of development, which is that long-term environmentally sound development must not exceed critical loads of the natural system, is ignored by most contemporary societies.[7]

The concept of sustainable development leads to an entirely new holistic or systemic view of development, which implies that economic, social and ecological development should be interpreted as a fragile entity whose should not be separated or traded off against each other. Yet it is important not to misunderstand this entity as being in harmony. A few exceptions notwithstanding, the relation between the three components is characterised by conflict and tension due to differing dependencies and dynamics.[8]

Implementing Sustainability

If economic and social development is to be oriented towards the carrying capacity of the natural environment, this necessarily requires a corresponding change in current life patterns still dominated by growth-centred economic progress and economic rationality. An environmentally unsound economy counteracts its own rationality because in the long run it destroys what it is living from (SRU 1994b: 9). Accordingly, a fundamental transformation presupposes an economic and social development that spurns waste of resources and degradation of environmental functions (SRU 1994b: 9, 46 f.). The model of a 'circular economy' (Pearce and Turner 1990: 35) and the principle of precaution are essential elements of the core idea of SD, pointing towards the way in which a transformation of the prevailing path of human development can be achieved.[9]

If an economy is to become viable over a long time horizon, it can no longer be designed as a linear but as a circular economy harmonising the production processes with natural cycles. This means that the long-term capacity of nature to provide resources and to receive material released after production and consumption has to be incorporated into economic accounting. This can be expressed by the following general rules of decision and action (SRU 1994b: 47):

- The use of a resource must not exceed its rate of regeneration or the rate of substitution of all of its functions (preservation of resources).

- The release of material or substances must not exceed the receptive capacity of environmental media.

This aspect of SD has to be accompanied by an effective precautionary protection of the health and life of mankind (SRU 1994b: 48). The principle of precaution mainly includes two issues: On the one hand, humanity must be protected against substance-related risks even before a manifest danger has arisen. On the other hand, it contains the obligation to preserve the natural living conditions. The principle of precaution thus offers a third rule of action in the concept of SD (SRU 1994b: 10):

- Dangers and excessive risks to human health from anthropogenic impact are to be avoided as early as possible.

Two more indispensable guidelines of SD are the polluter-pays principle and the principle of co-operation. The first principle entails that the costs of environmental degradation have to be paid by the persons or organisations who caused the degradation. This rule not only includes a method of cost or burden sharing, it may also serve as a as criterion for measuring economic efficiency when environmental policy instruments are employed. The second principle may be viewed as a procedural rule indicating that whenever possible political action should be oriented towards a consensual achievement of environmental goals.[10]

Any environmental policy striving to implement adaptive resource management[11] has to act within the framework of colliding or conflicting economic, social and ecological demands. This intermediary function has to be supported by an integration of environmental policy in all sector policy areas before a sustainable strategy of development can be followed (SRU 1994b: 48). Correspondingly, a modern environmental policy needs to define ethical, legal, economic and ecological criteria for environmentally sound action.[12] It is also necessary to develop adequate procedures to appraise the goals of environmental policy and regularly monitor the crucial parameters of critical levels, critical loads or critical structural changes. This approach has to be completed by a variety of competing or complementary environmental policy instruments resulting in a toolbox of measures referring to the personal (the individual) or structural level (the system).[13] This understanding of SD implementation can be exemplified by studying the analytical process leading to a Baltic 21.[14]

The Creation of a Baltic Agenda 21

Regionalisation in Baltic Europe has reached a critical stage calling for the implementation of a comprehensive Baltic Agenda 21 (Stålvant 1993b: 140 f.). Baltic 21 is primarily considered a political process. It has to do with engaging people in the communities, at all different levels of decision-making. However, the political process cannot come to fruition unless it is supplied with analytical information from a continuous monitoring and evaluation of the environmental and social systems. In order to provide a knowledge base for subsequent political negotiation, a parallel analytical process is necessary.[15] Figure 11.1 tries to identify, in principle, the main steps involved in the analytical assessment of SD.[16]

The analytical process begins with a look at the current situation followed by an extrapolation of present conditions and foreseeable scenarios for the region into the future, assuming trends continue as more or less 'business-as-usual.' Here the currently accepted principles of markets, private investments and competition are the fundamental engines of development. These conditions determine macro-type driving forces such as demographics, the scale and structure of economic activities, urbanisation and globalisation. These simply explain the pattern of life of the Baltic Sea region and its inhabitants.

Every one of these driving forces will have certain repercussions at the micro-level, within the different sectors of society. Sector assessments must be carried out to identify development trends and main environmental pressures within each sector. Integrated tools are needed to identify pressures across sectors. These environmental pressures may relate to the input, the natural resources, such as forests, soils and minerals, or the output, the environmental loads, such as air and water pollution and changes in land-use. Environmental pressures lead to ecological and social impacts or stress in different media. Different sectors have their own distinguishable influences on ecological systems in and around the Baltic Sea, on human health, on biodiversity etc. To describe and measure these impacts, bio-physical and socio-economic indicators are helpful. With such

Figure 11.1: The analytical process behind a Baltic Agenda 21

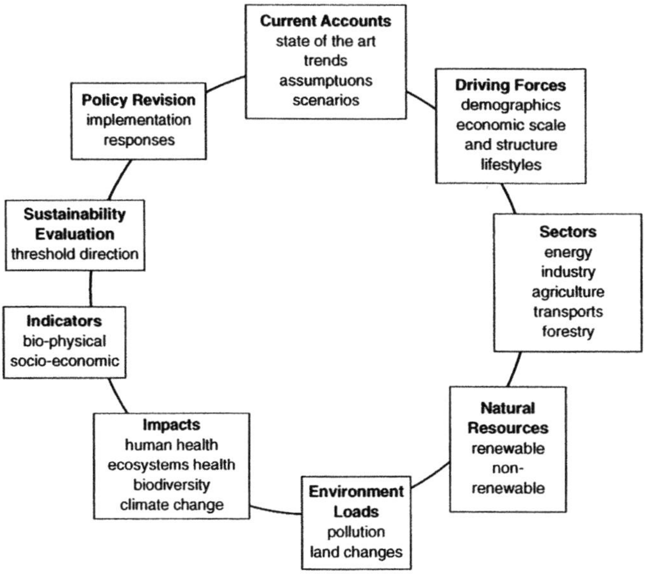

Source: Kristoferson and Stålvant (1996: 12)

indicators, it is possible to make a sustainability evaluation to determine whether certain ecological thresholds have been exceeded and in what respects society in the Baltic Sea states is moving on a sustainable or a non-sustainable path. The evaluation will then be used as an input for the political decision-making and action process, with possible subsequent policy revisions of a legal or non-legal nature, which may be reflected in the adoption of an implementation plan. Such a plan might result in proposals for policy changes, new conditions and future scenarios, and the process will start over again.[17] An open and thorough analytical process may support far-sighted political resource management by continuously monitoring and evaluating regional development from a sustainability perspective.[18]

As described above, the analytical process towards a Baltic 21 naturally has to decompose the complex regional system into various elements and sectors with the aim of gaining insight into their structure, functional behaviour and interlinkages. Implementation needs to put the parts together again. Because of its integrative, multi-sector character, internationally concerted spatial planning appears to be one of the best suited political instruments for this task, not only in the BSR,[19] if it is able to establish a 'friendly' competition among the riparian states' planning authorities for the best solution.[20]

Spatial Planning in the Baltic Sea Region

This section intends to link the Baltic 21 process to modern spatial planning concepts by isolating common evaluation criteria. It also provides an overview of the pan-Baltic spatial planning initiative VASAB 2010.

Demands upon Riparian-wide Spatial Planning

According to a widely used definition, the role of spatial planning is to promote long-term (sustainable) socio-economic development while preventing its harmful environmental impacts.[21] The aim is to create a more rational organisation of land-use in order to balance demands for socio-economic development, while improving the quality of life of the inhabitants and protecting the environment.[22]

Spatial concepts normally do not have any binding power. Spatial planning rather focuses on establishing rules of rational space management. Most spatial planning is of a strategic nature, aiming to elaborate ideas and strategies. It facilitates the decision-making of future private and public investors by providing them with information about the most desirable forms of land-use. In this context, the democratic process plays a central role.

Spatial planning presupposes a multi-sector approach. The involvement of local and regional authorities in the planning and implementation process is a vital element in the national planning system. Spatial planning refers to the methods used largely by the public sector to influence the future distribution of activities in space. It has at least four important tasks:

- to co-ordinate regional development with the aim of ensuring careful management of natural and cultural resources as well as promoting an efficient urban settlement system and infrastructure network;
- to improve the specific opportunities and potentials for socio-economic development in all regions;
- to co-ordinate the spatial impact of other sector policies in order to enhance socio-economic development and ensure spatial cohesion;
- to diminishing disparities between regions and to provide equivalent living conditions for citizens (unless these can be provided by market forces).[23]

In order to compare pan-Baltic spatial planning with the proposed concept of sustainability, I shall examine the characteristics of the environmental action programme listed in the Baltic 21 report:

- open-ended commitments,
- broad understanding of 'soft' and 'hard' elements of environmental transition,
- priority identification and concrete actions,
- specification of time horizons,
- incorporation of economic aspects and
- participation of a mixed set of actors with different status.[24]

VASAB 2010: The Vision

On 21 August 1992, representatives from the ministries responsible for spatial planning of countries around the Baltic Sea met in Karlskrona and agreed to jointly prepare a spatial development concept, 'Vision and Strategies around the Baltic Sea 2010.'[25] Despite the fact that the BSR is not clearly delimited by natural borders, the participating countries (Belarus, Denmark, Estonia, Finland, Germany, Latvia, Lithuania, Norway, Poland, Russia and Sweden) belong totally or partially to the Baltic Sea drainage area.[26]

At a Conference in Tallinn, 7-8 December, 1994 the ministers for spatial planning adopted the report 'Towards a Framework for Spatial Development in the BSR.' It outlines a spatial development perspective for the BSR and provides a useful basis for further strengthening and harmonising national and regional spatial planning policies (Kristoferson and Stålvant 1996b: 35 f.). The VASAB 2010 initiative has yielded spatial development guidelines compatible with the efforts of EU, Central European Initiative and the Barents Sea Council. Baltic Sea region ministers have urged the EU member states to take the VASAB 2010 into consideration when preparing the European Spatial Development Perspective (ESDP).[27]

For the further co-ordination of the proposed common actions, the ministers appointed a Committee on Spatial Development for the BSR (CSD/BSR) under circulating chairmanship, following the rotation practised by the Council of the Baltic Sea States (CBSS).[28] The CSD/BSR's obligation is to prepare proposals for continuation of the VASAB 2010 into the future, with emphasis on the build-up

Figure 11.2: Comprehensive integrated map of 'Vision for the Baltic Sea Region 2010'

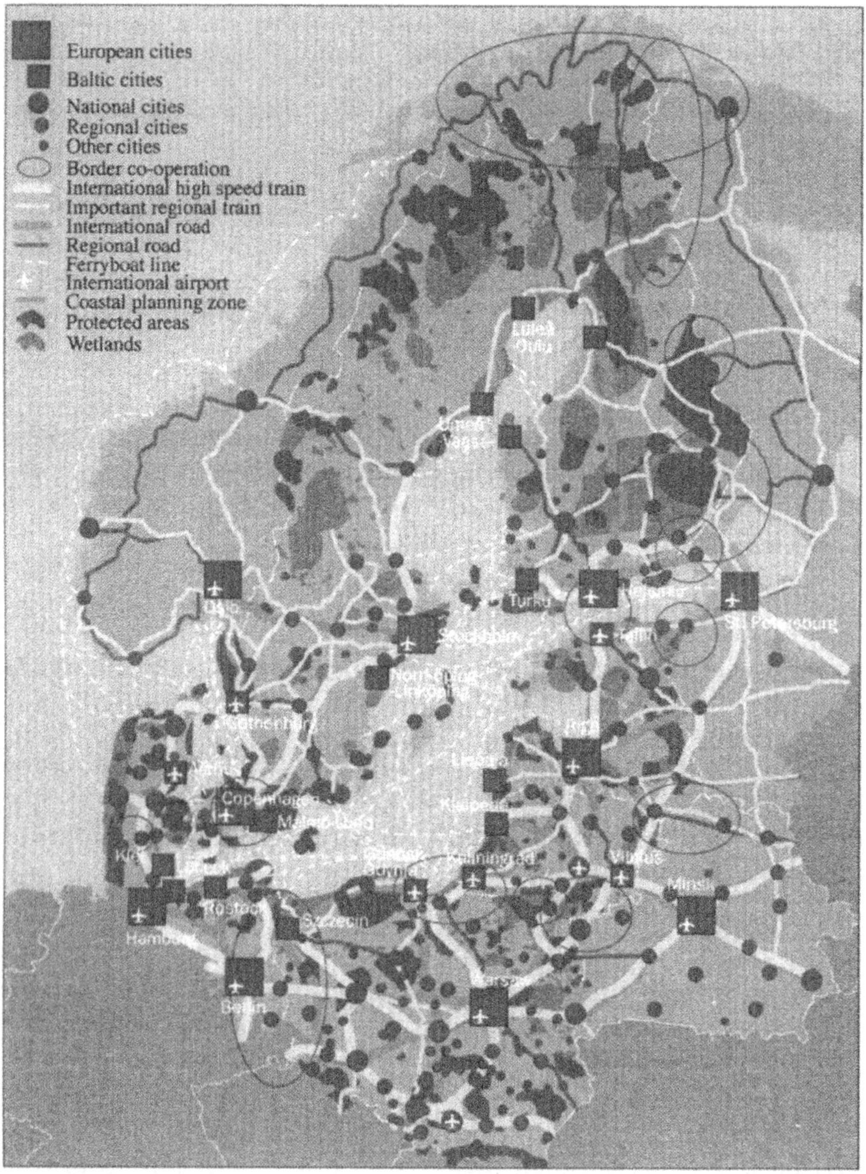

Source: VASAB (1995: 1)

of institutional arrangements and co-operation with other regional organisations, particularly the EU, the Council of Europe and the CBSS.[29]

The BSR comprises large areas of unique and unspoiled natural value due to long-standing environmental protection or to simplistic agricultural practices.

But it is also characterised by severe environmental damage through uncontrolled industrial pollution and careless disposal of urban and industrial wastes (HELCOM 1996b). Four basic values, incorporating the notion of SD and aiming at the improvement of the quality of life, consequently constitute the 'heart' of VASAB 2010 (Westermann 1995: 109 f.):

- development beyond economic prosperity and growth,
- economic, social and environmental sustainability, since development must not deprive future generations of their chances,
- freedom, as it implies the possibility to choose in accordance with individual/regional preferences,
- solidarity, the characteristic of a caring society, sharing benefits from development.

The 'vision' for a sustainable spatial system[30] in the Baltic Sea area encompasses the following four elements, also visualised in Figure 11.2:

'The Pearls': Environment-friendly cities and urban networks promoting spatial cohesion, reducing spatial discrepancies in living standards, providing conditions for efficient use of development potentials. The urban system consists of a Baltic ring of European cities, a network of Baltic cities, playing an important role in cross-Baltic integration, national cities, complementing the Baltic Cities network, and a number of regional cities.

'The Strings': A mobility and communication network plus energy supply system that promotes integration and spatial cohesion within the BSR, protects the environment and improves accessibility to services and job opportunities.

'The Patches': Areas supporting dynamism and quality of life, such as border areas that are instrumental to exchange between nations, areas of tourist importance, coastal zones with special needs and natural and cultural areas of special importance.

'The System': Comprehensive spatial planning in action, contributing to harmonisation and spatial cohesion across borders, based on the principles of subsidiarity, participation and transparency and contributing to the co-ordination of sector and regional planning.

VASAB 2010 Revisited: From Vision to Action

During 1995-96 the main work of the CSD/BSR has focused on implementation of the common framework for riparian-wide spatial planning. A number of priority actions were approved in Vilnius in April 1995. Pilot projects and some common actions have consequently been carried out according to a division of responsibility among the participating countries (VASAB 1996a: 2 f.).

Current Challenges to VASAB 2010

Many challenges and opportunities have emerged that are likely to affect VASAB 2010:[31] Baltic Sea co-operation is becoming more active at all levels, not least as a consequence of the Baltic Prime Ministers' meeting at Visby in May 1996. The CBSS work has been intensified and strengthened. Transregional collaboration is beginning to produce substantial and concrete results (Stålvant et al. 1996). Usually the various forms of co-operation also tackle spatial problems which call for sector integration. Such cumulative pressures sustain VASAB 2010 and, in turn, feed a spatial planning perspective into the overall process.

Work on a regional Agenda 21 for the BSR was simultaneously initiated by the ministers of spatial planning and the ministers of environment. Sustainable development is a fundamental concept both for Baltic 21 and for VASAB 2010 because it implies not only economic development and environmental protection but also balanced spatial development. In the view of VASAB officials, therefore, Baltic 21 should only be prepared in a concerted action between different interest groups such as environmentalists, spatial planners and regional economists.

Common spatial planning in the BSR should be treated as a learning process leading to an exchange of knowledge, synergy effects, human capital formation and mutual understanding. The same holds true for the co-operation among spatial planning authorities at local, subnational, and national levels.

The work in this direction has to be seen in the light of the expected enlargement of the EU towards the East because spatial planning encompassing the whole of the Baltic Sea area may help to prepare the associated countries for future integration into the EU (Treuner 1995: 178-84). Also the INTERREG II C programme is specially tailored to the needs of multilateral co-operation on spatial planning (Kommission der Europäischen Gemeinschaften 1996a: 1-7). Yet the BSR is still considered as a separate unit within the INTERREG II C framework.[32]

BSR integration in economic terms means, among other things, growing spatial interdependence of regions, which cannot develop in isolation.[33] This trend motivates spatial planning authorities to launch cross-border projects. It also initiates a regionally oriented approach to spatial planning which has to find a balance between regional co-operation and competition within a framework of a new division of labour.[34]

Priority Actions

The following list of common priority actions was agreed upon by VASAB 2010 countries in 1996:

- spatial and regional development of the TEN (Trans-European Networks) transport corridors,
- strengthening of the urban system,
- development of trans-Baltic tourism in areas lagging behind,
- cross-border co-operation with a spatial planning component,
- exchange of knowledge,

Figure 11.3: Pilot projects and common actions of VASAB 2010

Pilot project and common actions	Time horizon	Responsibility	Other participating countries
1. Transport Corridors as zones of accelerated development			
Orscha-Minsk-Brest	Finished in 1996	Germany	Belarus
Tampere-Helsinki-Tallinn-Riga (THTR)	1995-96	Finland	Latvia, Estonia, Lithuania (observer)
Karelia-Atlantic (Petrosavodzk-Vaasa-Umeå)	1995-96	Finland	Karelia, Sweden
Katowice-Gdynia-Karlskrona (Trans European Motorway, TEM)	1996-97	Poland	Sweden
2. Urban system			
Luleå-Haparanda-Tornio-Kemi-Oulu city co-operation		Sweden/Finland	
3. Specific areas			
Tourism development of German-Polish border region	Finished in 1995	Germany/Poland	Kaliningrad (observer)
Transborder co-operation between Latvia, Lithuania and Belarus	1995-96	Germany	Latvia, Lithuania and Belarus
4. Exchange of knowledge			
Compendium of planning legislation (linked with EU compendium)	1995-96	Estonia	All the riparian countries
Seminar on national strategic planning concepts	Stockholm, 6-8 Sept. 1996	Sweden	All the riparian countries
5. Planning system			
Common recommendations for spatial planning in the BSR coastal zone	Finished in 1996	Denmark	All the riparian countries

Source: VASAB (1996a: 3 f.)

- common recommendations for spatial planning of coastal zones,
- multimodal transport centres,
- preparation of a training programme for spatial planners,
- examination of the spatial impacts of new forms of telecommunication,
- preparation of a BSR spatial planning compendium and a multi-language glossary for spatial planning,
- improvement of port hinterland infrastructure,
- development and protection of valuable natural and cultural landscapes (VASAB 1996a: 2 f.).

As witnessed by pilot projects, workshops, seminars and international agreements ready to be signed, as in the case of the recommendations for spatial planning of the coastal zone (Committee for Spatial Development 1996: 1-5), some of these endeavours have moved forward. The list of the most successful VASAB 2010 pilot projects and common actions in 1995-96 is presented in Figure 11.3 and will be discussed in the next section.

Record and Critical Analysis of VASAB 2010[35]

Most of the priority projects described in the preceding section have been executed on a bi- or trilateral basis, with resources provided by the participating countries. VASAB 2010 applications for EU financing have not proved to be very successful. The important barrier has apparently been a lack of co-ordination between TACIS, PHARE, INTERREG II C and Structural Funding procedures. A more comprehensive approach on the part of the EU would considerably improve the efficiency of co-operation between EU and non-EU countries. It would also stimulate greater interest (beyond verbal declarations) among the responsible authorities of the CIS and would facilitate a learning process aimed at the transformation of spatial planning systems according to modern EU standards. Action by the EU member states and the European Parliament to alleviate the problem is urgently recommended, but EU officials have already indicated that for the time being, no new funding in addition to the already existing programmes is being contemplated.[36]

On the other hand, VASAB has not so far supplied detailed figures about estimated programme costs in contrast to HELCOM, which very early indicated expected JCP expenditures of up to 18 billion ecu from 1993 to 2012 in addition to a clear assessment of related measures (HELCOM 1996a: 5 f.). If VASAB is to succeed with its application for EU funding, it will have to quantify its financial demands exactly.

Urban Network and Balanced Settlement Structure

A balanced settlement structure of urban and rural areas is an essential element of sustainable development. Key issues in the development of rural areas are the decentralisation of settlements, businesses and administrative activities (Engelhard 1994: 113 f.). After VASAB's Third Ministerial Conference, a pilot project on city co-operation (Luleå-Haparanda-Tornio-Kemi-Oulu) was launched and executed. It demonstrated what benefits might result from co-operation between cities in servicing their hinterlands as well as from a functional division of labour, namely an exchange of experience and harmonisation of the main aspects of the cities' development.

The VASAB action plan proposes that work on the Baltic urban network should start in 1997. The results of studies made by the spatial research institutes' network are of great importance in this context.[37]

Practical experience must be considered a necessary precondition at the initial stages of city network co-operation. Networking is especially promising for shaping sustainable settlement patterns. Existing examples from Polish-German (Slubice-Frankfurt) or Swedish-Finnish (Luleå-Haparanda-Tornio-Kemi-Oulu) cross-border co-operation as well as certain national experiences show what short-term practical results can be achieved. Unfortunately, this aspect is not specified in detail by the new VASAB report.

It is suggested that the urban network initiative should be executed at two levels simultaneously:

- by research on the strengths and weaknesses of different types of settlement, their development potentials, and criteria for the assessment of the present function of cities and surrounding settlements;
- and by joint seminars of experts, representatives of cities and of VASAB 2010, aimed at the development of a harmonised strategy of a balanced settlement structure, city networks and networks of medium and small towns and rural settlements.

A constant link and regular feedback should be ensured between the levels. Experts and the VASAB 2010 representatives should mainly perform the role of facilitator and moderator, guiding cities and towns in the preparation of their own strategy (VASAB 1996c: 6 f.).

The Mobility Network: Regional Impact Assessment of the Transport Corridors

The development of the transport network in the Baltic Sea area is under the responsibility of the Conference of the Baltic Ministers of Transport. The G-24 initiative[38] and political and financial engineering exert a strong influence in developing the concept of the so-called 'Great European Corridors.' Four of them are of major importance to the BSR. One goal of VASAB 2010 is to initiate co-operation with the Conference and G-24 and to provide a spatial framework for the BSR transport networks. In particular, spatial planning for infrastructure development should take into account the impact on the socio-economic development and the natural environment of the adjacent areas because there is both a positive and negative correlation between transport corridors and regional development:

- 'strings' enhance economic development by increasing mobility opportunities, attracting human and physical capital, and improving accessibility;
- at the same time intensive development of transport corridors may jeopardise the preservation of non-renewable resources – particularly the natural environment. It may also contribute towards the deprivation of the social or cultural identity and stability of local societies (VASAB 1996c: 7).

How to solve this fundamental conflict is one of the most serious challenges for the regional implementation of sustainable development. The building of transport corridors must therefore be accompanied by strict regional impact assessments. Fortunately, such assessments are rapidly gaining importance in the Baltic Sea area.

The VASAB action plan recognises that spatial planning must shift its attention from mere infrastructure building to analyses of settlement structures, green area systems, and alternative, multimodal forms of transport, in order to reconcile the socio-economic development of the areas adjacent to communication lines with the preservation of their natural resources and landscape as well as protection of the environment (see also Engelhard 1994: 114 f.). Yet spatial planning in the BSR so far is neither endowed with binding power nor can it rely on clear political priorities in line with the SD principles listed above. It may thus help to bridge the interests of subnational, local, and national actors, but more probably it will be overruled due to economic pressure.[39]

According to VASAB representatives, meaningful results gainsaying this deficiency have so far been achieved by four pilot projects on transport (Tampere-Helsinki-Tallinn-Riga, TEM/TER, Brest-Minsk-Orsha and the Karelia-Atlantic corridor or Blue Way). They were launched with a view to demonstrating how transport corridors could be used for sustainable regional development. These projects provide guidelines on how to balance environmentally sound economic development, which also respects the quality of life, the cultural heritage and other human needs, on the one hand, and road, water, and railway transport, on the other (VASAB 1996c: 8).

There is said to be a growing demand for multiplying the results achieved so far by using the same approach and methodology in other parts of the BSR and to encourage similar work on the following corridors:[40]

- Riga-Warsaw (the southern part of the Via Baltica – transport corridor No 1,[41]
- St Petersburg southwards to corridor No 1, with a possible extension to Hamburg (Via Hanseatica),
- South Finland-Petersburg-Moscow (northern part of corridor No 9),
- Szczecin southwards (A 3) and the ferry lines to Ystad, Malmö and Copenhagen,
- Berlin-Moscow from Orsha eastwards, and from Brest westwards.

CSD/BSR members maintain that one of the key issues for spatial development in the future is maritime transport and the corresponding port hinterland connection, with a focus on multimodal transport centres. This is particularly important due to the fact that ferry traffic across the Baltic is the busiest in the world. However the expected development of these connections has now been slowed down by insufficiently developed land-based infrastructure, particularly in the southern and eastern parts of the BSR. The combination of maritime transport with road, railway and port development is an important goal for Baltic spatial planning. Yet the fundamental dilemma of sustainable spatial planning also prevails in this sector: How should environmentally friendly modes of transportation be promoted in an environment of growing competition among urban centres? VASAB still has no answer. To come up with one will require further quantitative research that includes long-term assessments of the effects of (tele-)communication innovations on transport and settlement structures (VASAB 1996c: 9).

Specific Land-Use Areas

One of the main assets of the Baltic Sea area is its nature. As the coastal zone is particularly vulnerable, the Committee for Spatial Development has proposed several projects under the umbrella of the 'Common Recommendations for Spatial Planning of the Coastal Zone in the BSR' (Committee for Spatial Development 1996: 1-5). In the northern and eastern parts of the BSR there are regions where pristine forests, lakes and other biotopes are an important resource which can be used to stimulate the development of these areas.[42] Sustainable tourism (eco-tourism) is one of the most frequently chosen alternatives of development in this part of the BSR.[43]

Sustainable Tourism

The challenge of SD in specific types of area (patches) is again how to maintain the existing high standard of the environment and biotopes whilst using these assets as a main leverage for development. To achieve this, the VASAB process needs to establish a constant working dialogue between spatial planning and environmental protection which takes the demands of the local population will be taken into account (VASAB 1996c: 9 f.).

A possible solution paving the way for sustainable tourism is outlined in the new VASAB report:[44] The first step is to make an inventory, classify, and evaluate the natural landscape and cultural heritage. This should be done jointly by ecological experts, specialists on cultural heritage and spatial planners. The next step is comparison and evaluation that highlights the economic and cultural value of the natural landscapes. The aim is to prepare a comprehensive description of landscape metrics as a tool for spatial planning.[45]

Since the development of eco-tourism is a priority for many Baltic countries, VASAB 2010 should also encourage the creation of a network of areas of natural landscape and cultural heritage which would form a Baltic Belt of Green Corridors – an attractive complex of landscape favourable for both tourists and permanent residents. The network of Baltic green areas is expected to create job opportunities, improve the accessibility of remote or peripheral areas, while doing less harm to the environment.[46]

The concept of Baltic Marinas produced within the Polish-German tourism development project is claimed to be of great interest for all countries along the southern and eastern Baltic coast and is therefore expected to encompass not only Poland and Mecklenburg-Vorpommern[47] but also Kaliningrad, Lithuania, Latvia, Estonia and St Petersburg. The idea is to establish a network of marinas suitable for yacht sailing and located at one-day sailing distance from each other. The development of water sports and prosperous sea-side resorts and centres located in the lake districts of Baltic Sea countries is believed to hold a great potential for increased local wealth. VASAB 2010 wants to promote an international agreement between cities and towns with marinas in order to stimulate this form of tourism (VASAB 1996c: 10).

Cross-Border Co-operation Projects

Two cross border co-operation projects with a spatial planning component have been conducted under the VASAB 2010 umbrella so far, i.e. the spatial development framework for the Polish-German border area and Latvian-Belarussian-Lithuanian cross-border co-operation. Both projects appear to have demonstrated both future potentials and actual benefits (VASAB 1996c: 11 f.).

The Polish-German project is aimed at setting an example for other border areas in Europe. The European Commission regards the German-Polish cross-border co-operation as one of the most resounding successes in transforming spatial planning in Europe. It permits the external frontier of EU to develop into an area of co-operation facilitating the desired integration of Poland into the Union.

The responsibility for the project rests with the Polish and German ministries for regional and physical planning.[48] The resolution 'Spatial Planning Concepts for the Area along the German-Polish Border' was adopted by the Commission in May 1995. The bilateral initiative involves three topics: protection of natural potentials and rehabilitation of damaged areas, promotion of a decentralised settlement structure and development of the technical infrastructure. The joint spatial development project has no legally binding character. It is rather a vision offering guidance to the municipalities and other public players and private investors. Implementation of the concept is now taking place and falls into the responsibility of public authorities.

Also the trilateral Latvian-Lithuanian-Belarussian project supported by the German government seems to be gaining momentum after the period of stagnation. This project is of particular importance for the cohesion of the BSR since it covers an area that is still effectively divided by borders. Among the main advantages of this project are transfer of know-how in the field of modern spatial planning and activation of local authorities in the peripheral Belarussian, Latvian and Lithuanian regions. In the view of the national and local authorities of Latvia, Lithuania and Belarus, the project should be continued.[49]

The System of Spatial Planning: Exchange of Knowledge

The need of more knowledge was highlighted as a VASAB 2010 priority by the Third Ministerial Conference (Bächtold et al. 1994: 224-26). All the VASAB 2010 pilot projects have played a key role in the exchange of knowledge and transfer of modern know-how in the field of spatial planning. They have also been useful in the marketing of VASAB 2010 ideas and approaches. The Polish-German spatial planning dictionary may serve as an example of the concrete results achieved in the exchange of knowledge.

A seminar on National Strategic Spatial Planning Concepts in the BSR was organised by the Swedish National Board of Housing, Building and Planning (Boverket) in September 1995 in Stockholm. The background was a growing demand for an exchange of knowledge, since most of the VASAB 2010 countries had already developed their own national strategic planning documents and the others wanted to do so. However, there still is a great need to develop VASAB 2010 work in the form of training and technical assistance for BSR spatial planners at subnational and local level (VASAB 1996c: 12 f.).

For this reason it was also decided to begin work on a BSR compendium of spatial planning legislation as one of VASAB 2010's top priorities. It is expected to attract attention from the EU due to the similarity of VASAB 2010 and EU work in this field. Currently VASAB 2010 is also engaged in the preparation of the BSR INTERREG II C Operational Programme.

If VASAB 2010 is to maintain its important role in the field of information exchange, it will need thorough scientific monitoring and research in all its priority areas. This work has to be integrative and interdisciplinary in order to handle multi-sector spatial planning and sustainability problems, but it is advisable to shift the emphasis from static and qualitative studies to quantitative ones that include dynamic aspects.[50] Another would be to inform the public about the important issues of spatial development to increase the effectiveness and acceptance of decisions. VASAB 2010 should also facilitate professional contacts between spatial planners and serve as a source of important information for them. This can be accomplished by linking existing data-bases and designing them according to the needs of spatial planners.[51]

The Contribution of VASAB 2010 to a Baltic Agenda 21

The analysis of VASAB 2010 shows that, in principle, its concept, structure and process are consistent with a Baltic Agenda 21 and will probably contribute to its success. VASAB 2010 commitments allow for flexibility while at the same time identifying priority actions, responsibilities and time horizons. The spatial planning initiative is open to broad social participation, and its emphasis on knowledge transfer along with regional impact assessments stands for a mix of 'soft' and 'hard' instruments of environmental rehabilitation. The influence from HELCOM is obvious, and many elements from environmental institutions can be retrieved in the official VASAB statements (Hjorth 1992, 1994: 11-31).

However, in contrast to the well-established HELCOM process it is apparent that VASAB 2010, though already initiated in 1992, is still in its infancy. In comparison to HELCOM and its long record of mainly ecological monitoring, VASAB's foundation of scientific research is still weak. This may explain why many of the envisaged actions appear declamatory and void of concrete substance. The deficiency is indicated by a very unsatisfactory incorporation of economic aspects especially regarding EU funding and the participation of international financial institutions. Nowadays it is widely accepted that international environmental co-operation and resource management can only succeed if economic institutions are involved from the start and if, wherever possible, environmental policy makes use of market mechanism incentives and refrains from imposing restrictive laws (Klemmer 1994: 19; Zylicz 1995: 146 f.).

Many conflicts between economy and ecology still remain unsolved or are not evaluated according to the sustainability rules listed at the beginning of this chapter because they lack an adequate hierarchy of politically accepted goals to guide decisions. This is even more the case for multi-sector supranational spatial planning, and for VASAB 2010 in particular. Until now no common, sector-integrating and binding rules or procedures have been established on how to handle existing or potential land-use conflicts between competing interest groups, especially concerning the expansion of the transport network and the necessary transformation towards sustainable agriculture. There is reason to fear that the pressure on infrastructure investments exerted by, among others, the EU with its vision of TENs will outweigh the concern for sustainable settlement and land-use patterns (Haber 1994: 13). Unless VASAB 2010 finds a way out of the dilemma created by its dependence on EU financial support, on the one hand, and the need to free itself from the spatial development concepts favoured by these funds, on the other, the idea of sustainable development in the Baltic Sea area through common spatial planning could remain a vision.

But sustainable spatial planning in the BSR is a long-term enterprise. It is therefore advisable not to expect too much too soon.

Notes

1 The author wishes to express his thanks to Carl-Einar Stålvant of the Centre for Research on Natural Resources and the Environment and Mr Jacek Zaucha and Mrs Agnieszka Zaboklicka of the VASAB Secretariat in Gdansk for valuable comments and kind support.

2 Taken from Declerck (1996: 2). The results of the CBSS meeting in Kalmar are summarised in N. u. (1996).

3 The concept of SD was first mentioned in the report 'Our Common Future' or 'Brundtland-report' published by the World Commission on Environment and Development in 1987. For the German reprint, see Hauff (1987).

4 Even the economic sciences increasingly make use of the sustainability concept. From their point of view it changes the growth paradigm of economic development. Ecologically

sustainable growth then means consistency of economic growth and preservation of the natural environment. Sustainable economic growth requires that the sources of income, i.e. labour, capital and natural resources, are preserved in quantity and quality even after the societal processes of production and consumption (SRU 1994b: 45). An economical interpretation of SD is given by Klemmer (1994: 14-19).

5 From Latin 'rete' (net).

6 The author follows the notion of SD as presented by SRU (1994a: 170).

7 See SRU (1994b: 9, 47) or the brilliant ecological findings of Holling (1995: 20-25) on the relation between the natural and the cultural system as expressed by 'barriers' and 'bridges.' Jansson and Velner (1995: 349-59) apply these results chronologically to the difficult process of shaping environmental institutions in the BSR.

8 This opinion is put forward in SRU (1994b: 9, 47) and Holling (1995: 25-28).

9 SRU (1994b: 48). Haber (1994: 13) shows a more sceptical attitude regarding the possibilities of a societal turnaround towards sustainability. He claims that the cultural development of mankind, particularly since the industrial stage, has irreversibly affected natural systems. Thus SD should concentrate on diminishing the most harmful effects.

10 A short explanation of the polluter-pays principle and the principle of co-operation can be found in Hansmeyer and Schneider (1992: 10).

11 The term adaptive resource management is used to describe a societal learning process ideally leading to a reconciliation of ecosystems and socio-economic systems in space and time. For further explanations see Holling (1995: 28-34 and Gunderson et al. (1995), in particular pages 530-32.

12 The difficulty of this task becomes obvious in Klemmer (1994: 16-19), who comments on the derivation of criteria for economic sustainability.

13 More details concerning the implementation of SD in SRU (1994b: 50-176) or SRU (1994a: 171-79).

14 The following is based on Kristoferson and Stålvant (1996a: 13) and Kristoferson and Stålvant (1996b: 11).

15 Hjorth (1994: 23-26) has outlined the key role of (scientific or non-scientific) epistemic communities in the creation and diffusion of ecological knowledge.

16 The figure does not capture decision-making processes and decision dilemmas, its value is heuristic.

17 For a similar approach see SRU (1994a: 170-79) and the figure in the same article on p. 177.

18 The historical record of ecosystem management in the BSR by Jansson and Velner (1995: 309-49) reveals periods of promising progress and serious set-backs.

19 Engelhard (1994: 103). Bächtold et al. (1994: 218 f. and 226 f.), on the other hand, warn not to expect too much from spatial planning and plead for a realistic assessment of its possibilities.

20 As the author intends to explain in his doctoral dissertation (in preparation), every process of regionalisation has to find its own characteristic mix of integrative, co-operative and competitive elements which must be permanently revised if competitive pressures from within or outside the regional system increase to a critical level and initiate change, either by learning or by destruction of the former order. This not always harmonious process is, of course, also reflected in most of the spatial planning projects presented in this chapter. These thoughts are analogous to the concept of 'infinity loops' or 'adaptive cycles' of ecosystem dynamics introduced by Holling (1995: 20-25). See also Stålvant (1993a: 67-70).

21 Alternative definitions of the term spatial planning are given by Bächtold (1994: 216 f.) or Schaller (1994: 256).

22 This section refers to VASAB (1996c: 5). Implications of SD for spatial planning and related problems of operationalisation are presented in Marx (1994: 16-22) and Brösse (1994: 40-42).

23 This is in line with the 'Stockholm Declaration of Sustainable Spatial Development Policy in the Baltic Sea Region' (VASAB 1996b: 1-3), the main objectives of the Treaty on European Union (Title I, Article B and Title XIV, Article 130a) and the Principles for a European Spatial Development Policy adopted by the Informal Council of Ministers responsible for Spatial Planning in the EU member states in Leipzig, September 1994.

24 The characteristics are listed in Kristoferson and Stålvant (1996a: 56). Key principles of the HELCOM JCP can be compared in HELCOM (1996a: 5 f.).

25 The basic report is VASAB (1994). Other sources commenting on the subject are Löwendahl (1995) and Westermann (1995).

26 See VASAB (1994: 4). The limitation is identical to the ones of HELCOM JCP and Baltic 21, see HELCOM (1996a: 4) and Kristoferson and Stålvant (1996b: 3).

27 The Nordic dimension together with VASAB results are incorporated into the recent EU report on spatial planning (Kommission der Europäischen Gemeinschaften 1995: 228-37).

28 VASAB 2010 and CSD/BSR are served by a three-person Secretariat located in Gdansk. Its task is to advancethe approved actions, assist in the preparation of the BSR ministerial meetings and CSD/BSR meetings, organise the continuous concertation process with other institutions and to co-operate with international and regional programmes dealing with spatial and regional development in the BSR. It proposes and follows research and pilot projects and publishes information on spatial planning in all the countries participating in the programme. See VASAB (1996a: 6 f.).

29 European spatial development policy after Maastricht is analysed by Selke (1993) and Treuner and Foucher (1995).

30 A theoretical explanation of spatial systems similar to the VASAB approach is provided by the regional economist Schätzl (1992: 21-24).

31 For this enumeration, see VASAB (1996c: 2 f.); Kuklinsky (1995: 1-8) and Joenniemi and Stålvant (1995: 38-50).

32 Veggeland (1995) points out that strategic spatial planning in the whole of northern Europe, including the Barents region, is going forward. A strategy for the North Sea region, the North Sea 2000+ Programme, is being developed. Work on the European Spatial Development Perspective is progressing towards a policy-oriented concept. A strategy of spatial development for the seven largest Baltic islands, 'The Baltic Sea Islands: A Common Strategy for the Future,' prepared according to VASAB 2010 methodology was presented at the Visby meeting. It will be the task of VASAB 2010 to provide links and initiate interaction between these programmes.

33 This increasing spatial interdependence is, for example, revealed by trade flow changes, see Jäger-Roschko (1995) or – for a more sceptical outlook on economic integration – Peschel (1993).

34 Intensified competition for freight and passengers between the numerous Baltic ports may illustrate the point.

35 The section is based on an early version of the new VASAB report 'From Vision to Action' and refers to VASAB (1996c: 4-13).

36 Whether EU funding will actually be based on principles of sustainability remains an open question.

37 The results of the VASAB 2010 seminar in Vilnius, December 1995, devoted to this subject, should be followed up.

38 G-24 is an intergovernmental mechanism established in 1989 for co-ordinating assistance to transition countries in Central and Eastern Europe. The Commission of the European Communities acts as the group's secretariat. The name alludes to the 24 Western countries that were members of the OECD in 1989.

39 This concern is expressed by Finke (1994: 134 f.) and Jansson and Velner (1995: 371 f.), using the example of the Øresund crossing. The need for infrastructure investments is stressed by, for instance, BCCA. See Martens (1995: 30 f.).

40 There is also a need for the VASAB 2010 to assess the impact of transport corridors complementary to the trans-European networks (TENs). This is important with regard to the development of specific types of area (patches), e.g. located outside urban networks and TEN development zones. The subnational mobility systems should be assigned the same role (at the subnational level) as played by TENs on the European scale. See Foucher (1995: 157).

41 The Second Pan-European Transport Conference, held in Crete in 1994, endorsed nine multimodal transport corridors in the CEE and CIS countries.

42 As SRU (1996a: 84-97) points out, it is essential that concepts of sustainable land-use in rural areas should go hand in hand with a new orientation of agricultural policy towards extensification incentives and (financial) compensation for ecological performance of agriculture and forestry.

43 See VASAB (1996c: 9) or, for the case of Mecklenburg-Vorpommern, Benthien (1995: 49-51).

44 For the implementing procedure, see also Engelhard (1994: 109).

45 It will be interesting to observe the exchange of experience between two similar pilot projects, the first executed within the ESDP, and the second within the VASAB 2010 framework.

46 The idea of a network of ecologically valuable landscapes is also proposed by Engelhard (1994: 108).

47 The Baltic Marinas concept for Mecklenburg-Vorpommern is worked out in Holst and Mathes (1994: 208-17).

48 The German-Polish Spatial Planning Commission was established on 2 July 1992 and is made up of representatives from the national ministries, the German regions of Mecklenburg-Vorpommern, Berlin, Brandenburg and Saxony and the Polish provinces of Szczecin, Gorzow, Zielona Gora and Jelenia Gora.

49 Many other cross-border projects, mainly of a bilateral nature with an important spatial planning component, have been executed in the BSR. The CSD/BSR has prepared a list of 30-40 such projects of potential benefit to the whole BSR.

50 See Schaller (1994: 256-61), who proposes to combine GIS methods with scenario techniques to support a well-defined spatial planning hierarchy reaching from the strategic to the local level. Further research demands in this field are listed in Finke (1994: 136-41). An example of how spatial planning research might be carried out is the derivation of principles and targets for SD in the coastal zone of Mecklenburg-Vorpommern. See Holst et al. (1994) and Holst and Mathes (1994).

51 Distribution of information via the Internet and the already established BALLERINA system of environmental information in the BSR (including the Baltic 21 homepage) looks very promising. This allows for open, public participation in development and planning work as access to the Internet is growing rapidly in the BSR.

References

Bächtold, Hans Georg, Berwert, Adrian, Buchmüller, Lydia et al. (1994). 'Sustainable Development und Raumplanung.' Arbeitsmaterial der ARL:212, pages 214-230. Hannover.

Benthien, Bruno (1995). 'Entwicklungskonzepte für dünn besiedelte ländlich-periphere Räume – Probleme und Lösungsansätze in Mecklenburg-Vorpommern,' pages 45-51 in ARL (ed.). *Raumordnung und Raumforschung im Ostseeraum.* Hannover.

Brösse, Ulrich (1994). 'Dauerhafte, umweltgerechte Raumentwicklung.' Arbeitsmaterial der ARL:212, pages 24-68. Hannover.

Committee for Spatial Development in the Baltic Sea Region (1996). 'Common Recommendations for Spatial Planning of the Coastal Zone in the Baltic Sea Region,' adopted at the Fourth Conference of Ministers responsible for Spatial Planning and Development in the Baltic Sea Region, Stockholm, 22 October 1996, pages 1-5.

Declerck, Joris (1996). The Baltic Sea Cooperation: Outline of Presentation by Joris Declerck, European Commission, at the European Conference, The Baltic Sea Cooperation, Bonn, 16 December 1996, pages 1-8.

Engelhard, Dieter (1994). 'Dauerhafte, umweltgerechte Raumentwicklung (insbesondere siedlungs- und infrastruktureller Ansatz).' Arbeitsmaterial der ARL:212, pages 99-118. Hannover.

Finke, Lothar (1994). 'Dauerhafte, umweltgerechte Raumentwicklung aus ökologisch-planerischer Sicht, insbesondere der des Naturschutzes.' Arbeitsmaterial der ARL:212, pages 119-155. Hannover.

Foucher, Michel (1995). 'Vorrangige Raumentwicklungsmaßnahmen für den gesamten europäischen Erdteil,' pages 155-158 in ARL (ed.). *Aufbruch zu einem Neuen Europäischen Raum. Bericht einer AEDAR.* Hannover.

Group of Focal Points (1994). *Vision and Strategies around the Baltic Sea 2010: Towards a Framework for Spatial Development in the Baltic Sea Region.* Third Conference of Ministers for Spatial Planning and Development, Tallinn, 7-8 December.

Gunderson, Lance H., Holling, C.S. and Light, Stephen S. (1995). 'Barriers Broken and Bridges Built: A Synthesis,' pages 489-532 in Gunderson, Lance H., Holling, C.S. and Light, Stephen, S. (eds.). *Barriers and Bridges to the Renewal of Ecosystems and Institutions.* New York.

Haber, Wolfgang (1994). 'Nachhaltige Entwicklung – aus ökologischer Sicht,' *ZAU*:7(1), pages 9-13.

Hauff, Volker (ed.). *Unsere gemeinsame Zukunft. Der Brundtland-Bericht der Weltkommission für Umwelt und Entwicklung.* Greven.

HELCOM (ed.) (1996a). *Protection of the Baltic Sea: Results and Experiences.* Report for the Baltic Sea States Summit in Visby, Sweden, 3-4 May. Helsinki.

HELCOM (ed.) (1996b). *The State of the Baltic Sea Marine Environment.* Report for the Baltic Sea States Summit in Visby, Sweden, 3-4 May. Helsinki.

Hjorth, Ronnie (1992). *Building International Institutions for Environmental Protection: The Case of Baltic Sea Environmental Cooperation.* Linköping Studies in Arts and Science:81. Linköping.

Hjorth, Ronnie (1994). 'Baltic Sea Environmental Cooperation: The Role of Epistemic Communities and the Politics of Regime Change,' *Cooperation and Conflict*:29(1), March.

Holling, C.S. (1995). 'What Barriers? What Bridges?' pages 3-24 in Gunderson, Lance H., Holling, C.S. and Light, Stephen, S. (eds.). *Barriers and Bridges to the Renewal of Ecosystems and Institutions.* New York.

Holst, Mathias, Billwitz, Konrad and Strunk, Peter (1994). *Leitbilder und Ziele für eine umweltschonende Raumentwicklung in der Ostsee-Küstenregion Mecklenburg-Vorpommern. Bestandsaufnahme und Bewertung.* Texte des Umweltbundesamtes:32/94. Berlin.

Holst, Mathias and Mathes, Ulrike (1994). *Leitbilder und Ziele für eine umweltschonende Raumentwicklung in der Ostsee-Küstenregion Mecklenburg-Vorpommern. Szenarien, Leitbilder und Instrumente.* Texte des Umweltbundesamtes:33/94. Berlin.

Jansson, Bengt-Owe and Velner Harald (1995). 'The Baltic: The Sea of Surprises,' pages 292-372 in Gunderson, Lance H., Holling, C.S. and Light, Stephen, S. (eds.). *Barriers and Bridges to the Renewal of Ecosystems and Institutions.* New York.

Jäger-Roschko, Olaf (1995). 'Zukünftige Handelsverflechtungen im Ostseeraum – Projektionen auf der Basis eines Regressionsmodells,' pages 37-44 in ARL (ed.). *Raumordnung und Raumforschung im Ostseeraum.* Arbeitsmaterialien. Hannover.

Joenniemi, Pertti and Stålvant, Carl-Einar (1995). 'Baltic Sea Politics: Achievements and Challenges,' pages 9-53 in Joenniemi, Pertti and Stålvant, Carl-Einar (eds.). *Baltic Sea Politics: Achievements and Challenges.* Stockholm.

Klemmer, Paul (1994). 'Nachhaltige Entwicklung – aus ökonomischer Sicht,' *ZAU*:7(1).

Kommission der Europäischen Gemeinschaften (1995). *Europa 2000+: Europäische Zusammenarbeit bei der Raumentwicklung.* Luxemburg.

Kommission der Europäischen Gemeinschaften (1996a). 'Mitteilung an die Mitgliedsstaaten über die Leitlinien für die von ihnen aufzustellenden Operationellen Programme im Rahmen der Gemeinschaftsinititiative INTERREG für transnationale Zusammenarbeit auf dem Gebiet der Raumordnung,' *EG-Amtsblatt*:8(7).

Kommission der Europäischen Gemeinschaften (1996b). *Mitteilung der Kommission. Initiative für den Ostseeraum.* Brüssel, 10 April, pages 1-9.

Kristoferson, Lars and Stålvant, Carl-Einar (1996a). *Baltic 21: Creating an Agenda 21 for the Baltic Sea Region.* Main Report, Stockholm Environment Institute, Stockholm 1996.

Kristoferson, Lars, Stålvant, Carl-Einar (1996b): 'Baltic 21: Creating an Agenda 21 for the Baltic Sea Region, Executive Summary.' Stockholm, Stockholm Environment Institute.

Kuklinski, Antoni (1995). 'The Transformation of Baltic Europe: Research Priorities (A paper for discussion),' pages 1-8 in Kuklinski, Antoni (ed.). *Baltic Europe in the Perspective of Global Change: In Memoriam of Jean Christophe Öberg.* Europe 2010 Series:1. Warsaw.

Löwendahl, Bo (1995). 'Towards a Framework for Spatial Development in the Baltic Sea Area,' pages 152-168 in Kuklinski, Antoni (ed.). *Baltic Europe in the Perspective of Global Change: In Memoriam of Jean Christophe Öberg.* Europe 2010 Series:1. Warsaw.

Martens, Axel (1995). 'Entwicklungsperspektiven des Ostseeraumes aus der Sicht der Baltic Sea Chambers of Commerce Association,' pages 28-36 in ARL (ed.). *Raumordnung und Raumforschung im Ostseeraum.* Arbeitsmaterialien. Hannover.

Marx, Detlef (1994). 'Überlegungen zur Frage nach den Umsetzungsmöglickeiten des allgemeinen umweltpolitischen Ziels "dauerhafte und umweltgerechte Entwicklung,"' pages 1-23 in *Raumforschung und Landesplanung.* Arbeitsmaterial der ARL:212. Hannover.

N.u. (1996). 'Fünftes Treffen des Rates der Ostseestaaten am 2. und 3. Juli 1996 in Kalmar: Kommuniqué,' *Bulletin*:66, 14 August, pages 716-720.

Pearce, D. and Turner, R.K. (1990): *Economics of Natural Resources and the Environment.* New York.

Peschel, Karin (1993): 'Perspectives of Regional Economic Development Around the Baltic,' pages 19-31 in Lundqvist, Lars and Persson, Lars Olof (eds.). *Visions and Stategies in European Integration: A North European Perspective.* Berlin.

Schaller, Jörg (1994). *Regionale Leitbilder für die nachhaltige Entwicklung von Teilräumen an zwei Projektbeispielen.* Arbeitsmaterialien der ARL:212, pages 250-288. Hannover.

Schätzl, Ludwig (1992). *Wirtschaftsgeographie 1: Theorie.* 4. überarb. u. erw. Aufl. Paderborn.

Selke, Welf (1993). 'Europäische Raumordnungspolitik nach Maastricht,' *Informationen zur Raumentwicklung*:9/10, Raumordnung in Europa, pages 577-583.

SRU (1994a). 'Dauerhaft-umweltgerechte Entwicklung – Leitbegriff für die Umweltpolitik der Zukunft,' *ZAU*:7, H. 2, pages 170-182.

SRU (1994b). *Umweltgutachten 1994.* Stuttgart.

SRU (1996a). *Konzepte einer dauerhaft-umweltgerechten Nutzung ländlicher Räume, Sondergutachten.* Stuttgart.

SRU (1996b). *Umweltgutachten 1996.* Stuttgart.

Stålvant, Carl-Einar (1993a). 'The Baltic Sea Area: An International Resource Region and a Test Case for Regionalism?' pages 49-71 in Joenniemi, Pertti (ed.). *Cooperation in the Baltic Sea Region.* Washington D.C., Bristol, London.

Stålvant, Carl-Einar (1993b). 'The Role of the Environment in the Regionalization of the Baltic Sea Area,' pages 117-142 in Sjöstedt, Gunnar and Svedin, Uno (eds.). *International Environmental Negotiations: Issues, Processes and Contexts.* Stockholm, Forskningsrådsnämnden och Utrikespolitiska Institutet.

Stålvant, Carl-Einar with the support of Westermann, Ralph et al. (1996). *Actors around the Baltic Sea. An Inventory of Infrastructures: Initiatives, Agreements and Actors.* Compiled for the Baltic Sea States Summit 1996. Stockholm.

Treuner, Peter (1995). 'Institutionelle und instrumentale Aspekte einer neuen regional ausgerichteten Entwicklungsstrategie für Europa,' pages 178-184 in ARL (ed.). *Aufbruch zu einem Neuen Europäischen Raum. Bericht einer AEDAR.* Hannover.

Treuner, Peter and Foucher, Michel (1995). 'Neue europäische Herausforderungen,' pages 94-107 in ARL (ed.). *Aufbruch zu einem Neuen Europäischen Raum. Bericht einer AEDAR.* Hannover.

VASAB (1995). *Vision and Strategies around the Baltic Sea 2010: Programme for a Multi-national Project.* Karlskrona.

VASAB (1996a). 'About the CSD/BSR and its activities.' Unpublished paper. Gdansk.

VASAB (1996b). *Stockholm Declaration on Sustainable Spatial Development Policy in the Baltic Sea Region.* Reprint of the Declaration adopted at the Fourth Conference of Ministers responsible for Spatial Planning and Development in the Baltic Sea Region, Stockholm, 22 October 1996, pages 1-3.

VASAB (1996c). *Vision and Strategies around the Baltic Sea 2010: From Vision to Action.* Preliminary version of the report Declaration adopted at the Fourth Conference of Ministers responsible for Spatial Planning and Development in the Baltic Sea Region, Stockholm, 22 October 1996, pages 1-16.

Veggeland, Noralv (1995). 'Der Ostsee- und der Barentsraum: Die nördliche Dimension,' pages 120-130 in ARL (ed.). *Aufbruch zu einem Neuen Europäischen Raum. Bericht einer AEDAR.* Hannover.

Westermann, Ralph (1995). 'Die Ostseeregion 2010. Zur Entwicklung eines Bezugsrahmens für die räumliche Entwicklung der Ostseeregion,' pages 101-117 in Gläßer, Ewald, Lindemann, Rolf and Venzke, Jörg-Friedrich (eds.). *Norden*:10, Nordica II, Regionale Studien zwischen Ostsee und Spitzbergen. Bremen.

Zylicz, Tomasz (1995). 'The Ecological-Economic Problems of the Baltic Sea,' pages 139-151 in Kuklinski, Antoni (ed.). *Baltic Europe in the Perspective of Global Change: In Memoriam of Jean Christophe Öberg.* Europe 2010 Series:1. Warsaw.

12 Transboundary Environmental Problems: Risk Analysis and Practical Lessons

Gunnar Sjöstedt

Introduction

Lately, environmental problems have often been referred to as elements of comprehensive security, or as new security issues, in the analysis of East-West relations in Europe. Paradoxically, environmental issues are at the same time increasingly becoming overshadowed by the 'old' military-security issues. These are now re-emerging on the political agenda in Northern Europe in connection with the projects of enlarging NATO and the European Union towards Eastern and Central Europe.

This chapter argues that in the struggle to establish sustainable, co-operative structures in Europe, it would be a strategic mistake to direct the attention away from transboundary, environmental questions. This proposition is valid also for co-operation and regime-building in the Baltic area.

Since the end of the Cold War, environmental co-operation has been facilitated by the asymmetrical relationship that has existed between, on the one hand, Central and Eastern European countries (CEECs) and, on the other, the European Union and Western European countries. This asymmetry is manifested by the substantial environmental aid given to CEECs and is partly due to the aspiration of CEECs to become members of EU and NATO, i.e. their position as applicants that have to demonstrate 'good behaviour.' CEECs have been granted exceptional treatment – less exacting obligations than EU member states in multilateral treaties, for example regarding acid rain (United Nations 1979).

It is, however, unlikely that this asymmetrical association between the EU and the CEECs will prevail in the long or even in the medium term. When the 'period of grace' is over for the CEECs with respect to transboundary, environmental issues, negotiations are likely to grow more cumbersome. Subdued conflicts of interest may manifest themselves more strongly. Dissimilar perspectives on environmental problems in different countries are likely to surface. The aim of this chapter is to assess the significance, and consequences, of such cross-country perceptional differences by looking at transboundary, environmental problems in the Baltic area through the lenses of risk analysis.

A Background Picture

In the 1990s further efforts have been made to strengthen the institutional and legal infrastructure for the co-operation between the nations in the neighbourhood of the Baltic Sea. Notably, the Council of the Baltic Sea States (CBSS) was created in 1992 and includes Denmark, Estonia, Finland, Germany, Iceland, Latvia, Lithuania, Norway, Poland, Russia, Sweden as well as the Commission of the European Union. The member states of the CBSS demonstrated the importance that they ascribe to this organisation by sending their heads of government to the Visby Meeting in June 1996. At the fifth regular Ministerial Meeting of the CBSS taking place in the Swedish city of Kalmar the following month, the foreign ministers of the Baltic Sea states followed up the Visby Declaration by approving three Action Programmes relating to democratic questions, economic co-operation and the environment (UD informerar 1997).

The Kalmar Action Programme for the environment rests on a solid basis of earlier co-operation. In his thorough examination of HELCOM, Ronnie Hjorth takes stock of 102 recommendations for various types of abatement measures to improve the environment in the period 1980-90; 44 related to land-based pollution, 41 to vessel-source pollution and 17 to clean-up operations (Hjorth 1992). In this final period of the Cold War, environmental co-operation between Baltic Sea states had a special significance due to its close, although diffuse, links to security policy (Bröms 1995).

The security dimension manifested itself in various ways. In the Cold War situation almost all kinds of international arrangements concerning the strategically highly important Baltic Sea had security implications in some way or other. Furthermore, the environment represented one of the few arenas where East-West co-operation could be developed at the time. Thus, the CoCom blockade of the Soviet Union and its allies curtailed economic exchange. However, the security dimension of environmental issues was not fully acknowledged in the public debate until after the end of the Cold War, when military issues had lost their dominant position on the agenda of international politics, at least temporarily.

Due to the recurrence of traditional high politics – military-security matters – in Northern Europe, there is a risk that other potential problems related to the inclusion of Central and Eastern European countries into the West European co-operative institutions, such as ecological problems, will once more be pressed towards the periphery of the political agenda. Such a development would represent a setback for those who want to secure a viable all-European integration project including CEEC nations. Preparedness with regard to environmental issues has to be kept high.

Environmental progress has certainly been achieved in the Baltic Sea area, which is indicated by reduced emissions of sulphur, phosphorus, CO_2 and other hazardous pollutants. However, the environmental problems in the Baltic Sea and its hinterland are far from solved. Much remains to be done. The cleaning of the heavily polluted areas in the earlier Soviet Union and other former Socialist states of the East has only started. The water quality in a large number of lakes and many rivers falling out into the Baltic Sea has be considerably improved. Special measures are needed to retain biodiversity in the Baltic Sea and on its shores, as many species are near extinction (Hjorth 1996).

A politically highly sensitive problem area is how the negative effect of agriculture on the environment is to be dealt with (UD informerar 1997). Furthermore, at any time a nuclear accident or other type of environmental disaster might occur.

Environmental Concerns: Critical Issue Attributes

In the literature there has been an extensive debate regarding the relationship between the environment and national security (e.g. Westing 1989; Bröms 1995). This debate has addressed the question whether environmental problems pertain to the sphere of high politics or not. To attribute security qualities to ecological concerns has essentially been a means to elevate their general status in international politics. There is a risk that this discussion may direct the attention of analysts away from other attributes of environmental issues than their security label, which may have a considerable impact on state behaviour.

Because environmental problems are usually of a transboundary nature, they tend to pull the representatives of several countries into negotiations. Bilateral, environmental agreements typically pertain to local ecological problems in a border area. Or they are extensions of a multilateral treaty as in the case of the 1986 Conventions on Early Notification of a Nuclear Accident and on Assistance in Case of a Nuclear Accident or Radiological Emergency respectively, that generated a number of such two-party agreements amongst the states in the Baltic Area (Sjöstedt 1993).

Public opinion and non-governmental organisations have been involved in environmental negotiations to an unusually high degree as compared to other international talks.

Usually, environmental problems are characterised by a high degree of uncertainty with regard to both causes and consequences. Often they can only be understood with the help of scientific models. The technical complexity of environmental issues requires the participation of delegates carrying quite different professional cultures, such as that of the career diplomat, natural scientist, engineer or international lawyer.

Acid rain water pollution in the Baltic Sea and other ecological problems are typically multi-dimensional in the sense that they are closely linked to other issue areas outside the environmental sector such as transports, energy, industry or agriculture. Parties engaged in negotiation on environmental issues often have 'negative perceptions of immediate outcomes.' Policy measures required by effective abatement strategies typically generate inescapable, easily discernible costs in the short term, whereas the associated benefits are diffuse, uncertain and accrue only in the longer term (Sjöstedt 1993).

The special or typical attributes of environmental issues on the agenda of international politics are important to consider because they contribute to condition patterns of state interaction in a fairly predictable way. For example, the special kind of uncertainty characterising environmental issues has given an important role in the negotiation or co-operation process not only to so-called 'epistemic communities' but also to scientific models and knowledge. Issue characteristics have an impact on how decisions are made by national governments and how joint commitments are built up in a bargaining encounter. Thus, in many cases international negotiation on environmental topics includes important elements of communication and management of risks. Often environmental policy-making is akin to a choice situation where an individual is considering a proposal for an insurance policy against fire: Is the prospect that a large fire will erupt in your house so likely that it motivates the substantive yearly premium that the insurance company asks for?

The Notion of Environmental Risks

A standard understanding of risk is a possible, negative outcome of an event or a strategy (for a discussion of different definitions of risk, see Drottz Sjöberg 1991). For example, if radioactive leaks into the surroundings of a military base, there is a risk of a greater frequency of cancer in that area.

A basic conventional formula to evaluate a risk is to multiply the negative value of an outcome, should it occur, with the probability of that outcome. This methodological procedure reduces risk assessment to a routine calculation. According to conventional theory the same approach should be applicable also to transboundary, environmental problems. However, recent developments in international risk research indicate serious flaws in traditional textbook methods of risk management, that are particularly stark when they are applied to transboundary, environmental issues (O'Riordan 1995). These problems typically require international solutions produced by collective decision processes involving two or more countries. In such contexts risk management immediately becomes something much more complex, diffuse and open-ended than conventional risk calculus, which presupposes that the assessment is made by one single homogenous actor.

The management of transboundary, environmental risks regularly involves a multitude of actors from several countries and often representing different professional cultures. Under these conditions it is unlikely that risks can simply be computed according to the textbook formula. The way risks will be coped with depends on how they are perceived and assessed by, and communicated between, the participants engaged in negotiations. Risk perceptions by the general public of the different countries and their participation in risk management processes may represent critical constraints for international agreements. A dilemma is that public participation cannot always be avoided and that sometimes it may even be a prerequisite for the effective implementation of an international agreement.

Empirical studies indicate that there may be great differences across cultures, be they ethnic or professional, with regard to perceptions of risks and how these are communicated (Douglas and Wildavsky 1982). For example, opinion studies indicate that Swedes tend to look at environmental issues in a somewhat different way than people from southern Russia (Drottz Sjöberg et al. 1993). One manifestation hereof may be diverging priorities between different kinds of environmental problems, say hazardous waste, river pollution, acid rain or climate warming. However, there also seem to be more fundamental cross-country differences pertaining to the basic way of thinking about risks and managing them.

Such differences also seem to exist between representatives of different professional cultures, for example politicians and natural scientists. For a scientist it may be quite natural to base a choice on a probabilistic assessment, which is very difficult for a politician to do because he or she needs to motivate decisions in terms of certainties: 'Unless we undertake these measures now, we will have to confront those problems and costs tomorrow.'

Thus, recent academic discussion and analysis indicate that the special problems of perceiving, assessing and communicating risks have to be seriously considered when transboundary, environmental regimes in Europe are negotiated and when they are implemented. This is necessary in order to avoid pseudo-conflicts and to facilitate processes of co-operation as far as possible.

Problems of Risk Perception and Communication

Risk perceptions are dependent on the 'substance' of an international, environmental issue. For example, hazardous waste on the ground is likely to be comprehended, and dealt with, somewhat differently than acidification of lakes caused by air pollution. It is perhaps less obvious that the way in which an environmental issue becomes transboundary may likewise represent an important condition for the perception, and eventually also the management of risks.

The basic transboundary syndrome is described in Figure 12.1 as the Flow Model. Its closest representation in the real world is pollution in an inland waterway passing through two or more countries. For example, the flow of pollutants of the river Oder begins in the Czech Republic, crosses the border with Poland and finally follows the border between Poland and Germany before it falls into the Baltic Sea.

Due to cumulative effects, water pollution becomes increasingly more severe as the river approaches the sea, unless riparian states undertake measures to clean the water. Another typical feature of the situation characterised by the flow model is that countries involved in a dispute tend to have either an upstream or a downstream position. The more downstream a country is located, the more it will be hit by the negative consequences of water pollution unless remedial action has been taken in upstream countries. The extreme upstream country will only be victimised by its own emissions of pollutants.

These circumstances tend to make upstream countries top dogs and downstream countries underdogs in their dealings with one another. Regardless of what the downstream country does in order to reduce emissions into the river, it cannot escape the hazardous emissions that have been let out from upstream countries. By contrast, the river transfers a portion of the pollution emitted in the upstream country to the territories of downstream countries. Furthermore, the upstream country can in theory stop all hazardous emissions into the river that are damaging to its own territory, whereas the downstream country cannot accomplish effective abatement without the co-operation of upstream countries. Accordingly, the relative upstream/downstream position of two countries involved in a negotiation will significantly influence their position and strategies.

Upstream-downstream relationships recur in all situations characterised by transboundary, environmental problems where, in a given pair of nations, one country exports more pollution to the other nation than it imports from it. This situation is, however, typically perceived quite differently depending on how pollution is produced in the upstream country, or countries. A distinction can be made between two types of situation that may be referred to as the Single-Source Pollution Syndrome and the Multi-Source Pollution Syndrome, respectively, as illustrated in Figures 12.2a and 12.2b.

Figure 12.1: The flow model of transboundary environmental risks

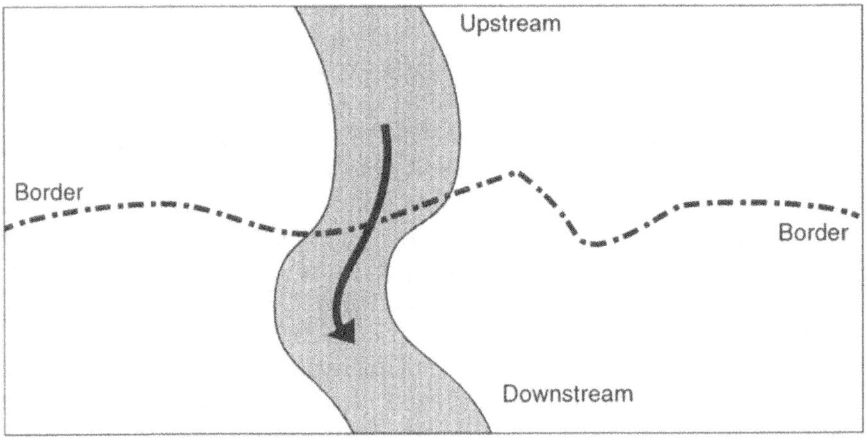

Figure 12.2a: The single-source transboundary model

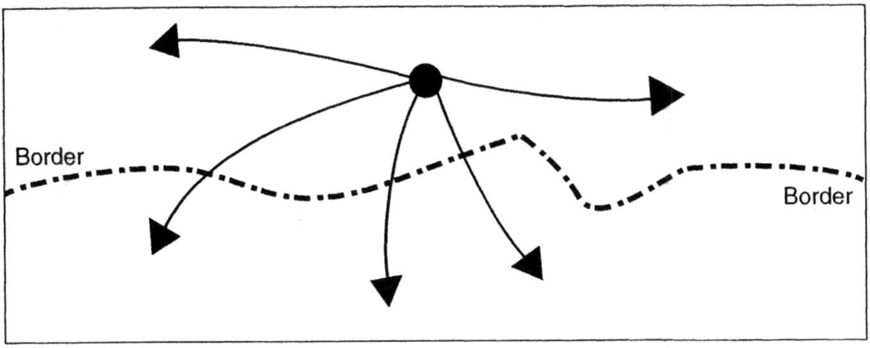

Figure 12.2b: The multi-source transboundary model

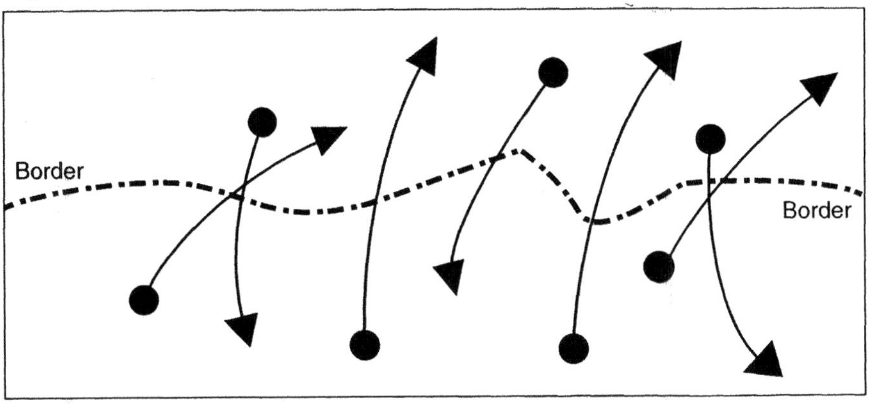

The Single-Source Syndrome: The Case of the Ignalina Nuclear Plant

A risk analysis pertaining to a nuclear plant is a complex mental operation, which may be carried out in quite dissimilar ways and with varying degrees of technical sophistication. Ultimately, the safety of a nuclear plant is dependent on the functioning of each of its constituent parts and their mechanical interaction. However, the 'human factor' intervenes in this systems interaction, adding unpredictable risks.

In an interview, Lars Högberg, Head of the Swedish Nuclear Power Inspection, suggests an approach to risk assessment which he refers to as the mapping of a risk picture, which is a variation of a probabilistic safety analysis. The objective is to evaluate the probability of chains of event that in the end may produce a nuclear disaster. This is a step-wise assessment. The first step represents the probability of an incident starting a critical chain of events. The second step captures the probability that the potential accident process will take particular directions depending on intervening factors like, say, malfunctioning individual components or systems. The last steps of the assessment pertains to the probability of the occurrence of various hazardous consequences and the probability that the perturbed part of the nuclear plant will be able to withstand these negative effects such as a fire.

Leaning on a similar rational risk assessment, Professor Gustaf Östberg, who is an internationally acknowledged expert on nuclear reactors, claims that it would be a perfectly viable option to extend the productive life of the Ignalina nuclear plant in Lithuania by making sound investments in safety measures: 'It should be technically possible to operate and control the safety of nuclear power stations using reactors of Soviet design satisfactorily, with proper considerations of the particular requirements' (Östberg 1995). The fate envisaged for Ignalina is, however, quite different.

In recent years Ignalina has often been portrayed as the main environmental threat in the whole Baltic area, which has to be eliminated at all costs. The basic reason for the strong international concern with Ignalina is the fact that its reactors are essentially of the same design as the Chernobyl reactors (the RBMK type) that have demonstrated their inherent weaknesses in a great disaster. It has also been reported in the media that Western experts have revealed flaws in security measures and routines in the Ignalina nuclear plant. The security problems connected with the Ignalina plant are, furthermore, no news as the Lithuanians became concerned with them already in the 1980s before the demise of the Soviet Union. Due to public protests the project of building a third reactor was interrupted in 1989 and formally cancelled four years later.

The widely signalled awareness of the technical deficiencies of the old Soviet RBMK-type of reactor indicates a wide consensus in the Baltic area about the need to close the two reactors in Ignalina. The Lithuanian government seems to be part of this consensus, as it has initiated a plan to this effect. According to this scheme, the production of nuclear energy in Lithuania will be phased out in the period 1998-2008 (Jankauskas 1995).

However, this ostensible harmony of interests evidently conceals underlying discrepancies with regard to how nuclear risks are really assessed in Lithuania and other states in the Baltic area. The decision by the Lithuanian government to close down the Ignalina plant was not an entirely independent choice. The European Union, the IAEA as well as certain neighbouring countries made efforts to influence the Lithuanian government to attain that result. Technical assistance was, for instance, given in order to enable a technical inspection of the two Ignalina reactors acceptable in the West. The European Bank for Reconstruction and Development (EBRD) supplied a grant of 33 million ecu to make further safety improvements possible in the Ignalina installation. However, as Dr Jankuaskas of the Lithuanian Energy Institute reveals, according to the Grant Agreement 'the Ministry of Energy is obliged to prepare a least-cost programme for the power sector development' (Jankauskas 1995). The real political message of this formulation was that the government of Lithuania should substitute other sources of energy for the electricity produced in Ignalina.

A totally autonomous Lithuanian energy policy for the 1990s would probably have pointed in a different direction; to invest more safety into the nuclear plant in order to extend its productive life span as far as possible. When Lithuania was still a Soviet republic, it could only afford to focus its nuclear risk assessment on the disastrous consequences of a reactor accident in case it happened. This bias, typical of risk assessment undertaken by people who are not technical experts, has seemingly also characterised the average foreign assessment of the risks of the Ignalina nuclear plant.

In Scandinavian, as well as other EU member states, the evaluation of the Ignalina risk has been made in the long shadow of Chernobyl: The main concern is to avoid the reoccurrence of a Chernobyl disaster (IAEA 1996). This means that in reality the risk of a disaster has been treated as if it were a near certainty, regardless of the safety measures undertaken.

A more difficult and sensitive energy policy situation after independence seems to have forced the Lithuanian authorities to partly reframe their perceptions of nuclear risks, particularly to increasingly consider not only the consequences but also the probability of a nuclear accident. When Lithuania was still a part of the Soviet Union, it had access to the overall Soviet network of energy distribution and would therefore become compensated for the reduction and eventual elimination of electricity production in the Ignalina plant. Following the demise of the Soviet Union, this situation was radically transformed. A Russian blockade of crude oil and oil products in 1990 highlighted the security motive for retaining domestic sources of electricity in Lithuania. For that reason the Ignalina plant has acquired a critical role in Lithuania's energy policy. It produces 87 per cent of the total amount of electricity supplied on the national market at the lowest cost (1993), except for the relatively small amounts coming from national hydro power plants (Jankauskas 1995).

The Multi-Source Syndrome: The Case of the Black Triangle

The problem of the so-called Black Triangle reflects a quite different situation: a multi-source pollution syndrome (see Figure 12.2b). The Black Triangle represents one of the worst polluted, and worst polluting, areas in Europe incorporating parts of Poland, the Czech Republic and Germany (the North-Eastern portion of the former German Democratic Republic). A large part of the pollution consists of sulphur dioxide (SO_2) emitted into the atmosphere due to the burning of coal for power and heat production. Some of these large quantities of SO_2 fall to the ground as acid rain in the neighbourhood of the sources that have emitted them. Significant amounts of SO_2 are, however, transported long geographical distances. For example, SO_2 from Polish sources has severely affected Germany, the Czech Republic, Denmark, Norway and Sweden (Kamieniecki and Salay 1994). Damage caused by acidification includes forest death, destruction of buildings and the annihilation of wildlife in lakes (NGO Secretariat 1992).

Although the emissions from the Black Triangle have been comparatively large, all countries in Europe have to some degree contributed to the downfall of acid rain. Therefore, the negotiations to deal with acid rain have been complex, protracted but eventually successful. Several international agreements have been concluded for the purpose of reducing SO_2 emissions significantly, notably the 1979 Convention on Long Range Air Pollution and the 1986 sulphur protocol. One condition for the success of the negotiations on acid rain, involving the quasi-totality of European nations, was probably the employment of a computer model (the RAINS model), that was able to sort out to what extent each participating country was a relative exporter or a relative importer of long-range air pollution (Alcamo et al. 1992).

The negotiations on acid rain were facilitated by the special treatment of the Central and Eastern European countries responsible for considerable shares of SO_2 emissions. Poland is a case in point as one of the largest polluters with emissions that were only surpassed by the former German Democratic Republic. Poland has recently accepted to reduce SO_2 emissions by 60 per cent by the year 2010. It did not make any commitments at all in the 1986 sulphur protocol, in which Western European countries pledged to reduce SO_2 emissions by 30 per cent before the end of 1993 based on 1980 levels (Löfstedt 1995).

This redirection of the Polish policy may be interpreted as increased harmonisation with the EU member states. However, in Poland there are many local environmental problems. Infant mortality is the third highest in Europe, and deaths caused by infections are the second highest (Osuch-Jaczewska and Baczynka-Szymocha 1992). A large number of these deaths and health problems are caused by heavy metal pollution, bad quality of drinking water and local air pollution reducing the strength of the human immune system (Löfstedt 1995). Löfstedt quotes a Polish policy-maker in the Ministry of the Environment: 'Local problems have to be prioritised over transboundary ones. ... We have serious local environmental problems. If we don't give priority to solving them, more people will die.'

In some cases, a risk-based approach has been furthered with the help of the US Environment Protection Agency. One example that Löfstedt refers to is the Silesia project which was set up by the municipalities of Katowice (Poland) and Ostrava (Czech Republic) and sponsored by the US EPA. The objective is to contribute to the reduction of air pollution in the Black Triangle. Löfstedt quotes a local policy-maker in Katowice: 'The Silesia project is a good example of the risk based approach. Rather than prioritising projects out of national bias, we are working together to find the local environmental problems that involve the highest risk' (Löfstedt 1995).

Conclusion

The full integration of Central and Eastern European countries into the European Union presupposes the solution of various social, economic, political and legal problems. Transboundary environmental hazards in Europe represent one of the critical issues likely to cause increasing difficulties in the future. One reason is that EU countries have come much further in coping with environmental problems. Also in an absolute sense, environmental destruction remains very serious in many places in the CEEC area.

CEEC integration into the EU will require a close and costly harmonisation with environmental and environment-related EU policies. EU-CEEC negotiations to attain effective co-ordination and integration may prove to be more cumbersome than is indicated by the East-West environmental co-operation accomplished during the first years following the end of the Cold War. It my well be that perceptions, as well as ensuing priorities, regarding environmental hazards will differ more between EU members and CEECs than has hitherto been the case.

No doubt, aid to CEECs countries has represented an important instrument in the search for a future all-European policy harmonisation in the environmental area. However, aid or other kinds of financial assistance are probably not sufficient to bring about environmental policy co-ordination. CEECs countries also need to become 'socialised' into the EU political culture.

One element would be the harmonisation of environmental risk perceptions and the establishment of viable procedures for effective risk communication. There is a danger that this process will prove to be more protracted and difficult than is usually anticipated. One should not forget that many of the Western leaders and administrations have long had an opportunity to harmonise their frames of reference to an extent that has not been possible in Central and Eastern European nations. For example, the OEEC/OECD has served as a highly significant instrument of co-ordination and building consensual knowledge for all Western European countries in a multitude of areas including that of the environment. Perhaps a substitute for this historical experience must now be invented to serve the co-operation between the EU and the CEECs.

References

Alcamo, J., Shaw, R. and Hordijk, L. (eds.). *The RAINS Model for Acidification: Science and Strategies in Europe.* Dordrecht, Kluwer Academic.

Bröms, P. (1995). *Environmental Security Regimes: A Critical Approach.* Research Report:23. Stockholm, Swedish Institute of International Affairs.

Douglas, M. and Wildavsky, A. (ed.) (1982). *Risk and Culture: An Essay on the Selection of Technological and Environmental Dangers.* Berkeley, University of California Press.

Drottz Sjöberg, B.-M. (1991). *Perceptions of Risk: Studies of Risk Attitudes, Perceptions and Definitions.* Stockholm, Stockholm School of Economics, Center for Risk Research.

Drottz Sjöberg, B.-M., Rumgantseva, G. and Martyvskova (1993). *Perceived Risk Attitudes in Southern Russia of the Chernobyl Accident.* Stockholm, Stockholm school of Economics, Center för Risk Research.

Hjorth, R. (1992). *Building International Institutions for Environmental Protection: The Case of Baltic Sea Environmental Cooperation.* Linköping Studies in Arts and Science. Linköping, University of Linköping, Department of Water and Environmental Studies.

Hjorth, R. (1996). *Baltic Environmental Cooperation: A Regime in Transition.* Water and Environment Studies. Linköping, University of Linköping.

IAEA (1996). *One Decade after Chernobyl: Summing up of the Consequences of the Accident.* Vienna.

Jankauskas, V. (1995). 'Present and Future Role of the Ignalina NPP: Economic Risks and Benefits,' unpublished paper for the Conference 'Transboundary Environmental Risk Management in an East European Context,' 20-22 August 1995 at the Swedish Institute on International Affairs.

Kamieniecki, K. and Salay, J. (1994). 'Environmental Profile of Poland,' in Kristoferson, L. (ed.). *Beauty and the East: An Evaluation of Swedish Environmental Assistance to Eastern Europe.* Stockholm, Stockholm Environment Institute.

Löfstedt, R. (1995). 'Transboundary Environmental Risk Management: The Case of the Burning of Coal in Poland for Heating and Electricity Purposes,' unpublished paper for the Conference 'Transboundary Environmental Risk Management in an East European Context,' 20-22 August 1995 at the Swedish Institute on International Affairs.

NGO Secretariat (1992). *The 'Black' Triangle: A General Reader.* (1992). Gothenburg, NGO Secretariat on Acid Rain.

O'Riordan. D. (ed.) (1995). *Perceiving Environmental Risks.* London, Academic Press.

Östberg, G. (1995). 'The Safety of Ignalina: West Meets East?', unpublished paper for the Conference 'Transboundary Environmental Risk Management in an East European Context,' 20-22 August 1995 at the Swedish Institute on International Affairs.

Osuch-Jaczewska, R. and Baczynka-Szymocha, H. (1992). 'Health Status of Children and Young People,' *Aura*:11.

Sjöstedt, G. (ed.) (1993). *International Environmental Negotiation.* Newbury Park, SAGE Publications.

Stockholms marina miljöövervakning (1994). *Östersjön: Årsrapport från marina miljöövervakningen.* Stockholm.

UD informerar (1997). No 6, March.

United Nations (1979). Convention on Long Range Air Pollution. New York.

Westing, A. (1989). 'Environmental component of comprehensive security,' *Bulletin of Peace Proposals*:20 (2).

13 European Transport Corridors along the Eastern Baltic Shores: International and National Interests

Garri Raagmaa, Raik Vürst, Kalle Pungas and Härmo Haljaste

Internationalisation and the Baltic Sea Area

As a result of negotiations held under the GATT and WTO, the whole world has accepted the new trend towards less trade protectionism, and in the last decades world trade has grown faster than the total output. International customs and free-trade unions have been and are being formed (e.g. NAFTA, LAFTA). The lessening or elimination of customs restrictions favour the rapid growth of trade.

As trade becomes global, the logistical chains are improved but also lengthened. Logistics is among the most important preconditions for successful business on a world scale. The tendency towards a united world trade system has also bolstered the practice of the global sourcing principle, which means that purchases of inputs are made where the price/quality relationship is the most favourable. The scale of international transport has increased considerably due to the widespread use of this principle and the development of just-in-time supplies.

In addition to changes in global logistics, many other processes underway in the Baltic Sea region have had an impact on the development of local or regional infrastructures and made conditions for transport extremely turbulent.

European integration is going forth: Finland and Sweden have joined the EU, and the Baltics and Poland are trying to get there by the next train. Part of the decision making concerning infrastructure investments in the Baltic region is being transferred to Brussels.

Secondly, the fall of the Iron Curtain at the beginning of the 1990s made direct communication possible between Eastern and Western citizens and businessmen in the Baltic Sea area. The reorientation of the economy towards the neighbours has caused major changes in the transport systems of the Eastern Baltic Sea countries in particular. Several joint projects of co-operation between the Baltic Sea countries are underway (the Council of the Baltic Sea States, VASAB and others).

Thirdly, after the crisis at the beginning of 1990s, the region's economy is improving and this is spilling over into increased freight and passenger transportation between the Baltic Sea countries.

Finally, changes in the ownership of the transport companies in Russia as well as the Baltic states create new conditions for micro-level operations and in the longer run for general logistics.

It is clear that where the interests of so many levels and actors meet, each country has to define its internal interest in order to participate effectively on the international scale. This is even more important in the Baltic Sea region, where the conditions for the development of railway and multimodal transport are totally different from those of other parts of Europe due to the low population density. In a similar vein, it is clear that international co-operation and participation of the EU in the implementation of projects are especially necessary in the Baltic states, whose ability to finance large infrastructure projects is very limited.

This chapter tries to evaluate the possibilities of completing various projected transport corridors on the Eastern shore of the Baltic Sea, not exclusively from the point of view of Brussels – which is a commonly adopted vantage point – but primarily in view of local circumstances and national interests. Against the background of transport policies, pressures and needs, the current and prospective bottlenecks of Via Baltica (= TEN 1, i.e. the Transeuropean Net No 1 as defined in EU planning documents) will be analysed and compared with other corridors.

The Transport Policy of the EU

The direction of EU policy is to realise the free movement of goods, services, people and capital in an area which currently includes approximately 380 million people. In the case of a widening of the EU towards the East, the common economic space could comprise as many as 500 million people. Free movement also requires free transport, and the single market has undoubtedly stimulated a rapid growth. Over the years 1984-89, transports within the individual EU countries increased by approximately 40 per cent, while a 44 per cent increase was noted for transport between the countries. There was a continous tendency to favour road transport, whose share increased from 69.1 per cent (1984) to 76.5 per cent in 1989. The corresponding development for railway transport was from 18.4 per cent to 14.4 per cent and for inland waterways from 12.5 to 9.1 per cent.

The majority (about three-quarters) of the EU freight load is north-south bound, while the east-west direction is only starting to develop. The possible transfer of production to Eastern Europe will increase the quantity of east-west oriented freight and influence the development of the transport hubs and chains.

The effort by the EU and its associates to develop the all-European highway, railway and combined transport network, with sea and air transport to be included in the future, is a very significant element in Europe's transition with vast influence on the surrounding countries. So Finland and Sweden as well as Central and Eastern European countries eager to join the EU have to adjust and harmonise their transport strategies with the EU policies.

Key Questions in the Development of Transport in the Baltic Sea Countries

If one compares the standard and potential of the transport systems of the Baltic Sea countries with those of Western Europe, two circumstances in particular put the former in a disadvantaged position.

- There is a higher cost of transport due to the distance to the most important markets. In addition, markets are rapidly growing in Southern Europe..The Scandinavian countries are facing many problems because of the over-exploitation of the north-south corridors in western Germany.
- There is great discrepancy between the developed and effective transport systems of Scandinavia and Germany and the out-dated and poorly equipped transport systems in the other countries of the area.

If handicaps due to geographical distance are to be overcome, it will be necessary to increase the effectiveness of transport and build shorter routes. In particular, it is necessary to surmount the following obstacles if a common strategy is to be put in place (Sitkowski 1995):

- The countries must agree on the identification of the major transport corridors of EU and local importance;
- adequately predict the increase in the quantity of transport;
- develop sufficient means of transport while minimising their environmental impact;
- estimate of the cost of the infrastructure;
- modernise the management of transport.

Under the VASAB project (Vision and Strategies around the Baltic Sea 2010) several suggestions have been made for developing transport co-operation (Löwendahl 1994):

1. To favour decentralisation, it is necessary to listen to regional associations and interests. Often the big international routes only strengthen the position of strong regions and central places. A good network of roads is one of the main factors ensuring decentralisation and regional balance.
2. Foreign investments in the development of international corridors need to be directed toward regional projects. The Baltic states must put pressure on countries in Western and Northern Europe who are primarily interested in furthering the all-European routes, and they must seek to attract assistance to the development of regional networks.
3. Borders should unite, not divide. International infrastructure will not function until certain obstacles at the borders disappear.

4. Rail transport must be promoted. Whereas the Western and Northern European countries have tried for years to enhance the competitive power of the railways, the Baltic states have not started yet.
5. Rail transport can be strengthened through co-operation between different means of transport. Central places located at the hubs of international and local highways and railways must be favoured for the freight transit. Such sites increase the importance of rail transport and make it possible for highway transport to take on the role of distributor-collector.
6. The greatest asset of the Baltic Sea countries – cheap and environmentally friendly sea transport – must be utilised to a greater extent. Though there are several projects for port development, they are hampered by the poor infrastructure of the ports' hinterlands. This diminishes the ports' competitive capacity.
7. The potential of inland water transport needs a more detailed investigation.
8. The rapid growth of highway transportation calls for means to forestall environmental damage and to consider the future of city transport. Supportive means and actions are needed to slow down the growth of highway traffic.
9. The environment must be considered when developing the transport corridors. Commercial integration increases traffic, which results in a higher rate of accidents and an increase in environmental damage.
10. The opportunities of the Baltic Sea countries to use alternative energy resources must be taken into account. The region is well supplied with oil and gas from Russia (oil pipes) as well as from the North Sea (tankers), but fuel supply will be more stable if it can be spread over more sources.

Changes in Transport during the Transition Period: Estonia's Example[1]

Changes in the Economic Structure and GDP

As we can see in Figure 13.1, the break-up of the Soviet Union was the strongest factor influencing the economic development of Estonia, resulting in a considerable fall in GDP. The GDP of Finland fell for the same reason. The recession in Sweden, mostly due to other factors, has been more restrained with a trough that appeared later than in Estonia and Finland. The strongest economic setback in the region took place in the years 1990 to 1992.

Trade volumes are connected with economic activity. The re-establishment of direct connections between the Baltic Sea countries coincided with the economic crisis. The trade turnover of Estonia with Finland and Sweden has been growing continuously since 1991, and there have been no particular fluctuations. As far as Russia is concerned, its share of trade has decreased – the absolute quantity of trade has nevertheless steadily increased. However, tensions and political ups and downs between Estonia and Russia have certainly limited the free commerce.

Figure 13.1: The dynamics of GDP in Estonia, Sweden and Finland, 1990-96, percentages

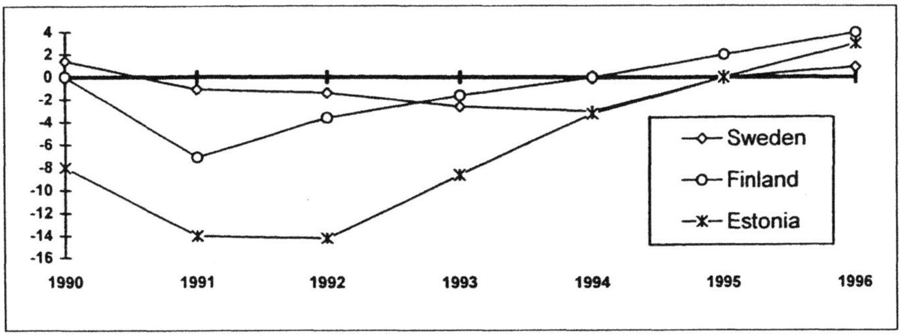

Estonia re-oriented its trade from the East to the West very swiftly during the years 1991-93. The share of ex-Soviet Union countries has dropped from more than 90 per cent to approximately 30 per cent today, while the share of the EU countries has increased to about 60 per cent. Similar trends, though on a smaller scale, have manifested themselves in the other Baltic states as well (see Figure 13.2).

The turn from an East to a West-oriented economy (or, in the case of Estonia, rather towards the Nordic countries) is most evident in the figures for tourism and travel services. For instance, in 1986 the travel volume between Tallinn and Helsinki was about 200,000 people. In 1996 the number had increased to over 5 million (25 times) exceeding the capacity of the Helsinki-Stockholm line. Tourists from the East have been primarily replaced by Finnish tourists. Also the target countries of Estonian tourists have changed considerably: from ex-Soviet Union countries towards primarily the Nordic Countries.

The great change in the flows of tourism is partly due to the reintroduction of

Figure 13.2: Distribution of Estonian imports and exports, 1995, economic value

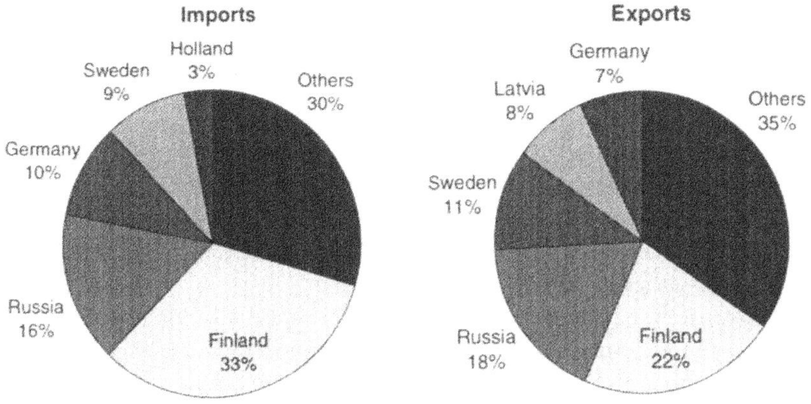

Figure 13.3: Tourists received in Estonia from Finland, Sweden and the CIS

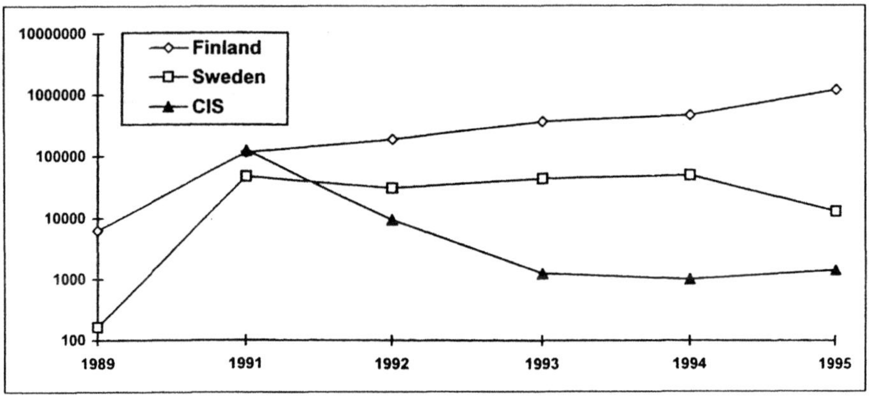

political barriers (complicated visa requirements between Estonia and Russia) but to an even greater extent to changes in people's values and identity. Tallinn's geographical proximity to the capitals of the Nordic countries combined with the great price differences is another important factor. There is a very large share of shoppers among the tourists. Business and other professional contacts have also played a big role in the increase (see Figure 13.3).

The Structure and Share of Estonian Transport Services in the GDP

With the increase in quantity, transport has turned out to be a very important aspect of the Estonian economy. According to the Bank of Estonia, transport accounted for 43 per cent of the service sector in 1995, representing however a drop from 56 per cent the year before. Transport services were exported for 4.3 billion and imported for 2.5 billion kroons. Services are playing a crucial role in balancing Estonia's foreign trade (see Table 13.1)

Table 13.1: Estonia's foreign trade balance, 1993-96, billion kroons

E/I of goods	1993	1994	1995	1996
Exports	10.6	16.9	21.0	25.0
Imports	11.8	21.5	29.1	38.6

In the same period, the export of transport services decreased by 12 per cent and imports increased by 7 per cent. The main reason for these changes was a reduction of the Estonian cargo fleet, causing the share of sea transit to diminish. Air cargo transit is insignificant.

Approximately one-fifth of the transport services consists of passenger carriage. Though the number of foreign tourists visiting Estonia has increased, it has not brought about a noteworthy rise in the figures for income stemming from exports of transport services. Competion due to the appearance of several non-local shipping companies in the Estonian market has caused ticket prices to fall. Seventy-two per cent of the international passenger services go by sea, 20 per cent by air.

Other services, i.e. loading and unloading, port and airport charges, dispatching, storage and so forth, showed a positive balance of 399 million kroons in 1995 (283 million in 1994).

Table 13.2 gives figures for the three main means of transport. Sea transports dominate, while the shares of road and air are 26 and 12 per cent, respectively.

Table 13.2: Estonian exports and imports by means of transport, million tonnes

	1994		1995	
	Exports	Imports	Exports	Imports
Road	0.5	0.3	0.6	0.4
Railway	1.1	3.7	1.2	4.2
Sea	2.7	0.7	3.5	1.1
Total	4.3	4.7	5.3	5.7

Traffic in Goods

According to the statistical reports, the quantity of Estonian goods traffic was 37.2 million tonnes in 1995 (92 per cent of the quantity in 1994) and 21.5 billion tonnes-km (67.2 per cent). Sea transport dominated with 76 per cent, while the figure for railway transport was 16.8 per cent, and road transport took care of 7.2 per cent of the total traffic in goods. So in a way, Estonia's transport system is still ecologically friendly (see Figure 13.4).

Figure 13.4: Goods traffic on Estonian railways, 1980-96, thousands of tonnes

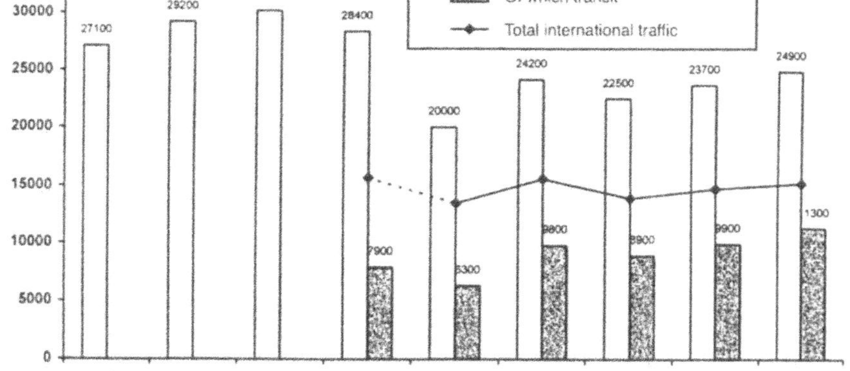

About 75 per cent of the quantity was carried by multimodal transport chains, 45 per cent by ship-train and train-ship chains, 20 per cent by ship-lorry and lorry-ship and 10 per cent by train-lorry and lorry-train chains. Combined transport of goods, i.e. transport by intermodal transport units (ITU containers, trucks or trailers on ships or trains etc.) made up about 1 million tonnes or 4.7 per cent of the total. Container goods made up 0.4 million tonnes only.

International surface transport – in total 16.8 million tonnes – was carried almost entirely by trains (91 per cent) and the remaining 9 per cent by trucks. The share of foreign trucks was approximately 22 per cent.

As one can see in Figure 13.4, carriage by Estonian railways has nevertheless decreased – and to a large extent been replaced by road transport. Nevertheless, transportation on the Estonian railways is surprisingly stable compared to Latvia and Lithuania, where the drop in the railways' share is considerable.

Public Estonian statistics on road carriers show a decrease to only 10 per cent of the number in 1980. The same trend is evident in Latvia and Lithuania. But figures are probably not reliable as they contradict a general impression of structural changes. The number of small enterprises and operators has increased, and certain carriers are probably concealed on purpose (the shadow economy is still considerable). A significant growth in the energy use of road transport also indicates a growing intensity of lorry transport. An increasing share of motor transport freight is international.

Finally, it may be observed that Estonian air transportation is insignificant, both in terms of quantity and economic value. Of the three capital city airports in the Baltic states, Vilnius registers the biggest freight loads.

Transit Trade

Transit trade is a most important aspects of Estonia's economy. In 1995 10.5 million tonnes of transit cargo was carried through Estonia, representing an increase of 1.2 million tonnes or 13 per cent on 1994. About 70 per cent of the freight loads passing Estonian ports was hence destined for transit. Almost 10 million of it (9.9) was carried by railway, 0.57 million tonnes by road. Hence, the transit freight was carried mainly by combined ship-train, namely 94.3 per cent. Only 30,000 tonnes or 0.3 per cent of the transit cargo – from one border station to another – was carried by lorry only.

The bulk of the growth of transit cargo was due to oil products (+60 per cent). The transit of fertilisers (+40 per cent) and dark metal (+4 per cent) also increased. The transit of grain is continuously diminishing (-46 per cent) (see Figure 13.5).

The quantity of transit cargo via Estonian harbours has been relatively stable in the last years, but there have been great changes in the direction and structure of the transit. Since 1995 there has been rapid change in favour of the west-oriented transit. Until 1995 Russia imported grain, making a use of Estonian transit. Now this trade has been replaced by a west-oriented oil transit *from* Russia. More than 60 per cent of the transit from Russia consists of oil products. This

Figure 13.5: Transit cargo flows via the eastern shores of the Baltic Sea

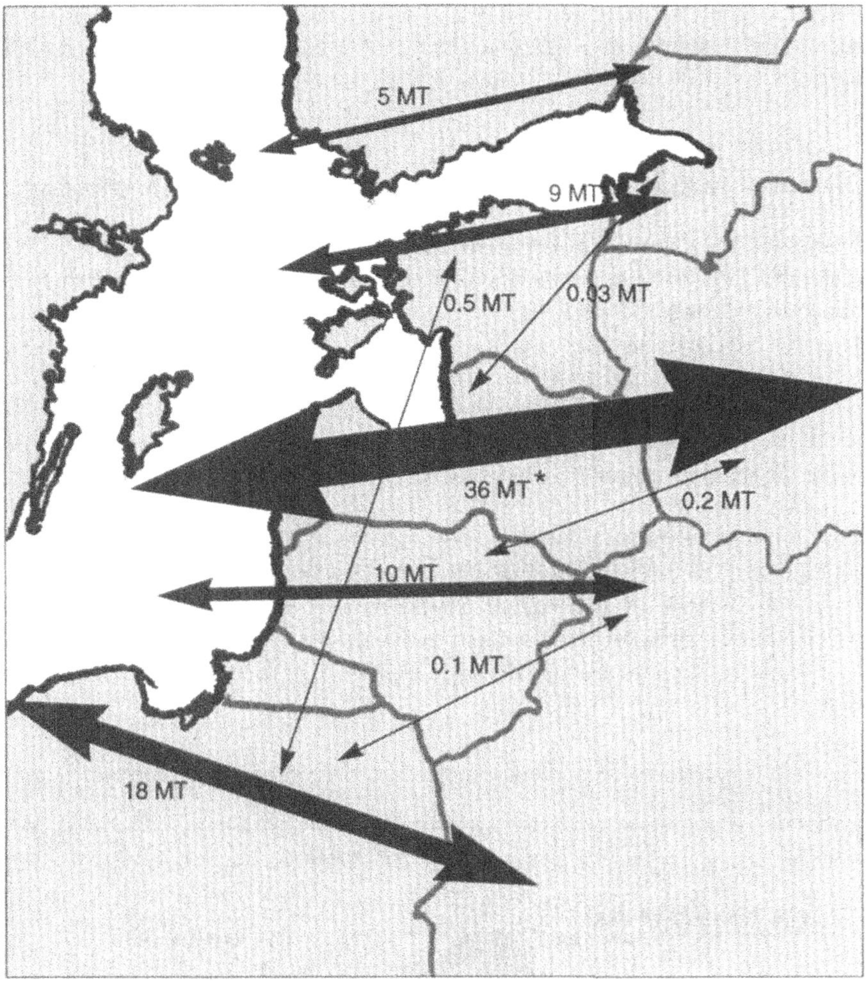

*Pipeline (crude oil) transport of about 20 million tonnes is included

development has caused a rapid growth of oil terminal capacity in the Port of Tallinn, coinciding with economic difficulties for the grain terminals.

One hundred per cent of the railway transit ran along the east-west corridor (Tallinn-Tapa-Narva (74 per cent) and Tallinn-Tapa-Pihkva railway routes). The north-south axis has a different character: sixty-nine per cent of all transit loads carried by lorry take this direction. Fifty-nine per cent is registered for the Tallinn-Pärnu-Ikla road, the Via Baltica.

Figure 13.5 shows that the vast bulk of the transit cargo through Estonia as well as through the other Baltic states is east-west oriented. The quantity which is still running north-south is relatively small and does not by itself provide any considerable reason for more actively pursuing the rail connection towards the south.

Low capacity and a modest actual use of the TEN I corridor – Via Baltica – apparently also suggest that there is no reason to improve the road within Estonia at the moment. Actully, there *is* a reason why the quantity of the cargo on the Via Baltica is so small, and we shall return to it in the next section.

National and International Interests in Tranport Corridors

Evaluating the Priorities of Estonian Transportation Policy

A number of factors have to be taken into account when modelling the transport networks of Estonia:

- The geo-economical location of Estonia with respect to the main areas of population density and centres of the EU and Russia;
- the very low average population density and the concentration of population in the main inhabited regions of Harju, Vöru and Tartu Counties (see Figure 13.6);
- sectoral and regional changes in economic structure;
- rapid growth in the number of cars, increasing the load on the roads;
- unemployment in the regions of the countryside and centralisation of economic activity and employment to the centres, leading to increased traffic/ mobility and congestion on the main highways, particularly in peak hours.

Figure 13.6: International transport corridors and Estonia's main population centres

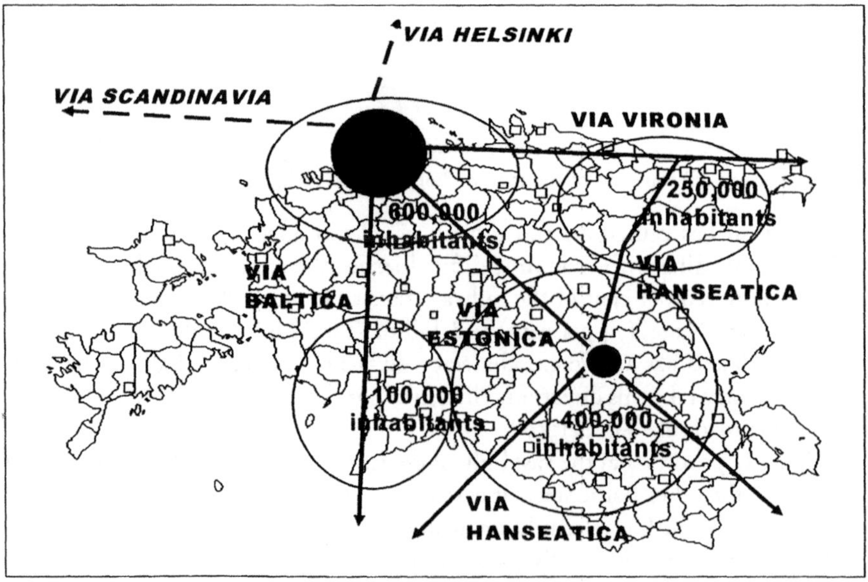

International co-operation is important for developing the necessary road network. In view of the desirability of improving the economy of the peripheries, one should be careful to predict future transport needs on the basis of static parameters. Estonia needs transport corridors also for domestic reasons:

- To raise the competitive power of the economy, to acquire faster, cheaper, ecologically more sustainable and safer connections between the different regions of the country and with the rest of the world;
- to narrow the discrepancy in level of development between the stronger and weaker economic areas, providing the latter with a direct, fast approach to Tallinn and international centres;
- to secure an optimal load on the roads and stimulate economic activity by involving local enterprises in projects.

When building these corridors, it is important to cover part of the investments through means from the EU or partner countries, thereby securing loans from foreign banks at favourable interest rates.

International Routes through Estonia
The following four transport corridors would be of primary importance for Estonia:

Tallinn-Tartu; Tallinn-Narva; Tallinn-Pärnu; Tartu-Jõhvi.

From an international perspective and based on the potential of inhabitants and the economic power of the country of departure/target, the main routes are:

- Via Estica (Stockholm-Tallinn-Tartu-Mid-Russia-Moscow);
- Via Hanseatica (St Peterburg-Narva-Jõhvi-Tartu-Valga-Riga-Kaliningrad-Gdansk-Berlin-Hamburg);
- Via Vironia (Stockholm-Tallinn-St Petersburg);
- Via Baltica (Helsinki-Tallinn-Pärnu-Riga-Warsaw).

If one combines the international routes with Estonian policies for regional development, the following corridors would be the most important:

Jõhvi-Tartu-Valga – Via Hanseatica; and Tallinn-Tartu-Koidula(Võru) – Via Estica.

The project receiving most international attention and finance has been the one least used but in the technically best shape – Via Baltica. In spite of pressures from the EU and Finland, co-operation between the Baltic states and Poland on the project has not been totally smooth.

More important for Estonia – with respect both to national traffic load and the traffic of international importance – are the highways connecting Tallinn with the inland (Tartu, central and south-eastern Estonia) and central Russia (Via Estica) and the corridor connecting the areas of concentration in the east with the biggest centres abroad – St Petersburg with Tallinn and Stockholm (Via Vironia). The main emphasis has been on the rail traffic, which determines the organisation of the transit flows. The EBRD (the European Bank for Reconstruction and Development) is also participating in the renovation of the railways. Since the summer of 1996, the public's attention has turned to the rebuilding of the Tallinn-Tartu road into a highway. So far, however, no international co-operation or financing has been found for the completion of this project.

The Hansa Road or Via Hanseatica, which would connect St Petersburg with Berlin and Hamburg via the Baltic states no longer commands any attention. Considering future just-in-time trade chains, however, this route may turn out to be the most important one by far.

Via Baltica
(Helsinki-Tallinn-Pärnu-Riga-Warsaw-Central and Southern Europe)

This is the TEN 1 corridor in EU terminology. The idea is to construct a land connection for the Scandinavian countries and Finland in particular with the markets of Central and Eastern Europe, which would be faster than ferry carriage and much cheaper than air carriage. It would be an alternative to the route from Northern Europe (Sweden) via Denmark and Germany and make a detour along overloaded highways and sea transports unnecessary. The distance is shorter (compared to the link with Central Europe through Denmark), and the route is competitive and cheap if environmental and fuel costs can be kept down.

In addition to the Baltic states, Finland in particular would derive advantages from Via Baltica, to some extent also St Petersburg and the regions of northern Russia. Sweden and Norway would also profit from it because it would provide them with an opportunity to keep in touch with their companies located in the Baltics.

There are, however, several problems with completing the route:

Some of these problems are of an economic nature:

- Five million Finns and half a million inhabitants of Tallinn do not make up a mass great enough to carry through the project.
- The goods dominating the exports of Finland are either very bulky – wood and paper, which would require maritime transport – or they are hi-tech, in which case companies would prefer air.
- The opposite flows to the distribution centres in Helsinki come from Western Europe through Sweden or by sea.
- Ferry carriage on the Tallinn-Helsinki and Tallinn-Stockholm routes is expensive. The route over St Petersburg and Sweden via Copenhagen is often preferred in Finland;

- Relatively large investments are necessary, particularly in Latvia, Lithuania and Poland.
- The poor quality of services and the weakness of joint marketing are obstacles to the exploitation of the route for tourism purposes.

There are political problems as well:

- The greatest problem is the waste of time at border and customs controls augmented by the behviour of a heavy-handed bureaucracy.
- Highway construction in Poland concentrates on the Berlin-Moscow route.
- The Baltic states cannot agree on pursuing common long-term interests.

To complicate matters even further, a number of technical difficulties must be mentioned:

- The difference in the width of the railway tracks in the Baltic states and Europe makes rail traffic expensive.
- The absence of a direct parallel rail connection; low speed due to poor technical conditions of the railways, restricting the use of rail transport for passengers and goods.
- The is a row of bottlenecks on the highways, particularly the exits from Tallinn, the approaches to Riga and the passing of the Lithuanian-Polish border.

Due to the problems just mentioned, the Via Baltica has not fulfilled the hopes, and the flow of goods has remained limited.

Estonia may choose to enhance the status of Tallinn as the logistical centre of the Nordic countries by opting for a land connection with the other Baltic states, Poland and Central Europe. It must, however, realise that economic and political competition among the Baltic states sets limits here. Moreover, western Estonia is much better developed than the eastern Estonian regions.

Via Vironia
(Scandinavia-Stockholm-Tallinn-Narva-St Petersburg-Northern and Central Russia)

The importance of this corridor does not need to be further explained. It is primarily vital for serving the Russian transit flowing through Estonia as well as for enabling the tourists to get to St Petersburg.

Multimodal, land-rail-marine, transport chains are possible. The competitor is the southern route of Finland. The advantages are navigation conditions, lower costs in terms of transportation, labour and environment in addtion to a better local awareness of conditions in Russia. The problems are mainly caused by political disagreements.

The road is in a relatively good shape, but the Narva bridge and the slow stretch between Narva and St Petersburg would need to be upgraded to highway standards. Investments to construct a double railway line have been planned.

The main problem has been a lack of interest on the part of authorities on both the Estonian and Russian side, reflecting their generally bad relations.

Via Hanseatica
(Northern and North-Western Russia-St Petersburg-Narva-Jõhvi-Tartu-Valga-Riga-Kaliningrad-Gdansk-Berlin-Hamburg-Western Europe)

The so-called Hansa Road has been less noticed until now. It represents the interests of Germany and north-western Russia. By creating better connections between the eastern regions and southern Estonia and old and new markets, it would be of great regional importance in Estonia. The route would reduce the travel time to one-third compared to maritime carriage.

Fast and safe connections are necessary for tourists from St Petersburg going to the traditional holiday resorts in eastern Estonia. The construction of a highway would also raise the competitive power of companies in eastern Estonia – an area which is currently economically depressed – by making it easier to reach the markets in St Petersburg and Germany.

Via Hanseatica is attractive to economic interests in Estonia and Germany who look forward to opening the markets of St Petersburg and gaining access to the resources of north and north-western Russia. The prospects of providing a safe connection for automobile tourists between Germany, the Baltic states and St Petersburg is also an important argument.

The companies of north-western Russia and eastern Finland should also be interested in gaining access to the markets of Germany. The northern republics and regions – St Petersburg and surroundings, Karelia, Murmansk and Arkhangelsk with surroundings, and eastern Finland – comprise about 15 million people.

Latvia might also be interested in seizing the opportunity to develop its peripheral regions in the north.

An alternative would be a route via Pihkva and the south-eastern corner of Estonia but it would require much larger investments from Russia and is therefore less likely. Besides, the St Petersburg-Tallinn-Stockholm route, i.e. the Via Vironia, is needed anyway.

On the basis of economic factors and regional policy interests, Via Hanseatica ought to be the second or third international priority

An alternative to Via Hanseatica is a route through Russia via Pihkva or via Belarus and Minsk merging with the Berlin-Warsaw-Moscow highway. The advantages of the route through Estonia are its short distance, better services and safer environment. To some extent, the St Petersburg-Vilnius-Warsaw railway may be a competitor.

As we see it, the main obstacle to the construction of this alternative route is a lack of public awareness.

In addition to a number of technical problems, there are major political obstacles to Via Hanseatica, such as the cold political relationship between the Baltic states and Russia; problems with the borders and the militarised Kaliningrad area in particular; and, as already mentioned, the fact that road building in Poland is primarily concentrated on the Berlin-Moscow route.

Estonia cannot complete this route with its own finances. One possibility would be to attract partners, in particular Germany and St Petersburg. Another option would be to seek area-wide co-operation within the Baltic states and Russia in an attempt to open Kaliningrad for the whole area.

Via Estica
(Scandinavia-Stockholm-Tallinn-Tartu-(Pihkva)-Moscow-Mid and Southern Russia)

The completion of this route is primarily in Estonia's interest because it would ensure a fixed connection between the two main settlements of Estonia, i.e. Tallinn and Tartu.

Faster travel should give an important boost to the development of enterprises in Tartu and the whole of south-eastern Estonia. It would also partly solve the housing problems in Tallinn, because a back-and-forth shuttle from Järvamaa and Paide to Tallinn (about 45 minutes) would then be realistic.

The project should also interest enterprises in Sweden and Norway (less so in Finland) as a fast and safe connection to the food-producing and consumer markets of mid-Russia. In addition it would provide and an opportunity to involve Estonian companies and give Russian enterprises a chance to flood the Scandinavian market with raw materials and other goods.

Via Estica would be a multimodal route involving both rail and road transport. It is also realistic to establish a distribution centre for south-eastern Estonia which would offer cheaper and safer storage facilities for Riga and Tallinn and which could absorb some of the skilled labour force of south-eastern Estonia.

Competing international routes would be the corridors of south and central Finland. The Finnish corridors, however, lack a number of assets, such as short distance, the possibility of bypassing the jams around St Petersburg, which are likely to get worse as a result of the growing number of cars, the longer ice-free period of the Estonian ports and the relatively cheap services (labour, energy, carriers, charges).

Another potential competitor is the route via the container port of Riga, which until now lacks regular and well-organised connections with Stockholm.

The project would be easier to carry out than Via Hanseatica or Via Baltica because there are less partners involved. This means that there are fewer differing interests to be considered.

The hinterland would be the 13 million inhabitants of Sweden and Norway with their companies willing to spread eastwards and their rich consumer markets, on the one hand, and central Russia and Moscow with about 30 million consumers and cheap production facilities on the other.

The problems, however, are considerable: political disagreements between Estonia and Russia; bureaucracy and slowness on the borders; technical bottlenecks on the roads including poor road quality in Russia; poor quality of rail transport in both Estonia and Russia.

The Tallinn-Tartu road is of national importance, and a number of strategic measures could be taken by Estonia alone.

Conclusion

Via Baltica, TEN 1, has secured its place on the maps of the EU. Still, the route has not found considerable support within the Baltic states for one obvious reason: most of the cargo flow is east-west oriented. Finland, Poland and the Baltic states are competitors in that field. Statistics show that the east-west oriented

Figure 13.7: Existing and coming transport corridors in the Baltic states*

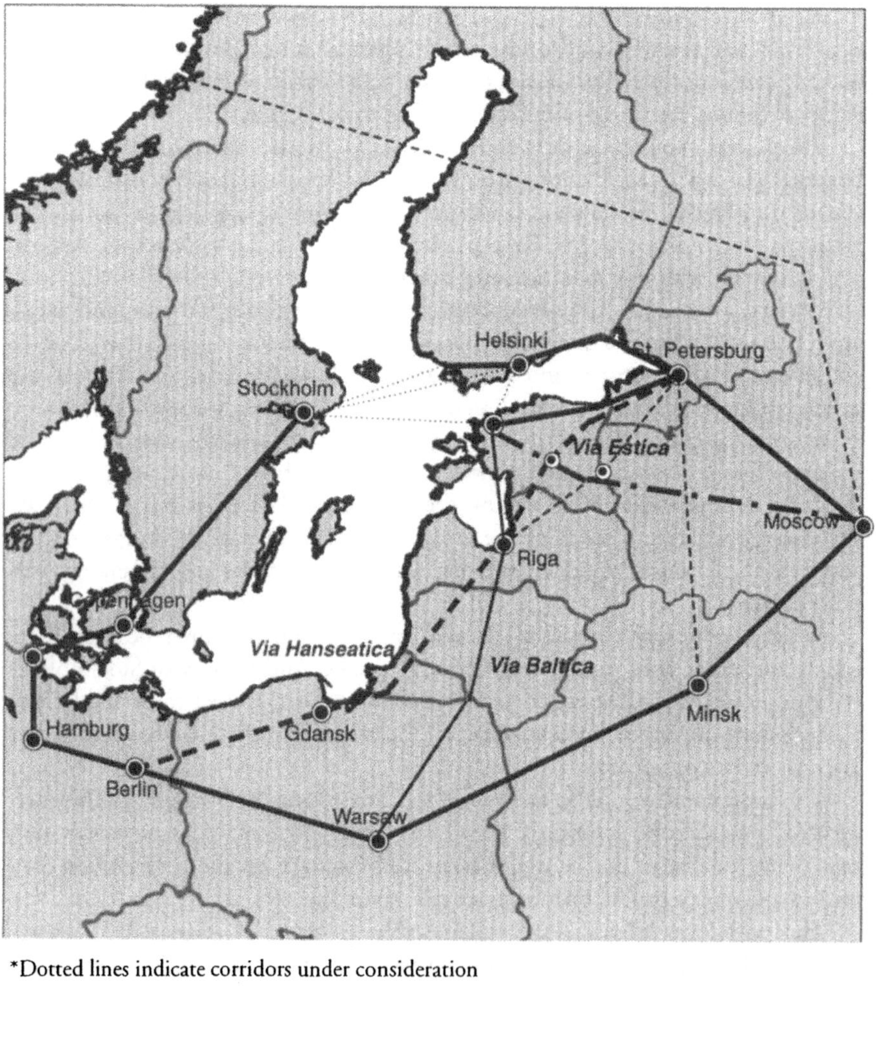

*Dotted lines indicate corridors under consideration

trade is increasing in spite of the cold relations of these countries with the eastern neighbours. This enables us to understand the interest of Finland, Poland and the Baltic states in furthering the east-west oriented transit routes.

Still, neither the goals of regional policy nor national traffic patterns can be ignored. Is is among Estonia's national priorities to secure better traffic between its main centres and to enable the national peripheries to get involved in the European transport networks.

The main obstacles to the development of Via Baltica and Via Hanseatica have been institutional problems: the customs unions, bureaucracy on the borders and so forth. As long as these obstacles have not been overcome, it is naive to speak about the completion of these routes and of increased cargo flows. Via Hanseatica and Via Baltica will save time for both cargo and passenger transports, but will require that political problems be solved first.

The limited capacity of Estonia's internal transport system is not only a domestic problem but an obstacle to wider Baltic trade. The transport policy of small states has to be international. Estonia, Latvia and Lithuania are very small countries and are therefore in need of relatively more international transport corridors and international co-operation for development.

A major problem is also the poor co-operation between sector ministries and tendencies towards narrow-mindedness in determining national goals.

There is a danger that we – the Balts – will fall asleep and end up competing only with each other.

Note

1 The sources of data cited in this section are listed in the references.

References

(Abbreviations: ESO, LSO and LiSO = the National Statistical Offices of Estonia, Latvia and Lithuania.)

Bizniss & Baltija (1996). 'Konkurents sadamate vahel hogustub,' *Äripäev*.9, February, p. 13.

European Commission (1994). *Europe 2000+: Cooperation for European Territorial Development.* Luxembourg.

European Logistics Consultants (1996). *Logistics in Europe: Division and Reality.*

ESO (1994-97). *Regional Statistics of Estonia.* Tallinn.

ESO (1995-96). *Estonian Statistical Yearbook.* Tallinn.

ESO (1995-97). *Estonian Statistics,* Monthly. Tallinn.

ESO (1995 and 1997). *Transport, Communications Yearbook.* Tallinn.

ESO (1995-97). *Transport, Communications Quarterly Bulletin.* Tallinn.

LiSO (1995-96). *Lithuanian Statistical Yearbook.* Vilnius.

Löwendahl, Bo (1995). 'Towards a Framework for Spatial Development in the Baltic Sea Area,' in Kuklinski, A. (ed.). *Baltic Europe in the Perspective of Global Change.* Europe 2010 Series:1. Warsaw, Oficy Naukowa.

LSO (1995-96). *Latvian Statistical Yearbook.* Riga.

Nordic Council of Ministers (1995-96). *Nordic Statistical Yearbook.* Copenhagen.
Rootsi Tötusliit/ Swedish Union of Industry (l997). 'Rootsi majandus on ahige,' *Äripäev*:8, February, p. 8.
Sitkowski, Andrzej (l995). 'The Restructuring Process in the Baltic Sea Region and the Transport Sector,' in Kuklinski, A. (ed.). *Baltic Europe in the Perspective of Global Change.* Europe 2010 Series:1. Warsaw, Oficy Naukowa.

14 Development and Implementation of Baltic Sea Pollution Commitments: The Case of Sweden

Ronnie Hjorth

Introduction

This chapter explores the Swedish implementation of Baltic Sea pollution commitments with an emphasis on the pattern of participation among various actor-groups.[1] There is a long history of Swedish commitments to the Baltic Sea environment, and the types of commitment implemented have changed over time. Hence the chapter initially specifies three main phases of Baltic Sea environmental co-operation, involving three different types of commitment.

The first phase covers the period between 1974, when the Convention on the Protection of the Marine Environment of the Baltic Sea Area, from here on referred to as the Helsinki Convention, was signed, and 1988, when the Second Ministerial Meeting was held. The Declaration signed at the 1988 meeting marks the beginning of the second phase, which ends in 1992 with the signing of a new Convention and Action Programme, the latter referred to as the JCP (Baltic Sea Joint Comprehensive Environmental Action Programme). The signing of these two documents in 1992 marks the beginning of the third phase.

> The division into phases is not based only on the dates of formal meetings. The character of Baltic Sea co-operation on pollution control actually changed on these occasions. The different phases are important because they are related to different types of environmental protection commitment. Since Sweden has played an active and often leading role in the activities under the particular regimes, the shifting nature of the commitments is important to recognise.

The implementation of Baltic Sea environmental commitments in Sweden has not been the subject of a special programme or organisation, but has been an integrated part of the national environmental protection policy. Hence, the task to be carried out in this chapter is not as simple as to study the activity of one particular authority. Nevertheless some areas and issues of Swedish environmental policy and politics are directly linked to Baltic Sea commitments, such as the building of waste-water treatment plants, the problem of nutrient discharges from agricultural production, and issues related to industrial pollution sources. Furthermore, Swedish environmental foreign policy in the Baltic Sea area has increasingly turned into an implementation commitment where Swedish authorities promote, support and actively assist implementation processes in neighbouring transition countries.

Commitments: The Three Phases

The First Phase, 1974-88

The 1974 Helsinki Convention was signed by Denmark, Finland, Sweden, Poland, the USSR and the GDR. Although ecological motives for international environmental co-operation were argued by scientists and codified at the 1972 Stockholm Conference (the United Nations Conference on the Human Environment) and elsewhere, it is undeniable that the signing of the Convention was also the result of détente politics. An indication of the symbolic value attached to the signing of the Helsinki Convention was its delayed ratification and entry into force.[2] During the 1980s, Baltic Sea environmental co-operation was pursued according to what has been labelled a scientific-technological strategy; an approach based on scientific evidence and technical solutions aiming at a gradual improvement of knowledge and technology while downgrading political aspects (Hjorth 1992).

Created in an atmosphere of 'peaceful coexistence' as superpower confrontation hardened, the ideological neutrality of the scientific-technological strategy made it more or less the only strategy available. Baltic Sea environmental regulation was oriented towards the co-ordination of national environmental policies according to fairly vague guidelines. Principles such as BAT (Best Available Technology) or BEP (Best Environmental Practice) were not yet applied, nor were the Precautionary Principle or other principles familiar in the mid-1990s. Furthermore, the first recommendations were vague in formulation and content, but were gradually improved during the 1980s by means of timetables, procedures for implementation, and pollution standards. The evolution of norms and rules was slow and strictly confined to advisory instruments. Financial instruments and other types of implementation support or enforcement mechanisms were not adopted until the 1990s, during the third phase.

The 1974 Helsinki Convention belongs to the first generation of multilateral environmental agreements and it shares many weaknesses with other agreements signed at about that time. One particular weakness of this generation of agreements is the lack of enforcement provisions. Implementation was handled by the contracting parties individually and through national institutions exclusively. This problem was particularly urgent for the Helsinki Convention, for two reasons: First, a gap in economic capacity and environmental awareness between Western Europe and Eastern Europe made the contracting parties heterogeneous, and no mechanisms or institutions were developed that could overcome such discrepancies. Secondly, the political context effectively closed the door for initiatives to bridge this gap. A strict interpretation of state sovereignty prevented attempts to expand the scientific-technological strategy to the output-side of the policy process (Hjorth 1992).

Acting as the host country for the United Nations Conference on the Human Environment in Stockholm 1972, Sweden founded its reputation as a state favouring increased international co-ordination and organisation of environmental policy. One way to follow up the Stockholm Conference was to negotiate regional environmental agreements for the Baltic Sea area. During the period between the signing of the Convention in 1974 and the ratification of it in 1980, Sweden and Finland both acted as hosts for the interim organisation. And during the 1980s, the two countries dominated Baltic environmental co-operation in terms of initiatives and representation (Hjorth 1992).

One way to prepare new recommendations was to designate the responsibility for preparation to different contracting parties – the so-called lead-party routine. In practice this was a voluntary undertaking, but it soon became the habit. During the 1980s, all contracting parties took on such a responsibility, except Poland and the German Democratic Republic. Sweden took the lead in three fields: Cadmium Discharges from Land-Based Sources; Cadmium and Mercury Containing Batteries and Waste-water from Urban Areas. Sweden thus accepted the responsibility for preparing recommendations in two of the prioritised fields, i.e. heavy metals and nutrients. Generally, the distribution of lead-party responsibility shows that the Western states took the lead in preparing new recommendations and that priorities reflected national interests. Denmark's responsibility in the field of agricultural pollution is one example, Sweden's responsibility for waste-water treatment – since Sweden was comparatively well advanced in this area – is another (Hjorth 1992: 227).

The statement made at the First Ministerial Meeting in 1984 further reveals the Swedish position as an advocate of a problem-solving approach. The Swedish Minister of Environment stated that 'In spite of our efforts, note that the protection of the marine environment in the Baltic demands much more united endeavours.' He argued in favour of a rational approach to problem solving on the basis of better information on discharges : 'Compilations of discharge data from the Contracting Parties can give an idea of the quantities discharged annually into the Baltic from natural sources and from human activities in industries, municipalities and agriculture. On the basis of such information realistic and meaningful assessments can be made of the possibility of a reduction of harmful emissions' (Hjorth 1992: 137 f.)

The statement indicates a view of environmental co-operation as input for decision-making rather than for implementation. It also signals a non-political approach to environmental policy co-operation; that environmental policy should be regarded as a scientific and technical issue rather than a political or moral one. This is one possible strategic approach to international policy co-ordination. Especially during the Cold War, keeping the environment at a 'low politics' level was more or less consensual. But as is shown below, such an approach may not only be regarded as an international strategy but also as a prominent element of the Swedish environmental policy style.

The Second Phase, 1988-92

In 1988 Baltic Sea pollution control co-operation was coming to a dead-lock. It became increasingly obvious that the many detailed provisions rendered very scant results. But the year 1988 also meant a turning point. One factor behind the change was political. The end of the Cold War suddenly appeared realistic.[3] Moreover, the opening up of Polish society confirmed the presumption that pollution control was really not improving in Poland.

The way to reforming environmental co-operation in the Baltic region and elsewhere was indicated in several documents; notably by the so-called Brundtland Commission report *Our Common Future.* The report became widely known for its popularisation of the concept of 'sustainable development' which was later applied in the Baltic region.

At the same time, the public debate on environmental issues intensified. In Sweden this debate secured the Green party a number of seats in parliament (Bennulf and Holmberg 1992). One of the much debated problems in concerned the death of seals in the Baltic Sea. Environmental pollution was thought to seriously diminish the seal population. Another major issue concerned the status of the Polish environment and how pollution from Poland might contribute to worsening the environment of the whole Baltic Sea area and not least in Sweden.

At the same time, a new generation of international agreements on pollution control were negotiated. The 1987 North Sea Conference led to a new approach to pollution control based on general quantitative policy goals and action programmes. A 50 per cent reduction of nutrient discharges between the years 1985 and 1995 was envisaged for the North Sea, and the implementation was to be monitored by a so-called Task Force steering group. The political initiative thus led to a new and different pollution control strategy and was considered a first step towards the renegotiation of several pollution control agreements of the first generation.

At the Second Ministerial Meeting of HELCOM in 1988, a similar strategy was initiated for the Baltic. At the meeting, which marks the beginning of the second phase, Sweden was one of the parties in favour of a new approach.[4] According to the Swedish Minister of Environment, the participants had to face the fact that 'we are not pursuing a sustainable development in the Baltic Sea area. The status of the marine environment clearly indicates that we have neglected our responsibility.' In the Minister's view, the damage to the marine environment could only be reversed over a long-term perspective, and 'the contracting parties must adopt a precautionary approach and not wait for full scientific proof of harmful effects before taking action to prevent and abate pollution.'[5]

This offensive, however, did not lead to major results at the meeting. But the activities in 1988 eventually led to a renegotiation of the Helsinki Convention. As a result of disagreements between the contracting parties on which strategy to follow, the four years between 1988 and 1992 were critical in the development of Baltic pollution control. The agreement finally reached in 1988 on a 50 per cent reduction of nutrients was of mere symbolic value since it did not indicate a time period (the reduction was supposed to be completed in 1995, but the baseline was not defined).

The next step in the development of Baltic pollution control was the 1990 Baltic Sea Conference in Ronneby, Sweden, hosted by the Swedish Government. The parties agreed to apply the precautionary principle, and the insufficient regulation adopted two years earlier was completed. The meeting also agreed to adopt an action programme for a 'decisive reduction of emissions in order to restore the Baltic Sea to a sound ecological balance.'[6] A so-called Task Force steering group was appointed to administer the programme. It was also agreed that a new Convention should be negotiated.

To sum up, the second phase entailed a fundamental change of strategy: As a result of a political initiative largely taken by Western countries,a new generation of environmental agreements came into being; and the 1989 political events in Eastern Europe and Russia opened the door to wider co-operation, financial assistance and joint enforcement efforts.

The Third Phase, 1992-

The starting point of the third phase of Baltic Sea pollution control is easily identified by the signing of the new Helsinki Convention in April 1992 and the Baltic Sea Joint Comprehensive Environmental Action Programme, JCP.[7] The new Convention includes a number of new provisions and stricter obligations. But the 1992 Helsinki Convention is more of an improvement of the objectives than of real measures, since it does not define obligations in terms of reduction rates or other effect-related criteria. Nor does the Convention involve financial or technological support (Ebbesson 1996). However, the JCP introduces a novel approach to Baltic pollution control, in particular, it symbolises a broadening of the commitments. Lasse Ringius has specified such an 'action-plan approach' including seven characteristics: (1) a set of policy, legal and regulatory reforms; (2) institution building and human resources development; (3) infrastructure investment for pollution control; (4) management of environmentally vulnerable areas; (5) support for research; transfer of technologies; more comprehensive understanding of critical problems; (6) public awareness campaigns and education; (7) strict time limits (Ringius 1996).

The central characteristic of the third phase is hence the creation of a 'transition regime,' i.e. environmental protection is explicitly organised in a way promoting system change and the marketisation process in the post-communist countries. The previous neutrality concerning economical and political aspects was thus superseded by an active commitment to the transition process.[8]

This process led to a new Swedish environmental foreign policy towards the

Baltic region. A two-level commitment developed. The traditional *demanding strategy*, i.e. attempts to persuade other contracting parties to enter into far-reaching agreements, was complemented by a *supportive strategy* involving aid and loans to transition countries.[9] Such a double commitment also became an element in the environmental foreign policy of other Western countries (e.g. Hiltunen 1994). In practice the two-level commitment involves, first, the domestic implementation of the JCP and, secondly, the promotion of implementation in transition countries through such means as education programmes, environmental aid and loans and joint ventures.

Thus, Sweden played an active role during the three phases and was one of the countries that sought to develop Baltic institutions functionally and structurally. A rationalistic practical and technical approach to problem solving has been a prominent element in this course. But Sweden has also been conscious of the political implications. The 1974 Stockholm Conference, the 1990 Ronneby Summit and, most recently, the Visby Summit in May 1996[10] are examples. On these occasions the environment has been in focus not only in its own right but has also as a symbol of Baltic solidarity.

Implementation: Convention and Action Programme

The Concept of Implementation

Before attempting to evaluate Sweden's implementation efforts, one has to reflect on what implementation could possibly mean during the different phases. What guidelines should states follow when implementing the Helsinki Convention?

The Convention – whether the 1974 nor the 1992 version – does not offer much in terms of detailed guidelines. Concerning land-based pollution, the basic provision stated in Article 6 is that 'the Contracting Parties shall take all appropriate measures to control and minimise land-based pollution of the marine environment of the Baltic Sea Area.' Dangerous substances such as DDTs and PCBs are 'black-listed,' which means that Parties should counteract their introduction into the Baltic Sea.

Other substances such as cadmium and mercury are considered less hazardous and are on the 'grey list' calling for 'urgent consideration' by the parties.

The only policy instrument available during the first and the second phase was recommendations: 'The Contracting Parties cannot become legally bound through the activities of the Commission even if its decisions and recommendations carry a considerable moral and political weight. ... The purpose, however, of adopting a recommendation is to submit a certain question to the Contracting Parties for study and implementation, if accepted.'[11]

New HELCOM recommendations are typically made by a party who has already incorporated the proposed measures in national policies and who can therefore offer good guidelines for other parties. The relevant question, however, is what impact such national experience can really have on other states.

The case of municipal waste-water treatment is illustrative. A comparative study of the implementation in Sweden and Poland shows that Sweden has had no problems keeping up with Baltic Sea commitments, whereas Poland has. In fact, a substantial reduction of phosphorus from point-sources was nearly implemented in Sweden before recommendations were passed on the subject (Löwgren and Hjorth 1991). In the 1990s, only two areas in Sweden did not comply with HELCOM standards and were thus treated as so-called hot spots (see below). In Poland, however, waste-water treatment remains a crucial area of pollution control.

Swedish reports submitted to the HELCOM secretariat in 1988 showed that many recommendations had already been implemented or were well under way to being implemented (Hjorth 1992: 247). Thus the early phase of Baltic Sea environmental co-operation does not appear to have had much independent and direct effect on Swedish national policies, at least for point-source emissions because these policies were already in accordance with domestic priorities. Nor did the Swedish initiatives lead to any appreciable results in other countries.

As for diffuse sources, however, the situation is somewhat different. Recommendations on nutrient discharges from agricultural production were issued during the 1980s and are still a prioritised area for HELCOM. Another type of emissions, which is not covered by specified HELCOM regulations, concerns atmospheric deposition from traffic.

According to a recent research report, no more than roughly 8 per cent of the nitrogen discharges and 25 per cent of the phosphorus discharges from all the countries into the Baltic Sea are coastal point-source emissions. The main part of discharges originates from diffuse sources, such as traffic and agriculture and upstream point sources (Stålnacke 1996). Furthermore, a recent report from the Swedish Environmental Protection Agency shows that the efforts to reduce the nitrogen discharges by 50 per cent have failed in Sweden (as in many other countries) (SEPA 1996). Recent research also indicates that the emissions of nitrogen and phosphorus from Swedish rivers into the Baltic Sea have been constant during the period 1980-93 (Stålnacke 1996). Thus even progressive countries like Sweden have had difficulties in limiting pollution of nutrients in accordance with international commitments.

The strategy to combat coastal point sources is not sufficient to control Baltic pollution. Yet it remains the dominant approach. The 'hot-spot' programme of the 1990s testifies to this. Although the treatment of hot spots in the area will contribute a lot to the environment of the Baltic Sea, and is indeed a costly affair, it cannot in the long run be the only strategy for cleaning up the Baltic.

Emplementing the JCP: The Third Phase

The third phase of Baltic Sea environmental co-operation is dominated by activities related to the JCP. As mentioned, the implementation of the action plan for Sweden and other Western parties is a two-level commitment involving both domestic implementation and the promotion of implementation in the transition countries and particularly their hot spots. As for domestic implementation, twelve such spots were located in Sweden. Five of them were in the northern part of the country in the drainage area of the Bothnian Sea and Bothnian Bay. Two municipal hot spots were located in the large cities, Stockholm and Gothenburg. Three hot spots were identified in southern Sweden, one was identified in the Sound and one in the Bornholm Basin. Finally two hot spots affect the Kattegat, the Laholm Bight and Skoghall north of Lake Vänern.

Table 14.1: Hot spots in Sweden

Site name	Type	Financing	Schedule
Rönnskärsverken	Industrial	Polluter pays	1993-2000
Husum Kraft Mill	Industrial	Polluter pays	Completed
Öststrand	Industrial	Polluter pays	Completed
Vallvik	Industrial	Polluter pays	Completed
Dalälven	Waste treatment	Government funds and polluter pays	Completed
The Sound	Agricultural	Local resources	1995
Skoghall	Industrial	Polluter pays	Completed
Gothenburg	Municipal	Local resources	1995-2000
Laholm Bight	Agricultural	Local resources	1995
Stockholm	Municipal	Local resources	1993-1998
Nymölla	Industrial	Polluter pays	1995
Bornholm Basin	Agricultural	Local resources	1995

Source: HELCOM. Third Activity Inventory, February 1995, p. 19

According to a 1995 HELCOM document, improvement was being realised in all Swedish hot spots, and in five of them recommendations had already been fully implemented (see Table 14.1). For all hot spots in Sweden, technical and financial aspects are fulfilled. According to the 1996 Lead Party Report on Combined Municipal and Industrial Discharges, the two municipal hot spots in Sweden can now be considered so-called cold spots, i.e. significant progress has been made in the form of technical development, institutional strengthening and reduced discharges (Lead Party Report 1996: 8).[12] The effluent values of the treatment plant in Gothenburg are 'well under existing HELCOM recommendations' (Lead Party Report 1996: 51 f.). Similarly, the hot spot in the Stockholm region is being eliminated, and that 'the new effluent values comply with existing HELCOM recommendations' (Lead Party Report 1996: 53). The report concludes that wastewater treatment in Sweden is well functioning (Lead Party Report 1996: 17).[13]

Participation: Consensus and Corporatism

Managing Baltic Sea Commitments: Goals and Means

In 1987 the Swedish government formulated two goals for international co-operation: first, that the protection of the Swedish environment required stronger efforts to influence the policies of other nations in order to reduce transboundary pollution flows; secondly, that Sweden share with other nations a common responsibility for the global environment (Swedish Government 1987-88).

The first goal is motivated by national interests. The two official strategies of Swedish environmental foreign policy mentioned above, i.e. to demand that other states take action and to support environmental investments in other countries, follow from this goal. Concerning the Baltic, it has been argued that the two strategies should be combined into an active environmental foreign policy involving both demanding and supportive means.[14]

The second goal is unclear as a practical guideline. It may be interpreted in terms of national interest when applied to such issues as global warming, where a non-specific future threat is perceived. The second goal is mainly of symbolic or ideological value, signalling a global approach to pollution control. For the Baltic area it means a commitment to support the development of a 'sustainable society' in the Baltic region and to promote educational and other activities in favour of 'sustainable lifestyles' and so on.

Participation at the International Level

The three phases of Baltic Sea environmental protection are also reflected in the international participation. During the first phase, 1974-88, it was exclusively governmental. Non-governmental organisations had no access to HELCOM. It was, however, possible to include non-governmental parties in the official country delegations.

As for Swedish official representation, the most important authorities were the Swedish Environmental Protection Agency, SEPA, and the Ministry of Environment, established in 1987.[15] SEPA has been the key institution for the formulation and enforcement of environmental protection policies and plays a key role as Sweden's representative in international fora (SEPA 1990).

Non-governmental organisations, ENGOs, were given access to HELCOM in 1989 when Greenpeace was invited to become an observer after an application made in 1987.[16] Since 1990 ENGOs have submitted a number of documents (Hjorth and Szrubka 1996: 64 f.). The ENGO representation is co-ordinated through the Coalition Clean Baltic, a federation of ENGOs. During the late 1980s, ENGOs participated in bilateral co-operation with Poland, and since the independence of Estonia, Latvia and Lithuania, various non-governmental and sub-governmental actors have become involved in environmental co-operation with those countries. The establishment of the JCP contributed to sub-governmental co-operation, but such efforts are being made even outside the JCP framework.

Participation by Sector Interests

Since 1967 Swedish environmental policy has centred on SEPA. According to Lundqvist (1996), SEPA has shaped a rationalistic an transparent environmental policy style, based on information exchange and negotiations between various interest groups.

Sector interests were given important positions on SEPA's executive board. They include powerful elites such as the Federation of Trade Unions (*Landsorganisationen*), the Swedish Federation of Industries (*Sveriges Industriförbund*), the Swedish Association of Municipalities (*Svenska Kommunförbundet*), and the organisation of consumer co-operatives (*Kooperativa Förbundet*). Landowner interests were represented by a high-level MP. However, no organisation of environmental interests was represented (Lundqvist 1996).

Today the Board no longer has the same element of interest representation. In an attempt to counteract corporatist tendencies in the Swedish central administration, several boards of this type were reorganised in the early and mid-1990s. Nevertheless, recent studies of the participation in the Swedish environmental protection administration show that some degree of indirect interest representation is still maintained and that the level of representation from non-governmental interest organisations remains low (Uhrwing 1995, 1996; Rothstein 1992).

SEPA retains its strong influence. The development of county administration and local environmental administration has, however, led to a shift in SEPA's role from policy implementation to policy formulation and evaluation. The responsibility for control and implementation enforcement is normally placed at the county level (*Länsstyrelsen*). The county administration of the twenty-four counties is led by County Governors (*Landshövding*) appointed by the Cabinet. 'Street-level' implementation is normally carried out by the 288 municipalities, and by 60 regional Water Councils (*Vattenvårdsförbund*) organised in accordance with drainage basins (Ejvegård 1986).

Consensus on a Technological Approach

Swedish policy style has been described as rationalistic and oriented towards reaching consensus (Richardson 1982). The establishment of SEPA was an attempt to organise a rational environmental protection administration. SEPA was given (and still keeps) the responsibility for co-ordinating research and planning in the environmental sector and for collecting, publishing and distributing information to the public, industry and public authorities. Although SEPA's role in the implementation phase has been reduced considerably in recent years, SEPA is more or less involved in every stage of the domestic environmental policy process and international co-operation.

SEPA was organised to administer environmental questions on the basis of scientific evidence rather than on the basis of moral or political considerations. One of SEPA's aims was to avoid a segmentation of environmental administration, to integrate policies concerning nature conservation, water management and air pollution into one central authority. The idea behind SEPA policy was to combine what Lundqvist (1971) has labelled 'long-term realism' and 'short-term activism.'

The long-term realism is based on the belief that economic progress is a precondition for successful environmental co-operation. Short-term activism is sceptical towards long-term planning. The problems of today should have priority and present-day knowledge should be guideline for activity (Lundqvist 1971). In a sense, the precautionary principle was recognised and practised already in the late 1960s.

Future policies were to be based on increased scientific and technical knowledge. The adoption of this particular 'ideology' rendered the environment more suitable for experts and specialists than for politicians. According to SEPA and the government, SEPA should draw up the guidelines for its own activities and not rely on political guidelines. As a consequence, SEPA became not merely an organisation for problem-solving and implementation of political goals but also a problem-defining authority (Lundqvist 1971: 138).

This profile, still maintained by SEPA, corresponds to the 'scientific-technological' character of the HELCOM organisation during the 1980s. HELCOM was shaped that way not only as a consequence of the Cold War but also due to the very limited knowledge of environmental problems during the regime's formative years. More knowledge and the sharing of it were necessary conditions environmental institutions at the time.

The Swedish commitment to develop the HELCOM organisation during its different phases is easily reconcilable with the domestic policy style. In Sweden, SEPA shaped environmental regulations based on consensus among major interest groups, and polluters (targets) were urged to take upon themselves voluntary tasks. Accordingly, Lundqvist (1996) has described SEPA's activities as follows: 'A climate was to be created where controllers and polluters would reason and take each others' arguments seriously. A key strategy was *information*. If only each side knew exactly what the other side wanted and why, the relations between controllers and polluters would lead to rational and balanced decisions. The keyword should be *trust*; polluters should be relied upon to execute agreed pollution control programmes and prescribed control measures – without day-to-day interference from regional or local environmental officers' (Lundqvist 1996: 290). Implementation was organised and to a certain extent carried out by the polluters themselves in co-operation with state authorities.

With the exception of issues related to energy production, especially nuclear power, a general consensus on environmental protection policy has been achieved. After examining the 'environmental discourse' in Sweden since the 1960s, Hedrén (1994) concluded that natural science and technical considerations dominate, whereas practical knowledge is downgraded. Furthermore, there is consensus among the major political parties. Only the Greens and the left-wing socialist party are taking a different position. The bigger parties 'are characterised by a kind of rationalistic optimism and great trust in technological solutions. ... This concept illustrates a primarily engineer-like attitude, characterised by scientific analyses, scientific prognoses, measurement and control programmes and, not least, a technologically based control of human activities' (Hedrén 1994: 285 f.).

There has thus been a considerable societal and political consensus on the goals and means of environmental protection, and the rationalistic approach has also been pursued in relation to Baltic Sea co-operation. According to Jamison, the impact of the environmental movement has been strong in the sense that it has been a political force affecting public debate. On the other hand, it has been 'subjected to a range of incorporation pressures that have made it difficult for an autonomous social movement to develop' (Jamison 1990: 13).

Environmental Corporatism

Although corporatism has been on the decline in many areas of Swedish politics during the 1980s (Lewin 1992), the essential character of a corporatist relationship has not yet weakened (Öberg 1994). Corporatism has been a way to build-up the welfare system in Sweden and has often been initiated by social democratic governments in an attempt to establish an effective administration of prioritised tasks (Rothstein 1986). This has also been the case within the environmental sector, for example in the field of land-use planning (Forsberg 1992).

Participation in the environmental policy process can be summed up as follows: (1) Participation from target groups takes place at national, regional and local levels. (2) The interaction between the state and sector and other interests can, furthermore, be characterised as corporatist.

One example is the Licensing Board for Environmental Protection. The Board administers a permit system for polluting activities, mainly industrial pollution, according to the 1969 Environment Protection Act. The permits are issued after 'negotiation' between the polluting company and 'public environmental interests' represented by SEPA. The process resembles a legal procedure where polluters are represented by legal experts and very often environmental expertise to support their case. At the other end of the table, SEPA's experts represent the public interest. The chairman is a judge, and the members of the Board possess environmental, technological and industrial expertise. Non-governmental interests are not represented. The role of SEPA in this process is somewhat peculiar since SEPA represents both public and government interests. Thus, on the one hand, SEPA represents public interests in specific cases. On the other hand, SEPA may issue general regulations steering the Board's activities (Loftson et al. 1993).

The politisation of environmental issues in the late 1980s leads one to think that environmental corporatism is on decline. It is not. The corporatist tradition has recently been relied on to implement recycling policies in Sweden. The central document is the 1993 Ecocycle Bill, whose aim is to promote a sustainable society (a goal in line with Baltic Sea Commitments in the 1990s). Whereas the state is responsible for issuing targets for reuse and recycling, industry is expected to provide the organisation and thus administer the closing of the ecocycle for various products and materials (Lundqvist 1996: 324). According to Lundqvist, the Ecocycle Bill 'amounts to nothing less than a system of ecological corporativism.' Lundqvist views the activities enforced by the Bill as a continuation of the strategy introduced in the late 1960s (ibid.).

Thus, consensus on a technological approach and environmental corporatism are complementary features of Swedish environmental policy and administration. The low degree of politisation and of ENGO influence is a consequence of that approach.

At the level of Baltic regional co-operation, the consensus on a technological approach is reflected, but not corporatism. The state-based regime of the first phase has been transformed into a more open and multilayered one. The role of ENGOs has developed continuously and particularly in relation to the JCP. At the domestic level, however, the structure of implementation and participation differs in accordance with national policy styles. For example, the Swedish pattern is to some extent repeated in Finland, whereas Poland has retained and developed institutions that were shaped before the transition, for example environmental protection funds.[17]

Conclusions

The implementation of Baltic Sea environmental commitments in Sweden have not been subjected to any special authority or procedure. Therefore the focus in this chapter has had to be on Swedish participation in the Baltic environmental protection institutions and on the participation of interest groups in the implementation of relevant domestic environmental policies.

Baltic Sea environmental commitments have always been a prominent field of Swedish environmental foreign policy. They are often initiated by Sweden (or other Western states) in areas where Sweden had already implemented or was about to implement policies that would satisfy the proposed commitments. Hence it has generally not been a very difficult task for Sweden to implement these commitments. The recent activities in relation to the JCP also show that Swedish implementation efforts have been successful.

Swedish policy proposals reflect the rationalistic and scientific-technological consensus that is characteristic of Swedish environmental policy and politics. Sweden's Baltic Sea policies have been oriented towards achieving working monitoring programmes, advisory recommendations, action programmes etc. Implementation is viewed as a joint enterprise between the state and the polluters. Often enforcement tasks are assigned to the polluter.

Participation in international co-operation as well as national implementation is organised in a state-centred, corporatist way, where state authorities have a central and often dominant position. Representation by power elites is ensured by sector participation. Sector representation is prominent both at the national and county levels. The participation of sector interests is organised according to a corporatist pattern. Representation by ENGOs is weak. In this respect the bodies developed during the third phase of Baltic Sea co-operation are not simply spillovers from national patterns. The ENGOs have been given voice and site in the implementation of Baltic Sea policy.

Notes

1 This chapter was originally prepared for the project Implementation and Effectiveness of International Environmental Commitments, IEC, at the International Institute for Applied Systems Analysis, IIASA. The views expressed here do not necessarily represent those of IIASA or its member organisations. I would like to thank Kal Raustiala and David G. Victor for their comments on earlier drafts. Carl Einar Stålvant has provided valuable suggestions during the editing of the final version.

2 It took six years until all the Contracting Parties had ratified the Convention in 1980, and a permanent organisation could be established. On the impact of détente, see Rytövuori (1980).

3 The impact of the Perestroika-Glastnost policies on Baltic Sea environmental co-operation was merely symbolic (Hjorth 1992).

4 Other parties advocating a reformed organisation were Finland, Denmark, and the Federal Republic of Germany.

5 Document. HELCOM 9/16, Annex 10, pages 90-92. For comments, see Hjorth (1992), pages 141-148.

6 Paragraph 2 of the 1990 Baltic Sea Declaration.

7 The 1992 Baltic Sea Declaration and Final Act of the Diplomatic Conference was signed by the Czech and Slovak Federal Republic, Denmark, Estonia, Finland, the FRG, Latvia, Lithuania, Norway, Poland, the Russian Federation, Sweden, the Ukraine, and the European Economic Community.

8 Background Document for the 1992 Baltic Sea Declaration. Conference Document No. 5/2, p. 4. On the regime change following this and other documents at the time, see Hjorth (1994).

9 These concepts were coined in a report of a special investigative commission to the Swedish government, SOU 1990:88. *Sveriges internationella miljösamarbete: nya mål och nya möjligheter.*

10 The Baltic Sea States' Summit Negotiation Committee issued three action programmes in the fields of 'increased people-to-people contacts and civic security,' 'economic co-ordination and integration' and 'strengthened environmental protection.'

11 Document: HELCOM 6/INF 9, 1985, Submitted by the Secretariat and based on document IC 5/14, 1978, Submitted by the Delegation of Finland. For further comments see Hjorth (1992: 87).

12 The full definition is as follows: 'Cold spot = Progress in the form of technical development, institutional strengthening and reduced discharges, is well under way. A Short-term Strategic Plan and a Long-term Strategic Plan, aiming at fulfilling applicable HELCOM Recommendations for municipal waste-water, has normally been developed and approved by appropriate national and financing bodies. Decisions on short-term programme implementation and financing have been made. Substantial construction work has often started. Further development has normally been viewed as a national responsibility.'

13 The same is stated concerning Denmark and Germany.

14 The strategies were drawn up in a committee report (Swedish Government 1990).

15 Before 1987 environmental issues were handled by the Ministry of Agriculture.

16 Hjorth (1992: 181) and HELCOM documents, HELCOM 8/8a/5 and 9/10a/1.l.

17 Concerning the Finnish case, see Storsved (1996). As for the Polish case, see Hjorth (1997). For an overview of the Nordic countries, see Christiansen (1996).

References

Baltic Sea Declaration. Background Document for the 1992 Conference. Conference Document No. 5/2.

Bennulf, M. and Holmberg, S. (1992). 'The Green Breakthrough in Sweden,' *Scandinavian Political Studies*:13, pages 165-184.

Christiansen, Peter M. (ed.) (1996) *Governing the Environment: Politics, Policy and Organization in the Nordic Countries.* Nord Report 1996:5. Copenhagen, Nordic Council of Ministers.

Ebbesson, J. (1996). '1992 Baltic Convention: Transition or Stand-still?' in Hjorth, R. (ed.). *Baltic Environmental Cooperation: A Regime in Transition.* Tema V Report 23. Linköping.

Ejvegård, R. (1986). *Korporatism, administration, aktårer och intressen: Analys och diskussion av några begrepp med anknytning till vattenvårdsproblematik.* Tema V Report 11. Linköping.

Forsberg, H. (1992). *En politisk nödvändighet. En studie av den fysiska riksplaneringens introduktion och tillämpning.* Linköping Studies in Arts and Science:74. Linköping.

Hedrén, J. (1994). *Miljöpolitikens natur.* Linköping Studies in Arts and Science:110. Linköping.

Hiltunen, H. (1994). *Finland and Environmental Problems in Russia and Estonia.* Foreign Policy Challenges:6. Helsinki, The Finnish Institute of International Affairs.

Hjorth, R. (1992). *Building International Institutions for Environmental Protection: the Case of Baltic Sea Environmental Cooperation.* Linköping Studies in Arts and Science:81. Linköping.

Hjorth, R. (1994). 'Baltic Sea Environmental Cooperation: The Role of Epistemic Communities and the Politics of Regime Change,' *Cooperation and Conflict*:29(1), pages 11-31.

Hjorth, R. (1997). 'Implementation of Baltic Sea Pollution Commitments in Poland: A Review of the Literature' in Victor, David G., Raustiala, Kal and Skolnikoff, Eugene B. (eds.). *Implementation and Effectiveness of International Environmental Commitments.* Cambridge, Mass., MIT Press.

Hjorth, R and Szrubka, W. (1996). 'The Role of International Organisations in
Baltic Environmental Cooperation' in Hjorth, R. (ed.). *Baltic Environmental Cooperation: A Regime in Transition.* Linköping Tema V Report:23. Linköping.

Jamison, A. et al. (1990). *The Making of the New Environmental Consciousness: A Comparative Study of the Environmental Movements in Sweden, Denmark and the Netherlands.* Edinburgh, Edinburgh University Press.

Lewin, L. (1992). *Samhället och de organiserade intressena.* Stockholm, Norstedts.

Loftsson, E., Hedrén, J., Hjorth, R. and Löwgren, M. (1993). *Svensk miljöpolitik.* Lund, Studentlitteratur.

Löwgren, M. and Hjorth, R. (1991). 'Water Pollution Control in Poland and Sweden: National Policies and International Cooperation' in Fenger, J. et al. *Environment, Energy and Natural Resources Management in the Baltic Region.* Nord 1991:48. Copenhagen, Nordic Council of Ministers.

Lundqvist, L. J. (1971). *Miljövårdsförvaltning och politisk struktur.* Lund, Prisma.

Lundqvist, L.J. (1996). 'Sweden' in Christiansen, Peter M. (ed.). *Governing the Environment: Politics, Policy and Organization in the Nordic Countries.* Nord Report 1996:5. Copenhagen, Nordic Council of Ministers.

Öberg, P.O. (1994). *Särintresse och allmänintresse: Korporatismens ansikte.* (Stockholm: Almqvist & Wicksell).

Richardson, J. (1982) (ed.). *Policy Styles in Western Europe.* London, George Allen & Unwin.

Ringius, L. (1996). 'The Environmental Action Plan Approach: A Milestone in Pollution Control in the Baltic Sea" in Hjorth, R. (ed.). *Baltic Environmental Cooperation: A Regime in Transition.* Linköping Tema V Report:23. Linköping.

Rothstein, B. (1986). *Den socialdemokratiska staten. Reformer och förvaltning inom svensk arbetsmarknads- och skolpolitik.* Lund Political Studies:21. Lund, Studentlitteratur.

Rothstein, B. (1992). *Den korporativa staten.* Stockholm, Norstedts.

Rytövuori, H. (1980). 'Structures of Détente and Ecological
Interdependence: Cooperation in the Baltic Sea Area for the Protection of the Marine Environment and Living Resources,' *Cooperation and Conflict*:XV, pages 85-102.

SEPA (1990). *Statens Naturvårdsverk och det internationella arbetet.*
SEPA (1996). *Kväve från land till hav.* SNV Rapport. Stockholm.
Stålnacke, P. (1996). *Nutrient Loads to the Baltic Sea.* Linköping Studies in Arts and Science:146. Linköping.
Storsved (1996) 'The Role of Expert Knowledge in the Build-up of an Environmental Administration: The Case of Finland' in Hjorth (ed.). *Baltic Environmental Cooperation: A Regime in Transition.* Linköping Tema V Report:23. Linköping.
Swedish Government (1987-88). *Miljöpolitiken inför 90-talet.* Regeringens propostion 1987/88:85 (Government Bill).
Swedish Government (1990). *Sveriges Internationella miljösamarbete: nya mål och nya möjligheter.* SOU 1990:88.
Uhrwing, M. (1995) 'Intresserepresentation i brytningstid.' Unpublished research report. Gothenburg University, Department of Political Science.
Uhrwing, M (1996) 'Att medverka eller icke medverka.' Unpublished research report. Gothenburg University, Department of Political Science.

15 Poland's Economic Recovery and Its Implications for Energy Use and Air Pollution

Jürgen Salay

Introduction and Background

Since the transition from centrally planned to market economy started in Central and Eastern Europe (CEE) in the early 1990s, the conditions for energy use have changed significantly. The former system left the countries in the southern and eastern Baltic region with a strong dependence on fossil fuels and an inefficient energy use, which made them exceedingly polluting compared to the countries of the western Baltic region. Are there any signs that this situation is improving? This chapter takes a closer look at Poland – the country in CEE where the transition started. The chapter reviews recent changes in Poland's energy use and air pollution against the backdrop of its recent economic recovery and discusses to what extent the Polish trends are discernible in other parts of the eastern Baltic region.

The rapid economic growth in Europe after World War II relied on a steadily increasing supply of energy. Both the centrally planned economies (CPEs) in Central and Eastern Europe and the market-oriented economies of Western Europe based their post-war economic development on an extensive use of coal, oil and natural gas. Until the 1970s, there was not much of a difference in the structure of energy consumption between these two economic systems.

The oil crisis in 1973-74 and the subsequent slowing of economic activity had serious implications for the future development of energy use in Europe. The drastic increase in the price of crude oil and other energy products forced the Western European countries to reconsider their energy policy. To mitigate the soaring costs of energy imports, governments attempted to replace oil with energy sources that appeared to be less sensitive to price fluctuations, e.g. nuclear power, while promoting energy conservation in industry, transportation and among households. In order to become less dependent on oil from the Middle East, oil imports were diversified. The oil crisis also created a boom for oil production in the North Sea, which became profitable as a result of the higher world market prices of oil.

The increase in energy prices thus accelerated the historic decline in energy intensity[1] in Western Europe resulting from structural and technological change.[2] The late 1970s and early 1980s was a period of the restructuring and rationalisation of West European industry, which had to cut production costs in order to remain competitive in the world market. The decline in the share of resource-intensive industry in total industrial production and the introduction of new technologies made the economies of Western Europe less energy intensive.

Because most countries in CEE satisfied their energy demand with domestic fossil fuels, and oil or natural gas from the USSR at subsidised prices, they were less affected by the surge in the world market price of oil in the 1970s. But in the beginning of the 1980s, the USSR cut down on its oil exports to other CEEs, mainly because of growing production costs at Soviet oil fields. This cut forced the Central and East European countries to intensify the exploitation of domestic coal and other fossil fuels since they could not afford to import oil from producers outside the socialist bloc (Salay 1991; Bethkenhagen 1987; The Economist 1985). The accelerated exploitation of domestic coal and other fossil fuels was costly. The intensified energy production in the CPEs demanded continued subsidies and an increasing share of the state budget. In the 1980s, the energy industry accounted for about a fifth of total state investments in the GDR and more than 10 per cent in Poland (Salay 1991: 25 f.). It became increasingly clear that this energy policy was not economically sustainable since energy prices were far below real production costs.

In contrast to Western Europe, Central and Eastern Europe never restructured the industry between 1970 and 1989. Since all essential resources were allocated by a central administration and enterprises operated under so-called soft-budget constraints,[3] they had few incentives to reduce production costs. The centrally planned economy was thus characterised by a consistent misallocation of resources. In addition to the system-inherent inefficiency, the underpricing of energy products and other raw materials resulted in a strong bias toward resource-intensive industry and a corresponding under-representation of light industry and services. Heavy industry continued to dominate industrial production and exports. While per capita energy use grew steadily in CEE between 1970 and 1986, it only increased marginally in Western Europe, North America and Japan in the same period.[4]

The combination of an inefficient economic system and a high share of energy-intensive industry explains why at the end of the 1980s, Central and Eastern Europe had an energy per GDP ratio that was several times higher than that of Western Europe.[5]

The inefficient use of energy and raw materials, the bias towards heavy industry in the national product mix, and the dependence on coal and other fossil fuels all contributed to place the CPEs among the world's most pollution-intensive countries. The pollution load was high also because of weak enforcement of environmental protection.[6] At the end of the 1980s, per capita emissions of sulphur dioxide (SO_2) in Poland, Hungary and Czechoslovakia were two to eight times higher than in Western Europe. Their SO_2 emissions per unit of GDP were more than ten times higher than that of Western Europe (Salay et al. 1993: 194).

Poland is an interesting case study of how energy use and air pollution has changed after 1989 in the Baltic region. There are several reasons for this choice. Poland was the first country in CEE to start the shift from centrally planned to market economy, and the first country in which economic growth returned after the strong recession in the initial phase of transition. Poland is extremely reliant on coal for its energy supply. In 1992, coal accounted for 77 per cent of Poland's total primary energy supply and for 97 per cent of its electricity production (International Energy Agency 1994: 163). As a consequence of its strong dependence on coal, Poland is among Europe's largest emitters of carbon dioxide (CO_2) and sulphur dioxide. It is also a significant source of transboundary air pollution to other European countries. Because it is one of Europe's largest emitters of sulphur dioxide, Poland's efforts to reduce its SO_2 emissions are highly relevant in the context of current European co-operation to curb transboundary air pollution. Poland's attempt to reduce the environmental effects of energy production is also illustrative of the challenges facing the energy industry in the former centrally planned economies in Central and Eastern Europe. All these features make Poland an interesting example of how economic transition is affecting energy use and air pollution.

Changing Conditions for Energy Use

The first half of the 1990s was a time of dramatic economic change in Central and Eastern Europe. Exposed to competition and free prices and deprived of direct subsidies from the state, the industry reduced its output sharply. In the first 3-4 years of transition, GDP fell by 17 per cent in Poland, 18 per cent in Hungary, and 21 per cent in Czechoslovakia (International Energy Agency 1994: 76, 107 and 164). Another reason for the decline in production was the breakdown of trade within Central and Eastern Europe, which traditionally had provided access to cheap raw materials and important export markets.

The collapse of the centrally planned economy in 1989-91 and the economic transition that followed had a profound effect on energy use in Eastern Europe. Because of falling industrial production and declining economic activity during the first years of transition, the Central and East European countries experienced the most drastic drop in energy use since World War II. While total primary energy supply (TPES) in the EU increased slightly between 1990 and 1993, Eastern Europe's TPES dropped by 20 per cent in the same period. Between 1988 and 1992 total primary energy consumption fell by 23 per cent in Hungary and 13 per cent in Czechoslovakia (International Energy Agency 1994: 76, 107). In Estonia, Latvia and Lithuania, it fell by about 50 per cent between 1990 and 1993. The sharp decline in the Baltic states' energy consumption is explained by a deeper fall in GDP than in Poland and by repeated shortfalls in oil and natural gas supply from Russia.

After the downfall of the communist regime in 1989, the conditions for energy use and pollution abatement in Poland have fundamentally changed. The new government deregulated energy prices by gradually lifting price controls and began to reorganise the energy industry. The administration of environmental protection was reorganised and a revision of laws and regulations was initiated.

The economic downturn in Poland in 1989-91 resulted in a significant decrease of energy use in all sectors. Total final energy use[7] in 1991 was 25 per cent below that in 1988 and the lowest since the mid-1970s. The main reasons for this large decline was the sharp fall in industrial output in 1990-91 and a huge drop in residential coal use because of higher prices.

Increasing energy prices also contributed to the drop in energy consumption after 1989, especially among households. With few exceptions, prices are no longer set by the state and subsidies have been abolished. As energy products were among the most subsidised goods in the CPEs, energy prices soared when price controls were lifted. Although most rises in energy prices have been phased in gradually, the overall increase has been considerable. In real terms, the price of coal, which dominates energy use in Poland, more than doubled between 1989 and 1993.[8] Between 1989 and 1995, the real price of electricity for industry rose by 50 per cent, while that for households more than quadrupled.

After the drastic slump in energy consumption during the initial phase of the transition, energy use is slowly increasing again as a result of recovering economic activity. Poland is now one of the fastest growing economies in Europe with the annual GDP growth averaging 5 per cent between 1993 and1996.

The drastic economic changes in Central and Eastern Europe in the 1990s make it difficult to collect reliable statistics to compare the structure of these countries' final energy consumption with that of the countries in Western Europe. However, some general observations can be made. Transportation and services account for a larger share of final energy consumption in Western Europe than in CEE. The established market economies in the West also tend to have a higher per capita consumption of electricity compared to the former centrally planned economies in the East. In CEE, the continuing shift from heavy industry to manufacturing and services, and increasing ownership of appliances in households will gradually increase per capita electricity consumption to levels approaching those in the West.

Although per capita levels of energy consumption are in the same range, there are large differences among the countries in the Baltic region with respect to energy efficiency. One measure of how efficiently energy is used in a economy is to calculate its energy intensity, i.e. energy use per unit of gross domestic production (GDP). Energy intensities are easy to calculate for individual countries. Unfortunately, comparing intensities across countries is not always as simple.

Before the transition, the energy intensities of the centrally planned economies were several times higher than those of established market economies in Western Europe. The most important explanation for this difference in energy efficiency was that energy prices were heavily subsidised in the centrally planned economies. Other reasons were the bias toward heavy industry, monopolistic energy supply systems and the lack of market discipline to encourage cost-effective investments that were typical in centrally planned economies. The legacy of the former system still burdens the countries of Central and Eastern Europe.

In Poland, the energy intensity in manufacturing increased during the sharp decline in output in 1990-91. This was a result of a low utilisation of productive capacity in industry. Despite higher energy prices, there was little evidence of energy conservation in industry in 1990-91. After the initial increase in energy intensity 1990-91, it dropped slightly in 1992. This may have been a sign that the rationalisation of production began to have an impact on energy use in industry.

There is a significant potential for improved energy efficiency in the Polish industry. Preliminary Polish data show that the decreasing energy intensity in industry which occurred in 1992 continued in 1993-95. Improvements in energy efficiency are likely to be faster in industry than in other sectors because of stronger market incentives and the effect of new capital investment.

Air Pollution in Poland

Poor air quality is a serious problem in several industrialised regions in Poland. Two types of air pollutant are particularly conspicuous: sulphur dioxide and particulates. They are considered the most urgent air quality issues in Poland. Nation-wide air quality data for 1990-92 show that SO_2 concentrations exceeded the Polish quality standard (24 hour limit, 200 mg/m^3) at measurement points in 15 of 49 voivodships (administrative regions), while particulate concentrations exceeded the standard (24 hour limit, 120 mg/m^3) at measurement points in nearly all regions (OECD 1995: 36, 41).[9]

Sulphur dioxide emissions into the air contribute to acidification of soils, waters and forests as well as corrosion damage to buildings. It is a principal factor in forest diebacks, reduced agricultural yields, and accelerated deterioration of historic buildings in Poland (Nowicki 1993: 105). According to various estimates, Poland's total emissions of SO_2 were 3.8-4.2 million tonnes (Mt) in 1988[10] – the third largest in Europe after the USSR and Eastern Germany in that year. Poland's SO_2 emissions per capita are among the highest in Europe (see Table 15.1). Calculated per GDP, emissions of sulphur dioxide in 1991 were more than two times higher than the average for the European Union.

Particulates from coal combustion and industrial processes contain soot, heavy metals and hazardous chemical compounds. Together with nitrogen oxides (NO_x) and hydro-carbons, they are the main sources of photochemical smog in urban areas, which is a serious health problem in several regions of the country. Emissions of particulates are also high by European standards. In 1988, Poland emitted about 2.1 Mt of particulates. Its per capita emissions were about 55 kg – more than five times higher than in West European countries (Klimont et al. 1993: 25).

Table 15.1: Emissions of SO_2 in selected European countries, 1991, total, per capita and per GDP*

	kt	kg/cap	kg/1000 USD
Poland	2996	74	6.9
Sweden	113	13	0.8
Germany	4430	56	3.3
France	1378	23	1.3
UK	3571	62	4.0
EU-12**	1568	45	2.8

* GDP at 1991 prices and purchasing power parities
** The 12 member states of the European Union in 1991

Sources: Author's calculation based on data from OECD (1995) and Norwegian Meteorological Institute (1995)

In 1988, more than 90 per cent of total SO_2 and more than 80 per cent of total particulate emissions in Poland came from power and heat production, including small boilers and stoves used in the residential sector (Klimont et al. 1993: B-2; Nowicki 1993: 105). Public power and CHP plants accounted for 55 per cent of all emitted sulphur dioxide and 39 per cent of total particulate emissions. Some of Poland's power plants are among the largest point sources of SO_2 in Europe. According to the emission inventory performed in eight Central European countries[11] by Klimont et al., 10 of the 25 largest emitters of SO_2 were Polish power plants. Outstanding among these was the 4,520 MWe lignite-fired power station in Belchatów in central Poland – the largest of its kind in Europe. The Belchatów plant emitted 342 kilotons (kt) of SO_2 in 1988; about as much as the total SO_2 emissions of Belgium in that year.

In 1990, the Polish government presented a policy paper containing a new national environmental protection programme which was adopted by parliament the following year.[12] The Ministry of Environmental Protection, Natural Resources and Forestry (hereafter MEP, the Polish acronym is MOSZNiL) was given the main responsibility for implementing the programme. The overall objective of the programme is to improve Poland's environmental situation by the year 2000. To achieve this objective, five fundamental measures were chosen:

1. revising the system of environmental laws and emission standards;
2. improving the enforcement of laws and standards;
3. increasing investments in environmental protection through environmental taxes;
4. reforming environmental management; and
5. enhancing education and social awareness of the environment.

Air pollution is a key target for the environmental protection programme. An important measure to improve air quality was adopted in 1990 when the MEP enacted an ordinance on air pollution regulation which revised the earlier system of standards for ambient air concentrations and emissions of air pollutants (Dziennik Ustaw Rzeczypospolitej Polskiej 1990).[13] With respect to stationary combustion processes,[14] such as power plants, specific permitted emission levels were introduced for SO_2, nitrogen oxides, and particulates.

In 1990-92, environmental management was decentralised. The voivodships now issue permits for industrial activities and set limits for permissible pollution levels. Penalties and fines for exceeding the limits are also decided by regional authorities. Each voivodship has a Department of Environmental Protection. Also in the early 1990s, several new laws regulating the environment and natural resources were adopted by the parliament. A law reforming the structure of the State Inspectorate of Environmental Protection (PIOS) was passed in 1991, subordinating it to the MEP in an effort to make it independent of local political influence (Dziennik Ustaw Rzeczypospolitej Polskiej 1991). The PIOS now consists of a network of regional inspectorates with headquarters in Warsaw. It is responsible for monitoring of air quality and is empowered to inspect any polluter or user of natural resources, including the right to close production in the case of a serious threat to the environment.

To increase investments in environmental protection, the system of environmental taxes has been revised. The tax system consists of fees for the use of natural resources, various fees for emissions of pollutants into air and water, as well as for waste disposal, and fines for emissions exceeding prescribed limits. The emission fees are paid per unit of emitted pollutant for each installation up to the emission limit set in the license. For emissions above prescribed limits, the polluter has to pay fines that are ten times higher than the fees per unit of pollutant. To make them more effective, fees and fines have been raised several times since 1990 to compensate for inflation (Zylicz 1992). Furthermore, in 1991, fees started to be collected four times a year from major polluters instead of the previous procedure which was only once a year for all polluters. Since then, fees have typically been adjusted at the beginning of each year. In 1996, the fee for emitting one metric tonne of SO_2 was 240 new zloty, PZN (about 100 USD). Fees in the heavily polluted Katowice and Krakow regions were twice as high (Dziennik Ustaw Rzeczypospolitej Polskiej 1995).

The revenues from fees and fines are collected in national and regional environmental funds, from which public investments in environmental protection are financed. As a result of the increased environmental charges, the volume of the funds' collected revenues and spent investments has grown significantly. In 1994, collected environmental fees and fines totalled 1,015 million PZN (about 400 million USD) (Glowny Urzad Statystyczny 1995: 372). Loans and grants from these environmental funds provided 41 per cent of total Polish investments in environmental protection in 1994. The amount of environmental fees claimed by Poland's environmental funds increased more than 15 times between 1990 and 1992 in real terms. Fees for air pollution accounted for 40-45 per cent of the total amount of environmental fees (see Figure 15.1). Calculated as a share of national income, Poland's total expenditures for environmental protection doubled from 0.5 per cent in 1987 to 1.0 per cent in 1994 (see Figure 15.2). This share is higher than that of many OECD countries (OECD 1995: 91).

Figure 15.1: Poland: fees charged by environmental funds, 1989-94, total and for air protection, at 1990 prices

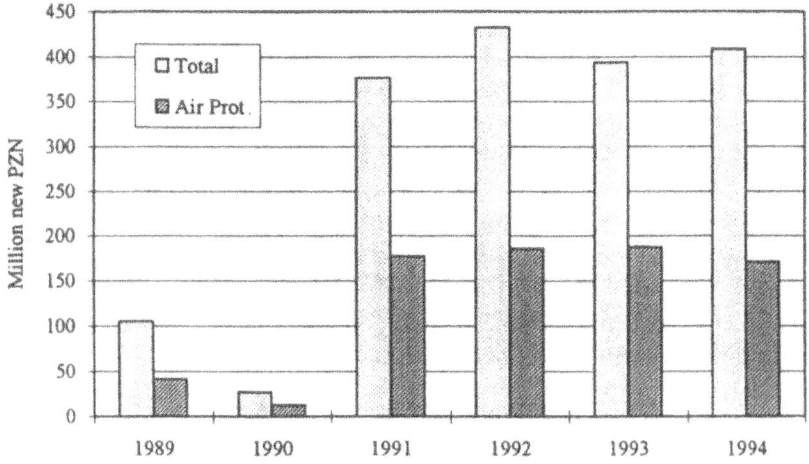

Source: Author's calculations based on data from Glowny Urzad Statystyczny (1995: 372). 1 Polish zloty (PNZ) = 0.95 USD (in 1990 prices)

Figure 15.2: Poland: investments in environmental protection, 1990-94, as share of GDP and total national investments

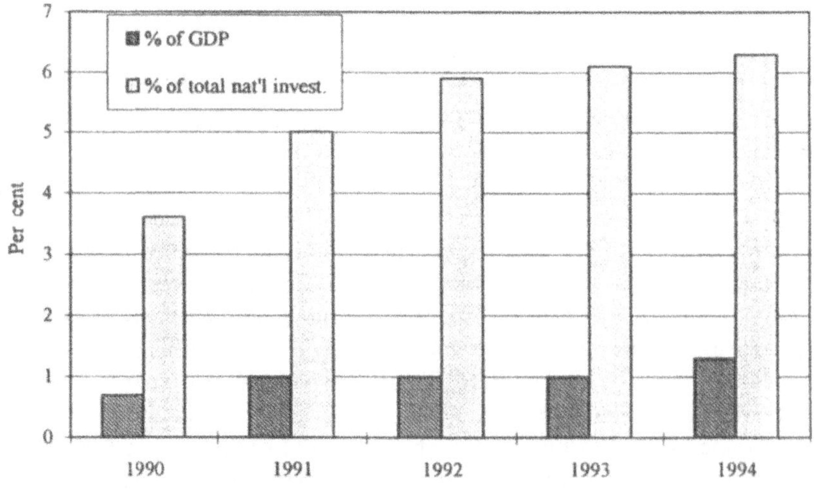

Source: Author's calculations based on data from Glowny Urzad Statystyczny (1995: 372). 1 Polish zloty (PNZ) = 0.95 USD (in 1990 prices)

Poland's objective to reduce its emissions of air pollutants is in line with an international agreement to reduce transboundary air pollution in Europe. In 1979, within the framework of the UN Economic Commission for Europe (ECE), the Convention on Long Range Transboundary Air Pollution (LRTAP) was signed by all European countries as well as the US and Canada. Several protocols on the reduction of various transboundary air pollutants have been added to this convention. A so-called sulphur protocol was signed in 1985. The signatories agreed to cut 1993 SO_2 emissions by 30 per cent compared to 1980 levels. In 1994, a new protocol on further reductions of European SO_2 emissions (also called the second sulphur protocol) was signed by twenty-six European countries. This protocol stipulates further reductions from the 1980 emission level by up to 80 per cent by 2000-2010 with individual reduction goals and deadlines for each signatory (*Acid News* 1994b: 10 f.).[15]

Poland did not sign the first sulphur protocol. However, when the environmental protection programme was adopted by the parliament in 1991, it set national reduction goals for certain air pollutants. Among its medium-term objectives is a decrease in emissions, with respect to 1980 levels, of sulphur dioxide by 30 per cent, particulates by 50 per cent and nitrogen oxides by 10 per cent by the year 2000 (OECD 1995: 39 f.; Pasierb 1992: 6). In recent years, Poland has taken a more active stance to the ECE Convention, and in 1994 it signed the second sulphur protocol, accepting to reduce its emissions of SO_2 by 37 per cent by 2000 and 66 per cent by 2010 (with respect to 1980 levels) (*Acid News* 1994b: 10).[16]

Poland's reduction goals are not only motivated by domestic air pollution problems. They are also a response to influence from other countries. Sulphur emitted in Poland is also deposited in its eastern and northern neighbour countries, which have soils that are very vulnerable to acid precipitation. It is estimated that about 500 kt SO_2 were transported from Poland to Russia, Ukraine, the Baltic states and Scandinavia in 1994 (*Acid News* 1995: 13).

Explaining the Drop in Air Pollution

In the period between 1988 and 1994, air pollution from industry and other stationary sources declined substantially in Central and Eastern Europe (Norwegian Meteorological Institute 1995: 17). In Poland, total SO_2 emissions fell from 4,180 kt in 1988 to 2,645 kt in 1994 – a reduction by 37 per cent (see Figure 15.3). The first reduction goal for SO_2 established by the Polish government (30 per cent below the 1980 level by the year 2000) was reached in 1992. Emissions continued to decrease in the following years, albeit at a slower rate.

The power industry is the dominant air polluter in Poland and is specifically targeted in the government's programme for air pollution control. This makes the power industry particularly interesting to study as a source of air pollution. Emissions of SO_2 from the Polish power industry fell by 22.5 per cent in 1990 and declined by a further 7.5 per cent in 1991, and by 9.4 per cent in 1992.[17] How was this fall in emissions possible? The fall in economic activity and electricity production in the early 1990s contributed, but other factors were at least as important in explaining the reduction in emitted SO_2.

The decreasing SO_2 emissions from electricity production after 1988 was a result both of the restructuring of the power industry and the government's new regulation of the air pollution control in 1990-91. The restructuring of the power industry included two kinds of measure to make power production more efficient: 'sticks' and 'carrots.' An important stick was the deregulation of coal prices, which increased the price of hard coal and made the fuel consumption of power and CHP plants more expensive. Because the price reform coincided with the reorganisation of the power industry, which made power plants independent, state-owned enterprises and gradually introduced hard budget constraints, it provided a strong incentive for power plants to minimise fuel costs and improve the efficiency of electricity generation. The carrot was provided by abolishing the central allocation of coal, which enabled power plants to purchase coal directly from the mines at prices and qualities that better suited their own needs.

As for the increase in plant efficiency, there is some evidence that the previous system of central allocation of hard coal in Poland made the power generation system less efficient, because it obstructed plants from choosing coal qualities that were optimal with respect to the performance of their boilers. A World Bank

Figure 15.3: Poland's SO_2 emissions, 1980-94

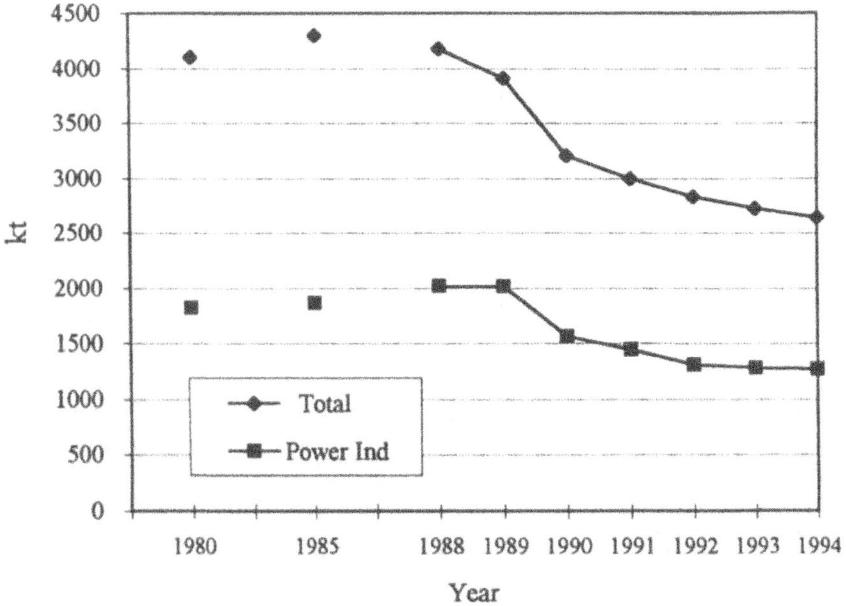

Sources: Centrum Informatyki Energetyki (1995) and Norwegian Meteorological Institute (1995)

survey of Polish industrial energy consumers in 1989 noted that plant managers complained about the delivery of hard coal of poorer quality than that for which the boilers had been designed (World Bank 1991: 50). The low-quality coal increased maintenance costs and the power plants' own consumption of energy, and reduced the efficiency of power generation. According to the Bank's estimate, at the end of the 1980s, more than 1,000 MW of power capacity were 'frozen' or underutilised in the Polish power industry because of these deficiencies, resulting in annual excess emissions of SO_2 amounting to about 400 kt. Apparently, it became possible for power plants to capture some of this 'inefficiency dividend' after the abolition of central coal allocation.

The new regulation of air pollution control introduced incentives for the power industry to reduce emissions. Like in the case of power industry restructuring, these incentives included both sticks and carrots. Stricter emission standards and reinforced environmental inspection, in combination with increased emission fees and fines, changed profoundly the working conditions for power plants. And the introduction of more rigorous procedures for obtaining licenses to operate boilers forced power plants to pay more attention to their emissions.

In several ways the power industry has adapted its behaviour to the government's stricter enforcement of environmental protection. Power plants have increased their efforts to monitor emissions in order to better manage pollution abatement.[18] Another reason for the monitoring of emission factors is that power plants want to check that they are paying the correct amount in emission fees and avoid fines.

Together with the restructuring of the power industry, the reform of air pollution control increased power plants' demand for high-quality hard coal. The easiest way for power plants to reduce emissions in the period 1988-94 was to use cleaner coal. To meet this demand, the government launched a fuel-enriching programme in the coal mining industry to reduce the content of rock and sulphur in hard coal from a selected number of coal mines (Nowicki 1991). The fall in coal consumption by other consumers after 1988 also increased the availability of high-quality coal for power plants. The improvement in the average heating value of coal for power generation demonstrates that since 1990, the power industry in fact used the opportunity to get better coal and that high-quality coal was available from the mines. As mentioned earlier, the utilisation of high-quality coal was also a way to boost the performance of power plants, which, in its turn, contributed to the lower SO_2 emissions of many plants.

The abolition of the centralised allocation of coal to power plants in 1990 enabled individual power stations to negotiate their own coal supply contracts directly with the mines. This change has created the basis for a competitive domestic market in coal supplied to the power industry. But because of considerable political opposition, the closing of unprofitable coal mines has been delayed. Subsidies from the state budget are still paid to the coal mining industry.[19]

Over a short period, Poland has changed from a static to a dynamic economy. The decentralisation of decision-making from one central planner – the state – to a growing number of independent economic actors has made it more difficult to discern the actual impact of various governmental policies on companies and other energy users. Energy use as such has not been the primary interest of policy-makers or managers. They have had other objectives, e.g. to reduce the state budget deficit by abolishing subsidies to the industry, to create a more efficient industry by lifting price controls and promote competition, or to reduce air pollution by increasing environmental taxes and improving pollution control. However, these financial, economic, and environmental policies have all significantly affected energy use.

The reform of air pollution control is particularly interesting in this context. In the view of the Ministry of Environmental Protection, the political measures that it imposed on the power industry have reduced air pollution. One indication that these measures are taken seriously is the industry's demand that emission standards and fees should be relaxed – a demand that would not be raised if there was no need to. But the reduction of SO_2 emissions can also be explained by factors that are unrelated to environmental policy. In other words, the reduction of SO_2 emissions is both the intended result of the government's political reforms, and the side-effect of the power plants' considerations and decisions in a market economy.

Prospects for Further Pollution Reductions

Poland's first reduction goal for SO_2 emissions, 30 per cent below 1980 emission levels by the year 2000, was met in 1992. Thus, during the first half of the 1990s, Polish air pollution abatement was successful with respect to this goal. However, it will be difficult and expensive to achieve continued reductions of SO_2 emissions. Sustained economic growth is likely to increase electricity consumption over the next 5-10 years, which will make it difficult to maintain SO_2 emissions at the current level. Additional improvements in coal quality and plant efficiency are not likely to compensate for increasing SO_2 emissions due to the expected growth in electricity demand.

After 1992, there has only been a marginal reduction of the power industry's emissions of sulphur dioxide. They fell by 35 per cent between 1989 and 1992 but only by 3 per cent between 1992 and 1994. To reach the reduction goal that Poland has accepted by signing the second sulphur protocol, i.e. 66 per cent of the 1980 level by 2010 – other solutions will be necessary for the power industry. Beside the installation of desulphurisation and other equipment to abate emissions, such measures may include fuel-switching from coal to cleaner sources of energy, the closing of the oldest and most inefficient plants, increased utilisation of combined heat and power production, and more efficient end-use of electricity and heat.

In the past few years, the power industry has started to prepare the installation of air pollution abatement technology at several power stations. Plant managers are apparently anticipating continued increases in emission fees. By the end of 1995, at least six larger power and CHP plants had launched investment projects to install fluidised bed combustion or desulphurisation equipment (Graczyk 1995).[20] The reform of environmental policy in Poland has made it easier for power plants to finance such investments. The national and regional environmental protection funds provide financial assistance in the form of loans and grants. The funds now play an important role in financing environmental protection and have helped boost environmental investments. Total investments in environmental protection increased by about 50 per cent between 1990 and 1994. Investments in air protection more than doubled in real terms between 1990 and 1994, and their share of total expenditures for environmental protection rose from about 30 to 44 per cent in the same period. In 1994, 36 per cent of all loans and grants given by the environmental funds were committed to air protection.

Estimates of the cost of meeting the 1998 emission standards in the Polish power industry range from 3 billion to 6 billion USD (OECD 1995: 118). Given the massive costs of desulphurisation technology in the power industry, it is important that cost-effective solutions are chosen. For example, the continuing installation of such technology at the lignite-burning power stations Belchatow and Turow seems reasonable because these two plants account for a major share of the power industry's total emissions. Together, they accounted for 39 per cent of total SO_2 emissions from the power industry and 30 per cent of its electricity generation in 1994 (Centrum Informatyki Energetyki 1995). None of the stations complied with the 1998 emission standards for sulphur dioxide. Belchatow was commissioned in the early 1980s and is one of Poland's newest power plants.

However, in the case of similar projects at other power plants, it may be less clear whether they are cost-effective with respect to the abatement costs, the technology chosen, and the age of the units. Such project proposals must therefore be closely examined and evaluated by the power industry and the environmental funds that contribute financial assistance.

Another important issue is whether the present system of public financing of environmental protection can be improved. As noted earlier, the revenues from environmental fees and fines are used by the national and regional environmental funds for investments in pollution abatement. The power industry, which is one of the major contributors to these funds, argues that it is paying more in fees and fines than it gets back in the form of loans and grants, and is attempting to influence the government to allocate a larger share of environmental funds for investments in the industry. It is possible that these demands will be met in one way or another. The power industry's participation in environmental protection sets an example for other branches of industry, so it is important for the government that power companies continue to pay environmental taxes. On the other hand, if an exception is made for the power industry, it give rise to similar demands from other sectors of the economy.

Continued monitoring of air quality and emissions, as well as improved enforcement of environmental protection will be crucial for the success of

Poland's ambitious air pollution abatement programme. The power industry argues that the present procedure for obtaining licenses and controlling emissions from each individual boiler rather than the whole plant is inflexible. It obstructs power plants from choosing cost-effective solutions for reducing their emissions of SO_2 and other pollutants. The industry has proposed a revision of the system of air pollution control in order to reduce its monitoring and abatement costs. Negotiations on how such adjustments could be made have started between representatives of the power industry and the Ministry of Environmental Protection.[21]

Trends in the Eastern Baltic Region

The 1990s have so far been a period of profoundly changing conditions for energy use in the Baltic region. The changes have been particularly dramatic in the eastern part of the region. Several factors are affecting the region's energy production and consumption.

One of them is the rate of economic growth. In Poland, after several years of declining energy use in the early 1990s, energy use is slowly increasing again as a result of growing economic activity. Poland's TPES is expected to grow by an annual rate of 2.5 per cent for the remainder of the 1990s. Even at this growth rate, Poland will still use less energy in 2000 than it did in 1988. In the case of the Baltic states, Belarus and Russia, the energy consumption will probably not reach the 1990 level before 2005. However, such forecasts are difficult to make. As noted, future energy consumption depends not only on the rate of economic growth, but also on structural changes and changes in energy intensity in various sectors of the economy. Decentralisation and privatisation have reduced the number of large state-owned enterprises and increased the number of small and medium-sized privately owned companies. At the same time, structural change toward less energy-intensive subsectors within the Polish industry continues.

The positive side of these developments is that they allow time for a policy reorientation from the short term to the long term. So far, the focus has been on securing energy supplies, especially in Estonia, Latvia and Lithuania. This is understandable, but decision-makers now urgently need to learn how the demand for energy is changing as a result of continuing structural changes in their economies.

Another important factor is the rising energy prices in Central and Eastern Europe. More expensive fuel imports and pricing reforms have led to a drastic increase in energy prices in Poland, the Baltic states and Russia. Households, which used to pay less than industry for their energy, are now charged more. Direct state subsidies have been phased out for all energy industries except district heating. For people in Western Europe it may be hard to understand the extreme hardships which the sudden increases in energy prices have imposed on Eastern European households. In the winter, costs of heating, hot water and electricity for a normal household in the Baltic republics may now account for up to a half of its monthly income. The corresponding costs for a household in Scandinavia are typically 5-10 per cent.

Increasing energy costs have become a serious social problem in the Baltic republics and Russia. Many households have difficulties paying their energy bills. Electricity and gas distribution companies and district heating companies have accumulated substantial debts owed by both households and industrial consumers. The non-payment of customers reduces the energy companies' revenues and makes it difficult for them to finance necessary investments in equipment for energy conversion and distribution.

However, the combination of economic reform, rationalisation of production and rising energy prices is having a positive effect on the efficiency of energy use. Poland's energy use per GDP fell by almost 20 percent between 1987 and 1993. The improved energy efficiency is partly the result of structural change. The growth of privately owned industry has led to a shift from heavy industry to less energy-consuming manufacturing and services.

The change in economic activity is also being accompanied by structural change. While the importance of industry in the energy economy will fall, as the shift from manufacturing toward services continues, the share of transportation in total energy consumption is likely to increase, mainly as a result of the growing number of private cars. The shift in economic structure in Poland and other former CPEs is gradually making them less energy-intensive. This process is further accelerated by the introduction of more energy-efficient technologies and the rationalisation and reorganisation of industry.

In the residential and services sectors, higher energy prices will motivate energy efficiency measures, but numerous barriers exist that will slow progress. Examples are lack of metering and frequent billing, unclear ownership rules and division of responsibilities for maintenance of buildings, and lack of financing. To find ways to overcome these barriers, so the potential for energy efficiency may be realised, is a critical task for managers and policy-makers.

Environmental concerns are resulting in stricter regulation of the energy industry both in Eastern and Western Europe. In many countries, the price of energy produced by fossil fuels typically excludes the environmental costs of using these fuels. Stricter environmental standards will increase the pollution abatement costs for power plants burning fossil fuels.

The development in Estonia, Latvia, Lithuania and Russia in the 1990s is similar to that in Poland. Total emissions have dropped markedly as a result of falling energy demand and reduced consumption of fossil fuels. However, it remains to be seen if these countries will be successful in controlling their emissions. Most power plants and other large emitters in Eastern Europe still lack equipment to control sulphur dioxide emissions. They also lack the necessary financial resources to invest in such equipment.

Other important means to further reduce air pollution in the Baltic region are improved energy efficiency and the switching from fossil fuels to less polluting energy sources, such as biofuels, wind and hydro power and natural gas. There are several institutional barriers that complicate the implementation of energy efficiency. Mixed ownership and unclear responsibilities for the maintenance of residential buildings often discourage the residents from investing in energy-saving equipment. There is also an information problem. Energy consumers are often not aware of the possibilities of making their energy use more efficient. Information campaigns in schools and at work might be helpful in presenting what options are available for reducing energy costs at home. Local demonstration projects, such as the renovation of residential buildings, are also important in order to explain the benefits of energy efficiency to the local population..

As regards renewable energy sources, an important barrier is the difficulty for small, independent energy producers to compete with the established energy companies. Several issues have to be resolved to give independent producers a strong and secure position in relation to larger producers so they can compete on equal terms. One issue is how the prices of electricity and heat are regulated. Other crucial questions are that the independent producers have free or cheap access to power grids, and that they have the same tax benefits as other producers of energy. For example, small district heat producers in Estonia and Latvia have recently faced increased competition from their national gas companies, which offer the households imported gas for heating at cheaper rates than the heat produced locally. In those cases where the district heat is produced from biomass, a switch to gas would be against the interests of the Estonian and Latvian governments, who want to reduce the dependence on imported fuels. Paradoxically, the same governments are owners of the national gas companies.

A large-scale introduction of renewable energy in the Baltic region requires that the external costs generated by the environmental impact be included in the price of fossil fuels. Environmental taxes on emissions of carbon dioxide or acidifying air pollutants will therefore be important to promote the utilisation of renewables.

Notes

1 Energy intensity refers to the amount of energy used for the service delivered, e.g. value added in manufacturing or km travelled in transportation. Thus, when the energy intensity of an activity decreases, its energy efficiency improves.

2 For a discussion of how structural and technological change affects energy intensity in industrialised countries, see Schipper et al. (1992). Long-term energy intensity trends in several countries are analysed in Nilsson (1993).

3 The concept of soft budget constraints, i.e. enterprises are compensated for increased costs by state subsidies and are therefore not forced to become more efficient, was introduced by the Hungarian economist János Kornai (Kornai 1986: 3-30).

4 Author's calculations based on data in National Accounts 1960-86 (OECD 1988, Vol.1: 16 f. and 150 f.). GDP at purchasing power parities and 1980 prices.

5 Comparing energy/GDP ratios of different countries is difficult. National energy statistics do not necessarily cover all energy consumption. Similarly, GDP data may exclude undocumented economic activity. GDP comparisons between countries which are diverse with

respect to climate, the type of economic system, and income levels are also problematic. For a discussion of methodological difficulties in comparing GDP levels of market and centrally planned economies, see Salay et al. (1993: 178).

6 For a valuable discussion of the reasons for environmental policy failure in the CPEs, see Zylicz (1994).

7 Final energy consumption excludes losses in energy conversion and distribution, e.g. in refineries, power stations and transmission lines.

8 Author's calculations based on International Energy Agency (1993-94).

9 Poland's air quality standards are stricter than equivalent standards applied in the European Union or the guidelines of the World Health Organisation. For example, concentrations of particulates were above national standards in nearly all of Poland's voivodships between 1990 and 1992, but in only half of them would the EU standards have been exceeded.

10 The higher figure is official data from the National Statistical Office of Poland submitted to the Economic Commission of Europe's European Monitoring and Evaluation Program (EMEP) and published in *EMEP/MSC-W Report* No 1/95 by the Norwegian Meteorological Institute. It is apparently based on sector fuel consumption and the assumed sulfur content of fuels used. The lower figure is from an emission inventory report made by a research group at the International Institute for Applied Systems Analysis (Klimont et al. 1993). The methodology used by the research group is described on pages 17-19 in the report.

11 The countries are Austria, Croatia, the Czech Republic, Italy, Hungary, Poland, Slovakia and Slovenia.

12 Poland's new environmental policy, its objectives and measures are described in Ministry of Environmental Protection, Natural Resources and Forestry (1991). See also Nowicki (1993) and Zylicz (1994).

13 This ordinance replaced an earlier ordinance on air pollution regulation from 1980.

14 Including public power plants, CHPs, heat-only boilers (HOBs), industrial auto producers and various small HOBs with a capacity above 0.2 MW.

15 For a background on the Convention on Long Range Transboundary Air Pollution and the sulfur protocols, see *Acid News* (1994a: 1 and 11-14).

16 By the end of 1996, Poland had still not ratified the second sulfur protocol.

17 Through the year 1990, the data on SO_2 emissions etc. also include public heat-only boilers (HOBs). In the period 1988-90, HOBs accounted for about 2 per cent of total SO_2 emissions from the power industry.

18 Personal communication from staff at Energopomiar, a Polish company specialising in service and maintenance of power stations, June 1993. This company experienced a significant increase in assignments from power plants including monitoring and control of air pollution after 1990.

19 For an analysis of the effects of the comprehensive restructuring on the Polish hard coal industry, see Radetzki (1994).

20 They include the two largest lignite-burning power plants, Turów and Belchatów, and several hard-coal-burning plants, among them Rybnik, Skawina, Jaworzno and Opole.

21 Personal communications from Polish Power Grid Company and Ministry of Environmental Protection, Warsaw, October 1995.

References

Acid News (1994a). No 1.

Acid News (1994b). No 4.

Acid News (1995). No 5.

Bethkenhagen, J. (1987). 'The Energy Economy and its Intertwining with CMEA' in *Rat für gegenseitige Wirtschaftshilfe: Strukturen und Probleme.* Bonn, Ostkolleg der Bundeszentrale für politische Bildung.

Centrum Informatyki Energetyki (1995). *EMITOR 1994: Emisja zanieczyszczen srodowiska w elektrowniach i elektroceplowniach zawodowych* (EMITOR 1994: Emission of Atmospheric Pollutants in Public Power and CHP Plants). Warsaw.

Dziennik Ustaw Rzeczypospolitej Polskiej (1990). No 15. Warsaw.

Dziennik Ustaw Rzeczypospolitej Polskiej (1991). No 77. Warsaw.

Dziennik Ustaw Rzeczypospolitej Polskiej (1995). No 153. Warsaw.

The Economist (1985). 'Comecon Survey.' 20 April.

Glowny Urzad Statystyczny (1995). *Ochrona Srodowiska 1995*. Warsaw.

Graczyk, A. (1995). 'Regulacja zanieczyszczen powietrza atmosferycznego a reformowanie polskiej elektroenergetyki' (Regulation of Atmospheric Air Pollution and Reform of the Polish Power Industry), *Energetyka*:9, pages 396-98.

IEA (International Energy Agency) (1993-1994). *Energy Prices and Taxes*. Paris. Various issues.

IEA (1994). *Electricity in European Economies in Transition*. Paris.

Klimont, Z., Amann, M., Cofala, J., Gyarfas, F., Klaassen, G. and Schöpp, W. (1993). *Emission of Air Pollutants in the Region of the Central European Initiative – 1988*. Laxenburg, International Institute of Applied Systems Analysis.

Kornai, J. (1986). 'The Soft Budget Constraint,' *Kyklos*:39, pages 3-30.

Ministry of Environmental Protection, Natural Resources and Forestry (1991). *Environment in Poland: Issues and Solutions*. Warsaw.

Nilsson, L. (1993). 'Energy Intensity Trend in 31 Industrialized and Developing Countries 1950-1988,' *Energy – the International Journal*:18, No 4, pages 309-322.

Norwegian Meteorological Institute (1995). *EMEP/MSC-W Report*:1. Oslo.

Nowicki, M. (1991). 'Power clean-up envisaged,' *Acid News*:1.

Nowicki, M. (1993). *Environment in Poland: Issues and Solutions*. Dordrecht, Kluwer Academic Press.

OECD (1988). *National Accounts 1960-1986*. Vol.1. Paris.

OECD (1995). *Environmental Performance Reviews: Poland*. Paris.

Pasierb, S. (1992). 'Review of Energy and Environmental Policies in Poland.' Report presented at the conference 'Energy and Environment in European Economics in Transition,' Prague, 17-19 June.

Radetzki, M. 1994. 'Poland's Hard Coal Industry: Prospects after Completed Restructuring,' *SNS Occasional Papers*:58, Stockholm, SNS.

Salay, J. (1991). *Östeuropas miljö: problem och framtidsutsikter*. Stockholm, Naturia.

Salay, J., Fenhann, J., Jaanimägi, K. and Kristoferson, L. (1993). 'Energy and Environment in the Baltic States,' *Annual Review of Energy and the Environment 1993*:18, pages 169-216.

Schipper, L., Meyers, S. with Grubb, M., Chadwick, M. and Kristoferson, L. (1992). *World Energy: Building a Sustainable Future*. Stockholm, Stockholm Environment Institute.

World Bank (1991). *Poland: Energy Market Development*. Washington.

Zylicz, T. (1992). *Environmental Taxes in Poland*. Working paper. Stockholm, Beijer International Institute of Ecological Economics.

Zylicz, T. (1994). 'Implementing Environmental Policies in Central and Eastern Europe' in Jansson, A.-M., Folke, C., Constanza. R. and Hammer. M. (eds.). *Investing in Natural Capital: The Economic Perspective*. Washington, D.C, Island Press.

16 The New Berlin: Towards the Sustainable Capital?

Christof Ellger and Kai Richter

Introduction

Berlin is undergoing a fundamental transformation process in terms of urban functions and economic base. This process is associated with profound changes in the built environment and the physical-ecological situation.

The transformation has three aspects: First, the political geography of Berlin is changing from a divided city with West Berlin forming a West German exclave surrounded by East German territory, to re-unification as one city which is also a Land (i.e. a Federal state). Around Berlin now lies the Land of Brandenburg – one of the five new East German Länder (see Figure 16.1). Secondly, profound socio-economic change is associated with the incorporation of former East Germany into the Federal Republic and its social system, which implies a change from 'real socialism' to a capitalist market economy. This is accompanied by a change in West Berlin's function from being a Western bridgehead and showcase supported by enormous funds from the West, to a more 'normal' city with normal processes of urban development, such as tertiarisation of central areas, selective gentrification and social decline. Thirdly, Berlin will have a new role as the future capital and government centre of unified Germany, which is reshaping the face of the city in a very fundamental way.

As with the Baltic Sea region as a whole, Berlin is – on a microspatial scale – faced with problems of East-West integration, which will have socio-economic as well as ecological implications. In that sense, Berlin is an interesting case study in the context of the Baltic Sea region.

Since the end of the nineteenth century, and especially during the 1920s, Berlin had become one of the largest, most lively and most modern urban centres in the world. With its dense networks of urban infrastructure (roads, railways, underground lines, telephone lines and even a pneumatic tubular postal system through the inner city), it acquired the nickname of 'fastest city in the world' and functioned as an advanced innovation centre in various fields of industry and cultural life. After fascist rule and the war – planned and started in Berlin – the city was divided and reduced to being a subsidised outpost of the West, on the one hand, and the capital of one of the smaller states of the Eastern bloc, on the other.

With its new position as German capital, the city and its region are expecting changes that will profoundly affect the city's environment. Infrastructure, such as the transport system, has to be modernised, expanded and prepared for a future context; new business functions and new housing needs must be accommodated in the urban structure. With all these changes occurring, Berlin has a unique chance to consider ecological necessities and targets as part of the grand project of developing into a metropolis of the twenty-first century.

Despite its new status as capital, the city will still have to find its future role. In many respects – population dynamics, employment, business control, communal financial resources – this role will not be very powerful. Berlin's centrality,

Figure 16.1: Berlin and Brandenburg, population 1990-96, millions

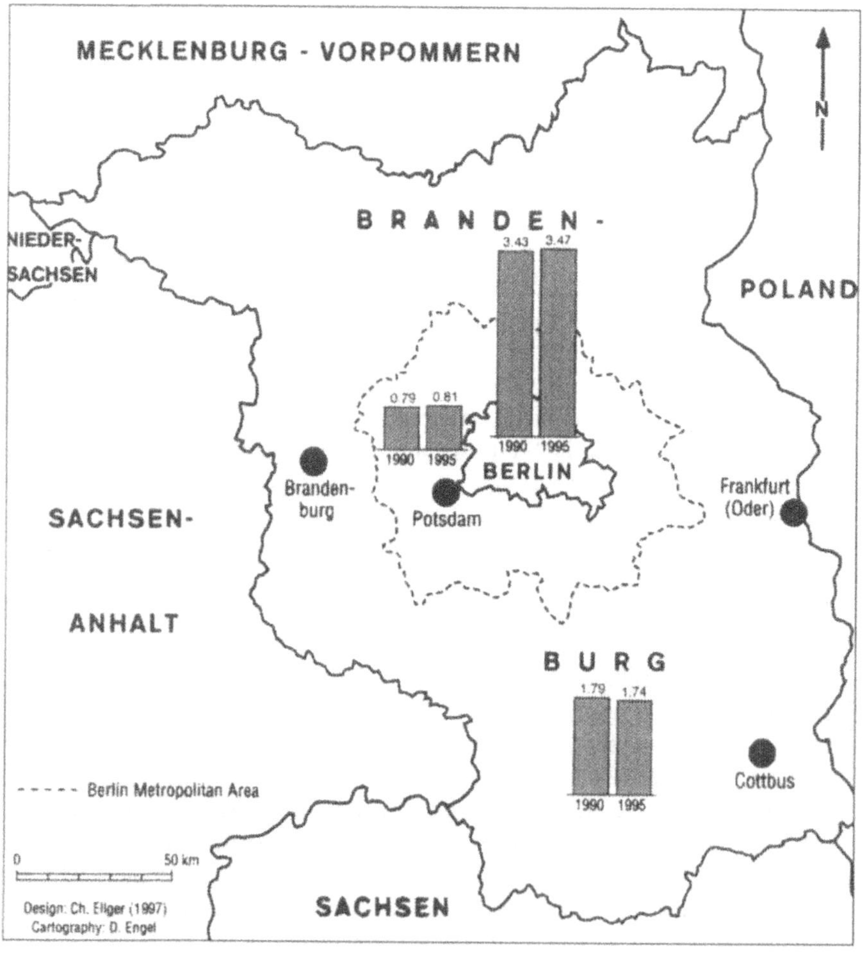

including its centrality for the Baltic Sea region, will therefore be rather limited. As a matter of fact, problems of urban economic development and management as well as urban finance are overwhelming at present. In the long run, however, slow growth may perhaps advance sustainable development in the wider region if the increasing social problems can be dealt with.

Berlin has inherited an urban structure which is most interesting and in many respects environmentally advantageous. There are a number of 'sustainability assets' in the urban tradition of Berlin which deserve consideration and conservation. Above all, the city still greatly benefits from an excellent public transport infrastructure, mainly set up during the inter-war years. It also posses a largely well-kept 'contained city,' which has come down to us as a result of the harsh geopolitical boundary around West Berlin and the restrained suburbanisation in and around East Berlin during the decades of division. It is consequently a dense metropolis with a very clear-cut urban edge, and within short distances people have access to a highly diversified pattern of multi-functional areas.

From an ecological point of view, the decisive question is whether the chances of a sustainable approach to metropolitan development are used or wasted. The politicians of the Senat, the Berlin city state government – since 1991 a 'great coalition' of the Christian Democrats and Social Democrats with a centre-right orientation – have constantly been proclaiming the importance of sustainability to Berlin's urban development. Berlin signed the climate alliance in 1991 and the Aalborg Charter (Charter of European Cities and Towns Towards Sustainability) in 1994. The city hosted the UN climate summit in the spring 1995 and another big OECD Conference on Sustainable Cities in 1996. But it remains to be seen whether these official events are followed by substantive political moves in Berlin. In addition, the continuing administrative division of the Berlin region into two Federal states makes planning in general and planning for sustainability in particular all the more difficult. In May 1996, an attempt to unite Berlin with the surrounding state of Brandenburg failed when a majority in Brandenburg (not in Berlin!) voted against an amalgamation of the two states in a referendum.

'Sustainable' is not simply a rephrasing of 'ecological' or 'environmental' since the Rio Conference of 1992, but stands for a highly demanding concept: man-made material flows and metabolism must be subjected to natural regeneration rates (for renewable resources) and to the preservation of natural capital (for non-renewable resources), in combination with efforts towards overcoming the fundamentally unjust relations on earth. Within the framework of the Agenda 21 process, sustainability is supposed to be approached both through international and national action and through local initiatives.

Like many other towns, but perhaps a little bit late, Berlin is only just beginning to set up a local Agenda 21 process to assess the problems and degree of unsustainability and to develop solutions. Activities first started in the city's 23 districts, where local environmental initiatives and district administrators work together. At the city-wide level, a wide range of NGOs have recently founded BLUE 21 (Berliner Landesarbeitsgemeinschaft Umwelt und Entwicklung), which is going to draw up a full-scale assessment of the environmental and development impact of the metropolis, trying to examine in particular non-local effects of Berlin's material turnover.

Berlin's planning for sustainability may draw on a considerable concentration of know-how in the field of urban ecology, which enables the city to compete on a world-wide scale. Among its many highly competent public institutions are the Federal Environmental Agency, which is, however, destined to move to Dessau in Saxony-Anhalt, the European Academy for the Urban Environment, the German Institute of Urban Affairs and university departments in various fields. Berlin also boasts a considerable number of private institutes with excellent reputations in fields such as transport and urban planning as well as strong grass-root groups involved in environmental issues.

The Economic and Demographic Situation in the 1990s

With unification and the euphoria of 1989 came predictions of vast increases in population as well as economic growth. It was expected that the metropolitan area with its roughly 4 million inhabitants would double by 2010.

So far, nothing of the kind has materialised. On the contrary, Berlin's population growth has been zero or even slightly negative over the last three years following a small increase which peaked at 3.475 million inhabitants in 1993 (see Figure 16.1). To some extent, non-German immigrants have counterbalanced Berlin's natural population loss, which is due to the city's very high proportion of old people and a death rate substantially exceeding the birth rate. However, large-scale in-migration from other parts of Germany or from abroad has not set in.

The surrounding area, i.e. the Brandenburg part of the Berlin metropolitan area, shows a small population increase due to some suburban development. Here the population has risen from 787,000 in 1990 to about 806,000 in 1995, but the increase does not come anywhere near the population figures of the 1930s. The rest of Brandenburg, sparsely populated for centuries, has lost inhabitants since 1990, accentuating the harsh contrast between centre and periphery in the Berlin-Brandenburg space: Population density in Berlin is 3905 inhabitants per km2, in the suburban fringe, i.e. the rest of the Berlin metropolitan area, the density is 180, and in outer Brandenburg it is down to 69. Again these figures show the degree of containment that still influences the population distribution in the Berlin region.

One reason for the non-existent in-migration boom must be sought in the employment situation, which is severe indeed (see Table 16.1). De-industrialisation is substantial, and a weak increase in service functions such as banking and producer services cannot make up for losses in manufacturing as well as retailing employment. This, of course, aggravates social polarisation. In East Berlin, manufacturing has experienced a dramatic break-down both in terms of employment and value added. But even in West Berlin, the unstable industrial structure of the 'island times' is not surviving the harsh winds of change. In March 1997, more than 260,000 inhabitants (15 per cent of the labour force and 7 per cent of the total population) are registered as unemployed.

Table 16.1: Employment in Berlin, 1991-95, in thousands

	1991	1995
Agriculture, forestry	11.1	11.4
Manufacturing, construction	482.5	371
Trade, transport	339.5	289.1
Other services	375.3	423.8
State, organisations	458.8	417
Total	1667.3	1512.3

Source: Senatsverwaltung für Wirtschaft und Betriebe

Nevertheless, growth anticipation remains strong as the move of the Federal parliament and government from Bonn to Berlin, now envisaged for the years 1999 and 2000, will stimulate new initiative. But a good deal of Federal administration will remain in Bonn, and other institutions will have to leave Berlin in recompense for its new role as government centre. It is very improbable that many corporate headquarters will move to Berlin at the expense of the now dominant control centres of Düsseldorf, Frankfurt, Munich, Hamburg, Essen, Stuttgart and Cologne, to mention only the most important. The corporate influx will be even slighter from other European centres.

This most plausible scenario, which is slow growth or even stagnation and decline in many sectors, will certainly mean future economic and fiscal problems. On the other hand, it may reduce some of the anticipated stress on the environment.

The Environmental Situation Today

A considerable reduction in the level of air pollution can be registered over the last 20 years, and especially so since the unification. As the world's leading brown coal (lignite) producer and user, the German Democratic Republic (GDR) was heavily affected by pollutants emitted by power stations and individual fireplaces. But West Berlin, too, relied very much on coal. Coal-fired stoves have always been typical of the extensive residential areas which date from the time of Berlin's big building boom between 1880 and 1910.

High levels of sulphur dioxide as well as dust concentration have characterised Berlin's air quality – on both sides of the wall. This was especially pronounced during the late 1980s, when the GDR increased the burning of its brown coal and brown coal products dramatically in a desperate attempt to save currency reserves.

Smog became a problem which necessitated restrictions on the use of cars and other energy processing units in West Berlin during winter smog alerts. This policy was scrapped in 1995. In East Berlin, the existence of a pollution problem was officially denied.

To a great extent, coal and brown coal have now been substituted by oil and natural gas or the use of heat from power stations. And, of course, industrial decay and the closure of factories have greatly contributed to a reduction of energy turnover and pollution in the Berlin region. In addition, power stations and heating centres are now being equipped with filter technology. Emissions of sulphur dioxide have consequently gone down to 15 per cent of the figures of the mid-70s, and measured dust levels have decreased by about 50 per cent between 1985 and 1995 (Senatsverwaltung 1997).

It becomes evident that total energy consumption as well as energy-related emissions of carbon dioxide – the 'climate gas' – reached a peak in the late 1980s, in fact in 1987. For that year, carbon dioxide emissions in Berlin are estimated at 31.9 million tonnes. Between 1987 and 1995, they have decreased by about 9 per cent to approximately 29 million tonnes, with strong oscillations, however, mainly due to differing weather conditions during the last few years.

With 1987 as the base year for the projected reduction of CO_2 emissions by 25 per cent by the year 2010, the aims set by the Berlin government with regard to its contribution to global climate protection do not appear very ambitious. A good deal of the work has already been done simply by the break-down of large parts of the Berlin-based manufacturing production, and by exchanging coal for other fuels. Undeniably, however, these developments have improved the environment considerably.

Nitrogen oxides are now the foremost problem in air pollution, together with CO and organic substances. They are mainly emitted by cars. Although technology has made cars much cleaner, and most of the old GDR cars (not so much the lorries) have disappeared from Berlin roads by now, the vast increase in transport volume (in kilometres per year) is virtually annihilating the progress in power station and motor engine technology. In addition, transport emissions are near the ground, affecting densely used parts of the urban fabric where human interaction is taking place. Along roughly 70 per cent of all major roads in the inner city, the EU orientation figure of 135µg/m3 for the NOx content is exceeded (Senatsverwaltung 1992).

With regard to water resources, Berlin is in a highly advantaged position. The city and parts of its region are built on a large water store of gravel sediments in the glacial valley (*Urstromtal*) of the river Spree. Therefore Berlin does not depend on long-distance water transport like most other urban agglomerations in Central Europe. More than half of the water raised for use in Berlin is near-surface water (Reichert 1994). This source needs constant renewal of its water reserves, which can be slack in summer, and depends heavily on water pumped from the brown coal mining district of Niederlausitz, further upstream. In addition, this method of freshwater production is, of course, very sensitive to toxic intakes so that waterworks in the vicinity of industrial premises or motor boat concentrations are constantly threatened by potential pollution.

The situation of the soil is a great problem, with large areas contaminated and a generally high degree of built-up and cemented urban land. The Berlin register for contaminated plots of land now cites about 5000 smaller or larger areas – an enormous task for decontamination and sanitation. And the problem is worse in many areas of Brandenburg, which had to bear the burden of the majority of military areas in East Germany. Many of them have suffered massively from oil and chemical pollution.

The amount of solid waste has actually decreased over the last few years, again predominantly in industry and business. Most of the refuse is dumped on waste tips in surrounding Brandenburg. This is a continuation of the bad practice set up in the times of the division, when the GDR received hard currency in exchange for relieving West Berlin of its waste.

Roughly a quarter of household and household-like waste is burnt in incinerators, which, in turn, produce aerial emissions. Plans for two new incinerators have been laid but are not carried forth at the moment, as the waste quantities, ironically enough, are not sufficient to fulfil the waste-dumping contracts with the Brandenburg waste tips.

The introduction of separate waste-collection schemes for dry-packaging material in the households, introduced on a national basis in Germany, has so far failed to reduce the volume of waste it was supposed to do.

For noise, too, traffic is the most important source. Emissions along major inner-urban roads are, again, drastically unhealthy. Traffic arteries also transect important recreation and natural areas on the outskirts. And there are still two inner-urban airports which impose heavy noise pollution on surrounding residential and industrial areas.

Major Determinants of 'Unsustainability' and Arenas of Action

Any full-scale assessment, be it qualitative or quantitative, of Berlin's distance from a sustainable situation is, of course, a very ambitious project. Nevertheless, the initiatives united in BLUE 21 will attempt an in-depth analysis, where all societal arenas are subjected to an examination of their ecological and world developmental impacts (Agenda 21, 1997). For the moment, only some summarising notes and selected sectoral glimpses on the sustainability question in Berlin can be presented.

With de-industrialisation and improvements in both heating and process energy supply for commercial users as well as households, transport is now the most important source of pollution and a dominant arena of action. In the context of urban structure and current spatial processes, and tightly combined to transport problems, urban sprawl is a second important facet of change in the

Berlin region. In addition, energy is wasted most in inefficient buildings, which means that ecological building and planning are also important in introducing a more sustainable metropolis.

Transport

The typical East German cars, Trabant and Wartburg, have practically vanished from Berlin streets. But it is not only the new availability of western cars which has led to a massive increase in traffic. The rediscovery of inner-urban and hinterland connections and the transport requirements of the 'service city,' reinforced by the role as prospective government centre, both strengthen this trend. This concerns passenger traffic as well as goods traffic, both on the inner-urban and on the inter-urban scale. Overall car traffic volume in West Berlin alone increased by 74 per cent between 1971 and 1993 (Senatsverwaltung, Umweltatlas 1996).

Despite Berlin's great heritage of urban public transport infrastructure, despite the underground (U-Bahn), the regional electrified railway (S-Bahn), trams (which, however, survived only in East Berlin) and buses, the dominance of individual car transport within the city is unchallenged. Based on the generous layout of the Prussian boulevards, car traffic was encouraged not only in West Berlin (whose poor 'imprisoned' inhabitants could not possibly be prevented from persistent use of their beloved cars) but also in East Berlin (where avenues where built that could never have been filled by 'Trabbis'). As a result, the modal split in Berlin leans heavily towards individual car transport instead of public collectivised means of transport. The relation between individual motorised transport and collective motorised transport is 60:40 in the inner city and 66:34 on the outskirts – not counting non-motorised modes of transport like pedestrian traffic or bicycles (Kutter 1994).

Although it is the express aim of the Berlin government to create a transport structure in the inner city of 80 per cent public and 20 per cent private transport, it does not look at all likely that this target will be met or that the burden of motorcars in the inner city will be relieved. On the contrary, new road construction ranks high among investment projects (see Figure 16.2).

In the inner city, a series of thoroughfares has been designated as an inner orbital road; as an important transect of this orbital road link, Oberbaumbrücke, the bridge over the upper river Spree, has recently been reconstructed and dedicated to motorcar traffic.

In addition, the motorway ring parallel to the railway ring is currently being expanded, and a new radial motorway will reach the inner city from the southeast, also linking the airport of Schönefeld with the city centre. All these measures will invite more car traffic into the central area. Most problematic, however, is the Tiergarten tunnel, a four-lane road tunnel designed for roughly 60,000 cars per day, which will bring car traffic right into the central area, creating great problems for the adjoining city quarters north and south of the tunnel.

Construction of more parking facilities in central areas, too, will further

Figure 16.2: Berlin's built-up area and major transport projects

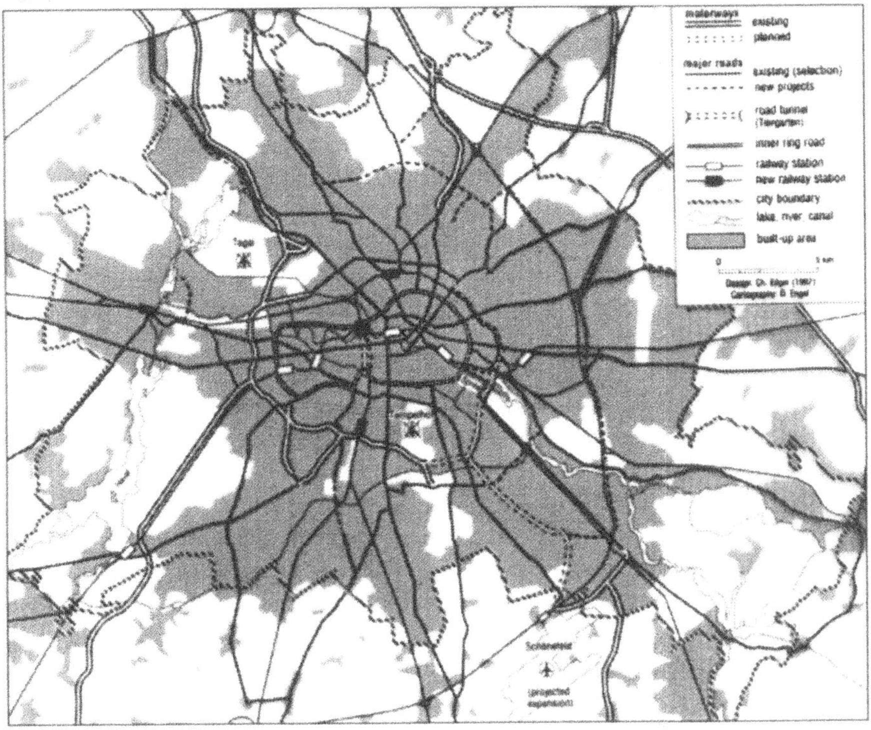

encourage car traffic. For decades Berlin enjoyed free parking. It now must be paid for in central areas, but pay parking schemes have so far increased the turnover of parking lots and encouraged the use of cars even further. All this will definitely lead to serious congestion in the near future – and only very indirectly to the realisation of something like the envisaged modal split.

More lanes reserved for buses, trams and bicycles have been promised for a number of years now, but so far very little has happened. Reconstruction of the S-Bahn network is slow, too. The circular line, which could become an excellent backbone for inner city traffic, is not reconstructed yet, nor are several radial connections.

Most of the money which goes into public transport infrastructure is destined for long-distance inter-urban traffic, culminating in a new railway station right in the city centre and in a new international airport as an enlargement of the existing airport at Schönefeld.

Instead of a decentralised model, with several railway stations for long-distance travelling, reviving the historic situation of pre-war times, a new grand central station is going to be built near the future government centre. This will link existing east-west traffic with a new north-south axis, to be built as a tunnel and also giving regional railway access to the largest new development site, the

Potsdamer Platz. Critics point to the heavy stress which will be put on this central 'government station' itself as well as the transport facilities leaving from there. An estimated 250,000 passengers per day will be directed right through the centre of town.

The logic of the central station, of course, lies in the offer of long-distance interconnections. However, passengers actually changing trains in Berlin will constitute only roughly 5 per cent of all users, because the origin or destination of most passengers will be a place within the Berlin region. On the other hand, the new station will certainly constitute a beautiful symbol for the future of rail transport in Europe. In addition, the important railway lines leading to and from Berlin are currently being renovated and expanded, among them a new high-speed line to Hannover and the Ruhr area.

Planning is under way for the 'Transrapid' – the magnetic high-speed system which shall, as a pilot and demonstration project, link Germany's two largest cities, Berlin and Hamburg. The project is scheduled to be completed by the year 2005, with a projected travelling speed of 400 km/h.

The Transrapid is much less a project of transport policy than a vehicle of industrial policy. It would be much cheaper and much more economical to expand existing railway connections to a high-speed link from Berlin to Hamburg – and hardly much slower in the end than the Transrapid. The intention is to demonstrate that the Transrapid will work and to attract foreign buyers. The system has some interesting aspects. Unlike the traditional railway system, the engine is part of the track and not of the moving vehicle, which saves energy during operation. But with the speed envisaged, the energy requirements are not lower than for advanced railway solutions.

Berlin's new role as government city as well as transport hub of east-central Europe will be further underlined by the development of a new international airport, replacing the two existing inner-city airports of Tempelhof and Tegel. After a long discussion, the existing airport site at Schönefeld was chosen as location. It is situated rather close to the city, in contrast to other potential sites further out in the southern Brandenburg periphery. The enlarged airport will relieve those inner city areas which are now suffering from air traffic to and from Tegel and Tempelhof, but bring more stress to the suburban south-east.

Finally, there are plan to expand the waterways to and from Berlin. Although, in theory, inland waterways may constitute an ecologically sound means of transport for bulk goods, there are vast problems. Particularly worrying is the destruction of unique fluvial ecosystems in the Havel transect west of Berlin, where the still near-natural river is transformed into a kind of canal, with artificial bed and increased flow speed.

It seems obvious from the number of parallel development schemes for transport that one major motive is to pump investment funds into the construction industry. This observation is certainly also relevant for public transport development within the city. For instance, the vastly expensive expansion of the underground system is preferred to a much less costly upgrading of the tram system.

The overwhelming role of the large-scale transport projects leaves little space for alternative ideas and projects. This is a great pity, because there are some very interesting and necessary initiatives. Among them is the car-sharing movement, which has a stronghold in Berlin: 'Stattauto' is the oldest and largest car-sharing institution in Germany. In spring of 1997, 3,200 people are sharing 140 motor vehicles, and membership growth is fast. With the opportunity of having a car when they really need it, participants can optimise their individual modal split, which reduces car ownership figures as well as car transport volumes. Stattauto estimates that each of its cars replaces five private cars and 42,500 car-kilometres per year.

The proportion of carless households is very high. Berlin still has considerably less motorised vehicles per inhabitants (0.403 in 1994, according to Kraftfahrtbundesamt) than any other large city in Germany, for instance Frankfurt (0.499) or Munich (0.563), and even less than the urban centres of eastern Germany, Leipzig (0.422) and Dresden (0.464). This is partly due to the economic structure of the city, with the overall importance of the public sector and administrative functions. But it is also a consequence of generally shorter routes to all kinds of facilities in the densely built-up and functionally mixed urban environment. This might be further strengthened through a policy in favour of 'transport avoidance,' i.e. a policy which would reduce the need to increase spatial interaction and distances and promote environment-friendly means of transport and discourage use of the private car.

The transport conflict is not only between different interest groups and lifestyles but also between political interests and opposing city government departments. The administration of environment and urban planning, currently held by the Social Democrats, is more dedicated to sustainability, whereas the transport department, held by the Christian Democrats and more in line with traditional technocratic approaches to transport policy, very much favours the use of the private car.

Urban Sprawl: The End of the Contained City

During the times of the division, Berlin remained a city with no or very little suburbanisation. In West Berlin, urban sprawl was blocked by the Wall. In East Berlin, state decisions on the use of land like the large-scale housing projects in Marzahn, Hohenschönhausen and Hellersdorf, but also in many inner city areas like Lichtenberg, led to the urban containment that is so specific to the city region's present-day situation.

This densely used and clearly demarcated city region with a decentralised structure, organised in 'cells,' each with a high degree of functional mix might have been an excellent starting-point for implementing sustainability.

Under the new socio-economic conditions, however, suburbanisation of urban functions and urban sprawl set in, and with this, functional segregation in the whole urban texture. Whereas suburban communal councils as well as investors and developers could start planning immediately after the fall of the

Wall and the unification, it took a number of years to establish state and regional planning to control land use changes in the suburban fringe and to restrict development of the historical railway axes linking Berlin and the central places of suburbia. The joint planning authority for the states of Berlin and Brandenburg did not take up its job before the beginning of 1996.

Of course, the local governments of the communes around Berlin want to capitalise from their location advantages and transform them into tax income from business or residential uses, luring away investors from the core city and elsewhere. Under these circumstances, substantial land-use changes have occurred in the suburban belt, making it one of the major investment areas of eastern Germany. Between 1992 and 1996, the suburban belt has increased its housing floorspace much more markedly than the core city of Berlin (see Table 16.2). Up to three-quarters of the annual floorspace production of Berlin were built in the Brandenburg part of the Berlin metropolitan area in 1994 and 1995, whereas there has been substantially less housing development in the rest of Brandenburg.

Table 16.2: Building activity in Berlin, the suburban fringe and the rest of Brandenburg, new floorspace and investment sums

		Berlin	Suburban	Rest of Brandenburg	Brandenburg
Floorspace housing (1000 m²)	1992	813.0	33.6	50.3	83.9
	1993	840.6	271.1	202.9	474.0
	1994	1000.4	760.8	572.1	1332.9
	1995	1327.7	975.9	633.3	1609.2
Floorspace non-housing (1000 m²)	1992	621.4	147.0	267.5	414.5
	1993	788.3	845.4	911.2	1756.6
	1994	944.7	1041.3	969.8	2011.1
	1995	1451.6	1008.3	881.6	1889.9
Building costs (million DM)	1992	4362	259	400	659
	1993	4958	1797	1724	3521
	1994	5767	2925	2589	5514
	1995	8502	3491	2686	6177

This residential development has been powered by massive tax relief for investors (buyers) in east Germany. Instead of paying taxes, affluent people could build or buy houses or apartments. Unfortunately, there are not enough tenants and users, and a good proportion of the new residential development in the Brandenburg countryside is empty. The decentralisation of residential investment, however, is not simply a problem of competition between Berlin and the surrounding municipalities. Berlin is building its own new residential periphery within the city boundary, with large-scale housing projects in, for example, Karow, Buch and Rudow.

Even more important than residential development is the construction of premises for non-housing purposes – industrial, commercial, leisure and office use – in the suburban belt. Large greenfield sites have been and are being developed for retailing, haulage, warehousing and so forth as well as for infrastructure projects, such as central goods transport centres, and some – not many – new manufacturing units. Berlin's non-housing new floorspace has more than doubled between 1992 and 1995, and at present one million m2 of non-housing floorspace is added to the existing stock every year. Service functions with extensive floorspace requirements, like mega-stores, furniture houses, storage capacities have been developed in the suburban belt around Berlin. This not only means substantial changes in land use, but also increasing distances in interaction patterns as well as further support for the use of cars, as most of the new locations are accessible only by cars. These 'non-integrated' service locations begin to threaten the survival of service functions in town. In some areas there, consumer-oriented service functions are beginning to thin out (Wawrzyniak 1996).

Ecological Building and Planning

The highest proportion of inefficient energy use stems from heating in the households and is due to insufficient insulation of buildings and the use of high-temperature energy, like electricity, for low-temperature purposes. Beside transport and consumption, construction – including renewal and refurbishment – is therefore the most important arena for action if sustainability is to be pursued.

With all the building going on in Berlin, is it ecologically sound? By now, the Berlin region has a fair number of model projects for energy-efficient building techniques (well-documented in Kosiol 1995). They concern both new buildings and refurbishment of the existing building stock. But in relation to the fact that 'green buildings' have been highlighted in the urban debate at least since the beginning of the 1980s, comparatively little has materialised, and the models remain exceptions. Investors in housing and buildings for other purposes are still rather hesitant in acknowledging the importance of ecological considerations. This is especially true when it comes to the environmental impact of production or transport, less so in terms of health effects on the inhabitants. The potential for energy-efficient techniques, active and passive solar constructions as well as for water-saving technologies is much greater than what has been realised, despite substantial subsidies from Federal and state government, for instance for active solar energy devices.

Some of the large new projects, however, have made more efforts to use ecological building techniques. The prime commercial development project on Potsdamer Platz, for offices, shopping arcades, leisure and cultural facilities as well as residential use, will get its heat as well as cooling supply from a joint energy station, which is itself linked to a new heat and power station for the historical centre. And the new Federal government buildings in Berlin may become a model of sustainable building in the office sector. Parliament has decided that the refurbishment of the Reichstag and other buildings as well as the new construction projects for parliament and government in Berlin shall be ecological in the sense that energy efficiency shall be realised to a high degree. With insulation, heat-pump assistance, combined heat-and-power stations (even using regionally produced plant oil), and, in addition, the installation of extensive photo voltaic systems, all state-of-the-art techniques in ecological building will be employed on a large scale. This will turn the government buildings into a good case study for best practices in urban ecology. But the diffusion of these applications is still slow.

Planning and action for sustainability in cities, however, has to go beyond these reductions in energy turnover in buildings or in transport. From an ecological perspective, cities have become vast producers of entropy. They require fresh air, fresh water, external energy resources, raw and processed materials, on the one hand, and emit, apart from the material products and the information which they produce, waste in gaseous, liquid as well as solid form, as well as waste heat, on the other. Matter and water circulate over long distances.

The important change towards sustainability, now, lies in shortened paths, in closed cycles of organic and inorganic material as well as water within the city region (Ripl and Hildmann 1995). This would balance material flows as well as the temperature, as water, which is now quickly running off from urban territory, would be retained as much as possible and would cool the city through its evapo-transpiration in hot weather conditions. Wilhelm Ripl (e.g. 1996) has already contributed substantially to visions of this kind for Berlin. Among many other aspects, they would include the creation of a maximum surface of vegetation cover, both horizontal and vertical, a different sewage system and natural sewage treatment near the consumer and decelerated water run-off, combined with food production in gardens, fields or fish ponds.

Conclusion

The special eco-spatial situation of Berlin which the unified city has inherited from its past still offers an excellent chance for sustainable planning in a metropolis. But it does not seem as if this potential is being fully used. The 'compact city' with its small-scale functional mix is not being retained. Urban sprawl, transport expansion through a car-oriented transport policy, functional segregation as well as 'grand projects' for long-distance transport are transforming it into a 'normal' metropolis, with all the ecological drawbacks of conurbations of this size.

In addition, progress towards sustainability will certainly not be possible without solving the city's rising social problems which have come about as a result of the mounting economic crisis. Increasing unemployment and poverty are often highly concentrated in the former working-class quarters of the city, and a marginalised population there will not be won for any sustainability programme which needs their hearts and minds. Social integration is imperative. Over the last few years, the industrial recession in Berlin has supported the improvement of the environment to a certain extent, but it would be fatal to believe in such a strategy for the future.

Nevertheless, the 'soft metropolis' is still feasible. The idea of a city which saves energy and matter and is quiet and green does not necessarily have to be buried. But current political decisions, e.g. financial cuts for public transport or the complete privatisation of the city's electricity company, point in another direction. In this situation, international and inter-communal efforts towards sustainability policies become very important. The combination of the inter-communal Agenda 21 process and the inter-governmental Baltic 21 initiative, together with learning from best practice examples elsewhere, e.g. concerning sustainable energy policy in Scandinavian countries, may put more pressure on the Berlin government to strengthen its efforts.

References

Agenda 21 (1997). *Auf dem Weg in ein neues Jahrtausend.* Berlin, BUND, 2nd ed.

Kloft, Edith (1993). *Energie. Stadtökologische Exkursionen in Berlin.* Berlin, EAUE.

Kosiol, Barbara (1995). *Bauen und Wohnen. Stadtökologische Exkursionen in Berlin.* Berlin, EAUE.

Kutter, Eckhard (1994). 'Verkehrsvermeidung und Siedlungsentwicklung,' pages 253-82 in: Behrendt, S. und Kreibich, R. (eds.). *Die Mobilität von morgen. Umwelt- und Verkehrsentlastung in den Städten.* Weinheim und Basel, Beltz.

Reichert, Gerhard (1994). *Wasser. Stadtökologische Exkursionen in Berlin.* Berlin, EAUE.

Ripl, Wilhelm und Hildmann, Christian (1995). 'Die Stadt als energiedissipative Struktur – ein systemökologischer Ansatz,' *Schriftenreihe für Vegetationskunde*:27, Sukopp-Festschrift, pages 201-7.

Ripl, Wilhelm (1996). 'Zwischen Verdunstung und Kondensation. Nachhaltige Wasserwirtschaft,' *Stadtforum Berlin*:58. Sitzung am 6. September 1996.

Senatsverwaltung (Berlin) für Stadtentwicklung, Umweltschutz und Technologie (1992). *Luft- und Lärmbelastungen in der Berliner Innenstadt durch den Kfz-Verkehr.* Berlin:

Senatsverwaltung (Berlin) für Stadtentwicklung, Umweltschutz und Technologie (ed.) (1993, 1994, 1995). *Umweltatlas Berlin.* Vols. 1, 2 and 3. Berlin.

Senatsverwaltung (Berlin) für Stadtentwicklung, Umweltschutz und Technologie, Energieleitstelle (1995). *Energiebedingte CO_2-Emissionen in Berlin 1991 bis 1994.* Materialien zum Energiekonzept Berlin:7. Berlin.

Senatsverwaltung (Berlin) für Verkehr und Betriebe (ed.) (1995). *Verkehrsplanung für Berlin.* Materialien zum Stadtentwicklungsplan Verkehr. Berlin.

Senatsverwaltung (Berlin) für Stadtentwicklung, Umweltschutz und Technologie (1997). *Entwicklung der Schadstoffbelastung – Ergebnisse des Berliner Luftgüte-Messnetzes – BLUME.* Berlin

Wawrzyniak, Peter (1996). *Das Quartier Mierendorffplatz in Berlin-Charlottenburg: Funktionswandel und planerische Massnahmen.* Diplomarbeit. Berlin.

17 The Development of Kaliningrad in the Light of Baltic Co-operation

Malgorzata Pacuk and Tadeusz Palmowski

Changing Geopolitical Conditions

The Russian Kaliningrad enclave (or rather exclave between Poland and Lithuania) is a world-wide curiosity in political and legal terms. There is no formal act defining the legal international status of this area. Together with an arbitrarily defined hinterland of approximately 15,000 km^2, Königsberg was taken over by the USSR without any legally valid peace treaty with Germany. At their conference in Potsdam after the fall of Germany in 1945, the Allies agreed to leave Königsberg under Soviet rule until the signing of an official understanding specifying the territory's status. Due to the Cold War, an agreement with Germany was never signed. In 1990 the situation changed when Germany renounced its claim to the territory. Nevertheless, Germany's sovereignty has not been officially transferred to any other state.

After the deportation of Germans in the years 1945-47, the Kaliningrad District remained closed for foreigners until 1991. Unlike the rest of Central and Eastern Europe, the Kaliningrad District remained completely isolated from the Western world. Aeroplanes from the district flew only eastwards, international shipping was effected solely by Russian vessels, international railway and road lines broke off at the Polish border. This situation stemmed from Kaliningrad's strategic importance as home port for the USSR Baltic Fleet as well as a base for land and air forces constituting 'the second line.'

Until the end of the nineteen-eighties, this half-way military exclave did not seem to have any political existence. Then the situation changed dramatically. As a result of Lithuania's, Latvia's and Belarus' break with the Soviet Union, the district became separated from the Russia mainland – a fact which was cemented by the dissolution of the USSR on 8 December 1991.

A number of other geopolitical changes, primarily the unification of Germany , European integration, the perspectives of NATO's eastward expansion and the political and economic changes in Poland and Lithuania, led to discussions both in Russia and abroad on the future of the Kaliningrad District.

The District's parliament (the Duma) has emphasised that Kaliningrad is and shall remain an inseparable part of the Russian Federation. And official circles in all countries involved do not in fact question the district's status as a part of Russia. The German Federal Government bases its policy on Kaliningrad on Article 1 of the Agreement '2+4,' according to which the status of the Federal Republic of Germany has been established once and for all. Lithuania's foreign minister has issued an official statement reneging claims to the territory, and Poland has followed suit. At the same time, however, new attempts are being made to raise the Kaliningrad issue to the European agenda and to refer the district's problems to all-European round table talks. The President of Lithuania called for such a solution in his address to the UN General Council meeting in October 1994.

The result has been a clash between various political and economic perspectives and ideas concerning the future status of the Kaliningrad. Russia's concepts are not always consistent or clear, particularly in view of the interests of other countries bordering on the exclave. In any event, the continued existence of the district as a closed military area has become an anachronism.

The best solution, in our view, would be a concept that satisfies the interests of the whole region, Russia's as well as those of its foreign partners, allowing for a balance to be struck between state regulatory measures for regional development and the free self-organisation of the district. In view of the acceleration of European political and economic integration, the Kaliningrad's transformation should be oriented towards establishing a bridge between Russia and other European countries. Under such circumstances, the economic and political development of Kaliningrad might become a model of future relations between the Union and countries of Central and Eastern Europe.

Before venturing to develop a strategy for development of the district, one should not only consider the situation from the perspectives of Europe or Moscow. It is equally important is to look at the issue from a bottom-up perspective – to understand how the changing geopolitical situation affects every-day life and economic development. This is also the primary aim of this chapter. But first an overview of Kaliningrad's changing strategic importance.

Kaliningrad's Strategic Importance as a Russian Military Base

Geopolitical changes in Central Europe at the end of the eighties led to the withdrawal of Russian troops from Czechoslovakia, Germany and Poland. The majority of these troops – pending an ultimate decision as to their fate – was relocated in the Kaliningrad district, which was rapidly transformed into one of the most concentrated military regions of Soviet Union. The breakdown of the Russian Empire and the establishment of independent Baltic states further isolated Kaliningrad, and Russia lost its military bases and training ranges in the Baltic republics, which clearly augmented the military importance of Kaliningrad. With the independence of Lithuania, Latvia and Estonia, parts of the Baltic Fleet which were stationed in these republics were withdrawn to the Kaliningrad.

At the time, the district's military manpower was assessed to number 200-300 thousand soldiers.[1] This figure is only an approximations as the exact numbers are still classified by the Russian Defence Ministry. In the following years, a systematic reduction of military forces in the district took place as large numbers of soldiers were transferred to Russia, and existing units were transformed by decommissioning officers and transferring men of lower ranks to the reserve. Since 1993, the number of Baltic Fleet ships has been reduced to a third, and staffing has been cut by approximately 40 per cent since 1992. The Baltic Fleet and the 11th Guards Army have left 17 towns of the Kaliningrad district. Nevertheless, the Fleet Headquarters are still seated in Kaliningrad, and together with St Petersburg, Baltiysk remains the principal Russian marine base on the Baltic.

In 1994 a special defence district was formed in Kaliningrad with the objective of holding the area until the main forces from Russia might be deployed. This objective is immediately associated with war in the region, but who might the aggressor be? So far none has been identified. On the other hand, the military concentration in the district is still high enough to permit not only the repulsion of a single aggressor but the invasion of neighbouring Baltic states in conjunction with Russian forces from the mainland in a short period of time. Naturally, this eventuality creates uneasiness and keeps up strategic apprehensions.

It has been assessed that at present, 10 per cent of Kaliningrad's inhabitants are either military personnel or their families. Thirty-forty per cent of the district's economy depends on the defence forces and therefore directly on the state budget. The region's geopolitical transformation has had the effect of burdening the district further because the local authorities have been left with the costs of maintaining the army. Consequently, further military reduction to a level sufficient to defend the territory – and which corresponds to the reduced forces of neighbouring Baltic states – is a precondition for Kaliningrad's economic and social development.

Will the accession of new members to NATO affect Russian defence policies in the Kaliningrad district? Lately, the military forces in Kaliningrad have served the purpose of extracting concessions in the process of Poland's coming NATO membership. The military potential of Kaliningrad may also become a vehicle to exert pressure on neighbouring countries.

The only way, it seems, to a step by step reduction of the district's military potential is to develop mutual trust and political partnership and to convince Russia that the overall stability in the Baltic Sea region allows a gradual military reduction.

Economic Problems

The isolation of Kaliningrad from Russia has created serious difficulties in the economy, which has declined more sharply than in other parts of the Russian

Federation. On the one hand, we are witnessing the opening of the district's economy, and, on the other, there has been a drastic fall in the production of former key branches leading to a growing domestic crisis.[2]

The Kaliningrad district remains important for Russia in terms of natural resources. It has the biggest resources of amber in the world, with approximately 700 tons exploited annually. Crude oil, lignite, potassium and other natural resources are extracted as well.

Kaliningrad has also developed a complex fish industry. At the end of the eighties, the district supplied over 7 per cent of domestic sea fish and almost 6 per cent of tinned fish. Every tenth inhabitant of the district was employed in the industry. The remaining economic fields – among them machinery construction for both military and civilian purposes, the paper industry and agro-industrial activities – were less significant.

The Russian crisis has not only brought changes in economic development but has also affected the management system, culture and the way of life. The rapid growth in the costs of power and transport and the transformation of former internal relations to international ones have made numerous fields of industry, formerly developed within the uniform economy of the USSR, inefficient. In addition, production in Kaliningrad has faced competition from highly efficient Western companies and many local firms have been unable to stand up to such competition.. Local producers risk being eliminated not only from foreign markets but also from the domestic market.

Table 17.1: Production of selected foodstuffs, 1990-95, thousand tonnes

	1990	1994	1995
Meat	50	28	11
Meat products	15	11	8
Fat	13	5	3
Milk	143	51	26
Cheese	4	3	2
Margarine	10	2	0.4
Flour	270	83	54
Bread	132	92	76

Source: Annual Statistics 'Yantarny Ostrov Rossii.' Kaliningrad 1996

Price liberalisation has forced a considerable number of the inhabitants to spend their whole income on food, while those with the lowest income are threatened with malnutrition. The biggest fall in production was noted in 1995, when the value of overall industrial production fell by 31.3 per cent compared to 1993. The light industry fared dramatically worse with a decline of 71 per cent, machinery and metallurgy dropped 68 per cent and the grain milling and fodder industry 65 per cent.

Although natural conditions (climate and soil) favour animal husbandry, orchards and vegetable cultivation, the state of agriculture is critical. The agricultural policy is in a blind alley, and farmers are faced with poverty never encountered before.

Attempts to restructure bankrupt kolkhozes and sovkhozes (state farms) have been unsuccessful. One hundred and ninety-three stock and limited liability companies and 3,553 individual farms have been set up in the span of only a few years, but most of the individual farms have gone bankrupt due to lack of an adequate credit policy. Many farmers have left their farms and those remaining raise on average one cow and one and a half pig.

Table 17.2: Agricultural ownership structure in the Kaliningrad district, absolute figures

Form of ownership	1990	1995
Kolkhoz	73	9
Sovkhoz	112	2
Stock companies	-	193
Individual farms	-	3,553

Source: see Table 17.1

A serious threat to the district economy is the disintegration of the scientific and technical potential, which until recently used to solve problems not only in Kaliningrad but also in Russia. Today the situation has radically deteriorated. In the years 1993-95, financing for science plummeted as did the number of scientific staff.

Table 17.3: Employment in Kaliningrad, 1980-94, thousands of persons

Sector	1980	1990	1994
Total	425	435	398
in:			
Industry	136	132	100
Agriculture	57	51	48
Transport and communication	47	38	35
Building	33	42	35
Trade	40	39	47
Health services	24	29	30

Source: see Table 17.1

This significant production decrease resulted in a continuously growing unemployment rate especially in such towns as Swietlyj, Czerniachovsk and Gwardiejsk. The number of inhabitants with permanent employment is falling at a rate of 4 per cent annually. Whereas unemployment is estimated at 100,000 people out of a the total population of 926,000 in 1995, only 25,037 persons were officially unemployed in 1995.

The district's tax system is inadequate to the changing economic environment. Economic reform has been limited to the privatisation of land and property, but even in these fields it was not carried out consistently. The halting reforms hamper formation of a market for land, capital and technology, without which a market economy cannot develop. The problem of legal protection of ownership has not been solved. The lack of laws and regulations is conducive to an economic underworld, and crime has permeated practically all spheres of economic life – ownership relations, financing and banking, production, trade and services as well as international relations.

Economic reform has so far turned out to be a failure. The next few years will be decisive. There are two options: either the destructive processes prove to be irreversible and the region becomes a mass consumer of imported goods while delivering raw materials and cheap labour. The alternative – a difficult and slow process – may bring the process of economic degradation to a halt and counteract negative tendencies.

A Special Economic Zone in Kaliningrad District

For some time now, politicians in Kaliningrad had asked for special rights particularly in regard to taxation and duty-collection which might attract foreign investors. On 3 June 1991, these endeavours resulted in the establishment of a free economic zone called 'Yantar' and a system of legal provisions that differ considerably from those in the rest of the Russian Federation.[3]

The objective of establishing the free economic zone was to create the most favourable conditions for developing economic activity, in particular with the participation of foreign capital, as well as limiting the number of barriers which make international co-operation difficult. Among the plans were customs liberalisation, the creation of privileges for foreign investors, the reduction of limits on exports of profits in foreign currencies and so forth. It was assumed that the zone would lead to a break with economic isolation – also from neighbouring Poland and Lithuania – thereby solving the massive problems of regional development with the help of foreign capital. Unfortunately, the awaited investment boom did not take place.

According to Kaliningraders, there were some objective reasons for this failure. The unstable political situation in Russia, legislation inadequate to market economy requirements, continuous legal amendments and lack of an act establishing the zone and clearly defining its advantages.[4]

It is obvious that the free economic zone nevertheless provided an impulse towards the development of foreign economic exchange and brought the district to the attention of foreign investors. Though the Moscow head office showed a passive attitude, the Committee for the development of Yantar managed to attract investors from 42 countries to the Kaliningrad district. However, the fall in industrial and agricultural production continued.

A Presidential decree, effective as of 15 March 1995, lifting all import and export allowances and introducing uniform customs and taxes in the whole territory of Russia – including the Kaliningrad district – seriously complicated the functioning of the zone. Although representatives of the district administration have emphasised that this decision does not mean closing the free economic zone, some companies with foreign capital withdrew from the local market. Consequently, an act on the status of the district was eagerly awaited.

On 22 January 1996, the President of Russia signed a Federal act on the 'Kaliningrad District Special Economic Zone.'[5] This time the system has a more solid legal basis as it was implemented by a separate act, a change of which requires a period of minimum three years. The present law will, however, require further detailed specification, and no immediate impact on the socio-economic situation of the district can be expected.

International Economic Co-operation

The complete change in the geopolitical location of the district after the dissolution of the USSR has transformed many previously domestic problems to international issues. Many traditional relations with the Baltic states have been severed. The Kaliningrad district thus has to enter two markets simultaneously: the Russian market and the Baltic regional market.

During the years 1992-95, economic turnover from Kaliningrad's foreign trade increased from USD 145 million to USD 1,019 million. Export rose from USD 91 to 459 million. In 1995, the principal trading partners in terms of exports were Switzerland, Germany and Namibia, and in terms of imports Lithuania, Poland and Germany (see Table 17.4).

The share of the Baltic countries, Poland and Germany in Kaliningrad's exports in 1995 amounted to 16 per cent of the total, whereas their share of imports was 45 per cent.

Crude oil dominated in the export structure with 17,1 per cent, celluloid came next (14.2 per cent), followed by artificial fertilisers (10,5 per cent) and fish (8.1 per cent). Imports were dominated by coal and crude oil (12.0 per cent), fish (8.5 per cent), meat and meat products (6.6 per cent), beverages (2.8 per cent), plastics (2.6 per cent) and machines and electrical appliances (2.3 per cent).

The district administration's efforts to strengthen economic relations with foreign partners have brought measurable results. At the end of 1995, 1,062 companies with foreign capital were registered in Kaliningrad, including 362 wholly foreign-owned. The majority of the companies – approximately 360 – is Polish, with 97 wholly Polish-owned. Next comes Germany with 96 wholly owned companies, followed by 47 Lithuanian-owned and 24 Latvian-owned.

In terms of capital investment, France is in the lead with about 5 billion roubles. Next come Germany and Poland with about 3 billion roubles each. Even the Japanese have announced their presence by opening a shop, Electric Plaza, in the Kaliningrad town centre.

Foreign companies have undertaken activities in various fields. Over 50 per cent of total investment from abroad stems from a French engagement in a telecommunications company. The District Ownership Fund auctions stock packages of state enterprises covered by privatisation to foreign investors. In this way, German companies, among others, have invested in upgrading the equipment and technology of building and machinery industries, and Swedish companies, among others, in upgrading the production of freon gasses. Limited liability companies deal mainly in tourism and trade.

Economic relations with Poland are among the most dynamic. An understanding on co-operation signed by the Russian Federation and the Republic of Poland in 1993 may be considered the first step, facilitating co-operation between the north-eastern provinces of Poland and the Kaliningrad region. Within the framework of this understanding, some principles of co-operation within the fields of transport, communication and agriculture were developed. Currently, Polish entrepreneurs are, above all, engaged in wholesale and retail trade, transport, building, tourist services, car services and production of common consumer goods. However, the potential of Polish-Kaliningrad co-operation seems far from exhausted.

At present, exports to Poland account for merely 10 per cent of the district's foreign turnover with this country, whereas imports from Poland account for 90 per cent (see Table 17.4). Most wholly owned Polish companies are active in trade and brokerage and are not involved in production of goods or services.

As of today, the problem of Polish and foreign flag ship traffic through the Pilawska Strait to Elblag has not been solved though talks have been held on the subject of shipping in the bay. Visible progress has been made in co-ordinating

Table 17.4: Turnover in foreign trade, 1992-95, million USD

Country	Imports from			Country	Exports to		
	1992	1993	1995		1992	1993	1995
Total	54.0	76.0	560.0	Total	91.0	126.0	459.0
Lithuania	1.0	2.0	102.7	Switzerland	-	1.0	97.0
Poland	16.0	17.0	91.0	Germany	15.0	16.0	25.0
Germany	9.0	18.0	48.0	Namibia	1.0	2.0	20.5
USA	1.0	2.0	31.3	Holland	-	1.0	17.4
UK	1.0	1.0	29.3	Italy	7.0	7.0	16.0
Holland	-	0.3	23.4	Lithuania	-	4.0	15.9
Norway	-	0.1	14.7	Estonia	-	0.4	15.3
Italy	-	1.0	12.0	Austria	-	2.5	11.5
Latvia	-	1.0	11.2	Poland	14.0	17.0	9.0
Belgium	-	-	10.8	UK	-	4.0	7.1

Source: see Table 17.1

co-operation between Polish provinces in the north-east and the Kaliningrad district. Such collaboration, however, has not been regular or fully successful.

The agreement on cross-border co-operation between regions of Poland and the Kaliningrad district puts special emphasis on food processing, transport, banking, insurance, science and technology, education, culture, environmental protection and information exchange. However, there is no co-operation on such matters as land-use planning, which may be interpreted to mean that the parties do not think this is a suitable subject for cross-border co-operation, which is surprising.

According to Russian experts, the governor and his administration play a dominating role in Russian regions and also prepare agreements on cross-border co-operation. In the Kaliningrad region, apart from district authorities, local self-governing bodies also play a role. However, in practice and in spite of sound legal regulations, self-governing bodies have never assumed a leading position on the regional scene in Russia. Their competence concerning cross-border co-operation covers only issues of a clearly local character, and where more consequential issues are involved, the co-operation of district authorities is necessary.

Among the factors hampering cross-border co-operation, Russian observers point to the following:

1. A lack of stable Federal legislation taking into account the interests and expectations of regional authorities. In extreme cases, amendments to Federal laws often make it impossible to fulfil international commitments earlier made.
2. A weak regional budget. Expenditures exceed the budget by 20 per cent. As a consequence, only 150 million roubles (approximately USD 30,000) was designated for scientific research in 1996, and this practically halted Russian research in progress commissioned by the Polish-Russian Commission on the development of neighbouring border areas. Central authorities enjoy considerable freedom in budgetary decisions and the president of the Federation may introduce amendments during the budgetary year.
3. The lack of separation between the state administration and the political sphere. Due to this phenomenon, every Federal or district election may bring about and usually does bring about changes in the personnel involved in cross-border co-operation in the region. During presidential elections and elections for the post of district governor, the administration is practically incapable of dealing with cross-border affairs.

Other factors impeding more intensive cross-border co-operation between Kaliningrad and the neighbouring north-eastern Polish provinces include the poor state of roads on both the Polish and Russian side, and the problem that passenger trains do not run at the same speed. On the Polish side, the Gdynia-Kaliningrad connection has an average speed of 54 km per hour and on the Russian side 27.4 km per hour. Though existing facilities have been developed and additional ones opened, there are still too few border crossings to meet the needs of travellers, and border traffic increases faster than the construction of new border crossings (see Table 17.5).

Co-operation programmes developed within the framework of the First and Second Round Table Talks in Kaliningrad and Olsztyn cover, inter alia, activities to facilitate traffic at border crossings by upgrading existing sites and constructing new ones.

Although the development of economic relations with Lithuania[6], Latvia and Estonia met with problems at the initial stage, they are currently considered to be good. There is still much left to be done if a step-by-step transformation of this border area into a sphere of animated international relations is to be achieved. Progressive normalisation of relations with neighbouring countries should be in the interest of the whole region.

Transportation Links and Transit

In order to further the region's modernisation, it is necessary to link the Kaliningrad district with the European communications systems and adapt border formalities to west European standards. Problems connected with transport to and from the district have become the major factor complicating trade and increasing costs (see Figure 17.1).

No programme for transit from Russia to the district and back has yet been prepared that might bring down the rising customs barriers and other costs.[7] During the years 1993-94, Lithuania unilaterally introduced a range of customs and tariff restrictions, including transit deposits, police convoying of goods, the so-called railway carriage tariffs, which complicate the transport of Russian goods to the district.[8] New costs related to transit through the newly independent state

Table 17.5: Travellers between Elblag province in Poland and the Kaliningrad district, thousands

	Road border crossing (Gronowo)	Railway border crossing (Braniewo)	Sea border crossings (Elblag, Frombork)	Total
1980	2.9	0	0	2.9
1990	39.5	0.12	0	39.6
1991	112.2	5.5	0.57	118.3
1992	164.3	135.2	4.2	303.8
1993	103.8	161.4	13.9	279.2
1994	164.4	61.7	21.6	247.7
1995	684.6	53.8	19.4	757.9
1996	1,369.1	65.6	17.1	1,452.2

Source: Data from the Department of Regional Policy of the Regional Authorities in Elblag

have definitely decreased the competitiveness of products from Kaliningrad on the Russian market and increased the cost of imports. As a result, Russian losses have amounted to tens of millions of USD since 1995. In addition, the district ports of Kaliningrad, Baltiysk and Svetly are being down-sized due to loss of cargo.

The port of Kaliningrad – the only ice-free Russian port on the Baltic – has great potential for development. Among the plans is a project a new oil terminal. According to the assumptions of the port's development programme, the mass of cargo handled by the year 2005 should rise to 12.5 million tonnes. But several circumstances are hampering the port's transformation into an important cargo-handling terminal, such as insufficient technical facilities, underdeveloped communications networks, problems connected with border-crossings and the protectionist actions of Lithuanian authorities.

The amount of cargo handled fell from 5 million tonnes in 1992 to 3.5 million tonnes in 1994 and 3.3 million tonnes in 1995, which proves that the port was not prepared to compete with ports of neighbouring countries. Simultaneously, the ports of Lithuania, Latvia, Estonia and Ukraine handle the export of 2-2.5 million tonnes of Russian goods per month. In 1995 Kaliningrad's commercial port lost approximately half of its metal, coal, grain and crude oil cargoes to foreign ports

The unclear situation concerning transit through Lithuania forces the district administration to search for alternative solutions. For example, a ferry line

Figure 17.1: Kaliningrad district and Russian communication links

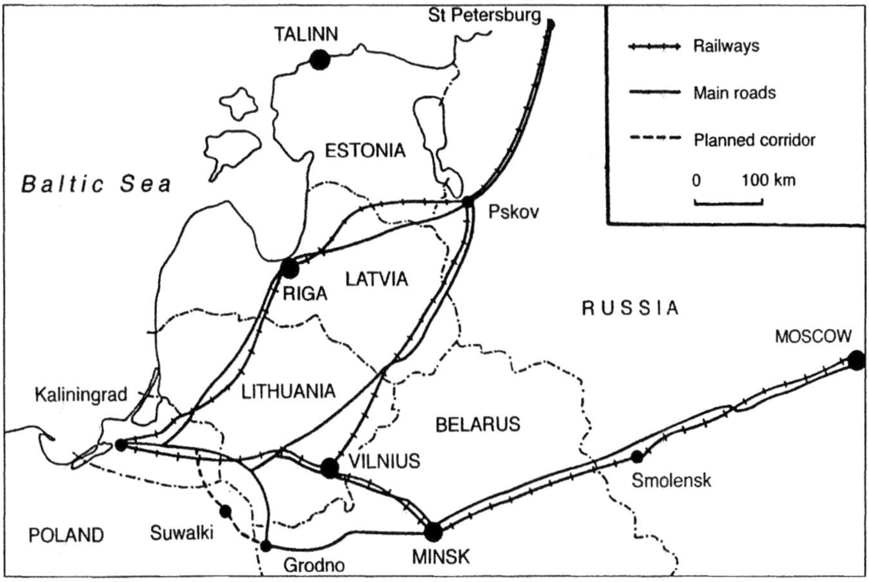

Source: Zverev and Gimbicki (1995)

between Kaliningrad and St Petersburg is envisaged. High hopes are also associated with the construction of a road from Kaliningrad through Elblag and on to Berlin, with a 40.2 km long section to the Polish border which will in future be linked with the international arterial road system, the Via Baltica.

The district currently has 24 border crossings – railway, road, air and sea borders. The Kaliningrad airport has obtained the status of an international airport. A new border crossing at Gusev-Goldap permits direct cargo and passenger connections between Kaliningrad and Belarus, circumventing Lithuania, through the Polish province of Suwalskie.[9]

The project of an alternative 'transit corridor' linking Kaliningrad with the rest of Russia, bypassing Lithuanian borders, was developed in the autumn of 1993 when Lithuanian authorities introduced a high transit tax and refused permission to transport scrap and entry of vehicles with military registration plates. According to a statement by the President of the Russian Federation, Russia and Belarus intend to reach agreement with Warsaw enabling them to build a corridor through Polish territory linking Russia and Belarus directly with the port of Kaliningrad. However, Poland has not received an official request concerning such a corridor.[10] According to representatives of Kaliningrad, the political implications that have worried the Poles are unwarranted as Russia and Belarus have not been considering an ex-territorial corridor.

Figure 17.2: Communication links between Kaliningrad and Poland

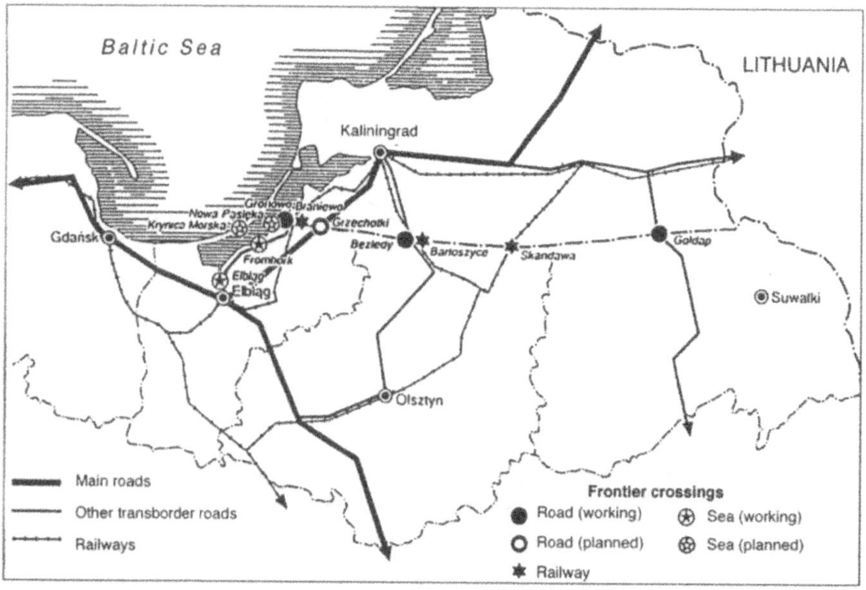

Source: Stasiak (1994)

Projections

Though at first glance the significance of this piece of land may seem marginal, its future is widely discussed in political and scientific circles in Russia as well as internationally and regionally. The need to solve the 'Kaliningrad puzzle' is unquestionable. Numerous, both optimistic and pessimistic scenarios – some still quite vague – exist on the possible future of the district.[11] Let us review a few of them.

A weak point in many scenarios is a lack of local perspective and negligence of bottom-up initiatives. Projections should put special emphasis on independence and self-reliance. Delegation of authority downwards from the central authorities may be considered a first step because all local and regional problems cannot be solved from the top.

One of the early proposals was to create a condominium comprising Russia, Germany, Poland and Lithuania to administer the district in order to bring it out of its isolation and slowly 'adapt it to life' (Dönhoff 1991).

The same author suggests that the region should become a model territory which brings Western and Eastern Europe together, with a free economic zone where Russians, Swedes, Poles, Lithuanians and Germans might trade, invest and live side by side in peace. The basic condition of this scenario is that Kaliningrad continues to belong to Russia, enjoys extensive autonomy and has its own currency (Dönhoff 1992).

Kaliningrad's former governor, J. Matoczin, has suggested that the district be transformed into a new Baltic republic as an autonomous formation within the Russian Federation and whose system of governance would be based not on elected but on directly appointed authorities. In relations with neighbouring countries, the local administration should enjoy wider authority and the territory should obtain certain economic privileges.

The scenario Euroregion Königsberg is – as a debate in the European Parliament showed – based on the perception that the district is isolated from the outside world and is declining in economic terms. For these reasons, it might become a political and military threat to the Baltic region. The establishment of a kind of Euroregion promoted by the European Union might help to avert this undesirable possibility. Within the framework of existing borders and in keeping with its membership in the Russian Federation, the district might become a bridge between Western and Eastern Europe, Belarus and the three Baltic states, provided that Kaliningrad's military forces be reduced to a level necessary for defence purposes. The European Union might assist in adapting military facilities to civilian purposes, introducing a new strong currency, establishing custom warehouses and so forth. The Kaliningrad district would thus become an experiment in economic reform and a starting point for further Western European endeavours in the Russian market.

The Borussii concept is an expression of a Lithuanian point of view. It would turn the district into a fourth independent Baltic state, where the number of inhabitants of Russian descent would fall due to migration back to Russia, whereas there would be a growing inflow of Lithuanians and Germans. German, Lithuanian and Russian would be the official languages. In the view of its author, this concept would thwart the alleged territorial pretensions of Russia, Germany and Poland (Venclova 1995).

The two most recent proposals should also be brought to light though they are mainly concerned with the economic sphere.

One is Euroregion Yantar – a Polish-Swedish concept. Apart from the Kaliningrad district and the district of Klaipeda, it would involve on the Polish side Elblag, Gdansk and Slupsk provinces, and on the Swedish side the communities of Kalmar, Karskrona, Jönköping, Växjö and Karlshamn. The aim is to facilitate regional co-operation covering not only the economic sphere but also cultural and educational exchange.

Russian spokesmen have shown much fear of Western economic and cultural expansion into Kaliningrad also on the part of the European Parliament. Russian policy is based on the belief that it is possible to introduce a special economic zone while maintaining a major military base in the district. The search for a solution to the problems of the Russian exclave is mainly a task for Russia and the Kaliningrad district themselves. Warsaw, Bonn, Stockholm and the European Union should base their policy towards Kaliningrad on the principles of the inviolability of existing borders, demilitarisation and economic development. Demilitarisation does not mean complete elimination of military forces but their reduction to reasonable level – which is termed 'mental demilitarisation' (Gnauck 1995).

According to the Polish geographer J. Zaleski (1993), a 'Baltic orientation' of Kaliningrad is the only reasonable solution to the district's problems. The authors of this chapter share this view. Though Russia is not prepared to contemplate such an outcome at the moment – at least not officially – perhaps it will be ready to do so in the future. It may come to realise that the only chance for the city and its hinterland is to give up Russian control and let the district become integrated into Baltic Europe. Such a solution would establish the Bay of Gdansk as one area of trans-border co-operation between Poland, Kaliningrad and Lithuania.

Notes

1 This created concern among the governments of the Baltic region. Such terms as 'stronghold' and 'garrison state' appeared. Approximations of the military manpower varied considerably – up to a difference of 500,000 men.

2 The economy of the district is thus divided into two sectors. One is associated with foreign trade and fares relatively well. The other – operating for the needs of the domestic market – cannot find its place in market economy and is based on financing from the budget. The coexistence of these sectors may lead to social conflict.

3 Yantar was established by a directive of the Chairman of the Supreme Soviet of the USSR 'On the economic and legal status of the free economic zone in the Kaliningrad district.'

4 The principal legal instrument defining the normative mechanism of the zone – 'Act on the Free Economic Zone Yantar'- is included in a resolution of the Council of Ministers of the Russian Federation. Consequently, it does not have the status of a proper law and has not been recognised by indivicual ministeries.

5 The reason why the Free Economic Zone was transformed into a Special Economic Zone seems obvious. Work on the free zone had been in progress for a long time, and in order to accelerate events, the Kaliningrad district administration, gave up the term free economic zone. In this way it became unnecessary to tie the Kaliningrad act to the general document on free economic zones, the fate of which still remains open.

6 The Kaliningrad region obtains up to 80 per cent of its power supply and raw materials from Lithuania or deliveries through its territory. This situation leads to a extreme dependency on the state of Russian-Lithuanian relations and gives rise to some economic problems.

7 According to data from 1994, 17 separate documents are required in order to carry cargo from Moscow to Kaliningrad.

8 Particularly the problem of military transport through the territory of Lithuania to Kaliningrad is complicated, though military transports are reported to constitute only one per cent of the total carriage and transport of military staff, arms and equipment make up a fraction of one per cent. The issue of Russian military transport, however, arouses storming political emotions.

9 The development of transport infrastructure should be seen as an activating factor in the Kaliningrad-Poland border co-operation.

10 On 30 March 1996, the President of Poland definitely rejected the project of establishing a transit corridor because this solution would infringe on Polish sovereignity. In line with common European practice, transit will have to take place on existing roads, and the inhabitants of Kaliningrad and Russia will be able to cross the territory of Poland subject to normal border procedures and administrative regulations of, for example, heavy vehicles.

11 A few examples are: Industrial Warehouse Kaliningrad, Baltic Revolving Shield, Military fortress, Russian (European) Hong Kong, Albania on the Baltic, Autonomous German Republic.

References

Annual Statistics (1996a). 'Yantarny Ostrov Rossii.' Kaliningradskij Oblastnoy Komitet Gosudarstvennoy Statistiki. Kaliningrad.

Annual Statistics (1996b). 'Mladshy Syn Rossii.' Kaliningradskiy Oblastnoy Komitet Gosudarstvennoy Statistiki. Kaliningrad.

Biuletyn Kaliningradzki (1994-96). Osrodek Studiow Wschodnich:1-12. Warsaw.

Dönhoff, M. (1992). 'Co zrobic z Königsbergiem?' *Tygodnik Powszechny*:37.

Dönhoff, M. (1991). 'Kondominium w Krolewcu,' *Polityka*, 30.11.

Fyodorov, G.M. and Zverev, J.M. (1995). *Sotsial'no-ekonomicheskoye razvitiye Kaliningradskoy Oblasti v novych geopoliticheskikh usloviyakh*. Kaliningradskiy Gosudarstvenny Universitet.

Gnauck, G. (1995). 'Kto widzi chmury nad Kaliningradem,' *Biuletyn Kaliningradzki*:5 (Polish translation from *Kaliningradskaya Pravda*, 4.05.1995).

Marianski, A. (1993). *Litwa, Lotwa, Estonia*. Warsaw, PWN.

Marciniak, K. (1995). 'Specjalny Kaliningradzki Obszar Obronny,' *Przeglad Morski*:7-8.

Müller-Herman, E. (ed.) (1994). Königsberg/Kaliningrad unter europäischen Perspektiven. Bremen, Verlag H.M. Hauschild.

Stasiak, A. (ed.) (1994). *Problemy wspolpracy przygranicznej pomiedzy Polska i Obwodem Kaliningradzkim Federacji Rosyjskiej*. Warsaw, IGiPZ PAN.

Sylwestrzak, A. (ed.) (1994). *Ustroj prawny Obwodu Kaliningradzkiego*. Gdansk, Wydawnictwo UG.

Szachraj, S. (1994). 'Kaliningrad-Königsberg-Krolewiec. Jak umacniac zachodni przyczolek Rosji?' *Biuletyn Kaliningradzki*:8 (Polish translation from *Nezavisimaya Gazeta*, 26.07.1994).

Tielatnikov, A. (1995). 'O koncepcji bezpieczenstwa gospodarczego enklawy kaliningradzkiej,' *Biuletyn Kaliningradzki*:5 (Polish translation from *Kaliningradskaya Pravda*, 18.05.1995).

Trusewicz, I. (1994). 'Wolnosc skrepowana. Strefa ekonomiczna Jantar w Kaliningradzie,' *Rzeczpospolita*, 14.12.1994.

Venclova T. (1995). 'Borussja – czwarta republika baltycka,' *Biuletyn Kaliningradzki*:4 (Polish translation from *Kaliningradskaya Pravda*, 26.04.1995).

Zaleski, J. (1993). *Razem czo osobno? Przyczynek do koncepcji baltyckiej wspolnoty regionalnej*. CUP, Biuro Planowania Regionalnego, Sopot.

Zverev, J.M. and Gimbicki, K.K. (1995). 'Kaliningradzki Obwod Federacji Rosyjskiej w nowych warunkach geopolitycznych,' *Przeglad Geograficzny*, T.LXVII, z.3-4.

Part III

Transborder Regional Co-operation

18 Cross-Border Co-operation after World War II

Viktor Frhr. von Malchus

Politico-Historical Background

Borders may be natural occurrences or the result of human activities, in which case they are historically explicable spatial structures. From the patchwork of historical regions of the 18th and 19th century, nation states were developed in the 19th and 20th century. Due to wars, borders were drawn between the nation states which separated many historical European regions and led to the phenomenon of peripheral location: settlement, economy and transport facilities became less developed in border regions than in the nation state centres. Particularly in the first half of this century, border regions were usually structurally underdeveloped areas which, for military reasons, were also insufficiently developed with regard to roads and rail connections (von Malchus 1975).

With its crimes, tragedies, destruction and new borders, World War II contributed considerably to the fact that, where it was possible, i.e. in the Western European democracies, people in border regions refused to carry the burdens of the legal, administrative, political, economic and social difficulties connected with borders and sought solutions through many and diverse forms of co-operation (AEBR 1981/1995).

As a result of the nation states' different policies particularly in the administrative, economic, cultural and social fields, the state borders had turned into strong barriers, which were further reinforced by natural boundaries such as rivers, lakes, oceans and mountains. After 1945, political ideologies and the power ambitions of military blocs entirely sealed off state borders, particularly between East and West, or turned them into Iron Curtains. People in border regions, the scars of history, stood back to back, and the desire to implement cross-border co-operation increased in all parts of Europe.

The Most Important Objective: To Overcome the Historical Scars

The most important objective of European cross-border co-operation remains the reduction of border barriers and obstacles including natural barriers. Since the 1950s, attempts have been made to achieve these aims in Europe through international, regional and municipal policy.

People in border regions wanted to live like people in the hinterland. However, all too quickly they realised that, due to lack of authority, they were incapable of achieving their aims in the regions and local communities. Where possible, therefore, they began establishing cross-border umbrella associations to solve a number of the problems caused by nation states:

- administrative and planning law – due to different administrative structures and planning methods;
- legislation on taxation, social affairs and culture, particularly with regard to competition, cross-border commuting, pensions, language education and acknowledgement of qualifications;
- extension of traffic routes and infrastructure for supply and waste disposal as well as the improvement of environmental conditions.

Left to their own devices, the citizens and communities in border regions were unable to improve these framework conditions. They needed the involvement of higher administrative levels and a shift in national policy. Since the 1960s, border regions have successfully pursued their objectives through the Association of European Border Regions (AEBR), the Council of Europe, the EU, the Nordic Council and national governments.

Developing Cross-Border Co-operation: Important Actors and Measures

The Contribution of the Council of Europe

From its beginning in 1949, the Council of Europe has pursued European integration and, in this context, tried to solve the problems of border regions. The co-operation between the members of the Council of Europe, including the Scandinavian countries, and territorial associations and authorities has taken place at several levels: the parliamentarian, regional, local and intergovernmental and ministerial levels. Several initiatives have been taken:

- In collaboration with the Association of European Border Regions (AEBR), the Council of Europe's Parliamentary Assembly and the Permanent Conference of the European Communities and Regions have organised six European Conferences of Border Regions: 1972 (Strasbourg), 1975 (Innsbruck), 1984

(Borken), 1987 (Sarragossa), 1991 (Rovaniemi) and 1994 (Ljubljana). A seventh conference is planned in 1998. These conferences have discussed the most important problems of cross-border co-operation, such as infrastructure, location of economic activities, the environment, nature conservation, cross-border commuters, culture, civil defence and emergency services.

- In the last 40 years, the Council of Europe's Parliamentary Assembly has passed many recommendations for the promotion of cross-border co-operation: the most important bases for these recommendations have been the European Framework Conference for the Improvement of Cross-Border Co-operation between Regional and Municipal Authorities and the 1980 Madrid Charter which was influenced considerably by the 1977 Agreement on Cross-Border Co-operation between Denmark, Finland, Norway and Sweden. Based on these recommendations, Belgium, Luxembourg and the Netherlands (1992), Germany and the Netherlands (1992), Italy and Austria (1993) and, among others, France, Switzerland and Germany (1996) have concluded agreements that enable communities to co-operate directly under public law.
- Moreover, many suggestions made by the European conferences and AEBR have been incorporated into the recommendations of the Council of Europe's Conference of Ministers of Regional Development and, most importantly, integrated into the European Charter on Regional Development (Charter of Torremolinos,1993) (von Malchus 1995).

The European Charter on Regional Development emphasises that nation states must agree on a policy of co-ordination and co-operation in border regions: 'The objective of such a policy must be to open borders, implement cross-border consultations on co-operation and the joint use of infrastructural facilities.' In accordance with the European Framework Conference on Cross-Border Co-operation between Regional and Municipal Authorities, nation states must ensure direct contacts between regions and communities affected.

Since the early 1990s, the Council of Europe has been active in the development of cross-border co-operation with and between countries of Central and Eastern Europe.

The European Parliament and the European Union

The European Community (EC) became interested in promoting cross-border co-operation relatively late. In the mid-seventies, the European Parliament's (EP) Committee for Regional Policy delivered several reports on cross-border affairs. The EP still holds the opinion that border regions are of particular importance for European integration and especially with regard to the rapprochement of the Union to the new Eastern European democracies and the promotion of co-operation between peripheral regions and third countries. A new EP report on border regions is currently under preparation for 1997 (Cranfield and Luechese 1996).

The European Commission received the many recommendations by the EP and AEBR with great reservations. However, since 1975 the cross-border effects of

EU funding have been considered in connection with in the regional policy of the European Regional Development Fund (ERDF). Moreover, in 1981 the Commission presented to its member countries a recommendation for the cross-border co-ordination of regional development programmes and proposed a number of border regions to be promoted within the framework of the ERDF. Since that time, the EC/EU has taken quite a number of initiatives to promote cross-border regional development:

- it has conducted trans-national studies;
- supported the development of cross-border action programmes;
- issued statements on the development of border regions in connection with the reports *Europe 2000* and *Europe 2000+*;
- taken a number of innovative initiatives within the field of regional development and development of regions based on Article 10 of the ERDF Regulations;
- approved the European joint initiatives Interreg I (1990-94) and Interreg II (1995-99) and set up guidelines for operational programmes which demonstrate that the Commission considers the solution of border-regional problems to be particularly important;
- initiated the EU joint initiative Interreg II C (1996).

The objective of Interreg is to support cross-border regional development and co-operation and help to prepare regions on the external borders of the Union for their future role in a strongly integrated community. These endeavours are carried out in close collaboration between the local, regional and national levels and the European Commission.

Since the early 1990s, the European Commission seems to have been paying more attention to resolutions by the Council, the European Parliament, the Committee of the Regions and individual member states. The Commission appears to have assumed a particular responsibility for cross-border initiatives and for improving trans-European networks which facilitate inter-regional co-operation.

Inspired by interventions from the European Parliament, the 1994 EU budget included for the first time an amount of 150 million ecu from the PHARE programme for the promotion of cross-border co-operation between regions of Central and Eastern European countries and neighbouring EU regions. The main objective is to encourage additional funding in connection with measures supported by the Structural Funds and in particular by Interreg. In the future it is of great importance to ensure a solid connection between PHARE cross-border co-operation and Interreg and to favour joint measures implemented by PHARE countries and member states. Moreover, the Commission is currently developing a new programme, CREDO, for the promotion of border regions in Central and Eastern Europe (Klein 1995). Additionally, after Finland and Sweden have joined the EU, it must be examined how PHARE, TACIS and the Structural Funds can be combined to promote measures with a regional dimension. In Scandinavia this applies particularly to the long border between Finland and Russia and to relations with the Baltic states.

The Nordic Council

Following the establishment of the Nordic Council in 1952, the Nordic Council of Ministers was founded in 1971 to ensure the practical implementation of decisions taken by the Nordic Council's Parliamentary Assembly. During the 10th conference of the Nordic Council in 1962, governmental co-operation developed a legal base through the Helsinki Agreement. At a later date, the Nordic countries committed themselves to close co-operation in the legal, cultural, social and economic fields as well as with regard to transport and environmental policy.

Under the leadership of the Committee of Senior Officials for Nordic Regional Policy (NERP), Nordic regional policy and cross-border co-operation gained a high standing.

The Nordic Council and the Nordic Council of Ministers were considerably influenced by issues raised in the 1950s and 1960s by the Council of Europe's Advisory Assembly. The ideas behind the Council of Europe's Framework Convention for Cross-Border Co-operation, which were, initially, not implemented by the Council of Europe, were implemented in the North. Regional cross-border co-operation was introduced as early as 1966 and later intensified along all Scandinavian borders. The framework was presented in the 1977 Agreement on Cross-Border Regional Co-operation between Denmark, Finland, Norway and Sweden. It stipulated that regional co-operation across borders could be implemented in the same manner as between regions and municipalities within the same country. Where necessary, each country promised to changes its legislation to remove obstacles to cross-border co-operation at local level. Moreover, as part of their planning, regions and municipalities were obliged to consider existing cultural, social and economic conditions in their partner communities on the other side of the border. The authorities of the contractual countries also promised to support the border communities in case of any problems arising in the course of their co-operation. Despite the fact that this agreement was concluded earlier, it clearly went beyond the subsequent European Framework Convention even though certain similarities and reciprocal influences can be seen (von Malchus 1986).

In addition to establishing a legal basis of cross-border co-operation, the Scandinavian countries have concluded many cross-border agreements and developed mutual plans to further Nordic co-operation, for example, since 1974, agreements on the prevention of cross-border environmental pollution and strain. The 1989-90 agreements on cross-border co-operation in the entire Baltic Sea area, also in regions where such co-operation used to be impossible due to the Iron Curtain, exceed by far the European Framework Convention. The Council of the Baltic Sea States founded in 1992 also deals with many areas of cross-border co-operation. It is particularly important to mention the expert conferences of the ministers of transport, environment and regional development, who have met several times.

The promotion of cross-border co-operation by the Nordic Council of Ministers can roughly be divided into two periods, corresponding with the developments in the rest of Europe: before and after 1989/90. In the period up to 1989, the number of Nordic cross-border regions increased from four to nine (Becker-Christensen and Buchwald 1977; Nordic Council 1989; Johannson 1991; Ramfelt and Nilsson 1996).

Cross-border co-operation was intensified as a result of the Nordic Council's regional policy action programme of 1979 which, for the first time, incorporated the promotion of border regions and instructed NERP to deal intensively and systematically with the existing and planned cross-border co-operation. In the years after 1986, the Nordic Council of Ministers developed a new approach: instead of funding programmes it started funding projects. From 1986 onwards, cross-border regions had to submit annual working programmes and financial plans to the Nordic Council. NERP then made the decision. In addition, cross-border associations were permitted to take projects for which the funds were allocated by the Nordic Council into their own hands.

In May 1990, the Nordic Council of Ministers established a new basis for cross-border co-operation. The regional policy co-operation programme for 1990-94 specifically incorporated cross-border regional policy. At the same time, a new dialogue was initiated between NERP and the border regions to ensure greater effectiveness of the work in individual regions. In November 1991, the Nordic Council of Ministers introduced new procedures for the period 1992-94 and issued new guidelines for future cross-border co-operation.

After a comprehensive discussion in NERP, the Nordic Council and the Nordic Council of Ministers, cross-border co-operation was also integrated into the 1995-99 co-operation programme on regional policy, which stressed the following areas:

- an effective exchange of information and experience between border regions and the Nordic Council of Ministers;
- reduction of costs for individual projects and concentration on one joint project in each region and
- joint and cross-border use of the infrastructure (for example, in education, science and health care).

In particular, the Council of Ministers emphasised that projects must be of Nordic relevance and it stressed the importance of scientific support and evaluation.

The Association of European Border Regions

The development of European cross-border co-operation was greatly stimulated through the foundation of the Association of European Border Regions (AEBR) in 1971. The AEBR keeps contact with the Council of Europe, the European Commission, the Council of European Communities and border regions. Moreover, it supports the Council of Europe in its attempts to improve cross-border co-operation through scientific analysis and organisational aid, and since 1971 it has held regular European conferences of border regions. In 1977, AEBR adopted its first statutes and, in 1979, it received status as official observer in the Council of Europe (AEBR 1996).

In 1979, the Council of Europe's Advisory Assembly and, in 1981, the Council of Ministers accepted the European Framework Convention for the Improvement of Cross-Border Co-operation of Territorial and Municipal Authorities (Madrid Charter), developed in co-operation with AEBR.

The AEBR Experts' Advisory Board, founded in 1979, develops sustainable and practical guidelines for cross-border programmes and economic development strategies and analyses the typical problems of European border regions. Based on this research, the AEBR has demanded a European Charter on Regional Development and has adopted a European Charter of Border and Cross-Border Regions. Since 1982, the AEBR has had the opportunity to co-operate with the Advisory Committee of Municipal and Regional Institutions in EU Member Countries. Membership of the AEBR increased from 10 border regions in 1970 to 24 in 1982.

Since the end of 1983, the AEBR has supported the preparation and implementation of the first regional cross-border development programmes. In co-operation with the AEBR, the EC Commission has gradually developed solutions to problems of border regions, which have become more and more important at the internal and external EU borders. In 1985, the AEBR was a founding member of the Council of European Regions (later: Assembly of European Regions – AER). In the late 1980s, the AEBR demanded a European cross-border regional development and transport policy on all European borders.

In its scientific research, the AEBR has always stressed that the problems in border regions are obstacles to the internal market and European integration. This recognition by the EC and later EU was the basis of Interreg I (1989-94) and Interreg II (1995-99), to whose development the AEBR contributed considerably with expert knowledge. Between 1990 and 1995, financial assistance from the AEBR project Observatory for Cross-Border Co-operation (LACE) provided the Association of European Border Regions with growing opportunities to give all border regions expert and technical support. The number of AEBR members increased to over 50. By 1996, the number of European border regions in the member countries of the Council of Europe had increased to 120.

After the 1989 democratisation in Central and Eastern Europe and the subsequent enlargement of the EU, cross-border co-operation in Europe has become more important. New border regions have developed with crucial assistance from the AEBR. In 1995, the AEBR adopted the amended Charter of European Border Regions, which was translated into the most important European languages. Within the framework of the LACE programme, the AEBR published a Practical

Guide to Cross-Border Co-operation, which was immediately sold out and, in 1997, translated into several official EU languages (AEBR 1995; in spring 1997, a reworked version of the LACE Guide was published as an EU document in several EU and Central and Eastern European languages).

In 1996, the EU Commission entrusted the AEBR with the LACE project Technical Assistance and Promotion of Cross-Border Co-operation in the context of Interreg II (TAP). In 1997, the AEBR will organise a seminar in Copenhagen on the future assistance of border regions in collaboration with the Nordic Council of Ministers and the Øresund region.

Cross-Border, Inter-Regional Co-operation

A Need to Differentiate

As a rule, the positive effects of cross-border and inter-regional co-operation are due to its contribution to:

- European integration;
- economic and social cohesion;
- improved communication, extension of interconnections, development of networks;
- development of new labour markets and
- preparation of the entry to the EU of new members.

Crucial for the length, success and type of co-operation will be:

- the involvement of the local population;
- the participation of all political levels (European, national, regional, local);
- the involvement of all authorities, organisations, associations etc. on both sides of the border;
- the structure and funding of joint cross-border organisation.

Because these conditions are only found in traditional cross-border co-operation, it is advantageous to distinguish between co-operation which includes all aspects of life for a long period, on the one hand, and co-operation (between national, regional and local authorities) in specific sectors and among a select number of actors for whom institutionalisation is less important, on the other. This differentiation will also be of significance in the Scandinavian countries (Cranfield and Luechese 1996).

Problems and Successes of Cross-Border Co-operation

Between 1995 and 1999, a total of 59 operational programmes will be implemented within the framework of Interreg II A, of which some 15 programmes (25 per cent) in Scandinavia. In contrast to the programmes in the rest of Europe, the Nordic Interreg programmes do not always correspond with traditional border regions assisted by the Nordic Council of Ministers. In some cases, the geographical area is much larger, and new areas have been added after the opening of the Central and Eastern European borders, such as Karelia, parts of the Barents region and St Petersburg.

Long distances in these sparsely populated regions and regions crossing sea borders (for example Kvarken and Mid-Norden) make the implementation of operational programmes difficult, as clearly pointed out in the Nordic Council of Ministers' evaluation of cross-border co-operation. But there have been additional problems (Ramfelt and Nilsson 1996):

- the projects have not always corresponded with the long-term development strategies of the border regions;
- the objectives of many projects have not been clearly formulated or have been changed during implementation;
- the cross-border objectives of individual projects have not always been clearly defined (some projects have followed clearly national objectives);
- the operational programmes have not been sufficiently based on socio-economic, cross-border analysis (analyses of strengths and weaknesses) and should have incorporated indicators from the start which would have made a continuous evaluation at a later stage easier;
- project managers have been insufficiently trained for their tasks.

Inter-Regional Co-operation as a New Approach

Since May 1996, the new initiative Interreg II C has tried to assist sustainable regional development in large European areas (European Commission 1995; 1996).The initiative is based on the Commission's documents *Europe 2000* and *Europe 2000+*, the conclusions of eight informal meetings of the European Community's ministers for regional development and further research on European regions. As published in *Europe 2000+*, the Commission (1994) decided to support regional development in large geographical areas, for example the North Sea and the Baltic Sea areas, if a minimum of three member countries supported such cross-border programmes. With the co-operation of Central and Eastern European countries, operational programmes for regional development are currently in preparation for large areas such as the Baltic countries and Poland.

It is a particularly beneficial aspect of the new initiative that trans-national co-operation with third countries will have priority. For Scandinavia, this implies co-operation with the Baltic countries, Poland and Russia. It remains to be seen whether such trans-national co-operations can also promote cross-border co-operation in the Baltic Sea and North Sea regions.

Important Aspects of Future Cross-Border Co-operation

Experience from European and Scandinavian cross-border co-operation has shown that future cross-border co-operation depends on five specific preconditions (AEBR N.a):

- solid and regionally based cross-border structures must be in place;
- cross-border co-operation should incorporate all spheres of life, but it is particularly important to cover the following areas: an increase of information flow between all border regions; extension of the infrastructure in the widest possible sense (including supply); economic and technological development and links, co-operation between small- and medium-sized companies, development of new relations between manufacturers and suppliers and the extension of cross-border labour markets; structural improvement in rural areas; promotion of democracy and measures in the fields of culture, education and social affairs;
- Interreg II A should be extended beyond 1999 and developed further because it is necessary to rethink unfinished projects. In future, more responsibility should be transferred to the regional actors (representatives of border regions), particularly with regard to programme conception (including the development of concrete measures), programme management, implementation and funding of programmes. The co-ordination of Interreg II A procedures with the PHARE CBC and TACIS programmes must be increased. After 1999, assistance should be granted to all regions along the EU's internal and external land and sea borders. The level of development in individual border regions must, of course, be considered when granting assistance.

The important criteria for assistance should be:

- the high quality of the operational programmes, which must be based on jointly developed, qualified analyses (development and implementation concepts) and, if needed, accompanied by regional subprogrammes with individual steering committees taking the concepts of spatial planning into consideration;
- the cross-border character of programmes must be stipulated in advance;
- there must be participation of local and regional public and private actors;
- there must be equal treatment of the partners in the decision-making bodies;

First and foremost, those attempts at cross-border co-operation which remain viable as cross-border structures (border regions) after EU funding is terminated should be particularly promoted.

In a network of border regions, solidarity between European border regions is of paramount importance to guaranteeing the transfer of knowledge and the exchange of experience; ensuring that the wealthy border regions help the poor ones; keeping alive the process of cross-border co-operation in all parts of Europe and promoting it for the benefit of European integration.

Most European and Scandinavian countries know that they cannot solve the many and diverse border problems without their neighbouring countries. In most cases, current cross-border co-operation is not strong enough to enable border regions to equalise deficits in development caused by borders and guarantee a balanced development on both sides of the border. A Europe without borders will continue to depend on cross-border co-operation.

References

AEBR – Association of European Border Regions (ed.) (1981/1995). *European Charter of Border and Cross-Border Regions*, of 20 November 1981 (amended on 1 December 1995 in Szczecin).

AEBR – Association of European Border Regions (ed.) (1995).LACE GUIDE: Practical Guide to Cross-Border Cooperation. Brussels. (Revised edition published as EU document in spring 1997).

AEBR – Association of European Border Regions (ed.) (1996). *25 Years of Joint Activities*. Gronau, Basle.

AEBR – Association of European Border Regions (N.a). 'Initial Thoughts on the Future Design of Cross-Border Cooperation After 1999.' Manuscript.

Becker-Christensen, H. and Buchwald, H. v. (1977). *Grænse-Kommunalt Samarbejde i Norden*. Aabenraa, Institut for Grænseregionsforskning.

Cranfield, M. and Luechese, A. (eds.) (1996). *Cross-Border and Inter-Regional Co-operation in the European Union.: Summary*. Luxembourg, European Parliament-Directorate General for Science (drafted by the Association of European Border Regions).

European Commission (ed.) (1994). *Europe 2000+*. Brussels, Luxembourg.

European Commission (1995). 'Guideline on Innovative Measures for Regional Development (Article 10 of the ERDF Regulations) 1995-1999.' Brussels, Luxembourg.

European Commission (1996). 'Communication to Member Countries on the Guidelines for Operational Programmes to be Implemented within the Framework of the Joint Initiative, INTERREG, for Trans-National Cooperation in the Field of Regional Development (INTERREG II C) of 8 May 1996.' Brussels.

Johannson, M. (1991). Pages 9-22 in Nordic Council of Ministers (ed.). Nordic Regions and Transfrontier Cooperation. Copenhagen.

Klein, R. (1995). 'Cross-Border Cooperation with regard to Regional Policy and within the Framework of INTERREG and PHARE,' *EUREG*:2, pages 48-52.

Malchus, V. Frhr. v. (1975). *Partnership on European Borders*. Bonn.

Malchus, V. Frhr. v. (1986). 'Summary and Perspectives of the Institutional Development of Cross-Border Cooperation,' pages 23-94 in *3rd European Conference of Border Regions*. Dortmund, ILS-Schriftenreihe, Vol. 0.032 (special publication in English, French and German).

Malchus, V. Frhr. v. (1995). Article, pages 437-43 in *Cross-Border Regional Development: Concise Dictionary of Regional Development*. Hannover, Akademie für Raumforschung und Raumordnung (ARL).

Nordic Council/Nordic Council of Ministers (ed.) (1989). 'Nordiskt gränsregionalt samarbete,' *Fakta om nordiskt samarbete*:9.

Ramfelt, L. and Nilsson, H.R. (1996). *Gränsregionalt samarbete i Norden*. NordREFO Working Papers 1996:5. Copenhagen.

19 A Norden of the Regions?

Harald Baldersheim and Krister Ståhlberg

The claim is often made that European integration is stimulating the emergence of a 'Europe of the Regions.' Regions are said to become more visible players on the European stage. The extent to which such a development is reality or an illusion may be a matter of debate (Balme et al. 1994; Bullmann 1994; Keating 1996; Kohler-Koch 1996). Nevertheless, we think it is of great interest to ask whether processes of regionalisation are also felt more strongly in the Nordic area now that three of five Nordic states are integrated in the European Union through membership and two states through the treaty of the European Economic Area (EEA). And if so, what are the impacts going to be?

The Nordic countries have usually been regarded as archetypically unitary states that developed into rather centralised welfare states after the Second World War . 'The passion for equality' is one of the characterisations that have been applied to the political culture of the Nordic countries (Graubard 1986). Such an attitude might be expected to favour strong central government rather than a tolerance for regional variation. However, the Nordic countries are also characterised by persistent centre-periphery cleavages and regional 'counter-cultures' (Lipset and Rokkan 1967) and a concomitant suspicion towards the national centres, perhaps more so in Norway than in the other countries of the area.

The centre-periphery cleavages were conspicuously present in the 1994 referenda on EU membership (Bjørklund 1996). Central regions saw opportunities in European integration, whereas integration was perceived as a threat in the peripheries. The existence of such regional contrasts might support regionalism in central as well as peripheral areas. It is therefore not unlikely that European integration will trigger new dynamisms among regions also in the Nordic countries. What these dynamisms might be like is the question that will be dealt with in this chapter.

However, before answering the question, it is necessary to get a clearer idea as to what the expression 'Europe of the Regions' might mean since there are a number of competing conceptualisations of the regionalisation process and its implications.

Europe has, for example, been portrayed as a continent composed of a mosaic of regions, characterised by contrasting economies, cultures and identities (Illeris 1993). When looked upon from a regional angle, Europe emerges as much richer in territorial variation than a comparison of nation states would suggest. In acknowledgement of this variety, national governments have often established regional political institutions that allow the expression of differing identities and interests, even drawing on this variety for the purpose of national development. However, this trend does not unfold in a uniform fashion or at a uniform pace. Institutional development in a regional direction and the emergence of regionalism take on different forms and unfold with varying force from country to country – from the decentralisation policies of Italy since the 1970s and France since the early 1980s to processes of federalisation in Belgium and Spain (Sharpe 1993).

The Nordic countries have been part of this trend towards institutionalising regional self-governments from the 1960s. In the 1990s, this mosaic of European regions is becoming more and more visible. Regions are acquiring the status of partners not only for national governments but also getting a voice in European institutions through the formation of the Committee of the Regions.

The Rise of the Regions

A stronger version of the Europe of the Regions thesis sees the emergent regionalism as a constituent part of the return of history in Europe, maybe even as a revenge of history (Harvie 1994). The waning of the Cold War has meant that the lid is taken off many regional aspirations. These are now allowed a freer rein to the effect that historical landscapes strive to regain ancient status, thereby sometimes altering the course of history.

This has been happening in the well-known national break-ups of Central and Eastern Europe, but the emergence of regional movements in Italy is also part of this post-Cold War trend. Spain offers another example of how the transition from dictatorship to democracy created opportunities for long-suppressed regional movements. Spain is also a promising model of how such movements may be accommodated through a well-thought-out process of gradual regionalisation that stimulates nation-building rather than blocking or breaking it (Agranoff 1996).The return of historical regions demonstrates the continued existence of a multi-layered, multi-cultural, heterogeneous Europe also inside the boundaries of many nation states. The dissolution of some of the unitary nation states in Europe suggests that the integrative capacities of the nation state may have been overrated, and that theories of nation-building have to be revised to capture elements also of deconstruction.

An even bolder vision of the Europe of the Regions is the claim that a Europe of the Superregions is emerging (Delmaide 1994). Superregions are collaborative patterns that cut across the existing national borders as well as the borders of the EU. The outlines of the superregions follow the logic of trade patterns and mutual economic dependencies driven by increasing international economic competition. The superregions are not necessarily distinct political-institutional entities but sometimes only vaguely discernible agglomerations of strategic alliances emerging in bottom-up fashion in the wake of economic necessities, formed by subnational governments (regional and local authorities), business and industrial associations, and civic actors.

This vision corresponds to the occurrence of some well-known regional projects such as the Baltic Conference, the North Sea Commission, or the Mediterranean co-operation. Other superregions painted on this canvas ('the Slavic Federation' or 'the Danube Basin') seem more fanciful entities, however.

The sum of these superregions is also a Europe of economic and cultural heterogeneity. This heterogeneity is a source of creativity and therefore of strength. European integration as evidenced by the EU project, as well as the waning of the Cold War, allow this heterogeneity to blossom more freely than before. Region-building across national borders is not seen as threatening the way it might have appeared in the days of superpower polarisation. However, this very heterogeneity that drives region-building and economic growth alike will also constrain the level of political cohesion and integration that is likely to be achieved on the wider European scene. A federal Europe similar to the USA is an unlikely outcome in this perspective. European integration is likely to mean something qualitatively different from a federation; and this difference is likely to be defined in large measure by its constituent regions.

For the Nordic co-operation some of the features of the superregion version of the Europe of the Regions may entail some disturbing prospects. The Nordic area is seen as being split between a 'Baltic League' and an 'Atlantic Coast' region, with Norway and Iceland collaborating primarily with the Atlantic area while Denmark, Sweden and Finland are pulled more in a Baltic direction. This is precisely what some observers have feared might happen in the new Europe, with Denmark, Sweden and Finland as members of the EU and Norway and Iceland outside. The new, vigorous co-operation around the Baltic Sea may be pulling the former three out of the pan-Nordic co-operation established in the 1950s, or may represent a competing project which might potentially weaken the interest of the Swedes and Finns in general Nordic co-operation.

The picture that emerges from an empirical investigation of the cross-border links of Norwegian counties demonstrates that the Atlantic links are indeed the most numerous ones. However, a good number of Baltic links also figure in the picture, and so does an Arctic orientation (Baldersheim and Litsheim 1996). A more likely development then, as far as Norway is concerned, is that the country will be torn between several regional projects.

A fourth version is the one much favoured by political scientists in the context of European integration: the notion of the emergent three-level game, in which regional actors become partners in decision-making alongside national governments and the European Union (Bullmann 1994, 1996). Some of those who support this notion perceive the current formal status of the Committee of the Regions as somewhat of a disappointment. The idea behind the three-level game is that regions increasingly seek to establish direct relations with Brussels, bypassing national governments with regard to the allocation of EU funds for regional development purposes. This may be more of an illusion than a reality but is nevertheless promoted by regional politicians seeking to enhance their own image (Keating 1996).

What is beyond doubt is that regions increasingly seek to further their own interests in Brussels independently of their national governments. In the 1990s, regional lobbying offices have mushroomed in Brussels (Marks et al. 1996). One of the leverages regions possess in the three-level game is related to the need for vigorous regional mechanisms to prepare the plans that are required in order to become eligible for Structural Funds support such that provided under the Interreg programme. Regional mechanisms are also required to spend the Structural Funds effectively. Regions also take part in other types of programme, such as those intended to promote scientific or educational co-operation. So the workings of EU institutions both intentionally and indirectly foster the emergence of a three-level game (Leonardi 1993).

May any of these trends of regionalisation be detected in the evolving territorial organisation of the Nordic states? Before any attempt is made to answer this question, a brief outline of the territorial institutions of Norden is necessary.

The Territorial Organisation of the Nordic Countries

The Nordic countries have long-established institutions of local and regional self-government as well as areas with home rule. The territorial subdivisions of national administration largely follow those of regional self-governments, with some exceptions, especially in Finland. The various units of territorial governance are identified in Table 19.1.

Three of the countries (Denmark, Norway and Sweden) have a two-tier system of local/regional self-government: municipalities and county councils, which are directly elected. The major services for which the second tier is responsible are hospitals, secondary education, and public transport and secondary highways. In Finland, these functions are managed through a system of special-purpose districts formed by collaborating municipalities. Directly elected county councils do not exist.

In the four largest countries, local and regional units of self-government form an important part of public administration, accounting for about 60 per cent of all public expenditures and employing nearly two-thirds of all public employees (Peterson 1994). The prominent position of the institutions of local and regional self-government points to the continuity of strong civic traditions in the administration of the Nordic countries also in the era of the welfare state. The civic tradition provides a counterbalance to the somewhat etatist orientation that is often attributed to the Nordic countries (Graubard 1986; Enzensberger 1987; Peterson 1994; Albæk et al. 1996).

In Denmark, Norway and Sweden, national district administrations largely correspond to the geographical boundaries of the county councils. These district administrations are co-ordinated by a district governor or prefect appointed by the central government. Finland also has this prefectural government. The prefect also has some powers of supervision in relation to municipalities. His powers of intervention in local government affairs are limited, since supervision is largely restricted to a legal review of local decisions. The largest municipalities are found in Sweden and the smallest in Iceland (average number of inhabitants 30,000 and 1.000 respectively). Local authorities are financed by local taxes (approx. 50 per cent), state transfers (approx. 25-35 per cent) and fees and charges (approx. 15-20 percent) (Oulasvirta 1992).

Table 19.1: The territorial organisation of the Nordic countries

	Denmark	Finland	Iceland	Norway	Sweden
Local self-government units	273 municipalities	452 municipalities	196 municipalities	435 municipalities	284 municipalities
Regional self-government units	14 county councils + capital area	about 260 intermunicipal units		19 county councils	23 county councils + 3 cities
National field administrations	14 counties	5 counties (excl. Åland)	23 counties	18 counties	24 counties
Home rule areas	Faroe Islands Greenland	Åland Islands			
Special districts				Spitsbergen (Svalbard)	
Intra-Nordic regional co-operation					
The North Calotte		*		*	*
Kvarken		*			*
Mid-Norden		*		*	*
Archipelago		* (Åland)			*
Arko				*	*
Bohuslän/ Østfold				*	*
Øresund (The Sound)	*				*
Bornholm/ Skåne	*				*
Western Norden	*(Faroe Islands, Greenland)		*		

* Indication of countries involved

Source: Compiled by the authors from official publications, 1997

For historical reasons Denmark and Finland have areas that have been granted extensive home rule, in the case of Åland since 1922, and in the cases of the Faroe Islands and Greenland since 1948 and 1978 respectively. Greenland has opted out of the EU despite Denmark's continued membership, whereas the Faroe Islands never joined the EC (Peterson 1994).

Finally, a series of vigorous regional cross-border ventures can be found in Norden (Östhol 1996; Johanson 1997). Several of those listed in Table 19.1 date back to the 1950s and 1960s. In the 1990s, a number of new initiatives have been added, stretching beyond the Nordic area as it has traditionally been defined. These initiatives include the Barents Euro-Arctic Council, the North Sea Commission and a host of collaborative ventures in the Baltic Sea area. On top of this, a large number of bilateral ties have been established between Nordic regions and their opposite numbers in other European countries. A survey of the bilateral cross-border relations of 18 Norwegian regions identified at least 70 agreements, reaching from neighbouring Sweden to more distant places like Bulgaria and Portugal (Baldersheim and Litsheim 1996).

In sum, Nordic territorial institutions reflect a careful balance between bottom-up and top-down approaches to governance. A civic culture valuing local and regional self-government represents an important tradition in all five countries. At the same time, the development of the welfare states has resulted in a standardisation of regional governance in the name of equality. Nevertheless, there is both scope for and a long tradition of regional-political entrepreneurship with regard to developmental initiatives. Will European integration give an impetus to the latter tradition and thus stimulate more regionalism in the Nordic countries? That is the question we will examine in the section below.

Reconstruction of the Developmental States of the North

In any international comparison, the Nordic countries are perceived as harmonious, unicultural and unitary states (Miles 1996: 5 ff.). We shall argue that despite this widely shared perception, a vigorous regionalisation process is taking place throughout the Nordic countries. These process may amount to the reconstruction of the Nordic states as developmental states, giving regions a much larger say in the use of public development funds. The reconstruction is occurring as a response to the need to achieve greater flexibility and legitimacy in the spending of such funds.

The mosaic version of regionalisation points to internal socio-economic variation in the nations as a result of demands for more voice in national decision-making and autonomy at regional level. To some extent we find this type of development in the Nordic context. Finland has previously lacked a distinct subnational administrative level with a solid local or regional democratic mandate. This administrative level has, however, been created as an a priori adaptation to the requirements of the structural policies of the European Union. The new joint municipal boards have been given full responsibility for the preparation of regional development plans for the Structural Funds, among these funds originating from the Community Initiatives. Formerly, such tasks were carried out by state authorities at the regional level (the state counties).

In Sweden and Finland, regional development issues have traditionally been entrusted to the state counties. According to a recent Swedish bill, development functions are to be transferred to secondary municipal institutions of various kinds. This initiative is in some cases related to the creation of larger regional authorities (Skåne, Kalmar and Western Sweden) (RP 1996/97: 36). In addition to these national initiatives, voluntary municipal co-operation is growing. One example is Mälardalsrådet, a voluntary regional council organised in the capital region and its surroundings. These developments are driven by the challenge of stiffer international competition. To deal with the enhanced exposure to international market fluctuations, regions develop strategic programmes analysing the strengths and weaknesses, opportunities and threats to the specific region.

A further indicator of the mosaic type of regionalisation may be the emergence of administrative reform strategies of a bottom-up nature and the formation of local and regional strategic partnerships. Over the last decade, the Nordic countries have attracted international attention for their experimental reform strategies. The most celebrated case has, undoubtedly, been the free municipality experiments whose aim is to reduce central government control over local and regional decision-making in order to enhance flexibility and adaptability (Baldersheim and Ståhlberg 1994). In the wake of these experiments, there has been growing interest among local and regional authorities in establishing networks and collaborative organisations (SOU 1996: 137; Kommunernes Landsforening 1996).

In the 1990s, the creation of 'strategic partnerships' between regions has proliferated. These initiatives have resulted, for example, in a surge of new development or technology centres. Usually, these are collaboratively maintained by private and public (local and state) actors. One example is the high-tech centre in Turku, Finland Its three components, Data City, Bio City and Electro City, are built on collaboration between the city of Turku, regional authorities, the two universities in the city, state agencies and private companies. Similar arrangements can be found in many development companies organised by collaborating local governmental authorities. In the case of Denmark, decision-making with regard to Structural Funds has been handed over to regional boards with both public and private partners (see below). A parallel solution is found in Finland. One of the institutional arrangements in the Swedish regional experiment, for example Jämtforum, in the county of Jämtland, is a forum for private-public partnership (RP 1996/97: 36).

The view of regionalisation as the return of history is based on the perception that regional aspirations has been suppressed, causing forceful, at times even violent, assertion of regional rights. On the Nordic scene, there have been no such outbursts, at least in modern times. But this does not mean that regional aspirations are in any way unfamiliar to the Nordic countries. The absence of forceful assertion gives evidence of a successful Nordic accommodation of such claims, as can be seen from the examples of Åland, the Faroes and Greenland with their home rule institutions, and Iceland, which became an independent member of the Nordic family after the war.

However, it cannot be denied that European integration has triggered some disagreements between regions and national governments. The resolution of some of these differences has been fairly dramatic. As already mentioned, Greenland left the EC in 1985, not wishing to go along with the rest of Denmark on the road to integration. Åland was granted a special status under Finland's treaty of accession to the EU. Furthermore, there is, particularly in Norway, some debate on the status of the Sami *Ting* (Assembly), but in this case – as in Finland and Sweden – the question does not primarily concern institutional autonomy but rather ethnic and cultural rights which are not necessarily linked to territorial integrity. It should not be overlooked, however, that recent Norwegian proposals to devolve further powers to the Sami of northern Norway have sparked tensions with already established local and regional authorities in the area.

All in all, the experience of the Nordic countries seems to demonstrate that European integration may result in a search for unique solutions for regions with particular historical claims, solutions that may not be available for other regional institutions.

According to the vision of evolving European superregions, ties of collaboration are knit across national borders. The Nordic countries have since long been part of this development. It is often overlooked that the post-war collaboration in the Nordic Council and the Nordic Council of Ministers somewhat confirms the superregion thesis. The co-operation is in itself an outstanding example of the continuing process and has resulted in an exceptionally tightly intertwined co-operative web, contributing to the functional integration of societies.

Since the 1970s, Nordic funds have been available for cross-border regional co-operation in the Nordic sphere. Even though the Nordic institutions have not, as a rule, been the initiators of the cross-border arrangements of this type, they have been a financial contributor to various cross-border projects (Johansson 1997).

In terms of resources, the North Calotte Committee is by far the largest of the cross-border regions (budget almost 30 million Danish kroner in 1994), whereas the West Nordic Committee and the Kvarken Council are medium-sized efforts (approximately 10-12 million Danish kroner). In comparison with these three, the rest of the cross-border regions are small ventures with budgets of 2-3 million Danish kroner. Among these we find the Archipelago Co-operation (Stockholm, the Åland Islands and the Turku archipelago region), Bornholm and south-east Skåne, the Østfold-Bohuslän Border Committee, the ARKO Committee, and the Øresund Committee. Today however, the resources of most of these cross-border regions have been vastly increased due to their successful attempt to achieve Interreg status. The foundation of this successful adaptation to European integration was built by the Nordic Council of Ministers.

In the immediate post-war years, the civic contacts of Nordic citizens through the Nordic associations became a driving force behind a surge for closer connections between Nordic municipalities. European integration has infused these already established networks with a new vigour. Over the last few years, project proposals have been mushrooming within these networks (Amtrådsforeningen 1996; Landstingen 1996; Tilastokeskus 1996).

Established Nordic co-operation may well be challenged by other super-regional projects in the area, for instance the Baltic and the Barents Sea co-operation, but so far it seems that the interests encompassed by these competing or parallel projects are more diverse than is the case with Nordic co-operation, and the co-operative tradition – perhaps even the co-operative and pragmatic culture – is largely missing. Therefore, these new initiatives are not likely to undermine established Nordic fraternity in the near future. The recent reorganisation of the Nordic Council, with the establishment of a committee to deal exclusively with Nordic-Baltic affairs, may in the long run even have a vitalising effect on the prospects of Nordic co-operation. This committee may, in fact, also be seen as a forum of cross-border regional co-operation with a region of particular importance to the Nordic area, i.e. the Baltic countries.

Conceptualising regionalisation as an emergent three-level game refers to shared interests between the central EU institutions and subnational regions of member countries. Indications of regionalisation along these lines are the establishment of direct channels of communication between regions and Brussels and cases of increasing tension between national and regional authorities, especially in the field of structural policy implementation. Experience in the unitary states of the North seems to confirm the regionalisation thesis.

After some initial hesitation, Nordic regions have entered the race towards Brussels. Since the early 1990s, a considerable number of Nordic regions have become members of the Association of European Regions and other European regional associations. Local and regional governments select candidates to Committee of the Regions. Increasingly, municipalities and regional authorities have strengthened their capacity for lobbying in Brussels. In some cases, their presence in Brussels is a result of regional cross-border co-operation and networking. One outstanding example is the Hanse-office of Schleswig-Holstein, which also houses representatives for Sydsam – a voluntary regional collaborative organisation in southern Sweden – the region of East Bothnia and the city of Vasa in Finland.

As might be expected, the restructuring of regional governance has not occurred without tensions. We have already mentioned that the joint municipal boards in Finland have taken over responsibility for regional development from state authorities. It is hardly surprising that the state county authorities did not look favourably upon this development. A similar confrontation can now be observed in Sweden in the wake of the government's proposal to transfer the responsibility for regional development planning to self-governing units (Fröjd and Åström 1996).

Tensions between local governmental authorities and the state have also emerged with regard to the administration of the Structural Funds. In Denmark, Finland, and Sweden, state authorities have tried to maintain control over decision-making related to Structural Fund projects. The regional authorities have, however, strengthened their positions. In Denmark, decision-making power over Structural Fund projects has been transferred to a regional board with private and public membership and whose secretariat is run by the regional (self-government) authorities. In Finland, regions have also acquired new powers. Recently, decision-making concerning the Interreg programme was handed over to the regional joint municipal boards. And, as already noted, the new regional experiments in Sweden include the transfer of some decision-making authority on the Structural Funds to the proposed new regional authorities, in addition to the transfer of planning authority from the counties to the municipal regional authorities (Amtsrådsforeningen 1996b; RP 1996/97: 36).

The tension between self-governing authorities and the state clearly reveals a pattern of an emerging three-level game. The EU's Directorate General XVI, responsible for regional policy, has consistently supported the regional level in its desire for more power over the Structural Funds. The Committee of the Regions has recently adopted a resolution evaluating experiences from the implementation of Structural Fund initiatives in the new member states (Austria, Finland and Sweden). The Committee is very critical, pointing out undue state interference or downright state monopoly with regard to important Structural Fund decisions, especially in Sweden.

Conclusions

It would seem that all four versions of the regionalisation trend discussed above may be observed in the Nordic area though the least likely version is that of historical regions asserting their claims for self-rule with renewed vigour. Otherwise, the regional mosaic is becoming more visible in governmental decision-making, and so-called superregions may be emerging.

It appears as if Nordic regions have entered the European three-level game with gusto. The consequence is a far-reaching reconstruction of regional governance. Among the examples so far is that Finland may finally get an upper tier of local or regional self-government, while Sweden takes the plunge into democratic administration of development funds at the regional level. In all countries, bottom-up processes of establishing developmental partnerships and cross-border strategic alliances are unfolding.

The totality of these changes may amount to a reconstruction of the Nordic developmental states on a regional foundation. The changes are, however, occurring in a typically Nordic fashion: through a step-by-step, experimental approach, not entirely without friction but with a pragmatic touch in conflict-resolution that reveals long civic traditions and the accumulation of much social capital

(Putnam 1993; Fukuyama 1995). The latter is a feature of the Nordic countries that probably will continue to play a decisive role after the reconstruction.

References

Agranoff, R. (1996). 'Federal Evolution in Spain,' *International Political Science Review*:17, pages 385-402.

Albæk, E., Rose, L., Strömberg, L. and Ståhlberg, K. (1996). *Nordic Local Government*. Helsinki, The Association of Finnish Local Authorities.

Amtsrådsforeningen (1996). *Danish Counties International Cooperation Projects*. Copenhagen.

Amtsrådsforeningen (1996b). *Opgavefordelingen mellem stat, amter og kommuner*. Copenhagen.

Baldersheim, H. and Litsheim, A.E. (1996). 'The Internationalization of Norwegian Regions.' Paper presented at the conference on Politics and Geography of Territorial Power Sharing, the Technical University of Wroclaw, 30 July-2 August 1996.

Baldersheim, H. and Ståhlberg, K. (eds.) (1994). *Towards the Self-Regulating Municipality: Free Communes and Administrative Modernization in Scandinavia*. Aldershot, Dartmouth.

Baldersheim, H. and Ståhlberg, K. (eds.) (1996). *Nordic Region-Building in a European Perspective: The Dynamics of Integration from Below*. London, Avebury (forthcoming).

Balme, R., Garraud, P., Hoffmann-Martinot, V. and Ritaine, E. (1994). *Le territoire pour politiques: Variation européennes*. Paris, L'Harmattan.

Bjørklund, T. (1996). 'The Three Nordic Referenda Concerning Membership in the EU,' *Co-operation and Conflict*:31, pages 11-36.

Bullmann, U. (1996). 'The Politics of the Third Level,' *Regional & Federal Studies*:6, No. 2, pages 3-19.

Bullmann, U. (ed.) (1994). *Die Politik der dritten Eebene. Regionen im Europa der Union*. Baden-Baden, Nomos Verlagsgesellschaft.

Delmaide, D. (1994). *The New Superregions of Europe*. N.Y., Dutton

Enzensberger, H.M.(1987). *Ach Europa!* Frankfurt am Main, Suhrkampf Verlag.

Fröjd, S. and Åström, J. (1996). *Regiondebatt och partiarbete i Västsverige*. Örebro, C-uppsats i statskunskap, Högskolan i Örebro.

Fukuyama, F. (1995). *Trust: The Social Virtues of and the Creation of Prosperity*. N.Y., The Free Press.

Graubard (ed.) (1986). *Norden: The Passion for Equality*. Oslo, Universitetsforlaget.

Harvie, C. (1994). *The Rise of Regional Europe*. London, Routledge.

Illeris, S. (1993). 'An Inductive Theory of Regional Development,' *Papers in Regional Science*:72, No. 2.

Johanson, J. (1995). *Europeiska regioner. Regionforskning i empirisk og normativ belysning*. Örebro Studies:13, University of Örebro.

Johansson, M. (1997). 'Similarities and Differences in Internal Nordic Co-operation' in Baldersheim, H. and Ståhlberg, K. (eds.). *Nordic Region-Building in a European Perspective: The Dynamics of Integration from Below*. London, Avebury (forthcoming).

Keating, M. (1996). 'The Political Economy of Regionalism' in Keating, I.M. and J. Loughlin, J. (eds.). *The Political Economy of Regionalism*. London, Frank Cass.

Kohler-Koch, B. (1996). 'Regionen als Handlungseinheiten in der europäischen Politik,' *Welt-Trends*:11, pages 7-35.

Kommunernes Landsforening (1996). *Opgavekommissionen – principper og tværgående temaer*. Copenhagen.

Landstingen (1996). *Landstingens engagemang i Östersjöområdet*. Stockholm, Landstingsförbundet.

Leonardi, R. (1993). 'The Role of Sub-National Institutions in European Integration' in Leonardi, R. (ed.). *The Regions and the European Community*. London, Frank Cass.

Lipset, M.S. and Rokkan, S. (1967). *Party Systems and Voter Alignments: Cross-National Perspectives.* N.Y., The Free Press.
Marks, G., Sharpf, F.W, Schmitter, P.H. and Streck, W. (eds.) (1996). *Governance in the European Union.* London, Sage.
Miles, L. (1996). 'Introduction' in Miles, L. (ed.). *The European Union and the Nordic Countries.* London, Routledge.
Östhol, A. (1996). *Politisk integration och gränsöverskridande regionbildning i Europa.* Umeå University, Department of Political Science.
Oulasvirta, L. (1992). 'Municipal Public Finances in the Nordic Countries,' *Local Government Studies*:18, pages 106-35.
Peterson, O. (1994). *The Government and Politics of the Nordic Countries.* Stockholm, Publica.
Putnam, R.D. (1993). *Making Democracy Work: Civic Traditions in Modern Italy.* Princeton, Princeton University Press.
RP 1996/97:36. *Den regionala samhällsorganisationen.* Stockholm.
SOU 1996:137. *Kommunalförbund och gemensam nämnd: Två former för kommunal samverkan.* Betänkande av kommunala förnyelsekommittén. Stockholm, Inrikesdepartementet.
Sharpe, L.J. (1993). 'The European Meso: An Appraisal' in Sharpe, L.J. (ed.). *The Rise of Meso Government in Europe.* London, Sage.
Tilastokeskus (1996). *EU-räporttisarja: Alueelliset menestystekijät.* Helsinki, International Business Statistics.

20 Spatial Development and Planning between 'High' and 'Low' Politics: Interreg II C in the Baltic Sea Region

Ib Jørgensen and Jan Nielsen[1]

Introduction

Nothing could be more true than this sober observation found in the proposal for the Baltic Sea Region Interreg II C Operational Programme (BSR/OP) sent by Denmark, Finland, Germany and Sweden to the European Commission's DG XVI in February-March 1997: 'At present, a considerable amount of activities are going on between countries in the Baltic Sea Region at national and sub-national level.' This particular quotation refers explicitly to activities concerned with regional policy, spatial development and planning but it could easily be extended to cover the entire complex of 'high' and 'low' political manoeuvrings which have the Baltic Sea region (BSR) as their focus of interest in the present period.[2]

Speaking about 'high' and 'low' politics,[3] it could sensibly be argued that transnational regional policy, spatial development and planning on a European scale, as now attempted by, in and through the EU, must be seen as part of an exercise in bridging or transcending the real and imagined gulfs between these two spheres of politics. We shall try to substantiate this assumption through a description and analysis of some decidedly innovative developments within EU policies.

A Brief History of Spatial Planning in the EU[4]

During the late 1980s and the early 1990s, a number of significant developments related to spatial planning began to materialise within the Union.

In Nantes in 1989 under the French EU Presidency, a series of informal meetings between ministers responsible for spatial planning was inaugurated. The Nantes meeting became the effective background for the Commission initiative which would lead to the document published in 1991 by Directorate General (DG) XVI, *Europe 2000: Outlook for the Development of Community's Territory.*[5] The net effect was that light was thrown on the need to adopt a more co-ordinated and holistic perspective on the spatial development of Europe as opposed to the mainly nationally oriented development policies financed by the Structural Funds. This was partly in order to ensure a more balanced integration within the Union, partly to attain the strongest possible position in the competition with other transnational entities like the USA (NAFTA) and Asia (ASEAN).

Following the 1989 meeting in Nantes, a whole series of informal meetings of planning ministers took place: Turin 1990, The Hague 1991, Lisbon 1992, Liege 1993, Corfu in June 1994, Leipzig in September 1994, Strasbourg 1995, Madrid 1995 and Venice 1996. In 1991 it was decided to establish the Committee for Spatial Development (CSD), a supranational institution consisting of senior civil servants from the Commission and from national ministries responsible for spatial planning. Eventually, the CSD would acquire a leading role in the development of a European Spatial Development Perspective (ESDP).

At the meeting in Liege 1993, it was agreed that an update of *Europe 2000 – Europe 2000+* – would have to be supplemented by a separate document stipulating the main objectives of spatial planning within the European Union, and it was suggested to baptise this document the European Spatial Development Perspective (Belgian Presidency 1993). Now the Commission and the informal group of ministers together with the CSD had effectively put spatial policy on the Union's agenda. The political principles of the ESDP were adopted in June 1994 in Corfu. 'It should be non-binding and be developed gradually in order to assist decision-making by offering more coherence on a EU-wide scale for all policies with a spatial or territorial impact' (Williams 1996: 221). Already three months later, in September 1994 in Leipzig, the informal ministerial meeting debated these issues again, one of the premises being that 'The differences in the level of development are growing – not so much between countries as between regions and the European sub-regions' (German Presidency 1994). It had to be realised that in spite of the growing sums allocated through the Regional Fund (and the two other Structural Funds, the Social and the Agricultural Fund), the actual development did not adhere to the principles and objectives hailed as the responsibility of EU policies, and as a consequence, the Leipzig meeting agreed upon the principles for the final ESDP. In the document *Principles for a European Spatial Policy* written by the CSD (1994), these principles were synthesised as follows:

- 'spatial development can contribute in a decisive way to the achievement of the goal of economic and social cohesion,'
- 'the existing competences of the responsible institutions for Community policies remain unchanged; the ESDP may contribute to the implementation of Community policies which have a territorial impact, without constraining the responsible institutions in exercising their responsibilities,'
- 'the central aim will be to achieve sustainable and balanced development,'
- 'it will be designed in accordance with existing institutions and will be non-binding on Member States,'
- 'it will respect the principle of subsidiarity' and

– 'each country will take it forward according to the extent it wishes to take account of European spatial aspects in its national policies.'[6]

In respect of political realism, and in spite of its many provisos and escape clauses, the ESDP seems to have a strong standing because of its quite long and arduous gestation process, which has led to a high degree of pre-established unanimity between the Commission, the planning ministers of the member states and not least the host of high-ranking national civil servants who have invested a considerable amount of work in preparing it.

Starting with the publication in 1991 of *Europe 2000: Outlook for the Development of the Community's Territory*, DG XVI initiated a number of transnational studies with the aim of providing the Commission with a better understanding of the differences in the spatial structures of the Union. Originally, the studies encompassed the following transnational regions: the Atlantic Arc, the North Sea, the Centre Capitals, the Continental Diagonal, the Mediterranean, and the Alpine Arc. 'The purpose was to stimulate new ways of thinking about spatial issues which were not inhibited by the mental confines of national boundaries and to encourage bottom-up development of inter-regional links' (Williams 1996: 102).

With the accession of Sweden and Finland to the Union, the Baltic Sea region has been added to the list of macro-regions, and thanks to the intergovernmental document *Visions and Strategies around the Baltic Sea 2010 (VASAB 2010)*, this region has swiftly acquired a kind of paragon status for the other transnational regions.[7] The group behind this development is the Council of Baltic Sea States involving 11 states around the Baltic Sea, including Belarus and Norway.

But one thing is to make academic and analytical studies of transnational regions and their individual characteristics and problems; another is to get representatives from these regions – be it public or private institutions, individuals or organisations – to work together on transnational spatial planning issues. This is where the Community Initiatives (CI) under the Regional Fund come in. In 1995 – at the request of the informal meeting of planning ministers in Strasbourg (Martin 1996) – the Commission decided to add a new strand to the Interreg initiative, Interreg II C concerned with transnational co-operation on spatial planning (EC/OJ 1996). The Interreg II C is divided into three elements: measures for spatial planning and transnational co-operation, spatial planning and transnational co-operation against flooding and spatial planning and action against drought. In order to get funding from Interreg II C, at least three contiguous states, hereof at least two member states, must be involved. Parties interested would have to forward letters of intent to DG XVI before 1 October 1996; final programmes were scheduled to be with the Commission by January 1997.

With the aim of introducing the Interreg II C initiative to the member states in a manner consistent with its intentions, the Commission, in association with the EU's Committee of Regions (COR), organised six regional planning seminars during 1996.[8] The penultimate of these meetings, the one in Edinburgh in

September 1996, brought together representatives from the North Sea and Baltic Sea regions.[9]

It is safe to say that one of the speakers listened to with the utmost attention was the Dane Henriette Bastrup-Birk, Principal Administrator at DG XVI, unit A3, responsible for spatial development and planning as well as interregional and cross-border co-operation. Ms Bastrup-Birk did not beat around the bush regarding the intimate relationship between the ESDP and Interreg II C: 'It should be noted that at the last meeting in Venice in May (1996), the European ministers responsible for spatial planning agreed that the new instrument provided by the Community Initiative, Interreg II C, should constitute the test-bed for practical measures relating directly to the objectives and approaches anchored in the ESDP.'[10]

The total contribution from the Structural Funds to Interreg II C is estimated at 415 million ecu, divided into 100 million for unspecified spatial planning, 165 million for spatial planning and flooding and 150 million for spatial planning and drought (Martin 1996).

Ms Bastrup-Birk made it crystal clear that the programmes which will receive funding must have as their basis a vision of the entire region and must be founded in a reliable organisational structure. Commenting, for example, on the activities of the actors in the North Sea region she said that 'there must be a readiness ... among these actors to display imagination and unconventional thinking in order to set up, sometimes even invent, appropriate organisational and institutional structures to translate this transnational strategy into practical measures.'

Regional Policy: The Structural Funds and Community Initiatives

With the Single European Act of 1986 and its declared new objectives of economic and social cohesion, structural and regional policy came to take a dominant place on the Community agenda and budget (Hannequart 1992). The Structural Funds today amount to roughly one third of the Union's total expenses, and Directorate General XVI, which is responsible for the administration of these large funds, has consequently become an increasingly visible and important partner of the member states, funding a large part of their national strategies and policies in regional development.

By far the major part of the Structural Funds is channelled through the European Regional Development Fund (ERDF) established in 1975 with the primary objective of supporting investment, infrastructure and small and medium-sized enterprises (SMEs) in disadvantaged regions; the European Social Fund (ESF) aimed at combating long-term unemployment, promoting occupational integration of young people etc.; and the European Agricultural Guarantee and Guidance Fund (EAGGF), supporting development and conversion of agriculture in rural areas.

These funds amount to roughly 27 billion ecu per year. About 40 per cent is earmarked for the ERDF, 25 per cent for the ESF, and most of the remainder is spent by the EAGGF.

Eighty per cent of the Structural Funds goes to Objective 1 regions through six designated areas in accordance with pre-established development criteria decided by the European Council and based upon the so-called Community Support Frameworks (CSF) for the member states worked out in co-operation between the Commission and representatives of national and regional authorities of the respective countries. It is a decisive point here that the CSF is a strictly national document and its preparation is primarily a question of collaboration between national and regional or local authorities based upon nationally accepted or acceptable development strategies and policies. In most cases, the allocation of EU Structural Fund resources is determined by national governments, however, any expenditure by the EU is supposed to be matched by public or private co-financing amounting to at least 50 per cent of the total expenditure.

In its granting policy DG XVI tries to influence the national projects so that they contribute optimally to the general EU objectives of economic and social cohesion, but so far DG XVI has not been able to add any specific European dimension to the combined regional development activities financed by the Structural Funds. It is this situation which the recent policy innovation Interreg II C is designed to come to terms with. The programme is launched within the framework the Structural Funds' Community Initiatives.

The Commission has the authority to decide about the allocation of around 10 per cent of the Structural Funds. One of its primary goals is to further European integration, and therefore it obviously has an interest in stressing the transnational dimension of EU policy.[11]

The largest of the Community Initiatives is the Interreg, which amounts to 3 billion ecu for the period 1994-99.[12] By far the biggest share of this amount, however, has been earmarked for Objective 1 areas, which by and large correspond to Ireland, Spain, Portugal, southern Italy and Greece. Interreg II is a combination of two earlier Community Initiatives, adopted in 1990, Interreg and REGEN. Their aim was to promote cross-border co-operation and assist isolated areas on internal and external EU frontiers, and fill gaps in energy networks. Thus, Interreg II A has been targeting cross-border co-operation (2.4 billion ecu), whereas Interreg II B (0.5 billion ecu) was designated for binding together energy networks (Williams 1996: 136).

According to Noralv Veggeland, Interreg II has had as its explicit objective to overcome the obstacles to regional co-operation represented by state borders, and it is supposedly the only programme where funds are channelled directly to collaborating regions rather than member states. The programmes are established in collaboration with regional and local authorities (Veggeland 1996). It may further be added that as an innovation, Interreg II A and B had provisions allowing for cross-border co-operation with regions of the Central and Eastern European countries eligible under the EU's PHARE programme, e.g. all the CEE countries that have, or are negotiating, formal association agreements with the EU. In the Baltic Sea region this pertains to Poland, Estonia, Latvia, and Lithuania (Williams 1996: 26).

In 1996 the Commission announced a new addition to the Interreg family, Interreg II C, which goes even further according to Commission's communication to the member states: 'In terms of its objectives, as well as its programmes, Interreg II C is entirely distinct from strands A (transnational cooperation) and B (selected energy networks), as much by the extent of the area covered and the types of partnerships which it seeks to promote as by the emphasis it places on the development of a strategic vision for the spatial planning of the areas in question' (CEC/OJ 1996).

The Transnational Regions Materialise, Or Do They?

The formation of transnational regions as new territorial units and the projected spatial planning according to the principles of the ESDP are genuine innovations in the EU toolbox. Transnational regions – if fully established – will be much more than the sum total of the constituent regions and their nation states. Transnational regions will have characteristics and present problematics inherited from the 'supplying' nation states complicated by the specific problems created by the attempt to unite a number of nation states into larger transnational configurations.

These new developments will invariably lead to changes in the traditional regional policies of the EU. So far, EU regional policy has taken as its point of departure the extant geography of nation states and their constitutional peculiarities, as witnessed by the fact that by far the larger share of the Structural Funds has been allocated in consideration of these national conditions, albeit subject to some very broad and flexible EU objectives like social and economic cohesion and sustainability. It is the bringing together of regional policy proper and spatial planning which adds a new quality to the prospective transnational regions.

In spite of their intimate connection, regional policy and spatial development, on the one hand, and spatial planning, on the other, have more often than not been carried out in separation from each other. Very broadly speaking, the first group of policies is about the deployment of various forms of financial incentives to more or less lagging regions and localities, whereas spatial and physical planning (*aménagement du territoire*) concerns the more technically oriented decisions as to the building of infrastructure, land use regulation, urban planning and so forth.

Its (apparently only seemingly) technical nature notwithstanding, spatial planning at national, regional and local levels has typically been facing more protest, strife and conflict than perhaps more consequential regional development activities. This probably has a lot to do with the almost metaphysical (some would say primitive and arcane) emotions attached to the territory.[13] This is not the place to start an elaborate philosophical exercise on this, but suffice it to say that the notion of security centred in the nation state is intimately related to the sovereign domain over a territory, an issue of growing attention these years (Tonboe 1996). There cannot be much doubt that it is this protective attitude towards the national territory which lies behind the many provisos and escape clauses with which the European Spatial Development Perspective most likely will be provided. A supranational territory seems an impossibility in the absence of some minimum of a federal elements. So far, however, federation seem to be a word *non grata* in official EU contexts. Nonetheless, we shall argue that it is precisely such supranational territories which the Commission, together with the informal ministerial meetings and aided by the CSD, is indirectly trying to construct through the attempt to link spatial planning and regional policy with the help of the financial instrument of Interreg II C, the planning instrument of ESDP and emerging new territorial 'polities,' namely transnational regions.

What we see is not a relation developing between the EU and nation states, with the sovereignty of the latter being more or less unquestioned, but a relation between nation states, transnational regions and the EU with some transfer of sovereignty to transnational regions, a form of partial sovereignty supported by EU intervention. It certainly would amount to a gross exaggeration to call these new formations 'mini-federations' with supranational bodies as an integrated part of the polity, but on the other hand we venture to say that, more or less explicitly, elements of federal thinking lie behind their invention. Expressed in the language of political science, the new transnational regions might be described as test-beds for a reconciliation between a statist (neo-realistic) and a neo-institutional (neo-functional) approach to integration.[14]

Of course, such an experiment is laden with potential conflict, not least the problem of the status of the transnational regions vis-a-vis the states whose territory they constitute part of. If our assessment here has a minimum of relevance, one would expect tensions between 'high' neo-realist and statist politics (concerning territory), and 'low'-politics, neo-institutional, neo-functional approaches (concerning first and foremost economic issues) to surface in the Operational Programmes which the prospective partners have been obliged to formulate and send to DG XVI in order to receive Interreg II C support.

The application from the Baltic Sea region might benefit from the Commission's April 1996 announcement of a Baltic Sea Region Initiative.

The Baltic Sea Region Operational Programme

'Linking the VASAB five-years accumulation of experience and knowledge with the Interreg II C programming in the BSR would be a strong asset for the programme. ... Another cornerstone is the full integration of the transition countries into the Interreg II C-programme and a third, encouragement of the local and sub-national level to participate in the process' (BSR/OP 1997).

More than anything else, this quote reveals how 'high' and 'low' politics are intermingled in the Baltic Sea Region Operational Programme (BSR/OP) which has been prepared in co-operation between the member states Denmark, Finland, Germany and Sweden – with Norway being a self-financing participant – and the transition countries in the Baltic Sea region. The member states have been represented by central state spatial planning and regional development authorities, but regional and in some countries local authorities have also been involved in the process.

Early on it was decided that the programme would cover the entire Baltic Sea region of EU member and non-member states. However, Interreg II C funding is only available for and expendable in member states, which is one of the roadblocks to the formation of a comprehensive Baltic Sea region: The EU funds made available for the transition countries, mainly under the PHARE programmes administered by DG IA (DG I being the Foreign Office of EU) cannot without further ado be used in tandem with Interreg II C. Provisions have been made to combine PHARE and Interreg II policy instruments (Christiansen 1997), but to our knowledge, this possibility has not, in effect, been extended to II C.[15] There cannot, however, be much doubt that some initiatives will be taken to make such combined efforts possible. According to an internal DG XVI Note (96340853 15/11/96), the issue was high on the agenda of a meeting in the Baltic Co-ordination Committee (BCC) in November 1996, but according to the BSR/OP, a satisfactory solution has not been found.[16] This is not only a simple matter of bureaucratic tinkering and accounting. It also has a lot to do with the various political and planning cultures which such a scheme must bring into a working collaboration.

It would have created great difficulties to establish a common programme involving the EU member states alone, because it is a precondition in the Interreg II C set-up that regional or local authorities are actively engaged in the programme. Here we confront the fact alluded to above, that the physical space covered by the Baltic Sea Region Operational Programme is only a small part of the territory of the Baltic Sea region, however it is defined. For the national authorities to back the programme, they must be in a position to assure their other regions and localities that the type of activity evolving in the region covered by the Operational Programme will not have harmful effects on their situation. Considering the relatively small amounts of money involved, this may not be too difficult seen from an EU perspective, whereas it is an entirely different question for non-member states.

In the first place, their political authorities will be much more alert to get as much value for EU money as possible. Not only in traditional economic terms, but also politically. This problem was revealed at the BCC meeting in November 1996. In the summary of the discussions attached to the DG XVI Note, one can read that during the debate on the prospects of combining Interreg II C and PHARE money, 'some Baltic countries expressed a concern that their national authorities should not be expected to accept automatically projects agreed by decentralised authorities amongst themselves.' Admittedly, this is not incontrovertible evidence, but we venture the interpretation that the reaction reveals some latent contradictions in the scheme which may later become a matter of contention, even in member states.

Variations in planning culture between EU and non-EU partners are also among the problems mentioned in the BSR/OP: 'Spatial planning has not been considered a priority in any PHARE and TACIS programme in the BSR... One reason for this situation is the weak position of spatial planning and other long-term and "soft" measures of development in the transition countries preoccupied by macroeconomic short- and medium-term problems.' We shall not try to elaborate on the unmistakably EU-centric stance of this observation, just note that it remains to be seen whether the position of spatial planning in the EU countries is strong enough to take on the challenges involved in constructing the new transnational regions in general, and the Baltic Sea region in particular.

The scale of the venture is far from enormous. According to the BSR/OP, the total budget is 46 million ecu, of which 24 million is EU financing from the ERDF, 20 million is national financing from member states and 2 million is private financing. The programme has been divided into three subprogrammes. Seventy-six per cent of the money available is earmarked for the promotion of a sustainable spatial development in the Baltic Sea region, including a Baltic urban

Figure 20.1: Interreg II C in Northern Europe

system and a balanced settlement structure; improving communication and energy through sustainable regional development; promoting integrated management of coastal zones and islands; and promoting sustainable development in other specific or sensitive areas. One might consider this the 'traditional' functional sectoral planning and development section of the programme.

Another 17 per cent of the budget is allocated for the promotion and updating of a spatial development strategy in the Baltic Sea region, including further development of spatial planning strategies and exchange of experience in the field of spatial planning and test projects. This, then, is the part of the programme where the more sensitive issue of the assembling of a new territorial unit, interfacing closely with 'high' politics would have to be confronted. Finally, 7 per cent of the funding is set aside for technical assistance to support transnational cooperation.

Implementation of the programme is planned to take place through the formation of a Monitoring Committee in accordance with EU regulations. Members will be member state representatives responsible for EU Structural Funds application and spatial planning, a representative of the regions from each member state, the chairman of the Steering Committee and a representative of the Commission. Each non-member state will have the right to send one consultative member.

The Steering Committee is of particular interest since it is suggested that it shall be assisted by national subcommittees including regional and local representatives and economic and social partners. These national subcommittees are supposed to form an organisation with a chairman, who will be a member of the Steering Committee. This could easily turn out to be one of the more tricky and difficult arrangements in the set-up. Furthermore, the Steering Committee shall be assisted by 'transnational sub-committees of thematic character, if necessary.' It is also an open question what might be implied here. New powerful groups or debate forums?

A common secretariat and a joint financial body will assist the Steering Committee, whose members, besides the national governmental representatives for regional policy and spatial planning, will be the chairman of the national subcommittees (one for each state); the chairman of the Monitoring Committee; representatives from Norway, Poland, Latvia, Lithuania and, if they agree to it, Belarus, Estonia and Russia; and finally, as an advisory member, a representative of the Financial Body. The latter will have as its central institution the Investitionsbank Schleswig-Holstein in Rostock in Mecklenburg-Vorpommern, which will be in charge of the financial administration of the EU funds in accordance with decisions made by the Steering Committee.

Conclusion

Will the attempts by the EU to institute a new kind of spatial planning for new territories described here lead to the desired improvements in the integration and development of the Union's territory – or territories – and how will these attempts affect the development in the Baltic Sea region?

In order to give a reasonable answer, we must first of all realise the magnitude of the challenge; the many other, and more powerful, dynamics at play; and not least the very modest financial scope of the activities, which mean that the short- and medium-term results are likely to be modest. But as one element among many others in the developing architecture of the European Union, the significance should not be underrated.

In this connection we would like to quote Philippe C. Schmitter. Referring to the multiple and incoherent provisions of the Maastricht Treaty, he points out: 'How ironic it would be if Eurocrats – normally so attentive with regard to identifying unintended consequences and so skilful at turning them into an expansion of their *compétences* – should discover that their preferred design for the Euro-polity was to be the accidental victim of their own efforts! The Maastricht Treaty opens for the institutionalization of diversity – for a multitude of relatively independent European arrangements with distinct statutes, functions, resources and membership, not coordinated by a single central organization and operating under different decision rules' (Schmitter 1996: 127). Or as peanut Charlie Brown once sighed: 'Now I'll go home and make my contribution to the general confusion.'

This may very well be the most significant accomplishment of the Baltic Sea region Interreg II C Programme but that need not be bad at all: if the quality of the confusion is high, something good may result eventually.

Notes

1 We thank the C.W. Obel Foundation for supporting our research leading to this chapter.

2 At the same time, one must also nod approvingly to an even more sobering *caveat*: since many of these activities and projects pertain to different sectors and various specific problems, an impact of their sum total is far from guaranteed. Effectiveness may be both hampered and improved.

3 'High' politics is understood as intergovernmental exchanges between sovereign territorial nation states mainly concerned with geopolitics (borders), security issues and peace-keeping. 'Low' politics being the more mundane day-to-day regulation of the economic, cultural and political interaction between corporations, enterprises, citizens and their organisations. The relationship between these two levels politics is a central issue for debate (e.g. Matlary 1993).

4 For a more comprehensive version of this section, see Jørgensen, Nielsen and Jensen (1996).

5 During the same period, DG XI published the so-called *Green Book on the Urban Environment*, and a number of member states issued planning documents emphasising the necessity of carrying out spatial planning with a European perspective. Particularly noteworthy was the Dutch contribution *Perspectives in Europe* (RPD 1991), but also the Danish document *Denmark Towards the Year 2018: The Spatial Structuring of Denmark in the Future of Europe* (MoE 1992) deserves mentioning in this context.

6 We cannot go into any details on this document here, but we would like to quote the proposed objectives for spatial development ,which have been condensed into three integrated components to be promoted by the ESDP:

- 'a polycentric urban system, as balanced as possible, discouraging excessive concentration around some large centres and the marginalisation of peripheral areas,'
- 'a network of environmentally acceptable and efficient infrastructure, strengthening the cohesion of the Community territory' and
- 'a European network of open spaces for the protection of natural resources, with protection areas classified according to their different functions' (CSD 1994).

7 'Substantial input for the development of the future spatial structure in the BSR has been made by the Ministers for Spatial Planning and Development in the BSR. It is evident that the VASAB co-operation has been of special importance for the three Baltic States and Poland in the transformation of their planning institutions. The VASAB process has also had an influence on the Commission's views on spatial planning in a larger Europe. It is therefore natural that the programme draws on experience from the VASAB process' (BSR/OP 1997: section 5: 'Conclusions' – emphasis added).

8 For practical reasons, the geographical areas covered were identical with the transnational regions of *Europe 2000* and *Europe 2000+* mentioned above (one seminar dealt with regions having a border with Central and Eastern Europe), but according to DG XVI (DG XVI 1996a), these regions 'are not the anticipated areas for the future Community Initiative INTERREG II C.' The same issue of the Newsletter further states that the meetings 'are intended for elected representatives and representatives of the local, regional, national and Community political institutions concerned and for those with an active economic and social involvement in regional planning.' As it turned out, these meetings came to function as an important legitimating backcloth to the Committee of the Regions' Opinion on Spatial Planning in Europe passed at its plenary in January 1997. This opinion is practically an all-out endorsement and propagation of the construct: transnational regions plus ESDP plus Interreg II C.

9 The authors attended the Edinburgh meeting, and quotations are based on tape recordings of speeches given at the plenary. The audience, 200 plus, was made up of representatives from local and regional authorities – the host being the Convention of Scottish Local Authorities (CoSLA) – as well as private and semi-private development institutions; COR members from the regions involved; national and Community politicians and civil servants.

10 We do not think it totally unwarranted to surmise that this development can be seen as an initial stage of making large parts of the Regional Funds subject to the principles of the ESDP, the more so since Commissioner Monika Wulf-Mathies, responsible for regional policy, has signalled a thorough revision of the criteria for the allocation of the funds after the termination of the present period in 1999 (DG XVI 1996b).

11 According to R.H. Williams (1996: 136) the Commission 'has sought to give CIs three distinctive features: a transnational and inter-regional character, bottom-up implementation and the opportunity to give the EU a high profile in the localities concerned.'

12 Williams (1996) describes the 13 Community Initiatives adopted by the Commission in 1994.

13 Clearly we are here dealing with the role of functional versus territorial constituencies/polities. According to Schmitter (1996), the founding fathers of the European Community, Jean Monnet et al., were deliberate neo-functionalists. Since then, however, 'the mix of functional and territorial constituencies/authorities at various levels has shifted significantly within the EC/EU, giving rise to the present uncertainty about the eventual outcome.'

14 'Functionalism and neofunctionalism were designed to explain economic and social processes, realism and neorealism were fashioned with security in mind' (Cornett and Caporaso 1992).

15 Actually, in a note (Brussels, 22 April, 1996) to Commissioner Wulf-Mathis from Director General Eneko Landaburu on the implementation of the Baltic Sea Region Initiative and the role of the Structural Funds, Mr Landaburu wrote: 'For 1997 and beyond, a decision has still to be taken whether to continue a joint facility between the ERDF and PHARE, or whether, as DG I now indicates is its preference, it would be better for each to go its separate way.' It

is not quite clear whether this refers only to administrative affairs, but at least it suggests some friction between the two DGs responsible for external affairs and regional policy respectively. See also Christiansen (1997).

16 'As far as PHARE is concerned it seems that in principle PHARE CBC Programme, PHARE Multi Country Cross-border Programme and ECOS-OVERTURE (BSPF) could be used to finance the spatial planning projects, *but in practice there seem to be considerable limitations to that. Especially there is no solution for concerted funding of projects executed jointly by PHARE, TACIS and EU countries*' (BSR/OP 1997: Part 4, section 'Coordination of EU-programmes in the BSR,' emphasis added).

References

Belgian Presidency (1993). 'For a Significative Step towards a Co-ordinated Planning of Europe's Territory.' Note of the Presidency regarding Regional Planning (discussion of 13 November). Conseil Informel 'Politique Regionale et Aménagement du Territoire,' Liège 12-13 November.

BMBau (1994). *European Spatial Planning: Informal Council of Spatial Planning Ministers in Leipzig 21-22 Sept.* Bonn, Bundesministerium für Raumordnung, Bauwesen und Städtebau.

BSR/OP (1997). INTERREG II C Baltic Sea Region – Operational Programme. 4 February. Unpublished manuscript.

Christiansen, T. (1997). 'A European Meso-Region?: European Union Perspectives on the Baltic Sea Region,' pages 254-92 in Joenniemi, P. (ed.). *Neo-nationalism or Regionality: The Restructuring of Political Space Around the Baltic Rim.* NordREFO 1997:5. Copenhagen.

Committee on Spatial Development (1994). 'Principles for a European Spatial Development Policy'. Committee on Spatial Development, Leipzig 4 October, in BMBau (1994), pages 2-20.

Cornett, L. and Caporaso, J.A. (1992) '"And Still It Moves!" State Interests and Social Forces in the European Community,' pages 219-49 in Rosenau, J.N. and Czempiel, E.-O. (eds.). *Governance without Government: Order and Change in World Politics.* Cambridge, Cambridge University Press.

DG XVI (1996a). 'Six Seminars on Regional Planning,' *Newsletter*.26, March. Brussels, DG XVI.

DG XVI (1996b). 'The Structural Funds after 1999,' *Newsletter*. 31, August. Brussels, DG XVI.

EC (1991). *Europe 2000: Outlook for the Development of the Community's Territory.* Brussels, DG XVI.

EC (1994). *Europe 2000+: Co-operation for European Territorial Development.* Brussels DG XVI.

EC/OJ (1996). *Official Journal of the European Communities,* 10 July, No. C 200, page 23.

German Presidency (1994). 'Conclusions Issued by the German Presidency...' in BMBau (1994), page 1.

Group of Focal Points (1994). *Vision and Strategies Around the Baltic Sea: Towards a Framework for Spatial Development in the Baltic Sea Region.* Karlskrona, The Baltic Institute.

Hannequart, A. (ed.). (1992). *Economic and Social Cohesion in Europe: A New Objective for Integration.* London, Routledge.

Jørgensen, I., Nielsen, J. and Jensen, O.B. (1996). 'INTERREG II C: A Loophole for Transnational Spatial Planning,' *Nord Revy*.5/6, December, pages 13-19. Oslo.

Martin, D. (1996). 'INTERREG II C: New Possibilities for Transnational Spatial Planning in Europe,' *IFHP Newsletter*.1. The Hague.

Matlery, J.H. (1993) '"And Never the Twain Shall Meet?": Reflections on Norway, Europe and Integration,' pages 43-63 in Tiilikainen, T. and Petersen, I.D. (eds.). *The Nordic Countries and the EC.* Copenhagen, Copenhagen Political Studies Press.

MoE (1992). *Danmark på vej mod år 2018: Danmarks fysiske og funktionelle indretning i fremtidens Europa* (Denmark Towards the Year 2018: The Spatial Structuring of Denmark in the Future of Europe). Copenhagen, Ministry of the Environment.

RPD (1991). *Perspectives in Europe.* The Hague, Rijksplanologische Dienst.

Schmitter, P.C. (1996). 'Imagining the Future of the Euro-Polity with the Help of New Concepts,' pages 121-50 in Marks, G., Scharpf, F.W., Schmitter, P.C. and Streeck, W. (eds.). *Governance in the European Union.* London, Sage Publications.
Tonboe, J. (1996). 'Territoriality: Displaced Power or Frustrated Identity?' in Elander and Källtorp (eds.). *Cities in Transformation – Transformation in Cities.* Aldershot, Avebury.
Veggeland, N. (1996). *Regionenes Europa – innføring i teori og praksis.* Oslo, Spartacus Forlag.
Williams, R.H. (1996). *European Union Spatial Policy and Planning.* Liverpool, Paul Chapman Publishing.

21 Transborder Co-operation along the EU's External Borders and the Turnabout of Regional Development Policies: A Mediterranean Perspective

Riccardo Cappellin

Introduction

The process of European integration according to a market approach mainly consists in the removal of the obstacles which hinder the integration of the national markets for goods, services, capital and labour. The abolishment of customs tariffs, the creation of the European Single Market, the free mobility of capital and the European Monetary Union represent various stages in this development.

According to an institutional approach, then, European integration is aiming towards a gradual transfer of legislative and administrative competencies from national authorities to the European institutions.

Both of these processes have a regional dimension, by transforming former international relations into a type of interregional relations. They also have an impact at the regional level because they create risks and opportunities for the economic development of the various regions and affect the powers and the financial resources of regional governments.

European integration also has a spatial character. The Common Market and the European Union have gradually come to include the United Kingdom, Ireland, Denmark, Greece, Spain and Portugal and recently Austria, Finland and Sweden. In the near future, they will be most probably be extended to the countries of Central and Eastern Europe.

Spatial models are also recurring in the debates on the centre-periphery concept (with Lotharingia or the 'blue banana' forming the centre) and the model of multiple circles with different speeds of integration.

According to a flexible geometry approach, however, the European territory can be interpreted as a set of overlapping transnational 'macro-regions' (Cappellin and Batey 1993), which are characterised by co-operation between the various administrative regions included in the same macro-region and by competition with regions belonging to other macro-regions. These macro-regions also represent complex networks of urban centres which perform complementary and competing roles on the European scale.

The Mediterranean basin and the Baltic basin are two such macro-regions, which include countries and regions both inside and outside the European Union. Other macro-regions are the Alpine region, Mitteleuropa, the Atlantic Arc and the capital regions in north-western Europe.

The European macro-regions may represent symbolic constructions. However, they are also based on an identification of the actual trends in the process of internationalisation. The latter is creating new forms of interdependence between neighbouring regions which were until recently almost completely separated by the divide between Western and Eastern Europe. The process of co-operation is a learning process which may in the near future enable the European macro-regions to develop a sort of 'soft' identity or a sense of belonging which is the prerequisite of a common development strategy and a common role in the European framework.

Thus, the experience of transregional co-operation in both Northern and Southern Europe indicates that the European macro-regions are different from cross-border agreements aiming at solving particular problems or reaching particular objectives. The defining characteristic of a macro-region is the existence of a common 'soft' identity determined by a sense of belonging to a common territory in a geographical, cultural and economic sense.

Macro-regions may represent a political space or forum for joint political action. They may also stimulate solidarity between the most developed regions in Western Europe and the less developed regions in Eastern Europe. Thus, macro-regions constitute a new framework for regulating the development of international relationships.

The emergence of European macro-regions clearly demonstrates that the European Union will not be a 'single' space but will be characterised by interregional networking. Moreover, the process of European integration is not leading to the withering away of the nation states, since the networks are overlapping and the existence of multiple or 'soft' identities is possible. Thus, each region is linked both to its respective nation and to a transnational macro-region or even several macro-regions.

The borders of the European Union in both Northern and Southern Europe are not made up of lines separating the countries which are increasingly integrated from others which, being outside of the Community, will face growing obstacles in their relations with a supposed 'Fortress Europe.' On the contrary, the borders are increasingly replaced by spaces or basins which encompass countries and regions both inside and outside the European Union and which are more and more integrated among themselves due to the general process of internationalisation. In fact, these transnational basins play the role of 'bridges' or 'interfaces' between the most central regions of the European Union and other groups of countries which belong to other parts of the European continent or to other continents.

Clearly, the development of transnational co-operation in both Northern and Southern Europe raises some common questions, such as whether transnational associations of regions should choose a large or small geographical framework, soft versus hard forms of joint institutions, a historical versus a forward-looking perspective or an inward- or outward-looking strategy. These questions deserve a common research effort.

The Development of the Mediterranean Regions of the EU

The economic development of the Mediterranean regions can no longer be identified as a question of industrialising economically backward areas (Cappellin 1995d). On the contrary, after 40 years of national industrialisation policies based on a 'fordist' model, and after the collapse of the industrial poles that took place from the 1950s to the 1970s, there is a need for a second phase of regional policy, which should aim at a 're-industrialisation' process to increase the supply of modern private and public services, create small and medium-sized firms and develop internationally competitive productions. Fiscal and financial measures should aim at a continuous increase of productivity rather than compensating for higher costs of inefficient local productions and defending them from international competition.

The decreasing importance of traditional agricultural activities in the economically lagging regions (Objective 1 areas in the EU regional policy) has led to a massive process of urbanisation in the largest metropolitan areas, such as Rome, Naples, Lisbon, Madrid and Athens. The need to develop the role of small and medium cities has only recently been recognised – as a result of the enormous economic, social and environmental problems of these large conurbations. A more balanced structure of the territory of the economically lagging regions seems a prerequisite or at least a complementary factor in order to strengthen the process of reconversion toward a more efficient and competitive economy.

Regional policies have often been a mere substitute for the inadequate level of other state investments in economically lagging regions. The endowment of transport and social infrastructure and the level of vocational and advanced education are still inadequate and represent obstacles to the less developed regions' ability to become economically, physically and socially integrated in the increasingly complex and sophisticated European production system. Investment in the creation and maintenance of infrastructure and public services becomes a crucial factor for the future, as it was during the early phases of industrialisation of the so-called 'basic' sectors.

Thus, it is necessary to evaluate the relative importance of explicit regional policies with respect to other investment policies, such as transport policy, other public work policies, industrial policies, research and innovation and technical and advanced education policies.

An important issue to be discussed is the relevance of policies based on the upgrading of infrastructure with respect to industrial policies more directly connected with the core of the economy and aiming to enhance the competitiveness of production in the international markets and in terms of technological development and innovation. This requires new instruments of industrial policy that are compatible with EU competition policy and will not cause distortions in the allocation of resources, as those applied in the past by traditional capital subsidies.

Relations with the Countries in Central and Eastern Europe

The economies of Central and Eastern European countries like the Czech Republic, Slovakia, Hungary, Slovenia, Turkey etc. are becoming increasingly interdependent with the European Union. Several of these countries will most probably join the European Union in the next decade. Due to spatial contiguity and strategic transport corridors these countries are tightly connected with Greece, Austria, Italy, France and Spain. This determines the need for national and EU regional policies to cover a wider area.

The economic prospects of some lagging regions inside the EU but on the periphery of its north-western core clearly depend on relations with neighbouring countries outside the Union. Thus, regional policies should consider not only the interregional relations between the core and periphery of the EU but also the role of peripheral regions in the Union's external relations.

The entry of countries to the south-east of the EU will move the Union's economic and demographic centre southwards. It is possible to indicate an axis of development going from the South-West (the Iberian peninsula) to the North-East (Mitteleuropa) including both the EU Objective 1 Mediterranean regions and the various countries in the Balkans. In this perspective, Southern Europe can exploit the enlargement of the internal European market to reduce its peripherality.

The industrial development of the European countries outside the EU can hardly be based on the final products which they used to export to the former USSR as the competition in the European market is too tight and the demand of the European consumer is too sophisticated for low-quality products. Therefore, a profound reconversion seems necessary towards intermediate products and modern subcontracting relations with large, and in some cases small, Western firms which are already established on the EU market. The spatial contiguity with EU countries makes it both possible and necessary to promote a tight integration of the industrial systems of Eastern countries with that of the EU and to abandon the myth of national self-sufficiency and of specialisation and leadership in specific sectors.

The relations between the EU's South European regions and the countries of Eastern Europe are apparently ones of competition, as the lower wage levels may redirect the flow of investments from the most developed regions of the EU. However, a change of perspective is needed because the Mediterranean Objective 1 regions are increasingly relying on endogenous industrial activities. In fact, an endogenous development strategy creates a need to define a wider international area in which to expand commercial, productive and technological ties. Moreover, whereas the relations between the Mediterranean Objective 1 regions and the central and most developed regions of the EU are largely characterised by dependence, their relations with countries outside the Union may be more active. Thus, it seems that the European countries outside the EU may represent both a strategic market for the exports of the Mediterranean Objective 1 regions and a pool of resources to be used through the decentralisation of some phases of production. Thirdly, the non-members, which show similarities to the recent technological and organisational level of Southern Europe, may be highly receptive to technological transfers in such fields as agriculture, tourism, infrastructure and light manufacturing.

An additional field where the transfer of know-how seems important is that of regional policy itself. In fact, the problems of industrialisation in the non-EU countries are very similar to those in the Mediterranean Objective 1 regions, and a strategy of endogenous development my be appropriate. Modern approaches to development policy and planning should be adopted in these countries to substitute both their traditional top-down Soviet-type planning and their naive trust in the market mechanism.

The Role of the Territory within a New Regional Development Policy

Interregional co-operation should not only be based on some type of homogeneity in the economic and social structure of the regions involved but also on a common development strategy (Cappellin 1992). In particular, regions both in Western and Eastern Europe should identify a complementary role in the actual world economy.

It is during periods of economic crisis rather than periods of quantitative growth that private and public actors focus their efforts on promoting structural or qualitative transformations of social relations, technologies and production systems. These changes may be the prerequisite of a new phase of development.

For example, in the case of the Italian Mezzogiorno, the degree of transformation is only partially revealed by the aggregate statistical indicators, which is rather similar to what occurred during the 1980s and 1990s in the regions of northern and central Italy. The industrial structure based on large publicly owned firms inherited from the regional policies of the 1960s is in a deep crisis, and new small and medium-sized firms are developing in completely different sectors. The fight against the Mafia has led to crucial results. The political representatives have been changed to a very large extent. The ideals and needs of the new generations have changed. Thus, the prerequisites to utilise the Mezzogiorno's endogenous resources seem to have been gradually created.

However, both in southern Italy and in the other Mediterranean Objective 1 regions, a radical reorientation of industrial policies is required (Cappellin 1995b).

The 'fordist' or 'proto-industrial' strategy of attracting branch plants of large outside firms operating in traditional, capital-intensive sectors such as the automobiles, chemicals and steel should be substituted by a new industrial policy which promotes the international competitiveness of local firms.

It is necessary to shift from a view of competitiveness based on low costs and salaries and various forms of financial support to the firms towards a market-oriented development strategy where competitiveness is based on product quality, the pace of adjustment to continuously changing consumer needs, increases in productivity, reducing the technological and organisational gap and tighter integration with the firms of more developed regions both at home and in other EU countries

There is a need for a transition from a 'financial approach to development' based on investments in productive capacity, to a new 'networking strategy' similar to the one adopted in the most developed regions of the European Union. This implies co-operation in production, technology and marketing as well as tighter vertical and horizontal integration among the industrial firms and the development of a system of modern services, all of which will allow the firms in economically lagging regions to become integrated in the networks that link the firms of the most developed regions in Europe. This also implies a need to 'reinvent government' by establishing relations between national, regional and local public institutions, particularly in the area of regional development.

Dynamism in productivity and ability to compete internationally are fundamental criteria when choosing a development strategy for regions tightly integrated in the European economy.

A faster pace of productivity increase should be promoted not only within the individual firms, but also in the whole territorial system in which the firms are embedded.

The factors of competitiveness are not only 'hard' ones like the cost of labour, capital incentives and the exploitation of scale economies, but also 'soft' ones which create a favourable environment for the development of the local firms such as the dynamism of the local economy, the availability of specialised suppliers, the local entrepreneurial culture, the development of human resources, relations with trade unions, the strength of local co-operation and the efficiency of public institutions.

Regional policy should give high priority to the improvement of traditional and modern infrastructure, renewal of the urban environment and large-scale management of the regional territory.

In particular, one needs to take into account that modern industry should be integrated at the national and international level and that this requires new investments in the sectors of transport and logistics. The crucial factor is not the cost of transportation, but rather the time constraint in the relationships between the firms, which in a modern industrial system should allow increasing specialisation and 'just in time' forms of co-operation.

Thus, interregional co-operation in the Mediterranean basin should promote intermodal transport both in a north-south and east-west perspective between the Balkan countries and Italy. For example, the new container port of Gioia Tauro in Calabria, which together with Algesiras in Andalusia qualifies as one of the greatest transhipment ports in Europe, may allow the regions in Southern Europe to be linked with the intercontinental trade flows and to attract modern industries and services, which is quite different from the branch plants operating with traditional technology that were typical of the recent past. The development of transhipment activities may also promote co-operative with other port cities and regions in the Mediterranean basin.

Interregional co-operation between Western and Eastern Europe might focus on new areas such as exports and agreements on production (subcontracting) among firms of different regions, which may promote a tighter integration of the production system of peripheral regions in the European economy; technological innovation and the creation of new small and medium-sized firms, which may diversify the local production toward new activities such as logistics and modern services; the requalification of the territory in terms of new infrastructure and services to the citizens and the firms; research on new trends in the economic-territorial development at the interregional level and training of public officials win regional and local administration in the modern approaches to regional policy and territorial planning.

The Subsidiarity Principle and Regional Policies

These new development strategies are incompatible with centralist institutions and require greater local and regional autonomy. In fact, fostering economic development in backward regions requires the engagement of a variety of local actors and not only intervention by national governments or the European Union (Cappellin 1995a). An increasing number of functions, such as the supply of modern services and infrastructure, should be managed at the local level in the framework of organisations capable of associating public and private actors like chambers of commerce, universities, research centres and financial institutions. Thus, the legitimacy of national intervention in the field of regional policy is challenged by the appearance of new public and private actors.

International relations are no longer the monopoly of national institutions. Most economic and social actors have established extended international relations. Therefore, interregional co-operation has as its aim to involve regional and local governments in a sort of regional 'foreign policy.'

In this perspective, nation states and the European Union are responsible for creating an institutional framework that may facilitate co-operation with and among the regional governments, also at the transnational level. In particular, the regional policy of nation states and the European Union may create financial incentives to the development of certain forms of interregional co-operation.

Moreover, quite often the appropriate level for designing new projects and to implement them is not even the regional but the subregional level, such as provinces, metropolitan areas and associations established by contiguous municipalities. The participation of local or city governments in interregional co-operation appears crucial, especially whenever the urban centres play a role of nodes (gateways) in international networks that is greater than their role in their respective regions. This has been the historical experience the 'maritime republics' of Venice, Genoa and the Hanseatic cities.

The principle of subsidiarity should therefore be implemented also within regions (Cappellin 1997). The problem is not only to decentralise the power of national governments in favour of regional ones but also to make room for flexible mechanisms of co-operation between the various regional actors and the regional governments and between the latter and the local and urban administrations.

The functions of public institutions in modern regional policy should neither be the direct ownership or management of production and services nor legal regulation through framework laws or the creation of ad hoc high authorities. Rather, public authorities should play the role of an 'active interface' or 'system integrator' capable of integrating the policies of various regional actors, stimulating their projects through specific initiatives and facilitating their implementation through technical assistance.

The decisive task is the management of complexity and flexibility, and that requires public authorities to identify general goals or very broad strategies of development rather than many and detailed objectives. The goal must be to promote consensus and create synergy among the many different regional actors.

The role of national and regional public administration is not hierarchical control of the policies of private and public actors but rather to implement flexible mechanisms to govern the relations between public and private organisations.

This evolution is especially needed in those fields of regional policy where private firms, chambers of commerce, entrepreneurial associations and other collective organisations may co-operate with the national and regional administration. Among the examples are the management of technological transfers, the promotion of exports and tourism, the creation of infrastructure and the promotion of economic development in general.

According to the network paradigm, therefore, a new regional policy should explicitly adopt a 'transactional' approach as opposed to a 'prescriptive' one.

The Renewal of European Regional Policy

Traditionally, national and EU regional policies have been guided by a redistributive principle based on equity, solidarity, political consensus and concern for institutional cohesion. Thus, regional policies have been part of a welfare state policy with the aim of transferring resources towards less developed regions in order to sustain their per capita income levels and reduce migration and unemployment.

In a European context, regional policy has also had the role of compensating lagging regions for the disparities caused by European integration, which has reduced the possibility of using traditional economic policy instruments.

In contrast to these objectives, the perspective of endogenous development implies that regional policy should aim at a full and efficient utilisation of economic resources within the various EU regions and at promoting more growth and competitiveness in the whole EU economy. The primary instrument is to eliminate various bottlenecks which impede the participation of lagging regions in the international process of economic growth (Cappellin and Batey 1993).

This endogenous approach is clearly compatible with the regionalisation movement which is becoming more popular everywhere in Europe. In many countries power is decentralised in order to promote both democracy and economic performance.

Thus, there is the need to define a new institutional framework for the relations between the state and the EU institutions, on the one hand, and regional and local authorities, on the other (Cappellin and Batey 1993; Cappellin 1995a).

In fact, the EU's regional policy has furthered the development of regional institutions even in countries with little regional decentralisation. Moreover, it has promoted a new approach based on contractual agreements between regional and national institutions and private and public organisations. The EU's regional policy has also indirectly stimulated regional networking at the international level.

The regional policy of the EU does not seem to supplement national regional policies. Rather, it has reduced the latter to an auxiliary role with very little autonomy vis-a-vis the Union's regional policy. In fact, the principle of co-financing (additionality), the increase in the Union's regional policy budget and the constraints on national budgets have led to a concentration of national financing to the same policy sectors as chosen by the EU

However, the EU's regional policy has still to be adjusted to an effective adoption of the principle of subsidiarity, which implies a greater focus on issues which are of truly European relevance.

Contrary to the actual interpretation of the principles of co-financing and of partnership, subsidiarity calls for a clearer division of tasks. The demand for joint participation of the EU, states and regional and sometimes local government leads to inefficiency. The EU should concentrate on the design and financing of projects whereas national authorities should mainly be responsible for the utilisation of endogenous capabilities. Regional and local authorities should be the ones responsible for the implementation of projects in tight co-operation with national agencies and qualified private firms.

In particular, the EU's regional policy has up till now failed to establish a far-reaching European strategic programme similar to other initiatives such as the Single Market or the Monetary Union. According to the regulations of the European Structural Funds, the EU's regional policy is limited to the evaluation and selection of initiatives taken by national and regional authorities. This is clearly a rather passive attitude.

Defining regions according to Structural Fund Objectives in order to assign to them different parameters of financial support is only one way of classifying them. It prevents the identification of territorial problems at the interregional level. Moreover, the EU is still largely involved in a plethora of programmes having a weak local connection, as, e.g., most of the programmes in Objective 2 regions.

The Union's regional policy is still mainly organised according to the methodology of individual regional plans or Community Support Frameworks (CSF) covering each individual 'problem region' rather than according to more modern methodologies, aiming at 'strategic regional problems.' In fact, the Community Initiatives represent a minor share of total regional funds.

A greater role for the Community Initiatives would encourage the design of interregional programmes, whereas the present approach of the regional CSF is leading to case by case solutions and therefore fails to consider the aim of promoting the integration of individual regions into the total European economy.

The entry into the European Union of countries in Central and Eastern Europe will profoundly change the scale of regional disparities. The order of magnitude of the problem of convergence and cohesion will grow to such an extent that the aims and strategies of the EU regional policies will have to be dramatically reconsidered. Many South European regions currently eligible for support under Objective 1 will be excluded from this category or the ratio between the EU expenditure and the regional product will be changed substantially.

Regardless of whether EU regional policy will end up renouncing its aim of redistributing income and investments among the European regions, it should, in my view, concentrate on other objectives. The enlargement of the EU to Central and Eastern European countries may imply that in future, the objective of EU regional policy should be to promote transfer of knowledge, pilot projects and the construction of major trans-European networks. The general aim should not be to reduce income disparities, which is best left to national regional policies. The objective of EU regional policy might be to improve the spatial, economic and technological integration of regions at the European level.

A policy of *amenagement* of the European territory may become more important than the traditional redistributive policies of the welfare state. In this perspective the territorial and urban-rural dimension might be recognised as a priority axis of intervention by the European Union, and territorial planning and urban-rural policies should be among the competencies of the European Commission.

The creation of networks between cities and regions on the European scale must conform to the principle of subsidiarity. EU intervention in the shape of top-down co-ordination must be avoided. Rather, its aim might be to lighten the transaction costs that impede co-operation among regions and cities and to promote innovative projects.

Cities are not impact areas of regional policies but rather institutions legitimised by their own constituency, which makes them partners in the institutional relations that also encompass the European Union, the nation states and the regions. Consequently, they are essential to the realisation of most EU plans.

The European Union's urban policy therefore faces the challenge of accepting the cities as an institutional partner in bargaining and co-operation. Secondly, an urban perspective on the organisation of the European territory is different from a regional perspective. Whereas the latter accentuates the dualism between regions that lag behind economically or are hit by industrial crisis, on the one hand, and more advantaged regions, on the other, an urban perspective stresses a multipolar dimension and highlights common problems of a strategic character.

Finally, a European urban policy requires organisational mechanisms that are different from the traditional procedures of the EU's regional policy. Based on the results of the 'innovative actions' taken in accordance with the Structural Funds' Article 10, it seems particularly desirable for the Commission to develop a 'Development Framework of the Community Territory' which may consider the organisation of networks in transport, energy and telecommunication and the access of small and medium-sized urban centres to these networks.

This does not imply that the Union's territorial or urban-rural policy should be based on rigid, top-down planning for each individual European macro-region, such as those defined in the study Europe 2000+ (European Commission 1994).

Due to its mainly strategic characteristics, a future Development Framework of the Community Territory should be capable of orienting the local administrations towards new initiatives like pilot projects, experimental programmes and exchange of experiences and of facilitate synergy between the Community and the local levels.

A new Development Framework should propose a strategy focused on the traditional and new problems common in various urban areas. It should stimulate local authorities and public and private organisations to present innovative projects to utilise the resources and the endogenous potential of the different urban areas in partnership with the European Union and the national governments.

In particular, Community financial resources should not be allocated *ex ante* to the individual regions on the basis of distribution keys determined by political criteria, as it now occurs with the instruments of the Community Support Frameworks, but only *ex post* on the basis of a competitive selection of projects presented by various local administrations.

A European territorial policy should thus combine the demands of long-term spatial planning with a respect for bottom-up decision-making.

Due to their top-down character, the Community Support Frameworks adopted in the Union's current policy in Objective 1 regions are not much different from the traditional regional macro-sectoral plans, which have led to neo-centralism at the regional level and have proved ineffective in mobilising local actors (Cappellin 1995c).

An increasing number of public functions, in particular the promotion of industry and the supply of modern services and infrastructure, should be managed by clusters of institutions and organisations at the local level, such as branch associations of firms, chambers of commerce, universities, research centres, banking and financial institutions.

EU regional policy must not continue to overburden the regional level since the enhancement of economic development requires mobilisation of a wide variety of actors. After all, the most appropriate territorial framework for operational interventions is at the subregional level of provinces and intercommunal associations.

Thus, there is a need to assign a greater role within the EU regional policy to such methods as:

- broad master plans of organisation of the European territory,
- networking among the various actors within the individual regions,
- networking between two or more non-bordering regions at the interregional level both within individual countries and at the transnational level,
- technical assistance by EU and national agencies,
- fiscal federalism and fiscal autonomy of local institutions.

A network approach leads to a discussion of the relevance of various principles that are currently at the base of the Union's regional policy: concentration on specific 'problems regions' rather than broad European regional problems affecting various regions simultaneously; co-financing of each initiative rather than a clearer division of tasks between national and regional authorities within the framework of an overall regional programme; planning with the instrument of the CSF rather than, e.g., strategic plans and planning contracts with individual firms or collective organisation.

Conclusions

Regions in the Mediterranean and Baltic basins face common challenges which underline the need to strengthen interregional transnational co-operation.

First of all, they both face the problem of promoting the transition from a command to a market economy of the countries and regions in Eastern Europe. This process may have different characteristics in different countries and in Northern and Southern Europe. The problem of developing forms of interregional co-operation, however, is largely common to both areas not least due to role which countries such as Germany and Italy play in the commerce and foreign investment of all countries of Central and Eastern Europe.

There is also a danger that a 'highway effect' will mean that peripheral regions both in the North and South of the European Union may be bypassed by tighter relations between the most developed regions of Western Europe and the capitals of Eastern Europe.

Thus, European integration should include the peripheral and less developed regions in Western Europe and make it possible for them to exploit new development opportunities through co-operative relationships with regions in Eastern Europe.

Moreover, the development of interregional co-operation both in Northern and Southern Europe points to a need of restructuring European regional policy. First of all, it is necessary to introduce a transnational perspective in regional policy. It is not enough to increase the productive capacity in economically backward regions. One must also strengthen their international competitiveness and particularly their links with foreign markets. Moreover, there is a common need to integrate the PHARE programme into a wider regional and interregional perspective in order to develop the Eastern European countries through technical assistance, training and new approaches to development similar to those already adopted by the EU.

Secondly, since interregional planning typically has a bottom-up character, it is necessary to revise the EU's approach to economic planning for lagging regions towards an approach based on strategic governance.

Finally, interregional co-operation might aim at promoting a sort of co-development of the border regions between Eastern and Western Europe, based on increasing economic, cultural, societal and territorial interdependence.

This requires not only a different industrialisation strategy within each region, focused on international competitiveness and co-operative forms of specialisation, but also an increasing EU focus on the integration of the whole European territory in accordance with the principle of subsidiarity.

References

Cappellin, R. (1992). 'Theories of Local Endogenous Development and International Co-operation,' in Tykkyläinen, M. (ed.). *Development Issues and Strategies in the New Europe.* Aldershot, Avebury.

Cappellin, R. and Batey, P. (eds.) (1993). *Regional Networks, Border Regions and European Integration.* London, Pion.

Cappellin, R. (1995a). 'Regional Development, Federalism and Interregional Cooperation' in Eskelinen, H. and Snickars, F. (eds.). *Competitive European Peripheries.* Munich, Springer-Verlag.

Cappellin, R. (1995b). 'Subsidiarity as a New Economic Strategy' in Steiner, M. (ed.). *Regionale Innovation: durch Technologiepolitik zu neuen Strukturen.* Graz, Leykam.

Cappellin, R. (1995c). 'A Market Oriented Regional Policy between Federalism and European Cohesion' in Froehlich, Z, Malekovic, S., Padjen, J, Polic, M and Svliek, S. (eds.). *Industrial Restructuring and Its Impact on Regional Development.* Zagreb, Institute of Economics.

Cappellin, R. (1995d). 'Mediterranean Multiregional Development: A European Policy to Foster North-South Cooperation.' Paper presented at the Round Table of the XVIth Italian Congress of the Regional Science Association, Siena, 30 October – 1 November.

Cappellin, R. (1997). 'Regional Policy and Federalism in the Process of International Integration' in Peschel, K. (ed.). *Regional Growth and Regional Policy within the Framework of European Integration.* Heidelberg, Physica-Verlag.

European Commission (1994). *Europe 2000+: Cooperation for European Territorial Development.* Luxembourg, Office for Official Publications of the European Communities.

22 Cross-Border Co-operation in the Barents Region

Hallgeir Aalbu[1]

Introduction

The Barents Euro-Arctic Region (BEAR) is the name of the new institutional arrangement established for the promotion of normalised relationships between Russia and the Nordic countries.[2] The aim of the BEAR includes contributing to social, economic and environmental development in the north-west of Russia, as this is seen as a prerequisite for political stability. The idea was launched by the Norwegian Foreign Minister in April 1992, and the region was established through a conference of foreign ministers in Kirkenes, Norway, in January 1993.

The initiative must be seen in the context of the new political situation developing after the end of the Cold War in 1989 and the fall of the Soviet Union in 1991 (Norwegian Ministry of Foreign Affairs 1993). The political situation on the northern fringe of Western Europe had for many years been stable but characterised by division. The area was subject to a heavy military build-up in the border area between two military blocs, and every country had a different security arrangement. The Soviet Union was one of two military superpowers; Sweden was neutral; Finland with an agreement with the Soviet Union; and Norway as a full member of NATO.

The borders between East and West in the Arctic had been almost completely closed for more than 70 years, with very limited direct cross-border communication. All major trade arrangements were agreed between Moscow and other national capitals. During these 70 years, one of the widest economic gaps to be found anywhere in the world between neighbouring countries developed. Now, with the borders open to more normal traffic, the security situation in the north demanded attention.

The Barents initiative is one of several attempts to develop structures for co-operation across the former East-West divide. This happened at the same time as the concept of regionalisation became accepted all over Europe, with an emphasis on the regional level as a counterweight to the strengthening of the international level. Unlike most other transnational arrangements at the regional level, however, the BEAR was to promote co-operation between national (and international) authorities as well as between regional ones.

Challenges in the Barents Region

The geographical area covered by BEAR consists of eight administrative regions, seven counties and one republic: three *fylker* in Norway (Nordland, Troms, Finnmark), one county (*län*) in Sweden (Norrbotten), one *län* in Finland (Lappland), and two *oblasts* (Murmansk, Arkhangelsk) and one *republic* (Karelia) in Russia.

The common feature of these administrative units is that a part of their territory lies north of the Arctic Circle. The Barents region covers more than 1.2 million square kilometres but has a population of only 4.4 million (compared with 3.2 million square kilometres and 367.7 million inhabitants in the EU-15). The Russian part of the Barents region has 76 per cent of the area and 79 per cent of the population. A drive through the Barents region from one regional capital to the next would involve a journey between the eight cities/towns of more than 6,000 kilometres (Aalbu et al. 1995).

Figure 22.1: The Barents region

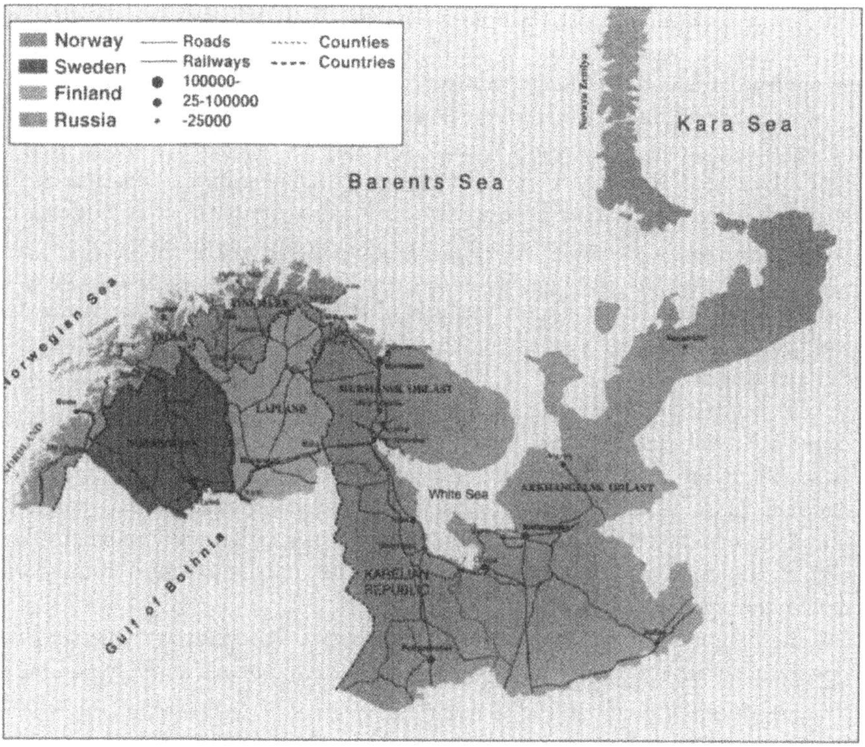

Source: Norwegian Foreign Office

This vast area at the northernmost part of Europe is richly endowed with natural resources such as fish, minerals, energy (hydroelectric, oil, gas) and timber. Substantial mineral and energy resources are still to be developed. Environmental conditions are generally good, with vast areas almost untouched by human development. However, there are also a number of heavily polluted areas and a serious potential danger caused by the poor state of the nuclear industry including nuclear waste in the Russian part of the region.

Within the Barents region, East-West trade expanded immediately after the political changes made it possible – despite the lack of convertible roubles, clear rules of trade and customs, security of private ownership, etc. Imports to Russia have been mainly consumer goods, whereas exports have usually been raw materials. Exchange has often been in the form of barter.

Undeveloped natural resources are obviously of interest to large multinational companies. Governments on both sides are also keen to promote investments to avert environmental hazards. The Russians are particularly interested in developing the transport infrastructure. And from a regional point of view, the increased activity creates opportunities for the border regions to become interfacing areas.

Interaction across the East-West borders in the region faces major obstacles.

- First, there is no common language in the area. Moreover, of the four national languages, three different language groups are represented. As a rule, interpretation services are needed.
- Secondly, cultural differences are significant, especially across the old Iron Curtain.
- Thirdly, the communications infrastructure is underdeveloped. All of the main transport corridors run north-south towards the national centres, and there are few east-west links, often of a low standard. However, telecommunications in Russia have been developed over the last few years. Telephone, telefax and e-mail are now working, even if the number of Russian subscribers is still limited. There are also daily flights between northern Norway and Murmansk/Arkhangelsk and between northern Finland and Sweden and Murmansk.
- Lastly, there are still substantial Russian tariffs on goods crossing the border, and travellers need a visa to pass through one of the two places (Storskog and Raja-Jooseppi) where border-crossing between Russia and the rest of the Barents region is possible. In 1994, 33,300 vehicles and 110,000 people passed through these two border stations between Russia-Finland and Russia-Norway. This can be compared with the almost 6 million vehicles that crossed the Swedish-Finnish border in the Barents region at Torneå.

Under these circumstances, developing new relations between Russia and her neighbours to the north-west is a ambitious challenge. The functional links between the different parts of the Barents region are poorly developed, especially between Russia and the other countries, but also between the northern parts of the Nordic countries, which are all at the periphery of their national economies.

The economic gap between East and West in this region might cause instability but it may also stimulate economic dynamism, as inequality and complementary, i.e. the degree to which different parts are compatible in terms of potential, are important for trade.

Nordic Transborder Co-operation in the North: Policy for Regional Development

The Nordic countries have a 30-year long history of formal, cross-border co-operation. At present, nine bi- or multinational committees are instrumental in promoting transnational integration at a regional level. Representatives of regional authorities are the key actors on these committees, which receive financial support from the Nordic Council of Ministers.

One of them, the North Calotte Committee, operates in the Nordic part of the Barents region. It was established in 1967, originally as a forum for co-operation between the regional authorities implementing labour market policies. In 1975 it became part of the Nordic regional policy programme, with the objective of enhancing regional economic development. A permanent secretariat was established in Rovaniemi, Finland, in 1980. A Swedish office was opened in Luleå (1980). A Norwegian office existed in Bodø from 1987 to 1996, when its tasks were transferred to the three county councils (Finnmark, Troms, Nordland).

During the 1980s, there was a decline of interest in Nordic cross-border co-operation, as the practical impact of such initiatives on regional development was not very impressive. Regional budgets were limited, and so was the number of possible co-operative projects. Moreover, the obstacles to cross-border trade could only be removed at the national level. Among the main impediments to east-west interaction is the fact that in all Scandinavian countries, the communication pattern is north-south.

The new international situation gave the North Calotte Committee an opportunity for revitalisation. The perestroika policy from 1985 opened new options for contacts with Russia, and with the end of the Cold War, the opportunities improved considerably. It was not long before businesses developed trade over the borders, and delegations of politicians and civil servants began visiting each other. In this situation, the North Calotte Committee was used as a informal forum to co-ordinate the different regions' bilateral contacts with Russia.

In the winter of 1991-92, the regional authorities in the Murmansk oblast raised the question of participation in the Committee and, together with Arkhangelsk, they were given observer status from 1992. This was decided by the Committee itself, without much consultation with the ministries of foreign affairs in the Nordic countries, and must be understood as an attempt to utilise the existing organisation for new tasks. There was even a suggestion to change the name to facilitate this enlargement (from the *Nordkalott* (North Calotte) Committee to the *Storkalott* (Great Calotte) Committee.

Clearly the North Calotte Committee wanted to incorporate the regional authorities in neighbouring Russia into the existing cross-border institution. However, this was not possible without approval from the constituent governments and from the Nordic Council. At the time, the Nordic Council of Ministers focused very much on intra-Nordic questions (this has since changed as the Council now also deals with Nordic-European relations) and had difficulties accepting the proposed enlargement. Also, the different ministries of foreign affairs were sceptical towards transnational institutions outside their direct control.

Instead, a different initiative to form common institutions with Russia came from Oslo.

The Barents Euro-Arctic Region: Policy for Regional Stabilisation

The concept of the Barents Euro-Arctic Region (BEAR) was developed in the Norwegian Ministry of Foreign Affairs early in 1992 and was launched in April that year. At the time, the NATO countries wanted to find new patterns of consultation with Russia, in a network of positive relationships (Jervell 1994). When it comes to relations with Russia, Norway has traditionally preferred multinational arrangements to bilateral ones. The Norwegian initiative must be interpreted as a continuation of this policy. Oslo wanted to reach a new multinational co-operative agreement that involved a number of Western countries and which might become part of Russia's policy towards Europe and of the EU's Northern policy. The name of the co-operative agreement, the Barents Euro-Arctic Region, reflects this ambition.

The BEAR was formally established in Kirkenes, Norway, in January 1993. The Kirkenes Declaration was signed by Denmark, Finland, Iceland, Norway, Russia, Sweden and the European Commission, and by observers from another six countries.

The Declaration is based on the aim that the establishment of the Barents region should 'to an essential part contribute to stabilization and success in the territory and the whole of Europe.' Former Norwegian Foreign Secretary Johan Jørgen Holst (1993) described its goals in three points:

- '*Normalization.* We wish to establish relations across the borders between the Nordic countries and Russia that are similar to the relations between the Nordic countries, and to the ties between the Nordic countries and other Western European countries.
- *Stabilization.* We wish to promote co-operation and stability by means of measures to counteract and reduce military tension, to reduce or eliminate

environmental threats, and to narrow the gap between the standards of living in the Nordic countries and Russia.
- *Regionalization.* We wish to create a multilateral framework for regional co-operation that will be attractive to states both within and outside the region, promote stability and establish a link between the Barents Region and the broader European process of restructuring that is currently taking place.'

Legitimacy and local enthusiasm for the BEAR were to be achieved through the support of a regional cultural framework, an emphasis on the shared history of the region (the 70 years of closed borders being viewed as a *parenthesis*) and by giving the regional authorities on both sides a distinctive role in the new institution.

The construction meant that the same Scandinavian regional administrations that were involved in the North Calotte Committee became active in the BEAR, but the wider international context was significantly different.

A Two-Tier Institution

The new institution has a two-tier organisation, with committees involving both national and regional institutions.

- The *Barents Council* includes the foreign ministries of Finland, Norway, Russia and Sweden. The chairmanship rotates between these countries on an annual basis. The European Community participates as the fifth full member. Other countries have an observer status. A Committee of Senior Officials from the ministries of foreign affairs prepares the meetings.
- Members of the *Regional Council* are the highest political or administrative leaders at the regional level. These are political leaders in Norway and Russia (Regional Mayor) and government civil servants in Finland and Sweden (County Governor). The chairmanship changes every second year. The indigenous population is also represented in the council. The *Administrative Regional Committee* undertakes the preparatory work for the Regional Council and includes administrative staff from the eight regional administrations. Ten permanent working parties for different issues assist this committee. The secretariat rotates with the chairman.

The structure involves a large number of people in the committees. The first years have been used to get to know each other and to review the challenges and opportunities of the different subregions. Due to the geographical and linguistic diversity, this has involved a significant amount of time-consuming travel and meetings.

There is no common funding of the activities of the BEAR. Each country covers its own meeting costs except that the host nation pays the costs of the Russian participants meeting outside Russia. Efforts to agree on common funding for proposed development projects have failed. Therefore, all projects have to apply for individual national financing. As a result, projects tend to be bilateral, involving one Nordic country and Russia, with most of their funding coming from the Nordic countries.

In Finland and Sweden, projects in the Barents region compete with other projects involving Eastern Europe. Norway allocates specific budgets for Barents projects, but they are limited compared with the total Norwegian spending on co-operation with Russia. In 1994, the grant for the BEAR represented about 10 per cent of the funds spent on co-operation in the Russian part of the Barents region.

Compared to other cross-border institutions, the two-tier structure of the BEAR is unusual. It combines a foreign policy perspective, where security, stability and environmental hazards are in focus, with a regional policy perspective focused on cross-border co-operation in fields like economic development, culture, education, indigenous population policies, communications and research.

There are some tensions between these two perspectives. The regional policy component can be seen as a continuation of the work of the North Calotte Committee and of its interpretation of the concept of 'regionalisation.' The mixed expectations attached to the BEAR – being an instrument of macro-political stabilisation and security *and* of regional development – are demanding. The first years of activity have achieved limited practical results that can be identified as the outcome of the work of the various committees (Aalbu et al. 1995). The lack of funds earmarked for projects has made it difficult for the Regional Council to implement desired initiatives to promote regional economic and social development. There is an obvious danger that an overly ambitious understanding of their task in terms of regional policy may create frustration among committee members expecting short-term results.

The Concept of Region

In the Barents Programme 1994-95, concepts like 'identity region' and 'functional region' are referred to when considering the strategic direction of the Barents region (Barentssekretariatet 1994). Such goals are, however, unrealistic in the short term and probably also in a longer term, given the distances involved both geographically and culturally (Aalbu and Wiberg 1997).

A 'region' can be several different things. Analytically it means an area where economic activity is integrated and internal contacts are more densely developed than those with the outside area. One may also talk about homogeneous regions with a common nature or culture. In administrative terms, a region is often understood as a unit at the subnational level.

In the Barents area, the concept of region has several different meanings. From the viewpoint of foreign policy, it is an area with co-operative institutions. From a European regional policy perspective, there is a tendency to define regions in terms of their eligibility for regional policy funding. In a regional development understanding, a region is frequently understood as an area where there are tight functional links between businesses.

These different interpretations of the regional concept also have bearing on the view of different participants about membership of the Barents region. Looked upon as a question of participation in the committees, there is a trade-off between the number of members and their functionality; however, in general new members are welcomed. Seen as a question of funding, more members mean reduced funds for each. While new subregions will want to join, the present members will tend to reject enlargement. From the point of view of regional development, a large region will tend to be less effective than a small one, not least because the economic functionality of the area will be weaker.

There has been continuous debate on the inclusion of new regions in the BEAR. At present, the common feature of the participating regions is that they all have a part of their territory north of the Arctic Circle. At an early stage, the region of Leningrad (Russia) was a candidate for membership. However, this was refused on the grounds that Leningrad lies far to the south of the Arctic Circle and is part of the Baltic Sea co-operation and therefore already included in the institutional network of cross-border regions.

The regions of Västerbotten (Sweden), Oulu (Finland), North Karelia (Finland) and the Komi (Russia) are observers in the Regional Council and have applied for membership. They are supported by their national governments but not by the present members regions, and the question seems to have caused a conflict between the Barents Council and the Regional Council (*Nord Revy* 1996b). This is not surprising given the two bodies' differing interpretations of region. According to the foreign policy view, a large number of participants is better than a few, whereas, from the regional policy perspective, enlargement would probably make it even more difficult to get results.

This again shows the difficulty of combining, within the same organisation, the goal of political stability with those of regional development – even if the achievement of the latter is an important precondition for the former.

Introduction of Interreg II Transborder Programmes

After Finland and Sweden joined the European Union in 1995, European regional policies were introduced to parts of the Barents region. One of these policies is Interreg II, which provides funds for cross-border co-operation.

In the area covered by the Barents region, there are now four Interreg II programmes:

- *Interreg Barents,* covering Finland, Sweden, Norway and Russia (the same area as the Barents region, but without Arkhangelsk and Karelia).
- *Interreg Nordkalotten,* covering Finland, Sweden and Norway (the same area as that of the North Calotte Committee).

- *Interreg Kvarken and Mittnorden*, covering Finland, Sweden and Norway (mainly situated south of the North Calotte area, but partly overlapping).
- *Interreg Karelen*, covering Finland and Russia (with Karelia from the Barents region).

These programmes are jointly funded by the participating national authorities and the EU, with the European Commission paying half the costs in the EU member states. European funding can only be spent in EU countries. Third countries can participate if they cover all the expenses themselves, and Norway has joined on these terms. Russia participates in the Interreg Barents programme on the expectation that part of Russia's national co-funding will be covered by European funding of other programmes. For the period 1996-99, the budgets for these programmes amount to 111 million ecu (*Nord Revy* 1996a).

These new cross-border programmes are based on separate institutional arrangements. Unlike the BEAR, the Interreg programmes all have specific budget allocations for a multi-annual period and common boards for project decisions. And, compared with the activities of the North Calotte Committee, the budgets involved are significantly higher. The funding of the North Calotte Interreg programme is more than three times the size of Nordic allocations for cross-border co-operation in the region (9 million ecu and 2.5 million ecu per year, respectively).

The most critical aspect of the various programmes will probably be the possibilities of national co-funding. Only projects with approved national co-funding will be implemented. In terms of funding, the main difference between the Barents Interreg programme and the BEAR agreement is that Finland and Sweden each pay 50 per cent of their costs for Interreg projects compared to 100 per cent for BEAR projects. In addition, the Interreg programme has a fixed budget, which the BEAR lacks.

A Complex Administrative Structure

It has been noted above that the BEAR was founded as a new institutional arrangement, but with many of the same features, organisation and actors that had been involved in the previous North Calotte Committee. With the introduction of Interreg, a third set of institutions was set up, again with many of the same organisations participating.

In all three systems, there are partnerships involving international organisations, national governmental bodies and the regions in question.

- At the international level, the Nordic Council of Ministers is the main organiser of Nordic cross-border co-operation. The EU was one of the founders of the BEAR, with expectations of EU financial support being provided to Russia. Interreg II has been set up in accordance with European Commission

regulations, with budgets decided by the EU and with 50 per cent financial support to participating member countries.
- At the national level, the BEAR is handled by the ministries of foreign affairs, whereas both the North Calotte Committee and the Interreg programmes are matters for national ministries responsible for regional policy.
- At the regional level, all cross-border co-operation is dealt with by those agencies at county level which are also responsible for the implementation of regional policy schemes. Since there is a limited number of individuals involved in such work, this creates good opportunities for strong connections between the different bodies.

It seems as if every new task demands it own institutional solution. The administrative structure is certainly becoming ever more complex, with an increasing number of bodies deciding on very similar types of regional development projects.

Necessary co-ordination can only be achieved at the local level, as it is at this level that the same actors operate. However, the possibilities for a bottom-up co-ordination of what are essentially top-down activities can be questioned. Even more importantly, there is a risk of too many programmes operating simultaneously within the same area, creating unnecessary competition for good, small-scale projects.

Conclusions

The BEAR is part of a broader pattern of new East-West institutions at the regional level which bridges the former Iron Curtain divide. Efforts have apparently been more successful at the international level than at the interregional one. This reflects the fact that the foreign policy task (providing an institutionalised framework for East-West co-operation) is easier to achieve than the regional policy objective (promotion of economic development).

The BEAR was only the second of three sets of transborder institutions established in the same geographical area. While the wind was taken out of the sails of the North Calotte Committee when BEAR was launched, the Interreg II programmes have become important competitors of the BEAR as they are better funded and better organised. The Interreg Barents programme has contributed further to the marginalisation of the existing Nordic cross-border co-operation and has also reduced the importance of the regional policy element in the BEAR.

The European Commission has played an important role in recent developments in several ways:

- The EU was a partner in establishing the BEAR as an institution with European ambitions, and its participation was necessary both to make the BEAR an interesting political channel for Russia and to obtain resources.

- The Interreg II programmes would not have existed without European co-funding as part of the financial transactions between the EU on the one hand and Finland and Sweden on the other. The size of the programmes is also determined by EU standards. They receive substantially more resources than any of the Nordic countries had been willing to put into cross-border co-operation. Also, the administrative framework is set by EU regulations, including multi-annual and common spending programmes and common decision-making bodies.

The Interreg programmes are larger, better planned and better monitored than previous cross-border co-operative initiatives. Because of EU rules, they have an administrative structure which has been advocated by the regional representatives in the Barents region but which has not gained support at the national level. In addition, because of their size, they attract more attention than the BEAR and the North Calotte Committee from applicants in municipalities, organisations and businesses.

The Nordic cross-border co-operation initiatives need time to develop a new and distinctive approach. The BEAR faces a similar challenge. As a large region with few functional economic links, the Barents region is a difficult target for regional policies, especially since funds are so limited.

However, the BEAR has an additional foreign policy task, and this is still important. The development challenges in Russia are of a scale that simply cannot be dealt with at the regional level. There is, consequently, a need for a framework for European-Russian co-operation at state level that can provide resources for the large-scale projects which are required in order to improve both environment and infrastructure. Furthermore, the future of the regional tier in the Barents region will depend on its ability to attract international financial resources to meet these great challenges.

Notes

1 This chapter is based on a research project funded by the Nordic Institute of Regional Policy Research (NordREFO). I would like to thank my fellow researchers Even Høydahl at the Nordland Research Institute, Ulf Wiberg at the University of Umeå, and Heikki Jussila at the University of Oulu for interesting co-operation. Thanks also to Douglas Yuill and John Bachtler at the European Policies Research Centre at the University of Strathclyde, Sverre Jervell at the Norwegian Ministry of Foreign Affairs and Anders Östhol at the University of Umeå for comments on drafts.

2 BEAR is the name of the institutional structure. The geographical area concerned is the Barents region.

References

Aalbu, Hallgeir, Høydahl, Even, Jussila, Heikki and Wiberg, Ulf (1995). *Å velge sine naboer: Barentsregionen som utenrikspolitisk og regionalpolitisk prosjekt.* NordREFO 1995:4. Copenhagen.

Aalbu, Hallgeir and Wiberg, Ulf (1997). 'How May Institutional Regionalization Promote Regional Development?' in Sondell, ?, Wiberg, Ulf and Dellenbrant, Jan Åke (eds.). *The Arctic Curtains.* Northern Studies. Umeå, CERUM.

Barentssekretariatet (1994). *The Barents Programme 1994/95.* Kirkenes.

Holst, Johan Jørgen (1993). 'The Barents Region: Institutional Solutions, Forms of Co-operation, Prospects.' Lecture at the Norwegian Academy of Science, 3 November 1993.

Jervell, Sverre (1994): 'Det euro-arktiske Barentssamarbeidet.' Paper at the conference on Trans-Border Regional Co-operation in the Barents Region, Kirkenes, 24 February 1994.

Nord Revy (1996a). No 1-2. Copenhagen.

Nord Revy (1996b). No 5-6. Copenhagen.

Norwegian Ministry of Foreign Affairs (1993). *Barentsregionen:Et regionaliseringsprosjekt i det nordligste Europa.* Aktuelle utenrikspolitiske spørsmål:1/93. Oslo.

23 Business and Politics in the Barents Region

Bo Svensson

The Barents Euro-Arctic Region, or the Barents region, is one example of how interregional co-operation might be used as a device for handling relations across the East-West divide in Europe. Apparently, the intention is to break up previous isolation and promote co-operation, exchange and interaction between societies on opposite sides of state borders. It is believed to have a stabilising effect and favour a positive development in the region.[1]

The formal establishment of interregional co-operation is a rather simple matter that demands little more than an agreement to work together on certain issues. For political co-operation to have an impact on the development of relations between societies is, however, a completely different matter. A closer examination of the potential of interregional co-operation must therefore be undertaken in the light of developments in the 'transnational society.'[2]

This chapter deals with transnational business seen as one aspect of the transnational society. The experiences of Nordic firms operating in north-western Russia (NWR) will lay the foundation for an elaboration on the scope and potential of the Barents region initiative as a development strategy.

A study of the perceptions of business representatives in Nordic firms with activities in north-western Russia is a source for better knowledge about the general business climate in the region.[3] Personal interviews were conducted in order to illuminate the conditions of transnational operations and how they affect the character of cross-border relations. For this purpose, firms involved in foreign direct investment (FDI) and new forms of investment (NFIs)[4] are considered more relevant than trade operators because of the long-term and substantial cross-border links they establish. The qualitative content of business relationships matters, since interdependent relationships between firm units on opposite sides of borders are an indication on the state of the transnational society.[5]

The empirical presentation which follows is structured along the lines of John H. Dunning's eclectical approach. The main focus is on the qualities firms may bring to new locations; the conditions which determine the potential and limitations of any location as a destination for transnational business; and the actual content of business relations (Dunning 1980, 1993; Dicken 1992).[6] Special attention will be devoted to the institutional and cultural setting affecting transnational business activities in NWR. Institutions, on the one hand, are the rules of the game and thus structure interactions, suggest certain solutions to societal problems and determine the course of action (Grafstein 1988; North 1990; Nørgaard 1996). Culture, on the other hand, provides actors with mental models, or taken-for-granted frames of reference, which they also bring into new institutional settings (Anderson 1991; Nørgaard 1996: 39-40). Transnational firms are here at the intersection between institutional and cultural settings, struggling to interpret them and to cope with the transaction costs they bring.

In the Barents region, where the institutional and cultural settings on opposite sides of the former Iron Curtain are vastly different, transaction costs are high and hamper transnational business. Knowledge about such complications is a necessary input to any discussion about the scope for interregional co-operation as a development strategy.

Transnational Business Opportunities

The empirical basis for the chapter was provided by interviews conducted with 30 firms from three countries – Finland, Norway and Sweden – with long-term ambitions in north-western Russia. Most of the firms are small and fall into the lower half of the small and medium-sized enterprise (SME) category (20/30), while the rest are split between larger SMEs and large transnational corporations (TNCs). The great majority of firms have their home base, or are subsidiaries of larger firms, located in the territory of the Barents region (21/30). A few are located on the fringes of the Barents region (4/30, while the rest, mainly larger TNCs have their headquarters in the Nordic capitals (5/30).

Most of the interviewees in SMEs are managing directors (18/30) and often also majority owners of their firms. In larger firms, they are division managers or vice presidents in certain subdivisions within the firm (6/30), project leaders for the firm's Russian operations (4/30), or people with market responsibility for the area in question (2/30).

When we look at owner-specific advantages internal to the firm, the possession of different types of knowledge and technology dominates heavily (23/30). Nearly half of the firms also mentioned networks and special knowledge or experience of Russia as a work place as a distinct advantage (13/30). Eight of these had a track record reaching back into the Soviet period, while the rest got started after perestroika had begun in the mid-1980s. Financial muscle and international experience were mentioned occasionally, both among SMEs and TNCs, whereas only the latter category mentioned brand names and reputation. Roughly half of the interviewees saw country of origin as an external advantage (17/30), mostly because it gave access to financial sources. All but one firm considered relative geographical proximity an advantage. Only a few, however, explicitly mentioned their northern location as a competitive advantage relative to firms from other parts of their own country. About one fourth perceived relative cultural nearness to be an advantage vis-a-vis competitors from other countries, including those mentioning living in similar climatic conditions.[7]

Although we are dealing with a small sample of firms, I will point to some differences between them when grouped according to country of origin, since this clearly seems to matter. While knowledge and technology are considered advantages by all firms, networks and knowledge/experience from working in Russia is a lot more common among Norwegian and Finnish firms, than among Swedish ones (1/9). Every Norwegian firm considers country of origin an advantage, while Swedish and Finnish firms are more hesitant (2/9 respectively 5/10). In general, Norwegian firms were more pleased with their home government backing. It is also more common that Norwegian firms consider relative cultural nearness an advantage. Experiences from the Soviet period were most common among Finnish firms (6/10), but were very unusual among Swedish and Norwegian firms.

Another way of describing the sample of firms is to look at the reasons for going transnational, which means that attention is shifted to the location-specific advantages of NWR as a destination for transnational business. Half of the firms, 15 out of 30, identified opportunities related solely to the market potential of north-western Russia or Russia as a whole. Cost and supply oriented activities were less common, being the driving force for 3 respectively 4 firms. The remaining firms (8) were driven by combinations of these, with a combination of supply and market oriented activities (6) being the most common. This means that if cases with combined opportunities are counted, 3 out of 4 firms were to some extent driven by market aspirations. Among these, however, it should be acknowledged that only one third were targeted at consumer markets, whereas the majority either provided business services for Russian and other foreign firms, or were engaged in technology transfer for the modernisation of Russian industry and infrastructure.

If we group firms that at least partly related to natural resources together – including both production, technological transfer and consulting – half of the firms (15/30) fall into this category. All but two, who had experienced substantial losses, saw great future potential for their business operations in Russia. Virtually everybody, however, expressed reservations on this optimistic outlook, pointing at certain negative location-specific features of Russia as a destination for transnational business. Not surprisingly, the overall picture is therefore that uncertainty about future developments prevails, which is a reason to examine the advantages and disadvantages of north-western Russia.

Perceived Institutional Complications

The institutional environment of NWR, in terms of legislation, regulations and the authorities responsible for the enforcement of these, seems to be a constant source of uncertainty to business operators. Somewhat paradoxically, both legislation that ought to be changed and legislation that is changed cause problems. However, problems arise not only from the legislation as such but are often created by implementing authorities.

The most telling examples on how legislation and authorities in charge can cause problems to the conduct of business are the customs procedures. Slow, costly, and frustrating routines seem to affect everybody bringing goods in or out of the country. At best, this has forced firms to work out their own procedures in co-operation with customs authorities. Occasionally this has not been achieved, which has made transaction costs almost unbearable.

One firm managed to bring clearance time down from ten days to one but still had to drive 250 kilometres from its Murmansk branch to the toll station just to deliver the necessary papers for customs clearing. Another firm speaks for those involved in production on the Russian side, and talks about the demand for detailed declarations on every job they are planning long before the actual clearing is accomplished. In these declarations every little component needs to be specified, otherwise cargoes might get stuck at the border customs for weeks. In these two cases, procedures are now swifter, but they remain demanding and troublesome, in particular when firms need to show flexibility towards customers. A third firm, however, reports that problems concerning clearance of input material appear to be growing. Clearance fees, and rent for storage during bureaucratic procedures, have often reached levels where they have exceeded the value of the goods in question.

It is no secret among interviewees that bad treatment of Western firms is a way for custom officers to increase their incomes, or perhaps compensate for salaries never paid. Since customs duties are channelled into the federal budget and seldom transferred back, inventiveness in terms of bureaucratic and awkward treatment of Western firms is a matter of survival at local offices. The same may be said of the behaviour of other authorities, for instance tax authorities. In their case, regular tax payments increase the federal budget, whereas fines remain a source of income for the local tax office.

As a consequence, local administrators seldom inform firms in advance. Instead they tend to fine them after some time and usually retroactively. In some cases taxes are summed up to more than 100 per cent as local authorities have kept adding new taxes on the project along the way. Coming on top of inflation, these expenses mean that calculated revenues are severely cut for many.

The effect on transnational firms is uncertainty and insecurity. To judge from the interviews, corruption and dishonesty by authorities pose a bigger problem than do outright criminal elements, i.e. the public Mafia is more troublesome than the private Mafia.

Without a doubt, these features of the NWR business environment hamper transnational business, and perhaps particularly the engagement of larger TNCs, which hesitate to make substantial investments. For the time being, they simply keep their eyes open and wait for things to change. Until that happens, there is always a chance that somebody comes along to explain that assets have been confiscated. Stable rules and legislation are required but also understanding about how Western firms operate.

Against this background, it is somewhat surprising that firms are generally reluctant to admit that they are discriminated against because they are foreign. Some even point out that Russian firms suffer from the same complexity and uncertainty, but on the other hand, Russian firms are perceived as being less concerned about conducting business in accordance with laws and regulations.

Perceptions of Business Culture

As mentioned, firms generally see relative geographical proximity as an advantage. In fact, only two of our SMEs appear to have considered expansion alternatives outside the Barents region.[8] It seems like many SMEs would not have had any foreign operations, not even in adjacent Nordic countries, if not for the sudden emergence of neighbouring Russia as an opportunity. Geographical distance, however, does not necessarily co-variate with cultural distance, and with few exceptions, there is a widespread reluctance to view cultural affinity as connected to geographical adjacency.

This section deals with the business culture of north-western Russia, as expressed by the interviewees. Many of the views are not very favourable for NWR and business people in the area, and might even seem to be permeated by prejudiced opinions. Before such a conclusion is arrived at, however, it should be taken into account that many of these interviewees are people who have spent a lot of time in NWR, struggling to realise their business interests in this unfamiliar environment. In the following, their opinions are presented in a rather unembellished fashion.

It should be pointed out from the beginning that firms' awareness of cultural differences varies considerably. Not surprisingly, firms with an international record, or with more than a few years of engagement in Russia, seem more alert to the importance of adjusting business conduct to the culture in question. Some stress the fact that one has to prepare oneself for a different culture, as when going anywhere else in the world, whereas others think that Russia is more alien than any other place. One interviewee in the latter category, who had just returned from India, concluded that India is much closer to home than Russia when it comes to business culture. Another mentions China where 'at least people look different to remind you of a different culture ... but with the Russians ... you think they understand, but forget that they have never heard about the basics.'

These are some of the most colourful opinions expressed among our interviewees, but perceptions of cultural differences are abundant.

To begin with, negotiations over contracts, and planning processes, are often considered very different from common Western practice. Once a project is identified, Russians tend to rush into detailed technical planning, covering several sectors even before preparatory investigations are finished and thoroughly evaluated. You also risk finding yourself deprived of returns from projects you have planned with Russian partners, while the project as such continues according to your plan long after you were excluded. Often formal and administrative procedures and signatures seem more important than the content of a contract, and sometimes the bargaining continues after the contract is signed, meaning that the actual contract is only to be part of the picture. As a result, negotiating processes tend to be very vague and difficult to grasp for many of the interviewees. It does not seem to occur to most Russians that there has to be economic returns in the end, which produces unrealistic business ideas and expectations.

In one way or another, a vast majority of the interviewees complain that Russians lack understanding of economic matters, which also makes them insensitive to the economic consequences of a their behaviour. A couple of them bring up issues of business ethics and morality, causing problems ranging from minor fraud and theft to outright plunder of foreign firms. Such problems do of course exist also in established market economic systems, but respondents seem to agree that the impact is different in transitory Russia. One who has suffered severely says that he has never met an honest Russian and that morality does not exist in the country. Another couple of respondents say that there is always someone who goes wrong in every project to gain personal advantage, which has to be taken into consideration.

Differences in business culture are often emphasised when relations between Western firms and their Russian partners and employees are discussed. Only in four cases do positive experiences with business partners seem to outweigh the negative aspects. The largest group (12/30) pointed to a mixture of positive and negative perceptions of their relationships with Russian partners, whereas nine firms expressed overwhelmingly negative opinions. In two of the most positive cases, relationships had developed over a long time, while the other two had moved into positive relationships rather swiftly. The two latter are of particular interest and we shall return to them.

Among the decidedly negative interviewees, sceptical views on Russian partners flourish, and illustrative stories are innumerable, including some remarkable examples of the dishonesty of business partners. In one case, the Russian chairman managed to manoeuvre an old friend into the position of puppet managing director. Most papers disappeared as did the chairman, whereupon a Russian auditor was called in only to mislay more papers. In the end, substantial values were lost. In another case, the Russian manager had packed the company truck with machinery and materials, which he sold before vanishing into thin air. According to a third sceptical voice, dishonesty among project participants must be taken for granted and taken into account when plans are made. Apart from dishonesty, unwillingness of Russians to take on responsibility and fulfil contractual obligations is mentioned as a problem.

In the group of firms with mixed impressions of Russian partners, negative opinions are frequent, but problems appear somehow manageable. It is a frequent perception that all Russians are not the same, making it important to identify the right persons within firms and organisations. One example may illustrate this view: 'In every organisation you really have to find out who is the promoter of Western technology and who is not. And if it seems that the key decision-makers are not, there is no sense in wasting your time.' These firms had often established contacts with several partners when they started operating in Russia, to choose the most appropriate after a period of trial and error.

If attention is shifted from Russian partners to Russian employees, interviewees seem slightly more positive. The respondents stress the technical skills of Russian employees and other contract workers. Their practical skills are on par with, if not better than, what may be expected in the firms' home country. Both workers and technical personnel in leading positions are well educated for what they are doing. Apart from this evaluation, however, few positive remarks can be found in the material, and again our interviewees do not hesitate to express their complaints. There is widespread opinion that things are often done in an awkward way. Poor understanding of quality demands and purposeful applications, lacking discipline and dishonesty are among the problems frequently mentioned.

The material contains an abundance of examples of how problems arise from differences in people's reasoning, perception, ways of doing things, values and beliefs. An overwhelming majority hold the opinion that Russians have a lot to learn, not least about economics, language and quality. They also think there is very little Western firms can learn in Russia except when it comes to particularities about Russian ways of doing things. Concerning business partners and employees, it is often emphasised that it will take time to change things and that it will require education. One interviewee, hardened after many years of experience, emphasises that no matter how hard one tries, there are still aspects of Russia one will not be able to understand:

'You may sit down and discuss customs duties and taxes, or discuss the printed framework, but in Russia a lot is unwritten, things you can't negotiate, put on the table or even talk about. ... There is a lot to watch out for, things that should be possible, but then anything can happen. ... It also depends on people – you might find somebody you are popular with... it is difficult to grasp. ...If you get such structures against you, things become complicated no matter what you do.'

Obviously, when counterparts with completely different backgrounds meet in business matters, routines become adventures into the unknown. Contracts and plans become matters of dispute or even worse, conflicts are not discovered because of misunderstandings, only to surface at later stages in the process. The most important lesson is that Russia is very different and that problems arise more frequently when differences are neglected. Harsh opinions among Western businessmen should in part be seen in this light, since they often express insensitivity and impatience with codes of conduct and taken-for-granted frames of reference different from their own.

Managing Uncertainty and Distrust

Considering the features of north-western Russia presented here, it is somewhat surprising that firms, with few exceptions, continue to develop their business activities and remain quite optimistic about future operations in NWR.[9] As will be discussed, however, the problematical nature of NWR as a location for transnational business has consequences for the qualitative content of business relationships.

At the time of the interviews, many firms were deeply engaged through subsidiary branches or joint ventures (16/30) , but many also operated on a contractual basis (12/30). Only two firms used subcontracting as their method of operation. For quite a few, however, the uncertain situation and related risks were too big to motivate substantial investments. In a number of cases, brave attitudes had either vanished or left few practical traces. Most firms found out that getting started in NWR demanded more time and resources than they had anticipated. Miscalculations derived from difficulties in finding reliable business partners and figuring out on what terms establishments could be made. As a consequence, several firms said that more time should be spent on projects in north-western Russia, while others emphasised the need for long-term commitments in order to learn how to do business in Russia.

Many respondents expressed hopes of trusting relations with partners and employees as well as with local and regional authorities. As has been noted, however, such relations are difficult to establish. Many firms also think that control is needed at every stage, which calls for a more or less permanent presence at the location. Not seldom does the quest for control derive from vast records of severe co-operation problems in joint venture arrangements. The following quotation captures much of what many have experienced:

'It did not seem to matter whether we owned 30, 60, or 90 per cent – the trend of affairs required that we were fully engaged all the time. Otherwise nothing, or negative incidents, happened when we were away. ... Our conclusion was that our commitment must be 100 per cent, otherwise we might just as well forget the whole thing. And apart from ownership control, Scandinavian management is necessary.'

There is thus both an ownership and a management aspect to the quest for control. In moments of reflection, three of the interviewees, whose Russian adventures had been marred by complications, expressed their belief that not enough effort had been put into the question of management and formal bureaucratic procedures. Russian partners had been entrusted with far-reaching responsibilities both concerning day-to-day matters and relations to public authorities but had taken neither task seriously enough. Experience from a joint venture had caused at least one firm to settle for a fully owned subsidiary when restructuring its Russian operations. Others had chosen similar solutions to the 'presence problem' and established small wholly owned subsidiaries. More often than not, operations were run at least partly with Russian personnel, whereas control remained at the head office.

Not all, however, is dark on the joint venture front. A few examples exist in the material where partners seem to have found each other, where trust has been established and where Russian partners fulfil their tasks according to agreements. These positive indications notwithstanding, it remains a fact that joint ventures have acquired a bad reputation and that many have avoided the joint venture construction after hearing stories of others.

In this connection, two Swedish firms, who sense that progress is constantly being made, stand out as interesting examples. Both are involved in manufacturing and both have decided to operate on a contractual basis. Their Russian counterparts contribute labour and buildings and run most practical matters concerning daily operations. The two firms are also fairly content with the way contacts with the authorities are handled. The Swedes contribute mainly machinery, input materials, market access and financing. Joint venture arrangements and anything but minor investments, have deliberately been avoided to limit risks. This means that nothing is jointly owned and that the Russian counterparts are kept at arm's length. Contract fulfilment is an absolute precondition for continued co-operation, meaning that there will always be new gains in the next round of negotiations.

The two firms have a very optimistic outlook on the future and are anticipating a growing engagement. Since firms in the West are in charge of ordering the goods, they can specify what quality they want without having to argue too much, but they are not relieved of the need to follow up on production to ensure that the right product is delivered. But doing so is probably a less sensitive matter.

However, regardless of what organisational solution a firm chooses, caution seems to be the only insurance against most problems, but it is not sufficient. One thing is obvious: firms that have adopted outright prospecting strategies and quickly manoeuvred themselves into substantial undertakings, have suffered great losses, or have even been thrown out at later stages as witnessed by a handful of the respondents. All in all, the conditions for entering NWR are not hopeless, but are far from ideal. As a consequence, business relationships tend to be fragile and require constant supervision if complete collapse is to be avoided.

Conclusion

For a number of reasons firms have been, and in most cases still are, careful not to get tied into business relationships that would be costly to abolish. It is obvious that firms, despite having identified extraordinary opportunities, have many reasons for not getting too deeply involved in north-western Russia. There seems to be a great market potential for different types of knowledge and technology. In addition, geographical proximity and relative cultural nearness are commonly perceived advantages. It also appears that there is a clear interregional dimension to transnational business in the Barents region, which is emphasised by the fact that many of our SMEs were not involved in foreign activities elsewhere. The first obvious conclusion is therefore that there is a scope for interregional co-operation. The question is whether such co-operation can do anything to improve the business climate, enabling the firms to take better advantage of the opportunities..

As we have seen, the unfamiliar institutional and cultural environment circumscribes any attempt to operate in a rational and goal-oriented fashion. Legislation and other regulations surrounding business activities are constantly changing or subject to unpredictable implementation by local and regional authorities. Institutional instability and complexity have led to higher levels of uncertainty and risk than is the case in other foreign locations. Although formal institutions are changing, often to the better, informal codes of conduct prevail among authorities and prevent institutional changes from being implemented. A second conclusion is therefore that the subnational layer of government involved in interregional co-operation needs to make policies and codes of conduct towards transnational business part of its own agenda for co-operation. Thus far there are few examples of this in the Barents region.

Firms also find the business culture of north-western Russia very difficult to understand. Relations with Russian partners and employees often suffer from misunderstandings and a lack of confidence. Much time and effort must be invested before things get started and revenues are realised, which proves troublesome particularly for SMEs. Interestingly, the cultural awareness of Norwegian SMEs is paralleled only by larger Finnish TNCs, which usually have decades of experience to fall back on.

Norwegian firms are also more satisfied with their government backing, probably because of the relatively generous provision of funding, which has been part of the Norwegian foreign policy in the area. This support has apparently given the SMEs the opportunity to get established in the NWR area with reduced economic risks, but may also have improved their ability to handle the Russian business culture. In order words, political efforts seem to matter.

The economic rationale for such measures may be questioned because they imply that to some extent, business operations become politically driven. However, if economic interaction in a certain area is considered politically important, then certain stimuli, not necessarily financial, to promote and assist the transnationalisation of firms could be an important element in interregional co-operation as a development strategy, and not just an aspect of foreign policy. This, in turn, it would knit transnational business closer to interregional co-operation and, in a sense, institutionalise business relationships. There are a few examples of this in the Barents region.

Without a doubt, it is very difficult for firms to handle the combination of institutional uncertainty and cultural differences, and truly interdependent relationships seldom emerge. Instead most firms stress that control over Russian operations is essential, which often seems to mean that relationships are either organised in an unequal manner or that engagements remain very limited. This is likely to increase the risk of cultural friction between Western firms and their partners and employees.[10] Unless measures are taken to come to terms with the difficulties stemming from the institutional and cultural features of NWR, truly interdependent business relations may not evolve, and as a consequence, the societal foundation for interregional co-operation is likely to remain fragile. The challenge for interregional co-operation is thus to assume a bridge-building and stabilising role in relation to transnational business.

In the Barents context, it cannot be denied that measures have been initiated at the interstate level, and not through initiatives at the subnational or interregional level. In other words, the regional tier of co-operation has not yet managed to play a role in relation to transnational business though there seems to be such a role to fill.[11]

Notes

1 See chapter by Aalbu in this volume for a fuller record of the Barents region co-operation. Comprehensive discussions on the Barents region and its early developments can be found in Bröms, Eriksson and Svensson (1994); Dellenbrant and Olsson (1994); and Stokke and Tunander (1994).

2 According to Karl Kaiser's definition, a transnational society is a system of interaction in a specific issue area between societal actors in different national systems (Kaiser 1971: 802).

3 North-western Russia is here used in a narrower sense than what is common practice and simply means the Russian part of the Barents region, i.e. Murmansk and Arkhangelsk oblasts, the Karelian Republic, and Nenets okrug.

4 FDIs are 'where a firm from one country buys a controlling investment in a firm in another country or where a firm from one country sets up a branch or a subsidiary company in another country' (Dicken 1992: 87). NFIs are nonequity and contractual forms of association, such as licensing agreements, franchising, subcontracting, management contracts and joint ventures (Stopford and Strange 1991: 16, 48).

5 Interdependent relationships are here understood as relationships that would be costly to break (Baldwin 1980: 484).

6 In Dunning's work, these aspects sum up to the OLI configuration, consisting of owner-specific advantages (internal and external); location-specific advantages; and internalisation (of business operations).

7 For reasons of discretion, firms will not be referred to by name, nor – for reasons of space – will they be provided with individual profiles. For more detailed presentations, see Svensson (forthcoming).

8 In both cases, geographical proximity proved decisive when choosing between different locations in Eastern Europe and Asia for manufacturing. TNCs are a different matter because of their broader international outlook.

9 Only 6 firms were pessimistic, or doubtful, about their future in Russia. The rest (24/30) were either optimistic or very optimistic.

10 The term 'cultural friction' is borrowed from Ekstedt and Henning (1994).

11 For a fuller analysis and elaboration on the relationship between interregional co-operation and transnational business, see Svensson (forthcoming).

References

Anderson, B. (1991). *Imagined Communities.* London, Verso.

Baldwin, D.A. (1980) 'Interdependence and Power: A Conceptual Analysis,' *International Organisation*:34(4), pages 471-506.

Bröms, P., Eriksson, J. and Svensson, B. (1994). *Reconstructing Survival: Evolving Perspectives on Euro-Arctic Politics.* Stockholm, ERU, Fritzes.

Dellenbrant, J.-Å. and Olsson, M.-O. (eds.) (1994). *The Barents Region. Security and Economic Development in the European North.* Umeå, Cerum.

Dicken, P. (1992). *Global Shift: The Internationalization of Economic Activity.* Second edition. London, Paul Chapman.

Dunning, J.H. (1980). 'Toward an Eclectic Theory of International Production: Some Empirical Tests,' *Journal of International Business Studies*:2, pages 9-31.

Dunning, J.H. (1993). 'Towards an Interdisciplinary Explanation of International Production' in Dunning, J.H. (ed.). *The Theory of Transnational Corporations.* London, Routledge.

Ekstedt, E., Henning, R. et al. (1994). *Kulturell friktion. Konfliktkälla och förnyelsekraft i en integrerad ekonomi.* Stockholm, SNS Förlag.

Grafstein, R. (1988). 'The Problem of Institutional Constraint,' *Journal of Politics*:50, pages 577-99.

Kaiser, K. (1971). 'Transnational Politics: Toward a Theory of Multinational Politics,' *International Organization*:25(4), pages 795-816.

North, D.C. (1990). *Institutions, Institutional Change and Economic Performance.* Cambridge, Cambridge University Press.

Nørgaard, A.S. (1996). 'Rediscovering Reasonable Rationality in Institutional Analysis,' *European Journal of Political Research*:29 (January), pages 31-57.

Stokke, O.S. and Tunander, O. (eds.) (1994). *The Barents Region: Cooperation in Arctic Europe.* London, Sage Publications.

Svensson, B. (forthcoming). *Interregional Cooperation and Transnational Business: The Case of the Barents Region.* Doctoral dissertation.

Stopford, J. and Strange, S. (1993). *Rival States, Rival Firms: Competition for World Market Shares.* Cambridge, Cambridge University Press.

Part IV

Political Integration, Territorial Governance and Security

24 Security around the Baltic Rim: Concepts, Actors and Processes

Kari Möttölä[1]

Introduction

The Baltic Sea region – or Northern Europe as a whole, where the Barents region and the European Arctic constitute the northernmost part[2] – is emerging as an international region with a distinctive agenda of security and co-operation and a developing pattern of interactions, alignments and institutions.[3]

The issue of security in the Baltic Sea region is shaped by the complexity of the concept of security itself, the multitude of internal and external actors and the variegation of their security needs and concerns, as well as the interaction of regional efforts with wider structures and the overarching European security process, and even the links between the region and its subregions.

This chapter will offer an overall assessment of security management and, on that basis, of future security generation for the Baltic Sea region. While the task at hand is to connect analytically and politically region and security in a particular case, regional security has to be evaluated in the broader framework of European transformation.

The significance of regionality in Baltic Rim security cannot be determined by a conceptual definition or a policy-making statement alone. In the end, the effect is established in practice, by actions and activities directed at security in the region, and by empirical evidence thereof. Regionality is part of a wider transformation in European security. The focus in this contribution will be on concerted or institutionalised efforts among states, as national-level policies are dealt with elsewhere in this volume. The objective will be to analyse and present the makings and workings of co-operative security, its content and institutional structure, in the Baltic Sea region.

While regions have of late gained popularity and prominence in the modelling of security policy,[4] they differ in their maturity and relevance as security formations and configurations. One of the challenges in analysing the Baltic Sea region is to determine its significance for Europe at large, the space covered by the Organisation for Security and Co-operation in Europe (OSCE). The scene around the Baltic Rim offers a rich mix of theoretical and political material for such an analysis. The principal question posed in this chapter is what kind of security space is emerging for the Baltic Sea region. An important part of the answer is provided by the analysis of the transition under way. In policy terms, the key question is whether, in effect, a programme for co-operation on Baltic Rim security is being outlined and implemented by states and institutions internal and external to the region.

Underlying the analysis of concepts, actors and processes in security policy making for the Baltic Sea region are two questions of general significance. One is the feasibility and sustainability of the concept of region in the context of security as part of the global order. The other is the scope and effectiveness of policies and processes dedicated to or targeted at regional security and the effects of regional security on the global order. The experience of the Baltic Sea region may be a test of the extent to which regionalism as a phenomenon and region-building as a policy may have a primary or subsidiary role in producing security for states.

Concepts

Security: Common, Comprehensive, Indivisible

The OSCE Security Model

The concept of security is patterned by the systemic change under way in the post-Cold War environment as well as by the opening up of societies to a broader range of risks and challenges of a domestic, transnational and international nature to fundamental values and basic structures. An outlook on security is adopted from, and its operationalised forms are sought in, the OSCE process aiming at 'a common and comprehensive security model for Europe in the twenty-first century,' which was launched by the Budapest 1994 meeting and further mandated by the Lisbon meeting 1996.[5]

The goal of the security model exercise is set as 'the development of a *common security space* based on the OSCE's comprehensive and co-operative concept of security and its indivisibility.'[6] The multi-dimensional concept covers international, national and subnational aspects of the envisaged security order.

In order to overcome the legacy of the Cold War division and to prevent a relapse to its inherent confrontation, such a common security space, by definition, should be free of old or new 'dividing lines.'[7] The goal of unification of a new Europe, set by the Paris Charter[8], is a stimulus to the policy of common security and a guiding determinant in the making of individual and joint security policies.

The *indivisibility* of security presupposes equality among states in the pursuit of their rights and responsibilities. All states have an inherent right to be free to choose or change their security arrangements. At the same time, states must not advance their security interests at the expense of others or make alliances in order to create spheres of influence over others. 'Grey zones,' where states are targets of competing influences or efforts of domination or where they are discriminated against, neglected or marginalised, constitute a threat to overall security and stability and undermine the unifying approach.

The *comprehensive* nature of security is defined by the OSCE as covering not only political and military factors but also respect for human rights as well as economic and environmental solidarity and co-operation.[9] The broad concept of security has led to an extensive use of policies that are designed to protect or create security for states and communities. Such a securitisation of international relations has brought about a recurrent discussion on the relative strengths of the narrow and broad concepts of security (Buzan 1997). As a consequence, military security tends to remain a category of its own both in theory and practice. Joining together military and non-military aspects of security in a mutually supportive manner is a specific challenge in the Baltic Sea context.

The policy of common security has a broader and deeper meaning in the post-division Europe than in the détente periods of the bipolar era, when it was primarily driven by the common interests of survival against military threats.[10] The achievement of a common security space in the new Europe is predicated on domestic and international transformation, where all states and institutions are participating in one way or another. Moreover, such a strategy of security through change is based on the allegiance of states to shared OSCE values, norms of behaviour and commitments.

While comprehensiveness and indivisibility are expressions of the end-goal in common security, *co-operation* is the method or operating principle for reaching and upholding those ideal conditions. The legitimacy and rationale of co-operation as a security policy strategy are based on the accountability of states to their citizens and each other for implementing the commitments adopted in a voluntary and transparent fashion. Co-operation is aimed, for the sake of solidarity, at assisting states in meeting the objectives of transition in accordance with the common values of democracy and the market economy. Co-operation is also aimed, in the name of accountability, at introducing joint action in cases of non-implementation or gross violations of the common standards. The dualism of support and compliance functions as the driving force behind co-operative security.

As exemplified by the OSCE, co-operative security is based on the inclusiveness of participation, the comprehensiveness of the agenda and the rule of consensus in decision-making whereby states conduct their concerted actions, individually, in groups or through institutions and organisations. The emphasis in co-operative security is not on enforcement action or sanctioning – they are more or less exclusively reserved for the UN system of collective security – but on exercising a long-term impact on the root causes of security problems, on promoting the prevention of conflicts and on enhancing the consolidation of stability through change. Moreover, institutions for co-operative or collective security are not entrusted with such hard competence or strong capability as are institutions for collective defence.

The agenda for co-operative security is broad and the circle of actors wide, consisting of states as well as international institutions to which they belong. Increased attention is devoted to co-operation and co-ordination among European, transatlantic and regional international institutions and organisations on the non-hierarchical basis of mutual reinforcement, complementarity and comparative advantage. Co-operative security denotes a multi-institutional order.[11]

Establishing security for the Baltic Rim is to be seen as a regional application of the concept of co-operative security. To fulfil the objective of the OSCE security model, all the states and subregions should be treated equally, all the dimensions of security taken into account, and the recreation of divisions or gaps avoided. A security space for the Baltic Rim with its specific regional architecture of actors and institutions is a contributing and constituent part of a European order for common security.

Developments since the lifting of the East-West overlay have revealed that security in the new Europe is increasingly defined, challenged and constructed locally and regionally. Drawing on the benefits of the overall security order, regional measures – undertaken by regional actors or targeted at regional conditions – are needed to ensure the indivisibility of security. While regional security processes may in many respects be a response to the general agenda in the transitional Europe, they produce and unravel their own variations of post-Cold War security management in response to specific problems.

Security Driven by Integration

While the conceptual and political implications of the inclusive policy making for common security in the OSCE space apply to the Baltic Sea region, it is the exclusive processes of political, economic and military *integration* and their implications that tend to govern the current scene. The European Union (EU) and the North Atlantic Treaty Organisation (NATO) adhere to the OSCE norms and principles and support the goal of a common security space, but the security benefits accrued to the privileged members make the two institutions powerful poles of attraction and dominant foci of the agenda in the Baltic Sea region. Due to their authority and capability, the EU and NATO are not only viewed as zones of stability in their own right; they are also vehicles for promoting stability outside their frontiers. On that account, the integrating institutions may be the most capable instruments of co-operative security, but they are not sufficient to ensure its indivisibility (Knudsen 1996).

Although the OSCE security model, as an expression of a value-based political, economic, social and military transformation, can be viewed as a peace-through-democracy strategy (Gleditsch 1995), it is the process of regional political and economic integration within the European Union that constitutes the core of the emerging democracy-based security order in Europe. Its political and economic membership criteria and its historic origins in the divided Europe make the EU an institution with an attractive capability and a unique authority for outsiders who are looking for solutions to their problems of security and prosperity.

The EU is producing security for the OSCE space and its subregions through support and partnership policies, pre-accession programmes and enlargement strategies. Although the EU's outreach activities aim at expanding the core zone of established democratic peace in Europe, the threshold to full membership is maintained high and demanding, and only a limited scope is left for purely political consideration in the determination of the fulfilment of the criteria by the aspirant countries. While maintaining the exclusiveness and conditionality of membership, the EU in its wider security role, acting directly or through international institutions such as the OSCE or the Council of Europe (COE) or financial institutions, is making a key institutional and functional impact on the evolving European order, globally as well as regionally (Miles and Redmond 1996).

The integration of the Nordic countries (Norden), rooted in common history and cultural affinity, is driven by political responsiveness, not by competent and capable institutions like the EU. Nordic integration, which is not self-sustaining but embedded within the EU/EEA in the functions covered by Union integration (acquis), offers to partners a link to the democratic core of nations in Europe. Such a link is established by the close Nordic-Baltic co-operation.

NATO has a security role as an exclusive institution for politico-military integration with its increasing outreach activities and evolving enlargement policies. While full membership in NATO is based on democratic criteria and viewed by aspirants as recognition of belonging to the democratic family of nations, NATO's decisions on enlargement are more likely to be based on political and geostrategic reasons than those of the EU. The wider room for political manoeuvre is due to the intergovernmental nature of NATO integration and its narrow scope of competence in comparison with the central role of supranationalism in the EU's integration and its deep political and socio-economic effects (Kugler 1996).

Parallelism in the EU and NATO enlargement processes may be uncertain, although there are connections both in time and substance. Both institutions maintain their autonomy in future decisions relevant for Baltic Rim security. While both the EU and NATO play key roles in pursuing common security for Europe based on the OSCE principles, they pursue policies of conditionality towards membership-seekers and other partners and maintain non-inclusive structures as composite parts of the overall security order. EU enlargement and NATO expansion may restructure in a complex way the institutional foundation of the Baltic Sea region in the long run.

It is significant for the future of Europe, and the Baltic Sea region as well, that because of its geopolitical and geoeconomical mass and its inherent great-power role, Russia cannot be viewed as embedded in either of the Western-originated institutions as a full member, even though both the EU and NATO pursue close and active partnership relationships with Russia. As the engagement of Russia in OSCE-wide co-operation is indispensable for the goal of common security, Russia's role is even more central in security management and generation for the Baltic Rim, where it is the preponderant local actor. As a great power located in the region, Russia is a kind of counterpart to the EU and NATO. Although

Russia does not offer an alternative as a focus of integration, Russia's reactions and policies will to an important extent determine the impact of the EU's and, in particular, NATO's policies on overall security in the Baltic Sea region (Baranovsky 1996; Legvold 1996)

Integration-driven security is a central part of the Baltic Rim scene, currently and for the foreseeable future. The EU-NATO-Russia triangle constitutes a framework for conditions to be met in establishing a common security space in the Baltic Sea region. Moreover, the interrelationship between inclusive co-operation and exclusive integration influences the effectiveness of security management. Multilateral regional co-operation must assert its place in security architecture.

Security Agenda for the Baltic Rim

A list of risks and challenges to security compiled by the OSCE,[12] caused by lack of implementation, non-compliance with or gross violations of the values, principles, norms and commitments adopted jointly, takes up military risks, political risks, risks to democracy, the rule of law, human rights and civil society, economic challenges, social risks, and environmental hazards. The task of the OSCE community is to generate and sustain co-operative action in response to non-compliance with the common principles and commitments or in support of their implementation. Post-Cold War or post-modern security policy making is a combined effort by individual states and inclusive, exclusive or regional groups of states and institutions, where the overall goal of a common security space functions as a yardstick of the policies.

The security agenda around the Baltic Rim reflects the challenge of common security that is being faced by the post-Cold War Europe at large, under the conditions of political change and economic transition (Maibach 1996). Efforts to enhance security in the region have to transcend a former politico-military divide and one of the widest socio-economic gaps in Europe and overcome civilian and military environmental risks and hazards of exceptional gravity. They have to deal with remnants of the Cold War military legacy and balance and stabilise the residual military potentials from the era of great-power confrontation. Co-operative policies are needed for coping with open political issues stemming from the Cold War and arising from its aftermath, such as those related to borders and minorities. Due to geopolitics and geoeconomics, the region has to cope with the implications of the key processes underlying and defining the overall European security development: the formation of Russia's great-power future, the deepening and enlargement of the European Union and NATO adaptation and expansion.

How states and substate actors as well as international and transnational institutions succeed in promoting and consolidating progress and stability for the Baltic Sea region – and the whole of Northern Europe – is in many respects not only illustrative of, but even critical for, the evolution of a common security space in the OSCE context. The *security agenda* is demanding:

- The Baltic Sea region is the scene of bilateral and multilateral support for political, economic and societal transition and environmental improvement in the north-western areas of Russia and in the Baltic states and Poland, channelled bilaterally and through regional and European multilateral institutions.
- Nordic integration has found a new relevance in exercising an external supportive and stabilising effect on the changes in the Baltic region and the neighbouring areas of Russia. Regional security is the main target of the newly enhanced foreign and security policy co-operation among the Nordic countries.
- Stability in the Baltic Sea region will be an important test of the effectiveness of the partnership, pre-accession and enlargement policies of the European Union, and of the introduction and implementation of a northern dimension of the Common Foreign and Security Policy (CFSP).
- The regional setting includes Russia, whose internal reform and external engagement are of vital significance for the security and unification of Europe in general. Moreover, Russia's position as a great power in search of a new role is a challenge to establishing security arrangements which would be balanced and equal and, at the same time, non-hegemonial and non-exclusive in the regional framework.
- The Russian question that agitates European politics in general is fuelled by Russia's unresolved relationship with its neighbours. In the Baltic Sea region, Russia's policies towards the three Baltic states, Estonia, Latvia and Lithuania, are driven by frustration over the status of ethnic Russians and the inconsistent functioning of the half-formed domestic political order of a nation seeking an identity.
- Progress on the consolidation of sovereignty and the international position of the Baltic states is an important indication of regional stability and a vital test of the indivisibility of security. The normalisation of Baltic-Russian relations and the integration of the Baltic states with European and transatlantic institutions are issues that have wide implications for international security and place high demands on the foreign policy capabilities of Estonia, Latvia and Lithuania.
- International attention in the areas of conflict prevention, dispute settlement and crisis management is focused on open issues in Baltic-Russian relations and on the development of the Kaliningrad region and its adjustment to a changed political and security milieu. Assistance programmes and missions of the OSCE and the Council of Europe play a practical and tested role in security management.
- Security around the Baltic Rim is tangibly affected by NATO enlargement, which will require a number of associated co-operative measures targeted at the region. The effectiveness of NATO policies aimed at post-first tranche stability will be tested, in particular, by the provision of reassurance for the Baltic states as well as consideration of the security interests of Finland and Sweden. NATO's arrangements aimed at meeting the security concerns of Russia will have direct implications for the security environment around the Baltic Rim

and test the implementation of equality towards the lesser countries of the region.

- NATO's adaptation of its structures and functions produces opportunities for co-operative security. Dual-purpose planning structures are opening up for partners in crisis management. An enhanced Partnership for Peace (PfP) and its regional applications will have a role to play in the promotion of stability in the Baltic Sea region. The Euro-Atlantic Partnership Council (EAPC) may offer regional sub-fora for a more structured and focused discussion of common interests.
- Military security around the Baltic Rim is being shaped by the restructuring that is under way nationally in allied and non-allied countries, as well as collectively within NATO. The outcome of military reform in Russia and the realignment and redeployment of its forces will shape the immediate security environment around the Baltic Rim. In the field of arms control, CFE adaptation in particular, the future of flank provisions and the issue of wider accession to the treaty affect the security environment of the smaller countries in the region.
- While security in the military field is organically linked with OSCE-wide or NATO-connected structures, regional arrangements can make a complementary contribution to the system of confidence- and security-building measures (CSBM) and play an initiating role in naval co-operation or provide a specific function in support of sovereignty management.
- Bilateral and regional initiatives are encouraged as part of the OSCE security model. The Baltic Sea region can act as an exemplary contribution to common security in all of Europe. On the other hand, the possibility of reconvening the Baltic Sea regional round table as envisaged in the follow-up mandate of the Stability Pact is explored within the OSCE context.

The agenda is not only a reflection of the multiple character of security challenges; it is an indication of a change under way on the Baltic Sea security scene from the immediate post-Cold War situation into a new phase, where significant aspects of the political and economic reforms are being concluded and a new post-transition perspective is opening up.

Region: Identity, Institutions, Functions

The concept of a *region* in international relations can be defined in a number of ways. A key criterion is that regions should be endowed with political dynamics of their own, driven by distinctive agendas, patterns of interactions and governed by specific codes of conduct or regimes. Region-specific or region-centred policies may be responses to the impact of global affairs and regions may also affect politics at the global level (Young 1996). Regions can be viewed as social systems of growing cohesion and homogeneity, on a scale extending from mere interdependence into organised co-operation, a civil society and an acting and capable subject in international relations (Hettne 1993).

The emergence of the Baltic Rim as an international region, filling an empty space offered by the dissolution of the bipolar order, can be approached as a scene of discourse, an effort of common governance or a series of actions by a constellation of players. Whether the region is based on identification, institutionalisation or functionalism, it is an cumulative and unfinished process of social and international change (Jukarainen 1996).

Regionalism or regionness around the Baltic Rim is occurring as natural regionalisation and as conscious region-building, and in both bottom-up and top-down fashions. There are subjective (history, culture, identity) and objective (geography, geoeconomics, geopolitics) factors that drive regionalisation. There are likewise political programmes of action and practical activities run by governments as well as subnational and substate actors that lead to region-building, and often in the form of new institutions (Saarikoski 1995).

Identity Formation

As a region based on positive self-identification, the Baltic Rim is derived from historical models and metaphors of unity, the most notable among them being the Hanseatic League which has given the region a strongly economic identity (Klinge 1994). The Baltic basin is perceived as one of the geoeconomical growth regions of Europe due to market, technological and infrastructural factors on the way toward fulfilling the potentials frustrated by the artificial division of the Cold War era (Kivikari 1996).

The regional approach to Baltic Rim security originated largely in academic and NGO discourses and parliamentary activities (Joenniemi and Wæver 1992; Jervell et al. 1992) as a precursor to intergovernmental and other institutional forms which have accelerated the rebirth of regionalism around the historical sea. The strength of a Baltic Sea identity and its effect on behaviour vary among states but may be strongest among subnational communities and within transnational networks (Perko 1996). The potential of togetherness is idealised and the region is presented in programmatic manifestations as an exemplary community able to introduce pluralistic social practices (e.g. peace zones or advanced minority regimes) or liberalist reterritorialisation (Securitas Baltica 1996: 8-13). An identity region is fused with a transregion (Wæver 1996) and finds its dynamics and, for many proponents, its legitimacy in the bottom-up model.

Identity formation can be also a top-down, government-driven and purposeful policy. The Baltic Rim world as a centre of identification is revisited and reconstructed in several developments. The close Nordic-Baltic relationship is a newly established subregional link based on historical and cultural affinity and transcending territoriality. Poland has reoccupied a position as a link between the Central European and Baltic worlds. The Hanseatic tradition has set forth an active contribution by the adjacent German Länder to the Baltic Rim community building, followed by the federal government. The adjacent areas of a democratic Russia, such as St Petersburg and Kaliningrad, are viewed as belonging to the Baltic Sea world, where Russia has its historic and geopolitical roots as a European power.

Institutionalisation

The institutional framework of the Baltic Sea region was most authoritatively and precisely determined by the establishment of the Council of the Baltic Sea States (1992) with the membership of Denmark, Estonia, Finland, Germany, Iceland, Latvia, Lithuania, Norway, Poland, Russia, Sweden and the European Union/Commission.[13] While the CBSS is a political construction by the central governments, under its umbrella and within the same geographic extension a proliferating set of subnational and non-governmental fora and networks has been created among counties, cities and other communities. The Baltic Sea States Sub-regional Conference is a main substate forum in the system of organisational pluralism (Joenniemi and Stålvant 1995; Hansen 1997).

The Barents Euro-Arctic Council (1993) with the membership of Denmark, Finland, Iceland, Norway, Russia, Sweden and the European Union/Commission delineates the other subregion that completes the overall North European region. While the BEAC is an institution run by the central governments, the Regional Council brings together the counties and the indigenous peoples of the Barents region in the spirit of devolution.[14] For Russia and the Nordic countries the CBSS and the BEAC form a closely linked whole in their conception of regional security and co-operation.

In addition to activities by dedicated multilateral regional institutions and among regional actors, the Baltic Sea region is reproduced in co-operation by states and powers external to the region, unilaterally, together with regional states, and in the work of international institutions.

The European Union, in designing Baltic and Baltic Sea strategies, is addressing the issue of regional co-operation in its common policies. The origins of integration within the EEC/EU context are based on a regionalist approach. The Baltic Sea region has emerged as a key geopolitical concept in the discussion of implications of NATO adaptation and enlargement and an important target of NATO's outreach activities. Regional and subregional initiatives are encouraged as part of the OSCE security model and the operational links such as round tables and administrative contacts between regions and the OSCE come under closer scrutiny. Russia is reconstructing a new Baltic and Baltic Sea policy in the changed domestic and international circumstances, and the leading Western powers are responding to expectations and demands by designing policy concepts for Baltic Sea regional security.

While the CBSS and the OSCE are inclusive intergovernmental institutions, the EU and NATO bring into the regional setting exclusionary policies. While both of them create a privileged and coveted community of states which covers only partly the Baltic Sea region, the process of integration is opening and may transform the institutional structure of the Baltic Rim in the long run.

Functionalism

Identity is a significant factor in explaining the revival of a Baltic Rim region, but it is not a sufficient engine for running the ensuing co-operation. Institutionalisation of the Baltic Rim is a vital underpinning of regional governance but the dynamics of Baltic Sea security are driven by a combined effect of functional processes and geopolitical interests with identities and institutions.

As a geopolitical delineation, the Baltic Rim has both historical and contemporary underpinnings. The Russian military and political withdrawal, followed by a diminished Russian military influence and the quest to secure its permanent geostrategic interests, have made the Baltic Sea region into a transitional zone. NATO's enlargement plans, combined with an effort to keep Russia together and involved in security co-operation as an equal, and the Russian responses to NATO's offers bring the element of power politics into the region. EU enlargement measures the dynamics of integration as a force of systemic change and democratic peace in the region and breaks historical patterns. The Baltic region is re-emerging as a zone located between the German and Russian influences. The Baltic Rim is becoming the context where the future influence of Nordism is determined.

Initially, regional co-operation for security around the Baltic Rim was dedicated to new challenges such as socio-economic instability, environmental damage, uncontrolled migration, refugeeism, international crime and narcotics smuggling. Lifting the Cold War overlay has freed the parties to tackle all the pressing problems of comprehensive security. Subsequently, the traditional aspects of politico-military security have emerged on the regional agenda. The approach favoured by the local actors remains the management of military security exclusively, initially or largely in the wider setting where account can be taken of the implications of, and the connections with, the Russian-NATO power balance.

Even though it is relatively weak as a formal international institution, the CBSS has been set up as a forum for dialogue, information, and co-ordination aiming at producing incentives for practical co-operation, not so much because of the common identity felt by the governments as with a view to the significance of 'low politics' for comprehensive security and the spillover effect of functionalism on transition and stability in the region. The chosen strategy behind regional institutionalisation around the Baltic Rim is non-military co-operation as a way towards comprehensive security.

As a result, in the context of the Baltic Sea region, security as a concept is present in all of its dimensions, 'soft' and 'hard' as well as 'broad' and 'narrow,' non-military and politico-military. The region is not a homogenous security area. There are subregions and states among which security levels vary or security deficits exist, and security agendas and concerns differ fundamentally from each other. There are states that view themselves as producers of security while others act predominantly as consumers or demanders of security. Consequently, both balancing and bandwagoning appear as security strategies among the smaller states. Implementing the principle of indivisibility is an accentuated challenge for co-operative security in the Baltic Sea region.

Actors and Processes

Co-operative Strategies

Security in the Baltic Sea region is promoted by a full spectrum of co-operative strategies targeted at the three main functional sectors of security policy: promotion of stability through transition, conflict management and maintenance of military-strategic stability.[15]

- *Stability policy* consists of measures in support of political, economic and military transition as the foundation for democratic and sustainable security. Stability policy is a long-term activity which addresses the root causes of conflict. Stability policy is a strategy of conflict transformation and, in a deep and structural sense, conflict prevention.
- *Conflict management* consists of co-operative actions responding to the various phases of the whole conflict cycle: early warning, conflict prevention by diplomatic and other means of international support, crisis management by political means such as mediation and other missions, military crisis management such as traditional or enlarged peace-keeping and humanitarian intervention, peace enforcement and military compulsion, and reconstruction and post-conflict rehabilitation.
- Policies devoted to *military-strategic stability* consist of separate or common defence arrangements aiming at dissuasion and deterrence and maintaining an adequate balance. Arms control and CSBMs are an integral part of military security policies. Co-operation in the area of military security deals with the management of residual strategic confrontation and the adjustment of defence restructuring with regional stability.

Actors as Centres of Gravity

Security in the Baltic Sea region is promoted by multilateral processes that gravitate around the exclusive Western-originated institutions related to integration (Norden, the EU, NATO) and the inclusive European, transatlantic and regional institutions related to co-operation (the OSCE, the COE, the CBSS).

Norden is a subregional security community based on deep socio-economic and cultural integration and close historical and identity-related affinity. The Baltic states (Estonia, Latvia, Lithuania) have responded to change by institutionalising their mutual co-operation in a somewhat similar fashion. Nordic-Baltic co-operation combines the diffusion of political and social practices that underpin transition to an established democracy and market economics with enhancement of the capability of the Baltic states to join the EU framework.

The idea of security through integration is pursued by the European Union towards Poland and the Baltic states as candidate countries in the framework of support, pre-accession and enlargement strategies. The thrust of the EU's common policies in the framework of the CFSP is on political and economic stability support as a way to integration. The Union is also active in enhancing regional security through the OSCE and the COE.

NATO's main and original role lies in the maintenance of military-strategic stability through common defence and deterrence. In addition to being a response to geopolitical shift, NATO enlargement is introduced as a strategy for promoting democratic stability. The co-operative activities of a 'new' NATO (NACC/EAPC/PfP) provide resources and capabilities for supporting military transition and also for co-operative crisis management.

The CBSS applies the concept of common and comprehensive security based on OSCE principles in the area of stability policy. The wider institutions, the OSCE and the COE, target concerted actions at transition support and conflict prevention in the region. The OSCE also offers a co-operative forum for arms control and CSBMs.

While integration is a core resource for co-operative security, the inclusive institutions are crucial as the symbols and frameworks for avoiding new dividing lines and creating a common security space. The competence, capability and authority of institutions determine their role and impact. An important factor is the principle of mutual reinforcement and complementarity of co-operative security-related institutions adopted within the OSCE, where the contribution of integration falls within co-operative security.

Membership of the EU and NATO is adopted as the priority solution by the transition countries for solving the pressing issues of broad and narrow security. The western integrating institutions are viewed as reliable security guarantors and efficient instruments of security policy. Co-operation within the OSCE and the CBSS is a complementary element in the security policy.

Russia is a key actor whose engagement will largely determine the effectiveness of regional multilateral stability policy. As a perceived source of instability, Russia is involved in political disputes that have drawn wide attention and efforts by the international community to resolve them. Russia will be preoccupied in the near future with establishing a reassuring military balance and stability in the vital north-western direction. Russia's relations with the EU and NATO will be of central significance for co-operative security in the region.

Processes Related to Integration

Norden as a Stabilising Force

In security and co-operation in Northern Europe, Nordic integration is a core process and a stabilising force. Throughout the Cold War era its external effects were limited. In the post-division situation, the institutions of Nordic integration and the policies of Nordic co-operation have been adapted to accommodate EU enlargement and to channel a Nordic influence towards security challenges in the vicinity.

The Nordic countries have found themselves in a homogenised security environment, where the differences in defence solutions (military alignment and non-alignment) play a lesser role in meeting the new problems of comprehensive security policy. The result has been intensified and structured co-operation among the Nordic governments focused on the neighbouring areas consisting of the Baltic Sea and the Barents and Arctic regions (Möttölä 1996b; Neumann 1996).

While the scope of foreign policy co-operation among the Nordic countries in the era of the Cold War division and confrontation was limited to the UN, development, peacekeeping and other primarily global issues, in the new Europe the Nordic countries have recognised the need for, and seized the opportunity of, concerting their policies on European transformation and integration, excluding only the issues of territorial defence.[16] The changes in Europe have produced the makings of a common Nordic foreign and security policy, where the traditional instrument of common positions has been supplemented by common assessments and co-ordinated or concerted actions, specifically on regional issues. The focus of the programmatic co-operation is placed on promoting stability through sovereignty, transition and integration support for the Baltic states.

In the immediate post-Cold War years, the Nordic agenda was dominated by such open and burning issues as political and economic change in Russia, the reconstitution of democratic institutions in the Baltic states, the withdrawal of Russian troops, the position of Russian-speakers in the Baltic states and the questions related to the Paldiski and Skrunda bases and the remaining Russian military personnel, as well as nuclear hazards related to civilian and military activity. Subsequently, the focus of joint Nordic positions has been shifted to the status of the Baltic states in EU enlargement policies, the development of regional multilateral co-operation and the EU contribution therein, together with continuing concern over the unresolved Russian-Estonian and Russian-Latvian border issues and a constant watch on the political and economic developments in Russia and their implications for regional security and stability.[17]

The Nordic capability to play an effective regional security role has been enhanced by a reform of decision-making and management mechanisms and an adjusted prioritisation of co-operation. The prime ministers have been given the responsibility for the overall political co-ordination and leadership of intergovernmental Nordic co-operation and the Nordic Council of Ministers has been made a flexible tool for concerting external activities.[18] Co-operation with the areas adjacent to the Nordic region (the Baltic states, north-western Russia, including Kaliningrad, and Poland) has been given a higher status as one of the three core areas of Nordic co-operation, together with intra-Nordic co-operation and co-operation within the framework of the EU/EEA.[19]

A newly adopted Nordic strategy document outlines joint Nordic measures to promote stability and transition in the adjacent areas (defined as Estonia, Latvia, Lithuania and north-western Russia, i.e. the St Petersburg area, Kaliningrad, the Republic of Karelia and the counties of Arkhangelsk and Murmansk).[20] While the overriding goal is to strengthen peace, democracy and stability in all of Europe by supporting democratic development, market economies, respect for human rights and the responsible use of resources in the region, a specific Nordic advantage or value added is sought in disseminating Nordic experience and Nordic values (such as the Nordic socio-economic model, labour market relations, local administration, NGOs and the knowledge of Nordic languages) through exchange scholarships and project programmes and the work of the Nordic information offices (in the Baltic capitals and, soon, in St Petersburg).

The allocation of joint Nordic resources to assist the adjacent regions, including projects supported by Nordic financial institutions through soft funding in the business, industry and environment sectors, is but one part of the regional impact of Norden, which also includes the Nordic countries' bilateral co-operation with Baltic Rim countries and subregions as well as their role in multilateral regional Baltic Sea co-operation and their contribution to the EU's northern policies.[21]

While the enlargement of Nordic integration to incorporate the Baltic governments and parliaments is not adopted as a model for re-establishing the historical connection,[22] institutional links have been established and reinforced between the Nordic countries and the Baltic states. The 5+3 pattern is applied in regular annual meetings between the Nordic Council of Ministers and the Baltic Council of Ministers at the foreign ministers' and defence ministers' levels as well as in the framework of meetings between the ministers representing the Nordic Co-operation Committee and the Baltic Co-operation Committee and in other functional areas. The Nordic Council and the Baltic Assembly have established contacts and held joint meetings and seminars. Baltic parliamentarians are invited to the sessions of the Nordic Council, which has set up a committee on matters related to the neighbouring areas (the Baltic region and Russia). The 5+3 institutional connection provides a constituent subregional structure in the Baltic Sea region.

The agenda of practical Nordic-Baltic co-operation consists of scholarship schemes, information and project activities supporting the development of democratic and civil society through training and education, NGOs, third and voluntary sectors, gender equality, public administration, regional and social equality, integration of aliens, and cultural activities and technical assistance leading to larger projects funded by Nordic financial institutions. Of special topical importance is co-operation on migration, asylum and refugee issues related to the Baltic countries' capabilities in border control.[23]

In their bilateral policies of advice and assistance for the Baltic states, the Nordic countries have introduced and implemented the concept of sovereignty support. Consistent and systematic support has been targeted at institutions vital to the development of a sustainable civil society and the maintenance of effective sovereignty by a normal democratic European state, such as responsible and effective local and central administration, higher education, the judicial system and police, the customs administration, the rescue services, the coast and frontier guards and the defence forces.[24]

A particular aspect of the Nordic countries' policies for enhancing stability in the Baltic countries has been support for the integration of the Russian-speaking populations in Estonia and Latvia. Financial assistance has been allotted to immigration authorities for handling residence and citizenship procedures and for language training programmes, media development and educational materials.[25]

In the area of foreign and security policy co-operation, the Nordic-Baltic connection is used for mutual consultation and the exchange of views on a range of European security issues with the focus kept on the development of the EU and the perspective of the Baltic states' accession to it. At the practical level, mutual benefit is found in sharing the Nordic experience of membership negotiations and accession with a view to providing Nordic assistance and advice to the Baltic states in their preparations. In addition to analysis of the substance of membership criteria, plans are prepared for close interaction, including 'twinning' between Nordic and Baltic ministries and administrations and other relevant institutions. While the enhancement of regional Baltic Sea co-operation is a priority, both the Baltic and Nordic governments note that it should take place 'in a comprehensive strategic perspective through involvement of the other significant subjects of international policy.'[26]

The institutional networks and the practical exchanges and interactions related to Nordic sovereignty, transition and integration support bring the Baltic nations closer to Norden and facilitate the diffusion of the Nordic model of society across the Baltic Sea. Despite the mutual interest and identity formation within a Nordic-Baltic region, integration of the Baltic states into Nordic institutions is not forthcoming or foreseen. For the Baltic states, Nordic-Baltic co-operation is no substitute for their integration with the primary Western institutions, nor are the Nordic countries prepared to dilute the integrity of Nordic institutions or shoulder an overdimensioned responsibility for regional security and stability. The Nordic countries remain, however, key players for the Baltic states' ambitions because of their established positions in European and transatlantic integration in the framework of the EU and NATO.

The European Union as a Baltic Rim Actor

The accession of Finland and Sweden has become a key factor and stimulus in the formation and development of a northern dimension in the European Union's common policies. The geographical enlargement of the territory to the North of Europe and to a common border with Russia, the strengthening of the Nordic component in the family of members and the embracing of the Baltic Sea have expanded and refocused the Union's agenda. A reinforced emphasis on Russia, a responsible concern for the Baltic states and a new perspective on the needs and opportunities of regional co-operation in the Baltic Sea and Barents regions call for increased political attention and resource allocation in all the pillars of the Union's common policies and joint actions. Community as well as CFSP and JHA instruments are to be put to use in constructing the Union's profile and role in the Baltic Sea region.

The Nordic member states have been instrumental within the EU in ensuring for the Baltic states equal treatment as applicants, which brings with it the benefits of the Europe Agreements and pre-accession co-operation with the Union. The Baltic states together with Poland are placed on the same starting line on the road towards the privilege of EU membership, where the outcome will depend primarily on their own achievements. Within the pre-accession strategy, their progress towards achieving membership capability is supported by the economic benefits of the Europe Agreements, a structured dialogue with the Union and White Book-based guidance for adaptation of their legislation to meet the standards of the EU's single market.[27]

The Nordic countries have been the main proponents of a more structured and effective EU policy towards multilateral regional co-operation in the Baltic Rim. The widely recognised interest among the member governments and the public has resulted in the Commission's Baltic Sea Region Initiative (1996), which outlines proposals for intensifying regional co-ordination and focusing on priority areas by taking full advantage of existing co-operation and structural programmes under the EU umbrella without a need for additional funding.[28]

The main items of the EU's programmatic policy of transition support in the Baltic Sea region are strengthening democracy and political stability, including the reconstruction of civil society; economic development, including legislative and administrative frameworks and infrastructures, energy supply and environmental practices; and the promotion of regional development and cross-border co-operation, also among subnational regions and local authorities and communities. An underlying theme in the EU's strategy is encouragement and support for co-operation among the countries of the region themselves. The EU pledges its support for strengthening the position of the CBSS, which has resulted in a more active role of the Commission on the body (such as the chairmanship of the CBSS economic working group and an active contribution to the CBSS action programmes adopted at Kalmar). As a general commitment to a sustainable support for regional processes, the EU is referring to 'the wider range of regional activities in Europe reaching from the Arctic to the Black Sea.'[29]

In its strategy for future relations with Russia adopted at the Madrid European Council (1995), based on the Partnership and Co-operation Agreement, the EU commits itself to establishing a substantial partnership with Russia in order to promote democratic and economic reforms and the respect of human rights and to consolidate peace, stability and security with the aim of avoiding new dividing lines and achieving the full integration of Russia into the community of democratic nations. The strategy has been followed by an Action Plan (1996), which lists practical measures and activities aimed at contributing to Russian democratic reforms, economic development, co-operation in justice and home affairs, a dialogue on security in Europe and co-operation in the field of foreign policy. The Action Plan codifies and registers the bilateral efforts of the members in their co-operation with Russia. There is no component in the programme specifically dedicated to the Baltic Sea – Russia is covered by the Baltic Sea Region Initiative – but its objectives are relevant for developments in Russia's north-western regions around the Baltic Rim and the Barents region.[30]

The resource instruments for the EU's stability policy are provided by the Phare and Tacis programmes as well as, indirectly, by European and international financial institutions where the EU carries weight. Phare has changed from an instrument of transition support into a vehicle for EU enlargement, as the grants-based technical assistance is, in effect, devoted to the construction of the required legislative, administrative and economic infrastructure in the recipient-applicant countries. In the perspective of Baltic Sea development, it is furthermore significant that Phare supports mutual and regional co-operation among the recipient countries and cross-border co-operation between EU and recipient countries and among Phare countries.[31]

The growing significance of the northern dimension in the EU's external interests is reflected in the allocation of Tacis funds. North-western Russia is a prioritised area in the Tacis programme (St Petersburg in the Baltic Sea region since 1992 and the Karelian Republic, Murmansk and Arkhangelsk in the Barents region since 1995). In addition, a Tacis-Interreg instrument can now be used for cross-border co-operation targeted at the areas adjacent to the Finnish-Russian border, the only land border between the Union and Russia, and Russia's Baltic Sea regions.[32]

In the area of CFSP, the European Union is engaged in an intensive and structured dialogue with its Europe Agreement partners, Estonia, Latvia and Lithuania, and Poland and its PCA partner Russia. In addition to pre-accession tasks and perspectives, the agenda with the Baltic states is dominated by Baltic-Russian issues and multilateral Baltic Sea co-operation. In the EU's regular meetings with Russia, issues related to Russian-Baltic relations and also Russia's relations with Ukraine and Belarus constitute a recurrent item together with broader European and international issues. It is of primary concern for the Union to follow Russia's reforms and its behaviour towards its neighbours.

The EU's policy of partnership and co-operation with Russia combines the objectives of ensuring Russia's participation in a unifying Europe on the basis of common principles and commitments and exerting the Union's influence as a political and economic force for projecting stability. The practical aspect of the Union's Baltic Sea policy concerns support for Russia's neighbouring regions.

The pre-accession and enlargement perspective governs the Union's relations with the Baltic states and Poland. It represents a model whereby security is attained through integration preceded by a policy of conditional support during the transition phase. The accession of Estonia, Latvia, Lithuania and Poland is addressed case by case. While the economic criteria are laid down in the EU rules, the political prospects are determined by the results of the Intergovernmental Conference (IGC). An additional argument is provided by a need to compensate destabilising effects of a first-tranche NATO enlargement with early accession of the Baltic states into the EU.

The question of dividing lines has to be considered as EU enlargement in the longer run may leave Russia as the only non-EU country in the Baltic Sea region. Russia's consensual attitude towards EU enlargement and the economic prospects it offers for Russia itself provide opportunities for using EU integration as an increasingly significant strategy for common security in the shorter and longer run.

NATO as a Partner and Military Co-operation in the Baltic Rim

NATO's dual role in providing the strategic underpinning as an 'article 5'-guarantor and the co-operative framework as a 'non-article 5'-partner is an essential part of the security scene in the Baltic Sea region. While NATO's current membership divides the region and the perspective of enlargement creates uncertainty, NATO's partnership network covers the whole region and provides a framework for wider military co-operation.

NATO's offer of practical politico-military co-operation within the framework of the Partnership for Peace (PfP) programme (1994) is aimed at supporting democratic control of the armed forces in transition countries and building up interoperability through planning and training for joint missions in crisis management among all the partners. Based on self-differentiation and bilateralism (16+1), active participation in the PfP programme is a necessary contributing factor for former Warsaw Pact countries to be admitted to the alliance, although it is not a sufficient or automatic condition for membership. An expanded political dimension has been created through the establishment of the Euro-Atlantic Partnership Council (EAPC), a new single framework for enhanced practical co-operation under the PfP.[33] Enhanced PfP aims at increasing the involvement of partners in joint activities, improving liaison with NATO command structures and developing regional co-operation within the PfP.

The Baltic states and Poland, as transition countries seeking NATO membership, and Finland and Sweden as militarily non-aligned countries are all early and active PfP partners. Together with Norway, Denmark and Germany, they participate in partnership exercises and other activities in the Baltic Sea region and elsewhere, whereas Russia has been a recalcitrant and passive PfP partner engaged in constructing a special relationship with NATO.[34]

While military co-operation around the Baltic Rim has been stimulated and provided with a common framework by the PfP, in many cases its roots are found in the overall opening of the international situation and it is linked with other co-operative efforts such as the Nordic countries' sovereignty support for the Baltic states. Moreover, the common normative foundation provided by the CSBM and other OSCE documents is being used for new regional initiatives in military co-operation.

The content and structure of military co-operation around the Baltic Rim offer a complex picture. PfP and 'in the spirit of PfP' activities take place in the multilateral framework with a varying line-up of participants, while training, supply of materials and transfers of technology are items in a network of bilateral co-operation, and special concerted efforts are aimed at setting up operational capabilities common to the three Baltic states.

Denmark has been an exceptionally active partner in military co-operation around the Baltic Rim. In addition to bilateral agreements in the field of military co-operation and contacts with Poland (1993), Latvia (1994), Estonia (1994), Lithuania (1994) and Russia (1994), Denmark is a party to the memorandum of understanding on trilateral military co-operation with Poland and Germany (1995). Co-operation consists of high-level visits and consultations, seminars, training, courses and other exchanges, assistance in defence management, participation in and arrangement of joint military and peacekeeping exercises and courtesy visits.

Finland has concentrated its bilateral efforts on assistance and advice for the development of Estonian national defence. After the initial period since 1992, when Finnish retired or reserve officers acted as advisers and instructors, from 1996 regular Finnish officers have participated in an enhanced support programme for the organisation, management, training and equipping of the Estonian defence forces, including assistance in planning and creating the mobilisation system for territorial defence. Since 1992, Estonian students have attended the Finnish National Defence College for officer training and the National Defence Institute for non-commissioned officer training. Higher officer training is being included in the programme. Material assistance has been limited to non-lethal equipment and decommissioned naval vessels. In the future, arms deliveries are possible in principle, in accordance with the established regulations for arms exports. Finnish-Estonian co-operation has been subsequently registered as a Finnish PfP activity. Finnish troops have participated for the first time in an exercise abroad in 1997 (Nordic Participants, in the spirit of PfP, Nordic Peace) and Finland is to host its first PfP staff-level exercise in 1998.

Finland has been involved in trilateral co-operation with Russia and Estonia in frontier surveillance and border checks in the Gulf of Finland since 1994. Finland has proposed co-operation among frontier authorities responsible for maritime safety, personnel and traffic surveillance and prevention of criminal activities to cover all the CBSS states. The Conference of the Border Control Authorities was established by the Baltic Rim states in Helsinki in May 1997. Areas of co-operation include the exchange of information and experience in border crossing surveillance and control arrangements, illegal migration, joint surveillance and exchange of experts.

Students from all three Baltic states have been undergoing officer training in Sweden. Sweden has assisted Latvia in organising a training system for conscripts. Courses on information output in crisis situations and voluntary defence have been held. Sweden has assisted in the environmental cleansing and phasing out of the former Soviet naval base at Paldiski, in Estonia, as well as in its subsequent conversion into a civilian community. Mine sweeping has been conducted around Paldiski and harbours in Latvia and Lithuania and the transfer of minesweeping know-how is part of educational support. Sweden has established a regional PfP training centre. The first PfP exercises hosted by Sweden are scheduled for 1997: Co-operative Banners (joint training of ground, naval and air branches, co-hosted with Norway), Co-operative Baltic Eye (sea and air rescue) and Co-operative Bear (humanitarian air transport).

Norway is an initiator of and party to a bilateral agreement with Russia on defence-related environmental protection and a trilateral arrangement with Russia and the United States on addressing pollution problems in the Arctic caused by military activity. Norway has hosted a first joint Nordic 'in the spirit of PfP' exercise (Nordic Peace, Troms 1997), benefiting from NORDCAPS (Nordic Co-ordinated Arrangement for Military Peace Support) co-operation for a joint Nordic crisis-management capability. In its bilateral programmes with the Baltic states, Norway has offered courses in the management of home guards and winter training of regular forces.

Germany maintains active military contacts with Poland and gives assistance in military training to the Baltic states. A trilateral German-French-Polish arrangement on military co-operation aims at the first joint naval exercises in the Baltic Sea in 1997. Germany is to host an 'in the spirit of PfP' maritime exercise (Open Spirit 1997) to which all the Baltic littoral states have been invited. The annual US-BALTOPS naval exercise is a demonstration of US presence and NATO engagement in the Baltic Sea, involving all the littoral states, including Russia.

Poland's position as a link is manifest in its trilateral arrangements (Poland-Germany-Denmark and Poland-Germany-France). To strengthen the Baltic connection, Poland is planning a joint peacekeeping battalion together with Lithuania. The Baltic states are active participants in the PfP programme. Lithuania hosted three exercises in 1996. Estonia hosted a first major 'in the spirit of PfP' exercise (Baltic Challenge 97) on combined peace operations.

As a rule, Russia's bilateral co-operation with Baltic Sea countries is limited to military contacts (visits and exchanges) with the Nordic countries, Germany and Poland. Russia has also participated in some PfP-related activities.

Multilateral Support for the Baltic States

The multilateral plan for support for the formation and training of a Baltic peacekeeping battalion (BALTBAT), consisting of three companies: one each from Estonia, Latvia and Lithuania and scheduled for deployment in 1998 for UN service, is based on the Nordic initiative and the subsequent Nordic-Baltic understanding on co-operation (1994) and on the agreement of the Baltic states (1994) on the establishment of the joint unit. The UK joined the Baltic and Nordic states as a signatory to the memorandum of understanding (1994) which established the framework for multilateral co-operation, and the United States, Germany, France and the Netherlands later joined the project. As part of the training phase, Baltic troops have been deployed for peacekeeping operations with Nordic units in Bosnia and Lebanon, a Lithuanian company and other Baltic units with the Danish battalion of the Nordic-Polish brigade in IFOR/SFOR, and an Estonian company with the Norwegian battalion in UNIFIL. The objective is to make the Baltic battalion capable of enlarged peacekeeping or demanding military crisis management.

A joint Baltic naval squadron (BALTRON) is being developed with multilateral technical support for mine-sweeping, maritime surveillance and search and rescue operations and peacekeeping operations with the aim of participation in a PfP exercise in 1998. Germany has acted as co-ordinator for BALTRON. A third Baltic joint project is BALTNET (Baltic Air Surveillance Network) which has the purpose of constructing a regional system linking civilian radar in the Baltic states and a defence radar in Lithuania. The United States is the main sponsor of BALTNET. The Baltic states have agreed on co-ordination, which will place the headquarters of BALTBAT in Latvia, the operational centre for BALTRON in Estonia and that of BALTNET in Lithuania.[35]

An independent multilateral group, mainly from NATO countries under British chairmanship, has been advising the Baltic defence ministers since 1995. The BALTBAT project has been organised under a political-level steering group, a military-level working group and a training and supervision team chaired by representatives of the contributing donor countries. Support activities for BALTRON and BALTNET are being organised in a similar fashion under a leading donor country and with the participation of contributing and recipient countries.

The Nordic countries, which have been at the forefront as donors and partners, wish to ensure the wider participation of Western countries and create a broader basis for material support by fostering a closer link between their support activities and the PfP programme.

Co-ordination of military assistance for the Baltic states, which has become a necessity, is the object of initiatives among the Nordic countries and those NATO countries which act as donors. The Nordic countries have been active in making proposals for co-ordination of military defence-related security assistance to the Baltic states in order to improve its effectiveness, avoid overlapping and respond to real needs. Finland has offered to act as co-ordinator for PfP assistance to Estonia. Norway and Denmark have taken initiatives to institutionalise the review, planning and practical co-ordination of security assistance to the Baltic countries among the donor countries. The United States – and France – supports enhanced co-ordination and expect the Nordic countries to take the lead. The Nordic states can provide sovereignty support but not – separately or jointly – security guarantees for the Baltic states.

Military assistance is part of the continued and accentuated need for security support to the Baltic states in view of future NATO enlargement and its implications.

NATO Enlargement as a Security Challenge

According to the enlargement doctrine, NATO is opening for new members not only to extend the security benefits of common defence and military integration, in the narrow sense of the security concept, but to provide increased stability and security for all of Europe. Prospective new members are required to commit themselves to the UN and OSCE principles in their international and, in particular, their neighbourhood relations. Their capability to settle ethnic or territorial disputes by peaceful means will be a factor in their acceptance into the alliance.

At the same time, the accession of new members should not weaken but strengthen NATO's effectiveness and cohesion and preserve its political and military capability to perform the core functions of common defence as well as the new missions related to crisis management and military co-operation. As NATO was approaching the decision to invite its first new members in the new Europe, the nature of enlargement as a continuing and indeterminate process was reaffirmed. No concrete commitments in time or names were given on how subsequent new members would step in through the open door.[36]

While PfP-related military co-operation is developing and proliferating around the Baltic Rim, the issue of the provision of security guarantees to new countries through full NATO membership divides the space and creates uncertainty about its future configuration. As Poland has been chosen for inclusion in the first tranche of enlargement with the Baltic states remaining in their role as applicants, and with Russia as a frustrated and potentially revisionist great power, NATO is faced with the task of creating a strategy to sustain and improve stability in the region (Asmus and Nurick 1996).

NATO is expected to maintain a close political relationship with the Baltic states in recognition of their bid for membership and reaffirm the open-door policy even though no specific commitments related to further tranches are forthcoming. Moreover, NATO will continue to assist the Baltic states in meeting the membership requirements through enhanced PfP and EAPC links and other bilateral political contacts that may be agreed upon. The Baltic states are expected to strive for an upgraded association-type relationship outside the EAPC framework that would place them clearly at NATO's doorstep. Meanwhile, in the perspective of the Baltic states, the United States will remain the main asset in the security reassurances short of membership to be provided by a continued and reinforced NATO engagement in the region.

The situation in the Baltic Sea region will be directly affected by NATO's response to Russia's security concerns and demands related to NATO enlargement. NATO has taken on itself the task of assuaging Russia's anxiety that it will be marginalised politically and militarily by NATO enlargement and of persuading the Russians that they will retain an influence over European security to which they are entitled. On the other hand, Russia is concerned over ensuring for itself the strategic space and defensive zone over which it has historically been accustomed to rule.

Most of the key issues in establishing a NATO-Russian security partnership are relevant for the Baltic Sea region. Russia's position in joint NATO-Russian decision-making (a voice vs. a veto) affects the issue of the future tranches of enlargement and the prospects for membership of the Baltic countries, which Russia has singled out as a last line of opposition. The security-policy freedom of choice of states in the region and Russia's room for manoeuvre as a regional power are connected with the principles and commitments adhered to in the NATO-Russian security accord (Founding Act). The question of the non-deployment of nuclear weapons, foreign troops and bases and military infrastructure to new member states in peacetime concerns primarily Poland. Another future issue is to what extent NATO is bound to change as an institution while undergoing enlargement and adaptation.

Among the NATO members, Denmark is a leading proponent of the Baltic states' early accession to the alliance. Finland and Sweden see themselves as partners of NATO in producing security and stability for the Baltic Sea region. Stressing the importance of NATO for stability, they pledge a close and active co-operation with NATO in the non-Article 5 area in the PfP/EAPC framework. While not seeking NATO membership, Finland and Sweden maintain their freedom of choice in security and defence arrangements and stress the importance to regional stability of respecting freedom of choice for the Baltic states. Moreover, the NATO-Russian security arrangement that is vital for managing the implications of enlargement should respect the OSCE principles and not be adopted at the expense of any other countries or create 'zones of influence, dividing lines or grey zones.'[37]

The Issue of Assistance to the Baltic States

The challenge of NATO enlargement has resulted in a number of initiatives and arrangements, based on NATO as well as other institutional structures, for organising the Baltic Rim security space by mixing stability-promoting political and economic actions with military measures.

Beyond NATO and its partnership instruments, other building blocks in international co-operation for Baltic Sea stability are non-military, such as the role of the OSCE, the contribution of the EU and the activity of regional fora. The Nordic countries, jointly and individually, and non-aligned Finland and Sweden in particular, are elevated to a key position, not only because of their close and workable connections with the Baltic states but also because of their will to support and facilitate the contributions of the multilateral institutions. The role of the Nordic and other regional players is vital also for the functioning of the PfP in the region.

The United States is envisaging close co-operation with the Nordic countries in its Baltic Action Plan, which combines a progressive development of NATO/PfP contacts with the acceleration of EU membership for the Baltic states and enhanced regional co-operation as well as a bilateral US engagement with the Baltic states based on a political document, void of the provision of military guarantee, to be negotiated. France is suggesting an arrangement between NATO and the Baltic states that would be supported by an active Finnish and Swedish contribution to the security of the Baltic states without providing military security guarantees.[38]

The task appears as one of concerting the interests of the Baltic states, Finland and Sweden and NATO, or leading NATO countries, and taking into account Russia's legitimate security interests, in a programme of action or an arrangement for enhancing security in the Baltic Sea region and the stability of the Baltic states in particular. No separate zone of security should be created where the Baltic states and the two militarily non-aligned Nordic countries would be isolated from the common security space. As military assistance to the Baltic states would be a central element in such a co-operative effort, and Russia is not – so far at least – among the donors, the co-ordination arrangement would be established outside the EAPC framework, while enhanced security-policy consultations could take place within the transparent EAPC framework. A NATO-Baltic states charter that would assuage fears of a NATO-Russian concert is among the ideas aired in the discussion. The underlying issue is one of burden-sharing among the Nordic countries and NATO countries that feel a responsibility for stability in the Baltic region. Another issue concerns reassurance – short of security guarantees – for the Baltic states flowing from the security-related assistance.

Security Implications of EU Enlargement and NATO Enlargement

Both the EU and NATO are security-related institutions that constitute zones of stability, possess instruments for promoting stability and appear as poles of attraction in the overall European architecture and in the Baltic Sea region. The two processes of enlargement are parallel in time but autonomous in decision-making and their various phases do not necessarily coincide, nor are they likely to. The processes are related to upholding a common security space, as the countries seeking either membership are doing so in order to integrate themselves into the core of Europe.

NATO enlargement is a challenge to political and military stability as well as to common security in the Baltic Sea region. As full integration with NATO is only foreseeable in the case of Poland, and accession to the EU by Poland or the Baltic states remains open – though in the case of Poland and Estonia more likely after the EU Commission's recommendation that membership negotiations should proceed – the issue of the parallel and mutual effects of the two enlargements becomes of particular relevance for Baltic Rim security.

The security implications of EU and NATO membership differ, and these differences are relevant for the future stability of the Baltic Sea region.

EU enlargement involves a security impact which is based on mutual political solidarity but it does not provide a defence assistance guarantee. EU membership will support the political and economic foundations of democracy and the market economy for Poland and the Baltic states and it is a necessity for their full integration into Europe. EU enlargement does not imply a strategic challenge for Russia but integrates Russia closer with Europe by the means of economic co-operation and political consultation. Enhanced efficiency of the CFSP and the enlargement of the EU's competence in crisis management will add to the EU's security role.

While NATO enlargement directly supports military considerations, and, indirectly, the transition to democracy and its consolidation in new member countries, the core impact of membership lies in the defence commitment and in military integration within the common structures. Russia's opposition to NATO enlargement, which is based on strategic considerations, is politically focused on the exclusion of the Baltic states from any future round of enlargement and militarily on securing a defensive zone on its western flank.

Regional applications of PfP/EAPC, coupled with the open door policy after the first round of enlargement, and the NATO-Russian arrangement will be instruments for managing the implications of NATO enlargement. In many assessments, the entry of the Baltic states into the EU is seen as a factor that would alleviate the uncertainty and frustration created by being left outside the first wave of NATO enlargement, while providing them with relevant non-military security benefits. EU enlargement and NATO expansion are complementary but not necessarily mutually reinforcing. A first-round 'double-no' – which has become the fate of Latvia and Lithuania after the EU Commission's announcement on 17 July that membership negotiations with the two countries will have to wait – creates a special challenge for stability and reassurance policy and a need for continued security support.

Processes Related to Co-operation

The CBSS as a Forum for Stability Support

The broad mandate of the Council of the Baltic Sea States (CBSS), an intergovernmental forum for guidance and overall co-ordination among the participating states, is in practice focused on the themes of its three working groups: assistance to democratic institutions, economic co-operation, in particular infrastructure and transportation, and nuclear and radiation safety. Another area of practical co-operation is the EuroFaculty support programme for university courses, which operates in the Baltic states with plans to extend its activity to Kaliningrad.

The work of the CBSS is directed at support for reforms and projects in transition countries and investment in a common economic infrastructure aimed at the revival of the Baltic Sea region as a dynamic economic zone.

The CBSS has an instrument for early warning and conflict prevention in the CBSS Commissioner on Democratic Institutions and Human Rights, including the Rights of Persons belonging to Minorities, established in 1994 after an initiative by Russia. Working in co-operation and co-ordination with the OSCE High Commissioner on National Minorities, the CBSS commissioner may make recommendations to individual governments and present reports to the CBSS on an extensive range of cases involving the social, political and cultural conditions of individuals and groups. The commissioner is free to choose his or her methods and may collect information, conduct surveys and receive communications from individuals, groups and organisations, but the impact of his or her recommendations depends solely on national governments and parliaments (Espersen 1996).

The first meeting of the heads of government of the Baltic Sea region, also attended by the President of the European Commission and the President of the European Council (Visby, 3-4 May 1996) has sharpened the political edge of multilateral regional co-operation. The Visby meeting emphasised the significance of civic security as an element in comprehensive security and focused future co-operation on three areas: increased people-to-people co-operation and civic security, economic development and integration and environmental protection. The leaders established a task force of personal representatives charged with reinforcing regional co-operation in combating organised crime. The Visby summit, which is to be followed by others, introduced the high-level political involvement of Russia and Germany in regional multilateral co-operation. Russia's full involvement in the work of the CBSS, which depends largely on the functioning of the centre-periphery relationship in the country, remains a key issue for the future. Another sign of increased politicisation is the establishment of an international advisory group by Sweden, as chairman of the Visby process, and the discussion on the need for a lead nation.[39]

Building upon the Visby results in the prioritisation of co-operation, the CBSS foreign ministers' meeting (Kalmar, 2-3 July 1996) adopted three action programmes, emphasising also the link with the EU Baltic Sea Region Initiative and the role of the Nordic strategy on support for the adjacent areas. The regional co-operation, with the CBSS as a centre of gravity that transcends the lines drawn by the EU and NATO, is picking up political dynamics and building links with other co-operative processes, including the OSCE security model.[40]

The OSCE as a Contributor to Regional Security

The Organisation for Security and Co-operation in Europe (CSCE/OSCE) has contributed to the transformation and stability in the Baltic Sea region with instruments of early warning and conflict prevention. Moreover, the OSCE has acted as a facilitator in the resolution of Russian-Baltic disputes stemming from the Soviet political, legal, ethnic and military legacy on Baltic territory. The presence of the OSCE in the Baltic Sea region will be felt in various forms, as the significance of regional co-operation and its links with overall European security are emphasised in the OSCE security model (Peters 1996).

Through their advice and recommendations, the OSCE long-term missions to Estonia (1992) and Latvia (1993), which were among the first to be established, have guided the governments and authorities towards adopting laws on citizenship and aliens that meet the UN, COE and OSCE standards of non-discrimination. In addition to the missions, the OSCE High Commissioner on National Minorities, and missions from the COE and the UN Human Rights Commission have at various times been involved in supporting and pressuring the Baltic states to settle the issue, which is of vital importance for their integration with the European core institutions. The legal basis is in place governing the status of the Russophone populations, predominantly of Russian ethnic origin, many of them registered as Russian citizens and the rest without any citizenship. It remains on the agenda of the OSCE missions in the field to observe and support the handling of applications for citizenship and residence permits and the overall task of the integration of Russian-speaking populations into Estonian and Latvian society.[41]

As the missions to Estonia and Latvia have concluded the main and acute parts of their original mandates, their termination has become an open issue. While Estonia and Latvia find their continued presence stigmatising and accommodating to the Russian needs of using the Russian ethnic issue as an instrument of pressure, their Western partners stress the significance of the missions as a Baltic contribution to co-operative security. As no exit strategy or precedent exists for terminating an OSCE mission, the threshold to such a decision remains high. The mandates of the missions as instruments of stability and early preventive diplomacy are broad enough to justify the continuation of their work.

The co-operation and assistance programmes of the Council of Europe for acceding countries and the mechanisms of the Parliamentary Assembly for monitoring the implementation of COE commitments have served the introduction and enhancement of democratic security in the Baltic Sea region. All the countries of the Baltic Sea region have become members of the COE, while Latvian, Lithuanian and, in particular, Russian compliance with its obligations remains under special monitoring.[42]

The OSCE (CSCE) offered a forum for establishing the political and normative framework for the complete withdrawal of Russian troops from the territories of the Baltic states, which took place on the basis of bilateral agreements in 1993 (Lithuania) and 1994 (Estonia, Latvia). Auxiliary agreements govern the status of Russian military pensioners in Estonia and Latvia and the OSCE representative participates in the governmental commissions handling residence permits in Estonia and social welfare benefits in Latvia. By participating in the joint Latvian-Russian commission, the OSCE is also involved in monitoring the implementation of the agreement on the dismantling and temporary lease of the former Soviet military early warning and air defence facility, the radar station at Skrunda.[43]

The Pact on Stability in Europe, an EU initiative in preventive diplomacy (1994-95) has provided incentives for settling border and minority disputes and developing good-neighbourly relations on the basis of OSCE principles in the countries that are candidates for EU membership. The Pact was later transferred to the responsibility of the OSCE, which remains entrusted with following its implementation. A number of agreements among Baltic Rim countries have been attached to the Pact. While the relevant OSCE principles provide the common normative foundation for settling border disputes between Russia and Estonia and Russia and Latvia, no third-party mediation mission has been established by the OSCE or any other outsider, and the negotiations remain bilateral in both cases.[44]

A Baltic round table was convened among the Baltic states, their neighbours and other countries responsible for regional security within the framework of the original Stability Pact process. Exploratory discussions are under way on reconvening the regional round table as an OSCE-connected forum for confidence and stability in the Baltic Sea region. The agenda of such a forum would cover various new security risks and obstacles to human and economic contacts. In a new situation, an OSCE instrument would have a dual role in conflict prevention and stability promotion.

Regional round tables are part of the growing interest and encouragement devoted to 'bilateral or regional initiatives aimed at developing relations of good neighbourliness and co-operation' within the OSCE security model process. The Lisbon meeting (1996) mandated the work towards defining modalities of co-operation between the OSCE and other organisations. The security model will deal with the contributions of regional institutions to overall security and stability and the means by which the OSCE can facilitate regional processes. Among the first steps are seminars and other measures for increasing information about regional institutions within the OSCE community. Consequently, contacts at the political and working level between the OSCE and the CBSS are to be part of the future security model.[45]

An early, informal post-Cold War forum for supporting the Baltic states in their reform and integration efforts is the 'Stockholm ad-hoc group,' consisting of the Nordic countries and leading EU and NATO states and the EU Commission. The activities of the group, which serves a consultative but not an operative role, have not been publicised.[46]

Military Openness and Restructuring as a Regional Strategy

The military situation around the Baltic Rim is stable and characterised by decreasing defence spending, restructuring of defence forces and assignment of new tasks, although the region remains strategically significant for European security. The growing military presence of NATO and the redeployment of Russian defence capabilities provide the framework for enhancing military stability.

Russia's need to secure its strategic positions in the north and the expectations of other states related to the Russian military future dominate the military security scene. Russian military reform is therefore of central significance for regional security.

The issue of increasing military stability and providing underpinning for broad security by region-specific CSBMs is under exploratory discussion within the OSCE framework. In addition to military CSBMs such as military contacts and exchanges of information, the list provided by Poland involves a broader approach related to strengthening civic security such as marine search and rescue and relief operations, maritime surveillance and preventing incidents at sea. Other measures suggested include specific border CSBMs, maritime CSBMs and military-civilian co-operation in fighting environmental hazards.[47]

The reconstruction of national defence forces creates preconditions for the Baltic states' participation in arms control, CSBM policies and international peace-keeping, also in the regional context. Nordic (training, material, peace-keeping) support for the development of the defence of the Baltic states has been of primary significance.

The balance of military capabilities is being determined within the framework of CFE adaptation. Russia's security concerns are focused on the Central European and flank zones, and the possibility of the accession by the Baltic states and Sweden and Finland to the Treaty has been discussed. Military stability in the north is thus linked with the overall regime of conventional arms control in Europe and Russia's security policy priorities and its perception of threats.

The Baltic Sea Region as a Security Space

Aspects of Common Security

Figure 24.1 provides an overview of the *functional relationships between the various aspects of the concept of security* and the creation of common security.

Figure 24.1: The concept of common security

Method	Criteria	Goal
Co-operative	Comprehensive Indivisible	Common security

Security co-operation in action – opening and setting the agenda, generating interactions and activities, managing conflicts and resolving disputes, and concluding and implementing arrangements and regimes – shapes the Baltic Sea region as a constituent element of the OSCE security space. Regional preoccupations lead to an agenda that largely reflects issues common to all of Europe, but regional and extra-regional actors and inclusive as well as restrictive institutions may influence the outcome.

A summary of *processes and instruments generating and managing security* is provided by Figure 24.2.

The main test of states and institutions engaged in security co-operation is their readiness and ability to adapt and change. Such flexibility is evident in the evolution of the agenda on new and contentious areas opened for security co-operation and in the spectrum of institutions available for security-seeking participants.

The agenda was initially dominated by efforts aimed at supporting political and economic transition and handling disputes emanating from the Soviet legacy. More recently, the scope has been extended to military co-operation in the form of assistance for the reconstruction of defence forces, activities related to the PfP and discussion of new confidence- and security-building measures. Furthermore, the approaching decisions on redefining the military-strategic balance and adjusting the pattern of deployments in the context of NATO enlargement and Russian military reform will have direct consequences for the Baltic Rim. Consequently, a full spectrum of security policy has been opened for region-based and region-targeted co-operation.

While it seems that the comprehensiveness of security is increasingly covered by institutionalised co-operation and other security policy making around the Baltic Rim, the greatest challenge to common security remains the assurance of its indivisibility. Equality in seeking security can never be guaranteed among

Figure 24.2: Generation and management of co-operative security for the Baltic Sea region

	Stability Policy	Conflict Management	Military-Strategic Stability
Issues	Political, economic and military transition	Borders, minorities, territorial integrity	Defence restructuring, military openness
Processes, Activities, Arrangements	Nordic strategy for the adjacent regions EU Baltic Sea Region Initiative (Phare) EU Action Plan for Russia (Tacis) EU pre-accession strategy COE co-operation and assistance programmes COE monitoring CBSS action programmes Visby follow-up Initiatives on Kaliningrad PfP (in the spirit of PfP) activities Military assistance and co-operation (establishment, transfers, management, training)	Implementation of withdrawal of Russian troops from Baltic states Arrangement on Skrunda Social guarantees for Russian military pensioners Adjustment and implementation of Estonian, Latvian law on citizenship, aliens Integration of Russian-speakers Estonian-Russian border regime Latvian-Russian border regime Transit to Kaliningrad	START I/II process Implementation of CFE flank provisions CFE adaptation NATO military presence (infrastructure, troops, nuclear weapons) on new member territories Re-allocation of NATO command structures Regional CSBMs Implementation of Russian military reform Reconstruction of Baltic states' defence forces Implementation of defence revisions of Baltic Rim states
Instruments, Institutions	Nordic Council of Ministers Nordic-Baltic (5+3) consultation forum EU CBSS Stockholm group Co-ordination of military assistance to Baltic states NATO/EAPC/PfP	OSCE missions HCNM CBSS commissioner OSCE Baltic round table OSCE mechanisms EAPC mechanisms Provision of good offices, mediation	JCF/CFE negotiation forum OSCE Forum for Security Co-operation OSCE regional round table NATO-Russia Joint Council NATO political and military structures

states that are not equal in military and economic strength. The practical test of indivisible security lies, therefore, in the provision of equal opportunities to participate in security co-operation and in genuine freedom to choose and change security arrangements.

The indivisibility of security is promoted by a security architecture that offers effective channels for states to attend to their security interests in accordance with the principle of freedom of choice. Although opportunities for states' participation and influence-seeking have grown, structural obstacles caused by membership criteria or dividing lines have become a central issue in security relations around the Baltic Rim.

The CBSS, as the principal regional forum, and the OSCE together with the COE, as active contributors to handling issues in the region, provide an inclusive normative and political framework for co-operation that supports the political and economic development in transition countries and in the region as a whole. Moreover, they provide instruments that have been used with a certain success for early warning, conflict prevention and dispute resolution, and the OSCE offers a forum for regional arms control. The inclusive institutions have an important function in bringing Russia together with its neighbours for discussion and practical co-operation. In the area of military-strategic stability, the regional security environment is strongly affected by bilateral great-power arrangements (START) and a negotiation process (CFE) in which a number of Baltic Rim countries are not participating, as well as by NATO enlargement, which is evolving in Central Europe, while the propensity to use inclusive or open-ended fora (OSCE/FSC regional round tables) for military confidence and security in the region remains tentative.

Norden, the EU and NATO have recourse to readily available resources and effective capabilities for undertaking and sustaining stability policy. They can also act as initiators and contributors in the OSCE engagement in conflict management, while NATO is the principal player in arms control and strategic restructuring. As exclusive institutions that are inviting new members, the EU and NATO have to engage their partners, the Baltic states, Poland and Russia in a close relationship that contributes to overall security in the region, while maintaining sovereign control over their enlargement decisions. Norden is working together with the Baltic states and Russia. The EU is using pre-accession instruments to support the Baltic states and Poland and partnership programmes to involve Russia. As NATO's instruments for partnership (PfP, EAPC) are enhanced and operationalised further, their role in regional security is taking shape. At the same time, NATO is faced with creating special relationships that satisfy the expectations of the membership seekers and meet the demands of the main opponent of enlargement. Informal ad hoc arrangements for security assistance to the Baltic states by Western and Nordic states offer an intermediate solution that helps to ameliorate traditional security concerns without creating a prejudice towards NATO enlargement or a challenge to Russia. Satisfactory or reassuring access to the benefits of the exclusive or restrictive institutions remains a key issue for the future of common security.

Layers of the Security Space

To help tabulate the security developments around the Baltic Rim conceptually and analyse them operationally, the security space can be divided into *layers*. The Baltic Sea region is constituted and transformed as a security space by a spectrum of co-operative processes that are amalgamated in *three subsystems* – a security complex, a security community and a security regime. The dynamics of co-operation and the interdependence between the layers and their relative growth determine the development of common security among the actors and shape the security order of the Baltic Sea region as a whole.

The constitution and transformation of the security space in the Baltic Sea region are presented in Figure 24.3.

Figure 24.3: Constitution and transformation of the security space of the Baltic Sea region

Security	Russia-NATO Russia-Baltic states-Poland Russia-NATO-Finland-Sweden	Traditional security
Security community	Norden, EU Baltic Council	Asecurity
Security regime	CBSS, OSCE, COE NATO/PfP	Comprehensive security
Security order	Baltic Sea region space OSCE space	Common security

In a *security complex*, states, which are bound together by the interdependence of their welfare and security, cope with the problems of traditional security that involve not only threats against their physical survival or political integrity but also perceptions and expectations concerning the viability of their freedom of choice and the sustainability of their sovereignty as decision-makers and actors.

In the post-Cold War environment, the danger of war or direct military threats have subsided, but the issue of 'hard' security has not disappeared from the agenda. Due to their military potential, Russia and NATO – or, in effect, the United States – are engaged in an inherent geostrategic competition and regard the maintenance of military balance and stability in the Baltic Sea region and Northern Europe as part of the wider European scenario. Moreover, as its military power position is an essential remaining component of Russia's great-power influence, the north-eastern area is a sensitive front line of defence. Russia's possible use of power politics is a recurrent aspect of its relations with the Baltic states, where sources of a deterioration of relations remain, not only as a result of the open issues of minorities and borders but also due to the political-psychological legacy of history. The Baltic states find themselves in a geopolitically and historically sensitive position between an assertive Russia and a Germany which tends to prioritise its new eastern partnership with Russia.

An emerging special NATO-Russian security arrangement has led the two non-candidates for NATO membership, Finland and Sweden, to counter the spectre of a sphere of influence that would narrow their choices. More tangibly, Finland and Sweden warn against a grey zone over the Baltic states that would deprive the newly established sovereign actors of their freedom of choice, destabilising the security environment in the region.

Poland, although a front-runner for NATO membership, has to be wary of jeopardising its full benefits and it is also heavily affected by Russian-Baltic tensions. Poland and the Baltic states perceive NATO membership as a solution to the existential question of traditional security, but the composition of the first tranche – with Poland invited, and the Baltic states left waiting – will make NATO enlargement as much a problem as a solution to security and stability in the region.

Traditional security in the Baltic Sea region is largely about current aspirations related to the full exercise of freedom of choice and future expectations regarding the full benefits of indivisible and common security. The future of traditional security in the Baltic Sea region is governed by the fact that problems and concerns related to Russia as an uncertain great power are not amenable to regional solutions. The presence of NATO and the United States has become an essential aspect in regional security bargaining. Statesmanlike resolutions are called for in settling the issues between Russia and its north-western neighbours. As the dissolution of the Cold War confrontation has ameliorated the security dilemma between Russia and the Western powers, new prospects exist for conflict resolution and stability management. The leading actors have to combine the promotion of their wider interests with the enhancement of regional stability by giving reassurance to the Baltic states, by providing a full opportunity for participation by Poland and by reinforcing the contributions of Finland and Sweden.

The issues of traditional security are not dealt with in a vacuum or without co-operative instruments. There are processes of integration and institutionalisation in the space of the OSCE and the Baltic Sea region that tend to change the nature of the security issue and transcend or mitigate the security dilemma among states. The deepening of integration and strengthening of institutionalisation are key factors in the transformation of the security space from a pure security complex during the Cold War into a security order upheld by a common purpose and action towards common security.

In a *security community*, where states are bound together by political, institutional or functional integration, military or power-political conflicts are excluded among the participants and the issue of traditional security has been transcended by asecurity. The absence of traditional security issues, however, does not exclude the existence of economic, environmental or societal problems.

Norden is a long-standing zone of stability and a model of a pluralistic security community. The Nordic version of integration is not likely to be applied more widely in the region, however, as the European Union has embarked upon enlargement as a pole of attraction and an instrument of stability and welfare. The interrelationship among the Baltic states, although their mutual co-operation has not been as effectively legislated and institutionalised as in the EU or based on historical harmonisation as in Norden, constitutes a further element reaching beyond traditional security to the area of desecuritisation in the Baltic Sea region.

The Nordic-Baltic (5+3) connection is a bridge that facilitates the preparation of the Baltic states' deeper involvement in European integration and strengthen the stability in the region as a whole, although no security guarantees in the traditional sense are provided by the Nordic countries as a group.

The Nordic countries are the main proponents of the northern dimension of the European Union, which they see as a political and economic burden-sharing issue among the members. EU enlargement to incorporate Poland and the Baltic states is a focal point of security policy making around the Baltic Rim whose significance will only be increased by the uncertainty and length of the transitional period likely to ensue after the conclusion of the IGC in 1997. The credibility of the security-through-integration doctrine will be put to the test by the management of EU enlargement in the coming years. If membership remains in sight, the readiness of the candidate states to rely on other forms of security co-operation as well will possibly be strengthened. If the membership expectations are frustrated or rejected, they may turn into an inward-looking nationalism that would freeze further integration with Europe or a backward-looking policy that might prevent the normalisation of neighbourly relations with Russia.

NATO is perceived as creating or imposing a security community among its members – Germany being a model case and Turkey-Greece a more questionable one – but it is based on a narrower concept of security than is EU integration. The uncertainty of NATO enlargement in the region beyond Poland may lead to a complicated game with EU and NATO enlargements as instruments of reassurance toward those seeking security in the institutions of originally Western integration. Institution-shopping and timetable-handling may become part of the political competition. A key issue in enhancing integration-based security is the engagement of Russia in co-operation and partnership that promotes common security and avoids divisions; the task in the case of Norden-Russian and EU-Russian relations differs from efforts aimed at reconciling Russia's political ambitions with NATO expansion. The Russian-NATO council brings an element of traditional security into the joint (16+1) consultation inside the NATO structures.

In a *security regime*, international institutions induce norm-consistent and co-operation-seeking behaviour among the participants and help them to overcome the inherent collective action dilemma. Differing in their degree of formalisation and robustness, international regimes are social institutions based on agreed principles, procedures and programmes that govern the interactions of states in specific areas. The effectiveness of regimes in helping states to solve their problems, or the impact of regimes on the outcomes of international relations in general, are broad issues of theory and practice. Institutions have a key function in the formation of actor expectations towards increasing confidence in absolute gains from co-operation and dispelling fears of desertion by partners. As a result of regime-building, participants converge to seek common solutions and take collective action.

The Baltic Sea region is densely covered by international institutions and organisations – regional, European and OSCE-wide, intergovernmental and transnational – that promote co-operation in various areas of comprehensive security. New challenges to 'soft' security are met by the CBSS and a large number of subregional and substate institutions and networks around the Baltic Rim, the OSCE and the COE with their instruments, as well as NATO/EAPC/PfP. The Nordic-Baltic (5+3) connection is an engine of regional co-operation. The EU acts as a leading force through European and regional organisations. Russia is a participant in all of the inclusive institutions. The United States is involved in regional politics inside the OSCE and NATO and at the margins of the regional organisations.

The effectiveness of international institutions and organisations active in the Baltic Sea region presents a complex picture for the future. The CBSS may become an increasingly important facilitator of problem-solving in practical areas, in particular if the Visby process continues to strengthen collective political will, and if the participants, Russia in particular, devote sufficient attention to this regional institution. The OSCE and the COE continue to provide frameworks for collective action in early warning and conflict prevention by the wider European community of states. With post-Soviet disputes resolved and no acute conflicts in sight, the regional instruments of the OSCE – round tables of the Stability Pact as well as in the field of arms control and CSBMs – may become more useful, in particular once the issues related to the security role of Russia and the evolution of EU and NATO enlargement have reached a greater clarity and predictability and the OSCE security model has provided more effective modalities for inter-institutional co-operation. Regional activities in the NATO/EAPC/PfP framework can make a growing contribution to the new culture of military co-operation that is emerging as part of common security in the OSCE space at large. The key to the future lies not in new institutions but in effective and rational use of the existing ones. While the CBSS cannot compensate for the benefits of EU membership or provide rules of co-operation separate from the legitimacy offered by the OSCE, the dynamics of such regional institutions as the CBSS and such regional applications as round tables are essential for the future identity of the Baltic Sea region as a security space.

A *security order* provides common direction and purpose to co-operation among states. Within the OSCE, the objective is defined as a common security space which is based on the OSCE principles and commitments and created through inter-institutional co-operation and mutual reinforcement. The OSCE objectives also apply to the Baltic Sea region. Common security is enhanced by integration and regime-building that help states to attend to their security needs in an equal manner (indivisibility) and over a wide array of issues (comprehensiveness). There is a growing regional element, viewed not only as regional instruments but also as region-specific policies, which provides the Baltic Sea region with an identity in security generation and management.

In the area of traditional security, solutions to region-specific problems are largely dependent on wider power constellations and security arrangements.

Regional instruments are fewer or lagging behind, but even traditional security issues are affected by the outcomes of the integrated community and the institutionalised regimes in the totality of the security order in the Baltic Sea region. The webs of interdependence and the habits of co-operation will, in the longer term, enhance the consolidation and condensation of the common norms and principles. The link between the layers of security formation (complex, community, regime) should be strengthened to mitigate the impact of traditional security problems and promote their negotiation and resolution. While the membership of integrative institutions remains restrictive, security benefits for outsiders flow from pre-accession co-operation with the EU and enhanced partnership with NATO as well as from solidarity within the OSCE institutions.

In *conclusion,* a programme of future security co-operation can be projected for the Baltic Sea region as an outcome of a complex and evolving set of regional and wider processes. In the Baltic Rim, the concepts of region and security meet as a result of the progress of pragmatic co-operation. Whereas the effectiveness of regional or region-specific instruments in providing security remains to be tested, their credibility will increase together with the effectiveness of European integration and the inter-institutional co-operation in the OSCE space. Even though we are living in a more benign security environment, the role of Baltic Rim EU and NATO members will become increasingly crucial, while the readiness of the leading members to use regional structures as a burden-sharing device will grow. Developments around the Baltic Rim will therefore help to determine the validity of the concepts of region and regional security in future international relations in Europe.

Notes

1. Statements of fact and opinion are those of the author and do not imply endorsement by the Finnish Government.
2. This chapter is devoted to the Baltic Sea region, but in terms of security, Northern Europe is a relevant unit of analysis in particular for the Nordic countries. Moreover, Russia's role is even more central in the Barents region and the Arctic region. The area around the Baltic Rim is defined here as a region in the European context, while in a global context it could be defined as a subregion of the OSCE region.
3. The concept is defined and analysed in a practical case in Young (1996: 9).
4. See 'Multi-Layered Integration: The Sub-Regional Dimension, An Interim Report with Recommendations addressed to the Chairman-in-Office of OSCE and OSCE Participating States' (October 1996) by the Institute for East-West Studies.
5. CSCE Budapest Document 1994: Towards a Genuine Partnership in a New Era. Budapest: CSCE (Chapter VII of Budapest Decisions): 20; OSCE Lisbon Document 1996 (Lisbon Declaration on a Common and Comprehensive Security Model for Europe for the Twenty-First Century), pages 6-9.
6. Fifth Meeting of the Ministerial Council. Chairman's Summary. Decisions of the Budapest Ministerial Council Meeting. Budapest: OSCE; the place of the security model process in a wider context is analysed in Möttölä (forthcoming 1997).
7. Lisbon Declaration, page 6.
8. Charter of Paris for A New Europe (1990). Paris, CSCE.

[9] The concept is originally defined in CSCE Helsinki Document. The Challenges of Change. (Helsinki Summit Declaration, para 21), page 9.

[10] A perspective on the original concept of common security designed by the Palme Commission, is provided by Blechman (1996).

[11] The principle of mutual reinforcement is originally defined in Helsinki Summit Declaration (1992, para 24), page 24; further work on the practical modalities for co-operation between the OSCE and other organisations is mandated in Lisbon Declaration (para 11), page 8.

[12] Contained in The Security Model Discussion 1995-1996. Report of the Chairman-in-Office to the Lisbon Summit (30 November 1996). Annex 1. Risks and Challenges to Security in the OSCE Area (REF.S/82/96). Lisbon, OSCE.

[13] Declaration of Conference of Foreign Ministers of the Baltic Sea States. Copenhagen, 5-6 March 1992.

[14] Declaration of Conference of Foreign Ministers in Kirkenes 11.1 1993. Co-operation in the Barents Euro-Arctic Region; Protocol from the constituent meeting of the Region Council – Barents Region – the Euro-Arctic Region. Kirkenes, 11 January 1993.

[15] This framework is used in Möttölä (1996a). The focus here is on concerted and joint policies, while national policies are dealt with in other chapters in this volume. On the operative concept of security policy, see also Keatinge (1996).

[16] Based on communiqués from the Nordic foreign ministers' meetings. A doctrinally more developed statement was given in Helsinki, 5 May 1992 (see Möttölä 1996b: 157 f.).

[17] Communiqués from the Nordic foreign ministers' meetings, 1991-1997.

[18] The reform was based on a report by a working group of personal representatives of the prime ministers: Statsministrarnas personliga representanter för nyvärdering av det nordiska samarbetet. Rapport till statsministrarna i de nordiska länderna (1992).

[19] Nordic Co-operation in a New Era. Nordic Co-operation – assessed against the background of the results of the referendums held in Finland, Norway and Sweden on accession to the European Union. Proposals on Nordic Co-operation in a time of change: goals, content, form. Nordic Council, Nordic Council of Ministers (February 1995).

[20] The strategy is based on a report by a working group appointed by the Nordic Council of Ministers: Proposal for a Nordic Strategy for the Areas Adjacent to the Nordic Region. The Nordic Working Group's Report. Helsinki, 10 June 1996; see also Arbetsprogram för Nordens närområden 1997. Copenhagen, Nordic Council of Ministers.

[21] The Nordic countries' total development aid to the adjacent areas, 1989-95, amounts to DKK 7,500 million, of which about a third has been allocated to Russia, with Poland, Estonia, Latvia and Lithuania sharing the rest approximately equally.

[22] A reluctance towards a close security integration of the Baltic Sea region as a whole is shown in Knudsen and Neumann (1995). A survey of elite attitudes in Estonia, Latvia and Lithuania shows a high preference for Germany both as a model of political and economic development and a partner for co-operation, while the Nordic countries are viewed as a proper model but do not rank as high as preferred partners for co-operation, see Steen (1997). The United States and Russia are considered important partner countries but not examples of development to be followed.

[23] Based on material from the meeting of the Nordic and Baltic co-operation ministers, Brussels, March 1997.

[24] Concerning the case of Sweden, see Sweden and the Baltic Countries. Co-operation for Security, Democracy and Development. Stockholm, Ministry of Foreign Affairs (1996).

[25] For example, a recent parallel decision by Finland and Sweden to support language training of the Russian-speaking population in Estonia and Latvia and the development of border control in Latvia and Lithuania, see Press Release by the Finnish Ministry of Foreign Affairs, No. 71, 18 March 1997.

[26] Press release by the Ministry of Foreign Affairs of Latvia, Riga, 20 August 1996.

[27] The criteria for accession are set down in the conclusions of the Copenhagen European Council (1993) and the pre-accession strategy in the conclusions of the Essen Summit (1994).

28 'Baltic Sea Region Initiative,' European Commission, Brussels, 10.04.1996; on the evolution and instruments of the EU's Baltic Sea strategy, see Christiansen (1995). Total EU assistance in grants for the Baltic Sea region in 1990-94 was ecu 517 million and projected for 1995-99 is ecu 950 million.

29 The lines are drawn in the conclusions of the Dublin Summit (December 1996) and indicate a more active approach also towards the Barents region.

30 The EU's strategy towards the Russian Federation was published as the annex 'Future relations between the European Union and the Russian federation' of the conclusions of the Council on 20 November 1995. The Action Plan was concluded by a working group in April 1996.

31 Total Phare assistance (technical assistance in grants) in 1990-95 was ecu 5,200 million of which Poland received about 25 per cent and the Baltic states about 5 per cent; Phare assistance projected for 1996-99 is ecu 6,600 million. The indicative programme of Phare cross-border co-operation (enhancing co-operation in border regions between member countries and Phare recipient countries, notably border crossings, also co-financed by INTERREG programmes) for the Baltic Sea region for the five-year period 1995-99 is annually on average ecu 14 million (Estonia 3, Latvia 3, Lithuania 4, Poland 4); Phare funds for cross-border co-operation between Germany and Poland are ecu 52 million annually on average for 1995-99. (The Phare Programme Annual Report 1995, Brussels: European Commission, 23.07.1996; Phare cross-border co-operation programme, published by the European Commission).

32 The total sum of Tacis funds (technical assistance in grants) allocated in 1991-1995 was ecu 2,250 million (for Russia ecu 790 million) and projected for 1996-99 ecu 2,220 million (for Russia ecu 600 million together with other Tacis programmes ecu 1000 million). Tacis cross-border co-operation programmes cover St Petersburg, the Leningrad oblast, the Karelian Republic and the Murmansk oblast; funds for 1996 were ecu 30 million. (The Tacis Programme Annual Report, Brussels: European Commission, 22.07.1996; European Community Tacis Programme, 1997 Cross-Border Cooperation Programme, November 1996).

33 NATO Partnership for Peace. Brussels: NATO, 10 January 1994. Proposal for enhanced PfP and an Atlantic Partnership Council was made by the NATO foreign ministers meeting on 10 December 1996.

34 Information on PfP activities and other items of military co-operation is gathered from various primary and secondary sources not identified here separately. It is not exhaustive but intended to reflect continuing trends.

35 Agreement on co-ordination was published in a joint communiqué by the ministers of defence in Vilnius, 3 April 1997. On the most advanced case of multilateral assistance, BALTBAT, see Project Plan for the Support to the Formation of the Baltic Peacekeeping Battalion (BALTBAT) (February 1997); Memorandum of Understanding concerning Co-operation on the Formation of a Baltic Peacekeeping Battalion between ministers of defence of Denmark, Finland, Lithuania, Sweden, Estonia, Latvia, Norway and the United Kingdom, Copenhagen, 11 September 1994; Memorandum of Understanding concerning Nordic-Baltic Co-operation on the Formation of a Baltic Peace-keeping Battalion, Visby, 3 June 1994; Agreement concerning the Establishment and Formation of Joint Peacekeeping Unit, Riga, 13 September 1994.

36 Study on NATO Enlargement. Brussels, NATO (September 1995).

37 Finland and Sweden on the approaching enlargement of NATO, a joint article by Tarja Halonen and Lena Hjelm-Wallen, published in Helsingin Sanomat, Svenska Dagbladet and (abridged) The International Herald Tribune, 15 March 1997; speaking notes published by Finland and Sweden on a discussion with NATO Secretariat, 2 April 1997; on the assessments by the two countries of their security environment, see The European Security Development and Finnish Defence. Report by the Council of State to Parliament on 17 March 1997); Omvärldsförändringar och svensk säkerhetspolitik. Försvarsberedningens rapport inför 1996 års försvarsbeslut. DS 1996:51. On the discussion of traditional security challenges towards Finland and Sweden, see Dörfer (1996); Lindberg (1994).

38 'U.S. Weighs Security Pact With the Baltic Nations,' The International Herald Tribune, 29-30 March 1997; 'Chirac regt Charta zwischen dem Baltikum und der Nato an,' Frankfurter Allgemeine Zeitung, 19 February 1997.

39 Presidency Declaration, Baltic Sea States Summit 1996, Visby, 3-4 May 1996. The second summit is to be held in Riga but the timing remains open.

40 Action Programmes for the Baltic Sea States Co-operation, Fifth Ministerial Session, Council of the Baltic Sea States, Kalmar, 2-3 July 1996.

41 On the origins and development of the CSCE/OSCE missions, see Carlsson (1994); Allan Rosas and Timo Lahelma (forthcoming 1997), 'OSCE Long-Term Missions'; on the case of Estonia, see Timo Lahelma (forthcoming), 'The OSCE's Role in Conflict Prevention: The Case of Estonia.' Major tasks of the OSCE mission to Latvia continue to be monitoring the implementation of the law on citizenship (with the Naturalisation Board) and the law on non-citizens (former USSR citizens), following the issuance of non-citizen passports, facilitating the withdrawal of the remaining demobilised Russian military personnel, and participating on the Joint Commission on Military Pensioners, as well as working with individual cases and making field trips. Major items on the agenda of the OSCE mission to Estonia are passports for aliens, permanent residence permits, naturalisations, language exams for citizenship, and activities related to the integration of national communities, in particular the Ida-Virumaa Round Table, and the situation in the Narva/Ivangorod border area.

42 Having accepted new members from Central and Eastern Europe in rapid succession, the Council of Europe has been faced with a challenge in supporting and monitoring the implementation and adoption of membership obligations in practice. The Committee of Ministers, in principle, assesses all members regularly. In the post-Cold War situation, the Parliamentary Assembly introduced a procedure for monitoring compliance by new members with their obligations; more recently, the function is being transmitted to a new monitoring committee. Among the new members in the Baltic Sea region, Poland was admitted earlier and Estonia has passed the special procedure, while Latvia, Lithuania and Russia remain to be assessed.

43 For an extensive account of the role of the OSCE in the Baltic Sea region, see Peters (1996). Kaliningrad may become an increasingly central item for stability policy co-operation in the future, see Wellmann (1996).

44 Pact on Stability in Europe. Paris 1995. At the request of Russia, and in agreement with Estonia, Finland undertook in April-May 1997 a study of the possibility of using its good offices in the bilateral discussions.

45 Lisbon declaration on the security model stresses the importance of 'bilateral or regional initiatives aimed at developing relations of good neighbourliness and co-operation.' The role of regional institutions and processes was discussed at an OSCE seminar in Vienna, June 1997.

46 On the role of the Stockholm Group, see Peters (1996: 233); the group has the same kind of role as 'friends of the Baltic states' as efforts aimed at co-ordinating military assistance to the Baltic states.

47 Regional arms control was discussed in an OSCE seminar in Vienna, 10-12 July 1995. Exploratory talks led by Poland on a Baltic Sea regional table have not led to a concrete outcome. On military security in national and multilateral policies around the Baltic Rim, see Krohn (1996).

References

Asmus, Ronald D. and Nurick, Robert C. (1996). 'NATO Enlargement and the Baltic States,' *Survival*:38(2), pages 121-142.

Baranovsky, Vladimir (1996). 'Russia,' pages 164-82 in Krohn, Axel (ed.). *The Baltic Sea Region: National and International Perspectives.* Baden-Baden, Nomos Verlagsgesellschaft.

Blechman, Barry (1996). 'Common Security as Seen from the 1990s,' pages 93-108 in Knudsen, Olav F. (ed.). *Strategic Analysis and the Management of Power: Johan Jørgen Holst, the Cold War and the New Europe.* London, Macmillan.

Buzan, Barry (1997). 'Rethinking Security after the Cold War,' *Cooperation and Conflict*:32(1), pages 5-28.

Carlsson, Staffan (ed.) (1994). *The Challenge of Preventive Diplomacy: The Experience of the CSCE.* Stockholm, Ministry of Foreign Affairs.

Christiansen, Thomas (1995). 'EU Perspectives on the Future of the Baltic Sea Agenda,' pages 93-108 in Joenniemi, Pertti and Stålvant, Carl-Einar (eds.). *Baltic Sea Politics: Achievements and Challenges.* Stockholm, the Nordic Council.

Gleditsch, Nils Petter (1995), 'Democracy and the Future of European Peace', European Journal of International Relations 1(4): 539-571.

Dörfer, Ingemar (1996). *Sverige är inte neutralt längre.* Stockholm, Timbro.

Espersen, Ole (1996). 'Human Rights Protection in the Baltic Sea Area: The Commissioner of the Council of Baltic Sea States on Democratic Institutions and Human Rights Including the Rights of Persons Belonging to Minorities,' *Helsinki Monitor*:7(2), pages 52-64.

Hansen, Erik (1997). 'Part I. The Baltic Sea Region,' pages 9-22 in Hansen, Erik (ed.). *Cooperation in the Baltic Sea Region, the Barents Region and the Black Sea Region.* A documentation report. Fafo-paper 1997:4.

Hettne, Bjørn (1993). 'Neo-Mercantilism: The Pursuit of Regionness,' *Cooperation and Conflict*:28(3).

Joenniemi, Pertti and Stålvant, Carl-Einar (1995). 'Baltic Sea Politics: Achievements and Challenges,' pages 9-54 in Joenniemi, Pertti and Stålvant, Carl-Einar (eds.). *Baltic Sea Politics: Achievements and Challenges.* Stockholm, the Nordic Council.

Jukarainen, Pirjo (1996). 'Euroopan alueiden identiteettipolitiikka' (The Identity Politics of European Regions), *Kosmopolis*:26(1), pages 21-40.

Keatinge, Patrick (1996). *European Security: Ireland's Choices.* Dublin, Institute of European Affairs.

Kivikari, Urpo (1996). *The Legacy of Hansa: The Baltic Economic Region.* Helsinki, Otava.

Klinge, Matti (1994). *The Baltic World.* Helsinki, Otava.

Knudsen, Olav F. and Neumann, Iver B. (1995). 'Subregional Security Cooperation in the Baltic Sea Area: An Exploratory Study,' *NUPI Report*:189.

Knudsen, Olav F. (1996). 'Bound to Fail? Regional Security Cooperation in the Baltic Sea Area and Northeast Asia,' *NUPI Report*:566.

Krohn, Axel (ed.) (1996). *The Baltic Sea Region: National and International Perspectives.* Baden-Baden, Nomos Verlagsgesellschaft.

Kugler, Richard L. (1996). *Enlarging NATO: The Russia Factor.* Santa Monica, CA, Rand.

Lahelma , Timo (forthcoming): 'The OSCE's Role in Conflict Prevention: The Case of Estonia.'

Legvold, Robert (1997) 'The "Russian Question,"' pages 42-71 in Baranovsky, Vladimir (ed.). *Russia and Europe: The Emerging Security Agenda.* Oxford, Oxford University Press.

Lindberg, Steve (1994). *Hotbilder för Finland: Säkerhetspolitisk förändring och kontinuitet.* Åbo, Åbo Akademis Förlag.

Maibach, Marcia (1996). 'The Baltic Security Agenda and Emerging Framework of Cooperation,' pages 263-82 in Krohn, Axel (ed.). *The Baltic Sea Region: National and International Perspectives.* Baden-Baden, Nomos Verlagsgesellschaft.

Miles, Lee and Redmond, John (1996). 'Enlarging the European Union: The Erosion of Federalism?' *Cooperation and Conflict*:31(3), pages 285-309.

Möttölä, Kari (1996a). 'Security in Northern Europe: Combining and Reinforcing National, Regional and Wider European Policies,' pages 88-103 in Orrenius, Anders and Truedson, Lars (eds). *Visions of European Security: Focal Point Sweden and Northern Europe.* Stockholm, Olof Palme International Center.

Möttölä, Kari (1996b). 'Nordic Security Policy Co-operation: A New Regional Role in the Making,' pages 150-70 in Bauwens, Werner et al. (eds.). *Small States and the Security Challenge in the New Europe.* London, Brassey's.

Möttölä, Kari (forthcoming 1997). 'The OSCE: Institutional and functional developments in an evolving European security order' in Bothe, Michael, Ronzitti, Natalino and Rosas, Allan (eds.). *The OSCE and the Maintenance of Peace and Security.* The Hague, Kluwer Law International.

Neumann, Iver B. (1996). 'Nordic Cooperation in a Homogenized Political Setting,' *Cooperation and Conflict*:31(4), pages 417-32.

Perko, Susanna (1996). 'Itämeren alueellistumisen kahdet kasvot' (Regional Cooperation in the Baltic sea Region), *Kosmopolis*:26(1), pages 41-51.

Peters, Ingo (1996). 'The Organization for Security and Co-operation in Europe,' pages 224-48 in Krohn, Axel (ed.). *The Baltic Sea Region: National and International Perspectives.* Baden-Baden, Nomos Verlagsgesellschaft.

Rosas, Allan and Lahelma, Timo (forthcoming 1997). 'OSCE Long-Term Missions.'

Saarikoski, Vesa (1995). 'Regional Alternatives: The Breaking of the Europe Between?' pages 228-56 in Archer, Clive and Jalonen, Olli-Pekka (eds.). *Changing European Security Landscape.* Tampere Peace Research Institute, Research Report:63.

Securitas Baltica (1996). *Security in the Baltic Region.* Helsingfors, Söderström.

Steen, Anton (1997). 'Baltikum i internasjonal politikk: førbilder og samarbeid,' *Internasjonal Politikk*:55(1), pages 79-92.

Wæver, Ole (1996). 'Confidence Between Two Modern Empires? The Baltic Sea Region in the 1990's,' in Securitas Baltica. *Security in the Baltic Region.* Helsingfors, Söderström.

Wellmann, Christian (1996). 'Russia's Kaliningrad Exclave at the Crossroads: The Interrelation between Economic Developments and Security Politics,' *Cooperation and Conflict*:31(2), pages 161-83.

Young, Oran R. (1996). *The Arctic Council: Marking a New Era in International Relations.* New York, NY, The Twentieth Century Fund.

25 Military Command Structures in the Baltic Sea Area

Bertel Heurlin

Introduction

In observing the emerging security environment of the post-Cold War era, what role do military command structures play in the Baltic Sea area? For that matter, why is it important to identify and analyse military command structures at all? And what is be to understood by military command structures? What is substance and what is symbol ? Military command structures are also reflections of relations between states. How important are alliance relations involving military command structures in terms of integration? These questions form the theme of this chapter.[1]

First and foremost, military command structures, i.e. the organisation of the management of military forces in peacetime as well as in wartime, reflect both the general and the specific existing security order in a given area. In terms of military scenarios and operations (including the execution of military exercises), these structures are an expression of 'planning for the future.' In the final analysis, military command structures are based upon the overall political structure of the international and, consequently, regional system. As such, they reflect the relative capabilities of the main powers along with their impact on the positions and possibilities of the minor powers. These structures also tend to reflect the general processes for the states in the system, i.e. the continuous competition and socialisation, which implies an imitation of the successful countries in the hard game of international politics (Waltz 1979). Certainly, military command structures are also by-products of geopolitical conditions and technological developments. In addition, by mirroring the infighting between strata, groupings and units inside the armed forces, they fall subject to organisational and bureaucratic struggles as well (Halperin and Kanter 1973). Multinational command structures are, however, mainly an outcome of intergovernmental bargaining.

Analysing military command may, under certain conditions, be a boring and laborious affair. Due to the long-term perspectives of military planning, command structures tend to be rather static and conservative. Like huge oil tankers, they can be slow to change course and difficult to manoeuvre; and like tankers, they may also suddenly sink and disappear. Certainly, due to the effects of time-lags and the fact that politics is constantly in a state of motion, one must use caution in attempting to draw a direct correlation between the current security situation and the existing military command structures. It is quite characteristic that during the Cold War, military command structures hardly changed at all.

By contrast, over a very short span of time from 1990 to 1991, fundamental transitions occurred politically as well as organisationally. Practically overnight, the Warsaw Pact disappeared and with it a solid, centralised, hierarchically and bilaterally organised military command structure. In spite of a transformed strategy, however, NATO's basic command structures continued without fundamental changes. New NATO-invented organisations such as the North Atlantic Co-operation Council (NACC) and later Partnership for Peace (PfP) were added and expected to fertilise future changes (NATO Handbook 1995).

Comprehensive changes in the military command structures are currently under way. NATO is on the verge of completely rethinking its role and organisation, a process which certainly influences the military commands. Consequently, it is necessary to identify and analyse this transformation – in particular in the Baltic Sea area, where changes in NATO have affected the entire region. In fact, due to the fundamentally new security environment, all Baltic Sea countries have been forced to rethink and change their military command structures. The Baltic Sea has become a cohesive area of operation. But now as before, it cannot be defended with maritime forces alone. Therefore land, sea, and airforce command structures have to be 'joint,' i.e. composed of all military services. The aim of this article is to identify, analyse, explain and even forecast – in very general terms – the development and role of military command structures in the Baltic Sea area.

Generally, the following levels of dynamics are included in the analysis: - command structures as an expression of subordinated international systemic transformations, as outcomes of intergovernmental negotiations based on the national interests and the relative position of the states involved, and, finally, as results of bureaucratic politics. It is a general observation, at least nationally, that the lower the command-structure level, the more pronounced will be the clashes between the military service and bureaucratic interests in the political game.

To date, rather few analytical pieces addressing this specific topic have been published. Consequently, it has been necessary to gather information through various interviews with civil servants, politicians and officers of different positions in NATO and in the countries involved. Internal reports have proved useful in identifying problems and verifying information. Scholarly and informative journals, along with other written sources, have provided valuable information about the political implications of the process.

Assumptions

The chapter's basic assumption is that due to the transformation of the international and regional system – a transformation which may be characterised as unipolar, with the United States as the lone surviving superpower – security is no longer indivisible, but rather, has become divisible (Hansen 1995; Heurlin 1995). This shift has caused critical changes in the strategies of the states and in the role of military forces. In post-Cold War Europe, military forces are, paradoxically, used in a more military way, i.e. in open wars or in an intervention mode aimed at establishing stability and containing islands of conflict. During the Cold War, their main purpose was to fight a virtual war based on nuclear weapons and the constant introduction of new weapons systems (Heurlin 1997b). This strategy presupposed the concept of an indivisible security in Europe.

The United States now has a new role of not only being the 'pacifier' of Western Europe but of all of Europe, and this has consequences. Unipolarity means increased regionalisation, and in certain cases also subregionalisation. In order to avoid being subjected to negative consequences of the new divisibility of security, most states will flock around the superpower in an attempt to demonstrate that precisely their region or environment is crucial to world stability and peace. The reason is simply that due to limited resources, the superpower, the US, is influenced by the threat of exhaustion (Heurlin 1996). To ease this threat, the United States is establishing a network of selected allies willing and able to execute the common 'new world order' policy. This is the case in the Baltic Sea area, where Denmark is pursuing a politico-military policy and Sweden a politico-economic-cultural policy.[2]

In this sense of a wider understanding of security policy, the United States is a Baltic Sea state.

Admittedly, this interpretation is attempting to explain broad tendencies only. Regionalisation and decentralisation may certainly be analysed in many different ways, not to mention the variety of views among the main actors. I have preferred to state this rather simple superior analytical point of departure because it convincingly suggests the rules of the new international game.

This is the main reason why the Baltic Sea area must be considered more secure than ever in terms of the absence of mutual military threats from major powers (Hansen and Heurlin 1997).

The new 'militarisation' of the military forces is a fundamental reason why military command structures are an important and interesting target for analysis. Military structures have gained new prominence as a political factor in the security of Europe, its regions and subregions. Subordinated to the rationale of the NATO alliance, these structures must still be able to function as effectively as possible in terms of being cost-effective and appropriate. While it is one thing to function effectively in theoretical terms and within the rationale of the common strategy, it is quite another to do so in practical terms, dealing with an intergovernmentally organised alliance which will always reflect national priorities even though it is integrated during wartime. This implies, for instance, that from a purely military logic, NATO headquarters will generally have many more officers than are required because each state is eager to be widely represented. The states want to maximise their influence where it matters most. And in the late 90s, military structures matter as a source of influence. Thus, multinationality has considerable political virtues, but it also involves costs in terms of reduced military efficiency.

In most cases, NATO members consider headquarters on national soil to be a valuable asset that provides political, economic and military leverage. Hosting a NATO headquarters necessarily equates with political influence and hence with a chance to become a real player in the political game. An HQ also means jobs and financial profits. Militarily, it is seen as providing insurance against 'being abandoned.' The potential negative effects – internally driven political problems between government and population, and the fear of being subjected to entrapment (Snyder 1984) – while certainly there, will play only a minor role due to the new security order in Europe, where NATO, as mentioned, now functions as a US-Western European security overlay for the whole of Europe.

The Baltic Sea Area: Old and New Conditions

Like in the rest of the world, the transformation which has taken place in the Baltic Sea area as a result of the end of the Cold War is profound. The main reason has been the voluntary demise of the Soviet Union. First it gave up its Third World empire and engagement, then – as a consequence of the change from the Brezhnev Doctrine to the Sinatra Doctrine – it renounced its Eastern European empire, including the Baltic republics and, finally, Russia was established as an independent state following the Soviet Union's dissolution. Russia, though recognised as the successor state of the USSR, was recreated as an Anti-Soviet Union by virtue of its take-over of the Western norms and organising principles of democracy, individual freedom, human rights and market economy. Despite its insistence that these values be referred to as 'global' norms and ideas, the reality is that Russia has copied the winning Western coalition.[3]

The Baltic Sea, formerly a Soviet-dominated area with a heavy military force ready for immediate counterattack in a western direction, is now (with a slight exaggeration) a 'NATO lake.' All countries in the area are members of the NATO-organised Partnership for Peace institution and many are engaged in 'in the spirit of PfP' bilateral or multilateral military activities. Furthermore, all are either members or observers of the NACC and, as such, are anticipated to participate in the new Atlantic Partnership Council, an organisation envisaged to take over the functions of the NACC and, partly, the PfP. In respect to the Western European Union (WEU), an organisation now recognised as being the European pillar of NATO, the Baltic states and Poland are associated partners while Sweden, Finland and Denmark are observers.

This new security architecture is lightyears away from a Cold War situation characterised by a centralised Warsaw Pact, bilateral control by the Soviet Union, by a situation where Finland – through the 1948 Pact of Friendship, Co-operation and Mutual Assistance with the USSR – could be assessed an Eastern-oriented neutral and a Sweden which was a Western-oriented neutral due to secret arrangements with NATO. The German Democratic Republic (GDR) and the Federal Republic of Germany (FRG) were heavily militarised with a combined total of 1.5 million soldiers and 10,000 nuclear warheads. They were both front-line states opposing each other. Denmark pursued a non-provocative policy vis-à-vis the USSR, with no nuclear weapons and no stationing of foreign military forces. In the event of war, however, Denmark was to be nuclearised in a very short time from NATO depots close to the Danish border (SNU 1996).

Russia had two very strong military districts in the area: one in Leningrad and the other in the Baltics. Militarily, Poland and the GDR were entirely integrated with the Soviet armed forces, and the command structure was clear: the USSR functioned as the undisputed centre. Despite the prevailing concepts of neutrality and 'Nordic Balance,' there was no doubt about the Cold War bipolar division of the area: the apparent military stability was combined with a deep sense of mutual animosity and an open political conflict.

Today, however, all this has changed. Despite the recent controversy over the enlargement of NATO, the basic relationship among all states – including Russia – is one of partnership. The existing organisational structure of unipolarity implies a process of regionalisation and subregionalisation. Depending on the perspective, the Baltic Sea area can be considered a region or a subregion (this makes a difference in military terms, as we shall see in the following section). NATO now has a close to dominant influence in the area. This development has the benign implication that never before have the Baltic Sea states lived in so positive a security situation. Bipolarity had the effect of leaving the countries in an extremely exposed and threatened position. During multipolarity (which characterised the world structure through the end of World War II), the small states were left with no security guarantees whatsoever as they had to constantly adhere to the changing alliances of the pole-countries. One of the outcomes of this structure was the elimination of the independence of the Baltic states in 1940.

This cannot happen today. The US military involvement in Europe, in combination with the magnetic function of the EU, have set the rules of the game: security for small and middle powers must be achieved through hard work (with no possibility of freewheeling) by flocking around the unipole (the United States) and by co-operation and partnership in a regional context (Heurlin 1996). These are the structural political prerequisites for the operational field of military activities and structures.

NATO: The Main Actor in the Baltic Sea

One of the primary reasons why NATO was not dissolved at the end of the Cold War was its function as the military connection between the US and Europe in taking care of the internal security among the allies. A militarily fragmented Europe was not in America's interest, and the European countries needed a heavily US-involved NATO in order to continue the great project of European integration. Thus, NATO has now become accommodated to the new environment. The new NATO is no longer a collective defence organisation directed against a defined enemy. The threat now is chaos, instability or Europe's past. Consequently, its primary goal is to avoid hyper-nationalism, neo-nationalism and independent, nationalistic military forces. The tool used to achieve this is a military integration on many levels: training, exercises, peace-keeping, peace-enforcing, and perhaps most importantly – as the basis of these activities – military command structures.

New NATO is founded on a new strategic concept – new also by virtue of the fact that it was a strategy open to the public and accepted by all countries (including France). The new NATO developed fast: at an organisational level with the NACC and Partnership for Peace; and at an operational level with the decisions to operate in a non-Article Five mode out of the area of the NATO countries, followed by the NATO-led involvement in ex-Yugoslavia through IFOR and SFOR.

This concept – like all major initiatives and strategically relevant changes – was an American invention. One of NATO's primary instruments, the combined joint task force (CJTF), is, firstly, combined, which refers to the claim that two or more nations must be involved. Secondly, it is joint, which means composed of units from different military services such as the navy, the army and the airforce. Thirdly, 'task force' implies a unit which is put together for a certain period of time, for a specific task, and is disbanded once the task is accomplished. The concept was introduced in order to cope with the political and strategic environment in Europe characterised by islands of conflicts or strategic 'ghettos.' Left uncontained, not to mention untreated, such hot spots would have a negative impact on the stability in Europe.

The CJTF concept is in many ways new and unique also in the context of command structures. Task forces have always been temporary command-and-control arrangements employed by ad hoc coalitions. NATO is now aiming at a permanent institutionalisation of the multinational task force notion.

There is no detailed official definition of CJTF, but the following will summarise the idea: a multinational, multiservice, task-tailored force consisting of NATO and possibly non-NATO forces, capable of rapid deployment to conduct limited-duration, primarily peace-keeping or peace-enforcing operations beyond Alliance borders, under the control of either NATO's integrated military command structure or the WEU, authorised by NATO. It has to be added that Article Five operations are not excluded.[4]

Headquarters for CJTF are defined by a NATO policy co-ordinating group as 'a deployable, multinational, multiservice alliance HQ of variable size, formed to command and control CJTF for contingency operations including peace-keeping.'

From its introduction, until its provisions became adopted by the foreign ministers at the June 1996 Berlin meeting, the CJTF concept was intensely discussed. According to assessments by some analysts and participants, divided views primarily between the French and the Americans evolved into an infighting which threatened the cohesion of the organisation. However, implementation proceeded under the 1996 compromise – but not without emerging disagreements.

Precisely what are the main aims of CJTF? First of all, to be included in command structures that are flexible enough to meet the new challenges and to maintain forces of increased mobility for military operations outside the collective defence obligations according to Article Five. The basic premise is the establishment of a nucleus staff derived partly from dual-hatting personnel within existing NATO commands, and partly from personnel of participating PfP countries.

The CJTF concept is part of the major transformation of the military command structure. In 1994 NATO's Military Committee commenced a so-called Long Term Study which dealt with the military implementation of the strategic concept (MC 400) and, subsequently, the command structure. The main problem has been in determining what tasks belong to what level of command. Secondarily, there has been the issue of how to reduce NATO headquarters. Decisions have already been taken to reduce the number from some 65 to 20 major headquarters. The Committee has come to terms with the replacement of the present four-level structure : 1) Major NATO commands, 2) Major Subordinate Commands, 3) Principal Subordinate Commands, 4) Subordinate Principal Subordinate Commands, with a new three-level structure broken down according to: 1) strategic commands; 2) regional commands; and 3) subregional commands. On the strategic level, no changes will occur. There will still be two commands – SACEUR (the allied forces in Europe) and SACLANT (the allied forces in the Atlantic) – whose military chiefs will remain Americans. SACLANT will have three regional – and no subregional – commands. A decision has yet to be reached as to whether SACEUR shall have two regional commands (with the Alps as the dividing line) or three (as in the present situation with a South , Central and Northwestern command). Since almost all countries support the two-commands solution, it appears the likely outcome.

There are, however, critical underlying problems due to the existence of a Western European power triangle of the dominant military powers of France, Germany and the UK, each with its different agenda and position. Naturally, each country wants to avoid losing its relative position. This begs the question of how to cut the European command structure so that the three countries are separated. The present structure of Germany in one region (Central) and the UK in another (Northwest) used to be acceptable due to France's non-participation in the military structure. With France back in NATO, however, the situation has dramatically changed. A French-British joint command is not acceptable to

Germany; similarly, a French-German solution is not acceptable to the UK. This dilemma, which remains to be solved, has major implications for the Baltic situation as it will reflect how Europe will be 'sliced' militarily, involving not least the US strategic preferences.

The third level of command will consist of two types of headquarters: Component Commands (CCs) and Joint Subregional Commands (JSRCs). The CCs, contrary to their present functions, are conceptualised as region-wide commands for particular either maritime or air matters while the JSRSs will remain conceptualised for more localised matters. The Military Committee is attempting to make these two concepts compatible, with the strength, position and functions of the two command structures still under discussion. With respect to the Baltic Sea area, however, one thing is clear: that the joint command, BALTAP, in Karup, Denmark, will remain the headquarters for the collective defence (Article Five) of the Baltic approaches and the Baltic Sea area. The name will likely be changed to 'Subregional Command Northeast,' and it will remain a combined and joint command, i.e. consisting of several countries and military services (see Figure 25.1).

The basic question concerning the command structures in the Baltic sea area will be how the non-Article Five activities (PfP, CJTF) can become incorporated

Figure 25.1: NATO's new command structure (not officially confirmed)

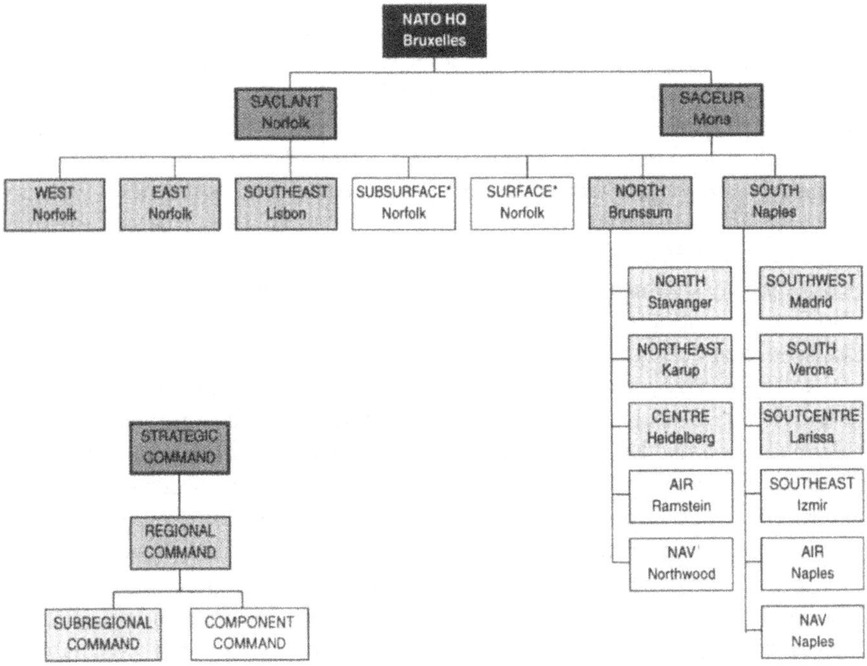

into the military command structures. The issue is a crucial one because these new command structures set the framework for the future as they are expected to adapt to the new challenges – primarily the enlargement of NATO and the intensification of partnership co-operation.

Contrasting Conceptions of Command Structure

Two main models of command structure can be identified: 1) one which emphasises the idea of a centralised organisation where decisions are taken at a high, central level and where small, costly and superfluous headquarters are abandoned; and 2) a concept which emphasises a decentralised, flexible structure and a multiple bi- and trilateralisation which supports subregionalisation and smaller, more flexible headquarters.

The first model is supported by most of the NATO countries and a majority of NATO institutions. This model is also – for different reasons – supported by the non-NATO, PfP partner members. The United States is generally split. On the one hand, it emphasises the centralised concept of keeping the decision-making process under strict control. To the US way of thinking, the CJTF concept and the required command structure can only to be realised at the regional – and not subregional – level. The US refers to the common understanding that CJTF operations are comprehensive endeavours. NATO will, at the most, be capable of running two CJTF activities at the same time: one large and one small. The larger endeavour might encompass up to 100,000 men; the smaller one is defined as a combined and joint operation up to a division size of air and naval forces of approximately 10,000-30,000 men.

On the other hand, the United States – at least in the case of the PfP – is supporting the regional, decentralised model. Regionalised PfP – including a permanent partner element attached to subregional command – is seen as an acceptable solution.

France and Spain, on the one hand, are both reluctant to allow too much decentralisation and multiple bi- and trilateralism. As new members of NATO's integrated command, they do not want to see Central and Eastern European partners at the same level of influence on the military command structures as themselves. France, however, also supports a regionalisation in the direction of an enhanced European Security and Defence Identity (ESDI), which implies a more flexible command structure aimed at avoiding American influence on military activities.

Most of the other countries, including the UK, Germany, Norway and some NATO commands, support the centralised, non-subregional model based primarily on either geopolitical or bureaucratic factors. There are plans to set up JSRCs in Karup – with Denmark as the marketing actor. Also Heidelberg and, due to its very specific geostrategic position, Norway are possibilities. This geostrategic reasoning, however, is invalid for the UK who rejects the notion that it might be attacked on a scale low enough not to involve the rest of the Euro-Atlantic area.

The CJTF Concept in Practice

How, in greater detail, can we assess the CJTF concept as analysed according to the two models? As previously mentioned, we are dealing with one notion addressing a large CJTF, and another referring to a small CJTF.

Common to both models is the fact that CJTF HQ should not have an independent structure but, rather, should be part of the existing and coming NATO command structure. Furthermore, the identified need for HQs with CJTF nuclei numbers between two and four. The Long Term Study had also referred to the possibility of small-scale CJTF headquarters to take care of less comprehensive operations.

There are claims that a CJTF can only be managed at a higher level of command structure because a CJTF deployment of forces is foreseen as having a certain size and level of operation and, therefore, is necessarily based on a huge HQ which cannot be reduced to a small nucleus. Applied to the Baltic Sea area, this indicates that Karup will not be the HQ used for CJTF nuclei. Since the CJTF is not a standing arrangement but, rather, a capability which is embedded at a given level, activated through augmentation, and in need for many assets, the HQ must be large. Experience – primarily through the operations in ex-Yugoslavia – has shown that comprehensive and complicated deployment is needed to bring an efficient and decisive halt to a serious crisis, with the argument being that it is very difficult to envisage an operation which would be insignificant enough to justify only a very small CJTF deployment. Within this context, therefore, Karup has no possibility.

The 'small' option claims that it is appropriate to deploy CJTF capacities at a subregional level. The litmus test should be the results of recent and coming exercises. The argument is sustainability and the need to rotate staffs. If CJTF nuclei are appointed only at the regional level, the Alliance will have insufficient CJTF nuclei to provide the necessary sustainability. Furthermore, in terms of flexibility, since operations always differ in size and complexity, NATO needs an HQ that can cater to all kinds of operations. In terms of cost effectiveness, it is argued that CJTF nuclei at the subregional level will not exceed the recent financial ceiling due to the double-hatting system for officers and the fact that partner-officers are being financed by their countries.

PfP: Functions and Possibilities

Another crucial problem – also with reference to the above model – is the relation to PfP. PfP has been referred to as having the function of a 'geopolitical eraser.' Every time a NATO enlargement draws new lines, PfP is supposed to step in and erase those lines. Dividing lines may also be drawn, however, as part of the tendency towards regionalisation. Another characterisation, the notion of 'self-differentiation,' refers to the principle that it is up to the individual partners to decide how close they want co-operation with NATO to be. With these concepts as a point of departure, we can again identify a centralised and a decentralised, subregionalised model.

This is certainly the case in the Baltic Sea area where one can see different visions and activities. The centralised model is exemplified by the Finnish military policy, which maintains very close relations with Estonia in regard to the delivery of weapons and training of military personnel. In terms of the military command structure, however, Finland is certainly not a supporter of regional solutions. First, Finland has no interest in any visions of establishing a Nordic-Baltic command structure. In the Finnish view, a position with a specific Nordic military relationship to – and military responsibility for – the Baltic countries is certainly not rewarding. Finland wants its security relations to Russia embedded in a larger context and as close to the European-Atlantic centre as possible. This is the reason for both Finland's EU membership and its insistence that relations to NATO be as close to the centre – with HQ in Mons, Belgium and Washington – as possible. Very little in the way of Finnish understanding is geared to exert influence through an intermediary such as Denmark.

This means that on the issue of CJTF, Finland supports the idea of a regional – and not subregional – arrangement. The same holds true for PfP arrangements and activities. Any subregionalisation of PfP activities – with the exception of membership – is not in accordance with the general Finnish strategy of being as close to NATO as possible. For reasons that are politically self-evident, the non-NATO member Finland has no official policy as concerns possible NATO membership for the Baltic countries.

Considered a main player in Baltic Sea military co-operation, Denmark, though certainly attempting to widen the role of the PfP 'eraser' function, is also using the regionalisation concept. By employing its comprehensive network of various bi-, tri-, and multilateral agreements as an argument for the virtues of subregionalisation, Denmark is exerting a 'bottom-up' influence on the internal NATO decision-making processes. For 1997 Denmark has planned more than 200 military activities on a bi- and trilateral basis inside – or 'in the spirit of' – PfP. Denmark maintains close military co-operation with the Baltic states, training Baltic personnel in peace-keeping, integrating Baltic troops directly in Danish peace-keeping units and conducting bilateral visits and exercises. Denmark also has military agreements with Russia, and bi- and trilateral agreements with Poland (including Germany). Furthermore, Denmark has sent PfP expert missions to the Baltic states in order to assist in the preparation of the PfP presentation document and the specific defence planning process.

As concerns arguments and general support for accepting the Baltic states as part of the first round of NATO expansion, Denmark is certainly in the forefront. However, there is no possibility of this solution. The American statement is that the 'door will remain open' to the Baltic states. Realising that the membership-now strategy has failed, it is Danish policy to try to establish a certain category of aspiring countries in the region, using the PfP co-operation as a tool. The concept goes under the label of Super PfP (or PfP-Plus) and aims at a reduced NATO membership 'encompassing everything except Article Five activities.' A crucial factor in this policy is, precisely, the military command structures. Within this notion, the goal is to provide increased participation in decisions concerning PfP. This goal is implemented through a decentralisation of PfP and an involvement of partners at all possible levels, including the military command structures of NATO. BALTAP, for example, will be replaced by JSR Northeast in carrying out planning and implementation of non-Article Five activities.

Furthermore, the Danish policy is to institutionalise the political dialogue, set up NATO information offices in the Baltic countries and keep the US involved there, particularly with respect to the Baltic action plan (still under development) and the possible Baltic charter. The involvement of Nordic and Western countries shall be a supplement to – and not a substitution for – the embedding of the Baltic countries in NATO.

In conclusion, Danish policy attempts to contribute to the enhancement of PfP by establishing 'Permanent Partner' elements in relevant headquarters of the new command structure. In the Danish view, it is possible to have such elements 'inside the fence, but outside the wall,' while still fully respecting Article Five planning and exercises conducted by NATO members only. Denmark also attempts to designate the relevant subregional headquarters, such as the coming Northeast HQ – as NATO headquarters with a CJTF nucleus. The Danish position appears to be that they should be used for smaller CJTF operations or for the support of CJTF headquarters in large-scale operations.

We have presented two contrasting views of the directly involved Baltic Sea countries. How, then, to assess the basic positions of the great powers concerning the Baltic Sea region?

Basic Positions of the Powers

The United States considers itself a European power and thus aims for stability and security in Europe. Europe is viewed as being part of a global 'forward defence' of a United States with no specific enemies except the so-called rogue states[5] and a variety of regional chaos and unrest. NATO command structures must be cost-effective and militarily efficient. The US wants them to be large but also has an interest in a subregionalisation of the Baltic Sea area where client states may conduct stability-promoting activities. Consequently, Denmark, as a member of NATO, may play a crucial role.[6]

France has come to realise that, with regard to defence, the only working body in Europe is NATO. France is therefore back in NATO – because of the new European security structure, because of its need to bind and balance the new Germany and because of budget constraints. Nonetheless, France – as previously mentioned – is aiming at the European Security and Defence Identity and the possible role of the WEU in a CJTF framework. This may, in fact, be achieved by emphasising European-only CJTF activities. As a primarily south-looking country, France has limited interests – and no specific priorities – as concerns the Baltic Sea.

Germany, on the other hand, *is* closely linked to the Baltic area. Its general interests favour the continued embedding of the Baltics into NATO, and seeing its closest neighbours, primarily Poland, embedded militarily in the same way. NATO integration is Germany's tool for not being considered threatening in any way. Due to its historical stigmatisation, as well as its new role as power centre for the whole of Europe, Germany is very reluctant to exert any significant influence on the command structure in the Baltic Sea area. This is reflected in the change of the command structures in 1993, whereby the Central command was extended to comprise Denmark and therefore, also partially BALTAP. Germany operates through trilateral military arrangements. In the case of Poland, Germany is cooperating with Denmark, which is acting as the small, politically legitimising partner.

The United Kingdom finds itself is in a mixed position. During the latest change of command structures, the UK was tied closer to NATO because the Northwest command implied the integration of all British forces. Concerning the connections to the continent, the UK is still reluctant to accept that be too close. On the other hand, the UK knows that is precisely where the influence lies. NATO, therefore, represents a most important link. The former UK-US special relation is withering away. In general, the UK expresses a very modest interest in the Baltic Sea with no very clearly pronounced priorities in terms of military command structures.

For Poland – among the first new members of the new NATO – the existing and emerging military structures are of vital significance. Poland is heavily involved in PfP activities as well as activities 'in the spirit of the PfP.' Among Poland's involvements are trilateral military arrangements with Denmark and Germany and France and Germany. These arrangements cover only the western part of Poland, however. Regarding the future command structure, no NATO headquarters are foreseen on the territory of the new member states. Poland will presumably enter into the coming Northeast Subregional Command as concerns the Polish navy. Army forces will be organised according to a German-Polish-Danish corps and will consist of three divisions, the Danish division, the Polish 12th division and the German 14th division. For political and geostrategical reasons, the HQ for this corps will probably be moved from Rendsburg to Potsdam. It becomes fairly evident that Poland, as a middle-rangking power in a crucial environment, will have interests extending far beyond a role in the Baltic Sea area. The Polish navy is not impressive in size, and Poland is mainly a military land power, which will probably be attached to the command structures in primarily Central Europe (see Figure 25.2).

Russia has serious and well-publicised problems with her command structures.

The reduction from the dominant Soviet military position in the Baltic Sea to the new Russian position of having only the Leningrad and Kaliningrad military districts is quite remarkable. Militarily, Kaliningrad has obtained a more independent status. The military commander has full control of the 40,000 armed troops in the area (in peacetime, the 10,000 border troops are, however, under Moscow's direct command). Though Russia is a PfP member, it has been increasingly reluctant to participate in activities. This implies that attempts at further regionalisation of the Russian areas in the Baltic Sea region (previously supported by regional military leaders) have now yielded to Moscow's increasingly centralised control. Fundamentally, Russia is against any enlargement of NATO and consequently has no priorities in regards to the NATO military structure. In Russia's eyes, the WEU and its new position in the CJTF concept is not a problem or challenge.

The Baltic States

The positions of the Baltic states are also mixed. Their main interest is in having the most intimate relations with – and membership of – NATO (or military structures close NATO). Any military relations with Russia (also via the PfP) are, for the time being, problematic and, especially for Lithuania, out of the question. With respect to the Nordic countries, binding permanent military structures are only considered negative if they have a 'side-tracking' effect. The main target is the European centre. But as the Baltic countries have now been informed that

Figure 25.2: Major headquarters and divisions stationed in Joint Subregional Command (JSRC) Northeast's area of geographical focus

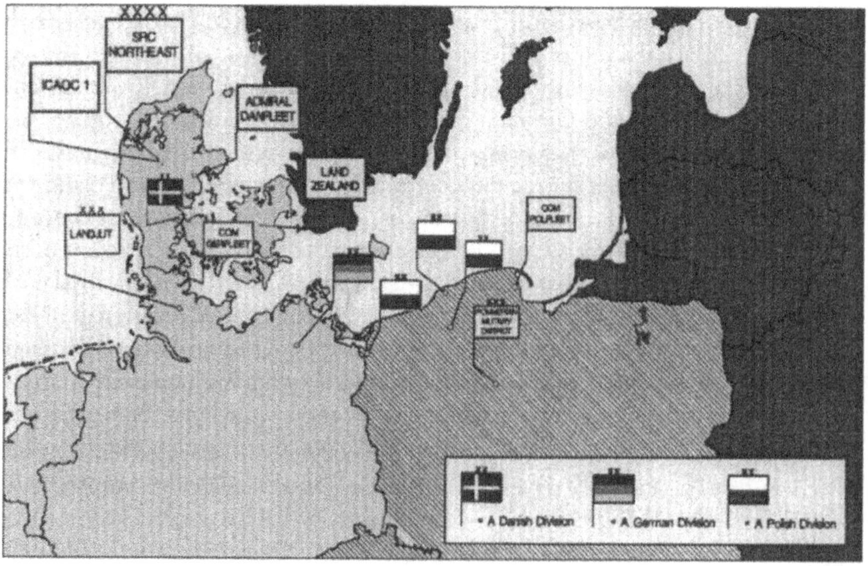

they will not be invited to join the Alliance in the first round, they are exploiting the possibility of getting as close to NATO structures as possible, even if only in a subregional context via countries which are playing the role of Baltic states spokesmen like Denmark.

In general, the Baltic countries are as different as the Nordic countries. Their relations are subordinated to the logic of limited co-operation among small states. Nevertheless, because of the specific security environment, there are gains to be achieved through multilateralism. BALTBAT, for example, has been a success, which is expected to be followed up by a naval co-operation project, BALTRON, and a common air surveillance system, BALTNET.

BALTBAT has Denmark as its main co-ordinator, and the main host country is Latvia. BALTRON is supposed to get Germany as the main co-ordinator with Estonia as the main host. The United States is expected to co-ordinate BALTNET, whose primary host is anticipated to be Lithuania. To these projects, the common partnership arrangements are to be added. Also as mentioned, Denmark is aiming at establishing common – including bilateral – military structures which are as close to NATO structures as possible.

The mixed positions are demonstrated by the temptation of the individual Baltic countries to break with the co-operative notion that has been more or less constructed from outside. In February 1997, for instance, Lithuania declared itself a Central European country in line with Poland, thus disowning its Baltic country connection. All in all, despite their need to please Russia, the Baltic countries are doing their utmost to become most intimately integrated into NATO or command structures close to it.

Conclusion

One of the points in the present chapter has been the notion that military command structures have permanence, inertia and immobility, and thus normally lag behind politics. The present planning and negotiations about command structures in the Baltic Sea area clearly demonstrate this. It is impossible for organisational structures to fully cope with a moving target, i.e. the present security dynamics. Though the future – and even near-future – European security environment is unpredictable in many ways, enduring command structures are in the process of being decided. One way to solve this problem is to establish structures which are not only sustainable but flexible enough to meet new challenges in a reasonable fashion. Thus, flexibility along with mobility, regionalisation and increased military integration are the key concepts, as pointed out.

However, this will not erase or harmonise the different priorities and policies of the individual states. Intergovernmental co-operation will produce solutions which are not in accordance with a more narrow military organisational logic. All involved actors are, however, recognising this price of military integration.

There are certainly bureaucratic politics at play, especially in cases where reductions are required, as in the military command structure. But bureaucratic politics also influences expansion or reconditioning, which is part of the recent development of the military command structure as NATO expands eastwards. Generally, however, as the NATO issue is high politics, on the top of the international agenda, military command structures are lifted into this sphere and are expected to remain there for some time. In this way symbol and substance are combined.

Can we make any forecasts about the development of military structures in the Baltic area? The detailed outcome of the present discussions and negotiations is not possible to foresee. What *can* be said is that as long as the United States, owing to its lone superpower status, remains as deeply involved in Europe as to consider itself a European power, the Baltic Sea, as an important but not central region, will be subjected to increasing military co-operation. This co-operation will be spelled out in flexible, regionalised military command structures which will be increasingly integrative and 'NATO-ised.' This NATO will be different, however, from the NATO of the Cold War.

Notes

1. I wish to thank Michael Winding for valuable and effective help with collecting data and information. Also thanks to colleagues from DUPI, the Danish Institute of International Affairs and to the important political and military actors who have served as invaluable sources.
2. Concerning competition between the Nordic countries in the Baltic Sea area, see Hans Mouritzen, 'Denmark in the Post-Cold-War Era' in Heurlin and Mouritzen (1997).
3. For a comprehensive survey of the US-Soviet relations around the end of the Cold War, see Garthoff (1994). For an assessment in more theoretical terms, see Heurlin (1997).
4. According to the official statement of the Atlantic Council of 4 December, 1996, the purpose of CJTF is to:
   - 'Provide flexible and efficient means to enable the Alliance to generate forces at short notice, providing rapidly deployable, multi-national multi-service Task Forces with dedicated Command and Control capability,
   - facilitate contingency operations in concert with nations outside the Alliance in situations not related to collective defense,
   - reflect the emerging European Security and Defense Identity, including the provision of separable but not separate military capabilities to the WEU.'
5. Identified by the United States as Iran, Iraq, North Korea and Libya.
6. The increased role of the Baltic area in American foreign politics is manifested by the decision to set up a post as Assistant Deputy Secretary of State for NATO enlargement, the Nordic countries and the Baltic Sea area

References

Atlantic News.

Archer, Clive (1996). 'The Nordic Area as a "Zone of Peace,"' *Journal of Peace Research*:33(4), pages 451-67.

Arter, David (1996). 'Finland: From Neutrality to NATO?' *European Security*:5(4/Winter) 1996), pages 614-32.

Barry, Charles (1996). 'NATO's Combined Joint Task Forces in Theory and Practice,' *Survival*:38(1), pages 81-97.
Bildt, Carl (1996). 'Norden och Baltikum i eget PFP blir naturlig bas även för samarbete med Ryssland,' *Fritt Militärt Forum*:3, pages 32-35.
Bitzinger, Richard A. (1996). 'The Nordic/Baltic Region: A New Strategic Significance?' *Defense Analysis*:12(3), pages 371-75.
B:son Uller, Lennart (1996). 'Sveriges försvar och Östersjöområdet,' *Fritt Militärt Forum*:3, pages 1-6.
Documentation from the Danish Ministry of Defence (1995). 'The Baltbat-Project.'
Documentation from the Danish Ministry of Defence (1996). 'Defence Cooperation around the Baltic Sea in 1997.'
Heurlin, Bertel and Mouritzen, Hans (eds.) (1997). *Danish Foreign Policy Yearbook 1997*. DUPI, Danish Institute of International Affairs.
Cornish, Paul (1996). 'European Security: The End of Architecture and the New NATO,' *International Affairs*:72(4), pages 751-69.
Dörfer, Ingemar (1996). *Sverige är inte neutralt längre*. Stockholm, Timbro.
Eyal, Jonathan (1996). 'NATO and European Security,' *Perspectives*: 6-7, pages 17-27.
Garthoff, Raymond L. (1994). *The Great Transition*. Washington.
Gordon, Philip H. (1996). 'Does the WEU Have a Role,' *The Washington Quarterly*:20(1), pages 125-40.
Goulden, John (1996). 'NATO Approaching two Summits: The UK Perspective,' *RUSI Journal*:December, pages 29-32.
Hansen, Birthe (1995). *European Security – 2000*. Copenhagen Political Studies Press.
Hansen, Birthe (1995). 'Unipolarity and the Middle East.' Unpublished PhD thesis. Copenhagen.
Hansen, Birthe and Heurlin, Bertel (eds.) (1997). *The Baltic States in World Politics*. Curzon Press (forthcoming).
Halperin, Morton H. and Kanter, Arnold (1973). *A Bureaucratic Perspective*. Readings in American Foreign Policy.
Heurlin, Bertel (1995). *Security Problems in the New Europe*. Copenhagen Political Studies Press.
Heurlin, Bertel (1996). 'The US Impact in European Security as We Approach the Year 2000,' pages 118-35 in Orrenius, Anders and Truedson, Lars (eds.). *Visions of European Security: Focal Point Sweden and Northern Europe*. Stockholm, Olof Palme International Center.
Heurlin, Bertel (1997). 'From Two to One Superpower.' Forthcoming.
Hunter, Robert E. (1996). 'The Evolution of NATO: The United States' Perspective,' *RUSI Journal*:December, pages 33-37.
Høy-Petersen, U. (1996). 'Combined Joined Task Force koncepten,' *Tidsskrift for søvæsen*:167(5), pages 279-89.
Knudsen, Olav F. (1996). *'Bound to Fail?': Regional Security Cooperation in the Baltic Sea Area and Northeast Asia*. NUPI Working Paper:566. Oslo.
Lejins, Atis (1996). 'The "Threat" of NATO Enlargement to the Security of the Baltic States,' *Kungl Krigsvetenskapsakademiens Handlinger och tidskrift*:200(3), pages 77-82.
Mandag Morgen (1997). *Hvad skal Danmark?: Visioner og provokationer om Danmarks rolle i det 21. århundredes Europa*. Copenhagen, Mandag Morgen.
McCalla, Robert B. (1996). 'NATO's Persistence after the Cold War,' *International Organization*:50(3/Summer), pages 445-75.
Moshes, Arkady and Vushkarnik, Anton (1997). 'Russia and the Baltic States: Between Coexistence and Cooperation?' *IWPS*:1, pages 77-100.
NATO Handbook (1995). Brussels, Nato Office of Information and Press. Reprinted edition, with amendments.
Reichel, Klaus (1996). "Nachdenken in Helsinki – Die Sicherheitspolitik Finnlands,' *Information Für Die Truppe*:12, pages 36-44.
Richthofen, Hermann Frhr von (1996). 'The Evolution of NATO from a German Point of View,' *RUSI Journal*:December, pages 39-44.

Rühle, Michael and William, Nick (1996). 'Partnership for Peace after NATO Enlargement,' *European Security*:5(4/Winter), pages 521-28.
Ruggie, John Gerard (1996). 'Consolidating the European Pillar: The Key to NATO's Future,' *The Washington Quarterly*:20(1), pages 109-124.
SNU, Det Sikkerheds- og nedrustningspolitiske udvalg (1996). *Grønland under den Kolde Krig.* Copenhagen.
Snyder, Glenn (1984). 'The Security Dilemma in Alliance Politics,' *World Politics*:36, pages 461-95.
Szlajfer, Henryk (1996). 'The Enlargement of NATO: A Polish View,' *RUSI Journal*:December, pages 49-54.
U.S. Department of State (1997). 'Report to the Congress on the Enlargement of the North Atlantic Treaty Organization: Rationale, Benefits, Costs and Implications.'
Værnø, Grethe (1996). 'Nordiske Sikkerhetsinteresser: Felles Interesser – Felles Politikk?' FHSFS Projekstgruppe 'Sikkerhet i Norden.' Hefte nr. 2/1996 i Forsvarets høgskoleforening, Studieutvalgets skriftserie.
Waltz, Kenneth N., (1979) (Reprinted with corrections 1983). *Theory of International Politics.*

26 CFE and the Baltic Rim

Jane M.O. Sharp

Summary-Introduction

This chapter explores the different interests of the Baltic Rim states in the Treaty on Conventional Forces in Europe (CFE). Four states – Denmark, Germany, Poland and Russia – are parties to CFE, as are all members of NATO and the former Warsaw Pact. Finland and Sweden, both neutral and non-aligned throughout the Cold War, are not parties to CFE. Estonia, Latvia and Lithuania, as member states of the former Soviet Union, were part of the CFE regime from Treaty signature in November 1990 until they achieved independence from Moscow in late 1991. At that time the United States insisted that the three Baltic states opt out of the Treaty. In retrospect the 1991 Baltic opt-out looks misguided, although at the time only Poland and Hungary raised any objections.

Although Mikhail Gorbachev and his Foreign Minister Eduard Shevardnadze were enthusiastic about CFE, Boris Yeltsin and the Russian military have never liked the Treaty. They claim that CFE was overtaken by events such as the collapse of the Warsaw Pact and the Soviet Union, and since early 1993 have repeatedly called for radical revisions. The non-Russian parties agreed that CFE should be adapted to new circumstances, but not until after the three year reduction period ended in late 1995. A Review Conference in May 1996 made several concessions to Russia at the expense of neighbouring states, and a CFE Adaptation Conference began in Vienna in January 1997. If the three Baltic states want to protect their interests vis-à-vis Russia they would be well advised to rejoin the CFE regime as soon as possible.

Gorbachev and the CFE Treaty

During the Cold War European security was thought to depend in large part on maintaining a stable military balance between two adversarial military alliances: the US-led North Atlantic Treaty Organisation (NATO) and the Warsaw Treaty

Organisation (WTO) dominated by the Soviet Union. Relations between the two blocs fluctuated between tension and detente, but diplomatic contacts were always maintained to make sure the Cold War did not erupt into real war. Arms control diplomacy was an important factor for stability during these years. The pace was plodding and incremental and the goals modest: to build confidence and trust between potential adversaries and to codify the status quo when balance had been reached in various indices of military power. Deep cuts in military forces were not anticipated through negotiation, though were sometimes achieved by unilateral actions. Agreements took years, even decades, to conclude and usually reflected rather than affected the state of East-West relations.

Mikhail Gorbachev changed all this when he assumed the leadership of the Communist Party of the Soviet Union in 1985. He used arms control as a tool to change relations not only between the Soviet Union and the West, but also between the Soviet Union and its WTO allies. Gorbachev was impatient with the pace of traditional diplomacy, and with the preoccupation of his military staff to codify parity with NATO and to prevent any intrusive inspection of Soviet territory.

Gorbachev's first innovation was to allow foreign inspectors onto Soviet territory to verify the Confidence and Security Building Measures negotiated at the 1986 Stockholm Conference of the pan-European Conference on Security and Cooperation in Europe. This new openness also facilitated the conclusion in 1987 of a Soviet-American Treaty banning intermediate range nuclear forces.

Gorbachev was especially impatient with the long running NATO-WTO negotiations towards mutual and balanced force reductions (MBFR) that had been under way in Vienna since 1973 with no tangible result. He believed the Soviet economy required deep cuts in military spending and suggested that instead of building up to parity, NATO and the WTO states would do better to build down. Specifically, Gorbachev said that which ever side was ahead in a particular category of weapons should be the one to make reductions. Gorbachev put this idea into practice in December 1988 at the United Nations when he announced unilateral withdrawals of Soviet troops from Central Europe.

Gorbachev's proposals rendered the MBFR talks redundant and more purposeful talks to limit conventional armaments began in March 1989. These produced the CFE Treaty in November 1990, which set equal ceilings for NATO and the WTO in tanks, armoured combat vehicles (ACVs), artillery over 100mm calibre, combat aircraft and combat helicopters. CFE mandated the destruction of some 50,000 pieces of treaty limited equipment (TLE) during a three year reduction period (1992-95), and established a regime of inspections and exchanges of information designed to make each alliance virtually transparent to the other, thereby removing the threat of surprise attack.

NATO and Central Europe judged CFE an unambiguous success and gave Gorbachev much of the credit. The problem, however, was that Gorbachev and his Foreign Minister, Eduard Shevardnadze, did not carry the Soviet military with them in their conciliatory overtures to the West. The Soviet General Staff did not veto the signing of CFE in November 1990, but did their best to sabotage the

Treaty and evade its provisions. Senior Soviet military officers resented CFE because more WTO equipment had to be destroyed than on the NATO side. As WTO and the Soviet empire collapsed, CFE became even more humiliating, codifying Russian inferiority vis-à-vis NATO, even if Russia remained the most powerful state in Europe. German unification in 1990, plus the desire of the three Baltic states and all the former European members of the WTO to join NATO, exacerbated Russia's sense of loss.

The Baltic Opt-out

It was to bolster Soviet interest in ratifying CFE that the US and Soviet delegates to the Joint Consultative Group (JCG) – set up to resolve ambiguities in compliance with CFE – decided not to include the independent Baltic states in 1991. Several smaller European states, especially in Central Europe would have preferred to keep the Baltic states inside the CFE regime. Poland, for example, argued that a Baltic opt-out would disrupt the unity of the region; that the Baltics would benefit from the transparency of the compliance regime; and that Baltic entitlements would be at the expense of the Soviet Union and therefore beneficial to the near neighbours (Nowak 1996: 241; Falkenrath 1996: 173-76).

At that time, the Balts themselves did not appear convinced of the benefits of joining the Treaty as independent states, largely because their main goal was distance from Moscow's influence after decades of Soviet occupation, and especially after the spate of violence perpetrated by Soviet OMON troops in January 1991. On the night of 12-13 January, Soviet OMON troops attacked the main Television transmitter in Vilnius, Lithuania, killing thirteen and injuring many more. On 20 January OMON troops also attacked the Latvian Interior Affairs ministry in Riga, killing several people (Jundzis N.a.; ISS Strategic Survey 1991-92: 16 f.). Not surprisingly then, in December 1991, President Vytautus Landsbergis argued against accession to CFE because he was 'unwilling to legalise the presence of Soviet troops' on Lithuanian territory (Clough 1991).

Others objected, fearing that a Baltic opt-out could encourage any additional states that might secede from the Soviet Union to also secede from CFE. Ambassador Lynn Hansen, head of the US delegation to the JCG, argued, however, that because the Western democracies never recognised Stalin's annexation of the Baltic states, they were in a different category from other Soviet states and would not set a precedent.

Lynn Hansen was more worried that having the Baltics remain in the CFE regime would complicate ratification and entry into force of the Treaty. For example, as parties to the Treaty in 1991 the Baltics could have claimed a share of Soviet equipment on their territory as well as inspection rights over military bases on Soviet territory. While acquiring these rights might seem good reasons for the Balts to adhere to the Treaty, Hansen feared that independent Baltic states would not be acceptable as CFE parties to the Soviet General Staff, who in any case never liked CFE and were always looking for an excuse to evade their CFE obligations. In 1991 Hansen judged that the main American interest was thus to move the Soviets towards ratification of CFE, and entry into force without delay.

Conditions of the Baltic Opt-out

Once Hansen and his counterparts had decided on the Baltic opt-out, Hansen visited all three Baltic states between 15-17 October, 1991, to let government leaders know they would not be part of the CFE regime and to urge them not to lay any claims to Soviet equipment on their territory. The Baltic leaders raised no objections. They were more interested in how the US could expedite the withdrawal of Soviet troops from their territories.

There were three parts to the Baltic opt-out. The first was a redefinition of the zone of application of CFE (Article II) to exclude the territory of the three Baltic states. In effect all that was then left of the old Soviet Baltic Military District was the Russian oblast of Kaliningrad now isolated from the rest of Russia by its Polish and Lithuanian neighbours. Secondly, the Soviet Union made a legally binding statement that as long as Soviet troops and equipment remained on Baltic territory, they would be subject to all provisions of the CFE Treaty, including information exchange, inspections, reduction and destruction obligations. In a separate statement the US assured the Baltic governments that they would be kept informed of all details of Soviet deployments on their territory – information to which the Balts had not been privy as Soviet republics. Thirdly, inspection of Soviet equipment on Baltic territory in accordance with CFE provisions would only occur with the consent and co-operation of the Baltic governments.

These three conditions were unanimously adopted by the CFE Joint Consultative Group meeting in Vienna on 18 October 1991. Poland and Hungary registered their objections but did not veto the agreement.[1]

The Baltic states soon began to rethink the wisdom of their decision to go along with the opt-out and asked if they could join the High Level Working Group which was established in December 1991 (at the suggestion of outgoing German Foreign Minister Hans Dietrich Genscher) to oversee the bringing into force of the CFE after dissolution of the Soviet Union.

Although Gorbachev announced the withdrawal of Soviet troops from central Europe in December 1988, it was 1994 before all Russian troops left Germany. There were various reasons for the delays, not least that there were often no barracks for the soldiers to return to in Russia.[2] The Baltics achieved independence in September 1991, and here again Russian troops did not leave until late 1994. In this case delays were due to Russian claims that the rights of Russian nationals were being abused, disputes over rights of residence for Russian military pensioners, and complaints that criteria for citizenship discriminated against Russian speakers. In Latvia Russia insisted on being able to use its radar base at Skrunda until 1998.

Russian Efforts to Revise CFE

Russia's unhappiness with CFE stemmed largely from the general sense of humiliation associated with the loss of East Germany, as well as the collapse of the Warsaw Pact and the Soviet Union. The need to find accommodation for Russian troops withdrawing from former Soviet bases in Central Europe and the Baltic states also highlighted Russian dissatisfaction with the zonal arrangements of the Treaty.

These zones were designed by NATO to prevent destabilising concentrations of Russian troops. Article IV of the Treaty defined the territory, and set equipment levels, for four zones, nested together like a Matrushka doll. Article V defined and set force limits for the outer Flank Zone. This arrangement permitted the movement of equipment away from, but not towards, Central Europe, thereby inhibiting surprise attack in what (throughout the Cold War) was considered the most vulnerable part of Europe. This arrangement suited the Central European states, but generated some anxiety in NATO flank states Norway and Turkey, who feared greater concentrations of Russian forces on their borders. These two states thus insisted during the initial CFE negotiations (1989-90) on adding restrictions about how much equipment could be kept in active units and how much in storage in the Flank Zone.

Russia complained, with some justification, that once the Soviet Union had devolved into its constituent republics in 1991, the zonal arrangements became discriminatory for Russia and Ukraine, the only state parties whose territory straddled more than one zone and who were restricted as to where they could deploy treaty limited equipment, even within their own national borders.

CFE provides for the convening of Extraordinary Conferences should changed circumstances require adaptation of the Treaty. Three such conferences were held during the early 1990s: in 1991 to settle disputes over Soviet data; in 1992 to adjust to the dissolution of the Soviet Union; and in 1993 to note the separation of the Czech and Slovak republics. In September 1993 Russia asked NATO to convene a fourth Extraordinary Conference to revise Article V of the Treaty, which set limits for the Flank Zone.[3]

The NATO states, who had devised the zones for sensible strategic reasons, were naturally reluctant to revise that aspect of the Treaty, even though the US, Germany and the UK expressed some sympathy for the Russian predicament. Turkey and Norway as the NATO flank states closest to Russia were the most resistant to changing Article V and the most anxious to maintain tight control on Russian forces.

Had NATO dealt with the Flank problem when Russia first raised it in 1993, all might have been well. In the event, however, the problem was allowed to fester until 1995, by which time Russia had moved even more equipment into the southern part of the Flank to conduct its war against Chechnya. Most NATO states were then reluctant to make any concessions on Article V lest they seem to condone Russian brutality in the Caucasus.

The result was that the CFE reduction period ended in November 1995 with Russia in violation of two key provisions: not only Article V, but also a politically binding commitment of June 1991 to destroy the equipment moved east of the Urals by the Soviet Union just before Treaty signature in 1990.

The CFE Review Conference

In the two week CFE Review Conference in May 1996, it was not possible to address major revisions of the Treaty, for example whether treaty limited equipment ceilings should be reduced overall and whether NATO enlargement required a change from group to national ceilings. The Review Conference focused primarily on papering over Russian violations; which meant, inter alia, bullying all state parties to accept yet another deal that had been pre-cooked in bilateral discussions between Washington and Moscow. Under pressure from the Clinton Administration the other CFE parties agreed to both reduce the size of the Russian Flank and increase the allocation of Russian tanks, artillery and armoured combat vehicles (ACVs) in the newly expanded Central Zone IV.2 (Final Document 1996) .

The Russian Flank, was reduced by redefining several oblasts as part of the Central Zone. Specifically, the oblast of Pskov in the north and the oblasts of Volgograd and Astrakhan, as well as parts of Rostov and Krasnador Kray in the south, were all redefined as belonging to Central Zone IV.2. In a similar gesture to Ukraine, the oblast of Odessa was transferred to Zone IV.3 (see Figure 26.1).

In the reduced Flank the Russian ceilings for tanks, artillery and ACVs remained the same as for the original Flank. Russian TLE ceilings were raised for the territory covered by the original Flank, but with some restrictions on where the extra equipment could be deployed. Russian ceilings for the old Flank territory were now set at 1,800 tanks (500 more than before), 2,400 artillery pieces (720 more than before), and 3,700 ACVs (720 more than before). Of the ACVs, no more than 600 may be deployed in Pskov, no more than 310 in the eastern part of Rostov, no more than 552 in Volgograd and no more than 552 in Astrakhan. Russia was given three more years to meet its new obligations, i.e. until May 1999, and allowed another easy opt-out in a unilateral Russian statement attached to the Final Document, namely, 'If the flexibilities listed in the agreement on the flank issue are not realised by 31 May 1999 the Russian Federation retains the right to use other treaty flexibilities discussed but not mentioned in the above arrangements.'[4] In exchange for these concessions Russia promised not to increase its current holdings in the old Flank from their May 1996 levels of 1,897 tanks, 2,411 artillery pieces and 4,397 ACVs.

Not surprisingly, the Russian Defence Minister, General Pavel Grachev, expressed himself well pleased and saw the NATO concessions as vindication of Russian demands for revision of the Flank ceilings. Many Europeans, however, feared that acquiescence in Russian violations set a dangerous precedent. Several

CFE parties were also irritated by another bilateral US-Russian deal at the expense of the security interests of small states contiguous or close to Russian territory: Norway and Turkey in NATO, as well as former Soviet states Moldova, Georgia, Ukraine, Azerbaijan and Armenia.[5]

Estonia, Latvia and Lithuania were also upset by the Final Document of the Review Conference, especially by the fact that Russian equipment in Pskov was no longer to be counted in the Flank limits. In June the Baltic Assembly's Foreign Affairs and Security Committee issued a statement that criticised Russian violation of CFE and complained that the US had not provided a reasonable explanation of the concessions made to Moscow.[6] This was the second time in the CFE context that the US had made concessions to Moscow at the expense of Baltic interests. Had the Balts been parties to CFE in 1996, they would at least have been able to raise their voices against the concessions.

Adaptation of CFE to Post-Cold War Europe

Three issues dominate the debate about adapting CFE to the new political realities in Europe: in the context of NATO enlargement, whether group ceilings should give way to national limits and whether the zonal arrangements need to be further modified; and whether CFE limits should be imposed on all the OSCE states throughout Europe.

Russian Opposition to NATO Enlargement

During 1995 several senior Russian foreign ministry spokesmen articulated seven conditions that would make NATO enlargement more palatable to Russia: no forward-based nuclear weapons; no forward-based troops; no hasty enlargement to upset the 1996 Russian elections; no permanent exclusion of Russia; new NATO members should remain (as France and Spain then were) outside NATO's integrated military command; no NATO exercises on former Warsaw Pact territory; and revision of the CFE Treaty. When Yevgeniy Primakov replaced Andrey Kozyrev as Foreign Minister he emphasised the 'no nukes no troops' conditions, but also spoke of no forward movement of NATO infrastructure onto the territory of new NATO states.[7] Russia also argued that the pan-European Organisation for Security and Cooperation in Europe (OSCE) should replace NATO as the main security organisation in Europe.

After the WTO and the Soviet Union collapsed in 1991, NATO adopted manifestly conciliatory policies towards all the former WTO states, including all the former Soviet republics, but NATO could obviously brook no outside interference in the running of its internal structures. An obvious way to assuage some of Russia's hostility to enlargement, however, was to pay more attention to requests to modify CFE. Paragraph 19 of the Final Document of the CFE Review Conference in May 1996 mandated the JCG to start a process 'aimed at improving the operation of the Treaty in a changing environment' and noted that 'the scope and parameters (of the process) should be defined as a matter of priority.' Accordingly, the JCG presented a document at the OSCE summit meeting in Lisbon in early December 1996, which laid out the aims and objectives, principles, scope and timetable for the adaptation of CFE (JCG Working Group B 1996).

The OSCE agreed that the CFE state parties should open negotiations to modify CFE in Vienna in mid-January 1997. Without making any specific promises or proposals, NATO agreed to review the following issues: the bloc-to-bloc structure of CFE; how NATO enlargement affects the CFE ceilings; the possibility of putting excess equipment into secure storage rather than destroying it all; and the possible extension of the scope of CFE to cover new states. NATO was not, however, prepared to limit new categories of weapons.

Group versus National Ceilings

The prospect of enlargement adds grist to the mill of those like France and Russia who want to move from group ceilings to national limits. In 1989-90, at the insistence of France, whose policy makers always dislike acting under any kind of alliance discipline, and Hungary and Poland, whose leaders were anxious to be free of Soviet influence, the 1990 CFE Treaty was de jure an agreement between individual states not alliances. De facto, however, CFE set equal ceilings on the heavy military equipment of NATO and the former Warsaw Treaty Organisation (WTO) in the Atlantic to the Urals area of application, and was widely perceived as a bloc-to-bloc arrangement. Once the WTO and the Soviet Union collapsed, the Russians thus began to claim that CFE had been overtaken by events.

France and Russia, who are the strongest advocates of national versus group ceilings, had not by late 1996 offered any specific proposals as to how national ceilings would work. In London, British officials asked how national limits would apply in the different zones and especially how they would apply to US holdings of TLE, since US territory is not within the Treaty area of application. In the Joint Consultative Group, Britain argued that the original rationale for zones – to avoid destabilising concentrations of forces in Europe – was still an important goal. Even though NATO caved in to the Russians over the Flank limits at the May 1996 Review Conference, Britain urged retention of the zonal concept in any revisions of the treaty structure. Thus in all NATO and JCG documents dealing with CFE adaptation, the British government has insisted on retaining a commitment to zonal arrangements.

Hungary, one of the strongest opponents of a bloc-to-bloc approach in the initial 1989-90 CFE negotiations, grew more cautious as an aspirant to NATO membership. In May 1996, Gabor Iklody, Deputy Head of the Department for Security and Co-operation in Europe in the Hungarian Ministry of Foreign Affairs, said that Hungary was prepared to change the bloc-to-bloc approach to CFE eventually, 'but this cannot be done now.'[8]

The 20 February Proposals
In time for Madeleine Albright's first visit to Moscow as US Secretary of State, NATO's High Level Task Force (HLTF) came up with a set of proposals for CFE modification, designed to meet Russian concerns. The key elements of the proposal were:

- the bloc-to-bloc nature of the Treaty would be abolished (to reflect NATO's interest in an undivided Europe) and each CFE party would now have a ceiling for its own national equipment levels;
- the flank regime as modified by the CFE Review Conference in May 1996 would be retained;
- apart from the flank zone, the former subzones would be replaced by a system of territorial ceilings designed to stop any destabilising build-up of forces;
- equipment ceilings in Central Europe (defined as the four Visegrad countries plus Belarus, Ukraine, and the Russian Military District of Kaliningrad) would be frozen at the level of current CFE entitlements, to demonstrate to Russia and the other CIS parties that NATO enlargement will not mean a build-up of Western forces in the new NATO countries;
- the current NATO-16 are willing to make substantial reductions from current entitlements, again to demonstrate that NATO enlargement need not mean an increase of NATO capability in heavy equipment;
- CFE should be open to other European states to join;
- the information and verification provisions should be enhanced to improve the transparency of the compliance regime (NATO High Level Task Force 1997).

The territorial ceilings, designed to permit states to have forces of other allies stationed on their territory, must not exceed current national entitlements for the so-called stability zone. Thus if these states wish (as the new NATO members may) to host NATO troops, they must give up some of their own national forces.

Ceilings may be temporarily exceeded for the purpose of conducting exercises, in which cases notification must be given to all CFE parties.

Should CFE be Harmonised throughout the OSCE Region?
One of the HLTF proposals was to expand the membership of the CFE regime, which has been on the agenda since 1992. As soon as CFE entered into force, the parties began to discuss how to harmonise the CFE regime throughout the territory of the OSCE, under the auspices of the Forum for Security Cooperation in Vienna. There has been little, if any, progress, not least because military planners in neutral states like Finland and Sweden are reluctant to accept the degree of transparency in the CFE compliance regime. The neutrals believe their national security depends on keeping their mobilisation plans secret. There seems to be a consensus, however, that as new states join NATO, they should also adhere to CFE. Those likely to join the alliance in the first wave in 1999 are already CFE

parties: Poland, Hungary and the Czech Republic. The only European states that still hope for NATO membership and are not already in the CFE regime are the Baltic and Balkan states. Of the latter, some of the former Yugoslavian states (Bosnia, Croatia and Serbia-Montenegro) are part of the post-Dayton arms control regime, which is modelled on CFE. Annex 1-B of the Dayton Agreement also provides for a wider Balkan arms control regime that might include states like Albania and Macedonia. Should all these states be accepted into the CFE regime, with NATO and all the former WTO states, there would of course be little need for a separate Balkan regime.

Security Options for Estonia, Latvia and Lithuania

Since achieving independence, the Baltic states have decided their future security requires them to join Western institutions. They are on track for joining the European Union, having signed Association Agreements, but this is a painfully slow process for former Communist countries who must adjust to a free market economy and strict environmental standards. Accession to NATO will also be slow as the Baltic states will not be in the next phase of NATO enlargement.

There are a number of reasons for this. The most disappointing from the Baltic perspective is that other NATO countries are only lukewarm about having them in the alliance. In NATO, only Denmark can be said to be enthusiastic about Baltic membership. Sweden and Finland as non-NATO states have no say in the matter, although both have expressed concern that to enlarge NATO without including the Baltics could undermine security throughout the region. It is not always clear whether these statements imply that the Balts should join NATO or that NATO should not be enlarged.

No-one in NATO would question that the three Baltic states have greater need for security guarantees than the three Central European states that are to become the next entrants: Poland, Hungary and the Czech Republic. Overriding Baltic desires and interests, however, are NATO anxieties about encircling the Russian oblast of Kaliningrad by NATO states and about unresolved minority and border disputes between Russia and the Balts. Russia has been quite shameless at playing on these NATO sensitivities, claiming that Baltic membership of NATO would be absolutely intolerable.[9] Some Russian publications even lay out specific scenarios for Russian re-occupation of the three Baltic states should they be accepted into NATO.[10] Others suggest the need for a corridor linking Kaliningrad with the rest of Russia (*The Economist* 1996).

These provocative Russian statements, combined with graphic TV reportage of the war in Chechnya, suggested to many that Russia after the Cold War was not so very different from the Soviet Union under Leonid Brezhnev. It thus heightened the desire of all Central Europeans, including the three Baltic states, to join Western institutions as soon as possible.

The major NATO powers did not handle Russian hostility to NATO enlargement at all well. By pandering to Russian concerns in a number of bilateral meetings, by turning a blind eye to Russian CFE violations and especially by condoning the Russian actions in Chechnya, Western leaders encouraged Russia to believe it was making headway with its anti-NATO campaign and generated ever more shrill objections to enlargement. As NATO's actions over the summer of 1997 testified, the Alliance did not sacrifice the interests of the three leading Central European candidates, but it did defer to Russia over the Baltic states at least for some time to come.

Already in Oslo in September 1996, to mention one example, US Defence Secretary William Perry announced that the three Baltic states were not yet ready for NATO membership. Perry was careful to leave the door open and emphasised that not yet did not mean never, but the Balts were disappointed nevertheless. In March 1997, at the US-Russian summit in Helsinki, Clinton apparently made no promises to Yeltsin about leaving out the Baltic states over the long term, though he probably repeated Perry's judgement that none of the Balts would be in the first round. Since Helsinki, however, the US has offered the three Baltic states a separate interim security agreement. As the Lithuanian Foreign Minister, Algirdas Saudargas, noted, the Balts naturally hope this proposed security pact 'would not be regarded as a substitute for NATO membership, but as a path towards membership' (Thomas 1997).

As NATO membership is not on the cards, the Baltic states will be looking for additional ways to strengthen their security. One obvious path to follow is enhanced co-operation with neighbouring states at all levels: political, economic and military. In all these areas the Nordic countries are very active, not only in helping the three Baltic states, but also in encouraging the three to co-operate more with each other and increase their trade with Russia. Inter-Baltic co-operation does not come easily after decades of Soviet domination, but all the Western democracies would feel more positive about the Baltics as partners if they first demonstrated regional co-operation. There are serious problems that need attention, such as fishing and oil exploration rights off their coastlines, so co-operation is essential (Girnius 1997)

In August 1996, the Swedish Prime Minister sought American support for Sweden's five part strategy for Baltic integration. This included more bilateral activities such as those in which Nordic countries train the Balts in peace-keeping and participate jointly in the Baltic Battalion (BALTBAT) in NATO's Implementation and Stabilisation forces in Bosnia (IFOR and SFOR). The second element of the Swedish strategy was to promote enhanced regional co-operation among all the Baltic Sea nations. The third was to promote EU membership for all three Baltic states. The fourth to encourage more activities under NATO's Partnership for Peace (PfP) programme. And the fifth was to increase the Baltic dialogue with Russia (Boustany 1996).

Sweden and Finland are both active in PfP, and some have suggested that the best model for the Baltic states would be to restructure their military forces according to the example of Finland and Sweden, two Baltic Rim states that joined the EU, but do not feel threatened by Russia and at least for the time being have retained non-aligned political and military defence postures (Asmus and Nurick 1996). Unfortunately, however, credible neutrality and non-alignment requires more robust defences and higher defence budgets than any of the Baltic states currently contemplate.

A better option might be to rejoin the CFE Treaty to benefit from the confidence-building aspects of the compliance regime.

The two options – that is following in the footsteps of Finland and Sweden, and rejoining the CFE – appear incompatible because Finland and Sweden have decided that the degree of transparency inherent in the CFE regime would undermine the secrecy and effectiveness of their mobilisation procedures. Nevertheless, for weaker states like Estonia, Latvia and Lithuania, greater transparency would be a worthwhile price to pay for belonging to a regime of rigorous inspection and information exchanges.

Notes

1 Statement of the Chairman of the Joint Consultative Group 18 October 1991, reprinted in *The Arms Control Reporter 1991*, page 407.D.83.
2 Russian troops did not leave Germany until late August 1994, see Shulte (1994).
3 Article V of the CFE Treaty defined the Flank Zone as the NATO territories of Iceland, Norway, Greece and Turkey; and the former WTO and Soviet territories of Bulgaria, Romania, Georgia, Moldova, Armenia and Azerbaijan as well as Russia's Leningrad and North Caucusus Military Districts and the Odesssa Military District in Ukraine.
4 Unilateral Russian statement of 31 May 1996.
5 Ukraine, Turkey, Georgia and Moldova registered their objections in unilateral statemets attached to the final document from the CFE Review Conference.
6 *Arms Control Reporter 1996*, page 407.B.541, citing Vilnius Radio on 9 June 1996.
7 Author interview with Primakov in Moscow in April 1996.
8 Cited by Fournier and Kokkinides (1996: 3 f.).
9 Yeltin's press service release on 'Long term guidelines on Baltic states,' ITAR-TASS News Agency, 11 February 1997, cited in SWB 42b/10.
10 Anton Surikov interview, 'Who Is Dying to Get under the Wing,' *Sovetskaya Rossiya*, 2 November 1995. Surikov was also one of the authors of a paper published by the Russian Institute of Defence Studies, reprinted in *Segodnya*, 20 October 1995.

References

Asmus, Ronald D. and Nurick, Robert C. (1996). 'NATO Enlargement and the Baltic States,' *Survival*, Summer, pages 121-42.

Boustany, Nora (1996). 'Sweden Seeking US Support for Baltic Integration Plan,' *International Herald Tribune*, 10 August.

Clough, Patricia (1991). 'Lithuanian Threat to Arms Pact," *The Independent*, 7 December.

The Economist (1996). 'Corridor Collywobbles,' 4 May, page 36.

Falkenrath, Richard (1996). 'The Baltic Settlement' in Kelleher, Catherine M., Sharp, Jane M.O. and Freedman, Lawrence (eds.). *The Treaty on Conventional Armed Forces in Europe: The Politics of Post-Wall Arms Control.* Baden-Baden, Nomos Verlagsgesellschaft.

Final Document of the first conference to review the operation of the Treaty on Conventional Forces in Europe and the Concluding Act of the Negotiation on Personnel Strength Vienna 15-31 May 1996, reprinted in The Arms Control Reporter, pages 407.D.87-97.

Fournier, Sami and Kokkinides, Tasos (1996). 'East-West Differences May Impede Progress at CFE Review Conference,' *Basic Reports*:52, 13 May.

Girnius, Saulius (1997). 'Back in Europe to Stay,' *Transition*:3(6), 4 April, pages 7-10.

IISS Strategic Survey 1991-1992.

JCG Working Group B (1996). '*Document adopted by the States Parties to the Treaty on Conventional Armed Forces in Europe on the scope and parameters of the process commissioned in paragraph 19 of the Fial Document of the First CFE Review Conference*,' 1 December 1996, Vienna.

Jundzis, Talavs (N.a.) 'Security Policy Trends in Latvia.'

NATO High Level Task Force (1997). *Basic Elements for Adaptation of the CFE Treaty.* HLTF (97) 2 (Final), 20 February 1997, Brussels.

Nowak, Jerzy M. 1996). 'The CFE Regime and Its Development: A Polish and Central European Perspective' in Kelleher, Catherine M., Sharp, Jane M.O. and Freedman, Lawrence (eds.). *The Treaty on Conventional Armed Forces in Europe: The Politics of Post-Wall Arms Control.* Baden-Baden, Nomos Verlagsgesellschaft.

Shulte, Heinz (1994). 'Germany's Unfond Farewell to the Russians,' *The Wall Street Journal*, 31 August 1994.

Surikov, Anton interview (1995). 'Who Is Dying to Get under the Wing,' *Sovetskaya Rossiya*, 2 November 1995.

Thomas, Richard (1997). 'US Moves to Quell Baltic NATO Fears,' *The Guardian*, 29 March.

27 Settled and Remaining Border Issues around the Baltic Sea

Tuomas Forsberg[1]

The Territorial Question

World history is often depicted in terms of a struggle over power which culminates in territorial changes. According to this view, when power relations change and empires fall, previously stable areas are hit by territorial turmoil and new border adjustments. The end of the Cold War and the disintegration of the Soviet Union were no exception: in the Baltic Sea area they resulted in German unification and the regaining of independence of the three Baltic republics. Other territorial questions emerged, some as a consequence of these changes of borders, some due to a reborn speculation in re-establishing other historical borders.

Alexander Sergounin has recently assessed that these territorial issues are not as important as some other issues but that they are still a potential source of dangerous tension (Sergounin 1997). Indeed, one might argue that after the end of the Cold War, territorial questions have played a minor role in the Baltic Sea region. Intellectually, the puzzle is not the existence of some territorial issues but rather their non-existence. Despite various possible reasons for making territorial claims, the Baltic Sea area has been relatively free from territorial conflicts, at least when compared to other border areas of the ex-Soviet Union and the Balkans.

There are generally three common explanations of why territorial disputes have not emerged. The first explanation is that there is no rationale for territorial expansion any longer. The fear of war is seen as minimal, or in any case, territory is not strategically important. In short, territory is not valuable for 'trading states' who benefit more from trade than from territorial control. The second explanation is that power relations, after all, do not give rise to territorial disputes. According to this view, potential claimant states have concluded that it does not benefit them to raise border questions because the other state would not budge. The third explanation is that post-nationalist identities and norms of territorial status quo are preventing disputes from arising. Those who are familiar with basic theories of international relations would – with some reservations – say that the first explanation is liberal, the second realist and the last constructivist. I think that all these theories may partly explain why territorial disputes have not risen in the Baltic Sea area. They are not exclusionary explanations but can be combined, at least to a certain extent.

A Legacy of Instability

Historically, borders in Baltic Sea area have been anything but stable. Attempts to gain hegemony by Danes, Germans, Swedes and Russians and the resistance against these attempts resulted in numerous wars and territorial changes in the course of the past centuries. Despite this belligerent history, the Baltic Sea area also provides one of the most famous example of successful resolution of a territorial dispute in the inter-war period, namely the Åland Islands question. Despite the contrary wishes of the islanders, the dispute was decided by the League of Nations in favour of Finland. Instead of self-determination, the decision was based on the principle of status quo.

Both World Wars brought about major changes in the Baltic Sea area. The inter-war period was characterised by territorial tensions. By contrast, the territorial status quo of the Cold War period was regarded as firm, but this belief proved to be an illusion. The situation changed drastically when the Soviet Union was dissolved and the prior territorial stability was gone. As compared to the aftermath of the First World War, the current process has been peaceful, and territorial questions have been less intense despite numerous potential issues of conflict.

A good example of the current territorial complexities in the Baltic Sea area which have been inherited from the past is the Kaliningrad area. It used to be a part of the former East Prussia, with Königsberg being the centre of the region for several hundreds years. The area was annexed by the Soviet Union at the end of the Second World War and was one of the decisive naval bases of the Soviet defence system. After the end of the Cold War, it has suddenly become a Russian enclave cut off from the main Russian territory. For historical and strategic reasons it would have been conceivable that Lithuania, Poland or Germany might have been interested in the area. None of these states, however, has presented any territorial claims, and very few people in these countries are actually arguing for border changes. But the location of Kaliningrad has not been without problems dealing especially with transit of Russian forces and cargoes. Russians accused the Baltic states of trying to isolate the area and proposed a permanent corridor. Whereas Belarus agreed in principle, both Lithuania and Poland rejected the proposal, which was quickly withdrawn. Lithuania allows Russian transits on a temporary basis. It has declined to sign a treaty but has accepted to extend the current regulation.[2]

The reason why territorial disputes have not emerged on a large scale is not to do with power relations alone. Were it so, one would have expected Germany lay claims on Kaliningrad or on Silesia in Poland. But it has abstained from any such moves. This has been seen as a major stabilising factor in the area, since especially the Poles would become anxious if there were any doubt about the German commitment to Oder-Neisse line.

Even more importantly, Russia has consistently insisted on the inviolability of present borders, despite the fact that millions of ethnic Russians now live outside Russian state borders. Moscow has been concerned about the Russian minorities in Estonia and Latvia, and it has constantly criticised the two countries for discrimination arguing that their citizenship laws deny the right of citizenship to many ethnic Russians or require them to learn Estonian or Latvian. Although the controversy has sometimes been regarded in terms of a territorial conflict since, for example, Estonia's north-eastern areas are overwhelmingly – in places more than to 90 per cent – Russian, Russia has refrained from any territorial claims. Despite minor border incidents and some speculations based on threats made by Russian nationalists such as Vladimir Zhirinovskiy, a territorial conflict seems unlikely. The fact that the Governor of the neighbouring the Pskov region belongs to the party of Zhirinovskiy has nevertheless created some worries among the Balts.

The Stance of the Baltic Republics

Lithuania has stated that it has no territorial claims on any of its neighbours, nor have any of the neighbours claims on Lithuania. As has often been pointed out, Lithuania is a beneficiary of the status quo because its present capital, Vilnius, was part of Poland before the Second World War. In 1991, Russia and Lithuania signed an agreement of co-operation on economic and socio-cultural development of the Kaliningrad area. The agreement included a clause on the integrity of the border, which is to follow the old German-Lithuanian border. Some controversy over the boundary demarcation emerged in the summer of 1996, because Lithuanians wanted the border to cross Lake Vistytis so as to allow Lithuanians to fish in it. Despite the hopes among some Lithuanians of some day 'recovering' Kaliningrad, the border is generally unchallenged and the demarcation problems have not been severe.

Lithuania has also confirmed its border against Belarus. At first, there was some concern that Belarus might raise a territorial claim stretching perhaps as far as Vilnius. The issue was discussed by the Belarussian parliament, but no demand was presented. Again, however, the exact delimitation of the border in USSR documents proved to be confusing and complicated. As the Lithuanian Defence Minister Audrius Butkevicius stated, 'the frontier of Belarus was drawn by Stalin with a thick red pen on a small map' (Reuters Library Report 1992).

As to Lithuania's borders in the north and south, serious conflicts were likewise avoided. For historical reasons there were fears in Lithuania that Poland might raise territorial claims. Despite several reassurances that Poland would respect Lithuania's territorial integrity, many Lithuanians did not believe that

Poland had buried the issue. In 1994, the countries concluded a treaty on friendly relations and good neighbourly co-operation declaring that neither had territorial claims on the other and would not have such claims in the future 'independently of the processes of the formation of their borders in the past' (Burant 1996). Finally, also Lithuania and Latvia decided to stick with their old border. This agreement was eased by the fact that they had solved their border problems already during the inter-war period. Although meetings held in 1993 revealed some problems, an agreement was achieved in March 1994.

Unlike Lithuania, Latvia and Estonia did raise territorial claims against Russia. Border questions have proved to be more enduring although less intense than was the question of the withdrawal of Russian troops from the Baltic states. The restoration of the Latvian-Belarussian border, however, has not involved any territorial problems.

Estonia has disputed two strips of land in the north-east and south-east, namely the Pechory and Ivangorod areas which were transferred to Russia at the end of the Second World War. These areas are small, and they are populated mainly by Russians. In the Pechory area there is a small Setu minority. It is also a railway junction as well as a site of a famous monastery. The dispute stems from the Estonian view which is enshrined in the constitution that the only valid border treaty between Estonia and Russia is the Tartu Peace Treaty of 1920. The border dispute has remained a persistent issue in Russian-Estonian relations, with Estonians demanding the recognition of Tartu Peace Treaty and protesting the unilateral demarcation of the border by Russia – a demarcation some Estonians have regarded as the technical equivalent of war. The dispute has also been manifest in several demonstrations organised by the Petserimaa movement and border incidents including a bicycle march of 2000 people trying to cross the border at Pechory. As a symbolic gesture, Estonia has also issued Estonian passports for inhabitants of these pre-war Estonian territories.

Since the areas are quite small and inhabited mainly by non-Estonians, the question is not so much to do with the territories as such as with the continuity of Estonian statehood from the pre-war era. After all, Estonians think that the inclusion of these areas into Estonia would increase minority problems and be rather costly. But they have not been willing to give up their view that the Tartu Peace Treaty is the only valid document which defines the Estonian-Russian border. In the Russian view, however, the Tartu Peace Treaty is not in force. Thus, Estonian claims are seen as unjustified and as signs of hostility towards Russia.

The negative attitude towards any border change is clear. In 1994 when Russians started their demarcation operation, President Yeltsin visited the border and declared that no single inch of Russian land would be given away. The Estonian government protested but also realised that it had few possibilities of preventing Russian measures. Estonian appeals to international organisations such as the OSCE and third parties failed.

The rightist Estonian government of the Isamaa party was also increasingly criticised for its stubbornness, which not only hampered good Russian-Estonian relations but also caused other harm both internally and externally. People such as the well-known Member of Parliament Jaan Kaplinski stressed that it would be better to have a border agreement on the basis of status quo than no border agreement at all. Public opinion was divided: although a majority still supported the territorial claims, there was also readiness to accept the present border. This was expressed by the approval of the statement 'the claims are justified but one can't argue forever.' Especially ethnic Russians were in favour of dropping the territorial demands.[3]

After the change of government in late 1994, under the leadership of Prime Ministers Andres Tarand and Tiit Vahi and with the support of President Lennart Meri, Estonia has been looking for an agreement with Russia. At the end of 1995, both parties agreed that they do not have territorial claims and that the present border will be preserved. Yet, although both parties took as their point of departure the idea that the present border is unalterable, it was not easy to agree on the principles upon which this agreement can be based. Thus, although the Estonians stated that they would not dispute the issue of whether the Tartu Peace Treaty and the legal succession were valid, they still stressed that this should be regarded only as the starting point of the negotiations.

The Russians have stated that they can only recognise the Treaty's 'historical value.' Although Estonians still have difficulties in accepting such an understanding of the Treaty, they were eventually ready to reach an agreement on the present border without mentioning the Tartu Peace Treaty. The Russians have underlined that one cannot go back to pre-war history. They do not want to recognise the Treaty's validity because it would leave the door open for subsequent claims of damages caused by the occupation, and it would also have implications for the minority question. Indeed, Russians have recently tried to link the minority question to the border agreement, insisting on a package deal which would guarantee more rights to ethnic Russians in Estonia.

After the meeting between Foreign Ministers Yevgeniy Primakov and Siim Kallas in Petrozavodsk, the parties announced that they were close to solving the dispute, but for the time being, Russia refused to sign any agreement if the minority question was not included (*Reuters World Service* 1996; *The Baltic Times* 1997b). Estonians were complaining that these issues did not belong together and argued that they had now done everything to solve the issue. The proposed border itself differed only slightly from the de facto border (*Postimees* 1997). There were some differences and inconsistencies in the respective maps of the parties, but this has not been seen as very problematic. One remaining problem, however, is the fact that the agreement still has many political opponents on both sides. Even if the border agreement is signed in the near future, its ratification is not guaranteed (Moshes and Vushkarnik 1997).

Latvia has laid claim the Abrene/Pytalovo area, which was part of Latvia in the inter-war period but was then transferred to the Russian Federation. As to the background and nature of the claim, the problem is very similar to the Estonian-Russian one. The area is small and the population consists of some 20,000 people, but it has some importance as a railway crossing. The population of the area is 98 per cent Russian, but Latvia demands its return on historical grounds. As with the Estonian reference to the Tartu Peace Treaty, the Latvian position is that the Latvian-Russian border is determined by the Riga Peace Treaty of 1920. The Russian point of view is that these claims are absolutely groundless (Bungs 1995; Dauksts and Puga 1995).

In 1992, the Supreme Council of the Republic of Latvia passed a resolution 'On the non-recognition of the annexation of the town Abrene and six oblasts of Abrene.' Latvian authorities also produced maps showing these areas belonging to Latvia. These implicit territorial claims were further confirmed in 1996 by the adoption of a 'Declaration on Occupation.' Despite these resolutions, Latvia long avoided taking up the issue directly with Russia. Nevertheless, following the Estonian example, Latvia started negotiations with Russia over the border issue in April 1996. It also seems that the success of the negotiations will depend on the signing of the Estonian-Russian agreement. Although little progress was made on the territorial issue during 1996, it seemed that a compromise was getting closer in February 1997 since Latvia was no longer insisting on the recognition of the Riga Peace Treaty (*The Baltic Times* 1997a).

It is worth stressing that Latvian-Russian relations have not been entirely deadlocked. Despite major difficulties in discussing the territorial issue, Latvia and Russia have been able to agree on visa freedom for residents of the border area, on co-operative guarding of their joint border and on building a joint railway border station (*The Baltic Independent* 1994). These agreements have stabilised and simplified the life in the border area. Now it seems that the remaining issues are regarded as technical.

Intra-Baltic Disputes

In addition to the Russian-Baltic border tensions, there have been numerous territorial disputes between the Baltic states mainly concerning maritime borders. Like Latvia and Lithuania, Latvia and Estonia have confirmed their land border principally as it was in 1940 by signing an agreement in 1992. Later, however, they had what was described as a 'bitter row' over their maritime border in the Gulf of Riga including the Estonian island of Ruhnu. The disputed area provides access to rich fishing waters. Fishing incidents have been regular, and both Latvians and Estonians have fished illegally in each other's territorial waters. Estonians and Latvians have accused each other of inflexible attitudes, and the Latvian Prime Minister Andris Skele has expressed pessimism. The parties were, however, able to solve the dispute in the summer of 1996 after a long series of negotiations.[4] In February 1997, the countries agreed that fishermen of both states should be permitted to fish in each other's territorial waters (*Transboundary and Environmental News* 1997).

Latvia's controversies over her maritime border and the sharing of oil resources with Lithuania, however, remain unresolved. Latvians think that the maritime boundary should continue the line of the land boundary, whereas the Lithuanians argue that the maritime boundary should follow the latitude of the point where the boundary meets the sea. The problem stems from the fact that the land boundary runs into the Baltic Sea at an angle that is very disadvantageous to Lithuania.

The countries tentatively agreed on their maritime boundary in 1994 largely on the basis of splitting the difference. Yet the border was not demarcated, and a decision by the Latvian government to allow American and Swedish oil companies to prospect for oil in the disputed area of the continental shelf sparked the border dispute anew. The Lithuanians were protesting because they regarded that the talks as unfinished. They have insisted that the border question must be resolved before negotiations on the potential sharing of the projected oil revenues commence. In April 1996, the parties were able to agree on a border protocol, but further talks on the establishment of economic zones were still needed.[5] Both parties declared their willingness to follow the UN convention of the Law of the Sea, but the difficulties in reaching an agreement were soon revealed by the fact that they were unable to determine the exact agenda of their negotiations (Girnius 1997: 23).

Lithuania has had similar problems with Russia over the demarcation of their maritime boundary. It is believed that oil may be found in this area as well. As the Lithuanian-Russian dispute is similar to the Lithuanian-Latvian one, the talks have been awaiting an agreement with Latvia. In practice, the parties have been very close to an agreement.

The maritime border questions in the north have been less complex. Although Estonia's decision to enlarge its territorial waters met with some disapproval in Helsinki, Finland followed Estonia's example, which left only a narrow free corridor for international traffic in the Gulf of Finland. The two countries also concluded an agreement over their maritime boundaries, which permits fishing in each other's economic zones but not in territorial waters. Moreover, Russia, Finland and Estonia have concluded a tripartite treaty over maritime borders.

The Karelian Non-Issue

One potential border issue which has not evolved into an open dispute is the Karelian question between Finland and Russia. Parts of Karelia, including the Karelian Isthmus with Finland's formerly second largest town of Vyborg, and some other minor areas such as islands in the Gulf of Finland were annexed by the Soviet Union after the Winter War in 1939, and the border was confirmed again in the peace treaties of 1944 and 1947. The latter treaties also transferred the harbour town of Pechenga by the Arctic Sea to the Soviet Union.

The basic treaty between Finland and Russia signed in 1992 stipulates the boundary as a border of good neighbourly relations according to the principles of the OSCE. The article was included in the treaty because a somewhat heated public discussion on the Karelian issue had emerged in Finland. This discussion dealt only with former Finnish territories, and not with the Republic of Karelia. Despite attempts by the Tartu Peace Movement (the Finnish-Russian Peace Treaty of 1920 was also concluded in Tartu) and the Karelian Alliance (which consists mainly of former residents of the area) to sketch models for the return of Karelia and keep the question alive, the domestic support gradually faded away as the potential costs of restoring Karelia and Russia's negative attitude became manifest. Even when the idea was discussed widely, only a minority of Finns showed willingness to open negotiations over the border issue, and throughout the debate, the government held firmly to the line that Finland has no territorial claims. This stand was most strikingly represented by the head of the general staff, Gustav Hägglund according to whom strategic factors mean that Finland should not take Karelia even if it were served 'on a golden plate' (Forsberg 1995).

As Hägglund's argument shows, one of the reasons why some territorial disputes have not been raised and why some of them have been solved has been the attitude that Russia is still a major power in the region which it is unwise to provoke. The conservative turn in Russian foreign policy since 1992 effectively ended most hopes that Russia would make concessions on territorial questions. The norms of the OSCE which stress the inviolability of borders are also internalised by the states in the Baltic Sea area. The existing disputes have to do with areas where the location of the border is unclear for historical and legal reasons.

The Impact of the EU and NATO

But perhaps the most important reason why territorial disputes have not flared up is that the European Union and Western states in general have adopted a policy line according to which the Balts should resolve all their outstanding border issues. The Balts have been told that if they want to boost their chances of early accession to the EU, they need to be considered as stable states, and stability implies uncontested borders. The former President of the European Parliament, Klaus Hänsch, for example, warned that the maritime border dispute between Estonia and Latvia might endanger their admission to the EU. His point was taken seriously. As one observer noted, 'clearly Hänsch's threat had created an environment in which an agreement, however flawed, had to be reached without delay' (Taht 1997: 25). Furthermore, according to the Estonian Foreign Minister Toomas-Hendrik Ilves, Estonia's unresolved border issue with Russia has been the main barrier to the next round of enlargement (*The Baltic Times* 1996). NATO has announced similar preconditions. In other words, both Estonia and Latvia have been under constant pressure from the EU and NATO to solve their border disputes with Russia (Moshes and Vushkarnik 1997: 95).

Although this Western policy has been acknowledged and welcomed by some Russians, it has also had the effect of making the Russians less willing to settle the border issues in an attempt to prevent Estonia and Latvia from joining NATO. Some Russians have also been suspicious that the Baltic countries will renew their territorial claims in the future once they have joined NATO.[6] So far the possible enlargement of the EU to the Baltic states has not caused similar worries; on the contrary, Russia has itself made overtures to Brussels.

The Baltic Sea Area Between Conflict and Co-operation

In the Baltic Sea area, disputes over land boundaries have been more linked to the past than to the future, whereas disputes over maritime boundaries have had more to do with the future exploitation of resources such as oil and fish. In the dominant view, open border issues have been regarded as the critical indicator of whether a relationship between respective countries is conflictual or co-operative. According to Alexander Sergounin, for example, official recognition of the territorial problems would destabilise the situation (Sergounin 1997: 348). Territorial claims often fuel suspicions and impede co-operation on other political, economic, social and cultural questions. Though the territorial conflicts in the Baltic Sea area are not likely to evolve into military conflicts, they are still not political issues that are easy to discuss unless considered as purely technical matters. Borders are emotionally loaded since they are linked to the very existence and identity of states. As the Estonian and Latvian disputes with Russia have shown, principles and symbolic values have often been more important than the actual territory in question.

In this sense, borders still have a lot to do with traditional concepts of sovereignty. The boundary between the Baltic states and Russia has even been fortified in order to control border crossings effectively. At the same time, however, the Baltic Sea area is also experiencing the trend towards the decreasing importance of border functions. The wish of Baltic states to integrate with the European Union underscores both trends, which are further strengthened by the unwillingness of the Nordic states to abolish visa regulations between themselves and Baltic states if their external borders are leaking.

The challenge to the Baltic states is therefore to establish borders which may prevent smuggling, sudden refugee flows, large-scale migration and the spread of crime but will encourage tourism, cultural contacts, trade and cross-border co-operation. Russia's plans to create free economic zones in the Baltic Sea area have offered one potential, but by no means problem-free alternative, which has, however, been badly implemented.

Though one should not diminish the successes achieved in concluding border agreements following the dissolution of the Soviet Union, some territorial issues are likely to remain open. If the end of the Cold War taught us anything, it is that beliefs in the eternal continuation of territorial stability and the absence of territorial disputes in international politics may be erroneous. After all, no border agreement can guarantee that new issues will not emerge. Yet, the consequences are not necessarily as bleak as one might assume, or to put it differently: the potential danger of territorial disputes is often exaggerated.

Territorial disputes are not necessarily warlike, and ethno-nationalism is not the only basis for territorial claims in an increasingly post-sovereign Europe. Territorial disagreements will not necessarily block co-operation in general. In some regions, transborder co-operation has been able to grow despite the existence of territorial claims. I also believe, perhaps naively, that interest in a territory which belongs to another state, if it is genuine, may equally well assume co-operative forms as confrontationist ones. If this is the case, one could imagine that even when some groups or states might find a particular border illegitimate or inconvenient, border areas might become nodal points rather than impediments to co-operation. But for the time being, we are still far away from such utopias.

Notes

1 I am grateful to Pertti Joenniemi, Olav F. Knudsen, Scott Kocher, Juris Prikulis and Peter Vares for providing material for this article. I have also greatly profited from using the database of International Boundaries Research Unit at the University of Durham.

2 The emergent literature on Kaliningrad includes, e.g. Smith (1993); Dörrenbacher (1994); Wörster (1995); Wellmann (1996); Joenniemi (1996).

3 See Bungs (1994); Jääts (1995). For the public opinion polls, see *The Baltic Independent* (1994).

4 BNS News Agency, 7 June 1996. http://www-ibru.dur.ac.uk/cgi.bin/data.pl.

5 Latvian Radio, 23 April 1996. http://www-ibru.dur.ac.uk/cgi.bin/data.pl.

6 See, e.g. *Izvestiya*, 5 March 1997; according to Orttung (1997).

References

The Baltic Independent (1994). 'Public Disagrees with Politicians over Border Issue,' 23-29 September.

The Baltic Independent (1995). 'Agreements Bring Detente to Border Relations,' 23 December 1994-5 January 1995.

The Baltic Times (1996). 'Estonia and Russia Debate Border,' 19 December 1996-8 January 1997.

The Baltic Times (1997a). 'Latvia Backs off Abrene,' 6-12 March.

The Baltic Times (1997b). 'Russia Says Nyet to Border Deal,' 16-22 January.

Burant, Stephen (1995). 'Overcoming the Past: Polish Lithuanian Relations 1990-95,' *Journal of Baltic Studies*:27(4).

Bungs, Dzintra (1994). 'Seeking Solutions to Baltic-Russian Border Issues,' *RFE/RL Research Report*:3(13), pages 25-32.

Bungs, Dzintra (1995). 'Seeking Solutions' in Forsberg, Tuomas (ed.). *Contested Territory: Border Disputes at the Edge of the Former Soviet Empire.* Aldershot, Edward Elgar.

Dauksts, Bonifacijs and Puga, Arturs (1995). 'Abrene,' pages 178-87 in Forsberg, Tuomas (ed.). *Contested Territory: Border Disputes at the Edge of the Former Soviet Empire.* Aldershot, Edward Elgar.

Dörrenbacher, Heike (1994). *Die Sonderwirschaftszone Jantar von Kaliningrad (Königserg). Bilanz und Perspektiven.* Arbeitspapiere zur Internationalen Politik:81. Forschungsinsitut der Deutschen Gesellschaft für Auswärtige Politik.

Forsberg, Tuomas (1995). 'Karelia' in Forsberg, Tuomas (ed.). *Contested Territory: Border Disputes at the Edge of the Former Soviet Empire.* Aldershot, Edward Elgar.

Girnius, Saulius (1997). 'A Year of Consolidation in Latvia,' *Transition*:3(2).
Jääts, Indrek (1995). 'East of Narva and Petserimaa,' pages 188-201 in Forsberg, Tuomas (ed.). *Contested Territory: Border Disputes at the Edge of the Former Soviet Empire.* Aldershot, Edward Elgar.
Joenniemi, Pertti (1996). 'Kaliningrad: A Region in Search for a Past and a Future.' Paper prepared for international colloqium on Kaliningrad, Ostsee-Akademie, Travemünde, 3-5 November.
Moshes, Arkady and Vushkarnik, Anton (1997). 'Russia and the Baltic States: Between Co-existence and Cooperation,' *IWPS*:1. Wallisellen, Institut für Wirtschaftspolitischen Studien.
Orttung, Robert (1997). 'Patterns of Regional Development,' *Russian Regional Report*:2(9), 6 March.
Postimees (1997). 'Kust hakkab kulgema Eesti kagupiir?' 6 February.
Reuter Library Report (1992). 'Lithuania Accepts Borders Sketched by Stalin.' 9 March.
Reuter World Service (1996). 'Estonia Says Near Border Deal with Russia,' 5 November.
Sergounin, Alexander (1997). 'In Search of a New Strategy in the Baltic/Nordic Area' in Baranovsky, Vladimir (ed.). *Russia and Europe: The Emerging Security Agenda.* Oxford, Oxford University Press.
Smith, Raymond (1993). 'The Kaliningrad Region: Applications of the Civic and Ethnic Models of Nationhood,' *Journal of Baltic Studies*:24(3), pages 233-47.
Taht, John (1997). 'Estonia Proves Itself,' *Transition*:3(2).
Transboundary and Environmental News (1997). Vol. 3(3), 1-15 February.
Wellmann, Christian (1996). 'Russia's Kaliningrad Exclave at the Crossroads: The Interrelation between Economic Development and Security Politics,' *Cooperation and Conflict*:31(2), pages 161-83.
Wörster, Peter (1995). 'The Northern Part of East Prussia' in Forsberg, Tuomas (ed.). *Contested Territory: Border Disputes at the Edge of the Former Soviet Empire.* Aldershot, Edward Elgar.

28 The Security Policy Doctrines in the Nordic and Baltic Countries: Stability and Change

Clive Archer and Øyvind Jæger

Introduction

Describing relations between states often depends on the right metaphor or simile. For many years the concept of the Cold War – with its strangely mixed symbolism[1] – was the dominant framework within which European states' relations were seen. The end of that period has challenged not only the agents of states and others acting across frontiers but the study of international relations in its search for a new representation of what is perceived to be happening. A number of concepts different from those used in the Cold War have been offered to allow a better understanding of the Baltic area. A discussion has arisen as to whether the Baltic Sea has now developed into a region and, if so, whether this has consequences for the area's security, however defined. It is the contention of this chapter that, since 1991, there has been a sort of dialogue of security agendas in the Baltic Sea area with, on the one hand, the Nordic states trying to externalise social peace and institutional co-operation and, on the other hand, the Baltic states internalising ethnic division and international conflict.

Whether the Baltic Sea area is a region has itself been a matter of some discussion. There is the wider question of whether Europe should be described as a region, and thus the Nordic area as a subregion and the Baltic as a proto-region (Wæver 1991: 105), or whether the Baltic is itself 'a European subregion' (Stålvant 1993: 61). Iver Neumann claimed that regions are, as Benedict Anderson described nations (1983), imagined communities whose existence is preceded by that of region-builders who 'disseminate this imagined identity to others' (Neumann 1994: 58), and he traced the attempts in the early 1990s by politicians from the various Baltic Sea countries to fashion the region in a way that had their own state at the centre (ibid.: 67-72). Another study considered that the regionalisation of the Baltic was leading to the establishment of regime-like patterns with 'sets of implicit and explicit principles, norms, rules and decision-making procedures around which actors' expectations converge in a given area of international relations' (Petersen 1991: 129, citing Krasner's definition of regimes). Others have considered the area to be 'a European mega-region' (Joenniemi and Stålvant 1995: 28) or potential 'meso-regions' with a host of common and co-ordinated institutions and activities (Lähteenmäki 1995: 278, using Cappellin's definition). These all recognise that there is now a *commonality* in the Baltic area – between the states and peoples there – that did not exist to any great extent in the Cold War period, and that this extends to a broad security agenda for what can best be called a region-in-the-making. The security approaches of two of the major elements that have composed the area – the Nordic countries and the Baltic states – will now be examined.

The Nordic Background

Even in the Cold War period, the Nordic states were not content just to follow the power politics agenda to which the East-West division seemed to condemn them.

The Nordic approach to security can best be described as liberal institutionalist[2], containing a number of elements aimed at creating – particularly in Northern Europe – an international society based on common norms and values, rather than just a system of states interacting purely on the basis of state interests. The following are key elements in this view:

- the means best suited to assist small states in creating an international society is support of international institutions such as international law, trade and commerce, and international organisations;
- there is also the recognition that small states could best survive if the institutions of both state and society are strong and effective (as in the Nordic states themselves) and some effort is given to 'state-building';
- there is an acceptance that international relations are not limited to intergovernmental relations and that non-governmental relations and organisations have a key role in improving state-to-state relations;
- while accepting the importance of military power, there is also a belief that good economic relations and other 'low political' links could eventually neutralise the necessity for 'force-based' relationships;
- attention is thus paid to a number of 'low political' issues between states – migration, organised crime, minority questions, economic relations – as solving or lessening these could contribute positively to the creation of a security community in the region.

This is not to say that power relations were shrugged off. An awareness of the power relations in the Baltic led Finland and Sweden to recognise the Soviet Union's presence in the Baltic states, contrary to the set of beliefs set out above. Furthermore, liberal institutionalism has manifested itself slightly differently the five Nordic states.

During the latter part of the Cold War period, the Nordic states readily embraced – and developed – concepts of *common security.* Indeed, Olof Palme – the Swedish prime minister – chaired the international independent commission that made the concept of 'common security' more widely used and accepted, and an important contribution was made to the Palme report by Johan Jørgen Holst, a Norwegian academic who subsequently became Norway's defence minister and then its foreign minister.

The core of the concept of common security is the notion that security is not a 'zero-sum game,' which means that one state's security can be enhanced without other states suffering. This had very much been the idea behind the sort of restraints that the Nordic countries had introduced during the Cold War period. It was not that these countries tried to deny the power politics nature of the Cold War divide, it was just that they tried to ameliorate its impact in Northern Europe by giving consideration to each other's feelings (and to those of the Soviet Union) in their security policies.

Both the aims and the means of the defence policies of the Nordic states during the Cold War went beyond the purely military. In each of these small countries, a *comprehensive security* was sought in which the defence of society was stressed. A Swedish example was the emphasis given in official pronouncements on security policy to the need to preserve and develop 'our society politically, economically, socially, culturally and in all other respects according to our own values' (cited in Andrén 1975: 1). Concerning the means to defend the state and society, the Nordic states also took an expansive view. Again small states could not afford to rely just on their military for their defence, neither was this in line with the participatory nature of the Nordic societies. The concept of 'total defence' was adopted whereby both the military and civilian side of life would offer an integrated response to any attack (Forsvarskommisjonen 1992: 19). In the words of H.C. Hansen, the Danish prime minister in 1959, 'we must think not only of the military sector, but also of the civil, and the latter consists not just of civil defence, but the whole administrative, economic and psychological side of preparedness' (cited in Christensen 1983: 4).

The Nordic States after the Cold War

Ideas of common and comprehensive security emerged easily from an already existing wider understanding of security in the Nordic area. Concepts of security were developed rather than reconceptualised. After the end of the Cold War, the Nordic states started to adopt very much a liberal institutionalist view on international security that contained the elements of common and comprehensive security. The common security element can be seen in the wider Soviet and NATO approach at the end of the 1980s and early 1990s, when the common concern was controlling the arms race and, in particular, reducing the number of nuclear weapons. Indeed, the Danish political establishment showed concern at the end of 1989 that events in Eastern Europe might undermine the move towards common security and arms control and disarmament agreements (Archer 1994: 601 f.).

Swedish views of security have continued to be tied to ideas of common security, whereby potential adversaries could be brought closer together in the face of a greater threat, an approach that Mr Gorbachev seemed to accept. The report of the Parliamentary Defence Commission in Spring 1995 talked about 'common security built on solid political and economic relationships between democratic states' (Ministry of Defence 1995: 10) and continued the Cold War belief that any threat of aggression against Sweden would have a wider strategic aim. Planning for the total defence of Sweden was 'based on the principle that an armed attack against Sweden would constitute a part of a larger conflict between major powers' (ibid.: 14).

From January 1995, Sweden joined the European Union with its Common Foreign and Security Policy, and it stressed less its non-alignment and more its international commitments, such as participation in the NATO-led IFOR operation in Bosnia. Sweden's Parliamentary Defence Commission saw the country's security goals being based on support for peace-keeping and humanitarian missions and 'democratic, social, economic and ecological development' (Försvarsdepartementet 1995: 126). This fitted in well with a long Swedish tradition of support for peace-keeping and humanitarian efforts, though the operational context was switched from the UN to NATO.

Regional co-operation in the Baltic was a stated aim of Swedish security policy, with security co-operation with the Baltic states and their integration into the EU being important elements (Försvarsdepartementet 1995: 120). However, the Baltic, in security terms, was seen in a wider context. The Parliamentary Defence Commission maintained a global and European view of security, even talking about an 'increased risk' of security policy regionalisation of the Baltic,' confirming that it was 'a Swedish interest to counteract such security policy regionalisation' (ibid.: 121). A later parliamentary defence report stressed the need to include Russia and the Western powers in the various forms of co-operation in the Baltic Sea area (Försvarsdepartementet 1996: 128-30).

Finland, meanwhile, had made a more dramatic change in its security policy orientation as a result of the collapse of the Soviet Union. It cashed in its close relationship with the USSR for a more 'normal' link with the new Russian Federation and turned to the European Union for membership. The collective security of the UN was to be complemented by 'co-operative security' through European institutions – such as the OSCE, the Council of Europe and the EU – that would provide 'new forms of security policy co-operation, joint settlement of disputes and crisis management' (Ministry for Foreign Affairs 1995: 52 f.). This report also called for a 'broad and comprehensive concept of security,' including respect for human rights, consolidating the rule of law, economic co-operation, and protection of the environment, as well as the more usual military and political considerations' (Ministry for Foreign Affairs 1995: 19). Russia was still seen as crucial to Finland's security and the Baltic was a key area, but the means of achieving security had changed from direct dealings with one superpower to a broader-based approach through a variety on institutions. While the wider European institutions were given preference, a place was allowed for regional groupings and institutions, such as those in the Baltic (ibid.: 22). More recently, co-operation with Sweden both within the EU and on military matters has been stressed (European Security 1997: 35, 51 and 95; Archer 1997a).

The liberal institutionalist approach was most clearly seen in Norway's early consideration of post-Cold War security. The lack of a common international authority was seen as contributing to insecurity and unpredictability in international politics. In recognition of this, states 'have sought to reduce insecurity by attempting to establish a common authority. ... The tendency to international anarchy is sought to be counteracted by organising a comprehensive pattern of co-operation' (Forsvarskommisjonen av 1990, 1992: 37, authors' translation). Whilst accepting that a genuine international authority with a set of common rules and laws that every state followed all the time was unrealistic, the establishment of a level of norms and rules that most countries would want to follow and which none would oppose, was regarded as being both desirable and achievable (Forsvarskommisjonen av 1990, 1992: 37). At first the Norwegian government attempted to pursue its policies through membership of the EU, as well as through NATO, but the rejection of EU membership by their electorate in November 1994 led to a rethink. Instead, the Norwegians have sought both multilateral and more direct dealings with Russia and have stretched their 'comprehensive pattern of co-operation' far and wide, including Central America, the Middle East, South East Asia and Africa. Nordic co-operation in the Baltic provides just one element in this network, designed as it is to prevent a 'marginalisation' of Norway.

After their rather cautious consideration of the new security situation in early 1990, Danish decision makers made the greatest break with the past. Perhaps feeling much safer than their Nordic colleagues who were closer to the collapsing Soviet empire, by 1995 they had thoroughly rethought their strategic situation. In a report from the Danish Commission on Security and Disarmament, which was supported by a broad academic and political consensus, the Europeanisation of Danish foreign policy was noted, as was 'a marked regionalization in the form of large-scale involvement in the Baltic region' and an increased use of military means in the form of peace-keeping efforts and military co-operation with the Baltic states and Poland. A gradual democratisation of foreign and security policies was also seen (Danish Commission 1995: 6 f.). For Denmark, the security problem has not been marginalisation but that of making a contribution to European security that is distinct from – but is also accepted by – their EU partners. Danish Baltic activities have fitted the bill.

It seemed though the Nordic states were seeking to extend internationally those virtues that they had developed over the years in their own societies: dealing with conflict in a peaceful way; extending democracy; overcoming social and economic divisions; furthering environmental values. The Cold War had somewhat limited the opportunities for the furtherance of the 'Nordic model,' certainly to the Central and Eastern European states. The end of the period of confrontation not only brought possible new insecurities but also new ways to deal with them.

Eventually all the four main Nordic states came to stress the need to develop the aspects of international society which exists when a group of states 'conceive themselves to be bound by a common set of rules in their relations with each other, and share in the working of common institutions' (Bull 1977:13). While they had this in common, there have been nuances in their individual approaches. Of the four main Nordic states, Norway and Sweden have perceived their security 'menu for choice'[3] as changing the least, while Finland and Denmark have seen their choice grow substantially. Of these two, Finland has pursued the European option fairly single-mindedly, while Denmark has adopted a more regional approach, being content to see 'regime-like' patterns emerge in the area and a regionalisation process to evolve.

More generally, the Nordic countries have given support not just to the OSCE, but also to a range of regional institutions including those in the Baltic and Barents areas. The notion was to bring in new states, states undergoing political transition and, in particular, Russia to forums where security, in its more comprehensive sense, could be discussed. Sweden has been most reluctant to allow 'high security' matters to be included in these regional forums, with the Danes the most open about having all elements of security considered by the Baltic Sea states. Whatever the Nordic countries thought about security matters, they first had to deal with the security perceptions of the new Baltic governments.

The Baltic States Coming to Independence

In late 1991, sovereignty was bestowed on the Baltic states after the Soviet implosion had rendered Russian power projection a gleam of its former glare. Russia – temporarily, the Balts were soon to believe – had abandoned its claim to Baltic dominance.[4]

The popular fronts, established in late 1988 in the Baltic states (and later in other Soviet republics), were responses to the Gorbachev reforms and his emphasis on the involvement of the people in the process of change (Jæger 1993: 65). Although these movements did not originally challenge the Kremlin reforms, change in the Baltic republics harboured a westward thrust, representing a strategy of 'catching-up.' Reforms, and later secession, were seen as resulting from an urge to modernise by becoming more Western (Jæger 1993: 87-90; Jurgaitiene 1993).

The issues at stake in the initial phases of the independence struggle were greater economic autonomy within the USSR, self-rule in cultural matters and the correction of history. The latter, involving the denouncing of the Molotov-

Ribbentrop Pact, would establish that the Baltic states were illegally occupied and had not entered the Soviet Union voluntarily. The mobilisation process took a tint of national struggle and led to a gradual radicalisation of demands from that of autonomy to that of independence. When the Soviet Union ceased to exist, the Balts were left not just with a claim to state sovereignty but with the task of implementing it. The cultural entity of the nation was conflated with the political one of the state, much in line with romantic traditional nationalism (Jurgaitiene 1993). Linking state and nation was a powerful strategy that proved successful beyond all expectations. However, statehood came abruptly upon somewhat confused and unready populations, distrustful of the task of state-building. Both legitimacy and security were in high demand, and the process of state-building is still hampered by a combination of poor government and weak horizontal integration into society.

On the security side, neutrality was seen as a viable strategy for the Baltics in the lead-up to independence. However, in this period this option was more part of negotiating with Moscow, as de-militarising the Baltic-Scandinavian region would serve Baltic interests in removing Russian forces and installations from Baltic soil and could also be seen as legitimate in the general climate of European disarmament. Also 'Neutrality was estimated to be a feasible means for gradual transition from the state of a Soviet Republic to an independent country' (Haab 1997). It also led to the acceptance of a regional concept that would link at least the two neutral Nordic states and the newly emerging Baltic states.

However, neutrality soon gave way to a strategy of Western alignment, and by the time of independence, key figures in Baltic politics had abandoned the notion of neutrality (Haab 1993: 75). This was associated with the violent circumstances under which independence was achieved (the attempted Moscow putsch) and the conscious revival of the inter-war states with the reminder of the futility of neutrality. The idea of neutrality, however, was not immediately banished as Mare Haab advocated conditional neutrality for Estonia in her 1993 article, though in the same year Peeter Vares was to describe the notion as 'practically forgotten' (1993: 20). By 1997 Haab had turned her back on neutrality for the Baltics and Atis Leijins, Director of the Latvian Institute of International Affairs, proclaimed that 'neutrality is a discredited word today in the Baltics' (1994: 32).

The Development of Baltic Security Considerations

Fearing that Russian troops stationed in their countries could be instrumental in furthering Moscow's desire to undermine Baltic statehood, the troop withdrawal issue was given early priority in Baltic security policies. An explicitly Western-oriented foreign policy – with the expressed wish to join NATO and the EU – only came to the fore after the troop issue was solved (Haab 1997; Miniotaite 1997; Ozolina 1997). The delay was not helped by political infighting and inexperience (Vares 1993: 5-10).

Negotiations on troop withdrawal were rife with stalemate and accusations (Vares 1993: 16-18; Leijins 1994). As the Russian Federation developed its 'near abroad' policy, the stalemate was transferred to rows about Estonia's entry into the Council of Europe, accusations in the OSCE and the UN, all of which was only smoothed out with US intervention and the prospect of American aid to Russia being withheld.[5] This outcome seemed to prove the success of the Baltic strategy of multilateralising their security concerns, pursued since their declarations of independence. The aim of this 'conflict manifestation' has been to rally support by elevating internal or bilateral issues to a higher level and on to the 'high politics' agendas of international organisations such as the UN, the OSCE and NATO (Knudsen and Neumann 1995: 13). The Russian strategy has been to keep issues at a bilateral level where the asymmetry in Baltic-Russian relations would give Russia the upper hand. However, there are indications that the Baltic strategy of conflict manifestation has frustrated even liberal Russian politicians and has added to the Russian view of the Balts as trouble makers (Haab 1997; Knudsen and Neumann 1995: 20-22).

Furthermore, the strategy of conflict manifestation has tended to rule out options for subregional security arrangements. The Baltic governments have shown only limited interest in low-key conflict resolution at the subregional level. The exception has been that Estonia has accepted the idea in principle and that Lithuania has considered it as an approach to regulate military transit to Kaliningrad (Knudsen and Neumann 1995). By and large, however, there seems to be little incentive for the Baltics to use subregional institutions as this might distract Western interest from the Baltic states on the assumption that they are sorting their problems out fine. This is not how the Baltic governments see matters; hence their drive for NATO and EU membership. The Baltic states are even prone to compete with each other to find the shortest route to integration into Western and Transatlantic security structures. They will co-operate if that is what the West wants, or they will compete if necessary. Indeed the Lithuanian foreign minister made it clear that Baltic unity was 'a mere fiction that only exists in Western Politicians' minds' and looked to Poland for a possible means to take Lithuania into NATO (Miniotaite 1997).

The Baltic states have thus not shown a preference for Baltic arrangements involving security issues. They have come to these at the behest of Western countries as very much the second-best or interim arrangement to be tolerated on the road to NATO and the EU, the European and Atlantic solutions, though regional arrangements have also been deemed preferable to dealing with Russia bilaterally.

Notwithstanding NATO's Partnership for Peace programme (the PfP), the West is reluctant to project its power to the Baltic states for fear that minor issues will strain the strategic relations between the US and Russia (Asmus and Nurick 1996; Knudsen and Neumann 1995). Rather the West has stressed other means and types of security – as seen in the section on the Nordic states above – and, although this has received attention in the Baltic states, there remains little doubt there that Russia is still *the* danger to the Baltics.

The plight of the Baltic states lies in the possibility that the dividing line between the European self and 'the other' might be drawn west of their part of the Baltic, leaving them once again on the wrong side and therefore prey to 'the other.' Thus there is talk of 'a new Yalta' or 'a new Munich' in the Baltic security discourse (Necrasas 1996: 59; Miniotaite 1997; Vares 1993).

Furthermore, the 'enemy within' has emerged as a theme, especially in Estonia and Latvia, with the link to the external threat. There has been an exclusivity to legislation on citizenship in Estonia and Latvia and in property restitution and land ownership in all three states.[6] The National Security Concept (NSC) of Lithuania, and to a certain extent Latvia, stresses ethnic and cultural nationality. In the Lithuanian NSC, 'national demographic decrease,' 'dangerous infections' and the spreading of 'inhuman, violence-propagating pseudo-culture' are cited as potential internal threats to national security (NSC Lithuania, Chapter 10, Section 2). The Latvian NSC states that 'the goal of Latvian security policy is to maintain and develop ... the language, [and] national identity' (Section 1) and goes on to link the internal and external aspects of security by claiming that the 'ethnic situation and execution of the Citizenship Law can cause political, economic and social problems' which might then act as a pretence for 'neighbouring countries to interfere [with] Latvian internal affairs or to carry out aggressive actions' (Section 4.9).

The Baltic states' quest for European integration is part of their discourse of danger, delineating Russia as 'the other' and Europe as 'self.' With few exceptions, the security discourse in the Baltic states identifies an array of dangers emanating from Russia and threatening the gamut of Baltic security from sovereignty to ethnicity. Because identity is precarious and elusive and because state institutions are weak, faltering or lacking, the entire state project is perceived as vulnerable. The discourse of danger is instrumental in propping up state institutions, borders and identity, and can thereby alleviate the sense of vulnerability. To maintain state identity, the Baltic countries see the need to be firmly anchored in the West, but this implies a dividing line between East and West which, in turn, perpetuates insecurity. Russia has become the Baltic states' 'other' (Neumann 1993).

The Interaction of Nordic and Baltic Approaches

The Baltic states emerged into a Hobbesian world where it seemed that their existence could well be 'nasty, brutish and short.' Their governments' view of the world was moulded by both their wartime and post-war experience, with intransigence being one of the key political attributes of many of their leaders. As seen above, this attitude has changed little with the advent of the Russian Federation. Many Baltic politicians remained unconvinced that the Russian bear had had its claws drawn, and their experience of negotiating with the new Russian leadership, especially over troop withdrawals from their territory, did little to change their views.

In the early 1990s it was clear that the Baltic states had little military power compared to that of the Russian Federation. The most immediate way around this problem was to bring in outside power to assist the new fledgling states. Thus the Baltic governments decided that membership of NATO was desirable (Joint Statement 1996: 2; Helveg Petersen 1996: 7), with the expectation that this would give them the protection afforded by the North Atlantic Treaty's Article Five. This resort to collective defence did not fit in well with the more embracing Nordic security concepts. It also meant that, in the absence of NATO membership in the near future, the three states would be left in a security limbo, made more dangerous with the prospect of Polish membership of NATO. It is in this context that the Nordic countries have had something to offer their small neighbours.

From 1990, there has been a sort of security dialogue between the Baltic states and the Western states, with the Nordic countries in the lead. The Nordic states, together with Germany, have brought the three Baltic states – and Poland – closer to a new wider security agenda. However, there is an acceptance – not least in the Nordic states – that, because of their position and their mindset, the Baltic states will need to deal with 'traditional security threats' for some time.

First, all the Nordic countries have helped the Baltic states by giving 'sovereignty support' to assist their police forces, border controls and defence administrations 'to bring them up to the level required for safeguarding sovereignty and self determination' (Ministry for Foreign Affairs 1995: 23). For example, in December 1994 a fast patrol boat was transferred from Norway to each of the Baltic republics (FD faktablad 1995: 17). Secondly, there have been meetings of Nordic and Baltic prime ministers (the fourth was held in November 1996) at which they have planned co-operation in wider forums and also established joint task forces such as that to fight against criminality in the area (Udenrigsministeriet 1996: 5). Also seminars have been held between the defence ministers of the Baltic and Nordic states (FD faktablad 1995: 17).

The new security agenda has placed an emphasis on institutions and on regional solutions. The Nordic Council has served as model and stimulus for the creation of a Baltic Council between the three Baltic states, and a Danish-German initiative has led to the creation of the Council of Baltic Sea States, on which is represented the governments of all the Baltic coastal states, as well as Norway and Iceland. This has provided a wider forum for the Baltic states and the Russian Federation to discuss their mutual problems. Another useful instrument has been the OSCE and its Baltic Regional Table, established consequent to the European Stability Pact of March 1995 and which has dealt with minority and border questions in the area.[7] The OSCE itself has helped in monitoring the withdrawal of Russian troops from the Baltic states (Viksne 1995: 80).

The content of much of the discussion within the institutions covering the Baltic has been decidedly comprehensive. The Council of the Baltic Sea States has produced an Action Programme for Baltic Sea States Cooperation that has the aim of increasing people-to-people contacts and 'civic security' (against crime), economic co-operation and integration and strengthened environmental protection (Council of the Baltic Sea States 1996: passim). These elements were identified as the non-military elements of 'soft security,' which in itself was defined as 'all aspects of security short of military combat operations including the defence of the national territory' (Helveg Petersen 1996: 1).

The other – military – aspects of 'soft security' were addressed in the programme of co-operation undertaken within the and PfP, but also by the Nordic states in the way that they encouraged Baltic defence co-operation as a contribution to UN peace-keeping. A Baltic battalion was established and trained by the Nordic states and the United Kingdom (Haab 1995: 10). The Nordic-Polish brigade deployed as part of IFOR in 1996 contained contributions from the Baltic states folded into the Danish battalion (Hækkerup 1996: 11-13).

The Nordic states have also played a role concerning the issue of NATO membership for the Baltic countries. The latter are clearly attracted by the collective defence aspects of the Alliance and have rejected the alternative course taken – so far – by Finland and Sweden in their adherence to a policy of staying outside alliances. Norwegian practice has been to advise caution in relation to expectations about NATO membership (Brundtland 1996: 15-16). Denmark, in particular, has been an advocate of the Baltic states' membership of NATO. However, its ministers have made it clear that it should be a reformed, more open NATO that takes in the Baltic states and that an agreement should be reached between NATO and Russia first. In other words they foresee NATO becoming more of a co-operative security organisation in its relations with Russia, whereas Baltic leaders still see its value as a collective defence organisation *against* Russia. The extension of NATO to include Poland will do nothing to ease this dichotomy, and might even lead to greater pressure by Russia on the Baltic states to stay out of NATO.

The hope of the Nordics must be that sufficient agreement between Russia and NATO about the question of NATO expansion can be achieved and that the process does not just produce a new dividing line in Europe. Continued Finnish and Swedish absence from NATO will help to dispel such an idea. Meanwhile the Nordic countries are encouraging the Baltic states to deal with the very real threats to the fabric of their societies and to continue a political dialogue with all their neighbours in the regional organisations. In order to succeed, the Nordic states need not just a reasonable Russian-NATO relationship but also a willingness by the Baltic states to look to regional solutions while they are waiting for NATO. For many Baltic politicians, there is the fear that playing the regional game could be at the expense of their longer-term aims.

Conclusions

One idea expressed in some of the Nordic political science literature is that the end of the Cold War has seen the end of the Nordic region's special position in Europe, and that the Nordic states are now positioning themselves to be key players in the emerging Baltic region (compare Joenniemi 1991: 158-63 with Wæver 1991: 97-8 and Neumann 1994: 70-1). In security terms, this has been seen as the demise of those elements that made Norden unique, with a subsequent replacement of the Nordic region by the Baltic (Heurlin 1995: 57-8). In a Europe of low tension, though with 'islands of conflict,' the Nordic concept of being an area of low tension is no longer special, neither is the Nordics' small-state profile in a continent that has proliferated small states; the Nordic social welfare model has lost much of its attraction; and a unified Germany is 'the determining factor in Europe,' weakening 'the cohesion of the Nordic states' (ibid.). However, Heurlin admits that the death of the Nordic region will be only partial because of 'the lasting perception of Nordic identity' (ibid.: 58). Though this challenges the idea that regions can be constructed and deconstructed at will, it nevertheless presents a barrage of reasons why the Nordic region is destined to spend its declining years in a rest-home, perhaps doting on its new Baltic offspring.

The retirement party may be too early. The period from 1989 has indeed seen many of the trends mentioned in Bertel Heurlin's 'farewell presentation speech,' However, this is only part of the story and one that can be challenged. Both Neumann and Heurlin over-emphasise the geostrategic element in the creation of the Nordic region and place less credence on the popular and cultural aspects (though Heurlin gives culture as a reason for the region's continued endurance). The strategic elements presented an environment within which those forces favouring Nordicism could act, but their change or disappearance need not mean the collapse of the Nordic region. It should be remembered that the Nordic area uniquely consists of five nation-states[8] which form a security-community, in Karl Deutsch's terms, and, importantly, still regard each other as being something different – and closer to each other – than the rest of Europe.

The Nordic states have merely taken advantage of the change in the strategic environment to add the Baltic dish to their menu, and it is one that they are then happy to choose themselves for their security course and as a side-dish in the economic course. If regions are 'imagined communities,' much of the imagination concerning the Baltic region has been Nordic. Admittedly, an early start was made by Björn Engholm, that most Nordic of German politicians from the most Nordic of Länder, but since then it has been Nordic politicians, civil servants, military officers, bankers, academics and business people who have pushed the idea. The Finns got the parliamentary links going; the Danes have taken a lead in military co-operation; the Norwegians have helped with 'sovereignty assistance,' the Swedes have pressed political and economic co-operation; the Nordic Council tutored the Baltic Council; and the Nordic EU members have made sure the Baltic republics have not received unfavourable treatment from Brussels. The list is long. The Baltic region should not be regarded as a successor to Norden, and certainly not an alternative. It is a Nordic mission, tolerated by the Russians and Germans, welcomed by the Baltic states, and encouraged by the EU and the USA.

What has been seen over the past few years is the deliberate linking by the Nordic states of their security complex with that at the eastern end of the Baltic

Sea. Some Nordic countries have done this more openly and enthusiastically – indeed, Denmark has led the pack. It may fall increasingly on the shoulders of the Nordic states to fill the expectations gap that has grown with plans for the extension of NATO and the exclusion of the Baltic states from the first echelon of new members. It may prove difficult for Nordic politicians to persuade their Baltic counterparts to accept the liberal institutionalist agenda outlined at the beginning of this chapter. However, in the long run it could provide more security for the Baltic states than membership of NATO.

Notes

1 The appellation of 'Cold War' was a mixed one in the sense that while the War side denoted conflict, the epithet 'Cold' was used to denote the opposite to 'Hot War,' i.e. a fighting war. At the same time 'Cold' suggested an unfriendly relationship between the two sides (East and West), opposite to warm relations. However, once relations improved and the 'Cold War' 'thawed,' it did not move into a 'Hot War' or a 'Warm War,' but, sometimes, a 'Cold Peace,'

2 One writer has described liberal *internationalism* as 'an "inside-out" approach to international relations' whereby democratic society has an international analogue in the form of peaceful global order (Burchill 1996: 61). We have called the approach liberal institutionalism because of the special emphasis given international institutions by the Nordic states.

3 The expression is that of Bruce Russett and Harvey Starr (1992).

4 For accounts of the independence struggle, see Lieven (1993) and Trapans (1991).

5 Acting on a Congressional resolution in July 1992, the UN General Assembly passed a resolution concerning negotiations on 25 November 1992 (Vares 1993: 15-17; Haab 1997).

6 However, there has been some moderation to match EU regulations in preparation for membership.

7 For further details, see Archer (1997: 87-91).

8 Here the term is used to mean a state where the overwhelming bulk of the population – say, 90 per cent or over – are from one national group, and where an overwhelming bulk of that national group exists within one state.

References

Anderson, Benedict (1983). *Imagined Communities: The Origins and Spread of Nationalism.* London, Verso.

Andrén, Nils (1975). *Problems of Swedish Security.* Stockholm, National Defence Research Institute.

Archer, Clive (1994). ' New Threat Perceptions: Danish and Norwegian Official Views,' *European Security*:3(4), pages 593-616.

Archer, Clive (1997a). *Finland, Sweden, the IGC and Defence.* Brussels, ISIS Europe.

Archer, Clive (1997b). 'Security Considerations between the Nordic and Baltic Countries,' pages 81-100 in *Danish Foreign Policy Yearbook 1997.*

Asmus, Ronald and Nurick, Robert (1996). 'Enlargement and the Baltic States,' *Survival*:38(2), pages 121-42.

Brundtland, Gro Harlem (1996). 'Prime Minister Gro Harlem Brundtland. Address at the University of Vilnius, 19 March 1996.' UD informasjon:8. Oslo, Utenriksdepartementet

Bull, Hedley (1977). *The Anarchical Society.* London, Macmillan.

Burchill, Scott (1996). 'Liberal Internationalism,' pages 28-66 in Burchill, Scott and Linklater, Andrew with Devetak, Richard, Paterson, Matthew and True, Jacqui. *Theories of International Relations.* New York: St Martin's Press.

Christensen, Ivan (1983). *Totalforsvaret.* Copenhagen, FKO.
Council of the Baltic Sea States (1996). *Action Programme for the Baltic Sea States Cooperation.* Mimeo.
Danish Commission on Security and Disarmament (1995). *Danish and European Security.* Copenhagen.
European Security and Finnish Defence (1997). *Report by the Council of State to Parliament on 17 March 1997.* Helsinki, Oy Edita Ab.
FD faktablad (1995). 'Sikkerhetspolitiske rammebetingelser for Norsk forsvars- og sikkerhetspolitikk.' FD faktablad:03/1995. Oslo, Det Kongelige Forsvarsdepartementet.
Försvarsdepartementet (1995). *Sverige i Europa och världen.* Stockholm.
Försvarsdepartementet (1996). *Omvärldsförändringar och svensk säkerhetspolitik.* Stockholm.
Forsvarskommisjonen av 1990 (1992). Norges Offentlige Utredninger:12. Oslo.
Haab, Mare (1993). 'Is Neutrality a Foreign Policy Option for Small Nation States?' in Joenniemi, Pertti and Vares, Peeter (eds.). *New Actors on the International Arena: The Foreign Policies of the Baltic Countries.* TAPRI, Research Report:50. Tampere.
Haab, Mare (1995). 'Estonia and Europe,' pages 37-60 in van Ham, Peter (ed.). *The Baltic States: Security and Defence after Independence.* Chaillot Papers:19. Paris, Institute for Security Studies.
Haab, Mare (1997). 'Estonia,' Chapter 5 in Mouritzen, Hans (ed.). *Bordering Russia: Prospects for Europe's Baltic Rim.* London, Dartmouth.
Helveg Petersen, Niels (1996). *Danmark, NATO og Østersøen.* Det sikkerhetspolitiske bibliotek:10/1996. Oslo, Den Norske Atlanterhavskomite.
Heurlin, Bertel (1995). 'Security Problems in the Baltic region in the 1990s,' pages 55-75 in Joenniemi, Pertti and Stålvant, Carl-Einar (eds.). *Baltic Sea Politics: Achievements and Challenges.* Nord:35/1995. Stockholm, the Nordic Council.
Hækkerup, Hans (1996). 'A Multinational Force Culture,' *Enjeux atlantiques*:13, June, pages 10-13.
Joenniemi, Pertti (1991). 'Regionalization in the Baltic Area: Actors and Policies,' pages 147-65 in Joenniemi, Pertti (ed.). *Co-ooperation in the Baltic Sea Region: Needs and Prospects.* TAPRI, Research Report:42. Tampere..
Joenniemi, Pertti and Stålvant, Carl-Einar (eds.) (1995). *Baltic Sea Politics: Achievements and Challenges.* Stockholm, the Nordic Council.
Joint Statement of the Ministers of Defence of the Republic of Estonia, the Republic of Latvia and the Republic of Lithuania (1996). 23 January. Tallinn.
Jurgaitiene, Kornelija (1993). 'Romantic Nationalism and the Challenge of Europeanization: A Case of Lithuania' in Joenniemi, Pertti and Vares, Peeter (eds.). *New Actors on the International Arena: The Foreign Policies of the Baltic Countries.* TAPRI, Research Report:50. Tampere.
Jæger, Øyvind (1993). *Litauisk nasjonalisme – en moderniseringsstrategi.* NUPI, Research Report:176. Oslo
Knudsen, Olav F. and Neumann, Iver (1995). *Sub-regional Security Cooperation in the Baltic Sea Area.* NUPI, Research Report:189. Oslo.
Lähteenmäki, Kaisa (1995). 'Cooperation of the European Border Regions,' pages 257-83 in Archer, Clive and Jalonen, Olli-Pekka (eds.). *Changing European Security Landscapes.* TAPRI, Research Report:63. Tampere.
Leijins, Atis (1994). 'Latvia in a post Cold War world,' pages 31-55 in Snider, Don and Brundtland, Arne Olav (eds.). *Nordic-Baltic Security: An International Perspective.* Washington DC and Oslo, CSIS and NUPI.
Lieven, Anatol (1993). *The Baltic Revolution.* New Haven, Yale University Press.
Ministry for Foreign Affairs (1995). *Security in a Changing World: Guidelines for Finland's Security Policy.* Report by the Council of State to the Parliament 6 June 1995. Helsinki, Ministry for Foreign Affairs.
Ministry of Defence (1995). *Sweden in Europe and the World: Conclusions of a Report on Security Policy by the Swedish Parliamentary Defence Commission.* Stockholm.
Minotaite, Grazina (1997). 'Lithuania,' Chapter 7 in Mouritzen, Hans (ed.). *Bordering Russia: Prospects for Europe's Baltic Rim.* London, Dartmouth.

Necrasas, Evaldas (1996). 'Lithuania's Security Concerns and Responses' in Leijins, Atis and Bleiere, Daina (eds.). *The Baltic States: Search for Security*. Riga, LAI.

Neumann, Iver (1993). 'Russia as Central Europe's Constituting Other,' *East European Politics and Society*:7 (2).

Neumann, Iver (1994). 'A Region-building Approach to Northern Europe,' *Review of International Studies*:20(1), pages 53-74.

Ozolina, Zaneta (1997). 'Latvia,' Chapter 6 in Mouritzen, Hans (ed.). *Bordering Russia: Prospects for Europe's Baltic Rim*. London, Dartmouth.

Petersen, Nikolaj (1991). 'Regimes and Regionalization in the Baltic,' paages 128-46 in Joenniemi, Pertti (ed.). *Co-ooperation in the Baltic Sea Region: Needs and Prospects*. TAPRI, Research Report:42, Tampere.

Russett, Bruce and Starr, Harvey (1992). *World Politics. The Menu for Choice*. New York, Freeman. 4th ed.

Stålvant, Carl-Einar (1993). 'The Baltic Sea Area: An International Resource Region and a Test Case for Regionalism?' pages 49-71 in Joenniemi, Pertti (ed.). *Co-ooperation in the Baltic Sea Region*. London, Taylor & Francis.

Trapans, J.A. (ed.) (1991). *Towards Independence: The Baltic Popular Movements*. Boulder Co., Westview Press.

Udenrigsministeriet (1996). 'Nordgruppens Ugeoversigt.' Copenhagen, Ministry of Foreign Affairs.

Vares, Peeter (1993). 'Dimensions and Orientations in the Foreign and Security Policies of the Baltic States' in Joenniemi, Pertti and Vares, Peeter (eds.). *New Actors on the International Arena: The Foreign Policies of the Baltic Countries*. TAPRI, Research Report:50. Tampere.

Viksne, Ilmars (1995). 'Latvia and Europe's Security Structures,' pages 61-81 in van Ham, Peter (ed.). *The Baltic States: Security and Defence after Independence*. Chaillot Papers:19. Paris, Institute for Security Studies.

Wæver, Ole (1991). 'Culture and Identity in the Baltic Sea Region,' pages 79-111 in Joenniemi, Pertti (ed.). *Co-operation in the Baltic Sea Region: Needs and Prospects*. TAPRI, Research Report:42. Tampere.

29 Russia's Security Policies in the Baltic Sea Area[1]

Alexander A. Sergounin

Six years after the dissolution of the Soviet Union and the re-emergence of the independent Russian state, Russia is still searching its national identity. Moscow's security policies around the Baltic Sea Rim also reflect both domestic struggles and the lack of national consensus on fundamental question: what is Russia about?

Russian politicians and analysts acknowledge the positive effect of the end of the Cold War: the Baltic Sea area is no longer a sphere of global military confrontation between the two superpowers and their respective alliances. However, they disagree as to assessments of current and future security environment in the area. Some of them are rather optimistic and predict quick transformation of the region into a zone of co-operation and stability (Uspensky and Komissarov 1993: 83).

Most of the Russian observers, however, tend to draw alarmist conclusions and depict the situation in rather dark colours (e.g. Fadeev and Razuvayev 1994: 114). There are also some analysts who can be described as 'cautious optimists': they see numerous obstacles to peace and stability in the region, but they believe that – not very soon but at least in the foreseeable future – Russia and neighbouring countries will be able to create a co-operative security system in the Baltic Sea area (Baranovskiy 1996; Sergounin 1996a: 112-15; Moshes and Vushkarnik 1997: 99).

Perceptions of Threat

From the early Russian history up to now, there have been clashes between Russia's economic and security interests in the Baltic Sea area. In some periods, the region has been perceived as a 'window of opportunity' for economic co-operation with neighbours; in other periods, it has been seen as a 'window of vulnerability' given a Western expansion in the area.

In the Cold War era, the Soviet leadership regarded the Baltic Sea area as a potential theatre of military confrontation, and consequently a formidable military infrastructure was created in the region. At the same time, the area was considered relatively stable because Moscow controlled the Baltic states, Poland and East Germany were its allies, Finland and Sweden were neutral, and the NATO forces were counterbalanced by the Soviet Baltic Sea Fleet as well as by the WTO troops and navies. In addition, it was an area of rather intensive economic co-operation between East and West (especially between the Soviet Union, Finland and West Germany).

Paradoxically, the end of the Cold War triggered some processes which were interpreted by Moscow, along with positive assessments, as detrimental to its security interests in the region.

First, Russia lost two-thirds of the former Soviet Baltic coastline and access to the Baltic Sea was significantly reduced. Moscow lost almost all that it had persistently aspired for over several centuries.

Second, with the collapse of the USSR, Kaliningrad, an essential component of the Soviet defence system in the region, turned into an exclave with doubtful defence capabilities. Currently, Kaliningrad has the appearance of being a trap for the Baltic Sea Fleet rather than being Moscow's military outpost in the region. The plans to transform Kaliningrad from a Cold War bastion to Russia's Hong Kong seem ambiguous because of the lack of economic and political stability in Russia, a tug of war between local and federal governments, difficult relations with the Baltic states, as well as competition with St Petersburg (one of Russia's powerful regional players). Moscow is also very sensitive to any talk about possible secession of Kaliningrad either in the form of a 'fourth Baltic republic' or returning it to Germany (Petersen 1994: 272-3; SIPRI 1994: 178).

Third, the dissolution of the Warsaw Pact deprived Moscow of its most important strategic allies, i.e. Poland and East Germany.

Fourth, the collapse of the Soviet Union and WTO undermined the entire military structure in the north-western part of Russia. Moscow had to redeploy and accommodate troops withdrawn from Eastern Europe and the Baltic states. The system of military command, logistic support and management in the area had to be changed. The Russian strategic planners had to think over how to defend vulnerable regions given the geopolitical cataclysm as well as shortage of funds, personnel and ammunition.

Fifth, Russia failed to prevent the rise of unfriendly or even hostile regimes in the three Baltic states. From the very beginning, the latter aimed at withdrawing from the Russian sphere of influence and favoured a pro-Western orientation. In addition, the emergence of the newly independent states necessitated the creation of a new border control and customs system.

Sixth, the region's alliance system is shifting to the detriment of Russian strategic interests around the Baltic Sea Rim. NATO in a sense 'swallowed' East Germany. Poland is going to join NATO. The Baltic states applied for NATO membership as well. Currently, the Polish and Baltic armed forces do not constitute any serious threat to Russia's security, but once incorporated into NATO and modernised, they could pose a challenge. Having joined the EU and obtained

WEU observer status, Finland and Sweden are no longer neutral. At the same time, Russia is unable to create a strong military organisation within the CIS and thus counterbalance the eastward expansion of the Western security institutions.

Seventh, the secession of the Baltic states generated a number of new and acute problems which can be attributed to the 'soft security' domain: national minority rights, territorial disputes, smuggling, internationalisation of organised crime, terrorism and environmental issues. The Russian security institutions were unprepared to meet these new challenges.

There is consensus among different Russian schools of security thought as regards the identification of threats to Russian national interests in the region. However, these schools have different assessments of the significance of particular threats and the importance of the region for Russia. Similarly, their recommendations on how to cope with security challenges differ.

A majority of Russian analysts believe that the principal threats do not originate from the West but from the South or the East. For that reason the Baltic Sea area tends to be of declining strategic importance for Russia. Social, economic and environmental problems rather than military security issues will dominate the regional agenda in the foreseeable future. Russia should acknowledge the right of the Balts to choose their security and foreign policy orientations and seek a compromise with the West on the Baltic issues in order to have a free hand in the South and East (Arbatov 1994: 71; Moshes and Vushkarnik 1997: 99; Lukin 1994: 110; Zhirinovskiy 1993). Interestingly, even the 'Atlanticists' and the 'Eurasianists' – the two leading and competing currents in the early Russian security debate (1991-93) – tend to agree on this issue.

However, there are other experts insisting that Russia is able to cope with the threats from South and East, but what really needs attention is a new Western 'Drang nach Osten', i.e. NATO and EU enlargement. Therefore the Baltic Sea area becomes strategically important again. Russia is unable to block the Visegrad countries' joining NATO, but can and should stop NATO expansion towards the Baltic states. This school does not exclude the eventuality of military confrontation in the region. The sources of such a confrontation might be the Balts' joining NATO or their decision to deploy foreign troops and nuclear weapons on their territory. Moscow may also use military force to protect the Russian minorities or to resolve territorial disputes with the Baltic states (*Komsomolskaya Pravda* 1995; *Nezavisimaya Gazeta* 1996). This point of view is particularly popular among nationalists, the top military leadership, and to some extent the communists.

Two related paradigms – realism and geopolitics – currently dominate Russian security thinking. Language such as 'power balance,' 'national interests,' 'national security' and 'national sovereignty' is basic for the Russian strategic planners. This should not come as a surprise in the case of a country undergoing nation- and state-building. However, it rebuffs co-operative patterns of diplomacy such as transregional co-operation and multilateral institutions. The country's leadership is inclined to employ traditional instruments of security politics: economic sanctions, diplomatic pressure, military build-up, military threats and actual use of military force. It is no accident that current Russian foreign policy and military doctrines are designed in such a traditionalist-realist way.

A Conceptual Framework of Russia's Policy

No official document specifically outlines Russian security interests and policy in the Baltic Sea area. Moscow's Baltic doctrine can, however, be roughly constructed from some official documents, numerous declarations, speeches and interviews with high-ranking Russian officials.

Russia still lacks a national security doctrine. Instead, a foreign policy concept was presented by the Foreign Ministry in January 1993 (*Diplomaticheskiy Vestnik* 1993) and approved by the President in April 1993. A military doctrine was adopted by the President in November 1993.[2] The two doctrines often do not correspond to each other as regards threat perceptions and the role of military force in the country's foreign policy. The Russian Parliament also adopted a 'Law on Security' in 1992 but this law deals mainly with domestic issues and does not outline any comprehensive concept of national security (Supreme Soviet of the Russian Federation 1992). The draft of a 'National Security Concept of the Russian Federation' (Committee on National Security 1995) has been pending before the State Duma since 1995 but has been bogged down by partisan politics.

According to the foreign policy concept (1993), the Baltic Sea area is ranked fifth (as a part of Europe) on a list of fifteen priorities. Europe follows the CIS, arms control and international security, economic reform, and the United States; but it takes precedence over the Asia-Pacific region, South and West Asia, the Near East, Latin America and so on. However, this ranking can be misleading because the document mixes regional and functional priorities. Hence the real policy may differ from declarations.

The document stipulates Russian interests in co-operation with the Baltic Sea countries (such as Denmark, Finland, Norway and Sweden) in developing joint projects on trade, environment protection, radiation security, housing for troops withdrawn from the Baltic states and improvement of infrastructure.

The Baltic states are brought up in a special section. The concept sets seven tasks for Russian diplomacy, such as the creation of a legal basis for bilateral relations; signing agreements on Russian troop withdrawal and retaining the most important strategic facilities in the area; demarcation of borders and establishing customs check-points; securing Russia's access to transport communications and ports; protection of Russian-speaking minorities; creating multilateral institutions for co-operation on energy, communications, fisheries, the environment and the Kaliningrad free economic zone; and the use of regional institutions to put a pressure on the Balts (*Diplomaticheskiy Vestnik* 1993: 14).

Remarkably, the concept downplays the role of military force in international relations. The document does not identify the Baltic states as a source of threat. Rather, it is aimed at problem-solving and co-operation with the Balts. This is not accidental; at that time the document was drafted, Moscow nourished the hope of establishing good relations.

The military doctrine approved by President Yeltsin several months later reflects the next – and more complicated – stage of Russian policies towards the former Soviet Union (FSU) states. Moscow was concerned with national minority rights in the post-Soviet space, territorial claims raised by neighbouring countries and the increase in Western influence on the ex-Soviet republics.

The doctrine sorts out a number of sources of military threats with a bearing on the Baltic states: 'territorial claims of other states on the Russian Federation and its allies,' 'the suppression of the rights, freedoms and legitimate interests of citizens of the Russian Federation in foreign states,' 'expansion of military blocs and alliances to the detriment of the interests of the military security of the Russian Federation' and 'the deployment of foreign troops on the territory of states adjacent to the Russian Federation' (*Jane's Intelligence Review* 1994: 7). Consequently, the Russian armed forces may be used to protect Russian citizens abroad, to resolve territorial disputes and to prevent the rise of hostile military alliances and coalitions in Russia's vicinity.

In adopting the new military doctrine, Russia repealed the Soviet principle of no first use of nuclear weapons. The Baltic Rim countries paid attention to two exceptions from Moscow's promise not to use nuclear weapons against any state party to the Nuclear Non-Proliferation Treaty which does not possess nuclear weapons. According to the document, Russia will never resort to such means against them, unless: '(a) such a state, which is connected by an alliance agreement with a nuclear state, attacks the Russian Federation, its territory, Armed Forces and other services or its allies; (b) such a state collaborates with a nuclear power in carrying out, or supporting, an invasion or an armed aggression against the Russian Federation, its territory, Armed Forces and other services or its allies' (*Jane's Intelligence Review* 1994: 6).

Members of NATO, such as Denmark, Germany and Norway, undoubtedly fall under these provisions. So may Poland and the Baltic states if they join NATO or the WEU or 'support' any Western intervention in Russia or the 'near abroad.' This might occur, for example, if they provide the Western alliances with rights of passage or bases. Many Baltic Sea countries saw these provisions of the Russian military doctrine as evidence of Moscow's aggressiveness, signalling a return to imperialist policies.

With the success of Vladimir Zhirinovskiy in the December 1993 parliamentary elections, the domestic base for reform-oriented and pro-Western policies shrank. The government became more susceptible to nationalistic rhetoric and declamatory politics. For example, in January 1994, Foreign Minister Andrey Kozyrev called the Baltic states 'a source of threat to Russia,' invoking the lack of progress on negotiations on troop withdrawal from Estonia and Latvia and incidents between the Latvian 'Zemessardze' and Russian servicemen stationed in this country (Kozyrev 1994). At that time, however, the Russian leadership did not depict the Baltic states as a potential source of serious military threat.

A fundamental change in Russia's attitudes to the Baltic states has occurred since the December 1994 decision on NATO enlargement and the Balts' subsequent application for membership. From that moment, the Baltic states and Poland really fell under the definitions of military threat in the Russian military doctrine. However, Russia's security concerns declined once NATO made it clear that the Baltic states would not be granted early membership, and the Paris Charter has been signed to guarantee Russia's security.

At the Baltic Sea countries summit in May 1996 (Visby), Prime Minister Chernomyrdin proposed a model of Baltic Sea regional security based on co-operation in a number of areas such as the economy, energy, communications, conversion of the defence industries of the Kaliningrad and Leningrad regions, fighting organised crime and the development of transregional links (*Diplomaticheskiy Vestnik* 1996a). At the same time he ignored purely security issues (arms control and disarmament, deployment of armed forces, confidence-building measures, alliance politics and so on) as well as other important 'soft' security issues such as minority and religious rights, international terrorism, smuggling and territorial disputes. This made the proposal less realistic because a regional security system cannot be based merely on economics, police, border guards and transregional co-operation.

Probably he wanted to make an impression on the Baltic Sea leaders by indicating that Moscow interprets security in a broader sense. Nonetheless, this turn from 'hard' to 'soft' security issues is noteworthy: a message was sent that Russia is ready to go far beyond traditional considerations of security and favours a co-operative rather than confrontational model of regional security. However, as the initiative does not address the broader questions of security and fails to outline Russia's interests and principles of regional policy, it does not meet the criteria for being Russia's Baltic doctrine. Such a departure is still lacking.

Russian Military Presence

The Russian military presence in the region has declined over the past five years. The Baltic Military District (MD) has been abolished, and instead, the Kaliningrad Special District (KOR) was established. The KOR consists of the units from the Baltic Sea Fleet, the land forces and the air defence forces under the general command of Admiral Yegorov. The KOR also has the task of co-ordinating its activities with border guards and Ministry of Interior troops located in the Kaliningrad Region.

Unlike in Soviet times, the KOR departs from a defensive rather than offensive doctrine. According to Admiral Gromov, in peace time the KOR should mainly fulfil deterrent functions against potential aggressors, as well as protect Russia's economic interests in the area. In war time, the KOR aims at protecting the Kaliningrad Region and the bases of the Baltic Sea Fleet, as well as preventing enemy penetration to the eastern part of the Baltic Sea and the Gulf of

Finland (Gromov 1995). No offensive tasks are outlined for the district (even in war time). This is not surprising given the remote location of the KOR, the lack of logistical support and the current level of forces.

Between 1990 and 1996, the KOR reduced the number of its tank divisions from two to one, an artillery division was transformed into three brigades, an airborne brigade was dismissed, the number of surface-to-surface missile brigades fell from three to one, artillery pieces were reduced from 677 to 426, and the number of combat aircraft fell from 155 to 28. Over the same period, the Baltic Fleet reduced the number of its submarines from 42 (two strategic and 40 tactical) to six (all tactical) and the number of surface ships from 450 (39 principal combatants, 150 patrol and coastal combatants, 120 mine warfare, 21 amphibious and 120 support vessels) to 259 (31 principal combatants, 42 patrol and coastal combatants, 60 mine warfare, 8 amphibious and 118 support ships) (*Military Balance 1990-1991*: 39-40; *Military Balance 1996-1997*: 114-15, 118). Now the Baltic Fleet is comparable with German and Swedish fleets in terms of both quantity and quality.

In the years following the withdrawal of the Russian troops from Eastern Europe and the Baltic states, Russia temporarily expanded its military facilities in the KOR area to accommodate these forces. For example, the naval presence at Baltiysk (the main base of the Baltic Sea Fleet) was expanded to include additional conventional submarines and new barracks to house a 1100-strong maritime border guard unit (*Jane's Defence Weekly* 1993: 14). In addition to a motor rifle division stationed in the KOR, one more was redeployed from ex-Czechoslovakia. From 1990 to 1995 the number of tanks increased from 802 to 893 (850 in 1996), the number of armoured combat vehicles increased from 1081 to 1156 (925 in 1996), and the number of attack helicopters increased from 48 to 52 (*Military Balance 1995-1996*: 105; *Military Balance 1996-1997*: 14). This, however, did not alter the general tendency towards decreasing military capabilities of the KOR.

Despite the KOR's declining military potential, the Baltic states and Poland continue to express concerns about the high degree of militarisation of Kaliningrad and urge Russia to turn the tide. For example, in November 1994 the Baltic Assembly – the parliamentary body of the three Baltic countries – adopted a resolution calling for an international round table conference on the demilitarisation of Kaliningrad (*Baltic Independent* 1994b: 1). Moscow interprets such appeals as open interference in its internal affairs. According to ex-Foreign Minister Kozyrev, 'the Russian side will never and with no one discuss the "future" of the Kaliningrad Region and its status' (*Baltic Independent* 1994b: 1). Some quarters in Moscow do not even rule out the possibility of a remilitarisation of the KOR if NATO is expanded in the area.

More generally, the Russian leadership still considers Kaliningrad an important military-strategic outpost in the Baltic Sea region. Consequently, Russia's military presence will be kept at a significant level. For the time being, however, Moscow focuses on qualitative (modernisation) rather than on quantitative aspects of military programmes.

The Leningrad (Northern) Military District has also been provided with a more defensive configuration. Over the period 1990-96, the MD's number of motor rifle divisions fell from 11 to five, the number of tanks was reduced from 1 200 to 870, and the numbers of artillery pieces, multiple rocket launchers and mortars fell from 2 140 to 1 000 (*Military Balance 1990-1991*: 39-40; *Military Balance 1996-1997*: 115). The district's contingency planning was retargeted mostly to conduct non-offensive tasks.

All these changes have reduced the concerns of the neighbours. Many Western military experts believe that the lack of cohesion and precision of purpose makes Russia's forces in the region less effective (e.g. Viitasalo and Österlund 1996: 32-33). At the same time, the neighbouring countries consider the Russian potential as sufficient to create a significant threat to their countries' security in the event of the coming to power of an authoritarian regime in Russia.

Russo-Baltic Security Relations

Russia's security relations with the Baltic Sea countries follow three main patterns: low-key (formal) co-operation conducted basically through multilateral institutions; rather developed co-operation; and confrontation rather than co-operation. The first category includes Denmark, Germany, Norway, Poland and Sweden, the second encompasses Finland, and the Baltic states form the third category.

Russia's military co-operation with the first group of Baltic Sea countries focuses predominantly on joint military exercises, visits, exchanges within the framework of the NATO Partnership for Peace (PfP) programme and non-PfP programmes. In September 1994, Defence Minister Grachev signed agreements on military co-operation with Denmark, Finland and Norway during a visit to Copenhagen (*Baltic Independent* 1994a: 2).

Russia's security co-operation with Finland is traditionally more advanced and well-established than with other Baltic Sea countries. Since the Soviet era it has included even such a delicate matters as arms transfers. Interestingly, the two countries used military-technical co-operation to resolve economic, financial and other bilateral problems. For example, late in 1995, Russia promised to repay part of its FIM 5.5 billion ($1.3 billion) trade debt to Finland by delivering three SA-11 'Gadfly' surface-to-air missile batteries. According to an agreement signed in Helsinki, the batteries, worth FIM 850 million, will constitute the first repayment of a long-standing debt left unpaid when the Soviet Union collapsed in 1991. Finland plans to use the batteries for defending the area of the capital Helsinki. The first battery was delivered in early 1997. As part of the package, Russia will also supply Finland with operational and maintenance training, spares and sundry items such as bullet-proof vests (*Jane's Defence Weekly* 1995: 9).

Russia's security relations with the Baltic states are far more tense than relations with other countries of the region. During the years 1991-94, the problem was one of withdrawal of Russia's residual forces. Lithuania adopted citizenship legislation which has satisfied Russia, Moscow and Vilnius reached an agreement on a quick withdrawal of residual forces, which was completed by 1 September 1993.

It was more difficult for Moscow to conclude agreements on troop withdrawal with Estonia and Latvia. Both sides, under pressure from domestic public opinion and hoping to gain more advantages, employed tough tactics instead of a pragmatic search for a compromise.

Finally, after lengthy and difficult negotiations, Russia reached agreements with Latvia (30 April 1994) and Estonia (26 July 1994), and the troops were pulled out of both countries by the end of August 1994. Small Russian contingents stayed behind to maintain the Skrunda radar station in Latvia for another five years and to dismantle nuclear reactors at the submarine training base in the Estonian port of Paldiski. The compromise was reached on the basis of mutual concessions. Russia had failed to force Estonia and Latvia to grant citizenship automatically to all Russian-speaking inhabitants, to postpone troop withdrawal for years, to get compensation for its military property and to keep strategically important naval bases in the region. Estonia and Latvia, on the other hand, had had to guarantee the social rights of Russian military pensioners and to provide them with residence permits, to give Moscow some limited access to base facilities (Skrunda radar station), and to abandon their claims to financial compensation for ecological damage caused by the Russian military.

In accordance with the 30 July 1994 agreement, Russia completed the dismantling of two nuclear reactors at Paldiski and handed over the former Soviet submarine training base at Paldiski to Estonia on 26 September 1995.

The issue of military transit between Russia and Lithuania caused much political controversy between 1993 and 1995. On 18 November 1993, Russia and Lithuania signed an agreement regulating the use of Lithuania's railway system and other transportation facilities for the withdrawal of the Russian troops from Germany up to 1995. Later on Lithuania tried to tighten its control over transit and avoid formal agreement with Russia on this issue. Moscow, however, wanted both a new accord on military transit and a comprehensive political agreement. In an attempt to compel Lithuania to sign new documents Russia doubled import duties on Lithuanian goods in 1994 and postponed the implementation of the 1993 trade agreement, which contained a most favoured nation status.

Finally, a compromise was reached. In January 1995 Moscow and Vilnius exchanged diplomatic notes by which Lithuania agreed to extend the current rules for Russian military transit to Kaliningrad until the end of 1995, and Russia stated that the agreement granting Lithuania most favoured nation status, signed in November 1993, had come into force (*Baltic Independent* 1995: 6). The agreement on military transit has since been extended on a yearly basis. Nevertheless, Lithuania has complained about numerous violations of its airspace by Russian aircraft.

After the completion of Russian troop withdrawal from the Baltic states in 1994, Moscow tried to provide its security relations with the Balts with a legal basis. In September 1994, Russia offered the Baltic states bilateral security agreements like those signed that month with Norway, Finland and Denmark. According to Defence Minister Pavel Grachev, another possibility was one multilateral security agreement signed by the three Baltic states and Russia (*Baltic Independent* 1994a: 2).

However, the prime ministers of the Baltic states, meeting in Riga on 13 September, had earlier stated that such a Russian proposal would be rejected because it was premature and because remaining problems must first be resolved.

Multilateral Institutions

Russia conducts its security policy not only through bilateral relations with the Baltic Sea countries but also through international organisations. There is no particular regional organisation that covers the Baltic Sea area's security issues. However, several regional institutions somehow touch upon 'soft security' problems. In addition, pan-European and global organisations are involved in discussions of the Baltic Sea regional security agenda.

Russia's position is that the OSCE – the institution in charge of preventive diplomacy and conflict management – should be a main leg of a European security regime including the Baltic Sea area. The Baltic Sea regional institutions can be useful addition to the OSCE in 'soft security' issues but cannot resolve 'hard security' problems. This position is partly explained by the fact that the OSCE represents the only European security arrangement where Russia is a member.

In particular, Moscow believes that the OSCE should play a major role in negotiating a new, improved, version of the Treaty, which should cover the entire Baltic Sea area. The OSCE also tackles some 'soft security' issues such as national minority rights and territorial disputes. In 1992, the Office for Democratic Institutions and Human Rights in Warsaw and the post of the High Commissioner on National Minorities in The Hague were established with active Russian participation. In 1993, OSCE missions were established in Estonia and Latvia to promote integration and better understanding between the communities in these countries.

However, the OSCE has some shortcomings. It does not provide security guarantees; decisions require nearly consensus (minus one state); the OSCE has no mechanisms to implement most of its own decisions. In particular, it does not have a military arm and hence is unable to conduct peace-keeping operations. In other words, the OSCE possesses diplomatic rather than military strength. For these reasons some Russian experts propose that the OSCE be transformed into a main collective security organisation on the continent, with a European Security Council (ESC) with permanent members possessing veto power and a number of rotating non-permanent members, representing smaller European and CIS states. Similarly, they would like NATO and WEU to be subordinated to the ESC and serve as its military arms in maintaining regional security (especially in peacekeeping operations) (Arbatov 1996: 248-49). Other OSCE member states (including the Baltic Sea countries), however, are rather critical of such an idea. Instead, they support NATO as a more effective security instrument.

Moscow also tries to use available NATO institutions such as the PfP and the North Atlantic Co-operation Council (NACC) initiatives. The PfP programmes in particular have developed into an important area for security co-operation in the Baltic Sea area. The PfP invites consultation with NATO if a PfP partner perceives a direct threat to its security. Although the PfP is not designed to be a mechanism for crisis management per se, consultations can send substantial political signals which could assist in crisis management. Most importantly, the PfP offers the establishment and development of military working relations not only with NATO but also with other participants. As mentioned above, under the aegis of the PfP programmes, Russia has participated in some naval exercises together with other Baltic Sea countries.

As for the NACC, it has developed into a flexible body of co-operation on political and security issues. Although the NACC cannot solve current regional security problems, it does provide a forum in which to address regional security issues and might contribute to crisis management at an early stage of a conflict. For example, NACC consultations had some success in cooling down part of the tension during the controversy between Russia and the Baltic states on troop withdrawal (Heise 1996: 212). Russia's more active participation in NATO activities is hampered by the dispute on NATO enlargement but may also be spurred in the same context.

From the Russian point of view, the Council of Baltic Sea States (CBSS) is the most important among the regional institutions. Some features of the Council resemble those of the OSCE. This makes the CBSS especially attractive to Russia. Moscow views the CBSS as an important forum for discussions of 'soft security' issues and it took an active part in establishing the post of a CBSS Commissioner for Human Rights and Minority Questions, which became Russia's key instrument in pressing Estonia and Latvia to comply with internationally recognised human rights standards.

In 1996, Moscow decided on a new political course towards the CBSS. As mentioned, at the May 1996 Visby Summit, the Russian Prime Minister proposed a scheme of regional security based on an extensive programme of co-operation in several areas such as economy, trade, finance, transportation, communications, conversion, ecology, border and customs control and fighting organised crime (*Diplomaticheskiy Vestnik* 1996a: 9-11). Chernomyrdin's initiative marked at least three important changes in Russian policy towards the CBSS: First, the status of the Council was essentially elevated in Russia's foreign policy. Secondly, Moscow sent a message to the CBSS member states that it is willing to broaden the Council's security agenda by highlighting environment and organised crime as important priorities. Finally, Russia indicated a willingness to provide the Council with organisational strength as the Prime Minister proposed to establish an International Secretariat and to carry out internal regulations to make the Council more effective.

Russia's initiative was well received by the Summit's participants, and some steps were taken to carry out the proposed programme. At the same time, many CBSS member states expressed reluctance towards a further widening the Council's security agenda.

Although formally, the Barents Euro-Arctic Council (BEAC), founded in January 1993, does not deal with Baltic region issues, Russia uses it as an additional channel of communications with the Baltic Sea rim countries (even with non-members of the BEAC). For example, during the BEAC fourth session in Petrozavodsk in November 1996, the Russian Foreign Minister Primakov met his Estonian colleague to discuss the draft of a Russian-Estonian agreement on border issues, as well as the rights of the Russian-speaking population in Estonia. In addition, Primakov used this forum to try to convince the Baltic Sea countries not to extend NATO to the region (*Diplomaticheskiy Vestnik* 1996c: 53, 68-9).

Moscow hopes to solve some of its ecological problems through the Helsinki Commission (HELCOM), which operates on the basis of the 1974 Baltic Sea Convention and the 1992 Convention. The HELCOM has elaborated an extensive 'Baltic Sea Joint Comprehensive Environment Action Programme' which identifies 132 ecological hot-spots, most of which are in the eastern part of the Baltic Sea area (Maibach 1996: 279). However, because of a lack of resources, the programme has not been implemented.

As a country with observer status, Russia works with the Baltic Round Table (BRT) consisting of the three Baltic states and Poland. The BRT operates within the framework of the Pact on Stability in Europe (also known as the Balladur Plan), which was presented to the EU in 1993, and adopted and handed over to the OSCE in May 1995 (Maibach 1996: 278). The Stability Pact aims at bilateral and multilateral settlements and agreements concerning good-neighbourly relations and minority and border issues among states applying for membership of the EU. Moscow hopes that the Baltic states' interest in the EU membership will facilitate the solution of remaining problems (in particular minority and border issues).

Neither Russia nor the other Baltic Sea rim countries believe that military security can be resolved at the level of regional security arrangements. However, contrary to Russia, which considers the OSCE a relevant instrument for achieving comprehensive European security, Poland and the Baltic states view NATO as the best option.

Alliance Politics

There were some illusions in the Russian leadership that with the end of the Cold War, military alliances had become obsolete and could be dissolved, as was the case with the Warsaw Treaty Organisation (WTO). However, for a number of well-known reasons, the alliance strategy turned out to be again in the focus of European politics by the mid-1990s.

The Baltic states' application for NATO membership has evoked Moscow's strong and negative reaction. Russian diplomacy argues that NATO enlargement is detrimental to both the fate of democratic reforms in Russia and regional security.

Moscow points out that joining NATO would not enhance the security of Poland and the Baltic states. On the contrary, it would inevitably force Moscow to perceive them as a potential military threat to Russia's security and therefore worsen their relations with Moscow. Russia has no intention (and capability) to attack current NATO applicants. The only real threat to European security originating from Russia is its internal instability. This perceived threat can be successfully met by non-military means such as enhanced economic and trans-regional co-operation targeted at the creation of an interdependency mechanism.

Russia also suggests that the East European countries might enjoy 'soft security' if they join the EU (and the WEU) instead of NATO. Moreover, the Nordic countries (such as Finland and Sweden) might enhance their military co-operation with the Baltic states. Moscow does not objects to the Baltic Sea countries' participation in these types of security arrangement.

Many Russian experts believed that a compromise with the West on NATO enlargement was possible. They proposed to delay NATO enlargement for some years and to limit it to the Visegrad countries and not to extend NATO to the Baltic states. They also suggested a special Russia-NATO charter to ensure Moscow's security (no further expansion to the CIS countries, no military bases and nuclear weapons on the territory of new members, continuation of the arms control dialogue and so forth) (e.g. Trenin 1995). As the Paris and Madrid accords demonstrated, some of the Russian suggestions have been accepted by NATO.

At the same time, and in response to NATO enlargement, Moscow initiated a new alliance politics of its own. First, Russia is developing a close security relationship with China including military-technical, defence industry and intelligence co-operation (Sergounin and Subbotin 1996). President Yeltsin and Foreign Minister Primakov even spoke about a strategic alliance with the PRC to counterbalance NATO's eastward expansion (*Jane's Defence Weekly* 1996: 10; *Jane's International Defense Review* 1996: 9).

Secondly, Russia fostered military integration within the CIS framework (especially with Belarus). Russia's efforts resulted in intensive programmes of military and military-technical co-operation, the creation of a joint air defence system, co-ordination of training programmes for military personnel, reaching bilateral and multilateral agreements on the use of military infrastructure and the airspace and waters of participating states and establishing and protecting a common border of the CIS (*Diplomaticheskiy Vestnik* 1995: 33-7; Sergounin 1996b).

It should be noted that military co-operation between the CIS member states often exists on paper rather than in reality. The process of Commonwealth military integration is far from completion. However, in the event of NATO enlargement (especially if the Baltic states join the alliance), Russia will likely encourage the CIS countries to form more effective military alliance. As former Defence Minister Pavel Grachev put it, if NATO does expand, 'we will no doubt form some defensive, military and political alliance of our own' (*Segodnya* 1995b: 2).

Russia and the Regional Arms Control Regime

In addition to the tensions between Russia and the Baltic states and the possibility of renewed confrontation between military blocs, the situation in the region is aggravated by the lack of a proper arms control regime.

The only international arms control agreement applicable to the Baltic Sea area is the CFE. Four Baltic Rim countries – Denmark, Germany, Poland and Russia – are state parties to this agreement. The Baltic states refused to abide by the Treaty because it was concluded at a time when they were a part of the Soviet Union. The CFE Treaty aims to reduce excess military equipment, essential for launching surprise attacks and initiating large-scale offensive operations. The agreement has thus played a positive role in the prevention of military confrontation and conflict in the area.

However, a number of post-Cold War developments have complicated the implementation of the CFE Treaty. The so-called flank issue has been the main bone of contention between Russia and most of the other parties. This issue was resolved by the Russian and American Defence Ministers. The Perry-Grachev compromise was later approved at the CFE First Review Conference in Vienna in May 1996. Along with some southern regions of Russia, the Pskov Region was excluded from the flank zone, whereas other parts of the Leningrad Military District were retained in this area (SIPRI 1996: 724).

The CFE Treaty also became a subject of indirect dialogue between Russia and NATO on the enlargement issue. Russia has complained that the ratio of its own conventional forces to those of NATO would worsen in the event of NATO extension (to about 7:10). At the same time, the accommodation of NATO newcomers in the CFE Central Zone would have to affect Germany. If the Treaty's 'groups of states' balance were to be retained, virtually no equipment could be based in Germany, which appears unrealistic.

By the way, Russia can choose a strategy of insisting on current limits imposed by the CFE Treaty to put NATO in an awkward position in the event of its expansion.

To avoid potential damage from NATO enlargement to the regional arms control regime, Moscow submitted a proposal to the OSCE Senior Council meeting in Prague in April 1995. According to Russia's initiative, a new CFE-2 Treaty should be concluded. It would provide for further cuts, 15-20 per cent below present CFE levels. The bloc limits should be replaced by national levels and quotas which should not exceed, and might possibly be lower than, the previous quantitative ceilings. A new treaty should include all OSCE states (i.e. the Baltic states, Finland and Sweden), and zone limits should be dropped or replaced by subregional limits based on a quite different approach (*Segodnya* 1995a: 3). Initially most of the CFE Treaty states reacted sceptically to the Russian proposal. However, the countries eventually agreed to revise the Treaty in exchange for Russia's consent to conclude the Paris Charter with NATO.

It should also be noted that the CFE Treaty is applicable only to land forces. Naval armaments are mainly excluded from the negotiation process. Unilateral measures have been taken to reduce naval armaments and naval activities, but they relate to obsolete weapons and cannot be a substitute for a real arms control regime. According to Volker Heise, the reason for the basic hesitancy of some NATO nations regarding naval armaments limitations in the Baltic Sea seems to be that if you initiate naval arms control in one of the seven seas, this might lead to restrictions on maritime flexibility in the other seas as well (Heise 1996: 219).

Along with the arms control regime, CSBMs are a very important element of any regional security system. According to the Vienna Document of 1994, the OSCE states should notify each other 42 days in advance of military activities involving more than 9000 troops or 250 battle tanks, 500 ACVs, or 250 self-propelled and towed artillery pieces, mortars and multiple-rocket launchers (100-mm calibre and above); or 3000 troops participating in amphibious landings, heliborne landings or parachute drops. Air forces are included in the notification procedure if at least 200 sorties by aircraft, excluding helicopters, are flown. Military observers may be sent to exercises conducted by 13 000 troops, or 300 tanks or 500 ACVs or 250 artillery pieces, mortars and multiple-rocket launchers (100-mm and above) or if manoeuvres foresee 3 500 troops taking part in airborne landings, heliborne landings or parachute drops (SIPRI 1996: 742).

As Russia has complied with these requirements, no complaint from the neighbouring states or the OSCE has been registered. However, the failure of the Vienna Document of 1994 to apply to naval military activities has led to some tensions in the region. For example, in October 1996, the Latvian Foreign Ministry protested against the crossing of its economic zone by a flotilla of Russian vessels led by the cruiser Pyotr Velikiy on its way from the Baltic Sea to Barents Sea (*Diplomaticheskiy Vestnik* 1996b: 63-4). Some Russian and Western experts believe that extension of the CSBMs to the sea could be useful addition to the Vienna Document of 1994 regime in the region (e.g. Goodby and Morel 1993: 262; Krohn 1993: 114-7).

Prospects for Regional Co-operative Security: Any Role for Russia?

Many Russian and Western analysts express an underlying fear that a new dividing line in security matters might be created both in the Baltic Sea area and in Europe. NATO enlargement, as well as the unpredictable domestic developments in Russia and in the CIS, and the existing economic and social imbalances between West and East obviously contain elements of conflict. In addition, any reliable organisational framework for a regional security dialogue is lacking. Under this circumstances, the role of each regional player becomes crucial.

Despite its economic and political weaknesses and the shift of its security priorities towards the south, Russia is still an important actor in the Baltic Sea rim space. It is obvious that it is practically impossible to create a co-operative security system in the region without Russia. However, it is still unclear whether Russia will play any constructive role in the creation of such a system.

This uncertainty mainly originates with Russia's continuing search for national identity both in the domestic and foreign policy realms. Moscow is still hesitant as regards which type of strategy – *Realpolitik* or co-operative security pattern – should be opted for. The Russian leadership still lacks a clear vision of the country's place and role in the European and global international relations systems. From the point of view of traditional power politics which currently dominates Russian security thinking, the Baltic Sea area is merely a 'flank' – and not a very important one – in the European 'power game'. 'Hard' security issues should be resolved at the 'continental level'; only 'soft' security could be covered by sub-regional arrangements.

However, these realist and geopolitical paradigms may very soon be challenged by the processes unfolding both in the Baltic Sea area and Europe. It appears EU enlargement and European integration – and not only NATO extension – now dominate the continental security agenda. NATO itself is changing its purpose and functions from military to political-military organisation charged with conflict management and peace-keeping rather than 'containment.' On the other hand, Russia will have to deal not only with pan-European institutions and individual countries but also with the 'Europe of regions.'

These developments give Russia opportunities both to join a pan-European process and to shift the focus of continental politics from geopolitical rivalry and 'hard' security to co-operative patterns. The Baltic Sea region, an area with established traditions of regionalised arrangements, with Denmark, Finland and Sweden as members of the European Union, and with the Balts and Poland on their way towards a closer relationship with the EU, is especially promising in this regard.

Moscow has already taken some positive steps to change its regional course. Russia no longer perceives the area as a zone of military confrontation with the West. It has downplayed the role of military force in solving regional problems except for some cases defined by military doctrine. Both Russian military presence and activities in the region have decreased significantly. Some progress in solving minority problems in Estonia and Latvia has been achieved. Territorial disputes have been kept at a relatively low level compared to other parts of the world. Russia and Estonia are close to the resolution of their border dispute. The countries of the region have agreed to co-operate on a number of 'soft security' issues such as environmental protection, military industry conversion and organised crime although the lack of money and co-ordination still prevents the realisation of some promising projects. An extensive network of global, pan-European and regional organisations exists; these engagements and institutions are not mutually exclusive and may be complementary in solving the Baltic Sea rim's security problems. Russian policy is conducive to the use of the EU and subregional institutions as alternatives to NATO as far as the Balts' security is concerned. As Chernomyrdin's initiative at the Visby Summit demonstrates, Moscow is tending towards redefining and broadening its security concept, as well as acknowledging the importance of subregional arrangements and transregional co-operation.

At the same time, a number of shortcomings must be overcome in the future. Russia still lacks a coherent, long-term Baltic doctrine. Moscow has failed to allay the Baltic Sea countries' concerns as to Russia's military strength in the region, its domestic instability and its external implications. Moscow has been unable to point to a proper and generally acceptable transnational organisation to cope with regional security issues. Russia and NATO have so far been unable to reach a compromise on the Alliance's extension to the Baltic Sea area. The anticipated NATO enlargement has led to the growth of Russia's 'hard security' concerns and to animated discussions on a possible military build-up in the region and the formation of a military alliance in the CIS context. Some countries, as well as some categories of weaponry, are not covered by the existing arms control regime; CSBMs are also underdeveloped in the area.

The negative trends can be averted if at least two interdependent aims are achieved – strengthening Russia's democratic system of government and creating a favourable and non-provocative international environment. With the completion of domestic reforms, Moscow will likely understand that co-operative rather than power-based or confrontational policies will better serves the country's national interests and its international authority. At the same time, other countries of the region should respect Russia's legitimate interests and concerns as regards NATO enlargement, minority rights and border issues. Potential elements of a favourable environment would be to delay or refrain from NATO extension to the Baltic states, improve arms control and CSBM regimes, give Western assistance to the conversion of the highly militarised Kaliningrad and St Petersburg regions, resolve the territorial and ethnic minority disputes in the area and develop transregional co-operation in various fields. In turn, this would encourage those forces in Russia who seek a balanced foreign policy. It would also assist Moscow in defining its national interests in the Baltic Sea area, as well as in choosing the appropriate conceptual framework and the tools for conducting security policies in the region.

Notes

1 This research was supported by grants from the Copenhagen Peace Research Institute and the Research Support Scheme (1996-97).

2 See an English translation in *Jane's Intelligence Review* (1994).

References

Arbatov, Alexey (1994). 'Russian National Interests,' in Blackwill, Robert D. and Karaganov, Sergey A. (eds.). *Damage Limitation or Crisis? Russia and the Outside World.* Washington and London, Brassey's, Inc.

Arbatov, Alexey (1996). 'The Future of European Security: Split or Unity?', *Visions of European Security: Focal Point Sweden and Northern Europe.* Stockholm, The Olof Palme International Center.

The Baltic Independent (1994a), 16-22 September.

The Baltic Independent (1994b), 18-24 November.

The Baltic Independent (1995), 3-9 February.

Baranovskiy, Vladimir (1996). 'Russia,' in Krohn, Axel (ed.). *The Baltic Sea Area: National and International Security Perspectives.* Baden-Baden, Nomos Verlagsgesellschaft, pages 164-182.

Committee on National Security, State Duma (1995). *Kontseptsiya Natsionalnoy Bezopasnosti Rossiyskoy Federatsii: Proyekt* [The National Security Concept of the Russian Federation: Draft], Moscow.

Diplomaticheskiy Vestnik (1993). 'Kontseptsiya Vneshney Politiki Rossiyskoi Federatsii' [The Foreign Policy Concept of the Russian Federation], Special Issue, January, pages 3-23.

Diplomaticheskiy Vestnik (1995), March.

Diplomaticheskiy Vestnik (1996a), August.

Diplomaticheskiy Vestnik (1996b), November.

Diplomaticheskiy Vestnik (1996c), December.

Fadeyev, Dmitri A. and Razuvayev, Vladimir (1994). 'Russia and the Western Post-Soviet Republics,' in Blackwill, Robert D. and Karaganov, Sergey A. (eds.). *Damage Limitation or Crisis? Russia and the Outside World.* Washington and London, Brassey's Inc.

Goodby, James E. and Morel, Benoit (eds.) (1993). *The Limited Partnership. Building a Russian-US Security Community.* NewYork, SIPRI/Oxford University Press.

Gromov, Feliks (1995). 'Znachenie Kaliningradskogo Osobogo Rayona dlya Oboronosposobnosti Rossiyskoy Federatsii' [The Role of the Kaliningrad Special District for the Russian Federation's Defence], *Voennaya Mysl:* July-August 1995, p. 11.

Heise, Volker (1996). 'The North Atlantic Treaty Organization,' in Krohn, Axel (ed.). *The Baltic Sea Area: National and International Security Perspectives.* Baden-Baden: Nomos Verlagsgesellschaft.

Jane's Intelligence Review (1994). Special Report, January.

Jane's International Defense Review (1996), September.

Jane's Defence Weekly (1993), 13 March.

Jane's Defence Weekly (1995), 16 December.

Jane's Defence Weekly (1996), 24 April.

Komsomolskaya Pravda (1995), 29 September.

Kozyrev, Andrey (1994). Statement, 19 January.

Krohn, Axel (1993). 'Naval Arms Control and Disarmament in the Baltic Sea Region,' in Joenniemi, Pertti (ed.). *Cooperation in the Baltic Sea Region.* London, Taylor and Francis.

Lukin, Vladimir P. (1994). 'Russia and Its Interests,' in Sestanovich, Stephen (ed.). Rethinking Russia's National Interests. Washington, DC, Center for Strategic and International Studies.

Maibach, Marcia (1996). 'The Baltic Security Agenda and Emerging Framework of Cooperation,' in Krohn, Axel (ed.). *The Baltic Sea Area: National and International Security Perspectives.* Baden-Baden, Nomos Verlagsgesellschaft.

The Military Balance 1990-1991 (1990). London, International Institute of Strategic Studies.

The Military Balance 1996-1997 (1996). London, International Institute of Strategic Studies.

Moshes, Arkadiy and Vushkarnik, Anton (1997). 'Russia and the Baltic States: Between Co-existence and Cooperation?', IWPS 1997:1.

Nezavisimaya Gazeta (1996a), 11 April.

Petersen, Philipp A. (1994). 'Kaliningrad: Transition From Garrison State,' *Jane's Intelligence Review*, December 1994.

Segodnya (1995a), 5 May.

Segodnya (1995b), 16 November.

Sergounin, Alexander A. (1996a). 'The Russian Dimension of Nordic Security: Hard Choices and Opportunities,' in *Visions of European Security: Focal Point Sweden and Northern Europe*. Stockholm, The Olof Palme International Center, pages 112-115.

Sergounin, Alexander A. (1996b). *On the Way to Integration: Military-Technical Co-operation between the CIS Member States*. Nizhniy Novgorod, University of Nizhniy Novgorod.

Sergounin, Alexander A. and Subbotin, Sergey V. (1996). *Sino-Russian Military Co-operation and the Evolving Security System in East Asia*. Nizhny Novgorod, University of Nizhny Novgorod Press.

SIPRI Yearbook 1994. New York, Oxford University Press.

SIPRI Yearbook 1996. New York, Oxford University Press.

Supreme Soviet of the Russian Federation (1992). *Zakon o Bezopasnosti Rossiyskoy Federatsii* [Law on the Security of the Russian Federation], Moscow.

Trenin, Dmitri (1995). 'NATO: How to Avoid Confrontation,' *International Affairs* (Moscow), Vol. 41:7 (July 1995), pages 20-26.

Uspenskiy, Nikolaj and Komissarov, Sergey (1993). 'New Stage in Cooperation in the Baltic Region,' International Affairs, Vol 39:2 (February 1993), p. 83.

Viitasalo, Mikko and Österlund, Bo (1996). *The Baltic: Sea of Changes*. Helsinki, National Defence College.

Zhirinovskiy, Vladimir (1993). *Posledniy Brosok na Yug* [Last Dash for the South]. Moscow, LDPR.

30 Poland's Security Policies in the Baltic Sea Area

Wojciech Kostecki

This chapter briefly describes the most recent events in Poland's security policies towards the Baltic Sea area. Basically, the whole year 1996 and the beginning of 1997 are covered; where necessary to show the dynamics, earlier circumstances and longer processes are included. The main issues concern Polish regional initiatives, military co-operation, approach to Kaliningrad and relations with Lithuania. Some background material is also provided in order to place the Baltic dimension in a wider perspective of sources and options for the overall Polish security policy.

Introduction

The 1989-91 changes in Europe: the collapse of communist governments in the Warsaw Pact countries and the dissolution of the Pact (together with the Council of Mutual Economic Assistance, CMEA), the reunification of Germany and the liquidation of the Soviet Union, had a double effect on Polish security policy. On the one hand, Poland obtained full rights – and responsibilities – attributed to a modern sovereign state. On the other, it had to cope with the new post-Cold War challenges of a transformed international environment that meant the disappearance of systemic bipolarity with its risks of global conflict and major war in Europe, and the clear friend-enemy pattern ('socialist camp' versus 'imperialist bloc'). Instead, Poland found itself on its own, surrounded by a completely new neighbourhood and guided by the necessity to introduce democratic and free market-oriented reforms.

In 1989 Poland had three neighbours: the USSR, Czechoslovakia and the GDR. Soon they were replaced by seven new states: Russia, Lithuania, Belarus, Ukraine, Slovakia, the Czech Republic and (reunited) Germany, and bilateral relations with them had to be arranged from scratch. This was particularly important in the case of Germany and Russia. From Germany it was necessary to obtain a reconfirmation of the Polish western border and a 'gateway to Europe.' With Russia there was a need to conclude a major treaty that would eliminate the dependencies characteristic of the former relations with the Soviet Union and ensure the withdrawal of Russian troops from Poland. And the desire to achieve 'the final confirmation' of the irreversibility of changes in the political system and to get the assistance necessary to transform and develop the Polish economy – contributed to the search for the closest possible rapprochement with the Western structures.

The principles of Poland's security policy under the new internal and international circumstances were summarised in 1992, that is after the political and economic reforms had been initiated and the first steps towards the Western structures had been taken. They referred to a broad understanding of security, respect for international law, and the significance of European integration and American presence in Europe.[1] They were adopted by the National Defence Committee and signed by President Lech Walesa, but not passed by Parliament.

The security policy based on these principles has been characterised by a noticeable level of continuity, although some changes – or adaptations – have also been visible (Kostecki and Wiberg 1996). They have concerned, among other things, the dilemmas of seeking NATO or/and EU membership and balancing the 'Western' (pro-integrationist) and 'Eastern' dimension of the policy. The most recent elaboration has set the following priorities: in the first place 'Poland's return to the Western World through integration with the European and Euro-Atlantic institutions' – which at the time meant the Atlantic Alliance; next 'building the best possible relations with our neighbours' – that is, first of all, with Russia; and only then 'regional co-operation serving to stabilise the region and to strengthen Poland's position' (Exposé 1996: 1097).

There are five major motives behind the so-called Euro-Atlantic option of the Polish security policy. Apart from the ideological premises and economic reasons mentioned above, as well as the historical lessons of a country for a long time subjected to the rivalries of neighbours, strategic and political-military considerations also matter. The latter concern, first, the geopolitical location of Poland between the stable Western Europe and the territories of the former Soviet Union, which experience a number of developments with uncertain results and potentially dangerous consequences for Polish security. Secondly, they are related to the fact that the present size and state of the Polish armed forces make it necessary and possible to search for political alliances.[2] Such events as the participation in several UN peace operations, the adjustment of the defence system to the Atlantic standards and military co-operation with NATO countries – especially Germany, France, Denmark and the US – are also to Poland's advantage.

The regional dimension of European co-operation is perceived in Poland as a component of building a pan-European security system. Another premise says that the foundation of the security of every country rests on good-neighbourly and co-operative relations with the immediate surroundings. Therefore Poland actively supports the co-operation in the Baltic Sea area but understands it as an element of step-by-step integration into the (West) European structures and an instrument of enhancing stability and confidence among the Baltic Sea states.

In the military domain, Poland sees the Baltic Sea as an open area but – according to the official sources – reserves itself the right to carry out defensive operations there if any threat exists (Cooperation). This declaration seems intended to serve propaganda purposes. Information discussed internally supports the view that in reality Polish naval forces have rather limited possibilities of undertaking large offensive actions. For instance, there are no means (neither mine-layers nor mines) nor plans to block the Strait of Pillau or the harbours of the Kaliningrad district in case of an armed conflict. What is anticipated is rather the protection of Poland's own near-shore communication routes. On the other hand, some internal games are apparently also involved since navy experts express great expectations concerning the envisaged NATO membership – namely, that among the Polish services, it is precisely the navy that will be given the most substantial tasks by NATO's military command.

In the face of NATO's eastward opening, Poland has stressed the necessity of taking into account the whole package of relevant issues: 'a NATO-Russian partnership,' 'the security situation of the three Baltic states and of the Ukraine,' 'the fate of the "Partnership for Peace" and the Alliance's relations with states which are not included in the first round of enlargement' and so forth (Address 1996b: 1260).

This position reflects the view that a gradual enlargement of NATO introduced together with improved relations with Russia and the Ukraine would make the whole process – and the Polish entry into the Alliance – smoother. If so, there is an obvious need to work out solutions for the states that will not be invited during the first round. An enhanced Partnership for Peace programme, a so-called PfP-Plus, may play such a role. Here, the Polish-Lithuanian 'enhanced partnership' is often mentioned. The Latvian Atlantic Partnership proposal of July 1996, on the other hand, has been interpreted in Poland as an unnecessary middle stage, which might slow down the accession process and give Russia the false impression that it is able to hamper NATO enlargement. However, another proposal concerning the Atlantic Partnership Council, put forward by the US in September 1996, has been welcomed on the assumption that it facilitates an appeasement of Russian fears.

Confidence and Security-Enhancing Measures: Towards Regionalisation

Poland, being a co-author of several proposals, has expressed its satisfaction with the successive codification and implementation of the confidence- and security-building measures (CSBMs) contained in the so-called Vienna Documents of 1990 and 1992. However, they have been perceived as the lowest all-European common denominator, and Poland has consequently argued in favour of concrete measures at the regional level.

The first Polish initiatives appeared at the CSCE Forum for Security Co-operation in Vienna in 1994 as 'illustrative regional CSBMs.' They concerned the following areas: exchange of military information, military contacts, prior notification of military activity, its observation and exchange of schedules, verification and inspections (Illustrative 1994). The aim was to arouse interest in Russia and other countries in a regional agreement and to expand CSBMs by also including naval forces into the exchange of information field.

The Polish initiative is explained by a wish to benefit from bilateral and multilateral co-operation around the Baltic Sea, including the economically and militarily important regions of the Russian Federation (Kaliningrad, St Petersburg) and by the fact that the Baltic Sea is going to become an 'inland sea' of the European Union. Despite the far-reaching differences in national security policies, the states of the area share a number of security concerns, like military disparities and imbalances, nuclear power risks, growing organised crime, and in the case of some of them – even domestic political and economic disturbances.

Therefore a considerable effort was made to convince all parties involved that implementation of the Polish proposal would not prejudice other states' interests. Polish diplomats tried to persuade the others that this was not a take-it-or-leave-it approach and was not intended to substitute the arrangements agreed earlier but to complement them. In other words, the aim was to support the OSCE efforts and, in addition, some of the measures might also fit in with the PfP activities. In sum, the idea was not to grant the Baltic Sea area some special status but to enhance confidence and security among states in the region. Consequently, the proposed label was changed from 'confidence and security building' (CSBMs) to 'confidence and security enhancing' (CSEMs) measures (Confidence).

In accordance with the assumptions just mentioned, Poland addressed the question of CSEMs for the Baltic Sea area twice in 1995. The food-for-thought paper, submitted to the European Union and former participants in the Baltic Table of the Pact of Stability and then presented during the OSCE Seminar on Regional Arms Control in Vienna (July), indicated the proper measures for bilateral and regional relations and identified a number of measures that were particularly applicable to the Baltic Sea region. On 17 October, representatives of the Baltic Sea states met in Warsaw to discuss the subject. The Polish side introduced new material suggesting four groups of desired measures: co-operation on the relief operations after natural disasters, accidents and so forth; enhancement of mechanisms preventing incidents related to military activity; and enhanced military contacts and co-operation, exchange of experiences and joint military training. Poland also proposed that CSEMs become a new area of activity for the Council of the Baltic Sea States.

The year 1996 brought rather weak feedback on these ideas. However, some signs of interest coming from Lithuania and Latvia, and from Sweden, the US and Holland were noted. In addition, two informal consultations were held in Vienna (29 March and 26 April) at the seat of the Polish Mission to the OSCE. Nevertheless, the debate among Polish experts continued. They underlined that the adoption of Vienna Document of 1994 means that the all-European domain of CSBMs has been substantially exhausted, and that regional initiatives may therefore be a reasonable path for further development. The Polish experts also pointed out that Finland, Sweden and the three Baltic states are not subjected to the CFE regime, and that any adaptation of the CFE Treaty may therefore not ensure stability for the region. The main motive, however, remained the same: to find a formula for Russia to participate in security arrangements around the Baltic Sea and to work out a solution for the Baltic states, which are not going to be accepted into the North Atlantic Treaty Organisation in the first round.

That is why experts advised to seek NATO impulses that might dispel the fears of the Baltic states (and Denmark) and, simultaneously, to negotiate a possible agreement in the framework of the OSCE Forum for Security Co-operation in Vienna – in order to gain Russian acceptance. It was stressed that the development of such NATO-Russian co-operation would add to the credibility of CSEMs and might limit the unpredictability of Russia's Baltic policy. Nor did the military circles want to be late. They worked on the enrichment of the CSEMs catalogue and called for a stronger involvement of military experts in the relevant discussions and negotiations (Building).

The Council of the Baltic Sea States: Looking for a New Mandate

In an attempt to find a suitable forum in which to develop and implement its initiatives on CSEMs, Poland turned its attention to the Council of the Baltic Sea States (CBSS). The CBSS had previously been assigned three tasks: the elimination of old ideological and political divisions and the resolution of disputes in the region; the facilitation of Poland's move towards the EU by providing patterns of multilateral co-operation; and support of democratic development and promotion of human rights.[3] Now a fourth task was suggested, namely to contribute to security and stability in the region. At the end of 1995, Poland proposed setting up a new working group of the CBSS. The group was to suggest and develop initiatives and make recommendations on enhancing confidence and security in the Baltic Sea area through both military and non-military measures (Confidence).

The concept stems from the general Polish approach to regional arrangements. Poland has had good experience with political collaboration in the framework of the Visegrad Group that facilitated the dissolution of the Warsaw Pact and the CMEA, and has been striving to extend this co-operation so as to join efforts aimed at achieving NATO and EU membership. The Polish government has advocated equipping another regional institution, that is the Central European Initiative with a mandate for political co-operation.

It should be noted that a role for the CBSS as a regional stabiliser had been envisaged from the very beginning. For instance, the declaration adopted at the Council's founding meeting in 1992 supported new democratic institutions in the region and various forms of co-operation there.

That is why Poland has suggested an extension of the CBSS mandate by adding a political dimension. Polish experts have emphasised that, in fact, the CBSS has already dealt with political matters such as the withdrawal of Russian troops from the Baltic states or the situation in Chechnya. However, the two major events in 1996: the Baltic Sea States Summit in Visby (3-4 May) and the Fifth Ministerial Session in Kalmar (2-3 July), did not bring support for the Polish idea. Before the latter meeting, Poland had issued a proposal to add a seventh domain of co-operation to the CBSS mandate, namely 'confidence, stability and civic security,' but could not get consensus.

Nevertheless, the Polish efforts brought some success in the non-military field. First, the issue of civic security was included in the Action Programmes adopted in Kalmar, marking a step forward in the co-operation of the Baltic Sea states because security issues were thus in practice introduced on the CBSS agenda though not formally accepted in its Terms of Reference. During the follow-up debate, Poland supported a Latvian initiative to establish a working group on civil security by stressing that existing bodies are either too specialised (the one dealing with organised crime) or not competent enough (the group on democratic institutions). Secondly, as Poland sees it, several issues of socio-political security and stability were in fact covered by the Programmes. In this context, it is significant that the following tasks were indicated: creation of a network of contacts between various communities, organisations and individuals; and better people-to-people understanding, especially through educational programmes, cultural co-operation and tourism.

The issue of organised crime has been of special Polish interest. Poland co-authored the proposal to launch regional co-operative projects against organised crime already in 1993. In 1994 and 1995, Warsaw hosted international conferences devoted to theft and smuggling of works of art, estimations of threats caused by organised crime and the possibilities of countering them. The Polish interest was confirmed by Prime Minister Wlodzimierz Cimoszewicz, who stressed that it was because of a Polish initiative that the Visby Summit established a task force to co-ordinate and direct actions in the field (Statement 1996a).

The Task Force on combating organised crime met as many as four times during the second half of 1996. Poland has accepted responsibility for preparing a report on the legal possibilities of multilateral efforts in secret surveillance of deliveries and sting operations. Moreover, following Task Force recommendations, the Polish representatives established bilateral contacts with their counterparts from Germany – senior officials of prosecutor-generals' offices and criminal bureaux (meeting in Lagow, 28-29 October), Estonia – senior officials of interior ministries, police, border guards, security services and customs officers (Warsaw, 18-19 November), and Sweden – senior officials of law-enforcement organs engaged in the fight against organised crime (Warsaw, 25-26 November).

Military Co-operation: A Ticket to NATO

As a consequence of its poor results on military CSEMs, Poland has put a lot of effort into military co-operation with its neighbours around the Baltic Sea. The co-operation has three dimensions: bilateral relations, the trilateral Polish-Danish-German undertakings, especially in a PfP context, and Poland's participation in the IFOR operations in Bosnia and Herzegovina within the structure of the Nordic-Polish Brigade.

The bilateral co-operation between Poland and other Baltic Sea states in the military domain has a solid legal basis. The relevant agreement with Latvia was signed in 1992, with Lithuania, Germany, Denmark and Russia in 1993, with Sweden in 1994, with Estonia in 1995. The number of common projects in 1996 grew to several dozens (for instance, with Germany – 88 items) and embraced high-level visits, working contacts, educational and sports enterprises, military exercises, exchange of information in various fields etc.; and last but not least, the concept of common units (for example the Polish-German one). All these endeavours have contributed to confidence building and therefore to security in the Baltic Sea area. However, it would be important to supplement them by more active co-operation with the Kaliningrad and St Petersburg districts.

The trilateral military co-operation between Poland, Denmark and Germany was initiated by the Danish side in 1994. A year later the Ministers of Defence from the three countries signed an agreement constituting the legal framework for such co-operation (meeting on Ærø Island, 16-17 August 1995). The decisions concerning common undertakings have been made during the successive (twice a year) meetings of the ministers, who have also used these occasions to discuss European security questions of common interest. Subunits from the 12th Mechanised Division constitute the main Polish troops taking part in the joint exercises. In 1996, the major events were: the command post exercise 'Baltic Cooperation 96' in Poland (Drawsko field training centre, 20-25 March), 'Baltic Endeavour 96' (Baltic Sea, 21-31 August) and 'Open Spirit' (German territory, 2-9 September).

From the Polish point of view, the Polish-Danish-German co-operation was desired also as an instrument to achieve interoperability with NATO forces – a task which Poland and NATO agreed on within the PfP framework. The most important elements of this co-operation consist of search and rescue operations, both at sea and in the air. They have been intended to prepare Polish units for participation in similar multinational operations led by NATO. Moreover, the trilateral co-operation has enriched the scope of the PfP programme by including certain CSBMs, like the opportunity for soldiers to become acquainted with each other, the mutual learning of military planning and management procedures, and mutual accommodation. According to Poland's ministry of defence, it would be useful to enlarge the command post exercises because they are less costly, and because the acquired skills are more effectively utilised by the professional officers than by ordinary soldiers, whose duties last several months only.

The Polish-Danish-German co-operation has been perceived as a vehicle for getting closer to NATO. Together with the Weimar Triangle activities and co-operation with the US, it has been a Polish priority and has contributed to regional stabilisation.

The decision to create the Polish Military Contingent within the framework of IFOR was made on 5 December 1995. On 18 January 1996, the first subunits set out for Bosnia, and on 5 February, the deployment of the Polish contingent was completed. The contingent (POLBAT) consisted of the 16th Airborne Battalion, which joined the multinational Nordic-Polish Brigade (NORDPOL-BRIG) together with units from Denmark, Finland, Norway and Sweden. The brigade was subordinated to the American 1st Armoured Division.

The significance of the whole undertaking has remained rather symbolic,[4] although the opportunity for soldiers coming from different milieus to adapt to each other has also mattered. When SFOR replaced IFOR in Bosnia, the number of Polish soldiers was reduced by one third.

In official rhetoric, the participation in IFOR and later SFOR has been perceived as 'evidence of the recognition of (Polish) aspirations to join the Euro-Atlantic security structures' and a test of 'the worth of (Polish) armed forces' (Address 1996a: 1011). The success of this mission has proved the capacity of the Polish Army to act within the NATO structure and has therefore constituted a step towards NATO itself.

The Kaliningrad Enclave: The Road Towards Desecuritisation

The essential issue of Polish security policy towards the Baltic Sea area has been the relations with the Kaliningrad district. This area was granted to the Soviet Union in 1945 by a decision of the Potsdam Conference, and it now forms a Russian enclave located within the territory of former East Prussia. After the dissolution of the Soviet Union, it is the only part of the Russian Federation that borders on Poland. The common frontier is 209 kilometres long, and following NATO enlargement – in the Russian perception – it may become a new dividing line in Europe. Units of the Russian Baltic Fleet, ground forces equipped with battle tanks and artillery, and air force and air defence systems are stationed there. The Russian military presence in the 'Kaliningrad Special Defence Region' (KOOR, formed in 1994) – in the direct proximity of Poland – can even be reinforced in a crisis situation.

On the other hand, there is a huge potential for mutually profitable co-operation, especially at the local level. Here the Russian 'window-on-the world' policy which originated with Gorbachev's perestroika, together with several opportunities brought about during the 1990s by new custom regulations, licensing policies and opportunities for foreign investment,[5] meets the economic needs of Poland's north-eastern provinces, which are relatively less developed. Poland therefore favours 'desecuritisation' of the relations with the Kaliningrad district, which implies supporting the area's transformation, removing considerations of hard security from the agenda, and reducing possible threats by increasing the scale of common undertakings.

The solid legal basis for such a transformation is provided by two major documents: the principal Polish-Russian Treaty on Friendship and Good-Neighbourly Co-operation, and the Agreement on Co-operation between the North-eastern Provinces of the Republic of Poland and Kaliningrad District of the Russian Federation (both signed on 22 May 1992). The latter obliges both parties to create favourable conditions for comprehensive economic and socio-cultural co-operation, including some measures belonging to a domain of civic security (information sharing and assistance in rescue operations at sea, ecological disasters, major incidents and epidemics etc.). The Polish-Russian Agreement on Trans-Border Co-operation (2 October 1992) and the Agreement on Bilateral Co-operation in the Military Domain (7 July 1993) are also relevant.

In 1996, the economic co-operation between Poland and Kaliningrad was labelled as 'revolutionary' in comparison with the previous 3-4 years (for details, see Statement 1996b). Since 1994, the Polish-Russian Council – a special body dealing with transborder co-operation in the region – has been at work. There have also been examples of military co-operation in the recent period: transborder co-operation between the Warsaw Military District and the Russian 11th Army, and seven cases of Polish inspection on the territory of KOOR and two Russian inspections in north-eastern Poland (within the framework of the CFE agreements).[6]

However, the Kaliningrad district still contributes to Polish security concerns. There is a considerable presence of military forces here, concentrated on a rather limited area. The number of uniformed personnel is currently estimated at some 60,000 men and consists of ground forces – 25,000, the Baltic Fleet – 38,000 and the border guards – 9,500.[7] Polish opinions on their combat readiness differ, but in general, the number of troops is estimated to be much higher than the Russian needs.

In any case, Poland would be interested in a further decrease in the level of forces in the Kaliningrad district. It is not clear, however, how such a reduction could be achieved. The proposals of some experts to introduce proper adaptations of the CFE Treaty are rather unrealistic since an opposite tendency prevails at the CFE-2 negotiations. The May 1996 adjustments seemed to have no consequences for KOOR (Joenniemi 1996: 11), nor, of course, did the January 1997 proposals to freeze the limits of Russian forces in Kaliningrad together with national limits for Poland, the Czech and Slovak Republics and Hungary, on one side, and Belarus and in part the Ukraine, on the other.

One should note that the Polish military point to the operational-strategic role of the Kaliningrad district, which makes their defence planning more difficult. They also suggest that they lack capabilities to oppose the Russian forces in case of an armed conflict.[8] There are several reasons for that. The military are trained – as everywhere – to predict the worst-case scenario even if it is not probable from the political point of view. The geographical location of Kaliningrad indeed enables it to control the navigation in the Gulf of Gdansk and launch ground operations in a south-western direction that could cut communication routes between Warsaw and the industrial regions of Silesia and Gdansk and Gdynia ports. The memories of 1939, when Poland was almost surrounded by enemy forces, are still alive – even if they may not be appropriate in the present international situation. Finally, the position of the Polish military may be interpreted as an element of pressure for more funds after suffering drastic cuts in defence expenditures for the last ten years.[9]

Hypothetically, Kaliningrad might become a base for nuclear weapons. Even now there are units with land- and ship-based tactical missiles able to carry nuclear warheads (although the presence of these warheads is not confirmed). But a more extensive deployment may be executed in future if a nuclear answer to NATO enlargement is decided on.[10] Such a risk has not yet been exploited by the Polish side as an argument in political debates, partly because of its speculative character, and partly because of a general endeavour to keep a low profile. However, in March 1997, President Kwasniewski – addressing the issue of a 'grand bargain' on the relations between an enlarged NATO and Russia – stated that if Poland is to remain non-nuclear, there should be no nuclear weapons in the Kaliningrad district either (interview in *Der Spiegel*, quoted from *Gazeta Wyborcza* 1997).

In sum, one can agree with the external, matter-of-fact oriented analyses pointing to the decline of Kaliningrad's military importance and instead concentrate on the district's potentially positive influence on regional stabilisation (Joenniemi 1996: 8-12 and others). Poland, for its part, has recognised the sovereign rights of the Russian Federation in the district and has adopted an active policy of co-operation. In particular, it has supported local initiatives and accepted a general policy aimed at calming down and desecuritising the bilateral relations. But historical lessons, long-lasting anti-Russian attitudes[11] and present assessments and interests mean that Kaliningrad remains an issue for Polish security policy.

'Corridor '96': Misunderstanding, Probe or Reminder?

The issue of the so-called corridor between Belarus and Kaliningrad may be seen by outside observers as having been played up by Poland. However, this was potentially the most dangerous problem for Polish security policy in the Baltic region in 1996. This is because Russian suggestions were interpreted as an attempt to limit Polish sovereignty and touched the most sensitive aspect of the post-Cold War Polish-Russian relations. The sharp reaction of Polish politicians – despite the strict principle of avoiding of any conflict because of the aspirations to join NATO and the EU – shows how far the consequences of this problem might reach.

The concept of a transport corridor and special conditions for Russian transit via Polish territory has been put forward by Russia since 1993,[12] although the idea itself has appeared somewhat blurred, and depending on the circumstances, different aspects of the proposal have been highlighted. The only positive Polish feedback to the Russians has come from the local authorities of Suwalski province whereas the Polish government has rejected the Russian proposals.

The issue became a matter of high politics when Boris Yeltsin, after a meeting with his counterpart from Belarus (Minsk, 27 February 1996), stated that both presidents would seek Polish acceptance to build 'a small bit of motorway' on Polish territory. Next day this idea was strongly opposed by Poland's Foreign Minister Dariusz Rosati and Deputy Prime Minister Grzegorz Kolodko and one day later, President Aleksander Kwasniewski described it as 'not acceptable.' The following week, Kwasniewski stressed that none of Poland's neighbours would be allowed to obtain a corridor or an exterritorial road. Facing the negative Polish reaction, the Russian side decided to soften the whole affair. Foreign Minister Primakov assured that the idea of a corridor existed only in the columns of the Polish press and that Russia wanted merely to make the most of the already existing border crossings and roads (visit to Poland, 15 March 1996).

The Polish objections to the Russian proposal may, again, be explained by the problem of attitude. First, in the eyes of Polish public opinion, any concept of a corridor put forward by an external power means an infringement of Polish independence and evokes associations to the German demands from the inter-war period. It is even more painful when introduced by Russia – the main opponent of the Poland's Western-oriented security policy. Secondly, the ruling left-wing coalition, paradoxically, felt that it had to react firmly in order to avoid accusations of compliance with or even submission to the wishes of the former suzerain.[13]

Later various arguments were advanced to justify the refusal. It was noted that the acceptance of the Russian proposals would imply considerable political and economic losses for Lithuania – the country which currently controls the transit to Kaliningrad – and consequently cause a deterioration of Polish-Lithuanian relations. Moreover, Polish national security would also suffer because the proposed motorway – not to mention a broader 'corridor'[14] – might be used by Russia for military purposes. Besides, it would separate Poland from the Lithuanian border, which would not be acceptable because of the strategic and political implications, including Polish commitments to the PfP programmes and future NATO enlargement.

After a period of culmination in February and March 1996, the Russian side stated that the question of an exterritorial corridor 'does not exist' and that the whole issue was a misunderstanding. Poland perceived the Russian proposal rather as a probe to test Polish sensitivity to renewed Russian power politics. Therefore it remained on the Polish agenda. In July 1996, a special consultation attended by political, military and economic experts from several ministries took place in Warsaw, and in January 1997, the Polish government discussed a draft statement of its standpoint on the issue. The statement again contained a rejection of any special facility or condition for Russian transit to the Kaliningrad district. In terms of the larger Baltic politics, the corridor issue served as a reminder that the security aspects of the Kaliningrad enclave, including its impact on the Polish-Russian relations, are still alive.

Poland-Lithuania: Between Aspirations and Realities

According to the official statistics from 1994, the number of people belonging to the Polish minority in Lithuania is 262,000 (7 per cent of the whole population). The Poles constitute large homogenous groups in the south-eastern part of the country. They live mainly in the Lithuanian capital Vilnius – about 108,000 (19 per cent of the population) and around Vilnius – about 60,000 (about 64 per cent), as well as in the regions of Soleczniki – 33,000 (78 per cent) and Troki – 19,000 (24 per cent). The Polish minority maintain their national identity – about 80 per cent of its members speak Polish fluently – and clearly express this identity through the educational system, Polish organisations (including a national political party), cultural undertakings, press and participation in the public life at the local level as well as in the parliamentary elections. The protection of minority rights is guaranteed by the Polish-Lithuanian Treaty on Friendly Relations and Good-Neighbourly Co-operation, signed on 24 April 1994 (came into force on 26 November 1994). These facts explain the importance which public opinion in Poland attaches to the situation of the minority and why it influences Polish policy towards Lithuania – to some extent even the security dimension of that policy.

After a period of tension in the early 1990s, the Polish minority question has basically been removed from the agenda of bilateral relations, which recently reached a new level of intensity,[15] confirmed by exalted rhetoric.[16] At the beginning of 1996, however, when speaking about the good situation of the Polish minority in Lithuania, Speaker Zych and President Brazauskas agreed that 'there are always problems which must be understood, approached matter-of-factly and resolved' (Chronicle 1996a: 1014). And half a year later, the head of the Polish-Lithuanian Parliamentary Group, Adam Dobronski, noted that the Polish minority was subjected to certain unfriendly actions by the Lithuanian authorities (Chronicle 1996c: 1184).

Among the issues that caused problems in 1996, one can point to the unsolved question of the spelling of Polish names. Article 14 of the Polish-Lithuanian Treaty of 1994 guarantees that persons belonging to the minorities have the right to 'use their names and surnames in the version used in the language of the national minority.' However, the next sentence says: 'Specific regulations concerning the spelling of names and surnames will be laid down in a separate agreement' (Polish-Lithuanian Treaty 1994: 29). This has still not been achieved. Besides, there have been discussions on changes of the administrative borders of

Vilnius to Polish disadvantage, problems of land reprivatisation concerning Poles, and cancellation of the special privileges of national minorities in the election law. On 31 December 1996, the Polish ministry of foreign affairs protested against a statement by the Lithuanian minister of education concerning his programme of eliminating the Polish language from schools.

The desire not to disturb the process of rapprochement to NATO, together with the wish to play the role of a Lithuanian advocate in this process, prevents Poland from going too deeply into exploiting these problems in bilateral relations. However, certain links can be traced. The first concerns the initiative put forward by President Brazauskas as early as the beginning of 1995 to form a joint peace-keeping battalion. Although the suggestion was officially welcomed in Poland, it was postponed (first till the end of 1997, and recently till the first half of 1998) with reference to organisational and financial problems – despite the Lithuanian interest in creating the battalion as soon as possible in order to add to the country's credibility as a Western partner and active participant in the Partnership for Peace. Instead, Poland presented the Lithuanian armed forces with several items of arms and equipment (armoured personnel carriers, trucks, small arms, 5 Mi-2 helicopters and 12 radar sets for the control of air space).

Secondly, Poland is rather hesitant when it comes to the institutionalisation of interparliamentary and intergovernmental collaboration. Far-reaching Lithuanian proposals, such as the recent one by Landsbergis to establish a joint parliamentary institution (21 February 1997) have not received a clear response.

Finally, it should be noted that Poland has certain reservations as to the aspirations of the Baltic states to become NATO members. Such reservations were unmistakable, for instance, when President Kwasniewski publicly declared that 'Poland will never oppose any *legitimate* membership application on the part of other states' (Address 1996b: 1260, emphasis added). The recent emphatic turn made by Lithuania – which is left in NATO's 'waiting room' – towards rapprochement with Poland (the would-be insider) means that Poland gains a powerful instrument of political influence on Lithuania and reserves for itself the right to make use of it.

Concluding Thoughts

Poland enjoys a special place in the security arrangements of the Baltic Sea area. Two main axes of the post-Cold War European development are crossing each other on its territory. This is a country lying exactly in-between: between an advanced, rather integrated and quite stable Western centre and lagging, loose-knit and potentially conflict-racked Eastern peripheries. It also constitutes a common link in a chain of several regional institutions: the Council of the Baltic Sea States, the Visegrad Group, the Central European Initiative. Moreover, Poland has been a part of the Baltic Table (with Estonia, Latvia and Lithuania), that is, of a body established by the Stability Pact – the common undertaking of the EU and OSCE to eliminate the grounds for local conflicts and instabilities in Central and Eastern Europe.

Poland's security policy in the Baltic Sea area has been subordinated to a general strategy aimed at achieving membership in the Euro-Atlantic structures. Various initiatives, with the Polish proposals concerning confidence- and security-enhancing measures on the top of the list, have been evaluated on the basis of three principal questions: Are they in compliance with the Polish pursuit of Europe? Are they also in the interest of NATO member states? Do they imply any obligations which NATO would not accept – and which might consequently arouse opposition against their author? In fact, Polish security policy in its Baltic dimension has been based on one more crucial criterion: to help draw Russia into the all-European security arrangements.

The importance which Poland has attached to Baltic co-operation grew when all Central and Eastern European states found themselves in the same situation: aspiring for membership of the European Union as soon as possible and waiting for the decision to launch negotiations. Also at the local level, the motivation for common projects intensified; patterns of transborder co-operation and the initiative to launch the Niemen Euroregion (Poland-Lithuania-Russia) testify to this.

Possible conflicts of interest have also been settled in accordance with the basic tenet of Polish security policy: do not harm the process of rapprochement to Western Europe. Two specific cases have confirmed this approach: the corridor issue and the Polish-Lithuanian minority question. In the first case, some Polish provinces might gain economically, but the state would lose out politically. The second case shows that certain bilateral problems do not appear on the agenda in order not to disturb the Polish road to Europe.

The Polish approach to the Council of the Baltic Sea States has revealed a tendency to institutionalise regional co-operation in the security domain. And the progress achieved in the joint military enterprises, especially those which have been undertaken together with Germany and Denmark, other Nordic countries and Lithuania, has confirmed Poland's desire to improve the co-operative dimension of military relations.

Some measure of diplomatic manoeuvring has characterised the attitude towards the most probable sequence of NATO enlargement: Poland first, the three Baltic states, that is Estonia, Latvia and Lithuania, afterwards. The preferable scenario has assumed reasonable flexibility: support for the others' aspirations – in order to maintain Poland's own influences; approval of a step-by-step strategy – not to provoke Russia unnecessarily and limit its own chances.

All these factors have helped Poland in its endeavour to play an active role in the Baltic Sea area and act as a real subject of international relations.

Notes

1 The relevant document defined 'modern national security' as one that 'includes political, military end economic problems, as well as ecological, social and ethnic issues' and stated that 'the Polish security policy complies with international law, especially with the law of the United Nations, as well as with the resolutions and decisions of the Conference on Security and Cooperation in Europe.' It also announced that 'membership in the European Communities is of fundamental importance' and that 'Poland is seeking links with existing defence alliances and security systems' (Guidelines 1992: 16).

2 The Deputy Minister of National Defence, Andrzej Karkoszka, stated in 1996: 'Poland – contrary to her Western (Germany) and Eastern (the Russian Federation) neighbours – is unable to provide for her own security, e.g. basing it on armed neutrality. It should be emphasised, however, that Poland possesses an economic and military potential which predisposes us to be a valuable member of the Alliance" (The Polish Vision 1996: 18).

3 Poland welcomed the establishment of the post of CBSS Commissioner on Democratic Institutions and Human Rights, Including the Right of Persons Belonging to Minorities. For a year (May 1995 – July 1996), Poland chaired a working group on these issues.

4 The NATO Secretary General, Javier Solana, named integration of Polish troops with the international brigade 'an example of how Allies and Partners, countries of Central Europe, NATO and the EU, can demonstrate operationally their commitment to a common cause' (Speech 1996: 1067).

5 It should be noted that the change of Kaliningrad's status from 'Free' to 'Special Economic Zone' by the federal law signed by President Boris Yeltsin on 22 January 1996, considerably limited the scope of local initiatives and independent foreign relations. However, there is still room for improvement of the economic co-operation between the district and its neighbours (Joenniemi 1996: 14-18).

6 No data are available on the consequences of the following provision taken from the agreement: 'The parties shall consider the possibilities of organising professional training for military officers placed in the reserves after service in the military forces of the Russian Federation in the Kaliningrad district' (Agreement on Cooperation between the Northeastern Provinces..., art. 12, para 2, in Stasiak and Komornicki 1994: XXVII, author's translation].

7 In fact, different data are available. The figures mentioned above are quoted from unpublished Polish military sources (Kaliningrad District). One will note that arithmetically they are not correct. Probably, the figure 60,000 concerns the number of men currently on the territory of KOOR, while some more stay at sea. (It should also be noted that Heurlin (in this volume) thinks the number of 'armed troops' is 40,000 – ed.).

8 The extreme position has been taken by two specialists who wrote (in a public source): 'The military potential gathered in the Kaliningrad district equals the Polish one in respect of quantity, but taking into account the level of technical quality of weapons and equipment exceeds it decidedly' (Dworecki 1996: 39).

9 See the figures and discussion leading to the conclusion that '(Polish) armed forces would not be in a position to oppose the aggression of a strong and modern armed state' (Ognik 1996: 131-32).

10 The threat was repeated in various statements by Russian politicians and military men in 1996 and, according to the Western press, appeared in recommendations made by Yeltsin's advisers (Biuletyn 1996: 22).

11 It is interesting that the opposite stereotypes have also survived. The Russian military presence in Kaliningrad is seen by some Poles, especially older ones, as an obstacle to a new German expansion eastward.

12 Unpublished background material from the Polish Ministry of Foreign Affairs enumerates 18 Russian initiatives between November 1993 and April 1996.

13 A few weeks before the corridor issue became known to the public, the Prime Minister nominated by the post-Communist party (Jozef Oleksy), was charged with collaboration with the Russian secret services.

14 According to some Polish experts, the 'corridor' in its maximum version, that is: a motorway, a railway, a gas pipeline and an energy line, would be about 500 meters wide.

15 President Aleksander Kwasniewski visited Lithuania on 5-6 March 1996; President Algirdas Brazauskas visited Poland on 19 September 1996 as did the newly elected President Vytautas Landsbergis on 20-21 February 1997; the Speaker of the Polish Parliament Jozef Zych called on the Lithuanian President Brazauskas on 12-13 January 1996, and the Speaker of the Lithuanian Parliament Ceslovas Jursenas visited Warsaw on 25-27 September 1996; Prime Minister Wlodzimierz Cimoszewicz met with his counterpart twice, on 19 April and 27 June 1996.

16 Prime Minister Cimoszewicz stated: 'We regard our contacts with the independent Republic of Lithuania as one of the most important elements of our foreign policy' (Chronicle 1996b: 1082). Speaker Jursenas announced: 'Today our contacts are such as never before in history' (Chronicle 1996d: 1237).

References

'Address' (1996a) by Aleksander Kwasniewski, President of the Republic of Poland, during the ceremonial sending-off of the Polish contingent of the IFOR, Cracow, 24 January. *Materials and Documents (MaD)*:5(1), pages 1011-2.

'Address' (1996b) by Aleksander Kwasniewski, President of the Republic of Poland, at the Royal Institute of International affairs, London, 24 October. *MaD*:5(10), pages 1260-4.

Biuletyn Kaliningradzki (1996). No. 6-7. (Published monthly by the Centre for Eastern Studies in Warsaw).

'Building of Bilateral and Regional Measures of Confidence and Security Enhancement (including the Baltic Sea region),' Unpublished material of MOD (in Polish). (Place and year not given).

'Chronicle' (1996a). *MaD*:5(1).

'Chronicle' (1996b). *MaD*:5(4).

'Chronicle' (1996c). *MaD*:5(7).

'Chronicle' (1996d). *MaD*:5(8-9).

'Confidence and Security Enhancing Measures in the Baltic Sea Region.' Polish 'invitation-to-discussion' paper. Duplicated material. (Place and year not given).

'Co-operation in the Baltic Sea Region.' Unpublished material of MOD (in Polish). (Place and year not given).

Dworecki, Stanislaw E. and Keson, Tadeusz (1996). *Konflikty zbrojne w Europie i na Bliskim Wschodzie. Analiza i komentarze* [Armed Conflicts in Europe and the Middle East: Analysis and Commentaries]. Warsaw, Department of International Security, Ministry of Defence.

'Exposé' (1996). By Dariusz Rosati, Minister of Foreign Affairs of the Republic of Poland, to the Diet of the Republic of Poland, Warsaw, 9 May 1996, *Mad*:5(5/6), pages 1097-1106.

Gazeta Wyborcza (1997), 28 March.

'Guidelines of the Polish Security Policy' (1992). *MaD*, No. 1, pages 16-18.

'Illustrative Regional Confidence- and Security-Building Measures Complementary to the Vienna Document 1992: Contribution by Poland to Possible Regional Arms Control Negotiations' (1994). FSC/CSCE Doc. 385, 22 June. Vienna.

Joenniemi, Pertti (1996). 'Kaliningrad: A Region in Search for a Past and a Future.' Background paper prepared for the international colloquium 'Kaliningrad: Future Prospects of the Region,' Ostsee-Akademie, Travemünde, 3-5 November, 1996.

'Kaliningrad District.' Unpublished material of MOD (in Polish). (Place and year not given).

Kostecki, Wojciech and Wiberg, Håkan (1996). 'Poland,' pages 157-84 in Mouritzen, Hans, Wæver, Ole and Wiberg, Håkan (eds.). *European Integration and National Adaptations: A Theoretical Inquiry*. New York, Nova Science Publishers.

Ognik, Halina (1996). 'Poland,' pages 129-40 in Krohn, Axel (ed.). *The Baltic Sea Region: National and International Security Perspectives*. Baden-Baden, Nomos.

'Polish-Lithuanian Treaty on Friendly Relations and Good-Neighbourly Cooperation, 1994, Vilnius, 26 April. *Zbior Dokumentow*, No. 2.

'Speech' (1996) by Javier Solana, Secretary General of the North Atlantic Treaty Organisation, at Warsaw University, 18 April. *MaD*:5(4), pages 1066-9.

Stasiak, A., and Komornicki, T. (eds.) (1994). *Problemy wspolpracy przygranicznej pomiedzy Polska i Obwodem Kaliningradzkim* [Problems of Trans-border Co-operation between Poland and Kaliningrad District]. Warsaw.

'Statement' (1996a) by Wlodzimierz Cimoszewicz, Prime Minister of the Republic of Poland, at a press conference after a meeting of the Prime Ministers of the Baltic Sea States, Visby, 4 May. *MaD*:5(5-6), pages 1086-7.

'Statement' (1996b) by Andrzej Zbucki, Commercial Counsellor of the Republic of Poland in Kaliningrad, at a press conference on the strategy of economic co-operation of the north-eastern voivodships of Poland, Warsaw, 6 May. *MaD*:5(5-6), pages 1087-8.

'The Polish Vision of the Pan-European Security Model' (1996). Main theses of the speech delivered by the Secretary of State, First Deputy Minister of National Defence, Dr Andrzej Karkoszka, at the meeting with military attaches accredited to Warsaw, 17 April. *Analizy. Syntezy*, No. 20. Department of International Security, Ministry of Defence.

31 Germany's Security Policies in the Baltic Sea Area

Axel Krohn

Introduction

At present, the political developments in Europe clearly indicate a shift towards a further Europeanisation of security, combined with an intensifying process of European integration – both having considerable impact on German political affairs. Besides, there are also clear movements towards regionalisation as well, i.e. 'a complex network of bi- and trilateral and other regional co-operation dealing, among other things, with various security and defence questions' (Danish Commission 1995: 7). This describes the basic political setting, where Germany has to define its security policy orientation.

However, already before the global bipolarity came to an end, German security policy was more than just preparation for military defence. The primary aim was to avoid conflicts by political and economic means, without having to refer to military forces. In this context, German security policy was oriented towards stability. Today, the mission spectrum of the German armed forces has been extended in comparison with the more or less static geopolitical and geostrategic situation of Germany during the Cold War era. The mission includes a larger geographical coverage and a broader military spectrum (Naval Forces Special Issue 1996: 15).

After the end of the bloc confrontation, Germanys security interests are basically directed towards two goals: first to embed the unified Germany into the European order by an intensified integration process and secondly to strengthen the stabilisation of the Central and Eastern European (CEE) Countries by enlarging the European Union and NATO (Schmidt 1996). These simultaneous processes of integration and enlargement are still a major task for German foreign and security policy.

The end of the bloc confrontation and the final unification force Germany to engage in a difficult political balancing act. German policies have to adapt to the new political situation in the CEE countries and Russia as well as to its complex domestic situation. Additionally, Germany is faced with Western countries' demands that it assume greater obligations in accordance with its economic and political strength. It is also aware of and sensitive to the fact that its European neighbours still harbour concerns that Germany might develop hegemonic tendencies.

However, Germany has made it clear that after unification, it would still remain a strong supporter of the European integration process. Possible fears of a Germany 'going national' have been dismissed by the country's outspoken adherence to multilateral structures.

Germanys strong support of a widening and deepening of the European Union should not only to be seen as an instrument to enlarge the European region of political, economic and military stability, but should also be understood as a means to minimise perceptions of a German hegemonial position in Europe. The German policy, however, involves problems, particularly as other partners in the EU have different priorities. The present discussion on issues ranging from economic and monetary matters to security policy makes it obvious that the EU has still a long way to go to arrive at the goal of a common foreign and security policy. Also Germany has no clear answer to the question of how to deal with the conflicting points of view.

The Security Policy Framework

After unification and the collapse of the Soviet Union, Germany has become one of the major middle-level powers in Europe. As one source has stated, with German unification in 1990, a littoral state disappeared from the Baltic map and a new European middle power re-emerged.

Germany has, however, shown little evidence of great-power ambitions in or around the Baltic Sea region. Instead it seeks to avoid the impression of a possible German expansionism. Therefore German foreign and security policy is focusing on multilateralism instead of bilateralism – making clear that Germany is one partner among others within the different initiatives.

Before inheriting a long stretch of Baltic coast line, Germany was basically involved as a gate-keeper to the Danish Straits. But as a result of German unification, NATO has also acquired a larger presence in the Baltic Sea region, without mentioning NATO's coming incorporation of Poland.

Until the beginning of the 90s, German perspectives on the Baltic Sea region were much in line with the general European view on Northern Europe, i.e. to the political elites in Brussels and Bonn, the region was hardly was on the political and economic map. While Nordic identity, Nordic integration and co-operation were constant factors within Scandinavian politics after the Second World War, Germany's interests were not specifically directed towards Northern Europe.

German political approaches to Northern Europe and the Baltic Sea region did not indicate that there was a special policy. In Bonn, Scandinavia was mainly understood as a separate entity in the north (Albrecht 1991: 140). At present, there is still no well-defined German perspective on future developments in Northern Europe and their possible impact on German foreign and security policy. So far, German political and economic activities are still basically directed towards the CEE countries and Russia, not towards the Baltic Sea region or Northern Europe. Only as far as the eastern Baltic is concerned have recent political developments in the region had an impact on German policy, which now recognises the new security interests of Poland and the Baltic states.

The collapse of the Soviet Union and the reshaping of the political map in Europe has forced Germany to take action and to adapt to the new situation. The Baltic Sea region as a link between the North European, the Central European and the East European countries is becoming more important and recognised by Germany in the field of politics, economy and security policy. The various activities in co-operation on military security are indicating an increasing German interest.

However, Germany's priorities are fundamentally determined by the process of European integration, developments in Russia, and transatlantic relations with the United States. This is a very complex foreign policy triangle. Germany is clearly in favour of closer integration, be it within the EU or NATO. Even though Germany has no clear answer to the 'double enlargement dilemma,' German politicians realise that tensions between Poland and Russia or the Baltic states would be counterproductive to integration. Therefore, stabilisation is considered to be a key task for the future. In this context, the Baltic Sea region and Northern Europe are located geographically and conceptually between Washington, Brussels and Moscow (Jann 1994: 182).

Germany's 'new Ostpolitik' is driven by security and economic logic. For Germany it seems obvious to look for markets which are still in need of 'traditional' German products such as machinery, steel, chemicals and automobiles and provide cheap labour as well, i.e. the developing countries in Central and Eastern Europe. Therefore Germany is a strong supporter of the extension of the EU to provide membership, markets and subsidies to the CEE countries (Kurth 1995: 384). This also includes a security policy, i.e. decisive steps in the direction of a common European defence via the WEU and the enlargement of NATO to the CEE countries.

While the Nordic countries have a somewhat 'traditional' foreign policy interest in the Baltic Sea region and Northern Europe, the present developments also put the region more into the political focus of Germany. But Germany is still avoiding any action that might fuel the impression that it would take a leading role in Nordic/Baltic issues.[1]

In March 1992, a new co-operative intergovernmental body was founded in Copenhagen, the Council of Baltic Sea States (CBSS).[2] Germany was among the founding members, as were the other Baltic littoral states and Norway (Larrabee 1993: 114). This initiative gained considerable public recognition, particularly in northern Germany. The CBSS shows that multilateral co-operation is perceived to be a viable approach to deal with present and future challenges in the region.

The Council seems so far to have had only a limited impact on major political developments in the Baltic Sea region. However, the recent meeting of the CBSS in Visby, held on 3–4 May 1996, ended with the signing of a document on economic co-operation, the fight against crime, and environmental protection (Imsa 1996). The future will show whether the CBSS can function as a viable body for further intensification of relations in the region.

Though Germany was a founding member and general supporter of the CBSS, its politics remains somewhat inconsistent, as it is not supporting any further institutionalisation, for example the establishment of a permanent office. Germany also saw to it that security was exempted from the agenda of the CBSS. This policy is probably fuelled by German anxieties of ending up with additional financial burdens in case the activities of the CBSS are expanded and intensified.

The new round of CFE (Treaty on Conventional Forces in Europe) negotiations, which started in January 1997, will have an impact on the eastern part of the Baltic Sea region and particularly for the Kaliningrad oblast, one of the area's 'hot spots.' Even though the present high concentration of military forces in the Kaliningrad oblast is not directly related to CFE implementation (Lachowski 1996: 773), it remains a concern for the neighbouring states. At present it is too early to forecast the results of the complex negotiations. However, the Kaliningrad oblast will probably be one of the regions where – due to NATO-Russian differences of opinion on a territorial/national or regional approach – the ceilings will be limited strictly. Kaliningrad is still a highly sensitive issue for Russia, and announcements to create a special defence region in the area to comprise large concentrations of ground forces, military aircraft, naval units and military installations, prompted anxiety about Russia's plans regarding the role and task of such forces (ibid.: 774).

Consequently, German policies towards the Baltic republics and particularly towards the Kaliningrad oblast are still rather sensitive and are pursued cautiously. Germany tries to avoid any impression that there might be a special German interest in turning back time and claiming territorial interests in the region. Instead it is officially made clear that there are no open territorial issues. One might well raise the question if it would not be helpful if countries like Denmark together with Sweden, Finland and Germany would develop a multilateral policy towards the Eastern part of the Baltic Sea region. Incorporating Germany into such a common foreign policy might help to overcome the obvious German difficulties.

If Germany should decide on a stronger build-up of its foreign policy engagement in the Eastern Baltic, it seems obvious that this might lead to competition with the Nordic countries, whose longer engagement and well-developed contacts in the region would have to compete with the substantial weight of the German economy. Denmark, for example, 'would therefore prefer Germany's energies to be directed towards other parts of Eastern Europe closer to home' (Petersen 1994: 19).

Even though the East-West confrontation has come to an end, Europe is still divided. Europe does not only remain divided between a region of 'assured security' (Rotfeld 1994: 206) and a region outside these security structures, but also between the economically integrated countries of the EU, and the 'others' that would like to become members of the EU sooner rather than later.

As mentioned, Germany is as strong supporter of a closer integration and a further enlargement of the EU. The German government believes that the two goals of deepening and widening of the EU can be achieved within the next decade. Britain and France have been reluctant because they believe that 'meaningful national positions continue to exist (Geipel 1995: 378). The Nordic countries Sweden and Finland, together with Denmark, might line up with these sceptics of the deepening agenda.

However, Norden is more varied, as Finland seems prepared to support the current process, i.e. being a candidate for the EMU, while Sweden is far more hesitant and Denmark has expressed her reservations. Even though the Scandinavian countries have not so far created a 'Nordic bloc' within the EU, the general context for German politics and efforts on European deepening and integration might change slightly in future, if the Nordic countries should decide to articulate a common voice on these issues. Also the German domestic support for 'grandiose visions of European integration is much weaker than some CDU leaders care to admit.'[3]

The current process of widening and deepening of the EU has impact on the future security policy in the region as well. The present American foreign policy is fuelling those voices who stress stronger European efforts to develop a European security system. The WEU, the oldest European defence partnership, was founded with the Brussels Treaty in 1948.[4] During the last several decades, the WEU has not had much weight in European defence issues since it has lacked the structures and the capabilities for military activities. This situation started to change after the Maastricht Treaty of 1991, in which the European countries agreed to establish a common foreign and security policy. After the meeting in Edinburgh in December 1992, where Denmark was granted special provisions, the Treaty became acceptable to the majority of the Danes as well (Petersen 1993: 13).

Germany strongly supports increased WEU activities and capabilities, but the present shortcomings of the WEU do not offer much political and military credibility to the idea of it becoming the European pillar of military security. Though NATO agreed to support the build-up of the WEU, thus far only the Eurocorps, the Multinational Division Central Europe, and the British-Netherlands amphibious task force are earmarked for the WEU. Despite various political statements, it seems clear to most of the European countries that a credible defence of Europe is, and will be, possible only with a substantial transatlantic link.

The low level of interest among most European countries to become members of the Eurocorps is a clear indicator of the WEU's lack of credibility. Basically, the Eurocorps remains a French-German undertaking, even though Belgium, Spain and Luxembourg have joined. The present German support of French positions in European security affairs could fuel further suspicions that German politics might intensify the German-French co-operation at the expense of the traditionally strong transatlantic ties.

The WEU has come up with a plan to establish a 'Hanseatic Corps' in the Baltic Sea which would protect the region's maritime safety and security. This standing Baltic Sea forces should comprise Denmark, Estonia, Germany, Latvia, Lithuania and Poland as founding members. The tasks would include border control, monitoring of fishing and environmental rules, shipping control and last but not least search and rescue (McEwan 1995). So far, however, the 'Hanseatic Corps' is very much in a preparatory stage.

German Military Potential in the Region

As a result of unification, Germany inherited a complete military force – air, land, and naval (for the following, see also Krohn 1996). However, most of the former GDR units have been scrapped or partly transferred to other countries. Due to budgetary constraints, further reductions are going to take place in the beginning of 1996. As it is outlined in the recent 'Bundeswehr-concept,' the overall strength of the German armed forces will not be more than 338,000 men. Due to changing military scenarios and budgetary cuts, the Chief of Staff of the German Navy formulated a concept of a smaller German Navy (Mann 1991). Though the perception of threat has disappeared, the existence of Russian forces is seen as a reason to keep up German military precautions. Some even see a specific role for Germany in securing the Baltic Sea (Poesze 1995: 4). However, the present German military security policy does not show any intention of filling the possible power vacuum in the region.

One of the major tasks will be shaping the armed forces according to future security tasks also outside NATO's area. As the European and international community is expecting a larger share of German man-power participation instead of just of supplying a check, German armed forces need to adapt to future needs. At present, the reduced service time for soldiers further complicates the issue of how a modern and highly sophisticated army can still be run with conscripts. A service period of 10 months hardly leaves enough time for the necessary training and exercise with modern electronic equipment and weapon systems.

However, even though the question of a professional army is widely discussed in the military, officially the present conscript system is dealt with as a holy cow not to be questioned in public, neither by the politicians nor by the Inspector General. Therefore it is hard to envision how the political and military elites will decide between technical needs and political wishful thinking. It certainly is a difficult question.

In this context, the German Minister of Defence Volker Rühe stated already in the German White Book 1994 that former tasks in the Baltic Sea region were no longer as necessary as before. The ability of German naval forces to participate in crisis-prevention and crisis-management operations had gained more importance

(Bundesministerium der Verteidigung 1994: 120). Due to the extended role of the German Navy to be deployable wherever the political interests of Germany require it, the regional focus on Northern Europe is diminishing. Besides continued operations in the North Sea and the Atlantic, the Mediterranean Sea gains more importance.

Still, the northern region retains its security importance. This is particularly due to developments in the Baltic area. They have created opportunities for permanent partnership with the other Baltic littoral states. 'More than any other maritime area the Baltic provides for the possibility to co-operate with navies of former Warsaw Pact countries within the framework of Nato's Partnership for Peace programme' (Naval Forces Special Issue 1996: 16).This becomes obvious from the increasing military activities and contacts outlined in the tables below.

As a result of the changes in Europe, the German Navy has developed a new 'stationing concept.' The total number of smaller and larger bases has been consolidated from fourteen to five major naval bases.[5] Up to one quarter of the German naval units will be stationed in the new German Federal state of Mecklenburg-Vorpommern. The fast patrol boats are already stationed in Warnemünde and will be followed during the next years by a new school for navy technicians in Parow near Stralsund. Also the 'Marineamt' is moving from Wilhelmshafen to Rostock (Boehmer 1995: 38). Under the new reorganisation, the Navy will maintain four big stations, i.e. Wilhelmshafen, for the North Sea, and Eckernförde, Olpenitz, and Warnemünde for the Baltic Sea. Other bases will get a reduced status, i.e. Flensburg, Kiel and Peenemünde.

Naval arms procurement during the next decade will basically be confined to the frigate F 123, of which the first was delivered in September 1994. Three more ships were to be delivered before the end of 1996. A new type of frigate, F 124, is planned for the year 2002. Further plans are to put a new submarine class 212 and new mine hunter/ -sweeper units into service (Hogrebe 1994).

Generally, present plans envision a reduction of the German naval forces from 183 units in 1989 to 93 in the year 2005, but probably the actual number will be even smaller. Approximately 40 per cent of the naval forces will be permanently designated for special tasks 'elsewhere' (Magenheimer 1995: 347-9).

Table 31.1: German major naval forces after 2005

Location	Navy composition
Wilhelmshaven	approx. 15 frigates, 2 auxiliary vessels
Eckernförde	approx. 8 submarines, 1 auxiliary vessel
Olpenitz	approx. 20 mine counter measure (MCM) vessels, 3 auxiliary vessels
Warnemünde	15 corvettes, 3 auxiliary vessels
Nordholz	approx. 10 maritime patrol aircraft (MPA)
Eggebek	approx. 45 fighter/bomber aircraft (FBA/RECCE)

The final composition of the German naval forces is still under discussion. Based on current trends, however, it appears likely that after the year 2005, the naval forces will comprise the major units and bases indicated in Table 31.1.

In addition the naval forces will include, among other units, several ammunition transporters, one sailing ship for training, intelligence gathering vessels and approximately forty helicopters for search and rescue and for deployment on the frigates. After the three destroyers at present stationed in Kiel have been decommissioned in 2002, Kiel will be further reduced but will retain its status as a small naval base not commissioned to a specific type of unit. Despite the cuts, the German Navy will remain the second strongest in the Baltic.

At present the fast patrol boats are stationed further east in new harbour facilities in the new Bundesländer. They are due to be replaced by 15 corvettes after the year 2000. Despite the changed political situation, the decision was made to replace the fast patrol boats with a bigger corvette type of about 1500 tons.[6] Due to their planned weaponry and speed, these ships are especially useful for 'out of area' operations. Procurement is not anticipated before the year 2007 (Burggraf 1994). Naval units are no longer just designated for German coastal defence, and with its enhanced capabilities, the corvette is not confined to operate in the Baltic (*Schiff & Hafen* 1994: 36). However, the main task of German armed forces is still national defence. In this context, the Baltic Sea still is a region of interest for German security. Consequently, a specific composition of naval forces with the primary task of conflict prevention and resolution in this region is still seen to be necessary (Jablonsky 1995: 20).

Close Military Co-operation

Despite different approaches to some aspects in European security, i.e. membership in the WEU, the perception of regional security in Northern Europe and the varying degrees of experience in international conflict prevention and resolution, there always was a German interest in co-operation in the region.

In the field of military security, the BALTAP Command serves as a good example (Petersen 1995). After the dissolution of the Soviet Union and the withdrawal of Soviet troops from Germany and the CEE countries, NATO began adapting to the new situation. One organisational result was the change of NATO's command structure. Not least as a result of German demands, the NATO regional border which ran through Germany was shifted from the river Elbe to the north. One might interpret this restructuring as driven by more than just military necessities. Until 1991 the Elbe border connected the defence of Schleswig-Holstein to Denmark and the Northern Region – supporting a Danish interest not to get too directly connected to the Central European Region.

BALTAP has been an instrument of close co-operation between the Federal Republic and Denmark in the defence of the Baltic land and sea approaches. Both Denmark and Germany wanted to keep the BALTAP arrangement, not only from military considerations, i.e. the unity of the Baltic defence, but also to continue the long-standing and stable co-operation between German and Danish armed forces. For Denmark BALTAP also means avoiding a possible decoupling from European issues. BALTAP has been especially attractive for Denmark because the C-in-C has always been a Danish officer and because the headquarters has been located in Karup, Jutland. After some discussion the following results came up with the inclusion of Denmark and BALTAP under the Central Region in 1994.

First, a Northwest Region was established with HQ in Britain, covering Britain and Norway, plus the naval forces from other North Sea countries (incl. Denmark). Secondly, the BALTAP command remains but is transferred to the Central Region. With respect to the naval forces under BALTAP, the COMBALTAP has to report to and is subordinated to the Northwest Region. However, the land and air forces are under Central command with a German commanding officer. As a result, BALTAP will in future have to co-ordinate its activities with two NATO regions.

'The decisive aspect, though, seems to be political symbolism. By and large, the new structure places Denmark more clearly in a Central European context; closer to Germany. Still, NATO remains of overwhelming importance for Denmark. Particularly as the USA is the geographically distant balancer which brings about a situation where Denmark becomes less dependent on Germany' (Heurlin 1996: 171). As long as the US is involved in European security issues, possible fears of an emerging Franco-German security policy can be minimised. Though for slightly different reasons, Denmark as well as Germany are strong supporters of a US commitment in Europe.

The bilateral as well as the multilateral military co-operation is further intensified. So far, the German military co-operation with non-NATO countries has focused on Poland. However, there are plans to intensify contacts with the Baltic states (Naval Forces Special Issue 1996: 88). The co-operation includes various fields of military training.

Common military exercises are of major importance as well. Between Denmark and Germany they take place under COMBALTAP in Karup (Denmark) and COMLANDJUT in Rendsburg (Germany). Among the yearly exercises, the Command Post Exercise (CPX) Chinese Eye 1994 and CPX Cold Grouse were of major importance. They were the first military exercises of the Multi-National-Divison Central.

German participation in the Partnership for Peace (PfP) exercises is also increasing.

Among others the following main military activities were conducted: Two exercises in 1994: Engineer Live Carbon Gap in Denmark (together with Poland) and the Field Training Exercise (FTX) Tatra in Poland. One exercise in 1995: SPESSART 95 in Germany, the first Polish/Danish/German exercise on German territory. Two exercises in 1996: Baltic Cooperation 96 in Poland with German/Danish/Polish troops, and Baltic Service 96, a tri-service exercise in Denmark in autumn 1996.[7] As joint trilateral Polish/Danish/German activities, the exercises BALTSAR 96, Baltic Endeavour 96 and Open Spirit 96 were conducted in 1996.

Summing up, we can state that beside meetings at the personal and expert levels in various specialised fields, great emphasis is placed on joint exercises which are conducted on a bilateral or multilateral basis. SAR exercises and exercises with mine countermeasures have been conducted with Poland and the Baltic states. A symposium on mine countermeasures was initiated by Germany and held in connection with the exercise Open Spirit. All Baltic littoral states were invited.

Table 31.2 gives an overview of the military contacts and co-operation between the German Navy and the Baltic republics and Poland.[8]

Table 31.2: Activities by the German Navy, annual programme for 1996

Estonia

Date	Activity	Location
2nd quarter	Expert meeting (advice on organisation and build up of naval staff and naval bases)	Estonia
13-15 May	Working visit of the Commander in Chief, German Navy	Estonia
25-29 Oct.	Naval visit (8 units of the mine warfare flotilla)	Tallinn

Latvia

Date	Activity	Location
13-15 May	Working visit of the Commander in Chief, German Navy	Latvia
6-10 Sept.	Naval visit (5 units of the mine warfare flotilla)	

Lithuania

Date	Activity	Location
13-15 May	Working visit of the Commander in Chief, German Navy	Lithuania

Poland

Date	Activity	Location
May	Exchange of SAR teams	Gdingen/ Glücksburg
June	Professional discussion on Hydrography	Poland
20-25 June	Polish naval visit to 'Kieler Woche'	Kiel
14-15 Aug.	Visit of German fast patrol boats	Poland
21-23 Sept.	Polish naval visit	Warnemünde
3rd quarter	Technical discussion on training and education for safety and damage control	Neustadt
3rd quarter	Technical discussion on training and education of combat divers	Eckernförde
15-19 Nov.	Visit of 5 units of the German mine warfare flotilla	Gdingen
	Professional discussion at admiral staff level	Germany
	Personal exchange programme (navy)	Germany/Poland

Source: BMVg – FüM III 1 – Az 04-06-00, 8.1.1996, Maßnahmen der Marine im Rahmen der Jahresprogramme 1996 mit MO-/SOE-/BALT- und GUS-Staaten

At present the question of the how and when of NATO enlargement is determining the discussion in Germany. Germany's position corresponds with NATO's actual decision to include Poland, Hungary and the Czech Republic. Whereas primarily Denmark has been supporting membership for the Baltic republics, Germany has chosen not to stress this wish due to Russian objections and has thus been in line with the general view in NATO.

At present, the area with the highest profile beside the Partnership for Peace activities, is to train and involve the three Baltic republics in peace-keeping operations within the United Nations. Denmark has played a rather leading role in co-ordinating the efforts of the Nordic states – together with some NATO countries such as the United States and Great Britain – in the build-up of a Baltic Peace-Keeping Battalion, BALTBAT. Germany's involvement in international peace-keeping operations is hampered by a lack of historical experience comparable of that of its Nordic neighbours. In addition, the issue has been complicated by a complex domestic struggle within the political elites in Bonn. Therefore German politics has favoured an 'IFOR type of security,' where Germany could provide the logistics and keep NATO and the US involved.

Recently the idea of a maritime Baltic Squadron (BALTRON) under German co-ordination and in close co-operation with Sweden has been suggested, and the decision was taken by the German ministry of defence to co-ordinate the establishment of a common naval unit from Estonia, Latvia and Lithuania. From 1998 the naval units will participate in PfP activities (*Kieler Nachrichten* 1997). However, tasks will be maritime border protection to prevent smuggling and illegal migration and to conduct mine sweeping in the Baltic Sea, rather than naval operations under a UN commitment (Eneberg 1997).

So far, Germany has been reluctant to offer any major military aid to the newly independent countries in the Baltic Sea region, particularly the Baltic republics – sometimes causing complaints about the stripping of armaments and communication equipment before the delivery of military systems. Apart from rifle ammunition and other surplus material from former GDR stocks, no weaponry has been delivered because Germany has done everything to avoid Russian irritation.

However, Germany seeks to support closer relations between the Baltic republics and European political institutions, e.g. the EU and the European and

Table 31.3: German-Baltic Sea bilateral security co-operation, 1995

Country	In Germany	In partner country	Total planned/realised
Estonia	6	4	14 / 10
Latvia	7	6	16 / 13
Lithuania	7	3	15 / 10
Poland	41	26	90 / 67

Source: BMVg SdB ZusArbOst, Bilaterale Kooperation, Bilanz Jahresprogramme 95, Az 32-01-10 vom May 31, 1996

transatlantic security organisations NATO and the WEU (Leutrum 1994: 358-59). In the absence of full membership for the Balts, various agreements, declarations, contacts and assistance schemes have developed during recent years as outlined in Table 31.3. Each of the Baltic republics has received assistance in the field of soft security, for example to develop police forces, as well as support for the border and coast guards.

Table 31.3 underlines the intensifying contacts between Germany and the Baltic republics, but the relatively greater importance of Poland as a security partner also becomes visible. Since 1995 the military contacts between Germany and the Baltic republics and Poland have been further intensified. In addition, Germany is beginning to give more military assistance to the Baltic republics.

The German and Latvian Ministers of Defence Volker Rühe and Andrejs Krastins have agreed to co-operate on the training and education of their navies. The first task has been the technical aid and assistance to the Latvian Navy in mine sweeping in the Gulf of Riga.[9] This mine hunting took place in connection with a similar operation by the Swedish Navy outside Estonia.

Two German officers have served as military advisers in Tallinn. Due to the financial constraints and the still somewhat unclear future tasks of the Estonian Navy, this proved challenging. For example, the advisers suggested a basic organisation of naval forces and prepared for the incorporation of two mine-sweeping vessels (KL 394) to be delivered by Germany.[10] The slow political decision-making process, however, turned out to be an impediment. Nevertheless, a decision was made not to incorporate the Estonian naval units into the coast guard (Piirivalve) but to maintain them as a maritime force and thus 'alliance capable.' Though it seems somewhat early to judge the results of the work of the German advisory group, it would seem to have provided a positive example of co-operation with the newly independent countries in the Baltic Sea region. Particularly as the Baltic republics will not be among the first new NATO members, it is important to make clear that they are not peripheral to European security interests. Military co-operation will be an important tool towards this end.

Still, at present Poland is the primary recipient of German assistance. Co-operation has expanded significantly, and a military co-operation agreement was signed in January 1993 (*Frankfurter Allgemeine Zeitung* 1993). Despite Polish interest in obtaining weapons from old GDR stores, Germany has not sold any stocks to Poland. Instead, there has been co-operation in the field of military and security policy. This co-operation ranges from the attendance of Polish officers at the General Staff Academy to varying assistance programmes, common training, and military exercises.

Germany has also given Poland considerable support for NATO membership. The fact that the retired German General Henning von Ondarza, the former NATO Commander in Chief Central Europe, became a consultant to the Polish government, strengthens the close relations.

The list of joint German-Polish military activities encompasses 67 different measures for 1995, and an additional 83 were planned for 1996. So far this constitutes the most intensive German co-operation with a CEE country. The activities have ranged from military training to expert meetings. Since 1991, 61 polish officers have undergone training in Germany. At present 19 officers are being trained in Germany and 14 more are expected in future.[11]

The co-operation is further strengthened by the Danish-German-Polish trilateral partnership in military and security policy. The Danish Minister of Defence Hans Hækkerup has stated that a further intensification of co-operation among German, Danish and Polish forces is in the interest of all three states and a means to generally enhancing co-operation in the Baltic Sea region (Hækkerup 1995). The trilateral agreement is the result of meetings between the ministers of defence in August 1995 on Ærø (Denmark) and February 1996 in Krakow and Zakopane (Poland). The trilateral co-operation will officially be ratified in 1997. It includes different activities, planned in advance and presented in a yearly programme. Among the envisaged joint activities is peace-keeping. An expert group established under the topic 'Peace-keeping Co-operation' is supposed to come up with suggestions for the yearly programme.[12]

The future position of the Baltic republics has also been discussed. As they will not be among the first new members of NATO, common agreement has been reached that it will be important to incorporate them, for example, by a

Table 31.4: Planned programme of military activities, 1997

Period	Activity	Type	Location/ Service	Host country
March	IPC	Exercise	tbd/Navy	Germany (Sweden)
8-10 April	MCM exercise Open Spirit	Symposium (open to all NATO and all Baltic countries)	Baltic/Navy	Germany
25-29 Aug.	NATO MCM exercise Baltic Endeavour	Exercise	Baltic/Navy	Germany
Aug.	MPC	Exercise	tbd/Navy	Germany (Sweden)
Aug.	FPC	Exercise	tbd/Navy	Germany (Sweden)
1-5 Sept.	MCM exercise Open Spirit	Exercise (open to NATO and all Baltic countries)	Baltic/Navy	Germany
tbd	Development of further friendship ties incl. signing of friendship agreement and 2 naval visits		tbd/Navy	tbd

Note: tbd = to be decided.
Source: Data taken from the calendar 'Trilaterales DEU-DAN-POL Jahresprogramm,' Fü M III 1, Bonn, Jan. 1997

regionalisation of PfP with subregional headquarters. The regional HQs could co-ordinate the PfP activities and allow the Baltic republics to participate.

The recent trilateral German-French-Polish initiative on security co-operation is another important initiative which connects the Baltic Sea region closer to Central Europe. The 4th trilateral meeting of the German, French and Polish ministers of defence took place in Warsaw on 2-3 February 1997. Besides agreement on closer military co-operation in training and exercises, the question of intensified arms co-operation was discussed. Possible trilateral defence co-operation on the French-German 'Euromissile' HOT 3 was considered, particularly as Poland seems not to be satisfied with the present performance of the 'Spike' system which they intend to buy in Israel. However, it may prove difficult for Poland to get out of the contract.

Obviously, military co-operation among all Baltic littoral countries is increasing,

Table 31.5: Planned programme of military co-operation and contacts, 1997

Estonia

Date	Activity	Location
10-13 Nov.	Expert meeting on press and information	St. Augustin
June-Sept.	Naval visit (possibly in connection with mine sweeping)	Open

Latvia

Date	Activity	Location
Open	Naval visit	Open

Lithuania

Date	Activity	Location
Open	Naval visit	Open

Poland

Date	Activity	Location
17-19 Feb.	Training (1 German, 1 Polish submarine)	Gdingen
Feb.	Working visit (preparatory meeting for LIVEX exercise)	Gdingen
3-6 March	Working visit Commander in Chief German Navy	Glücksburg
May	Exchange of personnel (SAR)	Glücksburg
2nd quarter	Delegation visit to naval academy 'Marineschule Mürwik'	Flensburg/ Mürwik
2nd or 3rd quarter	Expert meeting on incidents at sea agreement	Poland
23-26 June	Naval visit	Gdansk
27-30 June	Naval visit	Swinemünde
7-10 Aug.	Naval visit	Warnemünde
2-6 Sept.	Naval SAR, exchange program between RCC Glücksburg and RCC Gdingen	Gdingen
31 Oct.-3 Nov.	Naval visit	Gdingen

Source: BMVg, FüM III 1, Programm für die Weiterentwicklung militärpolitischer Beziehungen/ Militärischer Kontakte zwischen den Streitkräften, Bonn, Jan. 1997

and Germany is getting more involved. This growing engagement becomes obvious from in the calendars presented in Table 31.4 and 31.5 showing the various military activities and contacts between Germany, Poland and the Baltic republics planned for 1997.

Conclusion

Germany's interests are basically directed to the developments in Eastern Europe. Germany has become the major provider of Western assistance to the Eastern European countries, ranging from financial aid and material support to technical, administrative and economic know-how. So far, Germany has been transferring almost 50 per cent of the financial aid to the CEE countries (Schmidt 1996: 214). But there are limits to Germany's financial engagement in Eastern Europe. The main task will be reconstructing the former German Democratic Republic (GDR), which is proving much more costly than anticipated. As a result of these domestic problems, Germany has not demonstrated a capacity to play great power politics in European affairs or in Northern European security.

At present the general German policy remains located somewhere between its transatlantic responsibilities and an emerging European identity (ibid.: 217). It always was and still is a primary goal for German foreign and security policy to maintain and further develop the Atlantic Alliance and the European Union as complementary bodies. The fact that France has different perceptions on the structure and goals of future European security policy and that it is beginning to articulate its special interests might in the long run create a problem for German politics. It seems obvious that the other countries will observe German politics vis-à-vis French security interests very carefully. A stronger German support of French demands would certainly fuel suspicions towards the future development of the European security structure.

In particular, one should not underestimate the possible suspicions by the other Baltic littoral countries that the traditionally strong German commitment to transatlantic ties might weaken in future due to an intensified French-German security policy co-operation even in the Baltic Sea region.

A German contribution to a comprehensive security concept for the Baltic Sea region or the whole of Northern Europe does not exist. So far, Germany has reduced and redeployed its armed forces in the Baltic, according to the new political landscape in Europe and as part of the continuing co-operation process within the PfP and NACC.

How does Germany deal with the developments in the Baltic Sea region? Obviously, the political elites have no blueprint. So far there are some more or less important local initiatives such as the government of Schleswig-Holstein's 'Hanse Concept,' which focuses mainly on economic and cultural aspects. A consistent German policy strategy towards the Baltic Sea region which includes politics, economy and security policy is still lacking.

But obviously Germany is developing more activities in the BSR as it has started to recognise the importance of the security developments in the region. In this context, the German naval forces act as an important partner for the Baltic countries.

However, the CEE countries still receive the main bulk of German political interest and support. It seems likely that the new German 'Ostpolitik' will be continued in future, and a new German 'Nordpolitik' is not yet visible. Germany's Central and Eastern European policy focus leaves limited energy to be directed towards the North.

In fact, the 'Eastern European factor' is likely to become even more important in the near future. But as all Baltic littoral states share the same interests in stabilising the CEE countries, further intensified co-operation with Germany in the field of military security seems likely.

Notes

1 In this context, ideas to establish a Baltic Treaty Organization (BALTO) incorporating all Baltic littoral countries, aiming at a stronger integration of Sweden and Finland with the aim of safeguarding the Baltic Republics, seem rather speculative. First, the discussion on the division of labour in security matters is already going on between the countries in the region and, secondly, Germany would certainly not be interested in playing a leading role within such a 'Baltic mini-NATO.' The idea was brought forward by Alten (1996). For critics, see Zektri (1996).

2 Kukk (1994). For a general view on co-operation in the Baltic Sea region, see Joenniemi (1994).

3 Particularly the European Monetary Union (EMU) which means giving up control over the Deutschmark does not seem to be a done deal in domestic German politics. See also Geipel (1995: 378).

4 The founding members were Belgium, France, Great Britain, Luxembourg and the Netherlands.

5 H.R. Boehmer, Vice Admiral, Chief of Naval Staff, in an interview. See Naval Forces Special Issue (1996: 6-10).

6 The present fast patrol boats are about 350 tons.

7 See Bundesministerium der Verteidigung, Presseforum, Deutsch-dänisch-polnische Zusammenarbeit im militärpolitischen und militärischen Bereich. BmVg online, 7/17/96, p. 4, internet, http://www.bmvg. government.de/Presseforum/Pressemappen/M2Q1.htm

8 The information was partly provided by the German ministry of defence. The author is particularly thankful for the support from Fü M III.

9 BmVg, Bundesminister Volker Rühe vereinbart Ausbildungskooperation der deutschen und lettischen Marine mit dem lettischen Vertedigungsminister Andrejs Krastins. BMVg online http://www.bmvg.government.de./PM-96082200.htm, Sept. 19, 1996.

10 Marineberatergruppe Estland, Bericht über den Einsatz der marineberatergruppe Estland vom 26. März 1996 bis Jan. 20, 1997.

11 Bundesministerium der Verteidigung, Presseforum, Deutsch-dänisch-polnische Zusammenarbeit im militärpolitischen und militärischen Bereich. BMVg online, 7/17/96, p. 1, internet, http://www.bmvg. government.de/Presseforum/Pressemappen/M2Q1.htm

12 Bundesministerium der Verteidigung, Presseforum, Deutsch-dänisch-polnische Zusammenarbeit im militärpolitischen und militärischen Bereich. BmVg online, 7/17/96, p. 2, internet, http://www.bmvg. government.de/Presseforum/Pressemappen/M2Q1.htm

References

Albrecht, Ulrich (1991). 'German Policies in the Baltic Sea Region' in Wellmann, Christian (ed.). *The Baltic Sea Region: Conflict or Cooperation? Region-Making, Security, Disarmament and Conversion.* Proceedings of the TAPRI–PFK workshop, Kiel, December 1991.

Alten, Jürgen von (1996). *Weltgeschichte der Ostsee.* Berlin.

Boehmer, Hans-Rudolf (Vice Adm., Chief of Naval Staff) (1995). 'Die Zukunft der Marine,' *Europäische Sicherheit*:7.

Bundesministerium der Verteidigung (1994). *Weißbuch 1994.* Bonn.

Burggraf, Volker (1994). 'Korvetten: Neue Seekriegsmittel für die Marine,' *Soldat und Technik*:4/1994, pages 218-223.

Danish Commission on Security and Disarmament (1995). Danish and European Security, Summary. Copenhagen, http://www.isn.ethz.ch/dupi/dan-sec.htm.

Eneberg, Kaa (1997). 'Baltron fortfarande i sin linda,' *Dagens Nyheter*, 23 February.

Frankfurter Allgemeine Zeitung (1993). 'Militärische Zusammenarbeit mit Polen,' 26 January.

Geipel, Gary, L. (1995). 'Germany and the Burden of Choice,' *Current History*:94/November.

Hækkerup, Hans (1995). 'Die Zusammenarbeit im Ostseeraum: Dänische Perspektiven und Initiativen,' *NATO-Brief*, May 1995, pages 14-18.

Heurlin, Bertel (1996). Denmark: A New Activism in Foreign and Security Policy' in Hill, Christopher (ed.). *The Actors in Europe's Foreign Policy.* London, New York.

Hogrebe, Volker (1994). 'Marinerüstung und ihre deutschen Mindestkapazitäten,' *Marineforum*:5, pages 132-139.

Imsa, Edmunds (1996). 'A Baltic Region emerges in Visby,' *The Baltic Times*:8, 9–15 May.

Jablonsky, Walter (1995). 'Wer sagt denn, daß wir beispielsweise keine Ostseestreitkräfte mehr brauchen?' *Marineforum*:7/8/1995.

Jann, Werner (1994).' Common Security in the Baltic Sea Region: The View from the German Länder.' Common Security in Northern Europe after the Cold War, a report from the Olof Palme International Center Seminar, Stockholm, 18–20 March 1994.

Joenniemi, Pertti (ed.) (1994). Cooperation in the Baltic Sea Region. Washington.

Kieler Nachrichten (1997). 'Bundeswehr-Hilfe für die Baltischen Staaten,' 17 March.

Krohn, Axel (1996). 'Germany,' pages 96-116 in Krohn, Axel (ed.). *The Baltic Sea Region: National and International Security Perspectives.* Baden-Baden.

Kukk, Mare (1994). 'Ostseerat: Mitten im Teich,' *Nordeuropa-Forum*:1, pages 20-27.

Kurth, James (1995). 'Germany and the Reemergence of Mitteleuropa,' *Current History*:94/November.

Lachowski, Zdzislaw (1996). 'Conventional Arms Control and Security Dialogue in Europe' in: *SIPRI Yearbook 1995: Armaments, Disarmament and International Security.* Oxford.

Larrabee, Steven F. (1993). East European Security after the Cold War. Santa Monica, RAND.

Leutrum, Nortwin Graf (1994). 'Das Verhältnis der Bundesrepublik Deutschland zur Baltischen Region' in Meissner, Boris, Loeber, Dietrich, A. and Hasselblatt, Cornelius (eds.). Die Aussenpolitik der Baltischen Staaten und die internationalen Beziehungen im Ostseeraum. Hamburg.

Magenheimer, Kurt (1995). 'Umgliederung und Reduzierung der Bundeswehr,' *Österreichische Militärische Zeitschrift*:3/1995, pages 347-349.

Mann, Hans-Joachim (Vice Adm.) (1991). 'Die Deutsche Marine ist gut vorbereitet,' *Marine Forum*:1/2, pages 8-11.

McEwan, Gavin (1995). 'WEU Seaforce Proposed,' *The Baltic Independent*, 8-14 December.

Naval Forces Special Issue (1996). *Roles, Mission and Structure of the German Navy*, No. 5/1996.

Petersen, Nikolaj (1993). *Dansk Sikkerhedspolitik og den Europæiske Union.* Copenhagen.

Petersen, Nikolaj (1995). 'Denmark and the New Germany: Cooperation or Adaption?' in Auffermann, Burkhard and Visuri, Pekka (eds.). *Nordeuropa und die deutsche Herausforderung.* Baden-Baden.

Poesze, Jörgen (1995). 'Eine "Europäische Marine,"' *Marineforum*:5.

Rotfeld, Adam Daniel (1994). 'Europe: Towards a New Regional Security Regime' in *SIPRI Yearbook 1994: World Armaments and Disarmament.* Oxford.

Schiff & Hafen (1994). 'Bundesmarine: Der Inspekteur zur Lage und den Perspektiven,' No. 4/1994.
Schmidt, Peter (1996). 'Deutsche Sicherheitspolitik im Rahmen von EU, WEU und NATO,' *Aussenpolitik*:3/1996, pages 211-222.
Zektri, Sonja (1996). 'Wer wird Balto Generalsekretär?' *Frankfurter Allgemeine Zeitung*, 19 July.

32 'Internal' Security in the Baltic States

Joan Löfgren and Helena Mannonen

Introduction

Since regaining independence, the Baltic states have undergone dramatic transformations in state and society, accompanied by new patterns of economic and social inequality, shifts in legislation and changes in shared and legitimate norms. As a result, new challenges to the security of these states and societies have arisen, calling for revised notions of security among policy makers. Increasingly, notions of security are being employed which extend beyond traditional military meanings to include various 'inward-looking' aspects of security and which focus not only on the state, but on the societal – including collective and individual – dimensions of security. It is also increasingly acknowledged that these dimensions of an extended concept of security do not exist in isolation, but interact with each other and with more traditional, external forms of security. In the following discussion we outline some of the new challenges calling for extended concepts of security, in particular crime and minority issues, drawing examples from Estonia with some comparisons to Latvia and Lithuania.

Crime as a Security Issue

In all the former socialist countries of Europe, political and socio-economic change has been accompanied by increasing problems of crime in its various forms and the Baltic states are no exception. The increase in crime and the new publicity around it stand in contrast to the period of Soviet rule, when the level of crime was officially low. Yet in reality, many argue, Soviet society was 'secured' and silenced by repressive control and by norms based more on fear and apathy than respect for laws. In the event, the Baltic states have faced since independence striking changes in the level and nature of crime, while simultaneously having to rebuild shattered state institutions. It has also become essential for policy makers to address crime problems in light of potential accession to the EU. While no explicit criteria for EU membership exist concerning internal security in the broad meaning used here, the efficiency and legitimacy of the institutions and policies in that field and the co-operation carried on in the framework of the third pillar of the Maastricht Treaty are becoming increasingly important. Eventually the Baltic states must demonstrate that they will be able to be a part of the 'free and secure area' of the EU and to fully participate in the nascent co-operation and common policies in the field of justice and home affairs.

In the three countries, but especially in Estonia and Latvia, the number of crimes registered by the police increased rapidly during the years of 1988-92, with the highest crime rates recorded in Estonia. Although the trends, the pace of reforms and the circumstances in which they took place are different, the overall perception dominant among Baltic researchers in this field has been that after the collapse of the totalitarian regime, crime has been on the rise and that the state and societal control systems have been experiencing crises, confusion, and more than occasional corruption (McMahon 1995: 12).

The quality of crime in the Baltics also changed in the early 1990s. The significant increase in the number of violent crimes, more hidden forms of economic, organised and transnational crime and the simultaneous weakness of the legal justice system culminated in what some have called the 'wild East.' As information concerning crime gradually increased, crime also became a collective issue in a radically new way with heated discussions on specific cases and increasing public concern for the problem in the respective societies (e.g. Markina 1997: 1). Public perceptions of security, justice and crime, placed in a new economic and societal environment, were shaped by the media publicity around everyday crime situations, trials and scandals or criminal groups' violent methods (Raid 1997). In Estonia and Latvia, the crime issue also began to have some ethnic dimensions as the perception about the 'violent and criminal Russians' became popular. Recently, however, Baltic policy makers have attempted to de-dramatise these issues and to focus on concrete problem-solving.

Before discussing more specific crime statistics, it is important to keep in mind that while the official statistics can offer valuable information on the general trends in crime, they are based on those crimes reported to the police or registered by the police and are therefore an imperfect reflection of reality. A sizeable percentage of crimes in the Baltics, as in any country, probably go unregistered, creating a gap between registered and actual crime rates (re: Estonia, see Ahven 1996a: 84). The degree to which crime is reported can be seen as an important indicator of the public's attitude toward crime and the police and is an essential factor in the police's efficient and legitimate functioning vis-a-vis society. For example, in Estonia, notifying the police about crimes has decreased in recent years; a 1995 survey revealed that only 48 per cent of those respondents who were victims of crimes reported them to the police (Markina 1996: 1). It is estimated that only 20-40 per cent of victims of violent crimes or lesser crimes against property reported them to the Estonian police (Aromaa and Ahven 1995: 20-21). According to the same survey, the dominant motivation for not reporting was the belief that the police 'would not do anything anyway' or 'are unable to do anything' (together 50 per cent). In Latvia surveys have also shown that only an estimated 10-50 per cent of the actual crimes committed appear in the official statistics and almost half the victims thought 'the police would not be able to help anyway' (The protection of crime victims 1995: 66).

An Overview of Crime Trends in the Baltics

With this caveat in mind, we turn now to recent crime statistics: in Estonia, according to official statistics, the total number of recorded offences more than doubled from 1989 (19,141) to 1992 (41,254) (Estonian Police Board 1996), by which time new national legislative, executive and juridical structures were established, enabling the stabilisation of the crime rate to begin. By 1996, the crime rate dropped from the previous year by 11 per cent, but figures in January 1997 show an increase compared to the previous year (*Postimees* 10 February). It is perhaps too soon after reforms to predict whether the stabilising trend will continue or whether the increase at the beginning of 1997 points to a new, worsening trend.

In terms of the types of crimes committed, the decrease in recorded crime in 1996 took place in every crime category except economic crime (+27 per cent), severe injury (+2 per cent) and counterfeiting (+84 per cent). Compared to the previous year, the decreasing direction can be seen as considerable in the number of recorded homicides (-11,8 per cent), robberies (-16,8 per cent) and bribes (-55.5 per cent). When focusing on the offenders of the crimes solved, a decrease in three problematic groups can be seen as a somewhat positive sign. First, the number of those offenders who used firearms decreased by almost 30 per cent. The use of firearms remains high, however: 41 per cent of offenders used firearms in committing crimes and the high level of illegal arms remains a problem. Secondly, the high rate of juvenile delinquency, whose amount decreased during the year by 5 per cent, still totals over 20 per cent of all offenders. Thirdly, despite a decrease of 16 per cent in the number of previously convicted offenders, this group still makes up about 31 per cent of all offenders (Estonian Ministry of Internal Affairs 1997). Thus some positive changes can be seen, but the picture is mixed in Estonia.

The same kind of general crime dynamic has been taking place also in Latvia, where the recorded crimes increased rapidly in the early 1990s. The total number of crimes was at its highest in 1992 (61,871), amounting to a rate of 236 per 10,000 (Statistical Yearbook of Latvia 1996: 164), eventually dropping to 151.8 in 1996. Although the general trend showed a decrease, the number of economic crimes, robbery, smuggling and bribes increased considerably, as did the number of crimes committed by groups and offenders using firearms (Estonian Ministry of Internal Affairs 1997).

Compared to Estonia and Latvia, the Lithuanian crime rate in the early 1990s was lower and the increase slower, reaching in 1993 160.9 crimes per 10,000 (comparative data from Estonian Ministry of Internal Affairs). However, unlike the other two Baltic countries, the crime level in Lithuania has increased in recent years and Lithuania's crime rate has already surpassed Latvia's. Except in 1994, the number of recorded crimes has increased every year in Lithuania, totalling 68,053 crimes, a rate of 183.3 per 10,000 population in 1996. In 1996, the highest increases in Lithuania occurred in economic crimes, robberies, burglaries and severe injuries.

In general and in a longer perspective, the increase in recorded crime in all three countries has culminated in growth in crimes against property, totalling 70-90 percent of all crimes. The high level of severe violent crime (homicides, attempted homicide and inflicting severe injury) has also been worrisome in Estonia and Latvia (Ahven 1996b: 13). While in Estonia, the level of homicides began to decrease in 1995, the rate is still much higher than in most European countries (Estonian Police Board 1996), contributing to a widespread belief in a 'violence boom' (Aromaa and Ahven 1995: 7). The popular perception of homicide in Estonia is of killings among different criminal groupings. Yet data from crimes solved indicate more traditional contexts for homicide – domestic fights and heavy alcohol use.

Crime and Societal Change

Crime, especially as a security issue, cannot be understood in isolation but must be viewed against a background of the many economic and societal pressures occurring after independence was regained in 1991. It is also inherently linked to the capacities of the state, through its laws and security institutions, and the civil society, as a normative context, to resist crime. Put simply, during the Baltic states' transitions from Soviet rule, the old system broke down without a new one developing in time to replace it. Extensive socio-economic changes, the new opportunities and demands of the market economy, together with confused legal and societal norms resulted in a situation where the boundary between legal and illegal were often blurred in the economic, societal as well as administrative sphere. The previous coercive order disappeared, but elements of the past system still remained, such as the tradition of silent approval of informal and illicit activities (McMahon 1995). Furthermore, inherent difficulties of the transition period in creating new laws and systems to enforce them have allowed subjective and objective opportunities for criminal activities to expand.

While various interpretations have been developed to understand societal changes in post-socialist states, certain features of the transition are agreed upon by most scholars as essential for understanding crime and security in the Baltic republics. First, crime patterns have been shaped by an ideological and value vacuum in certain areas of society. Notwithstanding the goal of economic prosperity or survival, the shared societal and ethical codes necessary to back up the laws and regulations have to some degree been lacking. The demolition of the old stereotypes, of the cohesion based on state repression, but also of shared norms, together with the domination of individualism have contributed to an all-pervasive permissiveness and an understanding of freedom as freedom out of control and restraint (Leps 1992: 17).

Secondly, socio-economic disparities accompanying the transition to a market economy have had a variety of consequences concerning crime. In relation to the side-effects of the transition into market economy, i.e. lowered production, unemployment, 'spontaneous' privatisation, inflation and collapse of industry and agriculture (Ozolina 1996: 42), new social and economic strata have been emerging and have further polarised the societies into 'haves' and 'have-nots.' These categories are no longer strictly linked to social status or profession but to newly emerging routes to rapid economic gain that often involve sacrificing social prestige to 'grey' market activities, even to criminal action. For example, in the process of privatisation, a new class of owners and entrepreneurs has been born who have in many cases made their starting capital on the black market. Together with organised criminals, they also have attempted to launder illegally obtained money by investing it in real estate, trade, services and so forth (Leps 1992: 16). The societal basis of crime is also made up of the majority, the 'have-nots,' whose 'feelings of relative deprivation are accompanied by suspicion and sensitivity to injustice and corruption' (McMahon 1995: 7). Under these circumstances, the potential is high that the previously existing disrespect for the state, its laws, functionaries and property may spread, with worrisome implications for state and societal security.

Organised economic crime is considered the most severe crime problem in the Baltics, both for the law enforcement system to deal with and for the society to cope with. Despite the popular theme of the 'Mafia,' organised crime in the Baltics involves a series of criminal methods and activities, a network that is involved in large-scale smuggling, massive theft of state property, and administration of protection, extortion and prostitution networks. In addition to the threats to consumers, businesses and individuals, even the integrity of political and government institutions is put at risk by organised crime: police, judges and parliamentarians have allegedly been targets of bribery and other kinds of pressure from organised crime (McMahon 1995: 4).

Organised crime also has an inherent tendency to move beyond the borders of individual states, due to a need for the optimal investment of capital gains. Criminal networks also find it easier to evade action by the state by shifting the focus of their activities from one country to another. When large sections of the whole structure are outside of the respective state, it is more difficult for the investigative authorities to gain insight into these networks (Wettig 1995: 143).

Finally, crime has also been used as a tool of high politics. In any society, but especially one in transition, elements linked to crime and powerful criminal groups easily become scapegoats for much broader problems. This can also be true of relations between states and their populations, as crime is used as proof of the negative perceptions and stereotypes about others. From the Baltic perspective, for example, the 'ethnic' criminal groups may be seen as 'allies of Moscow' or as a problem stemming directly from Russia, while, from the Russian side, the 'ethnicisation' of the problem is proof of the perceived discrimination of the Russian minority (Goble 1997). The same dynamics are also working the other away round when Russia states that the criminal threat coming from the Baltic republics is an acute problem for the security of Russian society and citizens. Instead of desperately needed co-operation, this discourse has the potential of exacerbating distrust among the countries and limiting the ability of the political authorities to manage the situation (Goble 1997). Yet it is essential for the Baltic states and Russia to do so.

Problems in Policing

It can be argued that the problems being experienced by the police have occurred and are occurring both *despite* and *because of* major attempts at rapid reform (McMahon 1995: 8). The development of the police from a militia tradition to a modern police force has to be situated in the broader context of transformation and especially the processes of state-building. The legacy of Soviet practices, atomising the societal fabric to facilitate vertical integration and administrative and political control, encouraged individual and collective distrust towards the state and its servants, rather than the sense of communal solidarity which must be regarded as fundamental for state legitimacy and performance (Jæger 1997: 17). Such distrust directly affects the effectiveness of the police, which is essentially based on public trust and willingness to report crimes, co-operate and obey laws.

One of the greatest problems in policing faced by all three Baltic states has been the lack of financial and material resources. In the EU-European context, the difference between resourceful criminals, with their technical and border-crossing capabilities, and the police establishment suffering from scarce resources and from the limits of national boundaries, is considerable. In the Baltic countries this difference is striking. At the beginning of independence, everyday police work was severely hindered in all the three countries by the lack of material and technical means (cf. McMahon). The situation has strongly improved since, by the stabilisation and professionalisation of the new forces and by increased national resources and foreign aid. Low salaries and a low level of professional prestige, however, continue to be serious problems for the Baltic police forces.

The economic difficulties have been paralleled by, and interwoven with, legal, ethical and social ones. According to the Estonian expert Ando Leps (1992: 16-7), the transition time caused by the liberation from totalitarianism and transfer to market economy has hindered the consolidation of the new state, weakened legal and social control over the individual and enfeebled the structures of executive power. In such conditions, some officials have felt compelled to commit illegal acts, sensing that they have been left without control. The decisions they have made have often been oriented at achieving primarily political but also personal goals. All these circumstances have been a powerful stimulus for the development of corruption, the scope of which, according to Leps, has 'contained a real threat to a democratic law-governed society' and which reaches into various economic, administrative and governmental spheres. As one Estonian observer put it: 'The new political elite is adapting the non-democratic standards of the Soviet system to the cynicism of the market' (Ruutsoo 1997: 32).

These problems are compounded by the lack of public trust mentioned above. Leps, speaking of Estonian society, points out that 'people have been becoming convinced that the state is not in a position to protect them from crime, increasing violence and lawlessness' (1993: 1; quoted in McMahon 1995: 10). Such negative attitudes and experiences are in part a holdover from the Soviet-era militia, which discouraged respect for the law and law enforcement agencies.

Survey data support this rather critical view. According to the Baltics Barometer II study (1995), when asked 'would you expect fair treatment from the police?' 31 per cent of the ethnic Estonians and 34 of the Russian speakers answered 'not likely' or 'definitely not.' The answers from the Latvian respondents showed figures over 40 per cent in both categories, and Lithuanian, the negative answers amounted to about 50 per cent.

While dissatisfaction with and distrust in the police remain high, popular opinion about the professionalism of the Estonian police, for example, has improved due to the emergence of police personnel with modern training (Ahven 1996b. 87). Furthermore, progress can be seen in the percentage of recorded offences which were solved, increasing in Lithuania from about 29 per cent in 1990 to 41 per cent in 1996; in Latvia from about 40 per cent in 1990 to 44 per cent in 1996 and in Estonia from 27 per cent in 1994 to 33 per cent in 1996 (Statistical Yearbooks of Lithuania, Latvia and Estonia 1996).

Combating crime, increasing police effectiveness and striving for a secure community all require a strong legal basis. The Baltic countries have faced a massive revision and adaptation in their legal systems and criminal codes. Each of the Baltic states has repudiated the arbitrary and repressive legislation and procedures of the Soviet system. However, getting rid of the old and creating new, consistent legal norms has been a challenging task. Although the legal tools for combating crime are largely in place, harmonisation and implementation of the system are a continuing process, as is the creation of a co-ordinated ministerial crime policy.

Crime in the Baltic states has worrisome elements that must be taken seriously and are taken seriously by various state commissions, ministries etc. However, in the Baltic states, as in any other country, arguably the most challenging task is to avoid overdramatising crime. Many of the problems facing the police and through it, the state are broader than the institutional or legal aspects and are part of a larger context of societal change. Rapid changes have occurred in practically every area of society, whereas certain characteristics of the Soviet era have been held over. This applies not only to the societal factors influencing crime, but also to interethnic relations.

Minorities, Citizenship and Societal Security

Since 1991, the re-establishment and consolidation of democracy in the Baltics states have been the focus of international scrutiny by institutions from the Council of Europe and OSCE to the EU. As potential EU members, Estonia,

Latvia and Lithuania have to address the 'Copenhagen criteria' in order to demonstrate their readiness and ability to return to Europe as stable democracies. The European Council, meeting in June 1993 in Copenhagen, agreed that a candidate country may become a member when it 'has achieved stability of institutions guaranteeing democracy, the rule of law, human rights and respect for and protection of minorities, the existence of a functioning market economy as well as the capacity to cope with competitive pressure and market forces within the Union' (European Council 1993: 11). The Copenhagen criteria thus point to several areas to which the concept of security has been extended, from stable democracy to human rights and minorities.

How do the Baltic states currently rate in terms of certain key Copenhagen criteria? They have by now a proven record of stability in fundamental democratic institutions and the rule of law, and standard human rights concerns have generally been limited to the death penalty and prison conditions. Respect for, and protection of, minorities and related issues of citizenship, naturalisation and migration have been more problematic, however.

Minority issues are problematic in Europe today, partly because of a lack of consensus on what constitutes a minority. This lack agreement is reflected in the many epithets used in, for example, the Estonian discussion: minority, ethnic-minority citizens, Russian-speaking population, aliens, denizens, non-Estonians, foreigners, Soviet-era migrants, just to mention a few examples. In official policy, the Baltic states have generally defined minorities as citizens who belong to a cultural minority group, but de facto the international community has often expanded it to include non-citizens as well. At times, this has been a highly sensitive issue, affecting the threat perceptions of both native groups as well as Soviet-era immigrants.

It is helpful to recall just how dramatic demographic changes in Baltic societies were during Soviet rule (see Table 32.1).

As is clear from the data, both Estonia and Latvia had experienced a severe decline in the relative proportion of the native population by 1989, especially in Latvia, where ethnic Latvians were a minority in seven towns. In Lithuania, the

Table 32.1: The percentage of titular/native population in the Baltic states

	1939*	1959	1989	1996/7
Estonia	92.4%	74.6%	61.3%	64.6%
Latvia	77.0%	62.0%	53.7%	55.1%
Lithuania	83.9%	79.3%	79.6%	81.6%

* Includes data from 1923, 1935 and 1939

Note: data for years with no census available, e.g. since 1989, are reliable estimates based on the registration of births, deaths etc.

Sources: Öst 1994; 1996 Statistical Yearbooks of Estonia (p. 55), Latvia (pages 56-7) and Lithuania (pages 33-4); and *Estonia Today* 1996

indigenous population remained dominant, due to: a larger population and higher rate of population growth, the slower pace of industrialisation, which did not justify a large migrant labour force, and availability of labour from rural areas for urban industries. It is also important to stress that in Estonia and Latvia, the majority of non-native residents are Russians, whereas in Lithuania they are divided mainly between Russian speakers and Poles. The slight increase in the native population since independence is due in part to the withdrawal of Soviet military forces.

Partly in response to these demographic changes, varying citizenship policies have been adopted. Lithuania chose a 'zero option' approach, offering citizenship to practically all residents with little or no requirements (those applying later must fulfil more stringent criteria). Estonia chose a more restrictive approach, recognising pre-war citizens and their heirs, while instituting naturalisation for more recent immigrants which included residence requirements and a language exam. Latvia chose an even more restrictive approach, with stages in naturalisation according to age group in addition to language and residency requirements. In establishing such policies, Estonian and Latvian leaders faced an inherent challenge in promoting the social and political cohesion of their societies, given the large proportion of non-citizens remaining from Soviet rule.

Estonia and Latvia have both come under fire for inefficiency and bureaucratic delays in implementing citizenship and residence permit regulations. The situation in Estonia seems to have improved since 1996, when aliens' passports began to be distributed with increasing speed. Naturalisation, while slowing down after an initial wave, is proceeding at a moderate pace (in late 1996, 11,000 applications were pending; Rebane 1996). Recent surveys of Estonia show the percentage of ethnic Russians holding Estonian citizenship in north-eastern Estonia has grown significantly. In 1993 16 per cent of the Russians surveyed had citizenship, whereas in 1994 it had grown to 35 per cent and by 1996 to 49 per cent (Kirch et al. 1996: 6). Insufficient language ability continues to be a main factor hindering naturalisation, followed by practical and economic factors such as ease in crossing the Russian border.

In Latvia, the naturalisation process has been very slow. Since 1995 about 93,000 have become eligible for naturalisation, but only 7000, or 8 per cent, have in fact become naturalised (The Role of Naturalisation 1996: 2). A state-sponsored survey of ethnic Russian high school students who were eligible to naturalise in 1996 revealed the main factors hindering naturalisation: insufficient knowledge of the Latvian language or history, insufficient information, difficulties in obtaining the necessary documents and the high fee (The Results 1996: 4). The naturalisation process continues to be the target of criticism, and given sufficient political support, the system might be revised in the coming years.

In Lithuania, an estimated 95 per cent of the population chose Lithuanian citizenship during the implementation of the 'zero option' citizenship policy (Chinn and Kaiser 1996: 120). More recent immigrants must fulfil more stringent requirements for naturalisation.

Refugee and Asylum Policies

The Baltic states have also been developing a refugee and asylum policy. The main obstacle has been a fear that accepting applications for asylum would put an overwhelming burden on the state budgets and cause political problems with constituents, as occurred in Latvia even without such a policy. A related problem is the use of the Baltic territories for transit to other areas of Europe. Many of the migrants coming from CIS countries originate in the Middle East and Asia, attempting to travel through the Baltic states on their way west. They may have false documents, false visas or temporary tourists visas to some country of the CIS. There are also cases where such illegals hold documents certifying refugee status afforded in Moscow. One expert estimates that the majority of such transit migrants (about 60 per cent) travel without any personal documents (Sipaviciene 1996: 15). In the Lithuanian case, it is estimated that only about 50-60 per cent of illegal transit migrants are held back by the border control services. In Lithuania, about 17 per cent of transit migrants stopped at the border came from Afghanistan, 26 per cent from India, 17 per cent from Pakistan, 17 per cent from Sri Lanka, 11 per cent from Iraq (Sipaviciene 1996: 15).

Lithuania ratified the 1951 Convention on Refugees in 1995 (in effect 1996) and Estonia in early 1997. Observers expect Latvia to do so in the near future. In Latvia, local political controversies over social benefits to asylum seekers have complicated adoption of the Convention and the related implementation. Estonia's policy includes a narrow definition of asylum, for political not economic or humanitarian reasons, such as in wartime. In the Estonian parliament there was no major debate on the main principles, but instead on the social provisions, where Estonia decided to follow the more restrictive British approach (Nutt 1997).

Perhaps even more important for regional security are the series of return agreements which the Baltic states are in the process of concluding. Estonia has such agreements with Finland, Latvia, Norway, soon with Sweden, and a process is under way with Schengen countries, but not so far with Russia. Although Russia has ratified the 1951 Convention, its actual implementation is still in question.

With the return agreements and only moderate social provisions, Baltic leaders seek to balance responsibility for stopping the flow of illegal immigrants into the region with the acceptance of legitimate causes for asylum. Until full implementation is in place, it is difficult to evaluate their success, but Baltic policy makers expect the number of asylum seekers to stabilise at a moderately low rate. One expert estimates that social provisions by the Lithuanian state could likely accommodate up to 100 persons a year (Blazys 1996: 46-8), and in Estonia the number cited is up to 50 (Nutt 1997).

The main challenge for Baltic policy makers concerning asylum seekers is to reduce the incentives for transit migrants to use the Baltic territories as a way-station to their desired destinations elsewhere in Europe. While the numbers may be small in absolute terms, the social benefits provided might prove a great burden to small states over the longer term. And in the case of transit asylum seekers, it is unrealistic to expect their later integration as productive members of the Baltic societies.

Citizenship and Societal Security

Demographic transformation under Soviet rule together with restorationist citizenship policies have resulted in an unusually high proportion of the populations of Estonia and Latvia who do not currently enjoy citizenship of the country in which they live, i.e. they have the status of aliens. In addition, transit migrants and asylum seekers are joining already multi-ethnic societies, at least temporarily. What are the implications of these developments for the security of the Baltic states and societies? From the state perspective, security-as-sovereignty clearly puts citizenship on the agenda. And while instruments in international law provide that all persons have the right of citizenship, there is no such instrument in the field of human rights which recognises the right to a specific citizenship as a human right, i.e. there is no specific state which has the obligation to grant citizenship to any given individual (Pirjola 1995: 24). By the same token, states have the right to define the scope of asylum granted, departing from the minimum prescribed by the 1951 Convention.

Such legal justifications aside, the nature of the democratic system in any given state is bound to be affected by a large non-citizen population, who by definition does not enjoy a full range of political rights. From the individual perspective, many non-citizens in the Baltic states have felt their own security threatened by state rules they see as unfair or practices which are inconsistent. While such complaints may not fall within standard definitions of human rights abuses, they point to potential tensions between individuals and the state which could become a security issue.

At bottom lies the definition of the polity, and during their transition, the Baltic states have been in the unusual historical position of having to define their polities explicitly through the rules of citizenship. Their choices have ranged from a narrow definition of citizenship based on pre-war citizens and their descendants (restorationist approach) to a broad-based polity of long-term residents (zero-option approach). Estonia chose a conservative compromise solution, with a potentially broad-based polity at the local level and a much narrower one at the national level. In Latvia a narrower polity was instituted at all levels, and in Lithuania a broader polity was instituted at all levels. The degree of demographic change in each state played a key role in shaping notions of the polity which emerged in the early years of independence.

These Baltic citizenship policies were not, however, arrived at without heated debates, linked to broader tensions in interethnic relations. Drawing on Wæver's and others' notion of 'securitised' issues, it is helpful to consider which aspects of ethnic relations in the Baltics have been securitised, i.e. been dramatised in the security discourse as issues of absolute priority, presenting an existential threat. By labelling something a security issue, an actor has claimed the right to deal with it by extraordinary means (Wæver 1996: 106). Citizenship requirements in Estonia and Latvia became securitised both as a result of nationalist concerns and the concerns of the 'new minorities.' Nationalists perceived a threat from more moderate citizenship requirements, which would result in Russian speakers dominating the polity. In turn, the new minorities, mainly Russian speakers, saw their legal and political status, well-established in the Soviet era, threatened by citizenship and voting rules in the newly independent states. One man's restoration was another's disenfranchisement.

Ethnicity issues indeed became issues of survival during the Baltic transitions, in part because the Soviet system made ethnicity more salient than other identities such as class and citizenship. This tendency was further intensified by political entrepreneurs, who used ethnic identities for political gain, as the level of threat sensed by ethnic groups increased (Saideman 1996: 19). Eventually more radical nationalists in Estonia and Latvia came to dominate in the transitions and sought to restore the power of their national groups in the state.

Speaking more generally of such cases, if the state cannot protect the interests of all ethnic groups, then a particular group may seek to control the state, decreasing the security of other groups and decreasing the ability of the state to provide security for any group, whether it be economic, physical or political security – resulting in a type of security dilemma for the state (Saideman 1996: 23). Increasing security for one group implies a decrease in the security of another. As Baltic nationalist leaders instituted restrictive citizenship policies, many Soviet-era immigrants to Estonia and Latvia came to feel that their states were not protecting their interests but mainly the interests of ethnic Estonians and Latvians. In turn, nationalist elites justified this exclusion by defining the polity in terms of pre-war citizens: whose state was it anyway? The trade-offs may not actually have been zero-sum, with a loss for one group automatically bringing gain to another, but there was a strong perception that this was the case.

Some would argue that this security dilemma might easily lead to ethnic conflict, but that has not occurred in the Baltic states. Why not? First, the Baltic states may be becoming more and more impartial adjudicators of interest disputes, partly due to pressure from international institutions and bilateral relations with Nordic countries. Secondly, politicians from different ethnic groups are no longer able to mobilise solely around nationalist issues, but must demonstrate to constituents their ability to deliver economic and other benefits. Thirdly, as increasing numbers of Russian speakers are naturalised and become eligible to vote, Russian elite mobilising around dissatisfaction and isolation is less and less effective, partly since staying in Estonia is still considered a better alternative than returning to Russia. Finally, one could argue that the zero-sum trade-offs between ethnic groups are no longer taken for granted. Today what is good for Estonians is not necessarily bad for Russians. The current low level of interethnic tension is outlined in Table 32.2.

In spite of this overall low level of tension, one aspect of state-ethnic minority relations remains: trust in government is generally low in the Baltic states. For example, there has been at times a high degree of mistrust in the state's impartiality concerning naturalisation requirements. Russian speakers who are frustrated by confusing requirements and bureaucratic delays may easily blame the state for only making a show of naturalisation. So far this has not developed into open conflict but has had the potential of weakening democratic stability by alienating a large segment of the population from the state and the polity.

Aside from restrictions on political and legal rights, how well integrated are ethnic Russians in the broader Estonian society? In a 1996 survey in Estonia, the majority of Russians with Estonian citizenship felt that they have adapted to Estonian life and have fully conformed to it (69 per cent). The percentage among non-citizens was not as high, but significant: 49 per cent. Estonian culture seems to be rather close to the majority of local Russians irrespective of citizenship (75 per cent of citizens and 64 per cent of non-citizens). Actual cultural integration is, however, not proceeding as quickly as such positive attitudes might suggest. 'Most of the Russians living in Estonia are adapted to the local circumstances but actually are not prepared for a deeper cultural and political integration. As many as 90 per cent of the Russians agree that everyone in Estonia must know the Estonian language. Yet the real level of fluency in Estonian has not improved significantly among Russians for the last two or three years' (Kirch and Kirch 1996: 224 f.). Most observers describe the present situation as one of low tension but also of cultural isolation.

Table 32.2: Tensions in interethnic relations between Estonians and Russians, April 1992, February 1993 and March 1996, percentages

	Russians					**Estonians**
	Total	Tallinn	Narva	Ida-Viru (all cities)	Tartu	Total
			April 1992 (N=925)			
No tension	28	14	47	43	22	-
Some tension	36	38	33	33	41	-
Average tension	19	25	9	10	30	-
Above average tension	17	23	11	14	7	-
			February 1993 (N=867)			
No tension	39	40	46	42	33	53
Some tension	43	45	37	39	48	36
Average tension	12	11	9	10	14	8
Above average tension	6	4	8	9	5	3
			March 1996 (N=1300)			
No tension	62	73	33	49	71	64
Some tension	22	16	25	26	18	24
Average tension	13	8	34	20	7	7
Above average tension	3	1	8	5	4	5

Source: Kirsch, Kirsch and Tuisk (1996: 8)

What can be done to overcome some of this cultural isolation? To some extent it depends on deeply rooted cultural differences which cannot be easily transformed. But state policy can address factors such as education and language teaching. After an initial period of optimism about Russians learning Estonian, state officials now seem more realistic about which groups can be targeted successfully. More emphasis is now being put on educating younger generations than on older Russian-speaking immigrants, many of whom have few incentives for learning and maintaining a certain level of Estonian (Language Centre 1996). Officials in charge of developing the language strategy have highlighted the need to ensure that young ethnic Russians will be able to compete in the labour market after finishing school.

One major obstacle to expanding Estonian instruction in state schools is the lack of trained Estonian language teachers: only 1 in 7 are trained specialists. Other goals include improving curriculum and adult training focused on citizenship language exams. A sample test booklet was prepared in 1996 to assist citizenship applicants, and previous inconsistencies in administering the exam seem to be solved.

Asked if ethnic Russians consider the language exam unduly difficult, language policy officials pointed to a contrast between two major groupings: 1) those who are fluent in Estonian and passed the previous version of the exam and 2) the 100,000 or so citizens of Russia who have little interest in passing the language exam, either thinking it is too difficult or wishing to keep their Russian passports in order to travel easily across the border (Language Centre 1996). From the remaining population, a new wave of naturalisation could be anticipated, depending on incentives.

The complexities involved in ensuring the success of a state language strategy highlight the deeper and longer-term trends in society which are to some extent beyond the scope of a single state. And yet the minority and citizenship issues presented here will affect the long-term stability of democracy and can lead to challenges to the state by dissatisfied ethnic groups. In addition, the security of the region is affected since the 'minority problem' has been the focus of Russian foreign policy rhetoric on the 'near abroad' and the Russian Diaspora. For example, Estonian authorities claim that the Russian Federation has consistently pushed a policy of dual citizenship (not permitted by Estonia), by hindering efforts to confirm that holders of Russian passports have renounced their Russian citizenship before being naturalised in Estonia.

Estonia's border agreement with Russia has also been delayed in part because Russia is linking it to progress in solving 'human rights problems' among Russian citizens in Estonia. As Estonia moves closer to the EU, leaders consider it imperative to ensure that future citizens of Estonia – with the benefits an obligations as members of the EU – have strong loyalties that do not conflict with the aims and security of the Union.

Conclusion

The two major issues discussed above, crime and minorities, challenge narrower understandings of security, extending it to areas within Baltic states and societies not traditionally considered within the realm of security debates. Some of the problems facing Baltic leaders are transitional and can be addressed through reforms of state structures and well-targeted resources, whether from state budgets or international assistance. Other problems are more deeply rooted and can be addressed only partially by state policies: changes in norms and values, persistent cultural isolation of minorities, to name two examples. The persistence of these problems underscores the need for effective state policies which promote the internal security and stability of the societies, not only for the sake of EU accession, but for the countries themselves.

Moreover, the real test of security in the Baltic states seems to be the degree to which countries in the Northern European region and especially Russia and the three Baltic states are able and willing to work together in pursuing common interests and in solving the various problems that affect them all and can often not be resolved by unitary action. Here the extended security thinking, i.e. understanding security threats and security means beyond the statist military sphere, is essential. In addition to new problems, 'the new security agenda' thus also includes new kinds of possibilities and necessities for the Baltic countries in finding common ground for co-operation and community-building with the West and even more essentially, with the East.

References

Aromaa, Kauko and Ahven, Andri (1995). *Victims of Crime in a Time of Change: Estonia 1993 and 1995*. National Research Institute of Legal Policy. Research Communications:19. Helsinki, Yliopistopaino.

Ahven, Andri (1996a). 'Information on crime in Estonia,' pages 79-88 in *Estonian Human Development Report 1996*. Tallinn, United Nations Development Programme, Chapter Health and Personal Security.

Ahven, Andri (1996b). 'Rikollisuus Baltian maissa,' *Suomen Lähialueet*:2 /1996. Helsinki, Tilastokeskus.

Baltics Barometer II (1995). Rose, Richard Vilmorus Baltic Data House and EMOR: *New Baltics Barometer II: A Survey Study*. Studies in Public Policy:251. Glasgow, University of Strathclyde Centre for the Study of Public Policy.

Blazys, Ceslovas (1996). 'The Laws of Citizenship, Immigration, Emigration and Legal Status of Foreigners,' pages 41-48 in *Regional Seminar on Migration Legislation and Related Issues: Collected papers*. Helsinki, International Organization for Migration.

Chinn, Jeff and Kaiser, Robert (1996). *Russians as the New Minority: Ethnicity and Nationalism in the Soviet Successor States*. Boulder, CO, Westview Press.

Estonia Today (1996). Population by Ethnicity as of 1 January 1996. Electronic version, 16 October, pages 1-3.

Estonian Ministry of Internal Affairs (1997). Statistical data on crime in Estonia, Latvia and Lithuania in 1996.

Estonian Police Board (1996). 'Crime in Estonia in 1995.' Information about Statstics, 21 April 1996. Tallinn.
European Council (1993). European Council Meeting in Copenhagen, 21-22 June 1993: *Conclusions of the Presidency*. SN 180/93, Commission des Communautés Européennes, Secretariat General, Bruxelles, Section 7Aiii, p. 11.
Goble, Paul (1997). 'Crime and Post-Soviet Policy,' *The Baltic Times*:2(43), 23-29 January.
Jæger, Øyvind (1997). 'Securitising Russia: Discursive Practices of the Baltic States.' Unpublished draft.
Kirch, Marika and Kirch, Aksel (1996). 'Russians in Contemporary Estonia: from Adaptation to Integration,' *Proceedings of the Estonian Academy of Sciences, Humanities and Social Sciences*:45(2), pages 224-5 (English summary).
Kirch, Aksel, Kirch, Marika and Tuisk, Tarmo (1996). *Characteristics of the Ethnic and Social Development in Ida-Virumaa 1993-1996*. Tallinn, Institute of International and Social Studies, Work Group on Ethnic Policy.
Language Centre (1996). Interview with officials related to the State Language Centre in Estonia: Mall Pesti, Ave Härsing and Ilmar Tomusk, October 1996.
Leps, Ando (1992). 'A Brief Survey of the Criminogenic Situation in the Republic of Estonia, 1945-1992.' Tallinn, Estonian State Police.
McMahon, Maeve (1995). 'Crime, Justice and Human Rights in the Baltic States,' *Heuni Papers*:5. Helsinki, European Institute for Crime Preventation and Control.
Markina, Anna (1996). 'Organised Crime in Estonia.' Unpublished paper presented at the conference 'Internal Security and the Eastern Enlargement of the EU,' held at Finnish Police Academy, Espoo 15-17 November, 1996.
Nutt, Mart (1997). Interview with MP Mart Nutt, member of Constitution Committee of Estonian Parliament, 13 March 1997.
Öst, Anna-Carin (1993). 'Who Is Citizen in Estonia, Latvia and Lithuania?' in Dahlgren, Taina (ed.) *Human Rights in the Baltic States*. Advisory Board for International Human Rights Affairs, Publication No.6. Helsinki, Finnish Helsinki Committee.
Ozolina, Zaneta (1996). 'Latvian Security Policy' in Lejins, Atis and Bleire, Daina (eds.). *The Baltic States: Search for Security*. Riga, Latvian Institute of International Affairs.
Pirjola, Jari (1995). 'Remarks on the Migration Laws in Baltic States, Belarus, Russian Federation and Ukraine,' pages 24-30 in *Regional Seminar on Migration Legislation and Related Issues: Collected Papers*. Helsinki, International Organization for Migration.
Postimees (1997), 10 February.
Raid, Aare (1997). 'The Integration of the Baltic States into the EU.' Tallinn, unpublished manuscript.
Results (1996). 'The Results of the Opinion Poll Having Been Carried out among the Pupils of Educational Establishments Dec. 1995-Jan. 1996.' Report distributed by Naturalisation Board, Republic of Latvia, autumn 1996. Riga.
Role (1996). 'The Role of Naturalisation in the Process of Integration.' Document distributed by Naturalisation Board, Republic of Latvia, November 1996. Riga.
Ruutsoo, Rein (1997). Expert interview. In: Blom, Raimo (ed.). *Expert Interviews from the Baltic States*. Working Papers, B:37. University of Tampere, Department of Sociology and Social Phychology.
Saideman, Stephen (1996). 'The Dual Dynamics of Disintegration: Ethnic Politics and Security Dilemmas in Eastern Europe,' *Nationalism and Ethnic Politics*:2(1), Spring 1996, pages 18-43.
Sipaviciene, Andra (1996). *International Migration and the Baltic States: new Patterns and Policy*. Report prepared for Baltic Assembly/Nordic Council Seminar on Migration Issues Relevant to the Baltic Sea Area. Helsinki.
Statistical Yearbook of Estonia 1996. Tallinn, Statistical Office of Republic of Estonia
Statistical Yearbook of Latvia 1996. Riga, Central Statistical Bureau, Republic of Latvia.
Statistical Yearbook of Lithuania 1996. Vilnius, Department of Statistics, Republic of Lithuania.
Wæver, Ole (1995). 'What is Security: The Securityness of Security,' pages 222-54 in Hansen, Birthe (ed.). *European Security 2000*. Copenhagen, Copenhagen Political Studies Press.
Wettig, Gerhard (1995). 'A New Type of Challenge to European Security,' *Aussenpolitik*:46(2).

33 The Tackling of Minority Issues in the Baltic Sea Region in the Context of OSCE and CBSS

Hanne-Margret Birckenbach

The Baltic Sea region is rich in minorities.[1] This chapter presents a survey of the region's capacity to constructively tackle minority-related conflicts, provides information on the present state of minorities, and refers to a series of obstacles that hamper the Region's ability to improve minority-majority relations. Finally it focuses on the office of the Commissioner of the Council of Baltic Sea States (CBSS) and reflects on its contribution to overcoming the impediments to developing the region as a zone of peace.

Capacity for Coping with Conflicts

The region is better able to cope with minority issues than many other European areas. Regardless of the nature of the present disputes, open violence is relatively rare in all of the countries around the Baltic Sea. Intrastate and interstate war is absent. Minorities themselves act in a highly civilised manner when demanding rights. Non-violence has been generally accepted as the sole legitimate means of struggle. None of the minorities threatens the existence of their respective state, and state authorities usually remain within legal bounds in their treatment of minorities.[2]

The Region has developed good access to institutions and mechanisms which have been created in order to assist states in coping with minority issues nationally as well as internationally and at the governmental as well as non-governmental level. One example is the 'ombudsman,' a Scandinavian invention which has been exported to other countries within the region and beyond. The willingness to submit conflicts to international mediation has been more developed than in any other European area since the League of Nations assisted in the settling of conflicts over the Åland Islands and helped to establish exemplary legal protection of minorities in the Baltic states.

The Nordic countries have participated in various organs of United Nations and of the OSCE and contributed intensively to the evolution of the international human rights system. They now can build on getting a good return for the benefit of the region. The Nordic aspiration to make preventive diplomacy a consistent strategy, visible particularly during Sweden's chairmanship of the CSCE Council, and the application of this strategy to the conflicts over citizenship and related issues in Estonia and Latvia have already proved effective.

One of the latest innovations is the 'Commissioner on Democratic Institutions and Human Rights, including the Rights of Persons belonging to Minorities.' His office was set up by the Council of the Baltic Sea States (CBSS) and became effective after the Danish Government and Parliament had approved financial support for it in October 1994. Both locally and transnationally these institutions function as eyes, ears and voices against the maltreatment of minorities in order to increase their chances of becoming fully integrated into their societies without the pressure of assimilation .

The Present State of Minorities

The region's minority-related disputes pertain to a domestic as well as international agenda. Indeed, each country in the area has experienced disputes of its own over the rights of its minorities, and not a single riparian state can argue that its policy towards minorities is fully in line with internationally agreed human rights standards. This even holds for the Nordic countries despite their distinct reputation. Sweden, for instance, cannot be regarded as living fully up to its international legal obligations as long as the Tornedalen Finns lack a recognised minority status, and the removal of the special fishing and hunting rights of the Sami runs counter to the rights of indigenous peoples. Finland's treatment of immigrant groups obviously is not in line with Article 27 of the Covenant on Civil and Political Rights. Even Norway's overall record regarding human and minority rights has been questioned due to its insensitive attitude towards the Kven-Finnish minority, and Denmark pursues a policy of assimilation vis-a-vis migrant workers in breach of international law (Hannikainen 1996).

The situation of minorities differs from country to country though there is a general difference between East and West in the region. Despite the fact that it makes a difference in which part of the region a minority resides and which kind of political status is granted to it, some generalisations can be made.

Citizens: A State of Advanced Integration

Manifestly minority-related border conflicts among states have mostly disappeared around the Baltic Rim with the exception of Russian-Estonian and Russian-Latvian disputes. Despite the example of the Tornedalen Finns, minorities with obvious ties to the political majority in a neighbouring state are generally recognised as national minorities. Their treatment, however, varies and is not symmetric. Germans in Poland and 'Polonia' in Germany provide a good example. In contrast to the German laws concerning the Polish minority, the Polish laws grant the German minority a de facto guarantee of representation in Parliament. Although both Poland and Germany are firm in their rejection of dual citizenship, both minorities can obtain it. However, the process is much more difficult for Poles in Germany, who also have to pay high fees for this bureaucratic procedure, than for Germans in Poland. This minority has been intensively supported by the German government – not least through considerable financial aid – against many Polish reservations in order to avoid increasing numbers of ethnic Germans 'returning' from Eastern European countries. The current number of newcomers is more than 200,000 per year. Poland, however, shies away from risking any tension with the German government on the issue of the rights of the Polish minority because Poland needs German support for its application for EU and NATO membership.

Due to the advances of the rule of law, social welfare and civil society, indigenous groups living in the West can make their voices heard. Legally and politically, the Sami of Norway have gained a stronger position than the Sami of Finland or Sweden.[3] The Sami in Finland and the Frisians and Sorbs in Germany have achieved some improvements in the enforcement of their internationally agreed rights through the application of the 1994 Framework Convention on Minorities of the Council of Europe and respective amendments of constitutions and legislation. Kvens in Norway, however, have so far failed to do so.

Among the indigenous minorities in the eastern Baltic Sea region, only the Seto, who are not recognised as an indigenous minority by Estonia and whose villages lie in disputed territories, have recently managed to raise their voice transnationally, when their representatives in Estonia decided to join the Urepresented Nations and Peoples Organisation (UNPO), a world-wide organisation uniting stateless groups.

About 3,000 Seto live in the Petseri region on the Russian side, and about 5,000 in Estonia. They fear that they may become victims of an eventual agreement on the borders between Estonia and Russia which would confirm the division of 'Setoland' into a Russian and an Estonian part.

The situation of indigenous minorities living in just one country or in an area divided by national borders differs from that of the dispersed minorities, Jews and Romany, who were both targets of genocide during the period of national socialism. In the Baltic states many of the Jews belong to the Russian-speaking minorities. Those who can afford to do so tend to emigrate, mostly to Israel or the USA. Thus this minority, having survived the horrors of national socialism, is constantly becoming smaller and poorer. The situation of the Romany seems to be improving due to the attention paid to them in several OSCE discussions and by the OSCE's Office for Democratic Institutions and Human Rights (ODIHR) serving as a 'Contact Point for Roma and Sinti Issues.'

In its treatment of the Romany, Finland has become something of a model for Europe. Its constitution now recognises the cultural autonomy of the Romany. Finland's legislation has also provided for affirmative action to help the Romany especially in the field of housing and vocational training. Special manpower offices arrange employment training, and Romany children can be taught in their mother tongue.

In Germany, the crimes of national socialism still overshadow the life of about 70,000 Romany and Sinti. For many years they have lived a secluded life, hiding themselves from the public instead of claiming their rights and publicising their needs and aspirations. However, recently they have begun to appear in public and informing people about their language, culture, identity and lifestyle. In Schleswig-Holstein, where about 5,000-6,000 Romany live, their formal recognition as a national minority through an amendment to the state's constitution has been put on the agenda.

Generally, one can state that national minorities living in the Western European part of the Baltic Sea region experience better living conditions than those in the transition countries, i.e. Poland, Lithuania, Latvia, Estonia and the northwest of Russia, where the number of national minorities is greater, their share of the population is higher and the general living conditions tend to be inferior to those of the more homogeneous and prosperous West.

Of course, the 'silver curtain' has had an impact on the situation of minorities in the region. This also affects those social groups in a minority-like position which, like women, demand international standards of equality or, like children and old or disabled people, need a society which shows consideration for their particular difficulties and life circumstances. Whereas the Nordic countries still constitute a shining example in the sphere of women's progress in attaining political power, they do not find imitators in any other country of the region. Women in Germany have been losers in the unification of the German Democratic Republic and the Federal Republic of Germany. The situation of women in the transition countries has deteriorated considerably (UNICEF 1994).

Nevertheless, the general situation of minorities whose members are recognised as citizen of the country in which they reside appears rather good. The main problems have been identified and addressed by at least one or two countries playing the role of pioneers. In addition to the process of democratisation, the new opportunities for minorities to express their demands and the improvement of national legislation granting minorities affirmative action, minorities have benefited from both interstate co-operation and the emergence of the international human rights system. Sensitivity towards minorities has been particularly encouraged through the standards set by the United Nations, the OSCE and the Council of Europe. Further progress will very much depend on whether the civil society demands that governments implement these internationally agreed standards.

Aliens: The Making of Disenfranchised Beings

Very different from and far worse than the situation of minorities who enjoy citizenship, is the situation of groups whose members are not citizens of the country they live in and who may, at best, ask for naturalisation. Most states ignore their minority status and refer to international law which used to reserve this status to citizens. However, the OSCE has aspired to change this view, and it is obvious that the High Commissioner on National Minorities (HCNM) could not fulfil his duties, if he followed the traditional view in Latvia and Estonia.

When the Soviet Union ceased to exist, a new category of minority had appeared which had not been envisaged by the drafters of the relevant instruments of international law, i.e. residents who had lost their citizenship after major international upheavals. More than 50 million Soviet citizens migrated legally from one Soviet republic to one which became independent after the demise of the Soviet Union.

Although Russia and the new independent states have generally reached bilateral agreements granting such people the right to opt for either Russian citizenship or citizenship in the state in which they reside until the year 2001, the so-called 'Russians' face many problems. In May 1996, they were the subjects of a regional conference organised by the UN High Commissioner on Refugees (UNHCR), the OSCE and the International Organisation of Migration. All states bordering on the Baltic Sea participated. A programme of action was adopted, based on the principle of freedom of movement, a person's right to participate in elections in his or her place of residence and the right of citizenship in one of the successor states of the Soviet Union.

Estonia, Latvia and Lithuania, which do not perceive themselves as former Soviet republics, differ in their treatment of the 'Russians.' Whereas Lithuania has accepted them as its citizens, Estonia and Latvia have declared them 'non-citizens with a special status' and have adopted special legislation restricting their right to achieve naturalisation. This minority numbers more than one million.

Perceptions of the citizenship conflict differ among the parties, and most of the contradicting views seem to be legitimate, which indicates how different dimensions of peace, namely human and minority rights, national security and international stability have become interrelated in the region. From the Estonian and Latvian official point of view, the status of non-citizens results from a legitimate decision taken in the interest of national security. From a non-citizen's point of view, the decision is unjust and discriminating. In Russia's opinion, the stance taken by Estonia and Latvia is a massive violation of human rights, and the international community fears an escalation into violence and destabilisation. This is the reason why a strategy of preventive diplomacy has been pursued.

In recent years, a remarkable conflict transformation has been achieved through the assistance of international organisations. Conflict behaviour has remained free of open violence, and there has been a growing attitude in favour of dialogue and legislative reform. The United Nations, the Council of Europe and the OSCE have played decisive roles, and NGOs like the St Petersburg Minority Rights Group, the Swedish Helsinki Committee for Human Rights, the Helsinki Watch and the International Federation on Human Rights have contributed to this process.

International organisations have been able to build on a foundation which had already been laid during the period of pre-independence in the Baltic republics, when a culture of non-violence and a general acceptance of human rights had been developing. It has also been decisive that not just one but a variety of international organisations have been at work, thus guaranteeing a plurality of perspectives as well as unity in calling for integration of the minorities as the common goal. All actors have in some way benefited from their work. They have helped Estonia and Latvia rebut Russian accusations that they were massively violating human rights, and they have been instrumental in counteracting the idea of moving non-citizens out of the country as proposed by various political leaders in the two countries. This, in turn, has calmed emotions both in Russia and among non-citizens. Though avoiding direct support for non-citizens, international organisations have secured political guarantees which have allowed the minorities to stay legally in their country of residence. The international organisations have also provided the international community, the conflicting states and local NGOs with detailed and shared information and have sent out missions that have helped in revising laws and observing their implementation. In this manner they have served as a resource against rumours and assisted the governments in better adjusting their legislation to human rights obligations and European standards.

Despite these comprehensive efforts, a final resolution of the conflicts has not been reached, and 1996 has even been a year of stagnation. Figures on naturalisation are low. The situation in the north-east of Estonia has remained crucial. Accusations and threatening statements continue to be exchanged between Russian and Estonian as well as Russian and Latvian politicians. Requirements for naturalisation, the provision of passports, and language laws continue to be the most disputed issues. It is mainly international assistance that has prevented the situation from deteriorating. For instance, disputes regarding restrictions in the Estonian local elections in October 1996 were successfully mediated, and the Latvians were made aware that a more restrictive law concerning non-citizens would have fuelled further dispute with international organisations.

The development of institutions encouraging at least dialogue within the civil society has remained slow. One of the few positive signals is the establishment of the Consultative Council of Nationalities by Latvia's president. It follows the Estonian model of a Presidential Round Table and started working in July 1996. Although the experience in Estonia has been that the Round Table has not resulted in an improved status of non-citizens, it has contributed to clarifying why the national non-citizenship policy is failing its aims. The Round Table mechanism is also helping to remove some of the taboos from discussions on the naturalisation process.

The aim to initiate debate within society may be furthered by the Latvian National Human Rights Office (LNHRO), which was given complete independence by Parliament in December 1996 in regard to such duties as informing and educating the public on human rights and investigating alleged violations of them. The office has dealt with individual complaints covering a variety of questions such as living conditions for asylum seekers and allegations of discrimination against non-citizens. Although the LNHRO tends to take the official Latvian view that non-citizens should not have the right to vote or be elected, to work in the service of the state or to own land or natural resources, it has nevertheless stated: 'The Office finds that the provisions of the laws of Latvia that only citizens may work in the following professions and trades: fire fighter, private detective, employee of armed security (organisations), ... crew member of airlines, holder of licence of a pharmacy and veterinary pharmacy, advocate, assistant advocate, employees of elected bodies of religious organisations, do not correspond to Latvia's international commitments in human rights and are unjustified' (LNHRO 1996: 2).

Foreigners in Western Europe

Socio-economic disparities as well as disparities regarding personal safety and individual freedom and greater ease of travel are important pull and push factors in migration to Western Europe. This issue has been widely debated in Western European countries, since the living conditions in Eastern Europe and in many third world countries have deteriorated due to war, economic and ecological disasters at the same time as even rich countries in Western Europe face economic difficulties and high unemployment.

Citizens of a foreign state are far from being treated equally. Whereas the situation of people who are citizens of an EU member state tends to improve with further steps towards EU integration, this is not so for non-EU citizens. Working migrants and, to an even greater extent, refugees and asylum seekers are the losers in European integration. International standards, on which Western countries mostly agree, often are circumvented, ignored or undermined. For example, Denmark has refrained from ratifying international conventions protecting migrant workers, whereas the German government has taken advantage of provisions to restrict them by amending laws and through bilateral contracts. Thousands of Turks, though economically well integrated in the country to which they have immigrated as workers or entrepreneurs, who pay taxes, contribute to the GNP and the social security system, lack a political voice. Germany, with some seven million foreigners among its 81 million residents, still shies away from accepting that it is a country of immigration.

Many countries have argued that the investigation of asylum applications and financial help to newcomers and refugees consume too many of their financial resources. The German Länder have stated that they will no longer tolerate the social and economic burdens of supporting the 350,000 Bosnians currently residing in Germany. Recently, the social-democratic government in Lower Saxony even broke the law by demanding that the district administrations cut the financial support for war refugees by 20 per cent, calculating that it is cheaper to pay only the few refugees who actually go to court than covering all of them.

The situation of Serbian deserters and refugees from Bosnia or other parts of former Yugoslavia provides a good example of how aliens are made into bargaining chips in international negotiations. Bosnian refugees who were granted 'temporary protection' are increasingly losing out as Western European states attempt to make the public believe that the Dayton Agreement lives up to its promises of safe return. In early December 1996, a repatriation agreement signed by the Bosnian and German governments removed the legal obstacles to forcible expulsion, and thousands of Bosnians were immediately ordered to leave the country. Despite information on the irresponsibility of this action, Germany began to deport them in March 1997.

The issue of asylum seekers in the context of negotiations on EU enlargement and visa-free travel provides another example of double standards, which also discredits the efforts of international human rights organisations. When the Baltic states were urged to provide refugees with a formal, minimum protection of human rights according to the 1951 Convention on Refugees, the primary purpose was not a concern for human rights. Rather, the Baltic states – aspiring as they are to EU membership and visa-free travel – have been told that their border control is not tight enough to prevent them from creating refugee problems for EU countries. Negotiations on the protection of refugees are primarily intended to prevent the 'plague' from spreading to the Nordic countries. The position of asylum seekers would have been better if the Baltic states had continued to object to an asylum system which will remain inferior to that of the Nordic countries and turn the Baltic states into a buffer zone between their Nordic neighbours and countries with a high rate of emigration.

It therefore seems that the positive assessment of the situation of minorities in the Baltic Sea region does not hold for non-citizens. Whereas their integration in Estonia and Latvia may at least have reached a good starting point, the prospects of majority-minority relations regarding non-EU working migrants, refugees and asylum seekers have been deteriorating. To a large degree, foreigners depend on international organisations to remind the states of their obligations to uphold human rights and act as mediators and protectors of the disenfranchised, but the international organisations have remained weak when confronted with the European Union and its desire to create a Fortress Europe. On this issue, however, some disagreement has arisen among EU members. For instance, the German initiative to restrict the criteria for recognising refugees is opposed by Denmark and Sweden, who reserve their right to grant refugee status to people who have been refused by other EU members.

Prospects and Present Challenges

In practical terms, the integration of non-citizens in the Baltic states is usually regarded as more urgent than a better treatment of aliens in Western European Baltic Sea countries. And if one looks at national security and internal stability, the most burning issue is undoubtedly the status of non-citizens in Latvia and Estonia. However, if the aim is to provide minimum standards of humanity, priority should be given to the status of refugees and asylum seekers in the region's

Western parts. Thus, a decision on priorities depends very much on one's perspective. More important is that minority-related disputes in and among different countries are interdependent and will be even more so in future.

The interrelation between the discriminatory treatment of non-citizens in Estonia and Latvia and foreigners in Western Europe illustrates the point. The existing and forthcoming bilateral agreements between the Nordic and the Baltic states on visa-free travel contribute to the discrimination of non-citizens, who must still procure visas. The interest of the European Union is as follows: It neither wants its own restrictive minority policy to become affected by arguments as to who may be regarded as belonging to a minority, nor is it prepared to support visa-free travel for people suspected of having too many ties to Russia. Instead of bringing its full political weight to bear in order to end the conflicts over citizenship, the EU has been hesitant to deal with the issue of non-citizens, which has largely been handed over to the OSCE.

When it comes to language disputes, international organisations usually focus on support for the lesser-used languages. In contrast to this practice, but according to Estonian and Latvian wishes expressed at the Baltic Round Table that was established as part of the Stability Pact, the EU and its members provide the countries concerned with financial aid to support the teaching of the national language. In so doing, they support the Estonian and Latvian decisions to transform their bilingual countries with Russian as the lingua franca into monolingual ones with Estonian or Latvian as the only national language. It is rather questionable whether this assimilation strategy will serve the EU's interest in achieving internal stability in the Baltic states.

Both Estonia and Latvia have been making use of the maltreatment of immigrants in EU countries in justifying their own discriminatory treatment of non-citizens. Nevertheless, non-citizens in Estonia and Latvia are better treated than immigrants in many EU countries like Germany, where foreigners do not have the right to become naturalised even if they fulfil the official criteria. Even investigations by the Council of Europe have confirmed the Latvian and Estonian claims. Instead of competing over who behaves worse than oneself, however, it would be better to focus on the common ground of current minority disputes, shared by all Baltic Sea countries.

- There is a shared illusion of a future of homogeneous societies as a model for achieving social cohesion. However, ethnically, culturally, linguistically and in terms of religion, the region and the states belonging to it tend to become increasingly diverse, and a multitude of minorities will form a considerable part of the total population, as is already the case in the eastern Baltic Sea region. Thus, there is a need of policies aimed at preventing the potential for societal division from escalating into open hostility by motivating the various groups to strive for social and political integration.
- The dominant understanding of political participation ignores that in modern democracies, enfranchisement is not a gift to the people by a generous sovereign

but a mechanism that allows each person and each social group to feel responsible for the development of every other group and for the place where everybody lives and works. Participation works as a mechanism for integration in a situation where the homogeneity of a population is diminishing. Very few efforts have been made to provide persons carrying a passport of a foreign country or a non-citizen passport with a meaningful role in the decision-making process. Only Estonia and the Nordic countries grant local voting rights to all foreign residents regardless of nationality if they fulfil the condition of a minimum period to stay.

- The states bordering the Baltic Sea are unified in their tendency to protect minority rights only in so far as they deem them to be in accordance with the national interest. Subordination of human rights has remained the general approach. They are not appreciated as a value in themselves, and they do not function as the leading principles for politicians.
- As OSCE members, all Baltic Sea states have affirmed that minorities are a source of enrichment for European societies, but nowhere is this insight taken seriously. People have been left unaware of how minorities actually contribute to a better quality of life as well as to economic welfare and political understanding transnationally and domestically, or how they could do so if they were allowed to. It is rather illogical to say that initially the OSCE only referred to 'national minorities,' i.e. citizens of the respective country, because a person's contribution to a country's enrichment does not depend on his passport.

Despite this common ground, asymmetries exist. Whereas EU and NATO candidates experience some pressure to ensure certain standards, Western countries can more easily escape 'inconvenient' demands by minorities, they can more easily dodge international standards and steal away from coping with the effects of transnational migration. The institution that seems to have best understood the negative impact of these asymmetries appears to be that of the office of the Commissioner of the CBSS. The credit for having raised crucial questions among CBSS members is entirely his, and he may exert a beneficial influence in motivating the governments to widen the spectrum of questions on the official agenda.

The first reason refers to the construction of the Commissioner's mandate. Like the OSCE HCNM, the CBSS Commissioner is an institution that obtains its results with the help of recommendations and persuasion and not through binding decisions. However, this institution is by no means a duplication of the OSCE HCNM or any other institution. As opposed to other monitoring organs, the Commissioner's mandate is not limited to human rights obligations already agreed upon by the member states. He may strive to obtain a higher level of protection of human rights than the one embodied in legally binding conventions or OSCE documents. He is allowed to act against the blindness towards problems that members of minorities have to face daily. He may deal with the rights of individuals belonging to any minority, whereas the OSCE HCNM deals only with minorities as groups and only in so far as tensions have been identified as affecting peace, stability or relations between OSCE states. Thus, the Commissioner may continue his work when the mandates of other monitoring organs end.

With respect to activities, one finds, secondly, that the office of the CBSS Commissioner operates in accordance with a more Nordic style, which means that it is more sensitive to the issue of gender and more open to the public. The Commissioner's journal 'Mare Balticum' is a milestone in providing the public with information on the concerns of an international office. After a very short period of existence, the office can already point to a few positive developments, although one would hesitate to call them real progress regarding human rights. For instance, the Commissioner has reminded member states that even if they face financial difficulties, they remain obliged to uphold human rights and are not allowed to treat asylum seekers like criminals and to arrest and imprison them. As a result, the new Swedish Migration Bill transfers the responsibility for persons detained under the Aliens Act from the police to the civilian Swedish Immigration Board. As a result, asylum seekers will not be detained together with suspects or convicts. The availability of information on rules and procedures regarding naturalisation will be improved by Denmark following recommendations which the Commissioner made in a study on citizenship laws and in his Annual Report for 1995-96. Norway has already published information on criteria and procedures for obtaining Norwegian naturalisation in Norwegian, English, French, Polish, Turkish, Urdu and Vietnamese.

The Office has prepared a series of surveys dealing with the implementation of the UN Convention on the Rights of the Child, the Rights of Aliens and Non-citizens, the Right of Access to Information, and local self-government. Among the recommendations one finds a statement by the Commissioner that persons residing legally in a country should become 'integrated in the society in as many ways as possible, i.a. by having the opportunity to participate in political life.' Doubting whether any CBSS member state is currently ready for a reform which grants foreigners voting rights in parliamentary elections, he recommends 'that all members of the CBSS undertake to grant non-citizens the right to vote and to stand for public office in local authority elections, providing that the non-citizens fulfil the same legal requirements as apply to citizens and furthermore have been lawful and habitual residents in the state concerned for a period not exceeding 2-3 years prior to the election.' The Commissioner further recommends that the 1992 European Convention on the Participation of Foreigners in Public Life at Local Level, which comes into force after ratification by four Council of Europe member states, be ratified by all CBSS members (Commissioner 1996: 8 f.).

One should, however, keep in mind that compared to duties and expectations, the Commissioner's office is small. Due to his attempt to include in his considerations the so-called 'new' minorities, the Commissioner of the CBSS may face reservations by Germany as well as by the European Commission, which is a member of the CBSS and has equal status.

The final conclusion refers to the CSCE Charter For A New Europe, adopted in Paris in 1990. Since then the OSCE has advocated the view that human rights including the rights of minorities are basic elements of peace and security. Although the Baltic Sea region has adopted some advanced policies toward its minorities in so far as they are citizens of the country in which they live, this should not become a pretext for taking no further action. Minority-related tensions or even hostility among neighbouring countries, violations of agreed international standards, inequity towards people with different types of passport, and ignoring the needs of weak social groups remain severe problems in the region.

The vision of the Baltic Sea region as a zone of peace expressed by the OSCE may be undermined because of an inability to cope with the challenges identified by Dieter Senghaas: 'Peace in socially mobile, politizable and politizised modern societies is achieved by the interaction of the following factors: power monopoly and the control of the same by way of rule of law; by affect control resulting out of interdependencies; by democratic participation and endeavours for social justice and fairness as well as by a congenial culture of conflict based on these constituents' (Senghaas 1995: 3).

At present, non-violence as the sole legitimate way of addressing problems is not questioned in the region. Other essential factors, however, have come under pressure: the rule of law shows signs of eroding regarding migrants, asylum seekers and refugees. Social justice and equity for weak social groups has declined. The erosion of the welfare state, which has constituted the basic mechanism for social integration, may well jeopardise the integration of minorities. Social stress and hostility against aliens are threatening the region's 'culture of peace.' Political participation, once celebrated as essential for the New Europe, is actually declining if one keeps in mind the rising numbers of disenfranchised people. In Estonia and Latvia they constitute about 30 per cent of the population, and in Germany they already make up close to 10 per cent. There is no alternative to their integration.

Notes

1 Even international law has not agreed on a general definition of the term 'minority.' From a social science perspective, the term refers to people who define themselves as belonging to a minority in the sense of a non-dominant permanent group which identifies itself and can be identified by its distinction from others by certain characteristics, such as culture, religion, language or ethnic origin. A group is labelled a minority because of its structural position within the system of power, not because of numerical strength. This definition is in line with OSCE standards.

2 A few exceptions are reported from Germany, where the use of direct violence against asylum seekers has given rise to accusations by several NGOs such as Amnesty International, International Alert and Human Rights Watch/Helsinki since 1995. Physical attacks against foreigners in Germany are mostly of a private character, but they often receive indirect approval from a broaden spectrum of people. Direct violence against children and women at the so-called private level also remains an issue in many countries of the region.

3 The Swedish government recently has set up a Delegation on Indigenous People to promote the goals of the United Nations Decade of the World's Indigenous People. The delegation may function as a catalyst in closely following the work of drafting a Nordic convention on the Sami people.

References

Birckenbach, Hanne-Margret (1997). 'Preventive Diplomacy through Fact-Finding: How International Organisations Review the Conflict over Citizenship in Estonia and Latvia,' *Kiel Peace Research Series*:6. Münster/Hamburg/London, LIT Verlag.

Commissioner of the CBSS (1995). *First Report.* October 1994-May 1995.

Commissioner of the CBSS (1996). 'Right of Non-citizens, Residing Legally in the Member States of the CBSS,' *Survey Part 1: Voting Rights and the Right to Stand for Public Office.* February.

Hannikainen, Lauri (1996). 'Legal Status of Minorities, Indigenous Peoples and Immigrants and Refugee Groups in the Nordic Countries,' *Minorities and Conflicts*, pages 57-74. Mariehamn.

Human Rights Watch/Helsinki (1995). *Germany for Germans: Xenophobia and Racist Violence in Germany.* New York.

International Alert (1993). 'Racism and Xenophobia in Europe – Ways forward.' Report of a Consultative Meeting, 15.3.1993.

LNHRO, Latvian National Human Rights Office (1997). 'Activity Report for the Second Half of 1996 (1 July-20 December).'

Mackow, Jerzy (1995). 'Die Normalisierung der neuen alten Nachbarschaft. Zum aktuellen Stand der deutsch-polnischen Beziehungen,' *Aus Politik und Zeitgeschichte*:39, 22 September, 1995, pages 32-39.

Morokvasic, Mirjana and Rudolph, Hedwig (1995). 'Grenzen staatlicher Wanderungskontrollen im "neuen Europa,"' pages 113-131 in Rudolph, Hedwig (ed.). Geplanter Wandel, ungeplante Wirkungen. Berlin 1995.

Muiznieks, Nils (1997). 'Making Citizenship Work,' The Baltic Times:2(50), 13-19 March, page 23.

ODIHR (1996). 'Situation of Roma and Sinti in the OSCE Region.' Background material for the Review Conference, 1 October, 1996. (REF.RM/35/96/Add.1, 22 October 1996).

Regional Conference to address the problems of refugees, displaced persons, other form of involuntary displacement and returnees in the countries of the Commonwealth of Independent States and relevant neighbouring States. Geneva, 30-31 May, 1996. Programme of Action, CISCONF/1996/5, 11 June 1996.

UNICEF (1994). *Women and Gender in Countries in Transition: A UNICEF Perspective.* Regional Office for Central & Eastern Europe, Commonwealth of Independent States & Baltic States. October 1994.

Senghaas, Dieter (1995). 'The Culture of Peace.' Manuscript based on the author's translation of his publication 'Die Kultur des Friedens,' *Aus Politik und Zeitgeschichte*:43, 10 October,1995, pages 3-8.

North European and Baltic Statistics: Current Status and Development during the 1990s

Compiled by Jüri Köll,
Statistics Sweden, International Consulting Office

Introduction

Definition of the North European and Baltic Sea Area
The North European and Baltic Sea area, as used in this Yearbook, consists of the countries/regions around the Baltic Sea and the White Sea. Included are Denmark, Estonia, Finland with Åland, in Germany the three länder of Schleswig-Holstein, Hamburg and Mecklenburg-Vorpommern, Latvia, Lithuania, Norway, in Poland the ten voivodships (provinces) on the western and northern borders, in Russia the three regions at the Baltic Sea: Kaliningrad oblast, Leningrad oblast and St Petersburg city, and the three regions at the White Sea: Arkhangelsk oblast, Republic of Karelia and Murmansk oblast, and Sweden (see Figure).

The Size of the Area and Its Population
The total population of Europe is estimated at 726 million in 1994 according to UN World Population 1994. According to official statistics and special questionnaires filled in by the countries/regions for the purpose of this statistical survey, the population of the North European and Baltic Sea area was in 1994 55 million or 7.6 per cent of the total European population.

Of the 55 million inhabitants of the region in 1994, 23 million were living in the Nordic countries, 8 million in the Baltic countries, 11 million in the Russian regions, 6 million in the three German länder and 7 million in the 10 Polish voivoships (provinces).

In area Europe is the second smallest continent on the Earth and covers about 7 per cent of its land surface. Altogether the countries of Europe cover 11 million square kilometres. The area of the North European and Baltic Sea region is 2.46 million square kilometres or somewhat more than 22 per cent of the area of Europe.

The Nordic countries cover 1.22 million square kilometres, the Baltic countries 0.18 million, the Russian regions 0.94 million, the three German länder at the Baltic Sea 0.04 million and the ten voivodships in Poland 0.08 million square kilometres.

The population density in the North European and Baltic Sea region is 22.5 persons per square kilometre, for Europe as a whole the density is 32 persons per square kilometre.

The density in the Nordic countries is on average 19.2, in the Baltic states 44.8, in the included Russian regions 11.5, in the 10 included Polish voivodships 81.4 and in the three German länder 156.2 persons per square kilometre.

Figure: The North European and Baltic Sea area

The Choice of Information for the First NEBI Yearbook

The North European and Baltic Sea region consists of countries and regions with a very different historical background and thus also with very different demographic and economic characteristics. There area contains both countries and regions with market economies and others that are undergoing economic transformation. In addition, the transition countries/regions are at different phases of the transition process.

The NEBI area covers the Nordic countries with long democratic traditions and with governmental and economic structures developed over a considerable length of time, but it also contains the Baltic states, whose independence was restored only in 1990-91 and who are still in a process of rapid transition towards adequate open market and democratic structures. The German länder of Schleswig-Holstein and Hamburg are well developed and part of the European Communities from the beginning, whereas Mecklenburg-Vorpommern is a recent entrant still struggling with its GDR heritage. Poland, with its 10 voivodships included in this statistical survey, was among the first ex-command economy countries to embark on thorough transformation, whereas the included Russian regions started later and still have many of the old structures in place.

This heterogeneity makes it difficult to obtain comparable statistics over all countries/regions. The differences in economic structure, relative prices, the quality of goods and services and the standard of living make an over-all economic comparison very difficult not to say impossible at this stage.

The aim of this statistical section has therefore been to get some basic statistics from all the countries and regions included in the NEBI area, i.e. aggregated statistics about population, migration, economic structure, some indicators of consumption, foreign trade, and other foreign transactions and prices.

The focus is on comparison of the countries/regions to discover differences and similarities in levels, structures and rates of change during the first half of the 1990s and in particular whether the countries/regions have converged or moved further apart.

Population Change, Migration and Life Expectancy

In the Nordic countries, the western German länder, Poland and Kaliningrad there has been a population increase during the period 1991-95. The Leningrad region reports almost no population change. The other Russian regions, Mecklenburg-Vorpommern and the Baltic states report population decrease. In the Murmansk region, in Latvia and in Estonia the decline has been dramatic. In Murmansk the population fell 8.5 per cent between 1991 and 1995, in Latvia 6.0 per cent and in Estonia 5.1 per cent. All three areas experienced a huge net emigration over the period. In Murmansk the net emigration was 7.5 per cent of 1991 population, in Estonia 4.6 per cent and in Latvia 4.3 per cent. The three areas' emigration was particularly booming in the 1992 and 1993 but was also substantial in 1994 and 1995 (see Table 1).

The mean life expectancy at birth differs a lot between the constituent units of the North European and Baltic Sea region as do the changes during the 1990s and the differences between men and women.

While in 1995 mean life expectancy at birth varies between 72 and 76 years for men and 79 to 81 years for women in the Nordic countries and western German länder, the corresponding figures vary from 55 to 60 years for men and between 69 and 71 years for women in the included Russian regions. This is 16-17 years shorter for men and 10 years shorter for women than in the Western regions. Average life expectancy in the Baltic states is somewhat higher than in the Russian regions, 62 to 64 years for men and 73 to 75 years for women, but still 10 to 12 years shorter for men and 6 years shorter for women than in the West.

The differences between the NEBI area's Western parts, on the one hand, and the Russian regions and Baltic states, on the other, have widened considerably during the 1990s. In the Russian regions, average life expectancy decreased by 4.5 to 7.6 years for men and by 1.8 to 4.6 years for women, in the Baltic states by 1.7 to 3.1 years for men and by 0.5 to 1.7 years for women. Both in the Russian regions

Table 1: Net migration and total population change 1991-95, in percentage of 1991 population*

Net migration 1991-95		Total change 1991-95	
1. Leningrad	+4.9	1. Kaliningrad	+7.8
2. Hamburg	+4.6	2. Schleswig-Holstein	+3.4
3. Kaliningrad	+4.5	3. Hamburg	+2.4
4. Schleswig-Holstein	+4.4	(Åland	+2.4)
5. Sweden	+1.6	4. Sweden	+2.3
6. Denmark	+1.4	5. Norway	+2.3
7. Norway	+1.1	6. Denmark	+1.9
8. Karelia	+1.0	7. Finland	+1.8
9. Finland	+0.7	8. Poland, 10 regions	+1.6
(Åland	+0.7)	(Poland	+0.8)
10. Poland, 10 regions	-0.2	9. Leningrad	+0.1
(Poland	-0.2)	10. Lithuania	-1.1
11. St Petersburg	-0.7	11. Karelia	-1.9
12. Lithuania	-1.3	12. Arkhangelsk	-3.1
13. Arkhangelsk	-1.9	13. Mecklenburg-Vorpommern	-3.7
14. Mecklenburg-Vorpommern	-1.9	14. St Petersburg	-4.0
15. Latvia	-4.3	15. Estonia	-5.1
16. Estonia	-4.6	16. Latvia	-6.0
17. Murmansk	-7.5	17. Murmansk	-8.5

Note: The figures for Norway, Denmark and Schleswig-Holstein have been calculated on incomplete sets of data.

* General note: Throughout this statistical section, the following symbols are used:

*	Data not available
-	Magnitude zero
0 or 0.0	Magnitude less than half of unit employed

and in the Baltic states, the discrepancies in the longevity of men and women have increased dramatically. Poland is somewhere in between with increasing life expectancy for both women and men and with smaller differences between the two sexes

In both the Russian regions (with one exception) and the Baltic states, the average life expectancy has increased from 1994 to 1995 (see Table 2).

The Share of Food in Private Consumption

The proportion of the available resources for private consumption that is used for food tells something about the economic standard of the country or region. But the share is also affected by the relative prices. The main factor affecting the comparison in the North European and Baltic Sea region is the differences in the costs of living accommodation. In the Soviet era rents for flats were symbolic and bore no resemblance to the real costs of housing. That still affects the situation in the Eastern countries and regions because it has been impossible to drastically increase rents. It takes time to install an awareness of how high the costs of main-

Table 2: Average life expectancy at birth

Country/region	Average life expectancy in 1995 and change 91 to 95				Difference between men and women in years 1995
	men		women		
Schleswig-Holstein	73	*	79	*	6
Hamburg	72	*	79	*	7
Denmark	73	+0.5	79	+1.1	6
Finland	73	+1.5	80	+0.9	7
Norway	75	+0.9	81	+0.5	6
Sweden	76	+0.7	81	+0.9	5
Åland	73	+1.9	81	-0.6	6
Poland, 10 voivodships	67	+1.6	76	+1.5	9
Gdanskie	69	+2.6	76	+1.5	7
Poland	68	+1.7	76	+1.3	8
Estonia	62	– 2.7	74	– 0.5	12
Latvia	61	– 3.1	73	– 1.7	12
Lithuania	64	– 1.7	75	– 0.9	11
Arkhangelsk	57	– 6.7	71	– 3.7	14
Kaliningrad	59	– 4.5	71	– 2.3	12
Karelia	55	– 7.4	69	– 4.6	14
Leningrad	56	– 6.6	70	– 3.7	14
Murmansk	58	– 7.6	70	– 4.6	12
St Petersburg	60	– 4.5	72	– 1.8	12

Note: For Mecklenburg-Vorpommern we lack information. For Schleswig-Holstein and Hamburg we only have figures for 1986/88. The change in Finland is for 1990-95 and in Norway for 1991-94.

tenance and periodic restructuring really are. The low share of spending on food in Western countries and regions is partly a result of the high prices of living-space and also of the way in which taxation affects rents.

According to household budget surveys, food accounted for between 45 and 54 per cent of the Russian regions' total private consumption in 1995. The proportion had increased by 11 to 21 percentage units since 1991.

In Latvia and Lithuania, the proportion was 41 and 45 per cent, respectively, and had increased by 3 and 15 percentage points, respectively.

In Estonia and Poland (as a whole, figures at voivodship level are not available), the proportion was 31 and 29 per cent and had decreased by 6 and 3 percentage points from 1991.

In Mecklenburg-Vorpommern, the proportion was 24 per cent in 1994.

In the Western countries/regions, the share stood at 22 per cent as a maximum (see Table 3).

Share of Work-Force Engaged in Goods-Producing Activities

The distribution of employment by activity is available for all included countries/regions. For broad activity areas, the comparisons over countries are usually only marginally affected by the existing differences in classification standards and units used.

Table 3: Cost for food as a percentage of total private consumption

Country/region	% food in private consumption in year		Change in %-units from year
Arkhangelsk	45%	1995	+16%-units from 1991
Kaliningrad	54%	1995	+21%-units from 1991
Leningrad	54%	1995	+15%-units from 1991
Murmansk	49%	1995	+16%-units from 1991
St Petersburg	54%	1995	+11%-units from 1991
Lithuania	45%	1995	+15%-units from 1991
Latvia	41%	1995	+ 3%-units from 1991
Estonia	31%	1995	- 6%-units from 1991
Poland	29%	1995	- 3%-units from 1991
Mecklenburg-Vorpommern	24%	1994	*
Schleswig-Holstein	22%	1994	*
Hamburg	14%	1995	- 1%-unit from 1992
Denmark	20%	1995	- 1%-unit from 1992
Finland	20%	1995	- 1%-unit from 1992
Norway	18%	1995	*
Sweden	19%	1995	- 1%-unit from 1991
Åland	24%	1995	+ 3%-units from 1991

Note: Data from Karelia are missing. Data for the Nordic countries are from National Accounts or CPI-weights, for other countries/regions mainly from household budget surveys.

The split of the economy into a goods-producing and a services-producing sector gives a rough picture of the structure of production (see Table 4).

The Importance of Foreign Trade inside the NEBI Region

The foreign trade to and from all other countries wholly or in part included in the North European and Baltic Sea region can be calculated from the collected figures about foreign trade to and from the included countries and regions. No foreign trade statistics are compiled for the Polish voivodships, and we are therefore forced to use the foreign trade figures for Poland as a whole. In the case of Åland, only aggregated foreign trade statistics are available. Of all exports, the median percentage going to other countries in the area is 42 per cent, and the median imports from other countries in the area are 45 per cent of all imports. For the Nordic countries, the median values are for exports 38 per cent and for imports 43 per cent, for the Baltic states, 60 per cent for exports and 69 per cent for imports, for the German länder 18 per cent for exports and 38 per cent for imports, for the Russian regions, the figures are 43 per cent (exports) and 49 per cent (imports) and for Poland as a whole 49 per cent (exports) and 42 per cent (imports).

The available figures are given in Tables 5 and 6.

Table 4: Employed persons in goods-producing activities

Country/region	% work-force in goods production in 1995	Change in %-units 1992-95
1. Estonia	44	- 11
2. Latvia	44	- 8
3. Kaliningrad	43	- 8
4. Arkhangelsk	43	- 7
5. Karelia	42	- 7
6. St Petersburg	37	- 7
7. Lithuania	52	- 6
8. Murmansk	42	- 5
9. Leningrad	56	- 5
10. Hamburg	22	- 2
(Gdanskie	45	- 2)
(Poland	57	- 2)
(Åland	26	- 1)
11. Sweden	29	- 1
12. Poland, 10 voivodships	49	- 1
13. Norway	28	0
14. Finland	35	0
15. Mecklenburg-Vorpommern	35	0
16. Schleswig-Holstein	37	0
17. Denmark	29	*

Note: For Denmark, the figure for 1994 is used. The changes for Finland, Norway, Gdanskie and the 10 voivodships in Poland are for 1993-95.

Table 5: Exports to other countries wholly or partially included in the North European and Baltic Sea Area, in percentage of total exports

Country/region	1992	1993	1994	1995
Arkhangelsk	43.1	56.7	41.0	21.5
Kaliningrad	*	42.4	44.2	21.1
Karelia	*	*	47.8	35.6
Leningrad	*	38.3	87.7	81.1
Murmansk	*	*	40.3	44.9
St Petersburg	*	59.2	45.1	28.4
Estonia	70.2	77.2	77.9	75.5
Latvia	*	55.1	59.8	66.2
Lithuania	*	61.1	62.0	54.9
Poland	45.5	48.4	50.4	52.7
Mecklenburg-Vorpommern	31.0	42.0	20.7	24.2
Schleswig-Holstein	18.3	17.5	18.3	*
Hamburg	15.4	12.6	12.9	10.8
Denmark	43.9	45.0	44.6	45.1
Finland	40.8	38.3	40.8	39.1
Norway	31.8	29.9	29.8	31.9
Sweden	37.3	35.5	35.4	34.3

Table 6: Imports from other countries wholly or partially included in the North European and Baltic Sea Area, in percentage of total imports

Country/region	1992	1993	1994	1995
Arkhangelsk	29.2	31.6	39.2	*
Kaliningrad	*	84.8	70.6	44.1
Karelia	*	*	38.5	48.4
Leningrad	*	58.2	51.6	*
Murmansk	*	*	46.1	*
St Petersburg	*	56.9	47.0	*
Estonia	72.9	73.9	73.5	74.6
Latvia	*	64.4	65.8	71.7
Lithuania	*	72.6	70.0	65.1
Poland	41.6	44.0	41.4	42.2
Mecklenburg-Vorpommern	44.3	53.4	55.3	49.7
Schleswig-Holstein	42.2	35.9	35.1	*
Hamburg	10.5	10.2	10.2	10.5
Denmark	44.4	45.1	44.4	46.0
Finland	45.0	44.3	44.2	44.3
Norway	42.8	40.4	43.0	43.3
Sweden	41.6	40.0	40.8	42.8

Things to Keep in Mind When Comparing Dissimilar Countries

Any kind of comparison over countries creates problems. There may be different standards of how statistics are compiled, and different statistical units may be used depending on differences in the laws or in the practices of countries. The structure of society may differ. Cultural differences may cause problems because the same question put in different countries may be understood differently.

In this chapter statistics from Western market economies are compared with statistics from transition countries at different stages in the transformation process. Such comparisons may cause even bigger problems because of the special difficulties in compiling statistics during transition. The problems are mainly due to the rapidity of changes such as:

- the increasing proportion of market economy;
- the change to world market prices;
- the restructuring of the government sector or, as in the Baltic states, the build-up of a new government sector;
- the huge turnover of enterprises (starting and closing of enterprises) in the new unstable markets; and
- a great number of changes in laws, taxes, fees etc., affecting both the markets and the consumption trends.

The figures for the Baltic states are also affected by the currency reforms carried through in Estonia in June 1992, in Latvia in March 1993 and in Lithuania in June 1993 and by the extremely high export and import figures, which have reached upwards of 80-90 per cent of GDP in some years. It is very likely that considerable parts of the imports are re-exported unchanged. All differences in prices in and out affect the national accounts of these countries.

How fast the change to word market prices is carried through in the individual transition countries differs a lot. The increase in food prices, in energy prices and in the rents for flats exerts a heavy influence on living standards. How fast the prices are allowed to increase thus affect consumption, production and the restructuring of the economy and therefore the economic statistics of the country.

Country/Region Tables

Contents

The Baltic States
Estonia 563
Latvia 567
Lithuania 571

German Länder
Hamburg 574
Mecklenburg-Vorpommern 577
Schleswig-Holstein 580

The Nordic Countries
Denmark 583
Finland 586
Åland 589
Norway 592
Sweden 595

Poland
Poland 598
The 10 Voivodships 602
Gdanskie 604

Russian Regions
Arkhangelsk 606
Kaliningrad 608
Republic of Karelia 611
Leningrad region 613
Murmansk 615
St Petersburg 617

Country/Region: Estonia

Basic data

Total land and water area: 45200 square km, of which agricultural land: 32%, forest and woodland: 45%

Total population 1995: 1.48 million, of which 47% male, 53% female.

By age groups	0 - 19	27.4%	20 - 64	59.2%	65 -	13.4%

The total population decreased from 1.56 million in 1991 to 1.48 million in 1995

1000 of persons	1991	1992	1993	1994	1995
Total immigration	5.2	3.5	2.4	1.6	1.6
Total emigration	13.2	37.4	16.2	9.2	9.8
Net migration	- 8.0	- 33.9	-13.8	-7.6	- 8.2
Natural decrease	- 0.4	- 2.1	- 6.1	- 8.0	- 7.3

Average life expectancy at birth	1991	1992	1993	1994	1995
in years for men	64.4	64.5	62.5	61.1	61.7
for women	74.8	74.7	73.8	73.1	74.3

Food consumption as	1991	1992	1993	1994	1995
% of total private consumption [1)]	36.4	35.1	32.3	30.4	30.7
Cars per 100 persons [2)]	29	31	33	27	31

The number of dwellings in 1992 was 637 thousand, of which 62% was owned by state and local authorities. Of the 620 thousand dwellings in 1995 39% was owned by state and local authorities.

National Accounts

GDP in 1993 years prices in billion EEK and change in %:

1992	93/92	1993	94/93	1994	95/94	1995
24.1	-8.5%	22.1	-1.8%	21.7	+4.3%	22.6

GDP by field of activity, total in current prices

in billion EEK [3)]	1992	1993	1994	1995
Total at market prices	13.2	22.1	30.3	41.3
Agriculture, hunting, forestry and fishing	12.5%	9.9%	9.0%	7.1%
Mining, quarrying and manufacturing	23.4%	18.8%	18.2%	16.7%
Electricity, gas, water supply	4.1%	3.2%	2.9%	3.5%
Construction	4.6%	5.9%	5.6%	5.1%
Wholesale and retail trade	13.5%	15.2%	13.5%	14.5%
Transport, storage and communication	13.0%	11.1%	10.1%	9.1%
Public administration, education, health and social work	7.3%	10.5%	12.0%	12.9%
Other services	14.5%	15.2%	16.2%	19.0%
Total at basic prices	92.9%	89.8%	87.5%	87.9%
Taxes on products	8.8%	11.2%	13.4%	12.9%
Subsidies	1.7%	1.0%	0.9%	0.8%

GDP by expenditure, total in current prices

in billion EEK	1992	1993	1994	1995
Total at market price	13.2	22.1	30.3	41.3
Private consumption	54.4%	57.0%	58.9%	57.6%
Government consumption	15.8%	20.3%	22.4%	23.8%
Consumption of non-profit institutions	0.7%	0.5%	0.5%	0.5%
Gross fixed capital formation	20.9%	23.9%	26.4%	25.6%
Changes in stocks	5.8%	2.5%	2.5%	0.7%
Exports (FOB)	60.0%	68.9%	78.6%	75.8%
Imports (FOB) (-)	54.1%	73.1%	89.3%	84.0%
Statistical discrepancy	- 3.6%			

GDP by income, total in current prices

in billion EEK	1992	1993	1994	1995
Total at market price	13.2	22.1	30.3	41.3
Compensation of employees	47.5%	51.6%	56.1%	56.0%
therein wages and salaries	36.4%	39.1%	42.3%	42.4%
Consumption of fixed capital	4.9%	12.2%	11.0%	10.9%
Indirect taxes	12.2%	13.7%	15.1%	15.1%
Subsidies (-)	1.7%	1.0%	0.9%	0.8%
Operating surplus and mixed income	37.1%	23.5%	18.7%	18.8%

Changes in prices	1992	1993	1994	1995
Previous year = 100				
Consumer price index	1172	190	148	129
Producer price index for manufactured products	..	175	136	126

Foreign trade statistics

Total exports [4]	1991	1992	1993	1994	1995
Million EEK	510	5549	10636	16924	21040
of which to Russia	56.5%	20.8%	22.6%	23.1%	17.6%
to Finland	2.3%	21.1%	20.7%	17.9%	21.5%
to Sweden	0.5%	7.7%	9.5%	10.9%	10.8%
to Norway	0.0%	0.3%	0.6%	1.5%	1.8%
to Denmark	0.1%	2.4%	2.4%	3.4%	3.2%
to Germany	0.2%	3.9%	8.0%	6.8%	7.2%
to Poland	0.1%	1.9%	1.1%	0.7%	1.2%
to Lithuania	3.8%	1.5%	3.7%	5.4%	4.7%
to Latvia	7.6%	10.6%	8.6%	8.2%	7.5%
to EU-countries	0.9%	13.7%	17.8%	19.0%	54.0%
to CIS-countries	94.7%	34.9%	30.4%	30.3%	25.1%

Total imports [4]		1991	1992	1993	1994	1995
Million EEK		445	5128	11831	21509	29101
of which	from Russia	45.9%	28.4%	17.2%	16.8%	16.1%
	from Finland	2.0%	22.6%	27.9%	29.9%	32.6%
	from Sweden	0.8%	5.9%	8.9%	8.9%	8.5%
	from Norway	0.0%	0.4%	0.5%	0.6%	0.8%
	from Denmark	0.1%	1.7%	2.6%	2.6%	2.8%
	from Germany	0.8%	8.3%	10.8%	10.0%	9.6%
	from Poland	0.5%	0.3%	0.4%	0.6%	0.6%
	from Lithuania	6.3%	3.6%	3.3%	2.6%	1.6%
	from Latvia	5.1%	1.7%	2.3%	1.5%	2.0%
from EU-countries		3.0%	15.3%	23.3%	23.9%	66.0%
from CIS-countries		84.8%	40.1%	21.6%	20.5%	18.8%

Employment by activity

in 1000 employees	1992	1993	1994	1995
All activities	602	517	486	493
Agriculture, hunting, forestry, fishing	107	59	45	38
Mining, quarrying, manufacturing	173	141	127	130
Electricity, gas and water supply	15	12	15	16
Construction	38	33	32	34
Trade, hotels, restaurants	58	67	60	66
Transport, storage, communication	57	47	45	46
Private and business services, finance	47	49	48	52
Public administration, education health and social work	107	109	114	133

The number of active enterprises was 30 527 in 1995, 27 387 of which had private domestic owners, 1 981 had foreign owners and 1 159 were owned by state or local government. Almost half of all enterprises, or 14 075 enterprises, were in wholesale and retail trade.

285 enterprises had 200 or more employees, 3 742 from 20 to 199 employees, 8 988 from 5 to 19 employees and 17 512 less than 5 employees.

Foreign direct investment in Estonia

In 1992 the amount of 997 million EEK or 7.6% of the Estonian GDP for 1992 was invested by foreigners in Estonian enterprises. In 1993 the amount was 2 153 million EEK or 9.8% of the GDP for 1993, in 1994 2 819 million EEK or 9.4% of the GDP for 1994 and in 1995 2 313 million EEK or 5.6% of the GDP for 1995. For 1994 and 1995 together Sweden was the biggest investor followed by Finland and Russia.

Borrowing from abroad

In 1993 943 million EEK were borrowed from abroad or
4.3% of the Estonian GDP for 1993, in 1994 393 million EEK or 1.3% of GDP for 1994 and in 1995 612 million EEK or 1.5% of GDP for 1995.

Foreign aid received

In 1992 1 173 million EEK or 8.9% of GDP in 1992, in 1993 1 266 million EEK or 5.5% of

GDP for 1993, in 1994 1 268 million EEK or 4.2% of GDP for 1994 and in 1995 1 032 million EEK or 2.5% of GDP for 1995.

The number of vessels from abroad, arriving in Estonian harbours, increased from 4 455 in 1992 to 8 405 in 1995 and the number of passengers increased from 679 thousand in 1992 to 2 142 thousand in 1995.

Sources

Questionnaires filled in by the Statistical Office of Estonia.

Notes

1) From household budget survey data.
2) Registration of all cars and busses.
3) All bank services are distributed by activity.
4) The foreign trade figures for 1991 have been available and are included.

Country/region: Latvia

Basic data

Total land and water area: 64 600 square km, of which agricultural land: 39%, forest and woodland: 45%

Total population 1995: 2.50 million, of which 46% male, 54% female.

By age groups	0 – 19	27.0%	20 – 64	59.4%	65 –	13.7%

The total population has decreased from 2.66 million in 1991 to 2.50 million in 1995.

1000 of persons	1991	1992	1993	1994	1995
Total immigration	14.7	6.2	4.1	3.0	2.8
Total emigration	25.5	53.1	32.0	21.9	13.3
Net migration	-10.8	-46.9	-27.9	-18.9	-10.5
Natural increase	– 0.1	– 3.9	-12.4	-17.5	-17.3

Average life expectancy at birth	1991	1992	1993	1994	1995
in years for men	63.9	63.3	61.6	60.7	60.8
for women	74.8	74.8	73.8	72.8	73.1

Food consumption as	1991	1992	1993	1994	1995
% of total private consumption [1]	37.8	48.2	44.4	42.5	40.6
Cars per 100 persons [2]	*	*	*	13	17

The number of dwellings in 1992 was 961 thousand, of which 65% was owned by state and local authorities. Of the 952 thousand dwellings in 1995 54% was owned by state and local authorities.

National Accounts

GDP in 1993 prices in million LAT and change in %:

1992	93/92	1993	94/93	1994	95/94	1995
1723	-15%	1467	+0.6%	1476	-1.6%	1453

GDP by field of activities, total in current prices

in million LAT [3]	1992	1993	1994	1995
Total at market prices	1005	1467	2043	2361
Agriculture, hunting, forestry and fishing	16.5%	10.7%	8.4%	8.5%
Mining, quarrying and manufacturing	26.5%	21.1%	17.8%	16.8%
Electricity, gas, water supply	1.4%	6.8%	4.6%	5.1%
Construction	4.7%	3.9%	5.3%	6.7%
Wholesale and retail trade	10.8%	7.7%	8.7%	8.0%
Transport, storage and communication	16.6%	21.0%	18.1%	17.6%
Public administration, education, health and social work	6.2%	9.5%	11.2%	11.7%
Other services	10.8%	10.1%	14.5%	12.3%
Total at basic prices	93.4%	90.8%	88.6%	86.8%
Taxes on products	6.9%	9.2%	11.5%	13.2%
Subsidies	0.4%	0.0%	0.0%	0.0%

GDP by expenditure, total in current prices

in million LAT	1992	1993	1994	1995
Total at market prices	1005	1467	2043	2361
Private consumption	39.3%	52.3%	58.5%	59.2%
Government consumption	12.5%	22.1%	20.1%	20.7%
Consumption of non-profit institutions	0.1%	0.2%	0.2%	0.2%
Gross fixed capital formation	11.2%	13.8%	14.9%	16.6%
Changes in stocks	30.1%	-4.6%	4.3%	5.3%
Exports (FOB)	79.9%	73.2%	46.5%	47.1%
Imports (FOB) (-)	73.1%	57.0%	44.4%	49.1%
Statistical discrepancy	–	-	-	-

GDP by income, total in current prices

in million LAT	1992	1993	1994	1995
Total at market prices	1005	1467	2043	2361
Compensation of employees	37.4%	47.3%	45.9%	*
therein wages and salaries	27.3%	33.7%	32.9%	*
Consumption of fixed capital	1.5%	9.8%	12.5%	*
Indirect taxes	7.2%	11.7%	13.6%	*
Subsidies (-)	0.7%	0.7%	0.5%	*
Operating surplus and mixed income	14.1%	7.9%	8.9%	*

Changes in prices: Previous year = 100	1992	1993	1994	1995
Consumer price index	1051	209	136	125
Producer price index for manufactured products	2654	223	120	114

Foreign trade statistics

Total exports		1992	1993	1994	1995
Million LAT		*	676	553	688
of which	to Russia		29.6%	28.1%	25.3%
	to Finland		2.0%	2.4%	3.2%
	to Sweden		6.5%	6.9%	9.3%
	to Norway		0.3%	0.6%	1.7%
	to Denmark		0.9%	1.6%	2.0%
	to Germany		6.6%	10.5%	13.6%
	to Poland		3.0%	1.6%	2.5%
	to Lithuania		4.3%	5.5%	5.5%
	to Estonia		1.9%	2.6%	3.1%
to EU-countries			33.4%	39.2%	44.0%
to CIS-countries			46.6%	42.7%	38.3%

Total imports		1992	1993	1994	1995
Million LAT		*	639	695	960
of which	from Russia		28.5%	23.6%	21.7%
	from Finland		4.2%	8.5%	10.4%
	from Sweden		5.3%	6.4%	8.0%
	from Norway		0.1%	0.5%	0.8%
	from Denmark		1.8%	2.3%	2.9%
	from Germany		10.0%	13.5%	15.4%
	from Poland		1.0%	1.6%	1.9%
	from Lithuania		9.6%	5.9%	5.5%
	from Estonia		3.9%	3.5%	5.1%
from EU-countries			27.4%	40.6%	49.9%
from CIS-countries			38.2%	30.5%	28.2%

Employment by activity

in 1000 employees	1992	1993	1994	1995
All activities	1345	1245	1205	1189
Agriculture, hunting, forestry, fishing	269	243	232	220
Mining, quarrying, manufacturing	324	271	235	211
Electricity, gas and water supply	16	16	18	17
Construction	89	68	62	71
Trade, hotels, restaurants	187	187	198	191
Transport, storage, communication	105	108	106	105
Private and business services, finance	147	134	138	140
Public administration, education, health and social work	208	218	216	234

The number of active enterprises was 31 363 in 1995, 28 974 of which had private domestic owners, 599 had foreign owners and 1 790 were owned by state or local government. Almost half of all enterprises, or 14 872 enterprises, were in wholesale and retail trade.

387 enterprises had 200 or more employees, 3 480 from 20 to 199 employees, 8 135 from 5 to 19 employees and 19 361 less than 5 employees.

Foreign direct investment in Latvia

In 1992 the amount of 23 million LAT or 2.2% of the Latvian GDP for 1992 was invested by foreigners in Latvian enterprises. In 1993 the amount was 50 million LAT or 3.4% of the GDP for 1993, in 1994 173 million LAT or 8.5% of the GDP for 1994 and in 1995 274 million LAT or 11.6% of the GDP for 1995. For these four years Denmark was the biggest investor followed by USA and Russia.

Borrowing from abroad

In 1992 39 million LAT was borrowed from abroad or 3.9% of the Latvian GDP for 1992, in 1993 the figure was 138 million LAT or 9.4% of the Latvian GDP for 1993, in 1994 189 million LAT or 9.2% of GDP 1994 and in 1995 216 million LAT or 9.2% of GDP 1995.

Foreign aid received

In 1992 67 million LAT or 6.6% of GDP in 1992, in 1993 34 million LAT or 2.3% of GDP 1993, in 1994 62 million LAT or 3.0% of GDP 1994 and in 1995 19 million LAT or 0.8% of GDP 1995.

The number of passengers from abroad, arriving in Latvian harbours, increased from 11 thousand in 1992 to 50 thousand in 1995.

Sources

Questionnaires filled in by the Central Statistical Bureau of Latvia.

Notes

1) From household budget survey data.
2) Registration of all cars and busses.
3) All bank services are distributed on activities.

Country/Region: Lithuania

Basic data

Total land and water area: 65 300 square km, of which agricultural land: 54%, forest and woodland: 30%

Total population 1995: 3.71 million, of which 47% male, 53% female.

By age groups	0 – 19	28.6%	20 – 64	59.3%	65 –	12.1%

The total population has decreased from 3.75 million in 1991 to 3.71 million in 1995.

1000 of persons	1991	1992	1993	1994	1995
Total immigration	11.8	6.6	2.9	1.7	2.0
Total emigration	20.7	28.9	16.0	4.2	3.8
Net migration	-8.9	-22.2	-13.1	-2.6	-1.8
Natural increase	15.2	12.2	0.6	-3.7	-4.1

Average life expectancy at birth		1991	1992	1993	1994	1995
in years	for men	65.3	64.9	63.3	62.8	63.6
	for women	76.1	76.0	75.0	74.9	75.2

Food consumption as	1991	1992	1993	1994	1995
% of total private consumption	30.5	49.9	50.9	46.0	45.1
Cars per 100 persons	22	23	24	25	27

The number of dwellings in 1992 was 1 111 thousand, of which 20% was owned by state and local authorities. Of the 1 247 thousand dwellings in 1995 11% was owned by state and local authorities.

National Accounts

GDP in 1993 prices in million LIT and change in %:

1992	93/92	1993	94/93	1994	95/94	1995
15950	-30%	11108	+1.0%	11217	+3.0%	11551

GDP by field of activity, total in current prices

in million LIT	1992	1993	1994	1995
Total at market prices	3387	11108	16981	23829
Agriculture, hunting, forestry and fishing	11.7%	11.1%	7.4%	9.4%
Mining, quarrying and manufacturing	35.5%	24.8%	23.1%	25.9%
Electricity, gas, water supply	3.9%	5.6%	2.7%	3.0%
Construction	9.3%	7.8%	8.7%	6.7%
Wholesale and retail trade	4.5%	16.1%	23.1%	23.4%
Transport, storage and communication	8.1%	10.6%	9.4%	7.6%
Public administration, education, health and social work	6.4%	7.8%	9.3%	11.0%
Other services	20.6%	16.2%	16.4%	12.7%
Total at basic prices	...	...	...	...
Taxes on products	...	...	...	...
Subsidies	...	...	...	...

GDP by expenditure, total in current prices

in million LIT	1992	1993	1994	1995
Total at market prices	3387	11108	16981	23829
Private consumption	69.4%	69.1%	72.3%	69.4%
Government consumption	12.7%	16.4%	18.2%	19.8%
Consumption of non-profit institutions	-	–	0.1%	0.1%
Gross fixed capital formation	29.2%	24.3%	20.6%	21.4%
Changes in stocks	-20.3%	-1.6%	-5.2%	1.2%
Exports (FOB)	31.8%	86.1%	55.1%	53.6%
Imports (FOB) (-)	22.8%	94.3%	61.1%	65.5%
Statistical discrepancy	–	-	-	-

GDP by income, total in current prices

in million LIT	1992	1993	1994	1995
Total at market prices	3387	11108	16981	23829
Compensation of employees	37.9%	37.3%	41.8%	43.3%
therein wages and salaries	30.5%	29.8%	33.6%	34.9%
Consumption of fixed capital	11.2%	5.4%	5.8%	8.8%
Indirect taxes	11.2%	10.2%	11.3%	13.9%
Subsidies (-)	1.6%	2.4%	1.6%	1.2%
Operating surplus and mixed income	41.3%	49.5%	42.7%	35.1%

Changes in prices: Previous year = 100	1992	1993	1994	1995
Consumer price index	483	1263	289	136
Producer price index for manufactured products	437	2469	232	121

Foreign trade statistics

Total exports		1992	1993	1994	1995
Million LIT		*	8707	8077	10820
of which	to Russia		33.1%	28.2%	20.4%
	to Finland		0.9%	1.0%	1.1%
	to Sweden		1.8%	3.1%	2.5%
	to Norway		0.2%	0.6%	0.6%
	to Denmark		1.5%	1.7%	2.7%
	to Germany		6.8%	11.5%	14.4%
	to Poland		7.0%	5.0%	3.9%
	to Latvia		7.3%	8.4%	7.1%
	to Estonia		2.5%	2.5%	2.2%
to EU-countries			16.9%	25.8%	36.4%
to CIS-countries			57.1%	46.7%	42.3%

Total imports		1992	1993	1994	1995
Million LIT		*	9798	9356	14594
of which	from Russia		53.6%	39.3%	31.2%
	from Finland		1.3%	2.9%	3.3%
	from Sweden		1.1%	2.4%	2.8%
	from Norway		0.1%	0.7%	0.9%
	from Denmark		2.4%	2.6%	3.5%
	from Germany		9.6%	13.8%	14.3%
	from Poland		2.2%	4.0%	4.2%
	from Latvia		1.5%	2.7%	3.1%
	from Estonia		0.8%	1.6%	1.8%
from EU-countries			18.7%	26.4%	37.1%
from CIS-countries			67.5%	50.2%	42.0%

Employment by activity in 1000 employees	1992	1993	1994	1995
All activities	1855	1778	1675	1644
Agriculture, hunting, forestry, fishing	364	401	392	392
Mining, quarrying, manufacturing	505	424	340	306
Electricity, gas, water supply	31	33	38	42
Construction	169	127	111	115
Trade, hotels, restaurants	197	191	246	230
Transport, storage, communication	124	100	92	95
Private and business services, finance	174	214	159	151
Public administration, education, health and social work	291	289	298	313

The number of active enterprises was 63 241 in 1995. Almost half of all enterprises or 27 003 enterprises were in the wholesale and retail trade.

577 enterprises had 200 or more employees, 5 192 from 20 to 199 employees, 9 151 from 5 to 19 employees and 48 321 less than 5 employees.

Foreign direct investment in Lithuania
In 1995 1 604 million LIT or 5.9% of the GDP for 1995 was invested by foreigners in Lithuanian enterprices. For 1995 Germany was the biggest investor followed by USA and United Kingdom.

Borrowing from abroad
In 1992 227 million LIT were borrowed from abroad or 6.7% of the Lithuanian GDP for 1992, in 1993 324 million LIT or 2.9% of GDP for 1993, in 1994 350 million LIT or 2.1% of GDP 1994 and in 1995 429 million LIT or 1.8% of GDP 1995.

Sources

Questionnaires filled in by the Lithuanian Department of Statistics.

Notes

1) From household budget survey data.
2) Registration of all car and busses.
3) Imputed bank services, taxes on products and subsidies are distributed by activity.
4) Producer price index covers mining, quarrying and manufacturing.

Country/Region: Hamburg

Basic data

Total land and water area: 755 square km, of which agricultural land: 28%, forest and woodland: 5%

Total population 1995: 1.71 million, of which 48% male, 52% female.

By age groups:	0 – 19	17.9%	20 – 64	65.1%	65 –	17,0%

The total population has increased from 1.67 million in 1991 to 1.71 million in 1995.

1000 of persons	1991	1992	1993	1994	1995
Total immigration	79.1	91.4	89.2	77.5	75.1
Total emigration	57.7	67.4	70.7	70.5	68.7
Net migration	21.3	24.0	18.5	7.0	6.4
Natural increase	-4.9	-3.9	-4.4	-4.0	-4.4

Average life expectancy at birth		1986/88
in years	for men	71.8
	for women	78.6

Food consumption as	1992	1993	1994	1995
% of total private consumption [1]	15	15	14	14
Cars per 100 persons [2]	47	47	47	47

The number of dwellings in 1995 was 824 thousand.

National Accounts

GDP in 1991 prices in billion DEM and change in %:

1992	93/92	1993	94/93	1994	95/94	1995
113	- 0.3%	113	+2.1%	115	+2.1%	118

GDP by field of activity, total in current prices

in billion DEM [3]	1992	1993	1994	1995
Total at market prices	118	122	128	133
Agriculture, hunting, forestry and fishing	0.3%	0.3%	0.3%	0.3%
Mining, quarrying and electricity, gas and water supply	1.4%	1.4%	1.4%	1.3%
Manufacturing	15.7%	15.1%	14.7%	14.7%
Construction	3.6%	3.6%	3.5%	3.4%
Wholesale and retail trade, transport, storage and communication	22.1%	21.4%	20.8%	20.5%
Public administration, education, health and social work	10.2%	9.5%	9.3%	9.1%
Other services	40.9%	42.5%	43.6%	44.4%
Undistributed bank services	- 4.0%	- 4.2%	- 4.1%	- 4.1%
Total at basic prices	90.1%	89.6%	89.3%	89.7%
Taxes on products	9.9%	10.4%	10.7%	10.3%
Subsidies	-	–	-	–

GDP by expenditure, total in current prices

in billion DEM [4]	1992	1993	1994	1995
Total at market price	*	*	*	*
Private consumption				
Government consumption				
Consumption of non-profit institutions				
Gross fixed capital formation				
Changes in stocks				
Exports (FOB)				
Imports (FOB) (-)				
Statistical discrepancy				

GDP by income, total in current prices

in billion DEM [4]	1992	1993	1994	1995
Total at market price	*	*	*	*
Compensation of employees				
therein wages and salaries				
Consumption of fixed capital				
Indirect taxes				
Subsidies (-)				
Operating surplus and mixed income				

Changes in prices: Previous year = 100	1992	1993	1994	1995
Consumer price index [5]	105	104	103	102
Producer price index for manufactured products [6]	103	102	102	101

Foreign trade statistics

Total exports		1992	1993	1994	1995
Billion DEM		12.5	12.8	13.3	16.1
of which	to Russia	4.2%	2.1%	2.4%	1.8%
	to Finland	0.8%	0.5%	0.8%	0.7%
	to Sweden	2.2%	2.2%	2.3%	2.0%
	to Norway	0.9%	1.0%	0.8%	0.7%
	to Denmark	4.8%	3.6%	3.6%	3.0%
	to Poland	2.4%	2.7%	2.5%	2.2%
	to Lithuania	0.1%	0.3%	0.2%	0.1%
	to Latvia	0.0%	0.1%	0.2%	0.2%
	to Estonia	0.0%	0.1%	0.1%	0.1%
to EU-countries		55.4%	54.5%	53.7%	54.1%
to CIS-countries		*	*	*	*

Total imports		1992	1993	1994	1995
Billion DEM		52.2	47.2	48.7	44.9
of which	from Russia	1.8%	1.9%	2.0%	1.9%
	from Finland	0.9%	0.9%	0.9%	1.1%
	from Sweden	1.6%	1.8%	1.8%	1.0%
	from Norway	2.0%	2.2%	1.8%	2.2%
	from Denmark	2.9%	2.1%	2.5%	2.8%
	from Poland	0.9%	1.0%	0.9%	1.1%
	from Lithuania	0.2%	0.1%	0.1%	0.1%
	from Latvia	0.2%	0.2%	0.2%	0.3%
	from Estonia	0.0%	0.0%	0.0%	0.0%
from EU-countries		47.2%	42.3%	40.9%	36.7%
from CIS-countries		*	*	*	*

Employment by activity

in 1000 employees	1992	1993	1994	1995
All activities	946.9	935.7	927.6	918.5
Agriculture, hunting, forestry, fishing	7.6	7.5	7.2	7.0
Mining, quarrying, manufacturing, electricity, gas, water supply and construction	216.5	209.3	202.1	197.2
Trade, transport, storage and communication	256.5	249.0	241.1	235.3
Other services	291.4	296.9	304.0	308.2
Government, households and non-profit bodies	174.9	173.0	173.2	170.8

Of the 481 thousand foreigners visiting Hamburg in 1995 3 thousand were from the Baltic states, 10 thousand from Poland, 12 thousand from Russia and 89 thousand from the Nordic countries.

Sources

Questionnaires filled in by the Statistisches Landesamt Hamburg; and Statistische Berichte, Hamburg.

Notes

1) The percentages given are likely to be for food only, without beverage and tobacco.
2) All registered motor vehicles on 100 persons.
3) Undistributed bank services are not deducted from the separate activities but shown separately.
4) GDP by expenditure and by income are not available.
5) The consumer price index for Germany as a whole has been used.
6) Producer price index is without food and entertainment.

Country/Region: Mecklenburg-Vorpommern

Basic data

Total land and water area: 23 170 square km, of which agricultural land: 65%, forest and woodland: 21%

Total population 1995: 1.82 million, of which 49% male, 51% female.

By age groups:	0 – 17	22.5%	18 – 64	65.1%	65 –	12.5%

The total population has decreased from 1.89 million in 1991 to 1.82 million in 1995.

1000 of persons	1991	1992	1993	1994	1995
Total immigration	19.1	29.0	31.0	31.0	32.3
Total emigration	43.6	35.6	36.3	31.3	32.1
Net migration	-24.5	-6.5	-5.3	-0.3	+0.2
Natural increase	-7.8	-9.5	-10.1	-10.9	-9.4

Average life expectancy at birth	1991	1992	1993	1994	1995
in years for men	*	*	*	*	*
for women	*	*	*	*	*

Food consumption as	1992	1993	1994	1995
% of total private consumption [1]	*	25	24	*
Cars on 100 persons [2]	34	41	43	44

The number of dwellings in 1994 was 770 thousand.

National Accounts

GDP in 1991 years prices in billion DEM and change in %:

1992	93/92	1993	94/93	1994	95/94	1995
25.3	+3.3%	26.1	+7.4%	28.0	+5.9%	29.7

GDP by field of activity, total in current prices

in billion DEM [3]	1992	1993	1994	1995
Total at market prices	30.1	34.0	37.9	41.2
Agriculture, hunting, forestry and fishing	4.8%	4.0%	2.9%	2.9%
Mining, quarrying and electricity, gas and water supply	2.7%	2.2%	2.2%	2.3%
Manufacturing	12.3%	11.1%	10.8%	10.3%
Construction	12.4%	13.2%	15.7%	16.0%
Wholesale and retail trade, transport, storage and communication	14.1%	13.9%	13.6%	13.0%
Public administration, education, health and social work	30.7%	29.3%	27.0%	27.1%
Other services	22.9%	25.2%	26.3%	26.8%
Undistributed bank services	- 4.9%	- 3.7%	- 3.5%	- 3.2%
Total at basic prices	95.1%	95.2%	95.0%	95.3%
Taxes on products	4.7%	4.8%	5.0%	4.7%
Subsidies	-	-	-	–

GDP by expenditure, total in current prices

in billion DEM [4]	1992	1993	1994	1995
Total at market prices	*	*	*	*
Private consumption				
Government consumption				
Consumption of non-profit institutions				
Gross fixed capital formation				
Changes in stocks				
Exports (FOB)				
Imports (FOB) (-)				
Statistical discrepancy				

GDP by income, total in current prices

in billion DEM [4]	1992	1993	1994	1995
Total at market prices	*	*	*	*
Compensation of employees				
therein wages and salaries				
Consumption of fixed capital				
Indirect taxes				
Subsidies (-)				
Operating surplus and mixed income				

Changes in prices: Previous year = 100	1992	1993	1994	1995
Consumer price index [5]	115	111	104	102
Producer price index for manufactured products	101	102	103	104

Foreign trade statistics

Total exports		1992	1993	1994	1995
Billion DEM		2.58	2.89	2.59	2.58
of which	to Russia	20.0%	23.5%	6.4%	10.5%
	to Finland	1.5%	0.5%	0.7%	1.2%
	to Sweden	1.4%	1.4%	1.8%	3.3%
	to Norway	0.8%	8.0%	5.2%	1.3%
	to Denmark	4.7%	5.6%	4.7%	4.8%
	to Poland	2.6%	3.0%	1.9%	3.1%
	to Lithuania	*	*	*	*
	to Latvia	*	*	*	*
	to Estonia	*	*	*	*
to EU-countries		24.2%	25.1%	37.2%	38.9%
to CIS-countries		*	*	*	*

Total imports		1992	1993	1994	1995
Billion DEM		2.15	1.82	14.9	15.0
of which	from Russia	5.6%	3.2%	4.3%	5.8%
	from Finland	3.2%	5.8%	5.4%	1.0%
	from Sweden	7.6%	10.7%	13.5%	9.6%
	from Norway	5.6%	8.0%	8.0%	5.2%
	from Denmark	14.9%	17.9%	15.3%	16.2%
	from Poland	7.4%	7.8%	8.8%	11.9%
	from Lithuania	*	*	*	*
	from Latvia	*	*	*	*
	from Estonia	*	*	*	*
from EU-countries		49.7%	60.3%	60.9%	53.9%
from CIS-countries		*	*	*	*

Employment by activity

in 1000 employees	1992	1993	1994	1995
All activities	747.6	719.5	744.8	763.9
Agriculture, hunting, forestry, fishing	51.5	42.7	40.9	40.4
Mining, quarrying, manufacturing, electricity, gas, water supply and construction	210.5	203.7	216.0	223.6
Trade, transport, storage and communication	142.3	137.4	135.2	132.6
Other services	343.2	335.8	352.8	367.2

Of the 252 thousand foreigners visiting Mecklenburg-Vorpommern in 1995, 1 thousand were from the Baltic States, 4 thousand from Poland, 2 thousand from Russia and 41 thousand from the Nordic countries.

Sources

Statistisches Jahrbuch Mecklenburg-Vorpommern 1992-1996,
Statistische Berichte. Bruttoinlandsprodukt und Bruttowertschöpfung der Wirtschaftsberichte in Mecklenburg-Vorpommern 1991 bis 1995,
Statistische Sonderhefte: Entwicklungen in Mecklenburg-Vorpommern 1995

Notes

1) The weight of food and beverage in private consumption has been calculated on the basis of their weight in family budget surveys of medium income 4 person families.
2) The number of cars per 100 persons is based on the registration of passenger cars.
3) Undistributed bank services are shown separately.
4) GDP by expenditure and by income is not available.
5) Price indices used as CPI: Preiseindex für die Lebenshaltung aller privaten Haushälte in Mecklenburg-Vorpommern.

Country/Region: Schleswig-Holstein

Basic data

Total land and water area: 15 770 square km, of which agricultural land: 73%, forest and woodland: 9%

Total population 1995: 2.73 million, of which 49% male, 51% female.

By age groups:	0 – 17	18.6%	18 – 64	64.2%	65 –	16,0%

The total population has increased from 2.64 million in 1991 to 2.73 million in 1995.

1000 of persons	1991	1992	1993	1994	1995
Total immigration	*	148.7	*	116.2	114.8
Total emigration	*	116.2	*	99.4	93.9
Net migration	*	+32.5	*	+16.4	+20.5
Natural increase	-3.9	-3.2	-2.6	-1.5	-2.3

Average life expectancy at birth		1986/88
in years	for men	72.5
	for women	78.7

Food consumption as	1992	1993	1994	1995
% of total private consumption [1]	*	*	22	*
Cars per 100 persons [2]	*	50	51	51

The number of dwellings in 1993 was 1 120 thousand, of which 45% was occupied by the owners and 54% was rented.

National Accounts

GDP in 1991 prices in billion DEM and change in %:

1992	93/92	1993	94/93	1994	95/94	1995
93.1	-0.2%	93.0	+2.5%	95.4	+2.2%	97.4

GDP by field of activity, total in current prices

in billion DEM [3]	1992	1993	1994	1995
Total at market prices	97.1	100.0	104.8	109.3
Agriculture, hunting, forestry and fishing	2.4%	2.2%	2.0%	1.8%
Mining, quarrying and electricity, gas and water supply	3.1%	3.0%	2.7%	3.3%
Manufacturing	21.0%	19.9%	19.8%	19.3%
Construction	5.9%	6.0%	6.6%	6.4%
Wholesale and retail trade	10.7%	10.4%	10.0%	15,9%
Transport, storage and communication	6.4%	6.2%	6.1%	^
Public administration, education, health and social work	17.6%	17.4%	16.9%	16.8%
Other services	30.2%	31.8%	32.5%	33.4%
Undistributed bank services	-4.4%	-4.7%	-4.5%	-4.5%
Total at basic prices	92.7%	92.3%	92.1%	92.4%
Taxes on products	7.3%	7.7%	7.9%	7.6%
Subsidies	-	-	-	-

GDP by expenditure, total in current prices

in billion DEM [4]	1992	1993	1994	1995
Total at market prices	*	*	*	*
Private consumption				
Government consumption				
Consumption of non-profit institutions				
Gross fixed capital formation				
Changes in stocks				
Exports (FOB)				
Imports (FOB) (-)				
Statistical discrepancy				

GDP by income, total in current prices

in billion DEM [4]	1992	1993	1994	1995
Total at market prices	*	*	*	*
Compensation of employees				
therein wages and salaries				
Consumption of fixed capital				
Indirect taxes				
Subsidies (-)				
Operating surplus and mixed income				

Changes in prices: [5] Previous year = 100	1992	1993	1994	1995
Consumer price index	105	104	103	102
Producer price index for manufactured products	101	102	103	104

Foreign trade statistics

Total exports		1992	1993	1994	1995
Billion DEM		13.2	11.6	12.9	13.6
of which	to Russia	1.8%	2.3%	2.2%	*
	to Finland	1.0%	1.0%	1.0%	*
	to Sweden	3.0%	3.0%	3.2%	2.6%
	to Norway	2.3%	2.2%	2.6%	1.9%
	to Denmark	7.6%	6.6%	6.9%	6.4%
	to Poland	1.4%	2.0%	1.9%	2.2%
	to Lithuania	0.6%	0.2%	0.2%	*
	to Latvia	0.4%	0.1%	0.2%	*
	to Estonia	0.2%	0.1%	0.1%	*
to EU-countries		46.9%	45.0%	44.2%	51.4%
to CIS-countries		*	*	*	*

Total imports		1992	1993	1994	1995
Billion DEM		15.8	13.2	14.9	15.0
of which	from Russia	0.9%	0.7%	1.1%	*
	from Finland	4.4%	4.0%	4.3%	4.6%
	from Sweden	8.6%	9.2%	9.1%	10.4%
	from Norway	1.6%	2.7%	2.6%	2.7%
	from Denmark	24.8%	16.4%	15.5%	15.2%
	from Poland	1.8%	2.6%	2.1%	*
	from Lithuania	0.1%	0.1%	0.1%	*
	from Latvia	0.0%	0.1%	0.2%	*
	from Estonia	0.0%	0.1%	0.1%	*
from EU-countries		54.0%	47.3%	47.6%	62.9%
from CIS-countries		*	*	*	*

Employment by activity

in 1000 employees	1992	1993	1994	1995
All activities	1119	1111	1106	1108
Agriculture, hunting, forestry, fishing	59	52	53	47
Mining, quarrying, manufacturing, electricity, gas, water supply and construction	360	362	363	362
Trade, transport, storage and communication	262	266	262	323
Other services	568	566	567	525

The number of active establishments was 100.9 thousand in 1987, 26.9 thousand of the establishments were in trade and 33.7 thousand in services.

Of the 300 thousand foreigners visiting Schleswig-Holstein in 1995 3 thousand were from the Baltic States, 9 thousand from Poland, 4 thousand from Russia and 177 thousand from the Nordic countries.

Sources

Statistisches Jahrbuch Schleswig-Holstein 1993 and 1996 and Statistische Berichte Statistisches Landesamt Schleswig-Holstein.

Notes

1) The weight of food and beverages in private consumption is based on family budget surveys for medium income 4 person families.
2) The number of cars per 100 persons is based on the registration of passenger cars.
3) Undistributed bank services are shown separately.
4) GDP by expenditure and by income are not available.
5) Price indices for Germany as a whole are used.

Country/Region: Denmark

Basic data

Total land and water area: 44 500 square km, of which agricultural land: 59%, forest and woodland: 10% [1].

Total population 1995: 5.25 million, of which 49% male, 51% female.

By age groups:	0 – 16	19.8%	17 – 59	60.5%	60 –	19.7%

The total population increased from 5.15 million in 1991 to 5.25 million in 1995.

1000 of persons	1991	1992	1993	1994	1995
Total immigration	43.6	43.4	43.4	45.0	63.2
Total emigration	32.6	31.9	32.3	34.7	34.6
Net migration	10.9	11.5	11.1	10.3	28.6
Natural increase	4.8	6.9	4.6	8.6	6.6

Average life expectancy at birth	1990	1995
in years for men	72.0	72.5
for women	77.7	78.8

Food consumption as	1990	1992	1993	1994	1995
% of total private consumption [2]		21.3	20.8	20.0	19.9
Cars per 100 persons [3]	31				32

The number of dwellings in 1995 was 2 315 thousand, of which 52.4% were occupied by owners and 45.4% were rented.[4]

National Accounts

GDP in 1980 prices in billion DKK and volume change in %:

1992	93/92	1993	94/93	1994	95/94	1995
89.7	+1.1%	90.8	+4.0%	94.4	+2.4	96.7

GDP by field of activity, total in current prices

in billion DKK	1992	1993	1994	1995
Total at market prices	856	875	929	971
Agriculture, hunting, forestry and fishing	3.4%	3.2%	3.3%	3.6%
Mining, quarrying	0.9%	0.8%	0.8%	0.7%
Manufacturing	16.4%	16.4%	16.7%	17.3%
Electricity, gas, water supply	1.8%	1.8%	1.7%	1.7%
Construction	5.0%	4.7%	4.6%	4.8%
Wholesale and retail trade	11.1%	10.8%	10.6%	10.0%
Transport, storage and communication	8.1%	8.2%	8.3%	8.2%
Public administration, education, health and social work	20.1%	20.4%	19.8%	19.6%
Other services	21.8%	22.4%	22.5%	22.2%
Undistributed bank service	- 1.8%	- 2.1%	- 2.7%	- 2.5%
Total at basic prices	86.7%	86.6%	85.6%	85.7%
Taxes on products	17.3%	17.5%	18.1%	18.0%
Subsidies	- 4.1%	- 4.1%	- 3.8%	- 3.7%

GDP by expenditure, total in current prices

in billion DKK	1992	1993	1994	1995
Total at market prices	856	875	929	971
Private consumption	51.6%	51.7%	52.8%	52.7%
Government consumption	25.6%	26.3%	25.5%	25.0%
Consumption of non-profit institutions	0.7%	0.7%	0.8%	0.8%
Gross fixed capital formation	15.6%	15.0%	14.8%	16.0%
Changes in stocks	- 0.3%	- 0.8%	0.0%	1.3%
Exports (FOB)	36.1%	34.3%	35.0%	34.5%
Imports (FOB) (-)	29.3%	27.3%	29.0%	30.4%
Statistical discrepancy				

GDP by income, total in current prices

in billion DKK	1992	1993	1994	1995
Total at market prices	856	875	929	971
Compensation of employees	54.6%	53.7%	52.2%	52.8%
therein wages and salaries	*	*	*	*
Consumption of fixed capital	15.8%	15.9%	15.3%	14.8%
Indirect taxes	17.3%	17.5%	18.1%	18.0%
Subsidies (-)	- 4.1%	- 4.1%	- 3.8%	- 3.7%
Operating surplus and mixed income	*	*	*	*

Changes in prices: Previous year = 100	1992	1993	1994	1995
Consumer price index	102	101	102	102
Producer price index for manufactured products	*	*	*	*

Foreign trade statistics

Total exports		1992	1993	1994	1995
Billion DKK		240	233	255	264
of which	to Russia	0.5%	0.8 %	1.1%	1.4%
	to Finland	2.0%	1.9%	2.4%	2.6%
	to Sweden	10.5%	10.0%	10.3%	9.9%
	to Norway	5.7%	6.9%	6.4%	6.1%
	to Germany	23.7%	23.8%	22.6%	23.2%
	to Poland	1.3%	1.3%	1.4%	1.4%
	to Lithuania	0.1%	0.1%	0.2%	0.3%
	to Latvia	0.1%	0.1%	0.1%	0.1%
	to Estonia	0.0%	0.1%	0.1%	0.1%
to EU-countries		54.3%	51.6%	63.4%	64.6%
to CIS-countries		*	*	*	*

Total imports		1992	1993	1994	1995
Billion DKK		204	191	219	232
of which	from Russia	0.7%	1.2%	1.1%	1.1%
	from Finland	2.7%	2.9%	3.0%	2.9%
	from Sweden	10.8%	10.9%	11.4%	12.2%
	from Norway	5.4%	5.2%	5.0%	5.1%
	from Germany	23.1%	22.7%	21.8%	22.5%
	from Poland	1.3%	1.6%	1.7%	1.7%
	from Lithuania	0.2%	0.2%	0.2%	0.2%
	from Latvia	0.1%	0.3%	0.1%	0.1%
	from Estonia	0.1%	0.1%	0.1%	0.2%
from EU-countries		53.4%	52.3%	67.2%	69.7%
from CIS-countries		*	*	*	*

Employment by activity

in 1000 employees [5]	1992	1993	1994	1995
All activities	*	*	2585	*
Agriculture, hunting, forestry, fishing and mining, quarrying			133	
Manufacturing			463	
Electricity, gas and water supply			18	
Construction			139	
Trade, hotels and restaurants			440	
Transport and communication			172	
Business services, finance			278	
Public administration, education, health, social work and private services			921	

Source

Statistisk Årbog 1996 and previous years.

Notes

1) The area is for Denmark only, the Faroe Islands and Greenland are not included.
2) The estimate on food and beverage is based on the weight of food, beverage and tobacco in private consumption in National accounts.
3) Passenger cars only.
4) Only houses/flats where persons lived permanently.
5) Figures for 1 January, 1994.

Country/Region: Finland

Basic data

Total land and water area: 338 000 square km, of which agricultural land: 8%, forest and woodland: 68%.

Total population 1995: 5.12 million, of which 49% male, 51% female.

By age groups:	0 – 14	19.0%	15 – 64	66.7%	65 –	14.3%

The total population increased from 5.03 million in 1991 to 5.12 million in 1995.

1000 of persons	1991	1992	1993	1994	1995
Total immigration					12.2
Total emigration					9.0
Net migration [1]	13.0	8.5	8.4	2.9	3.3
Natural increase	16.1	16.9	13.8	17.2	13.8

Average life expectancy at birth	1991	1992	1993	1994	1995
in years for men	71.3	71.7	72.1	72.8	72.8
for women	79.3	79.4	79.5	80.2	80.2

Food consumption as	1991	1992	1993	1994	1995
% of total private consumption [2]		21.3	20.8	20.0	19.9
Cars per 100 persons [3]	38	39	37	37	37

The number of dwellings in 1994 was 2 352 thousand, of which 62.1% was occupied by owners and 28.2% was rented.

National Accounts

GDP in 1990 prices in billion FIM and change in %:

1992	93/92	1993	94/93	1994	95/94	1995
462	-1.2%	457	+4.4%	477	+4.2%	497

GDP by field of activity, total in current prices

in billion FIM	1992	1993	1994	1995
Total at market prices	477	482	510	546
Agriculture, hunting, forestry and fishing	4.5%	4.6%	4.7%	4.0%
Mining, quarrying	0.4%	0.3%	0.4%	0.3%
Manufacturing	19.4%	21.1%	22.1%	23.5%
Electricity, gas, water supply	2.3%	2.3%	2.4%	2.4%
Construction	5.5%	4.4%	4.6%	5.1%
Wholesale and retail trade	8.5%	8.3%	8.5%	8.2%
Transport, storage and communication	7.7%	7.7%	7.7%	7.7%
Public administration, education, health and social work	21.7%	20.6%	19.6%	19.2%
Other services	19.5%	20.9%	20.4%	19.8%
Undistributed bank services	- 2.2%	- 2.9%	- 2.8%	- 2.6%
Total at basic prices	87.2%	87.3%	87.5%	87.5%
Taxes on products	14.6%	14.4%	14.2%	13.5%
Subsidies	- 1.8%	- 1.7%	- 1.7%	- 1.0%

GDP by expenditure, total in current prices

in billion FIM [4]	1992	1993	1994	1995
Total at market prices	477	482	510	546
Private consumption	57.1%	57.1%	55.8%	54.2%
Government consumption	24.8%	23.3%	22.4%	21.8%
Consumption of non-profit institutions	*	*	*	*
Gross fixed capital formation	18.4%	14.8%	14.5%	15.1%
Changes in stocks	- 1.2%	- 0.8%	1.3%	1.3%
Exports (FOB)	26.9%	33.1%	35.8%	38.0%
Imports (FOB) (-)	25.6%	27.7%	29.4%	29.3%
Statistical discrepancy	- 0.5	+0.3	- 0.4	- 1.2%

GDP by income, total in current prices

in billion FIM [4]	1992	1993	1994	1995
Total at market prices	477	482	510	546
Compensation of employees	57.4%	53.5%	51.7%	51.5%
therein wages and salaries	45.4%	42.0%	40.1%	40.0%
Consumption of fixed capital	*	*	*	*
Indirect taxes	15.0%	14.8%	14.6%	13.8%
Subsidies (-)	- 3.6%	- 3.4%	- 3.1%	- 2.7%
Operating surplus and mixed income	*	*	*	*

Changes in prices: Previous year = 100	1992	1993	1994	1995
Consumer price index	103	102	101	101
Producer price index for manufactured products	102	104	102	103

Foreign trade statistics

Total exports	1992	1993	1994	1995
Billion FIM	107	134	154	175
of which to Russia	2.8%	4.5%	5.2%	4.8%
to Sweden	12.8%	11.1%	10.9%	10.1%
to Norway	3.5%	3.2%	3.2%	3.0%
to Denmark	3.6%	3.3%	3.4%	3.2%
to Germany	15.6%	13.1%	13.4%	13.4%
to Poland	1.5%	1.5%	1.7%	1.3%
to Lithuania	<0.1%	<0.2%	0.3%	0.3%
to Latvia	0.2%	0.2%	0.5%	0.6%
to Estonia	0.8%	1.4%	2.2%	2.4%
to EU-countries	53.2%	46.9%	46.4%	57.5%
to CIS-countries	*	*	*	*

Total imports	1992	1993	1994	1995
Billion FIM	95	103	121	126
of which from Russia	7.1%	7.6%	8.9%	7.1%
from Sweden	11.7%	10.2%	10.4%	11.7%
from Norway	4.0%	4.9%	4.8%	4.1%
from Denmark	3.4%	3.1%	3.0%	3.2%
from Germany	16.9%	16.4%	14.7%	15.6%
from Poland	1.3%	1.3%	1.3%	1.1%
from Lithuania	<0.1%	<0.1%	0.1%	0.1%
from Latvia	<0.1%	0.1%	0.1%	0.2%
from Estonia	0.6%	0.7%	0.9%	1.2%
from EU-countries	47.2%	46.5%	43.6%	59.9%
from CIS-countries	*	*	*	*

Employment by activity

in 1000 employees	1992	1993	1994	1995
All activities	*	2041	2024	2068
Agriculture, hunting, forestry and fishing		173	167	158
Mining and quarrying, manufacturing, electricity, gas and water supply		424	426	456
Construction		125	114	115
Trade, hotels and restaurants		304	297	300
Transport and communication		158	161	163
Business services, finance		209	202	220
Public administration, education, health, social work and private services		643	650	650

Source

Statistical Yearbook of Finland 1996, 1995, 1994, 1993

Notes

1) The figures for net migration for the years 1991-1994 are the difference between natural increase and the total population change.
2) The estimates on food, beverage and tobacco in private consumption are from National accounts.
3) Passenger cars only.
4) Consumption of non-profit institutions, consumption of fixed capital and operating surplus and mixed income have not been available in the sources used.

Country/Region: Åland

Basic data

Total land and water area: 6 800 square km, of which land 1 500 square km and water 5 300 square km.

Total population 1995: 25 200 persons, of which 49% male, 51% female.

By age groups:	0 – 19	24.3%	20 – 64	59.4%	65 –	16.3%

The total population has increased from 24 600 in 1990 to 25 200 in 1995.

Number of persons	1991	1992	1993	1994	1995
Total immigration	495	397	352	389	380
Total emigration	357	303	356	377	437
Net migration	138	94	- 4	12	- 57
Natural increase	68	47	88	42	80

Average life expectancy at birth	1991	1992	1993	1994	1995
for men	73.2	73.9	74.6	75.1	75.1
for women	81.7	81.0	82.6	81.8	81.1

Food consumption as % of	1990	1991	1992	1993	1994	1995
total private consumption [1]	21					24
Cars per 100 persons [2]		*	51	50	50	51

The number of dwellings in 1994 was 11 628, of which 6 847, or 58.9%, were owned by the occupier and 3 073, or 26.3%, were rented.

National Accounts

GDP in 1990 prices in billion FIM and change in %:

1992	93/92	1993	94/93	1994	95/94	1995
3.71	- 8.3%	3.07	+11.5%	3.42	+1.2%	3.46

GDP by field of activity, total in current prices

in million FIM	1992	1993	1994	1995
Total at market prices	3564	3343	3756	3823
Agriculture, hunting, forestry and fishing	4.4%	4.4%	4.5%	4.2%
Mining, quarrying and manufacturing	5.5%	5.7%	5.7%	5.8%
Electricity, gas, water supply	0.9%	1.1%	1.0%	0.8%
Construction	3.5%	2.9%	1.3%	2.0%
Trade, hotel and restaurants	7.4%	7.1%	6.7%	6.4%
Transport, storage and communication	38.4%	37.4%	42.2%	39.7%
Finance and business services	14.8%	14.2%	11.5%	13.8%
Public administration, education, health and social work	16.2%	17.1%	15.3%	16.1%
Others services	1.9%	2.9%	3.1%	3.2%
Undistributed bank services	- 2.9%	- 3.2%	- 2.7%	- 3.1%
Total at basic prices	90.1%	89.6%	88.6%	89.0%
Taxes on products	14.3%	14.1%	14.3%	14.3%
Subsidies	- 4.3%	- 3.7%	- 2.9%	- 3.2%

GDP by expenditure, total in current prices

in million FIM	1992	1993	1994	1995
Total at market price	3563	3343	3756	3824
Private consumption	41.4%	41.1%	31.8%	38.8%
Government consumption	20.6%	20.5%	19.4%	20.4%
Consumption of non-profit institutions	-	-	-	-
Gross fixed capital formation	29.1%	6.5%	25.3%	28.0%
Changes in stocks	- 3.5%	- 0.1%	- 0.9%	- 0.2%
Exports (FOB)	88.6%	96.1%	102.2%	95.4%
Imports (FOB) (-)	91.3%	70.3%	95.7%	91.5%
Other external transactions net	15.1%	6.2%	17.8%	9.1%

GDP by income, total in current prices

in million FIM	1992	1993	1994	1995
Total at market price	3563	3343	3756	3824
Compensation of employees	54.1%	53.1%	51.1%	53.5%
therein wages and salaries	42.6%	42.8%	39.4%	41.6%
Consumption of fixed capital	7.4%	13.4%	13.3%	12.4%
Indirect taxes	14.3%	14.1%	14.3%	14.3%
Subsidies (-)	4.4%	3.7%	2.9%	3.2%
Operating surplus and mixed income	28.5%	23.0%	24.2%	23.1%

Changes in prices: Previous year = 100	1992	1993	1994	1995
Consumer price index	104	101	102	100
Producer price index for manufactured products 3)	*	*	*	*

Foreign trade statistics

Total exports [4]	1992	1993	1994	1995
Million FIM	3157	3212	3842	3849
of which to Russia	*	*	*	*
to Sweden				
to Norway				
to Denmark				
to Germany				
to Poland				
to Lithuania				
to Latvia				
to Estonia				
to EU-countries				
to CIS-countries				

Total imports [4]	1992	1993	1994	1995
Million FIM	3254	2350	3595	3498
of which from Russia	*	*	*	*
from Sweden				
from Norway				
from Denmark				
from Germany				
from Poland				
from Lithuania				
from Latvia				
from Estonia				
from EU-countries				
from CIS-countries				

Employment by activity	1992	1993	1994	1995
All activities	11827	11580	11407	11038
Agriculture, hunting, forestry, fishing	1329	1219	1194	1137
Mining, quarrying, manufacturing, electricity, gas and water supply	1128	1129	1111	1133
Construction	689	624	598	595
Trade, hotels, restaurants	1622	1524	1461	1473
Transport, storage, communication	2240	2107	2166	2229
Finance and business services	982	851	841	855
Public administration, education health and social work and other services	3355	3466	3224	3213
Unknown	482	660	812	403

The number of persons arriving in Åland in 1995 was 1 121 thousand, 79% arriving from Sweden and 21% from Finland.

The number of overnight visitors was 179 thousand. They came from more than 80 countries. 86 thousand were from Finland, 79 thousand from Sweden, 3 thousand from Norway, 2 thousand from Denmark, 3 thousand from Germany. From the other countries around the Baltic Sea the number of visitors was between 8 and 181.

Sources

Statistisk Årsbok för Åland 1995 and 1996;
Nationalräkenskapsdata för Åland 1989-1993;
Inresande till Åland 1993-1996 och Inkvarteringsstatistik för Åland 1994-1996;
and tables provided by the Department of Statistics and Economic Research in Åland

Notes

1) The weight of food and beverages in private consumption is taken from the Consumer Price Index.
2) The number of cars per 100 persons is based on the registration of passenger cars.
3) Producer price index for manufactured goods not available.
4) Exports and imports by country not available.

Country/Region: Norway

Basic data

Total land and water area: 386 000 square km, of which agricultural land: 4%, forest and woodland: 33%

Total population 1995: 4.37 million, of which 49% male, 51% female.

By age groups:	0 – 15	20.7%	16 – 66	65.0%	67 –	14.2%

The total population increased from 4.27 million in 1991 to 4.37 million in 1995.

1000 of persons	1991	1992	1993	1994	1995
Total immigration	26.3	26.7	31.7	26.9	*
Total emigration	18.2	16.8	18.9	19.5	*
Net migration	8.0	9.9	12.8	7.4	*
Natural increase	15.9	15.4	13.1	16.0	14.9

Average life expectancy at birth	1991	1992	1993	1994	1995
in years for men	74.0	74.2	74.2	74.9	*
for women	80.1	80.3	80.3	80.6	*

Food consumption as	1991	1992	1993	1994	1995
% of total private consumption [1]					18.0
Cars per 100 persons [2]	38	38	38	38	39

The number of dwellings in 1990 was 1 751 thousand. [3]

National Accounts

GDP in current year prices in billion NOK and volume change in %:

1992	93/92	1993	94/93	1994	95/94	1995
784	+2.8%	823	+5.0%	870	*	926

GDP by field of activity, total in current prices

in billion NOK	1992	1993	1994	1995
Total at market prices	784	823	870	926
Agriculture, hunting, forestry and fishing	2.6%	2.6%	2.6%	2.4%
Mining, quarrying	12.1%	12.1%	11.6%	11.3%
Manufacturing	11.3%	11.5%	11.8%	12.6%
Electricity, gas, water supply	2.8%	2.6%	2.4%	2.6%
Construction	3.6%	3.1%	3.3%	3.7%
Wholesale and retail trade	9.9%	9.5%	9.6%	9.6%
Transport, storage and communication	9.7%	10.2%	9.9%	9.7%
Public administration, education, health and social work	16.4%	16.2%	15.9%	15.6%
Other services	23.7%	23.8%	23.3%	22.2%
Undistributed bank services	-4.3%	-4.0%	-3.6%	-3.2%
Total at basic prices	87.8%	87.6%	86.8%	86.5%
Taxes on products	12.1%	12.3%	13.2%	13.5%
Subsidies	-	-	-	-

GDP by expenditure, total in current prices

in billion NOK	1992	1993	1994	1995
Total at market price	784	823	870	926
Private consumption	47.6%	47.4%	47.5%	46.9%
Government consumption	22.1%	21.8%	21.3%	20.7%
Consumption of non-profit institutions	2.7%	2.6%	2.5%	2.4%
Gross fixed capital formation	19.9%	20.4%	21.1%	21.3%
Changes in stocks	0.7%	1.2%	1.5%	2.5%
Exports (FOB)	38.3%	38.4%	38.5%	38.3%
Imports (FOB) (-)	31.3%	31.8%	32.4%	32.3%
Statistical discrepancy				

GDP by income, total in current prices

in billion NOK[4)]	1992	1993	1994	1995
Total at market prices	784	823	870	926
Compensation of employees	49.5%	48.1%	47.8%	47.5%
therein wages and salaries	*	*	*	*
Consumption of fixed capital	*	*	*	*
Indirect taxes	12.1%	12.3%	13.2%	13.5%
Subsidies (-)	-	-	-	-
Operating surplus and mixed income	*	*	*	*

Changes in prices: Previous year = 100	1992	1993	1994	1995
Consumer price index	102	102	101	102
Producer price index for manufactured products	*	*	*	104

Foreign trade statistics

Total exports	1992	1993	1994	1995
Billion NOK	218	227	244	266
of which to Russia	0.2%	0.3%	0.4%	0.5%
to Finland	2.6%	2.5%	3.0%	2.7%
to Sweden	9.4%	8.7%	9.5%	9.8%
to Denmark	5.4%	4.4%	4.5%	5.0%
to Germany	13.2%	13.0%	11.5%	12.7%
to Poland	0.9%	1.0%	0.9%	0.9%
to Lithuania	0.0%	0.0%	0.0%	0.1%
to Latvia	0.1%	0.0%	0.0%	0.1%
to Estonia	0.0%	0.0%	0.0%	0.1%
to EU-countries	66.4%	78.3%	73.9%	77.2%
to CIS-countries	*	*	*	*

Total imports		1992	1993	1994	1995
Billion NOK		162	171	193	209
of which	from Russia	1.5%	1.4%	2.3%	1.8%
	from Finland	3.5%	3.3%	3.6%	3.9%
	from Sweden	15.4%	14.1%	15.0%	15.4%
	from Denmark	7.5%	7.4%	7.4%	7.5%
	from Germany	14.4%	13.5%	13.9%	13.8%
	from Poland	0.5%	0.5%	0.5%	0.5%
	from Lithuania	0.0%	0.0%	0.1%	0.1%
	from Latvia	0.0%	0.1%	0.1%	0.2%
	from Estonia	0.0%	0.1%	0.1%	0.1%
from EU-countries		48.8%	67.2%	68.7%	71.0%
from CIS-countries		*	*	*	*

Employment by activity in 1000 employees 5)	1992	1993	1994	1995
All activities	*	2004	2035	2079
Agriculture, hunting, forestry, fishing		111	107	106
Mining, quarrying		25	24	23
Manufacturing		292	303	308
Electricity, gas and water supply		22	22	22
Construction		116	119	126
Trade, transport and communication		158	165	170
Business services, finance		153	160	160
Public administration, education, health, social work and private services		775	784	803

Source

Statistisk Årbok 1996

Notes

1) The estimate on food and beverage is based on the weight of food, beverage and tobacco in CPI.
2) Passenger cars only.
3) Only houses/flats where persons lived permanently according to registration
4) Information about wages and salaries, consumption of fixed capital and operating surplus and mixed income have not been available in our sources.
5) Distribution on activities based on ISIC 1968.

Country/Region: Sweden

Basic data

Total land and water area: 450 000 Square km, of which agricultural land: 8%, forest and woodland: 54%.

Total population 1995: 8.84 million of which 49% male, 51% female.

By age groups:	0 – 19	24.6%	20 – 64	58.0%	65 –	17.5%

The total population has increased from 8.64 million in 1991 to 8.84 million in 1995.

1000 of persons	1991	1992	1993	1994	1995
Total immigration	49.7	45.3	61.9	83.6	45.9
Total emigration	24.7	25.7	29.9	32.7	34.0
Net migration	25.0	19.6	32.0	50.9	11.9
Natural decrease	28.6	28.1	21.0	20.4	9.5

Average life expectancy at birth [1]	1991	1992	1993	1994	1995
in years for men	74.9	*	*	75.3	75.6
for women	80.1	*	*	80.8	81.0

Food consumption as	1991	1992	1993	1994	1995
% of total private consumption	19.6	18.8	19.1	19.2	18.9
Cars per 100 persons [2]	42	41	41	41	41

The number of dwellings in 1990 was 4 043 thousand, of which 1% was owned by state and local authorities, 22% was owned by semi-public bodies, 49% by private persons, and 26% by private co-operatives and corporations.

National Accounts

GDP in 1993 prices in billion SEK and change in %:

1992	93/92	1993	94/93	1994	95/94	1995
1427	-2.2%	1395	+3.3%	1442	+3.6%	1493

GDP by field of activity, total in current prices

in billion SEK [3]	1992	1993	1994	1995
Total at market prices	1442	1446	1531	1645
Agriculture, hunting, forestry and fishing	2.0%	1.9%	1.9%	2.1%
Mining, quarrying and manufacturing	17.3%	18.1%	19.6%	21.5%
Electricity, gas, water supply	3.0%	3.0%	2.9%	2.8%
Construction	6.4%	5.5%	4.9%	4.5%
Wholesale and retail trade	9.1%	9.1%	9.4%	9.6%
Transport, storage and communication	6.2%	5.9%	5.9%	5.9%
Public administration, education, health and social work	21.5%	20.0%	19.9%	17.8%
Other services	22.3%	24.3%	23.6%	24.5%
Total at basic prices	87.7%	87.8%	88.2%	88.9%
Taxes on products	13.0%	13.1%	12.7%	12.0%
Subsidies	0.8%	0.8%	0.8%	0.8%

GDP by expenditure, total in current prices

in billion SEK	1992	1993	1994	1995
Total at market prices	1442	1446	1531	1645
Private consumption	52.5%	53.6%	53.0%	50.9%
Government consumption	27.9%	28.1%	27.2%	25.8%
Consumption of non-profit institutions	1.4%	1.5%	1.5%	1.4%
Gross fixed capital formation	17.0%	14.2%	13.7%	14.5%
Changes in stocks	- 0.5%	- 1.0%	0.5%	1.0%
Exports (FOB)	27.9%	32.7%	36.4%	40.9%
Imports (FOB) (-)	26.2%	29.1%	32.2%	34.6%
Statistical discrepancy				

GDP by income, total in current prices

in billion SEK	1992	1993	1994	1995
Total at market price	1442	1446	1531	1645
Compensation of employees	61.3%	60.0%	58.6%	56.9%
therein wages and salaries	44.6%	43.6%	42.9%	41.9%
Consumption of fixed capital	13.4%	14.1%	13.4%	12.6%
Indirect taxes	16.3%	15.6%	14.9%	14.4%
Subsidies (-)	5.5%	5.9%	5.3%	5.1%
Operating surplus and mixed income	14.5%	16.2%	18.3%	21.1%

Changes in prices: Previous year = 100	1992	1993	1994	1995
Consumer price index	102	105	102	103
Producer price index for manufactured products	99	105	105	110

Foreign trade statistics

Total exports	1992	1993	1994	1995
Billion SEK	326	388	472	568
of which to Russia	0.5%	0.7%	0.7%	0.9%
to Finland	5.2%	4.5%	4.8%	5.1%
to Norway	8.4%	8.1%	8.1%	8.5%
to Denmark	7.2%	6.6%	6.9%	6.1%
to Germany	15.0%	14.4%	13.3%	11.7%
to Poland	0.7%	0.8%	1.0%	1.3%
to Lithuania	0.1%	0.1%	0.1%	0.2%
to Latvia	0.1%	0.1%	0.2%	0.2%
to Estonia	0.1%	0.2%	0.3%	0.3%
to EU-countries	55.8%	53.2%	53.2%	56.9%
to CIS-countries	0.6%	0.8%	0.8%	1.0%

Total imports		1992	1993	1994	1995
Billion SEK		291	334	399	461
of which	from Russia	0.9%	1.0%	1.4%	1.2%
	from Finland	6.2%	6.2%	6.3%	5.9%
	from Norway	6.8%	6.4%	6.1%	7.1%
	from Denmark	7.8%	7.3%	6.8%	7.1%
	from Germany	18.6%	17.9%	18.4%	19.6%
	from Poland	0.8%	0.7%	0.9%	0.9%
	from Lithuania	0.1%	0.1%	0.2%	0.1%
	from Latvia	0.2%	0.2%	0.4%	0.5%
	from Estonia	0.2%	0.2%	0.3%	0.4%
from EU-countries		55.6%	55.2%	55.2%	70.6%
from CIS-countries		1.1%	1.0%	1.4%	1.2%

Employment by activity in 1000 employees	1992	1993	1994	1995
All activities	4209	3964	3928	3986
Agriculture, hunting, forestry, fishing	140	137	136	124
Mining, quarrying, manufacturing, electricity, gas and water supply	839	772	761	802
Construction	279	240	225	230
Trade, transport and communication	840	776	770	770
Private and business services, finance	696	669	689	721
Public administration, education, health and social work	1434	1364	1345	1337

The number of active enterprises was 563 thousand in 1995, 224 thousand of them were privately held and 210 thousand joint stock companies, 2 thousand were owned by state or local government. 20% of all enterprises, or 111 thousand enterprises, were in wholesale and retail trade and 29% in services. [4)]

2 thousand enterprises had 200 or more employees, 12 thousand from 20 to 199 employees, 44 thousand from 5 to 19 employees and 505 thousand less than 5 employees.

Sources

Statistical Yearbook of Sweden 1996 and 1995,
Foreign Trade Statistics

Notes

1) The figures on average life expectancy at birth are for the periods 1990-1994 and 1991-1995.
2) Passenger cars only.
3) Imputed bank services are distributed on activities.
4) All individuals and legal persons registered for value added tax and/or having employees are included.

Country/Region: Poland

Basic data

Total land and water area: 312 700 square km, of which agricultural land: 60%, forest and woodland: 29%

Total population 1995: 38.6 million, of which 49% male, 51% female.

By age groups:	0 – 19	30.9%	20 – 64	57.9%	65 –	11.2%

The total population has increased from 38.3 million in 1991 to 38.6 million in 1995.

1000 of persons	1991	1992	1993	1994	1995
Total immigration	5.0	6.5	5.9	6.9	8.1
Total emigration	21.0	18.1	21.4	25.9	26.3
Net migration	-16.0	-11.6	-15.5	-19.0	-18.2
Natural decrease	142.0	120.5	102.0	94.9	47.0

Average life expectancy at birth	1991	1992	1993	1994	1995
in years for men	65.9	66.5	67.2	67.5	67.6
for women	75.1	75.5	75.8	76.1	76.4

Food consumption as	1991	1992	1993	1994	1995
% of total private consumption	32.4	29.0	29.9	30.3	29.2
Cars per 100 persons	25.7	26.6	27.1	28.1	29.0

The number of dwellings in 1991 was 11.2 million, of which 30% was owned by state and local authorities. Of the 11.5 million dwellings in 1995 24 % was owned by state and local authorities.[1)]

National Accounts

GDP in current year prices in billion zlotys changes in % calculated in fixed prices: [2)]

1992	93/92	1993	94/93	1994	95/94	1995
115	+3.8%	156	+5.2%	210	+7.0%	286

GDP by field of activity, total in current prices

in billion zloty	1992	1993	1994	1995
Total at market prices	114.9	155.8	210.4	286.0
Agriculture, hunting, forestry and fishing	6.8%	6.7%	6.3%	6.6%
Mining, quarrying	3.4%	3.7%	4.4%	4.2%
Manufacturing	26.9%	25.2%	20.7%	21.0%
Electricity, gas, water supply	3.8%	4.0%	3.6%	3.7%
Construction	7.8%	6.5%	5.7%	5.2%
Wholesale and retail trade	13.1%	15.0%	13.1%	13.1%
Transport, storage and communication	6.2%	6.1%	6.3%	6.0%
Public administration, education, health and social work	14.1%	12.3%	11.5%	12.3%
Other services	13.9%	12.8%	14.1%	14.7%
Total at basic prices	95.9%	92.2%	85.8%	86.7%
Taxes on products	4.1%	7.8%	15.8%	14.7%
Subsidies	-	-	-1.6%	-1.4%

GDP by expenditure, total in current prices

in billion zloty	1992	1993	1994	1995
Total at market price	114.9	155.8	210.4	286.0
Private consumption	61.7%	63.0%	64.3%	63.7%
Government consumption	20.7%	19.5%	17.8%	16.9%
Consumption of non-profit institutions	0.8%	0.9%	0.9%	0.9%
Gross fixed capital formation	16.8%	15.9%	16.2%	17.1%
Changes in stocks	-1.6%	-0.3%	-0.3%	1.2%
Exports (FOB)	23.7%	22.9%	24.0%	24.9%
Imports (FOB) (-)	22.2%	22.0%	23.0%	24.8%
Statistical discrepancy	-	-	-	-

GDP by income, total in current prices

in billion zloty	1992	1993	1994	1995
Total at market prices	114.9	155.8	210.4	286.0
Compensation of employees	47.0%	44.2%	44.3%	*
therein wages and salaries	33.9%	31.6%	31.8%	*
Consumption of fixed capital				
Indirect taxes	14.0%	16.1%	17.6%	*
Subsidies (-)	2.4%	2.1%	2.3%	*
Operating surplus and mixed income	41.4%	41.8%	40.3%	*

Changes in prices: Previous year = 100	1992	1993	1994	1995
Consumer price index	143	135	132	128
Producer price index total [3)]	135	132	125	125

Foreign trade statistics

Total export		1991	1992	1993	1994	1995
Billion zloty		15.8	18.0	25.8	39.2	55.5
of which	to Russia	*	5.5%	4.6%	5.4%	5.6%
	to Finland	*	2.0%	1.4%	1.7%	1.5%
	to Sweden	*	2.5%	2.2%	2.6%	2.5%
	to Norway	*	1.2%	0.5%	0.7%	0.6%
	to Denmark	*	2.5%	2.9%	3.2%	3.0%
	to Germany	*	31.4%	36.3%	35.7%	38.3%
	to Lithuania	*	0.3%	0.3%	0.7%	0.8%
	to Latvia	*	0.1%	0.2%	0.3%	0.3%
	to Estonia	*	0.0%	0.0%	0.1%	0.1%
to EU-countries		*	58.0%	63.2%	62.7%	70.0%
to CIS-countries		*	8.1%	7.4%	8.3%	10.2%

Total imports		1991	1992	1993	1994	1995
Billion zloty		16.4	22.0	34.0	49.1	70.5
of which	from Russia	*	8.5%	6.8%	4.3%	6.7%
	from Finland	*	2.4%	2.0%	2.4%	1.9%
	from Sweden	*	1.9%	2.3%	2.8%	3.1%
	from Norway	*	2.2%	1.9%	1.7%	1.4%
	from Denmark	*	2.1%	2.4%	2.4%	2.2%
	from Germany	*	23.9%	28.0%	27.4%	26.6%
	from Lithuania	*	0.4%	0.5%	0.4%	0.2%
	from Latvia	*	0.1%	0.1%	0.0%	0.0%
	from Estonia	*	0.1%	0.0%	0.0%	0.1%
from EU-countries		*	53.2%	57.2%	57.5%	64.6%
from CIS-countries		*	10.6%	9.0%	11.7%	9.3%

Employment by activity

in 1000 employees [4]	1992	1993	1994	1995
All activities	15011	14761	14924	14968
Agriculture, hunting, forestry, fishing	4028	3938	4054	4046
Mining, quarrying	454	399	377	357
Manufacturing	3070	2986	3071	3103
Electricity, gas, water supply	254	257	269	269
Construction	1014	881	853	827
Wholesale and retail trade	1871	1982	1892	1903
Hotels and restaurants	164	170	176	186
Transport, storage, communication	913	823	844	838
Private and business services, finance	1129	1128	1122	1158
Public administration, education, health and social work	2114	2197	2265	2281

The number of active enterprises was 1 928 thousand in 1995, 1 904 thousand of them had private domestic owners, 13 thousand had foreign owners and 7 thousand were owned by state or local government. 44% of all enterprises, or 856 thousand enterprises, were in wholesale and retail trade. [5]

5 thousand enterprises had 200 or more employees, 35 thousand from 20 to 199 employees, 131 thousand from 5 to 19 employees and 1 757 thousand less than 5 employees.

Foreign direct investments in Poland[6]

In 1992 the foreign direct investment capital in Poland was 1790 million zloty, which is equal to 2.2% of the country's GDP in 1992. Countries in the North European and Baltic region had invested 45% of it. In 1995 the direct investment capital in Poland had increased to 15 129 million zlotys or 5.3% of GDP for 1995. 23% of it was invested by the countries in the North European and Baltic region. In 1995 the United States had the biggest part of the direct investment capital in Poland followed by the Netherlands and Germany.

Borrowing from abroad. [7]

Poland received foreign loans in the amount of 4 228 million zloty. That equals 1.5% of the GDP for 1995.

Foreign aid received
Foreign aid received in 1992 was 253 million US dollars, in 1993 68 million USD, in 1994 128 million USD and in 1995 244 Million USD.

The number of vessels from abroad, arriving in Poland harbours, increased from 10 453 in 1991 to 13 438 in 1995 and the number of passengers increased from 270 thousand in 1991 to 453 thousand in 1995.

Source

Questionnaires filled in by the Republic of Poland Central Statistical Office

Notes

1) Dwelling stocks occupied as of 31 December.
2) Constant price calculations for 1992 are made in 1990 prices and from 1993 on in the previous year's prices.
3) 1992 and 1993 gross prices include all taxes on products, 1994 and 1995 exclude VAT but include excise taxes.
4) Data on employment are given for 31 December and exclude people employed in budgetary units. The total employment including budgetary units in 1000 employees is: 1991: 15 772; 1992: 15 357; 1993: 15 118; 1994: 15 282 and 1995: 15 345.
5) The number of enterprises includes establishments of natural persons carrying out economic activity but excludes private agricultural farms.
6) Direct investment capital in Poland according to survey of enterprises.
7) Only loans received from direct investors.

Country/Region: The 10 Voivodships

along Poland's western border and northern coast.
Included are: Elblaskie, Gdanskie, Gorzowskie, Jeleniogórskie, Koszalinskie, Olsztynskie, Slupskie, Suwalskie, Szczecinskie and Zielonogórskie.

Basic data

Total land-and water area: 83 949 square km, of which agricultural land: 49%, forest and woodland: 36%

Total population 1995: 6.85 million, of which 49% male, 51% female.

By age groups:	0 – 19	32.2%	20 – 64	58.1%	65 –	9.6%

The total population has increased from 6.74 million in 1991 to 6.85 million in 1995.

1000 of persons	1991	1992	1993	1994	1995
Total immigration	1.3	1.7	1.4	1.9	2.0
Total emigration	6.3	4.1	4.1	4.3	5.0
Net migration	-5.0	-2.4	-2.7	-2.4	-3.0
Natural decrease	35.5	34.0	31.2	29.0	21.3

Average life expectancy at birth [1]	1991	1992	1993	1994	1995
in years for men	65.2	65.5	66.5	66.9	66.8
for women	74.6	75.1	75.5	75.6	76.1

Food consumption as	1991	1992	1993	1994	1995
% of total private consumption	*				
Cars per 100 persons	23	24	24	25	26

The number of dwellings in 1991 was 1 918 thousand, of which 45% was owned by state and local authorities. Of the 1 981 thousand dwellings in 1995 32% was owned by state and local authorities.

National Accounts, price indexes and foreign trade statistics are not compiled at regional level.

Employment by activity in 1000 employees [2]	1992	1993	1994	1995
All activities	2356	2276	2290	2293
Agriculture, hunting, forestry, fishing	*	454	441	428
Mining, quarrying	*	14	15	13
Manufacturing	*	489	494	502
Electricity, gas, water supply	*	50	51	50
Construction	*	137	131	134
Wholesale and retail trade	*	345	328	336
Hotels and restaurants	*	33	41	43
Transport, storage, communication	*	172	186	179
Private and business services, finance	*	184	192	194
Public administration, education, health and social work	*	397	411	415

The number of active enterprises was 344 971 in 1995, 339 993 of them had private domestic owners, 2837 had foreign owners and 1 449 were owned by state or local government.
44% of all enterprises or 150 765 enterprises were in wholesale and retail trade. 3)

863 enterprises had 200 or more employees, 7019 from 20 to 199 employees, 23 816 from 5 to 19 employees and 313 273 less than 5 employees.

Foreign direct investments capital in the enterprises of the ten voivodships were 2501 million zloty at the end of 1995. At the end of 1994 the amount was 1120 million zloty. Countries in the North European and Baltic Region had investments of 596 million zlotys in 1995 and 383 million zloty in 1994. Germany had the highest direct investments followed by Sweden and Denmark. 4)

The number of vessels from abroad, arriving in harbours in the region, has increased from 10 453 in 1991 to 13 438 in 1995, and the number of passengers arriving has increased from 258 thousand in 1991 to 416 thousand in 1995.

Source

Questionnaire filled in by the Republic of Poland Central Statistical Office

Notes

1) The average life expectancy at birth for the region is calculated as the median of the average figures for the ten voivodships.
2 Employment data from enterprise surveys, excluding employees in budgetary units.
3) The number of enterprises includes establishments of natural persons carrying out economic activity but excludes private agricultural farms.
4) Foreign direct investment capital according to surveys of enterprises.

Country/Region: Gdanskie

Basic data

Total land and water area: 7 394 square km, of which agricultural land: 51%, forest and woodland: 34%

Total population 1995: 1.46 million, of which 49% male, 51% female.

By age groups:	0 – 19	31.0%	20 – 64	59.0%	65 –	10.0%

The total population increased from 1.44 million in 1991 to 1.46 million in 1995.

1000 of persons	1991	1992	1993	1994	1995
Total immigration	0.5	0.5	0.4	0.7	0.6
Total emigration	2.8	1.9	1.6	1.5	1.7
Net migration	-2.3	-1.4	-1.2	-0.8	-1.1
Natural decrease	7.2	5.8	5.4	5.2	4.1

Average life expectancy at birth	1991	1992	1993	1994	1995
in years for men	66.5	66.9	68.0	68.4	69.1
for women	74.9	75.6	75.8	75.8	76.4

Food consumption as	1991	1992	1993	1994	1995
% of total private consumption	*				
Cars per 100 persons	22	23	25	25	27

The number of dwellings in 1991 was 408 thousand, of which 34% was owned by state and local authorities. Of the 423 thousand dwellings in 1995 26% was owned by state and local authorities.

National Accounts, price indexes and foreign trade statistics are not compiled at regional level.

Employment by activity in 1000 employees [1]	1992	1993	1994	1995
All activities	511	488	498	513
Agriculture, hunting, forestry, fishing	*	69	68	67
Mining, quarrying	*	1	1	1
Manufacturing	*	111	113	117
Electricity, gas, water supply	*	11	11	10
Construction	*	36	33	37
Wholesale and retail trade	*	73	75	81
Hotels and restaurants	*	8	12	11
Transport, storage, communication	*	50	52	49
Private and business services, finance	*	46	48	52
Public administration, education, health and social work	*	84	86	87

The number of active enterprises was 73 673 in 1995, 72 302 of them had private domestic owners, 900 had foreign owners and 230 were owned by state or local government.
42% of all enterprises, or 30 668 enterprises, were in wholesale and retail trade. [2]

227 enterprises had 200 or more employees, 1 758 from 20 to 199 employees, 7 081 from 5 to 19 employees and 64 607 less than 5 employees.

At the end of 1995, foreign direct investments in enterprises in Gdanskie (the figures include also the voivodship of Elblag) were 1 435 million zloty. At the end of 1994 the amount was 650 million zlotys. Countries in the North European and Baltic region had investments in the amount of 115 million zlotys in 1995 and 80 million zlotys in 1994. The biggest investor was Germany followed by Sweden and Norway. 3)

The number of vessels from abroad, arriving in Gdanskie harbours, increased from 4 012 in 1991 to 4 439 in 1995, and the number of passengers increased from 37 thousand in 1991 to 71 thousand in 1995.

Sources

Questionnaires filled in by the Republic of Poland Central Statistical Office

Notes

1) Employment data from enterprise surveys, excluding employees in budgetary units.
2) The number of enterprises includes establishments of natural persons carrying out economic activity but excludes private agricultural farms.
3) Foreign direct investment capital according to surveys of enterprises. Foreign direct investments for Gdanskie include the investments in Elblaskie.

Country/Region: Arkhangelsk

Basic data

Total land and water area: 587 400 square km, of which agricultural land: 1%, forest and woodland: 36%.

Total population 1995: 1.52 million, of which 49% male, 51% female.

By age groups:	0 – 19	29.9%	20 – 64	60.2%	65 –	9.9%

The total population decreased from 1.57 million in 1991 to 1.52 million in 1995.

1000 of persons	1991	1992	1993	1994	1995
Total immigration	46.7	43.1	34.2	35.6	34.7
Total emigration	55.9	50.7	39.6	39.1	39.1
Net migration	– 9.2	– 7.6	– 5.4	– 3.5	– 4.3
Natural increase	3.1	– 2.1	– 8.3	– 9.9	– 8.7

Average life expectancy at birth	1991	1992	1993	1994	1995
in years for men	63.8	60.6	57.3	55.9	57.1
for women	74.7	73.2	71.1	70.0	71.0

Food consumption as	1991	1992	1993	1994	1995
% of total private consumption [1]	32	40	40	42	45
Cars per 100 persons [2]	7	7	7	9	9

The general area of dwellings in 1991 was 27.0 million square metres, of which 74% was owned by state and local authorities and 26% by private persons. Of the 29.0 million square metres in 1995 45% was owned by state and local authorities and 40% by private persons. The average living space was in 1991 15.9 and in 1995 19.0 square metres per resident.

Changes in prices: Previous year = 100	1992	1993	1994	1995
Consumer price index	2769	1070	313	245
Producer price index for manufactured products	2755	901	478	284

Foreign trade statistics

Total exports		1992	1993	1994	1995
Million US$		122.6	129.6	309.9	436.5
of which	to Finland	0.5%	1.5%	9.6%	1.0%
	to Sweden	10.6%	10.5%	6.4%	5.5%
	to Norway	24.1%	11.6%	3.4%	1.0%
	to Denmark	4.4%	2.5%	1.1%	1.4%
	to Germany	0.7%	29.6%	18.6%	11.5%
	to Poland	2.8%	0.4%	0.5%	0.3%
	to Lithuania	*	0.1%	0.2%	–
	to Latvia	*	0.3%	0.5%	0.3%
	to Estonia	*	0.2%	0.7%	0.5%
to EU-countries		*	*	*	*
to CIS-countries		*	*	*	4.7%

Total imports		1992	1993	1994	1995
Million US$		95.8	99.0	88.2	*
of which	from Finland	12.6%	6.9%	14.3%	*
	from Sweden	0.8%	0.6%	3.6%	*
	from Norway	2.8%	1.0%	2.3%	*
	from Denmark	0.5%	0.9%	1.7%	*
	from Germany	11.5%	18.9%	12.2%	*
	from Poland	1.0%	2.9%	3.9%	*
	from Lithuania	*	0.1%	0.3%	*
	from Latvia	*	0.1%	0.6%	*
	from Estonia	*	0.2%	0.3%	*
from EU-countries		*	*	*	*
from CIS-countries		*	*	*	*

Employment by activity in 1000 employees	1992	1993	1994	1995
All activities	750	707	664	637
Agriculture, hunting, forestry, fishing	62	58	53	47
Mining, quarrying, manufacturing, electricity, gas and water supply	244	227	205	185
Construction	69	57	45	44
Trade, hotels, restaurants	67	68	67	65
Transport, storage and communication	88	86	83	80
Private and business services	66	61	60	59
Public administration, education, health and social work	154	151	152	158*

* From 1995 security services are included here.

The number of active enterprises was 9624 in 1995, 451 of which were owned by state or local governments, 8438 had domestic private owner or domestic mixed owners and 211 were wholly or partly owned by foreigners.

Foreign direct investment in the Arkhangelsk region
In 1993 0.1 million US$ in direct investments was reported, in 1994 0.0 million US$ and in 1995 2.5 million US$. In 1995 Germany was the biggest investor (1.7 million) among the listed countries, followed by the United States (0.1 million).

The number of incoming visitors from abroad was 660 in 1993, 286 in 1994 and 159 in 1995. Most were from Finland, Germany and Norway.

Sources

Questionnaires filled in by the Arkhangelsk region Committee of State Statistics

Notes

1) Food consumption as % of total private consumption from household budget surveys.
2) Registration of all cars and busses.

Country/Region: Kaliningrad

Basic data

Total land and water area: 15 100 square km, of which agricultural land: 54%, forest and woodland: 19%

Total population 1995: 0.93 million, of which 48% male, 52% female.

By age groups:	0 – 19	27.0%	20 – 64	62.2%	65 –	10.8%

The total population has increased from 0.89 million in 1991 to 0.93 million in 1995.

1000 of persons	1991	1992	1993	1994	1995
Total immigration	46.0	42.1	37.3	44.2	38.4
Total emigration	33.2	25.7	26.3	25.8	27.4
Net migration	12.8	16.5	16.5	18.4	11.0
Natural increase	1.6	- 0.6	- 4.2	- 6.1	- 4.7

Average life expectancy at birth		1991	1992	1993	1994	1995
in years	for men	63.4	62.1	58.5	57.1	58.9
	for women	73.7	72.6	70.9	69.8	71.4

Food consumption as	1991	1992	1993	1994	1995
% of total private consumption [1]	33	44	43	47	54
Cars per 100 persons [2]	9	11	13	14	16

The general area of dwellings in 1991 was 14.4 million square metres, of which 84% was owned by state and local authorities and 7% by private persons. Of the 16.6 million square metres in 1995 50% was owned by state and local authorities and 33% by private persons. The average area per resident in 1991 was 16.2 and in 1994 18.2 square metres.

Changes in prices: Previous year = 100	1992	1993	1994	1995
Consumer price index	1660	840	320	240
Producer price index for manufactured products	2400	970	330	250

Foreign trade statistics

Total exports		1993	1994	1995
Million US$		105.1	165.2	383.8
of which	to Finland	0.2%	1.8%	0.5%
	to Sweden	0.9%	1.2%	0.3%
	to Norway	2.4%	5.3%	0.9%
	to Denmark	0.4%	1.9%	1.0%
	to Germany	14.7%	16.2%	6.5%
	to Poland	16.6%	6.7%	2.3%
	to Lithuania	4.0%	5.0%	4.1%
	to Latvia	2.8%	5.1%	1.5%
	to Estonia	0.4%	1.0%	4.0%
to EU-countries		*	*	23.2%
to CIS-countries		*	*	14.1%

Total imports		1993	1994	1995
Million US$		34.6	136.9	555.9
of which	from Finland	2.9%	2.2%	1.9%
	from Sweden	-	2.3%	1.1%
	from Norway	0.3%	0.9%	2.6%
	from Denmark	0.9%	3.1%	1.3%
	from Germany	24.9%	13.6%	0.1%
	from Poland	47.7%	35.8%	16.4%
	from Lithuania	6.1%	9.2%	18.5%
	from Latvia	1.4%	3.4%	2.0%
	from Estonia	0.6%	0.1%	0.2%
from EU-countries		*	*	*
from CIS-countries		*	*	*

Employment by activities in 1000 employees	1992	1993	1994	1995
All activities	421	410	398	392
Agriculture, hunting, forestry, fishing	54	53	49	45
Mining, quarrying, manufacturing, electricity, gas and water supply	122	119	100	91
Construction	37	36	35	33
Trade, hotels, restaurants	39	38	47	48
Transport, storage and communication	36	35	35	33
Private and business services	38	34	33	35
Public administration, education, health and social work	95	97	100	107

The total number of enterprises was 20.3 thousand in 1995. 15.3 thousand of them had private domestic owners, 0.4 thousand foreign owners and 1.7 thousand were owned by state or local government. 37% of the enterprises were in trade or the hotel and restaurant business. 213 enterprises had more than 200 employees.

Foreign direct investment in Kaliningrad

In 1993 5.7 million US$ in direct investments was reported, in 1994 5.4 million US$ and in 1995 11.6 million US$. In 1995 the United States was the biggest investor (2.8 million) followed by Sweden and Switzerland (both 2.5 million).

Of the 40 thousand foreigners visiting Kaliningrad in 1995 24 thousand were from Germany, 5 thousand from Poland and 5 thousand from Lithuania.

Sources

Questionnaires filled in by the Statistical Office in Kaliningrad

Notes

1) From household budget surveys.
2) From registration all cars and buses.

Country/Region: Republic of Karelia

Basic data

Total land and water area: 180 500 square km, of which agricultural land: 1%.

Total population 1995: 784 thousand, of which 48% male, 52% female.

By age groups:	0 – 19	29.0%	20 – 64	61.0%	65 –	10.0%

The total population has decreased from 799 thousand in 1991 to 784 thousand in 1995.

1000 of persons	1991	1992	1993	1994	1995
Total immigration	28.5	25.5	22.1	22.4	21.9
Total emigration	26.8	23.5	21.7	20.8	19.9
Net migration	1.7	2.0	0.3	1.6	2.0
Natural increase	+0.7	– 1.8	– 4.8	– 6.5	– 6.0

Average life expectancy at birth		1991	1992	1993	1994	1995
in years	for men	62.1	59.7	56.2	55.0	54.7
	for women	73.8	72.0	70.8	69.0	69.2

Food consumption as	1991	1992	1993	1994	1995
% of total private consumption	*				
Cars per 100 persons	10	11	12	13	14

The general area of dwellings in 1991 was 13.9 million square metres, of which 87% was owned by state and local authorities and 13% was privately owned. Of the 14.9 million square metres in 1994 63% was owned by state and local authorities and 25% was privately owned. The average area per resident was in 1991 17.5 and in 1994 18.1 square metres.

Changes in prices: Previous year = 100	1992	1993	1994	1995
Consumer price index	2810	1032	331	249
Producer price index for manufactured products	3302	948	426	271

Foreign trade statistics

Total exports		1993	1994	1995
Million US$		341.0	380.8	633.0
of which to Finland		*	29.5%	21.8%
	to Sweden	*	3.1%	1.7%
	to Norway	*	1.2%	0.1%
	to Denmark	*	1.1%	0.5%
	to Germany	*	9.3%	6.3%
	to Poland	*	2.0%	3.8%
	to Lithuania	*	0.4%	0.4%
	to Latvia	*	0.7%	0.4%
	to Estonia	*	0.5%	0.6%
to EU-countries		*	54.5%	39.3%
to CIS-countries		*	7.7%	5.5%

Total imports		1993	1994	1995
Million US$		*	167.0	176.6
of which	from Finland		24.4%	31.4%
	from Sweden		2.9%	3.1%
	from Norway		0.1%	0.2%
	from Denmark		0.7%	0.3%
	from Germany		9.0%	12.4%
	from Poland		0.7%	0.3%
	from Lithuania		0.3%	0.3%
	from Latvia		0.2%	0.2%
	from Estonia		0.2%	0.2%
from EU-countries			60.3%	69.4%
from CIS-countries			28.4%	17.6%

Employment by activity in 1000 employees	1992	1993	1994	1995
All activities	402	380	373	371
Agriculture, hunting, forestry, fishing	27	25	24	22
Mining, quarrying, manufacturing, electricity, gas and water supply	128	124	110	102
Construction	42	40	36	33
Trade, hotels, restaurants	36	36	39	39
Transport, storage and communication	41	39	45	46
Private and business services	41	30	33	33
Public administration, education, health and social work	88	85	88	96

The total number of enterprises was 11.3 thousand in 1995. 7.4 thousand of them had private domestic owners, 43 enterprises had foreign owners and 1.6 thousand enterprises were owned by state or local government. 22% of the enterprises were in wholesale and retail trade.

Foreign direct investment in the Republic of Karelia

In 1991 1.7 million US$ in direct investments was reported, in 1992 4.6 million US$, in 1993 3.1 million US$, in 1994 13.7 million US$ and in 1995 16.0 million US$. In 1995 the United States was the biggest investor (5.4 million) followed by Sweden (3.0 million) and Germany (2.6 million).

Sources

Republic of Karelia in Figures; Concise statistical handbook 1996; State Committee of the Republic of Karelia on Statistics; and questionnaires filled in by the State Committee of the Republic of Karelia

Country/Region: Leningrad region

Basic data

Total land and water area: 8 391 square km, of which agricultural land: 10%, forest and woodland: 60% and water: 15%.

Total population 1995: 1.67 million, of which 46% male, 54% female.

By age groups:	0 – 19	26.7%	20 – 64	60.5%	65 –	12.8%

The total population has slightly increased from 1.666 million in 1991 to 1.668 million in 1995.

1000 of persons	1991	1992	1993	1994	1995
Total immigration	42.6	57.8	54.9	68.8	67.5
Total emigration	33.1	45.0	42.1	43.3	46.7
Net migration	9.5	12.8	12.7	25.4	20.8
Natural increase	– 4.8	– 9.4	- 18.0	- 20.1	- 18.4

Average life expectancy at birth		1991	1992	1993	1994	1995
in years	for men	62.1	59.7	55.7	54.7	55.5
	for women	73.8	72.6	70.4	69.2	70.1

Food consumption as 1991	1992	1993	1994	1995	
% of total private consumption [1]	39	50	50	51	54
Cars per 100 persons	*				

The general area of dwellings in 1991 was 31.4 million square metres, of which 77% was owned by state and local authorities and 23% by private persons. Of the 33.1 million square metres in 1994 67% was owned by state and local authorities and 33% by private persons. The average area per resident was in 1991 18.8 and in 1994 19.8 square metres.

Changes in prices: Previous year = 100	1992	1993	1994	1995
Consumer price index	2200	760	320	230
Producer price index for manufactured products	2510	950	380	260

Foreign trade statistics

Total exports		1993	1994	1995
Million US$		329.3	379.9	541.2
of which	to Finland	30.8%	74.9%	13.1%
	to Sweden	3.3%	0.6%	0.9%
	to Norway	0.2%	0.1%	0.6%
	to Denmark	-	-	55.8%
	to Germany	1.8%	1.8%	5.4%
	to Poland	0.2%	0.5%	0.2%
	to Lithuania	0.2%	7.9%	0.4%
	to Latvia	0.5%	0.5%	1.4%
	to Estonia	1.3%	1.4%	3.3%
to EU-countries		53.5%	10.4%	83.0%
to CIS-countries		*	*	3.7%

Total imports		1993	1994	1995
Million US$		56.9	87.4	*
of which	from Finland	22.0%	24.1%	*
	from Sweden	2.1%	1.1%	*
	from Norway	-	-	*
	from Denmark	-	-	*
	from Germany	30.2%	23.2%	*
	from Poland	3.2%	1.8%	*
	from Lithuania	-	-	*
	from Latvia	-	0.5%	*
	from Estonia	0.7%	0.7%	*
from EU-countries		*	*	*
from CIS-countries		*	*	*

Employment by activity in 1000 employees	1992	1993	1994	1995
All activities	728	713	668	678
Agriculture, hunting, forestry, fishing	99	102	95	95
Mining, quarrying, manufacturing, electricity, gas and water supply	236	229	198	191
Construction	73	70	58	59
Trade, hotels, restaurants	53	59	63	73
Transport, storage and communication	47	45	47	46
Private and business services	63	57	66	65
Public administration, education, health and social work	157	150	143	149

Foreign direct investment in the Leningrad region

In 1993 0.0 million US$ in direct investments was reported, in 1994 0.2 million US$ and in 1995 20.1 million US$. In 1995 Germany was the biggest investor (8.6 million) among the countries listed followed by Finland (0.9 million).

Sources

Questionnaires filled in by the Statistical Office in St Petersburg

Note

1) From household budget surveys.

Country/Region: Murmansk

Basic data

Total land and water area: 144 900 square km, of which agricultural land: 6%

Total population 1995: 1.07 million, of which 49% male, 51% female.

By age groups:	0 – 19	28.7%	20 – 64	65.6%	65 –	5.7%

The total population decreased from 1.17 million in 1991 to 1.07 million in 1995.

1000 of persons	1991	1992	1993	1994	1995
Total immigration	46.6	37.0	34.6	43.7	36.4
Total emigration	55.9	63.1	57.4	57.4	52.4
Net migration	– 9.3	-26.1	-22.9	-13.7	-16.0
Natural increase	4.6	1.0	- 3.2	- 3.5	- 3.4

Average life expectancy at birth		1991	1992	1993	1994	1995
in years	for men	65.3	62.4	59.1	57.0	57.7
	for women	75.0	73.6	71.1	69.7	70.4

Food consumption as	1991	1992	1993	1994	1995
% of total private consumption	33	42	42	45	49
Cars per 100 persons	*				

Changes in prices: Previous year = 100	1992	1993	1994	1995
Consumer price index	2230	840	340	230
Producer price index for manufactured products	5000	850	410	200

Foreign trade statistics

Total exports		1993	1994	1995
Million US$		515.0	587.2	851.5
of which	to Finland	*	8.7%	11.9%
	to Sweden	*	5.7%	8.1%
	to Norway	*	16.8%	17.8%
	to Denmark	*	5.1%	3.1%
	to Germany	*	3.8%	3.2%
	to Poland	*	-	0.0%
	to Lithuania	*	-	0.6%
	to Latvia	*	-	0.0%
	to Estonia	*	0.2%	0.2%
to EU-countries		*	-	34.2%
to CIS-countries		*	4.1%	1.7%

Total imports		1993	1994	1995
Million US$		149.0	176.3	299.5
of which	from Finland	2.9%	13.7%	*
	from Sweden	*	4.9%	*
	from Norway	*	15.5%	*
	from Denmark	*	2.2%	*
	from Germany	*	8.6%	*
	from Poland	*	1.0%	*
	from Lithuania	*	-	*
	from Latvia	*	0.1%	*
	from Estonia	*	0.1%	*
from EU-countries		*	*	*
from CIS-countries		*	*	*

Employment by activity in 1000 employees	1992	1993	1994	1995
All activities	568	520	493	470
Agriculture, hunting, forestry, fishing	13	12	11	11
Mining, quarrying, manufacturing, electricity, gas and water supply	173	168	152	146
Construction	81	53	48	42
Trade, hotels, restaurants	57	57	58	58
Transport, storage and communication	55	51	52	47
Private and business services	57	48	48	46
Public administration, education, health and social work	132	131	125	120

The total number of enterprises was 7.4 thousand in 1995. 6.3 thousand of them had private domestic owners, 0.2 thousand foreign owners and 0.9 thousand were owned by state or local government. 46% of the enterprises were in trade or the hotel and restaurant business.

Foreign direct investment in Murmansk

In 1995 3.8 million US$ in direct investments was reported. In 1995 the biggest investor was Germany (1.7 million) followed by Norway (1.3) and the Netherlands (0.9).

Of the 19 thousand overnight foreigners visiting Murmansk in 1995 4 thousand were from Norway and 3 thousand from Finland.

Sources

Questionnaires filled in by the Statistical Office in Murmansk

Notes

1) From household budget surveys.
2) Registration of all cars and buses.

Country/Region: St Petersburg

Basic data

Total land and water area: 606 square km of which water: 10%.

Total population 1995: 4.77 million of which 45% male, 55% female.

By age groups:	0 – 19	23.5%	20 – 64	62.8%	65 –	13.7%

The total population has decreased from 4.97 million in 1991 to 4.77 million in 1995.

1000 of persons	1991	1992	1993	1994	1995
Total immigration	103.9	69.9	67.0	79.2	80.4
Total emigration	113.0	89.3	83.3	74.8	72.6
Net migration	– 9.1	- 19.4	- 16.3	4.4	7.8
Natural increase	- 16.1	- 29.4	- 53.4	- 49.0	- 42.9

Average life expectancy at birth		1991	1992	1993	1994	1995
in years	for men	64.4	62.6	58.1	58.1	59.9
	for women	74.1	73.6	70.7	71.2	72.3

Food consumption as 1991	1992	1993	1994	1995	
% of total private consumption [1)]	43	62	55	56	54
Cars per 100 persons [2)]	6	8	10	11	13

The general area of dwellings in 1991 was 88.74 million square metres, of which 84% was owned by state and local authorities and 16% was privately owned. Of the 89.4 million square metres in 1995 63% was owned by state and local authorities and 37% by private persons. The average area per resident was in 1992 18.2 and in 1994 18.4 square metres.

Changes in prices: Previous year = 100	1992	1993	1994	1995
Consumer price index	2180	810	330	230
Producer price index for manufactured products	2090	850	390	240

Foreign trade statistics

Total exports		1993	1994	1995
Million US$		364.4	678.0	779.5
of which	to Finland	22.2%	13.7%	6.9%
	to Sweden	17.7%	2.8%	2.8%
	to Norway	0.1%	0.3%	0.3%
	to Denmark	1.8%	0.7%	0.3%
	to Germany	13.3%	12.1%	13.9%
	to Poland	2.3%	2.8%	1.9%
	to Lithuania	0.8%	4.5%	0.8%
	to Latvia	0.5%	5.1%	0.9%
	to Estonia	0.5%	3.1%	0.6%
to EU-countries		27.0%	36.7%	56.3%
to CIS-countries		*	*	10.8%

Total imports		1993	1994	1995
Million US$		249.1	363.5	*
of which	from Finland	15.0%	16.0%	*
	from Sweden	15.0%	5.6%	*
	from Norway	0.3%	1.0%	*
	from Denmark	5.5%	2.0%	*
	from Germany	19.3%	17.4%	*
	from Poland	1.1%	2.8%	*
	from Lithuania	0.4%	0.4%	*
	from Latvia	0.1%	0.2%	*
	from Estonia	0.2%	1.6%	*
from EU-countries		*	*	*
from CIS-countries		*	*	*

Employment by activity in 1000 employees	1992	1993	1994	1995
All activities	2387	2369	2353	2348
Agriculture, hunting, forestry, fishing	14	13	13	13
Mining, quarrying, manufacturing, electricity, gas and water supply	768	746	665	596
Construction	274	242	263	251
Trade, hotels, restaurants	203	239	273	348
Transport, storage and communication	228	224	227	219
Private and business services	188	196	230	240
Public administration, education, health and social work	711	709	680	680

Foreign direct investments in St. Petersburg
(No information about foreign direct investments was provided by the Statistical Office in St Petersburg.)

Of the 304 thousand foreigners visiting St Petersburg in 1995 49 thousand were from Germany, 25 thousand from Finland and 8 thousand from Sweden.

Sources

Questionnaires filled in by the Statistical Office in St Petersburg

Notes

1) From household budget surveys.
2) From registration of all cars and buses.

List of Abbreviations

ACV – armoured combat vehicle
AEBR – Association of European Border Regions
AER – Assembly of European Regions
ASEAN – Association of South-East Asian Nations
BALTBAT – Baltic Battalion
BALTNET – Baltic Air Surveillance Network
BALTRON – Baltic Naval Squadron
BAT – best available technology
BCC – Baltic Co-ordination Committee
BEAC – Barents Euro-Arctic Council
BEAR – Barents Euro-Arctic Region
BEP – best environmental practice
BLUE – Berliner Landesarbeitsgemeinschaft Umwelt und Entwicklung
BRT – Baltic Round Table
BSR/OP – Baltic Sea Region/Operational Programme
BSSSC – Baltic Sea States Subregional Co-operation
CAP – Common Agricultural Policy (EU)
CBSS – Council of the Baltic Sea States
CC – Component Command (NATO)
CDU – Christian-Democratic Union (Germany)
CEE – Central and Eastern Europe
CEEC – Central and Eastern European country
CEFTA – Central European Free Trade Agreement
CFE – Treaty on Conventional Forces in Europe
CFSP – common foreign and security policy (EU)
CIS – Commonwealth of Independent States
CJTF – combined joint task force (NATO)
CMEA – Council for Mutual Economic Assistance
CoCom – Co-ordinating Committee (of mostly NATO members to prevent the export of sensitive technology to Warsaw Treaty countries)
COE – Council of Europe
COMBALTAP – Commander Allied Forces Baltic Approaches (NATO)
COMLANDJUT – Commander Allied Land Forces Schleswig-Holstein and Jutland
COR – Committee of the Regions (EU)
CPE(s) – centrally planned economies
CPX – Command Post Exercise (NATO)
CSBMs – confidence- and security-building measures
CSCE – Conference on Security and Co-operation in Europe
CSD – Committee for Spatial Development

CSD/BSR – Committee for Spatial Development for the Baltic Sea Region
CSEM(s) – confidence- and security-enhancing measure(s)
CSF – Community Support Frameworks (EU)
DG – Directorate General (EU)
EAGGF – Agricultural Guarantee and Guidance Fund (EU)
EAPC – Euro-Atlantic Partnership Council
EC – European Community
ECE – Economic Commission for Europe (UN)
EEA – European Economic Area
EEC – European Economic Community
EFTA – European Free Trade Association
EMU – Economic and Monetary Union (EU)
ENGO – environmental non-governmental organisation
EP – European Parliament
EPA – Environmental Protection Agency (USA)
ERDF – European Regional Development Fund (EU)
ESC – European Security Council
ESDI – European security and defence identity (EU)
ESDP – European Spatial Development Perspective (EU)
ESF – European Social Fund (EU)
EU – European Union
FDI – foreign direct investment
FRG – Federal Republic of Germany
FTX – field training exercise (NATO)
GAO – gross agricultural production
GATT – General Agreement on Tariffs and Trade
GDR – German Democratic Republic
HCNM – High Commissioner on National Minorities (OSCE)
HELCOM – Helsinki Commission
HLTF – High Level Task Force (NATO)
IFOR – Implementation Force (NATO)
IGC – Intergovernmental Conference (EU)
IMF – International Monetary Fund
Interreg – Interregional co-operation initiative (EU)
JCG – Joint Consultative Group (NATO)
JCP – Joint Comprehensive Environmental Action Programme
JSR Northeast – Joint Subregional Command Northeast (NATO)
JSRC – Joint Subregional Command (NATO)
JSRS – Joint Subregional Command South (NATO)
JV – joint venture
KOOR – Kaliningrad Special Defence Region
KOR – Kaliningrad Special District
LACE – Technical Assistance and Promotion of Cross-Border Co-operation
LDLP – Lithuanian Democratic Labour Party

LNHRO – Latvian National Human Rights Office
LRTAP – Convention on Long Range Transboundary Air Pollution
MBFR – mutual and balanced force reduction
NACC – North Atlantic Co-operation Council
NAFTA – North American Free Trade Association
NATO – North Atlantic Treaty Organisation
NCLM – Nordic Common Labour Market
NEBI – North European and Baltic Sea Integration
NERP – Committee of Senior Officials for Nordic Regional Policy
NFI – new form of investment
NGO – non-governmental organisation
NORDCAPS – Nordic Co-ordinated Arrangement for Military Peace Support
NORDPOLBRIG – Nordic-Polish Brigade
NSC – National Security Concept (Latvia; Lithuania)
ODIHR – Office for Democratic Institutions and Human Rights (OSCE)
OECD – Organisation for Economic Co-operation and Development
OSCE – Organisation for Security and Co-operation in Europe
PfP – Partnership for Peace
PHARE – Poland and Hungary: Aid for the Restructuring of Economies (EU)
PIOS – State Inspectorate of Environmental Protection
PSE – producer's subsidy equivalent
RIIA – Regional Inward Investment Agency
SACEUR – Supreme Allied Commander Europe (NATO)
SACLANT – Supreme Allied Commander Atlantic (NATO)
SD – sustainable development
SEPA – Swedish Environmental Protection Agency
SFOR – Stabilisation Force (NATO)
SME – small and medium-sized enterprise
START – Strategic Arms Limitation Talks
TACIS – Technical Assistance to the Commonwealth of Independent States (EU)
TENS – Trans-European Networks
TLE – treaty-limited equipment (military)
TNC – transnational corporation
TPES – total primary energy supply
UK – United Kingdom
UN – United Nations
UNHCR – United Nations High Commissioner on Refugees
UNPO – Unrepresented Nations and Peoples Organisation
UR – Uruguay Round
USA – United States of America
USSR – Union of Socialist Soviet Republics
VASAB – Vision and Strategies around the Baltic Sea
WEU – Western European Union
WTO – World Trade Organisation (also Warsaw Treaty Organisation)

List of Figures

1.1 The economic geography of the NEBI area ... 9
1.2 The geopolitical position of the NEBI area ... 10
1.3 Russia's regional associations ... 17
1.4 Conceivable interactionist regimes ... 20
4.1 The size of the economy in terms of GDP, 1995 ... 56
4.2 GDP per capita, 1995 ... 57
4.3 GDP annual growth, 1980-93 ... 58
4.4 GDP per capita, 1993 and 1995 ... 58
4.5 The structure of the economy in terms of contributions to GDP by sectors, 1993 ... 59
4.6 Trade dependency, 1992 (for Latvia and Lithuania, 1993) and 1995 60
4.7 Export destinations from/to Baltic Sea countries, 1995 ... 61
4.8 Import sources to/from Baltic countries, 1995 ... 62
4.9 Strong and weak links in Baltic region trade ... 63
4.10 Frequencies of direct air connections, January 1994 ... 67
4.11 Frequencies of direct air connections, February 1996 ... 68
5.1 Main trade links, 2010 ... 79
5.2 Main trade links, 2010 ... 80
7.1 Industrial output, total capital investments and explicit environmental protection investments in the Murmansk region ... 100
7.2 Matrix of potential investment alternatives and their consequences ... 108
10.1 Share of enterprises of different size in total employment ... 149
10.2 Dominant markets of Estonian large privatised enterprises ... 153
11.1 The analytical process behind a Baltic Agenda 21 ... 167
11.2 Comprehensive integrated map of 'Vision for the Baltic Sea Region 2010' ... 170
11.3 Pilot projects and common actions of VASAB 2010 ... 173
12.1 The flow model of transboundary environmental risks ... 192
12.2a The single-source transboundary model ... 193
12.2b The multi-source transboundary model ... 193
13.1 The dynamics of GDP in Estonia, Sweden and Finland, 1990-96 203
13.2 Distribution of Estonian imports and exports, 1995 ... 203
13.3 Tourists received in Estonia from Finland, Sweden and the CIS . 204
13.4 Goods traffic on Estonian railways, 1980-96 ... 205
13.5 Transit cargo flows via the eastern shores of the Baltic Sea ... 207
13.6 International transport corridors and Estonia's main population centres ... 208
13.7 Existing and coming transport corridors in the Baltic states ... 214
15.1 Poland: fees charged by environmental funds, 1989-94 ... 240

15.2 Poland: investments in environmental protection, 1990-94 240
15.3 Poland's SO_2 emissions, 1980-94 242
16.1 Berlin and Brandenburg, population 1990-96 252
16.2 Berlin's built-up area and major transport projects 259
17.1 Kaliningrad district and Russian communication links 277
17.2 Communication links between Kaliningrad and Poland 278
20.1 Interreg II C in Northern Europe 317
22.1 The Barents region 338
24.1 The concept of common security 392
24.2 Generation and management of co-operative security for the Baltic Sea region 393
24.3 Constitution and transformation of the security space of the Baltic Sea region 395
25.1 NATO's new command structure 412
25.2 Major headquarters and divisions stationed in Joint Subregional Command (JSRC) Northeast's area of geographical focus 418

List of Tables

4.1 Exports to Baltic region countries, 1992 (or 1993 if not available) 64
4.2 Exports to Baltic region countries, 1995 64
4.3 Indicators of integration in Baltic region trade, 1995 65
4.4 Outbound contact opportunities, 1976, 1988 and 1992 66
4.5 Passenger flows by sea between Sweden and the Baltic Sea countries, 1970, 1980, 1990 and 1995 69
5.1 Foreign trade projections in the Baltic Sea area, optimistic scenario 77
5.2 Scenario comparisons 78
5.3 Significance and development of actual Baltic Sea trade 81
5.4 Sector trade shares, 2010, optimistic scenario 81
6.1 The significance of obstacles arising from the peculiarities of East-West trade during the Cold War 88
6.2 The appearance of problems in different forms of FDI 92
6.3 Foreign direct investment flows into emerging market economies in the Baltic Sea region 94
6.4 The investment ratings of emerging economies in the Baltic Sea region 95
7.1 Examples of pressure on the environment by economic activity in the Murmansk region 101
7.2 The structure of capital investment in the Murmansk region by source of financing 102
7.3 The structure of capital investment in the Murmansk region and Russia by type of ownership 103
7.4 Sectoral distribution of capital investment in the Murmansk region 103
7.5 Capital investment aimed at environmental protection in the Murmansk region 105
7.6 Annual volume of capital investment compared with potential sources of financing in the Murmansk region 106
8.1 Intra-Nordic migration balances between 1964 and 1988 in absolute numbers of migrants and percentages of total population 116
8.2 Potential receiving countries of the Baltic Sea area in terms of volume of labour market in the mid-1990s 120
8.3 Potential sending countries of the Baltic Sea area in terms of volume of labour market in the mid-1990s 121
8.4 Considerations about working abroad by age group in Visegrad and Baltic Sea areas 123
8.5 Some factors perceived as barriers to migration in Visegrad and Baltic Sea areas 123

8.6 Expectations of economic difficulties caused by three months' unemployment 124
8.7 Most wanted destination countries in Tallinn and St Petersburg . 126
8.8 Least wanted destination countries in Tallinn and St Petersburg . 126
9.1 The importance of agriculture 134
9.2 Agriculture, arable land, yields and level of support 135
10.1 Main partners in Estonian foreign trade 151
10.2 Share of foreign investments in Estonian enterprises, by country 152
13.1 Estonia's foreign trade balance, 1993-96 204
13.2 Estonian exports and imports by means of transport 205
14.1 Hot spots in Sweden 224
15.1 Emissions of SO_2 in selected European countries, 1991 238
16.1 Employment in Berlin, 1991-95 255
16.2 Building activity in Berlin, the suburban fringe and the rest of Brandenburg 262
17.1 Production of selected foodstuffs, 1990-95 270
17.2 Agricultural ownership structure in the Kaliningrad district 271
17.3 Employment in Kaliningrad, 1980-94 271
17.4 Turnover in foreign trade, 1992-95 274
17.5 Travellers between Elblag province in Poland and the Kaliningrad district 276
19.1 The territorial organisation of the Nordic countries 301
31.1 German major naval forces after 2005 509
31.2 Activities by the German Navy, annual programme for 1996 512
31.3 German-Baltic Sea bilateral security co-operation, 1995 513
31.4 Planned programme of military activities, 1997 515
31.5 Planned programme of military co-operation and contacts, 1997 516
32.1 The percentage of titular/native population in the Baltic states .. 528
32.2 Tensions in interethnic relations between Estonians and Russians 533

Index*

Åland Islands 4, 11, 14f, 302, 304, 438, 537
Aalborg Charter. *See* Charter of European Cities and Towns Towards Sustainability
ABB 118
Abrene 441f
non-recognition of annexation of 442
absolutist empires 13
acid rain (precipitation). *See* pollution
Action Programme for Baltic Sea States Co-operation. *See* Council of the Baltic Sea States
additionality. *See* European Union, Structural Funds
adjacent areas/regions. *See* Norden
Administrative Regional Committee 342
Advisory Committee of Municipal and Regional Institutions in EU Member Countries 291
Ærø 491, 515
affirmative action 540
Afghanistan 530
Africa 10, 453
'Agenda 21', 164, 253, 265; in Baltic Sea Region 163f, 166-9, 172, 179 265
'Agenda 2000', 8
agrarian structure 131f, 136, 140
Agreement on Bilateral Co-operation in the Military Domain 493
Agreement on Co-operation between the North-eastern Provinces of the Republic of Poland and the Kaliningrad District of the Russian Federation 493
Agreement on Cross-Border Regional Co-operation between Denmark, Finland, Norway and Sweden 287, 289
Agricultural Guarantee and Guidance Fund (EAGGF). *See* European Union, Structural Funds
agriculture 42, 52, 59, 80, 82, 97, 102, 131-44 *passim*, 145, 151, 155f, 170, 189, 218, 223, 271, 312, 327, 325
collective 131f, 135f, 145; exports 131; policy 134, 138, 143; pollution. *See* pollution; production 132, 138; productivity 131; sustainable 186
agro-industry 270
air
cargo 204; carriage 210; connections 67-9; pollution. *See* pollution; traffic 66; transportation 206; quality 237f, 245, 255
airports 69, 206, 257
Albania 432
Albright, Madeleine 431
Algesiras, Port of 329
Alpine
Arc 311; region 324
aménagement du territoire 314
America 415, 486, 507
Andalusia 329
Anderson, Benedict 449
Archer, Clive 23
Archipelago Co-operation 304
Arctic 363, 337, 379, 383
Circle 338, 344; ecosystems 100; environment 107; region 376; Sea 443
Arkhangelsk 17, 212, 338-40, 344, 376, 380, 551
ARKO Committee 304
armaments
conventional 424; naval 479
Armenia 429
arms
control 370, 391f, 394, 424, 452, 468, 470, 477-9, 481; control, regional 478; race 451; transfers 472
asecurity 396
Asia 310, 530
Asia-Pacific region 468
Assembly of European Regions (AER) 291
assimilation 538, 545
Assistance in Case of a Nuclear Accident or Radiological Emergency 189
Association Agreements 139, 314, 432
between Estonia and the EU 151
Association of European Border Regions (AEBR) 286f, 290-2
Experts' Advisory Board 291; Observatory for Cross-Border Co-operation (LACE) 291
Association of South-East Asian Nations (ASEAN) 310
Astrakhan 428

* The index does not cover notes, figures and tables. Non-English characters are treated as follows: Danish, Norwegian and Swedish å/Å as *aa*; Danish and Norwegian æ/Æ and ø/Ø as *ae* and *oe*, respectively; Estonian, Finnish, German and Swedish ä/Ä and ö/Ö as *a* and *o*, respectively; Estonian, Finnish and German ü/Ü as *u*.

asylum, asylum seekers 377, 530f, 543f, 547f
Atlantic
Arc 311, 324; Partnership Council 408, 487
Austria 14, 141, 287, 306, 323, 326
autarchy 12, 19, 41
autonomous territories 11
Azerbaijan 429

Balkan, Balkan states 326, 329, 432, 437
Balkanisation 20
Balladur Plan 386, 416, 476
Baltic
Action Plan 386, 416; Agenda 21. *See* Agenda 21; Air Surveillance Network (BALTNET) 384, 419; (land and sea) approaches 412, 510; Assembly 377, 429, 471; basin 334; Battalion (BALTBAT) 23, 383f, 419, 433, 459, 513; Belt of Green Corridors 177; charter 416; Conference 299; co-operation 96, 491, 511; Co-operation Committee 377; Coordination Committee (BCC) 316; Council 458, 460; Council of Ministers 377; defence co-operation 459; doctrine, Russian 468, 470, 481; environmental co-operation 219; Fleet, Russian 269, 466, 470f, 492f; Fleet, Soviet Fleet 267, 466; integration, Sweden's five part strategy for 433; Marinas 178; Military District, Russian 470; Military District, Soviet 426; naval squadron (BALTRON) 23, 383f, 419, 513; police forces 526; Prime Ministers' meeting at Visby (May 1996) 163f, 172, 188, 222, 388f, 470, 475, 481, 490; regional co-operation 229; regional trade 60, 65, 87; regions 57, 66; Round Table (BRT) 370, 390, 476, 545; Table (of the Pact of Stability) 488, 497; trade deficits 60; troops deployed with Nordic peacekeeping units 383
Baltic Rim 23, 33, 35, 37, 39f, 42f, 55, 68f, 78, 363, 465, 469
countries 33, 382; military co-operation around 381, 385
Baltic Sea 4, 70, 167, 188f, 191, 217, 220-3, 383, 408, 417f, 420, 443, 487f, 491, 508-10, 513, 551
Conference in Ronneby (1990) 221f; Convention 476; drainage area 169; Joint Comprehensive Environmental Action Programme (JCP) 217, 221-3, 225, 229, 476; pollution 217; Regional Initiative 379
Baltic Sea region 59
Interreg II C Operational Programme (BSR/OP) 309, 316f
Baltic Sea states (countries, also littoral) 188, 472, 474f, 477, 505, 509, 512, 516-8
Sub-regional Conference 372; Subregional Co-operation (BSSSC) 22
Baltic states (countries, republics, i.e. Estonia, Latvia and Lithuania) 7f, 15, 23f, 55, 57, 59f, 63, 69, 73, 75-7, 79f, 91, 127, 131-6, 140f, 143, 150f, 155, 200, 202f, 206f, 209-15, 241, 246f, 268f, 273, 279, 289, 293, 305, 369, 374, 376- 88, 390f, 394-7, 408f, 415f, 418f, 423, 425-7, 432-4, 438, 440, 442, 445, 449f, 452-9, 461, 466f, 469-79, 481, 487, 489f, 497f, 505f, 511-7, 521, 524, 526-8, 530-2, 535, 537, 539, 541, 544f, 551-5, 557
accession to EU 380, 521; annexation of 425; application for NATO membership 470; foreign attempts to gain hegemony over 438; inflation 76, 133; military assistance to 384, 387; military co-operation with Nordic countries 477; re-occupation by Russia 432; regaining independence 426, 437; relations with Russia 369, 456; sovereignty assistance for 460; status of ethnic Russians in 369; withdrawal of Russian troops from 390, 426f, 440, 455f, 458, 468, 472, 490, 529. *See also* Estonia, Latvia, Lithuania, Russia
Baltic-Scandinavian region 455
Baltiysk 269, 471
Bank of Estonia 204
Bank of Finland 96
Bank of Lithuania 51f
banking crisis 51, 95
system 39
bankruptcies 38, 40, 91, 133
banks 50-2, 149, 151, 209
commercial 39
Barents
area 12, 19, 376, 378-80, 454; co-operation 20; Euro-Arctic Council (BEAC) 169, 302, 342, 372, 476; Euro-Arctic Region (BEAR) 337-47 *passim*, 349-59 *passim*; indigenous peoples of 372; initiative 19; Interreg 345; Programme (1994-95) 343; region 8f, 19, 293, 338-47 *passim*, 349-59 *passim*, 363; Regional Council 342-4
Barents Sea 4, 104
Bastrup-Birk, Henriette 312
Belarus 169, 178, 212, 246, 267, 278f, 311, 318, 431, 438f, 477, 485, 493, 495
Belchatow 238, 245
Belgium 238, 287, 298, 415, 507
Benelux 79
Berlin 176, 209-13, 251-65 *passim*, 278
East 253f, 256, 258, 260f; meeting of foreign ministers (June 1996) 411; Wall 3, 18, 261f; West 251-65 *passim*

Berliner Landesarbeitsgemeinschaft Umwelt und Entwicklung (BLUE 21) 253, 257
Best Available Technology (BAT) 218
Best Environmental Practice (BEP) 218
bi- and trilateralism 413
biodiversity 143, 167, 189
biofuels, biomass 248
biotechnology 91
bipolarity 22, 409, 485, 503
Black Sea 379
Black Triangle 195f
black market 525
blue banana 323
Bodø 340
Bohuslän 304
Bonn 255, 504, 513
border(s)
  and customs controls 211, 377, 508, 544; crossing 278, 339; disputes over 390, 437-46 *passim*, 480; guards 470; incidents 439f; inviolability of 439, 444; maritime 442-5; protection 513; regions 285-95 *passim*; restrictions 135
Borken 287
Bornholm 304
  Basin 224
Borussii concept 279
Bosnia 383, 432, 452, 491f, 543f
  refugees from 543f
Bothnian Bay 224
Brandenburg 15, 251, 253f, 257, 260, 262
Bratislava 122
Brazauskas, Algirdas 496f
Brest 176
Brezhnev, Leonid 432
  Doctrine 408
Britain. *See* United Kingdom
Bröcker, Johannes 74
brown coal (lignite) 238, 245, 255f, 270
Brundtland Commission 220
Brussels 300, 305, 504f
  Treaty of 507
Buch 262
Budapest, meeting (1994) 364
Bulgaria 121, 302
Bundeswehr concept 508
bureaucracy 91, 211
  bureaucratic interests 406; politics 406, 419f
business
  climate (environment) 96, 147; culture 353f, 358; ethics 93, 354; small, private 145, transnational 349f, 358
Butkevicius, Audrius 439
Calabria 329
Canada 11, 241
capital
  costs 100; cultural 124; domestic 153; flight 104; flows 115; foreign 152, 154, 272f; goods 41; human 70, 176; investment 273; markets 39; private 153; social 306; stock 36, 108f; transfer 42
capitalism/capitalist system 13, 37, 89
carrying capacity 164f
cartels 39f
Caucasus 427
Central America 453
Central and Eastern Europe (CEE) 8, 200, 210, 233-6, 267f, 287f, 291-3, 298, 313, 323, 326, 332, 334-48 *passim*, 413, 498, 503, 505, 515, 517f
  countries 133, 139-43, 187f, 196f, 234, 313, 454, 503, 505
Central Europe 8, 371, 394, 417, 424f, 427, 431f, 505, 516
Central European Free Trade Agreement (CEFTA) 135
Central European Initiative 489, 497
Central European Region 510
Central Region. *See* North Atlantic Treaty Organisation
Central Zone. *See* Treaty on Conventional Forces in Europe
central banks 40f
centrally planned (regulated) economies (CPEs) 36, 55, 73, 233-48 *passim*
centre-periphery
  cleavages 297; concept of 323
Charter of European Border Regions 291
Charter of European Cities and Towns Towards Sustainability 253
Chechnya 427, 432f, 490
chemicals 328
  industry 148
Chernobyl 194f
Chernomyrdin, Viktor 470, 475, 481
China 87, 133, 353, 477
Christian-Democratic Union (CDU) 253, 261, 507
Cimoszewicz, Wlodzimierz 490
cities (towns) 66, 70, 332f
  medium and small 175; networks of 175; ports 202, 213, 329, 468; regions 126
citizenship 473, 528f, 531-4, 538
  discrimination against Russian speakers 426; dual 539; laws 389, 439, 472; legislation on in Estonia and Latvia 457; policies 529, 531; requirements 531f;

civic traditions 306
civil society 3, 12, 15f, 20, 47, 50, 163, 368, 370, 377, 379, 524, 540, 542
climate
warming 191; conditions 101
Clinton, William 433
Administration 428
co-operatives 136, 145f, 153
coal 233-7, 242-4, 256, 273
mines 243
Coalition Clean Baltic 225
coastal zones 171, 174, 177, 318
CoCom 188
cohesion 70, 178, 330, 332
economic 15, 57, 292, 310, 312f; social 314, 545
Cold War 12, 88, 119, 123f, 187f, 197, 220, 227, 267, 298f, 337, 340, 364, 368, 370f, 373, 375f, 391, 395f, 405-10, 420, 423f, 427, 432, 437f, 445, 449-54, 459, 465f, 476, 485, 494, 497, 503
cold spots 224
collectives 146
farms 132; workers' 50
collectivisation 131
Cologne 255
COMECON. *See* Council for Mutual Economic Assistance
Commissioner on Democratic Institutions and Human Rights. *See* Council of the Baltic Sea States
Committee for Spatial Development (CSD) 177, 310, 315
Principles for a European Spatial Policy 310
Committee for Spatial Development in the BSR (CSD/BSR) 169, 171, 177
Committee of Senior Officials for Nordic Regional Policy (NERP) 289f
Committee of the Regions (COR). *See* European Union
common agricultural policy (CAP). *See* European Union
Common Recommendations for Spatial Planning of the Coastal Zone in the Baltic Sea Region 164, 177
Commonwealth of Independent States (CIS) 150, 154, 174, 431, 467f, 474, 477f, 480f, 530
communications 82, 84, 148, 152, 318
infrastructure 70, 339
communism 13, 84
system 47; Manifesto 13; countries 432; governments 485; period 135
Community Initiatives. *See* European Union, Structural Funds
Community Support Frameworks (CSF). *See* European Union, Structural Funds
comparative advantage 41, 102, 110,
competition 39, 70
control 39; laws 40; policy 40, 326; rules 34; theory 39
competitive advantage 351
competitiveness 40, 92, 136
Conference of the Baltic Ministers of Transport 175
Conference of the Border Control Authorities 382
Conference on Security and Co-operation in Europe (CSCE)
Charter for a New Europe 548; Council 538; Forum for Security Co-operation 487
confidence- and security-building measures (CSBMs) 370, 374f, 381, 398, 424, 479, 481, 487f, 491
confidence- and security-enhancing measures (CSEMs) 488f, 498, 491
confidence-building 23, 470, 491,
conflict
behaviour 541; management 374, 394, 474, 480; prevention 369, 374f, 388-90, 394, 398
Consultative Council of Nationalities 542
Continental Diagonal 311
contractual freedom 38
conurbations 325
Convention on Long Range Transboundary Air Pollution (LRTAP) 196, 241
Convention on Refugees (1951) 530f, 544
Convention on the Protection of the Marine Environment of the Baltic Sea Area 217
Conventions on Early Notification of Nuclear Accident 189
convergence, European 115
Copenhagen 65, 67, 176, 210, 292, 505, 528
criteria. *See* European Union; European Council meeting (June 1993) 528
Corfu 310
corporativism/corporatism 226, 228f
corridors
to Kaliningrad 432, 438, 494-6, 498; transport 199-215 *passim*
corruption 24, 48, 51, 352, 522, 525f
Council for Mutual Economic Assistance (CMEA, also COMECON) 41, 55, 57, 76, 132f, 485, 489
Council of Europe (COE) 170, 286f, 289, 291, 367, 369, 374f, 389f, 394, 398, 452, 456, 527, 539-41, 545, 547
Advisory Assembly 289, 291; Conference of Ministers of Regional Development 287;

Framework Convention for Cross-Border Co-operation 289; Parliamentary Assembly 286f
Council of European Regions 291
Council of the Baltic Sea States (CBSS) 11, 18-20, 23, 163, 169f, 188, 199, 289, 311, 372-5, 379, 382, 388f, 391, 394, 398, 458, 475f, 488-90, 497f, 505f, 538, 547
Action Programme for Baltic Sea States Co-operation 458; Commissioner on Democratic Institutions and Human Rights 388, 537, 546f; economic working group 379
country risk rating 96
Covenant on Civil and Political Rights 538
credit 136, 147
and finance institutions 511; policy 52, 271
CREDO. *See* European Union
crime 24, 48, 51, 93, 95, 272, 352, 382, 445, 521-7, 535
code 527; economic 523f; fight against 506; international (transnational) 373, 522; organised 389, 450, 467, 470, 475, 481, 488, 490, 525
crisis management 374f, 381, 383, 385, 387, 452, 475
Croatia 432
cross-border co-operation 21, 25, 175, 275, 285-95 *passim*, 313, 340, 344-7, 379f, 445
Barents 337-47 *passim*; integration 12, 22; Nordic 340; programmes 70, 345; regional 3, 19, 22f, 25, 288, 304; regions 290, 344. *See* also transborder co-operation
culture/cultural 126f
and political integration 533; capital 124; co-operation 490; contacts 445; differences 94, 110, 554; distance factors 75; friction 359; heritage 176f; identity 176; integration 533; isolation 534f; landscape 143; obstacles 116; political 197; similarities 116; system 165
currency
convertibility 42; reforms 554
customs 53, 339, 355
procedures 352; restrictions 199
Czech Republic 191, 195f, 326, 427, 432, 485, 493, 513
Czechoslovakia 234f, 268, 485
Czerniachovsk 271

Danish
federacy 11; Straits 504
Danish-German-Polish trilateral partnership 515
Dayton Agreement 432, 544
DDT 222
de-industrialisation 254, 257
death penalty 528
decentralisation 90, 201, 407
defence
forces, reconstruction of 392; forward. *See* United States of America; industries, conversion of. *See* Russia, military conversion; total 451f
deficit spending 41
demilitarisation 280, 455, 471
democracy 47, 50, 91
process 168, 540; system 35
Denmark 4, 6, 11, 19, 57, 59f, 65, 69, 73, 76-8, 80, 91, 115, 120, 126, 148, 152, 169, 188, 195, 210, 218f, 299-304, 306, 309, 316, 323, 341, 372, 381-4, 386, 407-9, 412f, 415-7, 419, 423, 432, 453f, 459, 461, 468f, 472, 474, 478, 480, 486, 489, 491f, 498, 506-8, 510f, 513, 515, 538, 543f, 547, 551
armed forces 511; biotechnology 91; Commission on Security and Disarmament 453; food industry 91; military co-operation with Baltic States 384, 415; military co-operation with Germany and Poland 491; pharmaceutical industry 91; Unity of the Realm 11
dependency 5, 327
deregulation 39
desecuritisation 396, 492, 494
Dessau 254
détente 218, 365
Deutsch, Karl 460
Development Framework of the Community Territory. *See* European Union, Structural Funds
development
endogenous 326f, 331; perverse 12; regional 11-3, 99, 105, 110, 209, 268, 318, 343f, 346, 379; spatial, European 309. *See also* European Union, European Spatial Development Perspective; strategy 70, 328, 358; sustainable (SD) 99, 104, 108-10, 163, 165, 220, 310, 318
dictatorship 12
diplomacy, preventive 390, 538, 541
Directorates General (DG) I , IA, XVI. *See* European Union
disarmament 452, 455, 470
discrimination 525
disintegrationist factors 12, 20
dispute resolution 394
District Ownership Fund. *See* Kaliningrad
district heating 248

division of powers 35
Dobronski, Adam 496
Dönitz, Karl 16
double enlargement dilemma 505
Drang nach Osten 467
Drawsko 491
Dresden 261
Duma. *See* Russia
Dunning, John H. 349
Düsseldorf 255

early warning 388f, 394, 398
East Asia 10
East Bothnia 305
East Prussia 438, 492
East-West confrontation 506
Eastern Bloc 3, 252
Eastern Europe 36, 324, 326f, 329, 334f, 343, 408, 452, 505f, 517
  macroeconomic stabilisation of 74
Eastern Germany. *See* German Democratic Republic and Germany
Eckernförde 509
eco-tourism 177
Ecocycle Bill. *See* Sweden
ecological
  building 258, 263f; crisis 14; sustainability 99; systems 165
Economic and Monetary Union (EMU). *See* European Union
economic
  cohesion 15, 57, 292, 310, 312f; crisis 51; decline 101; growth 57, 70, 83, 117; imbalances 59; integration 10, 55-70 *passim*, 73, 85; rationalisation 101; reform 52, 272; transformation 74, 553; zones 443
economies
  circular 165; post-industrial 56; of scale 149; transitional 33
Edinburgh 311
  meeting (December 1992) 507
EIM International 155
Elbe 510
Elblag 274, 278, 280
electrified railways (S-Bahn) 258
Ellemann-Jensen, Uffe 18
emigrants 117
emigration 553
EMOR Ltd 155
employment 94, 110, 134, 136, 145, 148f
  distribution of 556; in agriculture 134
energy 39, 132f, 148, 189, 206, 318, 333, 339
  alternative 202; consumption 233, 235, 256; efficiency 264; networks 313; nuclear 104, 194, 227, 233; production 227, 234; reserves 9; solar 263; supply 163, 235. *See also* Poland, energy use and policy
Engels, Friedrich 13
Engholm, Björn 16, 18, 460
enterprises
  ownership of 146; small 145f, 206; small and medium-sized (SMEs) 146, 148f, 155f, 246, 294, 312, 325, 327, 329, 350, 358; state-owned 39f, 93, 102, 246. *See also* firms
entrepreneurship 145-58 *passim*
entropy or minimum information indicators 63f
environment 23, 91, 93, 107-9, 143, 163-265 *passim*
  awareness 143, 218; challenges 3; concerns 143; damage 100; degradation 14, 109; discourse 227; factors 93; harmonisation of policies 197; hazards (issues, problems, risks) 100, 368, 467; load 167; marine 219f, 222; movement 228; natural 164; non-governmental organisations (ENGOs) 225, 229f; policy 190, 197, 244f, 289; policy, Polish 233-48 *passim*; policy, Swedish 217-30 *passim*; pressures 167; protection 93, 100f, 104, 109, 143, 217, 234, 236, 238-41, 245, 389, 458, 506, 468; protection funds 239, 245; protection investments 101; rehabilitation 179; rural 142; standards 432; taxes 238f, 244; values 454. *See also* pollution
Essen 255
Estonia 4, 6-8, 11f, 15, 22, 25, 33, 37, 40-2, 47-9, 60, 65, 75f, 87f, 90, 95-7, 131, 133-6, 139f, 145-58 *passim*, 169, 178, 188, 202-15, 225, 235, 246-8, 269, 276f, 314, 318, 369, 372, 374, 376, 378, 380, 382-4, 389f, 415, 419, 423, 429, 434, 439-45, 455-7, 473-5, 480, 490f, 497f, 508, 513f, 521-4, 526-34, 538-42, 544-6, 548, 551, 553f, 556
  Association Agreement with EU 151; citizenship, legislation on 457; co-operation with Finland 382; Commercial Code 175f; Commercial Register 157; corporate taxes 147; defence forces 382; disputes over local elections 542; economic centralisation 145; elections 146; Export Crediting Fund 147; Finnish investments in 7; food production 148; foreign economic ties 150; forms of enterprise ownership 145; fuel prices 150; Fund for Crediting Agriculture and Rural Life 147; Fund for Crediting Small Enterprises 147; harbours 206; industry 145-58 *passim*; infrastructure 148, 156; Innovation Fund 147; Institute of Economics 155;

language 533f; language laws 542; Law on Entrepreneurship 146; Law on Taxes 147; monetary reform 151; Navy 514; OSCE mission to 389; police 522, 527; Privatisation Agency 37, 147; regions 211; Russian troop withdrawal from 390, 469, 473; Russian-speaking population of 527, 533; standard of living 15; status of non-citizens 541
ethnic
conflicts (disputes, tensions) 20, 384, 532; Germans 121, 539; groups 532, 534; identity 532; minorities 532; relations 527, 531; Russians 439, 441, 529, 533
ethno-nationalism 446
EU. *See* European Union
EU enlargement. *See* European Union
Eurasianists 467
Euro-Atlantic Partnership Council (EAPC) 370, 381, 385-8, 394, 398
Eurocorps 507
EuroFaculty 388
'Europe 2000' 288, 293, 309-11
'Europe 2000+' 288, 293, 310, 333
Europe Agreements. *See* European Union
European Academy for the Urban Environment 254
European Agricultural Guarantee and Guidance Fund (EAGGF). *See* European Union, Structural Funds
European Bank for Reconstruction and Development (EBRD) 52, 194, 210
European Charter of Border and Cross-Border Regions 291
European Charter on Regional Development (Charter of Torremolinos) 287, 291
European Commission. *See* European Union
European Community (EC) 75, 287f, 291, 302, 304, 342, 553
European Convention on the Participation of Foreigners in Public Life at Local Level 547
European Council. *See* European Union
European Economic Area (Space) (EEA) 11, 19, 33, 75, 87, 118, 297, 367, 376
European Economic Community (EEC) 115, 372
European Framework Conference for the Improvement of Cross-Border Co-operation between Regional and Municipal Authorities (Madrid Charter) 287, 291
European Free Trade Association (EFTA) 11, 33, 75
European integration 16, 33, 199, 267f, 286f, 291f, 295, 297, 299, 302, 304, 313, 323-35 *passim*, 399, 410, 486, 503-5, 507, 543
European Parliament (EP). *See* European Union
European Regional Development Fund (ERDF). *See* European Union, Structural Funds
European Security and Defence Identity (ESDI) 413, 474
European Security Council (ESC) 474
European Social Fund (ESF). *See* European Union, Structural Funds
European Spatial Development Perspective (ESDP). *See* European Union
European Stability Pact (March 1995) 458
European Union (EU) 8, 10, 11, 15, 16, 18-23, 33, 34, 43, 49, 70, 77, 87, 115, 118-21, 135, 138f, 141, 143, 148, 151, 158, 169f, 174, 178-80, 187, 195-7, 199-201, 203, 208-10, 214, 235, 279f, 286, 288, 291f, 294, 297-300, 302, 304, 309f, 313-7, 319, 323f, 326, 328f, 331-3, 338, 344-7, 366-8, 372, 374-80, 386-91, 394, 396f, 398f, 409, 415, 432-4, 444f, 452f, 455f, 460, 466f, 476f, 480f, 486, 488f, 494, 497f, 503-5, 507, 513, 517, 522, 526f, 534f, 539, 543-6
Association Agreement with Estonia 151; Association Agreements 139, 314, 432; Baltic Sea policy 380; Baltic Sea Region Initiative 379, 389; cohesion policy 25; Committee of the Regions (COR) 14, 16, 288, 298f, 306, 311; common agricultural policy (CAP) 8, 131-44 *passim*; common foreign and security policy (CFSP) 369, 374, 378, 380, 387, 452, 504, 507; Copenhagen criteria 528; core and periphery 326; CREDO 288; Economic and Monetary Union (EMU) 8, 323, 331, 507; enlargement of 8, 22, 33, 43, 70, 73, 139-43, 172, 187, 291, 332, 367f, 373, 375f, 380, 387f, 397f, 444f, 505, 507, 544; Europe Agreements 33, 379f; European Council 313, 388; European Council meeting in Copenhagen (June 1993) 528; European Parliament (EP) 174, 279f, 287f, 444; European Spatial Development Perspective (ESDP) 169, 310-2, 314f; integration 543; Intergovernmental Conference (IGC) 380, 397; Maastricht Treaty 16, 319, 507, 552; MacSharry reform 137; northern dimension of 378; Northern policy 341; Partnership and Co-operation Agreement with Russia 379; Poland and Hungary: Aid for the Restructuring of Economies (PHARE) 22, 174, 288, 294, 313, 316f, 335, 380; pre-accession programmes 367, 369, 379f, 394, 399; regional policy 314, 325, 330-4; relations with Russia 397; Single European Act

312; single (internal) market 33, 41, 43, 70, 291, 323, 331, 379; structural policies 25, 302; Technical Assistance to the Commonwealth of Independent States (TACIS) 22, 174, 288, 294, 317, 380; widening and deepening 507

Commission 25, 34, 178, 188, 287f, 291f, 309, 313-5, 318, 332, 341, 346, 388, 391, 547
Directorates General (DG) I 316; IA 316; XVI 306, 309, 311-3, 315f

Structural Funds 14, 137f, 140, 174, 228, 300, 303, 306, 310, 312-4, 318, 331, 333
additionality (co-financing) 331, 334; Community Initiatives 303, 311, 313, 332; Community Support Frameworks (CSF) 313, 332-4; Development Framework of the Community Territory 333; European Agricultural Guarantee and Guidance Fund (EAGGF) 138, 310, 312f; European Regional Development Fund (ERDF) 288, 310-3, 317 (ERDF Regulations, Article 10, 288, 333); European Social Fund (ESF) 310, 312f; Interreg 22f, 288, 293, 300,304, 306, 313, 347, 380; Interreg Barents 344-6; Interreg I 288, 291; Interreg II 288, 291f, 313, 344-7; Interreg II A 292, 294, 313; Interreg II B 313; Interreg II C 19, 172, 174, 179, 288, 293, 309-19 *passim*; Interreg Karelia (Karelen) 345; Interreg Kvarken and Mittnorden 345; Interreg North Calotte (Nordkalotten) 344; Objective 1, 137, 313, 325-7, 332f; Objective 2, 332; Objectives 5a and 5b 137; Objective 6, 137; REGEN 313
ex-Yugoslavia 23, 410, 414
exchange rates 42, 51, 77, 141, 150
exports, subsidisation of 138f
expropriation 36

farms
family 136; collective 132; co-operative 133; private 145f, size of 135; state 52, 131f. *See also* kolkhozes and sovkhozes
Faroe Islands 11, 302, 304
fascist rule 251
Federal Environmental Agency. *See* Germany
Federal Republic of Germany. *See* Germany
federalism 16, 298, 315
Federation of Trade Unions (Landsorganisationen). *See* Sweden
filter technology 256
financial and monetary policy regimes 117
financial institutions 329
Finland 4-7, 11, 14f, 18f, 23, 33, 60, 69, 76f, 87, 91, 96, 115-8, 120, 132, 141, 151, 154, 169, 188, 199f, 200, 202, 209-13, 215, 218f, 229, 288f, 299-306, 309, 311, 316, 323, 337f, 340-5, 347, 350, 369, 372, 378, 381f, 384, 386, 391, 395f, 408f, 415, 423, 431-4, 438, 443f, 450, 452-4, 459, 466-8, 472, 474, 477, 479f, 489, 492, 506f, 530, 538f, 551
border with Russia 380; co-operation with Estonia 382; farming 117; Finnish-Russian Peace Treaty (1920) (Tartu) 444; firms 351; Gulf of 382, 443, 470; investments in Estonia 7; military policy 415; Ministry of Labour 127; National Defence College 382; National Defence Institute 382; northern 339; urbanisation 117
Finnmark 338, 340
firms
Finnish 351; foreign, plunder of 354; limited liability 157; multinational 339; Norwegian 351, 358; publicly owned 327; Russian 351, 353; Swedish 351, 357; Western 352-5, 359; wholesale 149. *See also* enterprises
fiscal policy 40f
fishing
industry 270; stocks 104, incidents 442
flank zones 427, 430f
Flensburg 509
flexible geometry 323
food
consumption 132; industry 96, 152; production 148; subsidies 133
Fordism 115, 122, 325, 328
foreign relations index 156
foreign troops, deployment of 385
forest
death 195; industry 91f, 155
Fortress Europe 324, 544
Forum for Security Co-operation 431
Framework Convention on Minorities 539
France 15, 79, 273, 287, 298, 326, 383f, 386, 410f, 413, 416f, 429f, 486, 507;
co-operation with Germany 508, 511, 517; security interests 517
Frankfurt 175, 255, 261
fraud 354
free economic zones 272, 279, 445
free municipality experiments 303
free press 49f
freedom, individual 408
Frisians 539
front-line states 409

gas
natural 233-5, 248, 256; supply 148
Gdansk 95, 209, 494;
Bay (Gulf) of 280, 494
Gdynia 275, 494
gender equality 377
General Agreement on Tariffs and Trade (GATT) 137f, 199
Genoa 330
genocide 539
Genscher, Hans Dietrich 18, 426
geopolitics 467, 480
Georgia 429
German Democratic Republic (GDR) 3, 12, 124, 195f, 218f, 234, 237, 255-7, 409, 485, 517, 513f, 540, 553
German-French-Polish trilateral initiative 516
Germans, deportation of 267
Germany 6, 8, 11, 16, 19, 56f, 59f, 63, 65, 69f, 73, 76-80, 129f, 148, 169, 188, 191, 195, 201, 210, 212f, 251, 254, 257, 260f, 267f, 273f, 279f, 287, 309, 316, 334, 372, 381-4, 389, 395, 397, 411-3, 415-7, 419, 423, 427, 438, 458, 460, 466, 469, 472f, 478, 485f, 490f, 498, 503-18 *passim*, 538-40, 543f, 545, 547f, 551
armed forces 503, 508, 511; co-operation with Denmark and Poland 491; co-operation with France 508, 511, 517; Eastern 257, 427; expansionism of 504; Federal Environmental Agency 254; Federal Government 268; Federal Republic of (FRG) 251, 409, 540; German Institute of Urban Affairs 254; hegemonic position of 504; länder 16, 371, 543; Marineamt 509; military co-operation with Denmark and Poland 417, 511; naval bases 509; Navy, naval forces 471, 508-10, 512, 518; Nordpolitik 518; Ostpolitik, new 505, 518; Polish minority in 538; political elite 504, 513; regions 65; security interests 503; trade 7; unification 254f, 267, 425, 437, 485, 504, 508, 540; White Book (1994) 508; withdrawal of Russian troops from 268, 426, 510
Gioia Tauro, Port of 329
globalisation 118, 167
Gorbachev, Mikhail 423f, 426, 452, 454, 492
Gothenburg 224
Gothenburg-Landvetter 69
Grachev, Pavel 428, 472, 474, 478
Great Belt 84
Great Britain. *See* United Kingdom
Great European Corridors 175
Green party. *See* Sweden
greenfield investment. *See* investment
Greenland 11, 302, 304
Greenpeace 225
Gross Agricultural Production (GAO) 134
Gusiew-Goldap, border crossing 278
Gwardiejsk 271

Haab, Mare 455
Hækkerup, Hans 515
Hägglund, Gustav 444
Hague, the 310
Hamburg 4, 15, 84, 176, 209f, 255, 260, 551, 553
Hannover 260
Hanseatic
cities 330; concept 517; Corps 508; League 8, 371; new 18, 73; tradition 371
Hänsch, Klaus 444
Hansen, H.C. 451
Hansen, Lynn 425f
Haparanda 175
harbours 84, 206
Harju 156, 208
Havel, Vaclav 260
Hayek, Friedrich von 39
Heckscher-Ohlin-Samuelson equilibrium model of factor mobility 116
Hedrén, J. 227
Heidelberg 413
Heise, Volker 479
Hellersdorf 261
Helsinki 176, 203, 209f, 289, 382, 472
Commission (HELCOM) 164, 174, 179f, 188, 220, 222-5, 227, 476; Convention (1974) 218; Convention (April 1992) 221f; Watch 541; US- Russian summit 433
Heurlin, Bertel 460
High Commissioner on National Minorities. *See* Organisation for Security and Co-operation in Europe
Hiiumaa 156
Hitler, Adolf 13, 16
Hjorth, Ronnie 188
Högberg, Lars 193
Hohenschönhausen 261
Holland. *See* Netherlands
Holst, Johan Jørgen 341, 451
home rule 11, 302, 304
Homo Sovieticus 15
hot spots 14, 223f, 410, 476
housing 39, 91, 102f, 136, 125, 213, 261f
human rights 3, 34, 163, 365, 368, 408, 452, 475, 489, 528, 531, 534, 538
Hungary 234-6, 423, 426, 430, 432, 493, 513

Iberian peninsula 326
Iceland 11, 19, 188, 299, 301, 304, 341, 372, 458
Ida-Viru 156
identity 373, 378, 532
Baltic Sea 371; ethnic 532; European 517; national 465, 480; Nordic 460, 504; post-nationalist 437; region 343, 371; social and cultural 176; soft 324; state 445;
Ignalina, nuclear plant 194f
Iklody, Gabor 430
Ilves, Toomas-Hendrik 444
imagined communities 449, 460
immigrants 117, 529, 532, 534, 538
illegal 530; maltreatment of 545; Soviet-era 528. *See* also migration
Implementation Force (IFOR). *See* North Atlantic Treaty Organisation; Polish contingent of. *See* Poland
import
barriers 41; substitution 41; tariffs 134
income
support 143; transfers 141
indebtedness 95
India 353, 530
indigenous peoples/populations 342f, 529, 538f
in Barents region 372
infrastructure 3, 91,156, 163, 286f, 314, 333
bottlenecks 82; communications 70, 148; energy 148; institutional 136; rail and road 148; transport 325; social 100, 325
Innsbruck 286
Institute for Regional Research, University of Kiel 74
integration 12, 41, 47, 49, 70, 87, 315, 546
of aliens 377; Baltic Sea Region 87-97 *passim*; cultural 533; economic 10, 55-70 *passim*, 73, 85; European. *See* European integration; European and transatlantic 378; factors 12; measures of 63; Nordic 367, 369, 375, 377, 504; regional 11, 85; social 10, 264; strategy 70; transnational 9, 19; vertical and horizontal 328
intergovernmental co-operation 20
Intergovernmental Conference. *See* European Union
International Federation on Human Rights 541
International Monetary Fund (IMF) 41
International Organisation of Migration 541
Interreg. *See* European Union
interregional co-operation 329-30, 334f, 349, 358f
Inuit 11
Investitionsbank Schleswig-Holstein 318
investment 42, 52f, 84f, 96, 118, 353, 356f
foreign 3, 6, 70, 73, 147, 150, 152f, 272, 274, 326, 334; foreign direct (FDI) 6, 42, 85, 87-97 *passim*, 349; greenfield 93f; Murmansk region 99-111 *passim*; new forms of (NFIs) 349
invisible hand 38
Iraq 530
Ireland 313, 323
Iron Curtain 4, 73, 199, 285, 289, 339, 350
Isamaa party 440
islands of conflict 407, 410, 460
Israel 516, 539
Italy 287, 298, 326f, 329, 334
southern 313
Ivangorod 440

Jæger, Øjvind 23
Jäger-Roschko, Olaf 74
Jamison, A. 228
Jämtforum 303
Jämtland, County of 303
Jankuaskas, V. 194
Japan 151, 234, 274
Järvamaa 213
Jews 539
Jöhvi 209
Joint Comprehensive Environmental Action Programme (JCP). *See* Baltic Sea
Joint Consultative Group 425, 430
joint ventures (JVs) 88, 93-5, 110, 146, 150, 222, 356f
joint-stock companies 146, 157f
Jönköping 280
just-in-time 199, 210
Jutland 511
juvenile delinquency 523

Kaliningrad 7, 11, 17, 74, 76, 80, 96, 178, 209, 213, 267-80 *passim*, 369, 371, 376, 388, 418, 426, 432, 438f, 466, 470f, 473, 481, 485, 487f, 491-6, 506, 551, 553
condominium 279; corridor to 432, 438, 494-6, 498; District Ownership Fund 274; foreign trade 273; foreign-owned enterprises in 273; free economic zone 468; Military District 418, 431; Port of 277f; poverty 271; Round Table talks in 276; Special Defence Region (KOOR) 492f; Special District (KOR) 470f; Special Economic Zone 273; strategic importance of 268; transit to 278, 438, 473, 495f
Kallas, Siim 441

Kalmar 163, 188, 280, 379, 389, 490
  Action Programme 188; Fifth Ministerial Session in 490
Kaplinski, Jaan 441
Karelia 212, 293, 338, 344f, 443f
  Isthmus of 443; Republic of 7, 17, 376, 380, 444, 551
Karelian Alliance 444
Karlshamn 280
Karlskrona 169
Karow 262
Karup 412-4, 511
Katowice 196, 239
Kattegat 224
Kemi 175
Kiel 509f
Kirkenes 341
  conference of foreign ministers 337; Declaration 341
Kirov 17
Kirovsk, district of 107
Klaipeda 280
Koidula 209
Kola 104
kolkhozes 52, 271
Kolodko, Grzegorz 495
Komi, Republic of 17, 344
Königsberg 267, 438
  Euroregion 279
Kozyrev, Andrey 429, 469, 471
Krakow 239, 515
Krasnador Kray 428
Krastins, Andrejs 514
Kvarken 293
  Council 304
Kven-Finnish minority 538f
Kwasniewski, Aleksander 494f, 497

Lääne, County of 156
labour 39, 91, 110, 148
  cheap 511; costs 89; division of 8, 33, 41, 55, 74, 82, 84, 97, 119, 122, 175; division of, European 33; force 117, 119, 125, 146, 213; markets 3, 120, 122, 124, 292, 294; markets, Nordic 118; migrant (workers) 529, 543. *See also* migrants; mobility 115-27 *passim*; productivity 109, 131; protection 116; surplus 136
Lagow 490
Laholm Bight 224
land
  ownership 136; use 84, 167f, 180, 228, 262f, 275, 314
Landsbergis, Vytautas 425, 497
Lappland 338
Latin America 468
Latin American Free Trade Association (LAFTA) 199
Latvia 4, 6f, 11f, 14f, 22, 25, 33, 35, 40-2, 47f, 59f, 75, 87f, 90, 95, 97, 131, 133-6, 139f, 151, 155, 169, 178, 188, 206, 211f, 215, 225, 235, 246-8, 267, 269, 276f, 314, 318, 369, 372, 374, 376, 378, 380, 382-4, 388-90, 419, 423, 426, 429, 434, 439-45, 457, 469, 473-5, 479f, 487-91, 497f, 508, 513, 521-4, 527-32, 538, 540-2, 544f, 548, 551, 553f, 556
  citizenship, legislation on 457; constitution 35; Declaration on Occupation 442; Institute of International Affairs 455; National Human Rights Office (LNHRO) 542f; National Security Concept (NSC) 457; Navy 514; non-recognition of the annexation of the town of Abrene and six oblasts of Abrene 442; OSCE mission to 389; Presidential Round Table 542; relations with Russia 442; Russian-speaking population of 532; status of non-citizens 541; withdrawal of Russian troops from 390, 469, 473
Latvian-Russian joint commission 390
Law of the Sea 443
Lead Party Report on Combined Municipal and Industrial Discharges 224
League of Nations 438, 537
Lebanon 383
Lebed, Aleksander 95
Leijins, Atis 455
Leipzig 261, 310
Leningrad 16f, 344, 409, 470, 551
  Military District 418, 472, 478; province 96; region 553
Leps, Ando 526f
Lichtenberg 261
Liege 310
life expectancy 7, 553-5
lignite. *See* brown coal
Lisbon 310, 325
  OSCE summit meeting (December 1996) 364, 391
Lithuania 4, 11f, 15, 22, 25, 33, 37, 41f, 47-53 *passim*, 59f, 75f, 87f, 90, 95-7, 131, 134-6, 139f, 142, 151, 155, 169, 178, 188, 194f, 206, 211, 215, 225, 235, 246f, 267-9, 272f, 276-80, 314, 318, 369, 372, 374, 376, 380, 382-4, 388, 390, 418f, 423, 425f, 429, 434, 438-40, 442f, 456, 472f, 485, 488, 491, 495-9, 508, 513, 521, 523f, 527-31, 540f, 551, 554, 556
  armed forces 497; Democratic Labour Party (LDLP) 48f; elections 48-50, 53;

Energy Institute 194; national budget 51; National Security Concept (NSC) 457; Polish minority in 496, 529; poverty 50; relations with Poland 495; Russian-speaking population of 529; Stock Innovation Bank 51; violations of airspace 473; withdrawal of Russian troops from 390, 473
Ljubljana 287
Lotharingia 323
Lower Saxony 543
Luleå 175, 340
Lundqvist, Lars 226-9
Luxembourg 287, 507

Maastricht Treaty. *See* European Union
Macedonia 432
macroeconomic stability/stabilisation 34, 40, 133
MacSharry reform. *See* European Union
Madrid 310, 325
 Charter 287; European Council (1995) 379
Mafia 24, 327, 352, 525
Mälardalsrådet 303
Malaysia 87
Malmö 176
Malmö-Sturup 69
Mare Balticum (journal) 547
Marineamt. *See* Germany
market
 economics 5, 34-6, 38, 42, 47f, 52, 91, 133f, 150, 334, 408; economies 6, 8, 92, 145, 148; forces 169; mechanism 180, 327; order 35f; prices 150; systems 354
Marx, Karl 13
Marzahn 261
Matoczin, J. 279
Mecklenburg-Vorpommern 4, 15, 178, 318, 509, 551, 553, 556
Mediterranean 163, 311, 509
 basin 329, 334; co-operation 299; regions 325
Meri, Lennart 441
metropolitan areas 325, 330
Mezzogiorno 327
Mid-Norden 293
Middle East 233, 453, 530
migrants 115, 530
 quotas on 119; transit 530f; working 543f. *See also* labour
migration 3, 7, 10, 101, 103, 109, 115-22, 125, 127, 330, 373, 377, 445, 450, 528, 543, 546, 553
 flows 116; illegal 382, 513; pressure 119
militarisation 471
military
 aggression 4; balance 395; bases 425, 477; blocs 285, 337, 469; co-operation 472, 477, 486; confrontation 465, 467; forces, reductions of 424; integration 410; spending 424; tensions 341; threats 407. *See also* Baltic states, North Atlantic Treaty Organisation, Treaty on Conventional Forces in Europe, and individual countries

 equipment
  armoured combat vehicles (ACV) 471; attack helicopters 471; combat aircraft 471; French-German 'Euromissile HOT 3', 516; frigate 'F 123' 509; frigate, 'F 124' 509; Mi-2 helicopter 497; mine-sweeping vessels (KL 394) 514; missiles, surface-to-surface 471; missiles, tactical (Russian) 494; rocket launchers 472; SA-11 'Gadfly' surface-to-air missile batteries 472; submarine 'class 212' 509; submarines (Russian) 471, 473; tanks (Russian) 471f

 exercises 472, 491, 511, 514
  'Baltic Challenge 97' 383; 'Baltic Endeavour 96' 491, 512; 'Baltic Service 96' 511; 'BALTSAR 96' 512; Chinese Eye 511; Co-operative Baltic Eye 382; Co-operative Banners 382; Co-operative Bear 382; Command Post Exercises (CPX) 491, 511; CPX Cold Grouse 511; Field Training Exercise (FTX) Tatra 511; Live Carbon Gap 511; Nordic Participants 382; Nordic Peace 382f; Open Spirit 383, 491, 512; Polish/Danish/German exercise 511; 'SPESSART 95' 511; US-BALTOPS naval exercise 383

 formations
  American 1st Armoured Division 492; Baltic naval squadron (BALTRON) 23, 383f, 419, 513; Baltic peacekeeping battalion (BALTBAT) 23, 383f, 419, 433, 459, 513; British-Netherlands amphibious task force 507; Danish battalion (of NORDPOLBRIG) 383, 459; Danish division (of the German-Polish-Danish corps) 417; Estonian company with Norwegian battalion in UNIFIL 383; German 14th division 417; German-Polish-Danish corps 417; Hanseatic Corps 508; motor rifle divisions (Russian) 472; Multinational Division Central Europe 507; Nordic-Polish Brigade (NORDPOLBRIG) 383,

459, 491f; Norwegian battalion in UNIFIL 383; Polish 12th Mechanised Division 417, 491; Polish 16th Airborne Battalion 492; Polish Battalion (POLBAT) 492; Russian 11th Army 493; Russian Baltic Fleet 269, 466, 470f, 492f
minimum information indicator 63f
mining 100, 148
Ministry of Environmental Protection, Natural Resources and Forestry (MEP). *See* Poland
minorities 368, 388, 528, 532, 534f, 537-48 *passim*
and border issues 458; dispersed 539; German 539; indigenous 539; issues (disputes, problems, questions) 441, 450, 480f, 521, 528; Kven-Finnish 538f; national 469, 540; Polish 496, 529, 538; protection of 496, 528; rights of 35, 467, 470, 474, 481, 496; Russian 439, 467, 525; Russian-speaking 527, 529, 532f
Minsk 176, 212, 495
Mitteleuropa 324, 326
Modernity, Apotheosis of 13
Moldova 429
Molotov-Ribbentrop Pact 454
monetary stabilisation 40f
monopolies 39, 41f, 73, 90, 133, 136
Mons 415
Montenegro 432
mortality, infant 196
Moscow 65, 176, 209, 211-3, 455, 505
most favoured nation status 473
Möttölä, Kari 22
multi-party system 50
Multi-Source Pollution Syndrome. *See* pollution
multipolarity 409
Munich 255, 261
new 457
Murmansk (region) 7, 14, 17, 99-111 *passim*, 338-40, 352, 376, 380, 551, 553
budget 102; industry 102, 104, 106f; inflation 106; infrastructure 100; investments in 102, 104f, 107, 111; regional government 105-8; Regional Inward Investment Agency (RIIA) 111; resources 111
mutual and balanced force reductions (MBFR) 424

Namibia 273
Nantes 309f
Naples 325
Narva 207, 209, 211f
Narva Kreenholm textile plant 147
nation state 315, 324, 333
nation-building 25, 298
National Defence Committee. *See* Poland
National Defence Institute. *See* Finland
national socialism 12f, 16, 539f
nationalism 397, 410, 455, 467, 532
rhetoric 469; thinking 84
NATO. *See* North Atlantic Treaty Organisation
NATO-Russian security accord (Founding Act) 385
natural resources 95, 97, 110, 270, 339
renewable 110, 253
naturalisation 258f, 533f, 540-2, 547
nature
conservation 226; preserves 104
naval
armaments 479; arms control 479; bases 438, 473, 509; exercises. *See* military exercises. *See also* military formations
Near East 468
Nenets area 17
neo-functionalism 315
neo-realism 315
Netherlands 148, 287, 383, 488
networks
cities 20; functional 21-3
Neumann, Iver 449, 460
neutrality 409, 455
new democracies 24
new world order 23, 407
Niederlausitz 256
Niemen Euroregion 498
Nokia 118
non-citizens
political rights of 531; status of 541
Non-governmental organisations (NGOs) 225, 253, 371, 377, 541f
Non-violence 537
Norden 79, 82, 195, 201, 241, 247, 286, 289, 292-5, 367, 374, 394, 396, 460, 504, 507
areas/regions adjacent to 376f, 389; relations with Russia 397
Nordic
associations 305; bloc 507; co-operation 299, 305, 376, 453; Co-operation Committee 377; Co-ordinated Arrangement for Military Peace Support (NORDCAPS) 383; Common Labour Market (NCLM) 115-7; Council 11, 23, 286, 289f, 304f, 341, 377, 458, 460; Council of Ministers 289f, 292f, 304, 340f, 345, 376f; countries (states) 4-6, 14f, 24, 57, 59f, 63, 70, 108, 115f, 137, 201, 203f, 211, 265, 289, 297f, 300-4, 307, 337,

340-3, 347, 353, 367, 372, 375-9, 381, 383f, 386, 397, 416, 418f, 433, 445, 449-51, 454, 456, 458-61, 477, 498, 505-7, 513 532, 537f, 540, 544, 546, 551-4, 557; countries, neutral 455; cross-border co-operation 340; cross-border regions 290; identity 460, 504; information offices 377; institutions 378; integration 367, 369, 375, 377, 504; labour markets 118; languages 377; model 378, 454; regional policy 289, 340; regions 65f, 305; security assistance to Baltic countries 384; Social Security Convention 115; social welfare model 460; values 377; welfare states 14
Nordic-Baltic
(5+3) 397f; co-operation 367, 374, 377; command structure 415; meetings of prime ministers 458; relationship 371; understanding on co-operation 383
Nordicism/Nordism 373, 460
Nordland 338, 340
Nordpolitik. *See* Germany
Norrbotten 338
North America 234
North American Free Trade Association (NAFTA) 127, 199, 310
North Atlantic Co-operation Council (NACC) 406, 408, 410, 459, 475, 517
North Atlantic Treaty
Article Five, collective defence obligations according to 410-2, 416, 427f; activities (operations) 416, 410
North Atlantic Treaty Organisation (NATO) 4, 11, 21-3, 187, 269, 337, 341, 366-70, 372-5, 378, 381, 383-9, 391, 395-9, 405-20 *passim*, 423-5, 427-33, 444f, 451-3, 455f, 459, 461, 466f, 469f, 475-81, 486f, 489, 491f, 494, 497f, 503-8, 510f, 513-5, 539, 546
adaptation of 368, 372; Central Region 511; combined joint task force (CJTF) 410-8; command structure 381, 416, 510; Commander Allied Forces Baltic Approaches (COMBALTAP) 511; Commander Allied Land Forces Schleswig-Holstein and Jutland (COMLANDJUT) 511; Commander in Chief Central Europe 514; Component Commands (CCs) 412; depots 409; enlargement (expansion) of 23, 187, 267, 367-9, 372f, 375, 380, 384-8, 392, 394, 396-8, 409, 413-5, 418, 420, 428-33, 459, 467, 470, 475-9, 480f, 487, 492, 494f, 498, 505, 513; European pillar of 408; headquarters 408, 411, 416f; High Level Task Force (HLTF) 431; Implementation Force (IFOR) 383, 410, 433, 452, 459, 491f, 513; information offices 416; integrated military command structure 410, 413, 429; Joint Consultative Group (JCG) 430; Joint Subregional Command Northeast 416f; Joint Subregional Command South (JSRS) 412; Joint Subregional Commands (JSRCs) 412f; joint command Baltic Approaches (BALTAP) 412, 416f, 510f; Long Term Study 414; major commands 411; major subordinate commands 411; Military Committee 411f; Northeast Subregional Command 417; Northwest command 417; Northwest Region 511; out of area operations 410, 510; Principal Subordinate Commands 411; rapid deployment 410; regional commands 411; relations with Russia 385, 395, 459, 487, 489; secret arrangement with Sweden 409; Stabilisation Force (SFOR) 383, 410, 433, 492; strategic commands 411; strategic concept 410; Subordinate Principal Subordinate Commands 411; Subregional Command Northeast 412; subregional commands 411; Supreme Allied Commander Atlantic (SACLANT) 411; Supreme Allied Commander Europe (SACEUR) 411; United States involvement with 409f
North Calotte 345
Committee 304, 340-7; Interreg. *See* European Union, Structural Funds
North Karelia 344
North Sea 202, 220, 233, 311, 509
Commission 299, 302; countries 511; region 312
North-East Passage 9
North-Western Europe 324
Northern Europe 4, 324, 334f, 368, 375, 395, 450f, 504f, 509f, 535
Norway 4f, 7, 11, 15, 19, 57, 60, 65, 69, 73f, 76-8, 80, 115, 120, 169, 188, 195, 210, 213, 297, 299-301, 304, 311, 316, 318, 337f, 341-5, 350, 372, 381-4, 413, 427, 429, 451, 453f, 458, 468f, 472, 474, 492, 505, 511, 530, 538f, 547, 551
firms 351, 358; foreign policy 358; Kven-Finnish minority 538f; Ministry of Foreign Affairs 341; northern 304, 339; regions 302
Novgorod 17
Nuclear Non-Proliferation Treaty 469
nuclear
and radiation safety 388; hazards (risks) 376, 488; industry 339; power (energy) 104, 194, 227, 233; reactors 194f, 473; warheads 409, 492; waste 339; weapons 385, 407, 409, 429, 451, 467, 469, 477, 494; weapons, first

use of 469

Oberbaumbrücke 258
Objectives (regional policy). *See* European Union, Structural Funds
Oder 191
Oder-Neisse line 439
Odessa 428
OEEC. *See* Organisation for Economic Co-operation and Development
Øresund 84, 224
Committee 304; region 292
Østfold 304
Office for Democratic Institutions and Human Rights. *See* Organisation for Security and Co-operation in Europe
oil 80, 206, 233-5, 256, 270, 273, 445
and gas 102, 202; companies, American 443; companies, Swedish 443; crises 117, 233; exports 234; imports 233; market 53; pollution 257; production 233; resources 442; revenues 443; terminals 207
Olpenitz 509
Olsztyn, Round Table talks in 276
OMON, attack on Latvian Interior Ministry 425
Ondarza, Henning von 514
Organisation for European Co-operation and Development (OECD) 6, 135, 197, 240
Conference on Sustainable Cities 253
Organisation for Security and Co-operation in Europe (OSCE) 11, 23 363-70, 372, 374f, 381, 384, 386, 389-92, 394, 396, 398f, 429-40, 444, 454, 456, 458, 474-6, 479, 488, 498, 527, 537, 539-41, 545-8
Forum for Security Co-operation 489; High Commissioner on National Minorities (HCNM) 388f, 474, 541, 546f; missions 389f; Office for Democratic Institutions and Human Rights (ODIHR) 474, 539; Seminar on Regional Arms Control, Vienna 488; Senior Council meeting, Prague 478; summit meeting, Lisbon (December 1996) 430; Vienna Document (1994) 479, 488
Orsha 176
Östberg, Gustaf 194
Ostpolitik. *See* Germany
Ostrava 196
Oulu 175, 344
Our Common Future 220

Pact of Friendship, Co-operation and Mutual Assistance 409
Pact on Stability in Europe 390, 476
Paide 213
Pakistan 530
Paldiski (naval base) 382, 473
Palme, Olof (report) 451
Paris Charter 364
Parliamentary Defence Commission. *See* Sweden
Pärnu 207, 209
Parow 509
Partnership and Co-operation Agreement (EU-Russia). *See* European Union
Partnership for Peace (PfP) 11, 23, 370, 381-6, 388, 392, 394, 398, 406, 408, 410-8, 433, 456, 459, 472, 475, 487f, 491, 495, 497, 509, 511, 513, 516f
expert missions 415; in the spirit of 381-3, 408, 415, 417; PfP-Plus (Super PfP) 416, 487
peace
enforcement 374, 410; operations 486
peace-keeping 23, 374, 383f, 391, 410f, 415, 433, 452f, 459, 480, 513, 515
operations 474f
peaceful coexistence 218
Pechenga 443
Pechenganickel 106
Pechory 440
Peenemünde 509
perestroika 145, 350, 340, 492
peripherality 5, 326
peripheries 66, 209
Permanent Conference of the European Communities and Regions 286
Perry, William 433
Perry-Grachev compromise 478
Petrozadovsk 441, 476
Petseri region 539
Petserimaa movement 440
PHARE (Poland and Hungary: Aid for the Restructuring of Economies). *See* European Union
Pihkva 207, 212
Pilawska/Pillau Strait 274, 487
planned economy 145, 150
planning 12, 38, 93, 354
central 15; culture 316; dual-purpose structures 370; land-use 228; national 168; Soviet-type 327; spatial 168, 309, 311f, 314f, 318f; territorial 329, 332; urban 261, 314. *See also* territorial
Poland 3, 6, 8, 11f, 15, 22, 24f, 33f, 36, 40-2, 57, 59f, 63, 65, 69, 75-9, 82, 87f, 90f, 96f, 120, 127, 131-6, 139-41, 143, 155, 169, 178, 188, 191,

195f, 199, 209, 211, 213, 215, 218-20, 223, 229, 233-48 *passim*, 267f, 273f, 278-80, 293, 314, 318, 369, 371f, 374, 376, 379-83, 385-7, 391, 394, 396f, 408f, 415, 417, 419, 423, 425f, 430, 432, 438-40, 453, 458f, 466, 469-72, 476-8, 480, 485-98 *passim*, 504f, 508, 511-7, 538-40, 551, 553, 555, 557
anti-Russian attitudes 494; armed forces 486, 492-4; co-operation with Denmark and Germany 491; constitution 36; contingent of Implementation Force (IFOR) 492; energy use and policy 233-49 *passim*; environment 220, 233-49 *passim*; fossil fuels 234, 247f; German minority in 539; industry 234, 236; maritime provinces 4; military co-operation with NATO countries 486; Ministry of the Environmental Protection, Natural Resources and Forestry (MEP) 196, 238f, 244, 246; minority in Germany 538; minority in Lithuania 496; National Defence Committee 486; Navy, naval forces 487; north-eastern provinces 492; relations with Lithuania 495; relations with Russia 494, 496; State Inspectorate of Environmental Protection (PIOS) 239; withdrawal of Russian troops 268, 486
Polish-German spatial planning dictionary 179
Polish-Lithuanian
'enhanced partnership' 487; minority question 498; Treaty on Friendly Relations and Good-Neighbourly Co-operation 496
Polish-Russian
Agreement on Trans-Border Co-operation 493; Council 493; Treaty on Friendship and Good-Neighbourly Co-operation 493
polluter-pays principle 166
pollution 106, 110, 187-97 *passim*, 233-48 *passim*
abatement 236, 243, 245, 247; acid rain (precipitation) 187, 189, 191, 195, 241; agriculture 219; air 167, 191,196, 233-48 *passim*, 255, 257; air, transboundary 233-48 *passim*; cadmium 219, 222; carbon dioxide (CO_2) 188, 235, 248, 256; control 220f, 223, 225, 244; heavy metal 196, 237; industrial 171, 218; land-based 222; levels 239, 241; mercury 222; Multi-Source Pollution Syndrome 192; nitrogen 223; nitrogen oxides (NOx) 237, 239, 241, 256; noise 257; nutrients, discharges of 218, 220f, 223; oil and chemical 257; particulates 237-9, 241; phosphorus 188, 223; photochemical smog 237; reduction of 219, 221; second sulphur protocol 241, 244; Single-Source Pollution Syndrome 192; smog 256; standards 238, 243-5; sulphur dioxide (SO2) 188, 195f, 234f, 237-9, 241-7, 255f; sulphur protocol 241; transboundary 187-97 *passim*, 225; water 167, 189, 191
Polonia 538
Pomor trade 8
popular fronts 454
in Estonia 146
population
decrease 101; density 200, 208, 254, 552; growth 254, 529; structure 101
Portugal 15, 43, 302, 313, 323
post-sovereign Europe 446
Potsdam 417
Conference 267, 492
Potsdamer Platz 260, 263
poverty 50, 271
Practical Guide to Cross-Border Co-operation 291f
Prague 122, 125
Organisation for Security and Co-operation in Europe, Senior Council Meeting 478
pre-accession programmes. *See* European Union
precautionary principle 166, 221, 227
Presidential Round Table. *See* Latvia
price
controls 326; liberalisation 270; mechanism 38-40
Primakov, Yevgeniy 429, 441, 476f, 495
Principles for a European Spatial Policy. *See* Committee for Spatial Development
prison conditions 528
Privatisation Agency. *See* Estonia
privatisation 37, 39f, 50, 52, 93, 95, 97, 102, 132f, 136, 146f, 152-4, 156f, 246, 265, 272, 274, 525
vouchers 50, 147
Producer's Subsidy Equivalent (PSE) 134f, 138
productivity 39, 41, 89, 117, 127, 134, 136, 143, 328
property
rights 36f, 111; ownership status of 94; private 34, 36-8; public 36; restitution of 147, state, theft of 525
protectionism 42, 92, 134, 199
Pskov 17, 428, 429
region 439, 478
Purju, Alari 150
Pyotr Velikiy, cruiser 479
Pytalovo 441

railways 65, 83, 148, 200, 202, 205-7, 210-4, 260. *See also* traffic and transport
RAINS model 196
Raja-Jooseppi 339
realism 467, 480
recycling 228
refugees 543f, 548
Convention on 544; flows of 445
REGEN. *See* European Union
region(s)/regional
arms control 478; backward 329, 333, 335; balance 201; Baltic 57, 66; border 285-95 *passim*, -building 20, 22, 299, 364, 371; city 126; co-operation 127, 486; concept of 4, 343f, 364, 370; core 66; 'counter-cultures' 297; cross-border co-operation 305; cross-border, Nordic 66; development 11-3, 99, 105, 110, 209, 268, 318, 343f, 346, 379; development, sustainable 318; disparities between 169; distribution of enterprises 148; East European 65; economy 102, 105; equalisation 14; Estonian 211; European 65f, 70; expansive 70; functional 343; German 65; governments 323; historical 298; identity 343, 371; income gaps between 117; integration 11, 85; investment (policies) 102, 104f, 107, 111; Inward Investment Agency (RIIA). *See* Murmansk; lagging 325, 331; less developed 325, 334; macro- 311, 323f, 333; mega- 450; meso- 450; movements 298; policy 215, 343; Nordic 65f, 305; North European 65; North Sea 312; Norwegian 302; peripheral 178, 287, 297, 326, 329, 334; policy, EU 309, 331; policy, Nordic 289, 340; policy, transnational 309; resources 14, 100; Russian 6, 15, 75, 100, 379; security 475-7, 479f; South European 326, 332; specialisation 56; stabilisation 492, 494; super- 298f, 304. 306; transition 314f; unevenness of economic growth (disparities) 148, 332
regionalisation 18, 23, 297-307 *passim*, 342f, 371, 407, 409, 413, 415, 418f, 449, 503, 516
concept of 337; movement 331; of security policy 23, 397; perverse 20
regionalism 364, 371
regionalist movements 343
Reichstag 263
Rendsburg 417, 511
repression, by state 524
resources
allocation 38; human 127; management 180; natural 95, 97, 110, 270, 339; renewable 110, 253; rural 143; substitution 110
Ricardo, David 10
Riga 67, 176, 209, 211, 213
Gulf of 442, 514; Port of 213
Riga Peace Treaty (1920) (between Latvia and Russia) 442
Ringius, Lasse 221
Rio Conference (1992), 253
risk
assessment 190, 194; management 190; perception 191, 197, substance-related 166
rogue states 416
Romania 121
Romany 539f
Rome 325
Ronneby, Baltic Sea Conference (1990). *See* Baltic Sea
Rosati, Dariusz 495
Rostock 318, 509
Rostov 428
Rotterdam 84
Rovaniemi 287, 340
Rudow 262
Rühe, Volker 508, 514
Ruhnu, island of 442
Ruhr 260
rule of law 4, 24, 35, 368, 452, 528, 548
rural
areas 143, 155, 174; development 137, 142f; environment 142; resources 143; settlements 175
Russia/Russian Federation 4, 11f, 14-7, 23, 55-7, 59f, 63, 73f, 77, 80, 87-92, 95-7, 102-4, 107, 110, 120, 127, 133, 139, 150-4, 156, 169, 188, 191, 200, 202, 204, 206, 208-14, 235, 241, 246f, 268f, 272, 274, 278-80, 289, 293, 318, 337-42, 344-7, 350f, 353-6, 367-9, 371-3, 375-83, 386-92, 394-8, 408f, 415, 418f, 423, 425-34, 438-45, 452-4, 456-9, 465-81 *passim*, 485, 487-9, 491f, 494f, 498, 503, 505f, 508, 513, 525f, 530, 532, 534f, 539, 541f, 545, 551f
armed forces (military) 423, 469; Baltic doctrine 468, 470, 481; Baltic states, attitudes to 470; Baltic states, re-occupation of 432; Baltic states, relations (tensions) with 26, 380, 389, 396, 442; Belarus, relations with 380; central 213; CFE, violations of 428f, 433; citizens abroad 469; Constitution 104, 111; democratic reforms 379, 477; Diaspora 534; diplomacy 468; Duma (Parliament) 17, 468; ecological damage caused by military 473; economic associations 17; economy 101; elections 429; Empire 268; Estonia, border issues with 376; Estonia, citizens in 534; Estonia, naval bases in 473;

Estonia, relations (disputes) with 440, 538; Estonian-Russian Peace Treaty of 1920 (Tartu) 440-2; ethnic issue 390; ethnic Russians in Baltic countries, status of 369; EU, relations with 397; Finland, border with 380; Finnish-Russian Peace Treaty of 1920 (Tartu) 444; firms 351, 353; foreign enterprise in 95; foreign policy 444, 468; foreign troops, deployment in areas adjacent to 469; Kaliningrad, corridor to 432, 438, 494-6, 498; Kaliningrad, transit to 278, 438, 473, 495f; Latvia, border issues with 376; Latvia, naval bases in 473; Latvia, relations (disputes) with 442, 538; Law on Security 468; Law on the Protection of the Environment 101; Lithuanian airspace, violations of 473; military conversion 382, 470, 480; military doctrine 468-70; military pensioners 390, 426, 473; military personnel 376, 469; military reduction 269; military reform 370, 392; Ministry of Defence 269; Ministry of Interior 470; minorities abroad 439, 467, 525; National Security Concept 468; national interests 467; nationalists 439; NATO enlargement, hostility to 433; NATO, relations with 385, 395, 459, 487, 489; Norden, relations with 397; north-western 212, 337, 349-59 *passim*, 376, 380, 466, 540; north-western economic association 4; northern 210; Oblast Duma (Murmansk) 105; Partnership and Co-operation Agreement with EU 379; Poland, relations with 494, 496; regions 6, 75, 100; regions, north-western 15, 379; repeals non-first use of nuclear weapons 469; Russian speakers, in Estonia 156,377f, 389, 473, 476, 532, 533, 534; Russian speakers, in Latvia 377f, 389, 473, 532; Russian speakers, in Lithuania 529; Russian speakers, in the Baltic states 376, 468, 527, 532-4; security debate 467; security interests 468; security relations 472; security thought, schools of 467; sphere of influence 466; strategic interests 466; strategic planning 467; tanks, artillery and ACVs, ceilings on 428; troop withdrawals 268, 376, 390, 424, 426f, 440, 455f, 458, 468f, 472f, 486, 490, 510, 529; Ukraine, relations with 380; Western intervention in 469. *See also* Baltic states and individual countries

Russian-NATO council 397

Sajudis 47

Sami 304, 538f

Ting (Assembly) 304

Sarragossa 287

Saudargas, Algirdas 433

Saxony-Anhalt 254

Scandinavia. *See* Norden and Nordic countries

Schengen 530

Schleswig-Holstein 4, 305, 510, 517, 540, 551, 553

Schmitter, Philippe C. 319

Schönefeld, airport 258-60

second sulphur protocol. *See* pollution

security 70, 363

agenda 368, 449, 458, 535; architecture 409; assured 506f; Baltic Sea region 470; civic 388, 391, 458, 490, 493; co-operative 365f; collective 452, 474; common 451f; community 394, 396f, 450; complex 394f; concept of 22; environment 405f, 419, 465; extended concept of 521; generation 363; management 363; military 3; military, European pillar of 507; national 541, 544; order 398f, 408; policy 449-518 *passim*; policy structures 22; policy, regionalisation of 23, 452; regime 394, 397; regime, European 474; regional 470, 475-7, 479f; societal 3; soft 459, 467, 470, 474f, 477, 480, 514; structure, European 416; structures, Western and transatlantic 456; subregional 456; system, European 507; system, regional 405, 407. *See also* individual countries

Seimas 48f, 53

Senghaas, Dieter 548

Serbia 432

deserters from 543

Sergounin, Alexander 437, 445

services 109, 117, 145, 148, 204f, 123, 234, 328f, 333

public 39, 325; sector 557

Setoland 539

Setu/Seto minority 440, 539

Sharp, Jane 23

Shevardnadze, Eduard 423f

shock therapy 48

Silesia 196, 438, 494

Silver Curtain 540

Sinatra Doctrine 408

Singapore 152

Single European Act. *See* European Union

single-industry towns 107, 109, 111

Single-Source Pollution Syndrome. *See* pollution

Sinti 539f

Skåne (Scania) 304

Skele, Andris 442
Skoghall 224
Skrunda, radar station 376, 390, 426, 473
Slovakia/Slovak Republic 326, 485, 427, 493
Slovenia 326
Slubice 175
Slupsk, province of 280
Smallbone, David 155
Smith, Adam 10, 38
smuggling 445, 470
social democrats (Germany) 253, 261
social
capital 306; cohesion 314, 545; exclusion 122; integration 10, 264; justice 548; malaise 24; polarisation 254
socialism 90
in One Country 13
socialist
bloc (camp) 117f, 124, 234, 485; countries (regimes, states) 87f, 189, 521; economies 38; era 93, 155
Soleczniki 496
Sorbs 539
Sound, the. *See* Øresund
sourcing principle 199
South East Asia 453
Southern Europe 201, 324, 326f, 329, 334f
sovereignty
assistance 460; concepts of 445
Soviet Union (USSR) 3, 6-9, 12-4, 16, 24, 47, 69, 75, 87, 95, 121f, 123, 132f, 145f, 150, 188f, 194f, 202f, 218, 234, 237, 267, 326, 337, 408f, 423-30, 432, 437-9, 443, 445, 450-2, 454f, 465f, 472, 478, 485f, 492, 510, 541
armed forces 409, 424; atomisation of social fabric 526; August 1991 coup 12, 455; Baltic Military District 426; Baltic Sea Fleet 267, 466; Baltic states, annexation of 425; collapse 504f; Communist Party 424; defence system 466; economy 131, 424; Empire 19, 425, 453; era 555; Estonia and Latvia, minorities in 14; ex-Soviet republics 469; General Staff 424f; oil fields 234; Paldiski, naval base 382; republics 150; rule 524, 528f; successor states of 35, 40; system 35; troops and equipment remaining on Baltic territory 426
Soviet-American Treaty banning intermediate range nuclear forces 424
Soviet-type planning. *See* planning
sovkhozes 271
Spain 43, 298, 313, 323, 326, 413, 429, 507
Spatial Planning Concepts for the Area along the German-Polish Border 178
spatial
cohesion 169; fragmentation 20; governance 13; planning. *See* planning. *See also* European Union, European Spatial Development Perspective
special economic zones 96f, 280
Spree, River 256, 258
Sri Lanka 530
St Petersburg 6f, 17, 67, 74, 76, 80, 90, 96, 120, 122, 125, 176, 178, 209-13, 269, 278, 293, 371, 376f, 380, 466, 481, 488, 491, 551
Minority Rights Group 541
stabilisation, regional 492, 494
Stabilisation Force (SFOR). *See* North Atlantic Treaty Organisation
Stability Pact 370, 378, 497, 545
stability policy 374
Stalin, Josef 13, 16, 425, 439
Stalinist regime 15
State Inspectorate of Environmental Protection (PIOS). *See* Poland
state-building 450, 455
Stattauto (car-sharing) 261
steel 82, 328
Stockholm 15, 67, 179, 203, 209f, 212f, 224
ad-hoc group 391; Conference (1974) 222; Ministerial Conference on the Environment and on Spatial Planning (October 1996) 164; region of 224; United Nations Conference on the Human Environment (1972) 218f
Stockholm-Arlanda 69
Storskog 339
Stralsund 509
Strasbourg 286, 310f
Strategic Arms Limitation Talks (START) 394
Structural Funds. *See* European Union
Stuttgart 255
subregionalisation 407, 409, 413, 415f
subsidiarity 310, 330-2, 335
Suez Canal 10
sulphur protocol. *See* pollution
superpowers 407, 420
sustainability 99, 104, 109, 264, 314
assets 253; concept of 164, 169; in cities 264, metropolis 258. *See* also development, sustainable
Suwalskie, province of 278, 495
Sweden 4-6, 11, 14, 18f, 23, 33, 57, 59f, 68f, 73, 76-8, 80, 91, 115-8, 120, 126, 132, 141f, 151, 154, 156, 169, 188, 195, 199f, 202, 210, 213, 217-20, 222-5, 227, 229, 288, 299-303, 305f, 309, 311, 316, 323, 337-9, 341-5, 347, 350, 369, 372, 378, 381f, 386, 389, 391, 395f, 407-

9, 423, 431-4, 450, 452-4, 459, 466-8, 472, 477, 479f, 488-92, 506f, 513, 530, 538f, 544, 551
Association of Municipalities (Svenska Kommunförbundet) 226; Baltic integration, five part strategy for 433; Ecocycle Bill 228; Environmental Protection Agency (SEPA) 223, 225-8; environmental policy 217, 220; Federation of Industries (Sveriges Industriförbund) 226; Federation of Trade Unions (Landsorganisationen) 226; firms 351, 357; Green party 220, 227; Helsinki Committee for Human Rights 541; Immigration Board 547; Kooperativa Förbundet 226; left-wing socialist party 227; Licensing Board for Environmental Protection 228; Migration Bill 547; Ministry of Environment 225; National Board of Housing, Building and Planning (Boverket) 179; Navy 471, 514; Parliamentary Defence Commission 452; secret arrangement with NATO 409; Water Councils (Vattenvårdsförbund) 226; welfare system 228
Swietlyj 271
Switzerland 125, 273, 287
Sydsam 305
Szczecin 176

TACIS (Technical Assistance to the Commonwealth of Independent States). *See* European Union
Tallinn 67, 122f, 125, 148, 155f, 169, 176, 203f, 207, 209-13, 514
Port of 207
Tampere 176
Tapa 207
Tarand, Andres 441
tariffs 41f, 138, 151f
Tartu 156, 208-10, 213
Peace Movement 444; Peace Treaty (1920) (between Estonia and Russia) 440-2; Peace Treaty (1920) (Between Finland and Russia) 444
Technical Assistance and Promotion of Cross-Border Co-operation (LACE) 291f
Tegel 260
telecommunications 39, 90, 96, 151, 174, 333, 339
Tempelhof 260
territorial
conflicts (disputes) 437-46 *passim*, 469; control 437; governance 11; planning 329, 332; policies for rural areas 143; polities 315; state 13, 20. *See also* planning
terrorism 467, 470
Third World 408
Tiergarten Tunnel 258
Torneå/Tornio 175, 339
Tornedalen Finns 538
totalitarian
regimes 4, 14, 24, 522; states 13f, 24
totalitarianism 12, 526
tourism 172, 177f, 203, 211, 274, 327, 330, 445, 490
sustainable 177
Towards a Framework for Spatial Development in the BSR 169
trade 7, 10, 41f, 73-85 *passim*, 82-5, 88, 115, 472
agreements 135, 151; blocs 59; deficits in Baltic region 60; dependency 59; distortions 73; East-West 339; flows 73-85 *passim*; foreign 3, 53, 55, 73, 557; foreign, monopolies on 73; freedom of 38; liberalisation 42; obstacles to 70; patterns 65, 68, 74, 76; policy 151; transit 206, 210f; value density of 83; volume 60, 76, 202; wholesale and retail 148; world 199
traffic 73-85 *passim*, 223
air 65; ferry 69, 210; goods 258; highway (road) 84, 202; hubs 84; motorcar 258; passenger 69, 258; rail 84, 210f; routes 84, 286; sea 65; volume 258. *See also* transport
transborder co-operation 19, 280, 323-35 *passim*: 446, 493, 498. *See also* cross-border co-operation
Trans-European Networks (TENS) 172, 180, 200, 288, 332
transaction costs 332, 352
transatlantic relations 505, 507f, 517
transition/transformation
countries 3, 6f, 9, 90, 163, 218, 222f, 316, 375, 381, 388, 394, 540; economies 119, 121, 125, 127; policies 122; political and economic 392; processes 37, 132; regions 314f; zone 8
transnational corporations (TNCs) 125, 127, 350, 358
transport 9, 39, 82-4, 96, 148, 189, 257f, 328, 333
air 200; bottlenecks 82-4; bulk goods 82; car 258; container 82; corridors 176, 199-215 *passim*, 326, 339; emissions from 256; flows 74; freight 83; infrastructure 75, 325, 339; inland, water 202; multimodal 174, 176f, 200, 206, 211, 213; networks 180; personal 70; policy 325; public 253, 258f; rail 200, 202, 205, 214, 260; road 84, 200, 205f; sea (maritime) 84, 177, 200, 205, 210; systems

199, 252. *See also* traffic
Transrapid 260
transregional co-operation 324
travel
ease of 543; visa-free 544f
Treaty of Rome 115, 137
Treaty on Conventional Forces in Europe (CFE) 370, 391, 394, 423-34 *passim*, 478f, 489, 493, 506
Adaptation Conference, Vienna (January 1997) 423; Article II 426; Article IV 427; Article V 427; Central Zone 428; CFE-2 negotiations 493; CFE-2 Treaty 478; Extraordinary Conference (September 1993) 427; Joint Consultative Group meeting, Vienna (October 1991) 426; Review Conference (May 1996) 423, 428-31, 478; Russian violations of 428f, 433; treaty limited (ceilings on) equipment (TLE) 424, 428, 430f
Treuhand 37, 147
Troki 496
Troms 338, 340, 383
Turin 310
Turkey 326, 397, 427, 429
Turku 303f
Turow 245
twinned cities 21

Ukraine 150, 241, 277, 427-9, 431, 485, 487, 493
unemployment 52, 101, 103, 109f, 116, 118, 121, 133, 136, 148, 208, 271f, 312, 330, 525, 543
unipolar world order 23, 407, 409
United Kingdom (UK) 79, 323, 383, 411-3, 417, 427, 430, 459, 507, 511, 513
special relations with USA 417
United Nations (UN) 365, 376, 383f, 389, 424, 443, 452, 456, 459, 486, 513, 537, 540f
climate summit (spring 1995) 253; Conference on the Human Environment, Stockholm (1972) 218f; Convention on the Rights of the Child 547; Economic Commission for Europe (ECE) 241; General Council 268; High Commissioner on Refugees (UNHCR) 541; Human Rights Commission 389
United States of America (USA) 11, 23, 152, 241, 299, 310, 383-6, 395f, 398, 407-10, 413, 416, 419f, 423, 425, 427, 429f, 433, 456, 460, 468, 486-8, 492, 505, 511, 513, 539
Environment Protection Agency (EPA) 196; forward defence of 416; military involvement in Europe 409; NATO, involvement in 410; special relations with UK 417; strategic preferences 412
Unity of the Realm. *See* Denmark
universities 329, 334
Unrepresented Nations and Peoples Organisation (UNPO) 539
Urals 428, 430
urban
areas 136, 174; centres 323; ecology 254, 264; environment 261, 328; networks 18, 171, 175; perspective 333; planning 261, 314; policy 333; settlements 169; sprawl 261, 264; structure 252f; system 172, 317
urbanisation 116f, 167, 325
Uruguay Round (UR) 138
USSR. *See* Soviet Union

Vahi, Tiit 441
Vakaru Bankas 51
Valga 209
Vänern, Lake 224
Vares, Peeter 455
Vasa 305
VASAB 2010. *See* Visions and Strategies around the Baltic
Västerbotten 344
Växjö 280
Veggeland, Noralv 313
Venesaar, Urve 155
Venice 310, 312, 330
Via Baltica 176, 200, 207-11, 213-5, 278
Via Estica 209f, 213
Via Hanseatica 176, 209f, 212f, 215
Via Vironia 209f, 212
Vienna 487f
Documents 479, 487f; Organisation for Security and Co-operation in Europe, Seminar on Regional Arms Control 488
Vilnius 67, 171, 206, 212, 439, 496f
visa
regulations 445; requirements 204. *See also* travel
Visby 388f, 470, 506
Baltic Prime Ministers' meeting (May 1996). *See* Baltic; Declaration 163, 188; process 389, 398
Visegrad 122-5, 431, 467, 470, 477, 489, 497
Visions and Strategies around the Baltic (VASAB 2010) 163-80 *passim*, 199, 201, 311, 315
Third Ministerial Conference 175
Vistytis, Lake 439
Volgograd 428
Vologda 17
Vöru 208f

Vyborg 443

Wæver, Ole 531
Walesa, Lech 486
war 407, 485, 537
  fear of 437; virtual 407
Warnemünde 509
Warsaw 67, 176, 209, 212, 239, 488, 490, 494f, 516
  Military District 493; province of 95; Treaty Organisation (WTO) 381, 406, 409, 423-5, 427, 429f, 432, 466, 476, 485, 489, 509
Washington 415, 505
waste-collection 257
waste-water treatment 218f, 223f
water
  management 226; pollution 167, 189, 191; quality 189; resources (reserves) 256; -saving technologies 263
Wehrmacht 16
Weimar Triangle 492
welfare state 297, 300, 302, 330, 332, 548
West Nordic Committee 304
Western Europe 6, 10, 25, 47, 234f, 324, 327, 329, 334f, 341, 407f, 486, 543
Western European Union (WEU) 408, 410, 417f, 467, 469, 474, 477, 505, 507f, 510, 514
White Sea 551
Wilhelmshafen 509
Winter War 443
women's
  progress 540; participation in labour market 116
World Bank 52, 242
World Trade Organisation (WTO) 138f, 199,
World War I 12f, 438
World War II 12f, 131, 285, 297, 409, 438-40, 504
World Wars 126, 438

Yantar
  Euroregion 280; free economic zone 272
Yalta, new 457
Yegorov, Admiral 470
Yeltsin, Boris 423, 433, 440, 469, 477, 495
Ystad 176
Yugoslavia 432, 543

Zaleski, J. 280
Zakopane 529
zero option 529, 531
Zhirinovskiy, Vladimir 439, 469

About the Authors and Editors

Hallgeir Aalbu: Nordic Centre for Spatial Development (NORDREGIO), Stockholm and Copenhagen
Clive Archer: Department of Philosophy and Politics, Manchester Metropolitan University, England
Harald Baldersheim: Department of Political Science, University of Oslo, Norway
Hanne-Margret Birckenbach: The Schleswig-Holstein Institute for Peace Research (SHIP) at the Christian-Albrechts-Universität zu Kiel, Germany
Stefan Callsen: Institute for Regional Research, Christian-Albrechts-Universität zu Kiel, Germany
Riccardo Cappellin: Department of Economics, University of Rome 'Tor Vergata,' Italy
Vladimir Didyk: Kola Science Centre, Apatity, Russia
Christof Ellger: Institut für Geographische Wissenschaften, Freie Universität Berlin, Germany
Tuomas Forsberg: Department of International Politics, University of Wales, Aberystwyth, Wales
Härmo Haljaste: Faculty of Economics, University of Tartu, Estonia
Lars Hedegaard: Nordic Centre for Spatial Development (NORDREGIO), Copenhagen and Stockholm
Bertel Heurlin: Danish Institute of International Affairs (DUPI), Copenhagen, Denmark
Ronnie Hjorth: Department of Political Science, Linköping University, Sweden
Pertti Joenniemi: Copenhagen Peace Research Institute (COPRI), Denmark
Øyvind Jæger: Copenhagen Peace Research Institute (COPRI) and Norwegian Institute of International Affairs
Ib Jørgensen: Department of Development and Planning, Aalborg University, Denmark
J. Ilari Karppi: Department of Regional Studies and Environmental Policy, University of Tampere, Finland
Urpo Kivikari: Institute for East-West Trade, Turku School of Economics and Business Administration, Turku, Finland
Jüri Köll: Statistics Sweden, Stockholm
Wojciech Kostecki: Institute for Political Studies, University of Warsaw, Poland
Axel Krohn: Department of Political Science, Christian-Albrechts-Universität zu Kiel, Germany
Claus-Friedrich Laaser: Kiel Institute of World Economics, Kiel, Germany
Bjarne Lindström: Department of Statistics and Economic Research (ÅSUB), Mariehamn, Åland
Joan Löfgren: Tampere Peace Research Institute (TAPRI), University of Tampere, Finland

Lars Lundqvist: Department of Infrastructure and Planning, The Royal Institute of Technology (KTH), Stockholm, Sweden
Viktor Freiherr von Malchus: Association of European Border Regions (AEBR), Gronau, Germany
Helena Mannonen: Tampere Peace Research Institute (TAPRI), University of Tampere, Finland
Kari Möttölä: Finnish Ministry of Foreign Affairs, Helsinki, Finland
Jan Nielsen: Department of Development and Planning, Aalborg University, Denmark
Anders Östhol: Department of Political Science, Umeå University, Sweden.
Malgorzata Pacuk: Institute of the Economic Geography of the Sea, University of Gdansk, Poland
Tadeusz Palmowski: Institute of the Economic Geography of the Sea, University of Gdansk, Poland
Lars Olof Persson: Research Group on Regional Analysis (FORA), The Royal Institute of Technology (KTH), Stockholm, Sweden
Karin Peschel: Institute for Regional Research, Christian-Albrechts-Universität zu Kiel, Germany
Kazimira Prunskiene: Lithuanian-European Institute, Vilnius, Lithuania
Kalle Pungas: Institute of Geography, University of Tartu, Estonia
Garri Raagmaa: Institute of Geography, University of Tartu, Estonia
Ewa Rabinowicz: Departement of Economics, Swedish University of Agricultural Sciences, Alnarp, Sweden
Kai Richter: Institut für Geographische Wissenschaften, Freie Universität, Berlin, Germany
Jürgen Salay: Department of Environmental and Energy Systems Analysis, Lund University, Sweden
Klaus Schrader: Kiel Institute of World Economics, Kiel, Germany
Alexander A. Sergounin: Faculty of History, University of Nizhny Novgorod, Russia
Jane M.O. Sharp: Institute for Public Policy Research (IPPR) and Centre for Defence Studies at King's College, University of London, England
Gunnar Sjöstedt: Swedish Institute of International Affairs (SIIA), Stockholm, Sweden
Krister Ståhlberg: Department of Government, Åbo Academy University, Finland
Carl-Einar Stålvant: Centre for Natural Resources and Environmental Research, University of Stockholm and Södertörn Högskola (University College of South Stockholm), Huddinge, Sweden
Bo Svensson: Swedish Institute for Regional Research (SIR), Östersund, and the Department of Political Science, Umeå University, Sweden
Juhan Teder: Faculty of Economics, Tallinn Technical University, Estonia
Erik Terk: Estonian Institute for Futures Studies, Tallinn
Raik Vürst: Institute of Geography, University of Tartu, Estonia

Ralph Westermann: BalticNet and University of Cologne, Germany
Ulf Wiberg: Department of Social and Economic Geography, Umeå University, Sweden

List of Partners

The publication of The NEBI Yearbook 1998 has been made possible by generous grants from the following Partners:

Danish Institute of International Affairs (DUPI), Copenhagen
The Ministry of Foreign Affairs, Finland
The Ministry of Foreign Affairs, Norway
The Ministry of Foreign Affairs, Sweden
The Government of Åland, Mariehamn
Centre for Regional Science (CERUM), Umeå
Copenhagen Peace Research Institute (COPRI)
Federation of County Councils, Stockholm
Institute for East-West Tråde, Turku
The Kvarken Co-operation, Vasa
The Mälardal Council, Stockholm
Nordic Centre for Spatial Development (NORDREGIO), Stockholm
The Øresund Committee, Copenhagen
Ostee-Akademie, Travemünde
Schleswig-Holstein Institute for Peace Research (SHIP), Kiel
The Skärgård Co-operation, Mariehamn
Swedish Institute for Regional Research (SIR), Östersund

Batch number: 10755248

Printed by Printforce, the Netherlands